Unmasking the State

Unmasking the State
Politics, Society and Economy in Guyana • 1992–2015

Edited by
Arif Bulkan and D. Alissa Trotz

IAN RANDLE PUBLISHERS
Kingston • Miami

First published in Jamaica, 2019 by
Ian Randle Publishers
16 Herb McKenley Drive
Box 686
Kingston 6
www.ianrandlepublishers.com

© 2019, Arif Bulkan and D. Alissa Trotz
ISBN: 978-976-637-981-0

National Library of Jamaica Cataloguing-In-Publication Data

Names: Bulkan, Arif, editor | Trotz, D. Alissa, editor
Title: Unmasking the state : politics, society and economy in Guyana, 1992-2015 / edited by Arif Bulkan and D. Alissa Trotz
Description: Kingston : Ian Randle Publishers, 2019 | Includes index.
Identifiers: ISBN 9789766379810 (pbk)
Subjects: LCSH: Guyana – Politics and government | Guyana – Economic conditions | Guyana – Social conditions | Guyana – Race relations
Classification: DDC 988.1033 --dc23

All rights reserved. While copyright in the selection and editorial material is vested in Arif Bulkan and D. Alissa Trotz, copyright in individual chapters belongs to their respective authors and no part of this publication may be reproduced, stored in a retrieval system or transmitted in any form or by any means electronic, photocopying, recording or otherwise, without the prior express permission of the author and publisher.

Cover and Book Design by Ian Randle Publishers
Front Cover Art: Stanley Greaves, Abary Survey Pay Table (2013). Acrylic on Canvas © Stanley Greaves. Artist's Private Collection.
Printed and Bound in the United States of America

Table of Contents

List of Figures ... vii

List of Tables ... viii

Acknowledgements ... ix

Acronyms and Abbreviations ... xi

Introduction ... xv
    Arif Bulkan and D. Alissa Trotz

A. Constitutionalism, Democracy & Governance

1. Constitutional Architecture and the Production of Authoritarianism ... 1
   Arif Bulkan

2. Guyana's Public Financial Management Systems in the Post-Independence Period ... 37
   Anand Goolsarran

3. Uncontested Democratic Spaces: The Politics and Practice of Local Government in Post-Independence Guyana: 1992–2015 ... 62
   Esther M. McIntosh

B. Legacies of Racial Dysfunction

4. Politics and Underdevelopment: The Case of Guyana ... 91
   Tarron Khemraj

5. Crime, Ethnicity and the Political Impasse in Guyana ... 120
   Rishee S. Thakur

6. Between Despair and Hope: Towards an Analysis of Women and Violence in Contemporary Guyana ... 154
   D. Alissa Trotz

7. Race, Ideology, and International Relations: Sovereignty and the Disciplining of Guyana's Working Class ... 178
   Percy C. Hintzen

C. Insecurities of Neoliberalism

8. Local Impact of Global Change: Rice and Sugar in the History and Memory of Africans and East Indians in Guyana ... 209
   Wazir Mohamed

9. Poverty and Human Security in Guyana ... 236
   Clement Henry

10. The Myth of Free Education ... 269
    Diana Abraham

11. Growing Downhill? Contestations of Sovereignty and the Creation of Itinerant Workers in Guyanese Call Centres ... 297
    Alissa Trotz, Kiran Mirchandani, and Iman Khan

12. Consolidation and Implications of Discretionary Rule over Guyana's Public Forests, 1992–2015 ... 325
    Janette Bulkan

D. The Politics of Gender and Sexuality

13. Madness, Myth, and Masquerade: Cultural Patrimony and Violence Against Disabled Women in Guyana ... 369
    Savitri Persaud

14. Gender, Inclusionary Politics and the Electoral Quota in Guyana: Politics as Usual? ... 394
    Natalie Persadie

15. 'Push Ya' Body': Imaginaries of the 'Bush' and the Amerindian Body in the Guyanese State ... 429
    Shanya Cordis

E. Lenses of Hope: Alternative Engagements with the State

16. Lenses of Hope: Investigating the Social Economy as a Paradigmatic Shift Through the Wowetta Women's Agro-Processing Cassava Enterprise ... 455
    Hollis France

17. Inundated with Facts: Flooding and the Knowledge Economies of Climate Adaptation in Guyana ... 479
    Sarah E. Vaughn

18. Journeying Towards LGBTIQ+ Equality in Guyana ... 501
    Vidyaratha Kissoon

Contributors ... 525

Index ... 531

List of Figures

Figure 4.1:   The Colonial Underdevelopment Trap ... 100

Figure 4.2:   Inner Vicious Endogenous Cycle of Underdevelopment ... 102

Figure 4.3:   Outer Vicious Endogenous Cycle of Underdevelopment ... 102

Figure 4.4:   Reinforcement of Colonial Underdevelopment Trap ... 113

Figure 8.1:   Plan number 16852 dated March 31, 1973 ... 216

Figure 9.1:   Results of Three Poverty Studies in Guyana ... 240

Figure 9.2:   Poverty Rates by Region, 1993 and 2006 ... 240

Figure 9.3:   Box Plot for Human Security Scores ... 250

Figure 9.4:   Graph Depicting Levels of Human Security for Guyana ... 251

Figure 9.5:   Comparison between the Findings of the 2006 Poverty Study and 2013 Human Security Study ... 252

Figure 13.1: Traditional representation of the Old Higue at Mashramani 2014 ... 387

Figure 13.2: Young women don Old Higue costumes at Mashramani 2014 ... 388

List of Tables

Table 4.1:	Broad Indicators of Relative Economic Development	95
Table 4.2:	Broad Measures of Development, Inequality and Polarization	96
Table 4.3:	Source of Votes and Party Identification by Ethnicity	108
Table 4.4:	Hypothetical Lifetime Income Payoff from Bi-Communal Voting	111
Table 5.1:	Population Distribution and Allocation of Regional Seats	130
Table 9.1:	Summary Table on the 17-Indicator Instrument	246
Table 9.2:	Indicator Variables and Corresponding Factors	248
Table 9.3:	Syntax for Computing Human Security	250
Table 9.4:	Human Security Classifications	251
Table 9.5:	Mean Economic Security Scores by Region	253
Table 9.6:	Mean Food Security Scores by Region	253
Table 9.7:	Mean Health Security Scores by Region	254
Table 9.8:	Mean Personal Security Scores by Region	254
Table 9.9:	Mean Environmental Security Scores by Region	255
Table 9.10:	Mean Societal Security Scores by Region	256
Table 9.11:	Mean Political Security Scores by Region	256
Table 14.1:	Women's (Under-) representation in National Parliaments in the Independent Anglophone Caribbean	395
Table 14.2:	Available Party Manifestos with Specific Statements on Gender Issues in the post-1992 Period	405
Table 14.3:	Percentage of Women by Party holding seats in Parliament from 1966–2016	409

Acknowledgements

This collection of essays on the period following the 1992 transition to electoral democracy in Guyana has been almost four years in the making. Naively intending that it would be complete in time for the country's fiftieth anniversary of political independence in 2016, we did not anticipate how much work goes into curating and preparing an edited collection of this size for publication. While the final product contains 18 chapters, we began even more ambitiously in our attempt to cover themes and events, so that the overall project was even larger and more demanding than its current length would indicate. So, while we are considerably beyond our own deadlines, not to mention those of the publishers, we are at once relieved and thrilled to have finally reached the finish line.

This project would not have been possible without the generous support of many colleagues. To our contributors who have participated from the outset, those who contributed new work for the collection and those who consented to have their essays reprinted in the volume, we thank you for your unending patience and support through this process. Thank you also to the dozens of reviewers who generously reviewed the submissions, and whose care and rigour have immeasurably improved the quality of the volume. We owe an immense debt of gratitude to Carol Lawes, whose meticulous copyediting skills and professionalism have made all the difference. Thank you as well to Sergey Lobachev for a splendid and swift indexing job. Finally, we are deeply grateful to the incredible Guyanese artist Stanley Greaves, who upon hearing of the project immediately agreed that we could go through his art work, and whose acrylic on Canvas, *Abary Pay Table* (2013) graces the cover of this text.

The Ian Randle Publishers team has been extraordinarily supportive from the start, and we would like to especially thank Christine Randle who expressed enthusiasm for this project when it was just in proposal form and who was committed to seeing us through to publication.

In December 2018, a successful no confidence motion brought the life of the 2015 coalition government to a premature end, an outcome that has been challenged in the courts and, as this book goes to press, is headed to the Caribbean Court of Justice for a final determination of whether the motion was legally valid. In the midst of yet another political stalemate, we give thanks to those Guyanese who have steadfastly refused to toe one or the other two party line, those who have fought for an expansion of our political imaginations, often at immense sacrifice and risk to their personal lives and professional careers, in some cases even at risk of their lives. Many are still among us, and many remain in Guyana. We remain inspired by and dedicate this collection to their dreams and their struggles for what Martin Carter describes as 'a little freedom, different from this.'

Arif Bulkan
St Augustine, Trinidad & Tobago, April 2019.
Alissa Trotz
Toronto, Canada, April 2019.

Acronyms and Abbreviations

AFAPA	Aroaima Forest Producers Association
AFC	Alliance for Change
ALC	Amerindian Lands Commission
AML/CFT	Anti-Money Laundering and Countering the Financing of Terrorism
APNU	A Partnership for National Unity
ASCRIA	African Society for Cultural Relations with Independent Africa
BCL	Barama Company Ltd
CADRES	Caribbean Development Research Services Inc
CAP	Conservancy Adaptation Project
CARICOM	Caribbean Community
CARIFLAGS	Caribbean Forum for Lesbians, All-Sexuals and Gays
CDC	Commonwealth Development Corporation
CDO	Community Development Officer
CFATF	Caribbean Financial Action Task Force
CIA	Central Intelligence Agency
CIDA	Canadian International Development Agency
CPI	Corruption Perceptions Index
CTMP	Central Timber Manufacturing Plant
DFID	Department for International Development
DTL	Demerara Timbers Limited
EAB	Elections Assistance Bureau
ERC	Ethnic Relations Commission
ERP	Economic Recovery Programme
EU	European Union
EUTR	European Union Timber Regulation
FAA	Financial Administration and Audit
FAO	Food and Agricultural Organization
FATF	Financial Action Task Force
FCH	Feed, Clothes, and House Ourselves
FDI	Foreign Direct Investment
FIC	Forest Industries Corporation
FIU	Financial Intelligence Unit
FLEGT	Forest Law Enforcement, Governance and Trade
FMA	Fiscal Management and Accountability
FPA	Forest Products Association
FPTP	First Past the Post
GAIBANK	Guyana Cooperative Agricultural and Industrial Development Bank
GAPE	Guyana Association of Professional Engineers
GCC	Guyana Credit Corporation

GEA	Guyana Energy Agency
GECOM	Guyana Elections Commission
GEF	Guyana Equality Forum
GFC	Guyana Forestry Commission
GGMC	Guyana Geology and Mines Commission
GHRA	Guyana Human Rights Association
GIFT	Guyana Indian Foundation Trust
GIHA	Guyana Indian Heritage Association
GINRIS	Guyana Integrated Natural Resources Information Service
GLSC	Guyana Lands and Surveys Commission
GMC	Guyana Marketing Corporation
GMSA	Guyana Manufacturers and Services Association
GNBS	Guyana National Bureau of Standards
GRA	Guyana Revenue Authority
GRDB	Guyana Rice Development Board
GTU	Guyana Trans United
GT&T	Guyana Telephone and Telegraph
GUARD	Guyanese Action for Reform and Democracy
GUYSTAC	Guyana State Agencies
Ha	Hectare
HCV	High Conservation Value
HDI	Human Development Index
HPS	Head of the Presidential Secretariat
IACAC	Inter-American Convention against Corruption
ICAC	Institute of Chartered Accountants of the Caribbean
IFAC	International Federation of Accountants
IFMAS	Integrated Financial Management and Accounting System
IICA	Inter-American Institute for Agricultural Cooperation
ILO	International Labour Organization
IMC	Interim Management Committees
IMF	International Monetary Fund
IP	Indigenous People
IPA	Interpretative Phenomenological Analysis
IPSAS	International Public Sector Accounting Standards
IRO	Inter-Religious Organization
ITTO	International Tropical Timber Organization
IUCN	World Conservation Union
JSC	Judicial Services Commission
LAPOP	Latin American Public Opinion Project
LCDS	Low Carbon Development Strategy
LGBTIQ+	Lesbian, Gay, Bisexual, Transgender, Intersex, and Queer
LSS	Land Settlement Schemes
LTR	Lands, Territories And Resources

Mha	Million Hectares
MMA	Mahaica-Mahaicony-Abary Scheme
MSMNPA	Men Who Have Sex with Men No Political Agenda
NCN	National Communications Network
NCW	National Congress of Women
NDIA	Ministry of Agriculture and National Irrigation and Drainage Authority
NICIL	National Industrial and Commercial Investments Ltd
NPAS	National Protected Areas System
NPTAB	National Procurement and Tender Administration Board
NRDD	North Rupununi District Development Board
NREAC	Natural Resources and Environment Advisory Committee
NRMP	Natural Resources Management Planning
OAS	Organization of American States
ODA	Overseas Development Agency
PAC	Public Accounts Committee
PCD	Patriotic Coalition for Democracy
PNC	People's National Congress
PNC/R	People's National Congress/Reform
PPP	People's Progressive Party
PPP/C	People's Progressive Party/Civic
PRSP	Poverty Reduction Strategy Paper
REDD+	Reducing Emissions from Deforestation and Forest Degradation
ROAR	Rise, Organise and Rebuild
RRI	Rights and Resources Initiative
RSA	Representative Sample Area
SASOD	Students against Sexual Orientation Discrimination
SFEP	State Forest Exploratory Permit
SFM	Sustainable Forest Management
SIMAP	Social Impact Amelioration Programme
TIP	Trafficking in Persons
TPL	Toolsie Persaud Ltd
TSA	Timber Sales Agreement
TUF	The United Force
U-RAP	University of the West Indies Rights Action Project
UNCAC	United Nations Convention against Corruption
UNDP	United Nations Development Fund
UNFCCC	United Nations Framework Convention on Climate Change
UPR	Universal Periodic Review
USAID	United States Agency for International Development
UWI	University of the West Indies
WADN	Women's Agro-Processors Development Network
WEDO	Women's Environment and Development Organization

WGEC	Women and Gender Equality Commission
WPA	Working People's Alliance
WRI	World Resources Institute
WRSM	Women's Revolutionary Socialist Movement
WTO	World Trade Organization

Introduction
Arif Bulkan and D. Alissa Trotz

This collection examines the period following the transition to political democracy in 1992, when on October 5 Guyana held its first free and fair elections since 1964, paving the way for the 54 per cent win at the polls by the People's Progressive Party (PPP). This heralded the return from the political wilderness of its leader, Cheddi Jagan, who was sworn in four days later as president of Guyana. It was an historic moment for this elder political statesman, who at the height of the anticolonial period had represented the aspirations of a multiracial movement that centred the experiences of the ordinary people. That upon his death five years later and at a time of growing political turmoil, his funeral cortege would be spontaneously stopped in Buxton, now a predominantly African-Guyanese community, so that villagers could pay their respects, was a sign of the deep respect and affection with which he was regarded by Guyanese across the political divide.

This period of renewed optimism that was dubbed 'the restoration of democracy,'[1] was a far cry from the political turmoil that had gripped the country in 1953, when the British, backed by the Americans, suspended the recently enacted British Guiana Constitution, sent in troops, and jailed political leaders in response to the electoral success of a self-declared Marxist political party and the appointment of Cheddi Jagan as premier. The Secretary of State for the Colonies Oliver Lyttleton unapologetically disclosed at the time that 'Her Majesty's Government are not going to allow a communist state to be organised within the British Commonwealth.'[2] Accompanying the suspension was a slew of emergency measures, which heralded the restoration of executive powers in the governor and simultaneously nullified those of the newly elected members.

Arguably, however, the most damaging aspect of the campaign of external destabilisation orchestrated by the UK and US governments was the undermining of the multiracial aspirations represented by the unprecedented success of the PPP at the 1953 polls. To this end, they sabotaged the unity of the PPP by actively enabling the departure of Forbes Burnham, who established an alternative political party, the People's National Congress (PNC). The consequences for the country were catastrophic, heralding the fissure of the PPP along racialised lines, resulting in politically inspired violence that tore the coast apart and arrested nascent developments of national unity. This fragmentation stoked by external forces eager to ensure that independence did not lead to transformation, has been one of the country's more enduring and tragic legacies.[3] Independence would be eventually 'granted' in May 1966 under the more palatable (to the British and American governments) PNC, which managed to defeat the PPP only by a post-election coalition in 1964. Thereafter, the PNC remained in power for an uninterrupted 28 years through the manipulation of successive elections.[4] PNC rule evolved into a menacing and authoritarian period where democratic outlets were stifled and restricted. Fundamental human rights were routinely violated, and the worst of these excesses included the harassment, intimidation, persecution, and even assassination of anti-government activists at the height of the popular anti-dictatorial struggle.[5]

It was ironic, and telling, that Cheddi Jagan's eventual return to political power represented the culmination of the work of a well-organised network of local and diasporic Guyanese appeals to the international community that focused attention on the long history of electoral fraud. It also would not have been possible without the covert and overt assistance of the US government, with the Carter Center heading an elections observation mission to the country in 1992. The restoration of electoral democracy arrived on the heels of a series of reforms implemented by Desmond Hoyte, leader of the PNC and executive president after the death of Forbes Burnham in 1985, as part of a wider process of political and economic liberalisation. With the changed geopolitical realities at the end of the 1980s, there was no longer a Cold War impetus to support opposition to a PPP victory. In fact, and notwithstanding a declaration shortly after victory at the polls that the party remained committed to the principles of Marxism-Leninism (it continues to define itself as a left-wing political party), the incoming administration reassured Western donors by faithfully continuing and deepening the course of action initiated under President Hoyte in 1985, that would see Guyana reverse its ultimately failed attempt at co-operative socialism and rapidly open up the economy through a structural adjustment programme implemented under the auspices of the International Monetary Fund.

In a discussion of the fiftieth anniversary of Jamaican independence, the late economist Norman Girvan (2012) reflected on what he describes as the 'policy recolonization' of the Caribbean state via the requirements imposed by international financial institutions, suggesting that the term 'In-Dependence' might better reflect the contemporary economic and geopolitical realities facing the region. Girvan's disillusion with the post-independent Jamaican state stemmed from his sense that it had been completely gutted 'of its capacity to influence economic life'. But such an emphasis may well obscure precisely the reconfiguration of the state in the context of economic and political neoliberalisation.[6] Fundamentally loosening the state's grip on the economy has not, in the Guyanese case, necessarily meant that the state has surrendered all control (under co-operative socialism the state was the principal employer, which served as a significant modality of stifling discontent and opposition to what was effectively one-party rule). As several chapters in this volume elaborate, what has emerged is a system of free-market patronage in the years after Cheddi Jagan's death, described by Tarron Khemraj as an elected oligarchy moulding a supportive business class. Most of the post-1992 period has been dominated by President Bharrat Jagdeo, who replaced Janet Jagan (herself president between 1997 and 1999 after her husband's death). PPP rule under President Jagdeo has been described by economist C.Y. Thomas as 'a government for itself', referring to the use of state resources as a means of personal enrichment of the political elite and their close associates. As Arif Bulkan details, Jagdeo further concentrated executive power over all aspects of national decision-making during his 12 years in office, notwithstanding Cheddi Jagan's promise in his address at the opening of the sixth Parliament in 1992 to purge the worst excesses of the PNC era, by ensuring that '[o]ur nation [will] be rid forever of bureaucratic/command type government and bureaucratic/command type management.'

Analysts of the Caribbean have eloquently argued that to dismiss elections as simply bourgeois democratic rights is to miss the historic struggles of working peoples, and in the case of Guyana, to overlook both the decades of electoral fraud as well as the opposition to dictatorial rule that would see the country mobilised across racial and class lines for the first time since 1953, inspired by the example of Walter Rodney and the formation of the Working People's Alliance (WPA).[7] But it is also the case that elections, particularly in a Westminster system, supplant or subvert the impetus to ensure meaningful participation across social divides. This takes particular form in Guyana, where the return to elections 'free and fair and free from fear' also demonstrated the pernicious grip of racialised voting in the polling booth, a grip that would not be sufficiently loosened to threaten PPP rule for 19 years. Opposition declarations of commitment to a government of national unity involving all major political players disappeared once a winner had been declared, with President Jagan avowing in his address to Parliament that 'national and working-class unity and racial/ethnic cohesiveness' would instead be delivered under the leadership of the PPP–Civic (PPP/C).[8]

Racialised tensions have also been part of the political landscape of the post-1992 period, threatening the tentative alliances forged during the broad-based efforts at mobilisation in the final years of the PNC era. Amidst charges of racial discrimination under a PPP government, combined with a sense that a deterministic racial arithmetic could potentially permanently exclude African-Guyanese from political and economic power, such tensions have erupted during elections into violence against Indian-Guyanese. The violence has been product and producer of the cycle of racial mistrust and fear. In the face of a jailbreak in 2002 that terrorised Indian-Guyanese communities (and that also took aim at African-Guyanese who raised their voices in opposition), the government offered tacit support to a shadow grouping, the Phantom Squad, to bring the situation under control. The country would witness a wave of violence and fatalities, with African-Guyanese men comprising the vast majority of the hundreds killed over the next four or five years.

Those in power did not shy away from invoking racialised appeals during times of crisis. In July 2012, police confronted a large demonstration of women, children, and men from the bauxite mining town of Linden, protesting the removal of electricity subsidies from a community devastated by the decline and eventual privatisation of the bauxite industry over several decades. The confrontation resulted in the death of three men.

Editorials and other reports in the state-controlled media categorically refused a narrative that linked the crisis of economic collapse and social reproduction to the protest, portraying it instead as simply a pretext controlled by the opposition for African-Guyanese to legitimise anti-Indian aggression. (The 2011 elections had delivered the PPP a minority position in the national assembly – an unprecedented breakthrough given the racial political stalemate up until then.) These reports even went as far as to make direct references to the internecine disturbances of 1964 when Indian-Guyanese had been violently ejected from the area (see Trotz 2014). In this respect, then, the restoration of formal democracy did not necessarily imply substantive correction of the problems that had enabled the electoral fraud of the PNC era.

There are few book-length analyses of post-independence Guyana, and those that do exist tend to focus on or stop at the period of PNC hegemony.[9] This volume, while not an exhaustive account of the PPP years, fills a critical gap in our understanding of contemporary Guyanese political, economic, and social life. It presents a discrete period for analysis, though within a larger context where historical divisions, persistent constitutional manipulation, and systemic and institutional failures have produced successive periods of authoritarianism and corruption.

Constitutionalism, Democracy, and Governance

In his opening chapter, Arif Bulkan sets out to demonstrate the legal and constitutional architecture that has enabled authoritarian rule in Guyana. The 1980 Constitution – delivered via a fraudulent referendum – is a 'patchwork' of borrowings from socialist constitutions and the Westminster prototype, which resulted in a hybrid presidential system thrust awkwardly upon the inherited framework. An American-style president, where in one person was merged both the head of state and head of government, presides over a Westminster system, which is noted for its strong overlaps between the legislature and executive. Thus, the most potent aspects of each system were adopted while crucial safeguards were jettisoned, resulting in a hybrid product that is neither entirely parliamentary nor presidential, but instead strongly authoritarian. With control vested in the executive president over the cabinet, civil service, legislature, and ultimately his or her own party, no individual or entity possesses the legal backing to contradict or otherwise check such extensive power and privilege vested in this position.

Stridently opposed to the executive presidency when in opposition, once in power the PPP did not demonstrate a similar appetite to transform the constitutional framework, notwithstanding President Cheddi Jagan's commitment in his inaugural parliamentary address in 1992 to a 'new constitution fashioned by the Guyanese people'. A costly and extensive reform process precipitated by the post-election crisis of 1997 did little to realign these imbalances. By simply fiddling at the margins and instituting palliatives like weak commissions and strengthened rights regimes, at best the changes could only tinker with the manifestations of authoritarianism, not its causes. Bulkan documents how an already imbalanced power structure was reinforced under the presidency of Bharrat Jagdeo, through further miniaturisation of and outright disregard for the few constitutional mechanisms and processes that promote neutrality and transparency. This left the executive presidency with enormous unchecked powers, accountable to none – a state of affairs that inexorably led to rampant mismanagement, nepotism, and corruption.

The absence of public accountability in relation to financial management that Bulkan outlines is the subject of Anand Goolsarran's reflections. In 1992 the PPP inherited audited public accounts that were a decade in arrears. Goolsarran, who served as the auditor-general between 1990 and 2004, argues that this time-lag persisted, compounded by persistent and uncorrected flaws in reporting and a lack of co-operation with the Audit Office that hampered its ability to perform effectively and independently on behalf of Parliament in overseeing the financial audits of publicly funded entities in Guyana. While the period saw the establishment of several mechanisms – for instance the integrity commission and the passage of the Financial Administration and Audit (Amendment) Act – these were largely symbolic moves that promised and offered the appearance of financial accountability and openness, but which were never substantively implemented.

In her examination of the largely non-functioning local government system, the challenges identified by Esther McIntosh mirror those that undermine meaningful participation at the national level. Both post-independence governments – the PNC between 1966 and 1992 and the PPP/C between 1992 and 2015, following the restoration of formal democracy at the national level that returned the PPP to power – have overseen the miniaturisation of local democratic processes, leading to extremely low levels of citizen confidence in the effectiveness of engaging at this scale. Notwithstanding Article 13 of the Constitution which calls for the creation of an inclusionary democracy through the provision of 'increasing opportunities for the participation of citizens, and their organisations in the management and decision-making processes of the State, with particular emphasis on those areas of decision-making that directly affect their wellbeing,' local government elections were held only once under each administration, immediately after accession to power. Despite a formal commitment to decentralisation and acceptance of devolved government, specific action in this regard remained non-existent. McIntosh identifies the centrality of party politics as a key factor militating against the creation of a robust local democratic process, noting the impetus to non-cooperation between political parties on the question of local government reform. Consequently, coercion and patronage remain key in the distribution of resources to communities, reinforcing the centralisation of state power.

Legacies of Racial Dysfunction

Perhaps the most striking feature characterising regime change from dictatorship to electoral democracy is the continuity of authoritarian and unaccountable structures, patterns that cannot be understood outside of the context of a heavily polarised political landscape. Tarron Khemraj describes the post-1992 period as characterised by a system of elected oligarchy, in which the PPP moved towards an explicitly pro-business position while managing to retain control over its electoral base for four straight elections. He argues that the winner-take-all Westminster system takes particular form within Guyana – facing endogenous and exogenous development challenges from its insertion into the global economy, as well as the costs of draining and maintaining an extensive coastal system – where the competition for state power has historically been divided along racialised lines. Such division is institutionally entrenched by a constitution that, by foreclosing the possibility of post-election alliances, fosters what he refers to as a 'non-cooperative equilibrium,' in which fears of splitting the vote keep would-be party defectors in line in a contest for state power that seems resolutely zero-sum such as was the case for two decades of PPP rule. Ultimately, the centrality of ethnic mobilisation has tended to make Guyanese politics both relatively predictable and at times politically volatile, a theme taken up by Rishee Thakur in his discussion of what he terms low intensity violence with periodic eruptions that characterised elections in the post-1992 period.

Reflecting upon the crime wave that swept the country between 2002 and 2004, Thakur argues that this period of sustained violence (marked by the introduction of high powered weapons on the streets and fuelled by a transnationalised illicit economy in drugs and firearms) must be placed within a longer post-war history of internecine violence, although he is careful to suggest that it has so far not led to the upheavals and racial disturbances of the 1960s. The retreat to a winner-take-all approach dashed initial hopes for a government of national unity, with a stubborn racial arithmetic delivering a majority victory to the largely Indo-Guyanese supported PPP in elections held between 1997 and 2006. PNC-led opposition to the 1997 and 2001 results fuelled post-electoral protests and violence in those years by African-Guyanese, whose fears of being permanently shut out of the political system (and thus from access to racialised patronage networks via the state) spilled over into the streets, with Indian-Guyanese businesses and individuals being the principal targets of attacks. The clear ability of the PNC to shut down parts of the country brought the PPP to the negotiating table, delivering some limited electoral and constitutional reforms, but as Arif Bulkan's chapter indicates, the dialogue failed to accomplish a fundamental shift to a system of shared governance.

To be sure, privileging race as the dominant explanatory framework leaves little space to interrogate the processes through which (what Tarron Khemraj describes as) a bi-communal society, materialises or gets taken for granted. It also forecloses attention to how these ideas of difference are unevenly experienced. Focusing on the bodily and sexual assaults that clearly singled out Indo-Guyanese women in the aftermath of the 1997 and 2001 elections, Alissa Trotz explores how gender and sexuality are constitutive of racialised Guyanese identities, such that attacking women becomes key to underlining a community's inability to reproduce and defend itself. On the other hand, as letters to the media decrying the targeting of Indian women revealed, deeply heteronormative masculinist rhetorics of protection situate survivors as silent victims, whose bodies become the grounds for redrawing rigid boundaries around 'community'. Moreover, a selective focus (in this case, on inter-racial violence) renders invisible other forms of violence that also institute women as subordinate and inferior (like the violence – domestic and otherwise – that takes place within communities whose boundaries are reproduced precisely via the regulation of women). In asking how we might avoid approaches that reduce women to collateral damage by seeing racial difference as *a priori* and racialised conflict and violence as a given, Trotz turns her attention to some examples of anti-violence activism that address women as a diverse collectivity, draw attention to the interpenetration of structural and discursive violence, and foreground the gendered work of social reproduction as one way of elaborating a tentative politics of connection.

If it is important for academics to interrogate rather than unproblematically reproduce race as an unchanging given in the Guyanese landscape, Percy Hintzen's chapter takes up the question of whose interests are served by the narrative of racial dysfunction and distrust. Hintzen's interest is with nationalism's compatibility with the Caribbean's conscription into neocolonial relations. In Guyana, he argues, international intervention in the pre-independence period undercut incipient efforts at popular mobilisation that crossed race divides and potentially challenged the county's peripheral status in the international arena. During the years of the Burnham dictatorship, economic isolationism by the West reduced the country to a basket case while keeping the PPP – perceived as the more radical option – out of power. In the post-1980s, post–Cold War era, Hintzen argues that the 'idiom of race' in Guyana acts as a disciplining mechanism that focuses popular attention on securing control of the state for 'one's side', while appeals to the international community to verify elections, mediate conflicts between the dominant political forces, and shore up the local economy, in fact, work to secure the interests of global capital (for which the language of good governance, transparency, and democracy serve as alibis).

Insecurities of Neoliberalism

What then have been the consequences for everyday life of the increasing liberalisation of the Guyanese economy? Writing in the tradition set out by Walter Rodney's *History of the Guyanese Working People*, Wazir Mohammed takes an historical perspective to the question of the place of rice and sugar in the lives of African and Indian Guyanese. His analysis challenges reductive culturalist explanations of the division of labour in both sectors, reveals how differences between formerly enslaved and indentured workers were actively produced under colonial rule, and offers important new insights into the ways in which rice in particular was intertwined in the lives of firstly African and then Indian farmers as they sought to carve out spaces of autonomy from the sugar plantation. Mohammed's elaboration of a series of disempowering labour and land laws that were put in place in the immediate post-emancipation period to maintain the monocrop sugar industry, underlines the point Hintzen makes about the disciplining of the working people and the subjugation of the local economy to external interests. (As he notes, the emergence of rice on a large scale can only be understood against the context of the decline of sugar on the global market in the closing years of the nineteenth century). Nor has the shaping/disfiguring force of these externalities abated in the post-independence period. The historical overview, Mohammed argues, thus provides a context to locate the structural dislocations – unprecedented displacement of rice and sugar producers – engendered by economic liberalisation policies inaugurated from the mid-1980s.

In his assessment of vulnerabilities engendered by neoliberalism, Clement Henry cautions against an exclusive focus on income-based data as an indicator of poverty, focusing on the period between 1988 and 2013 that saw the introduction of structural adjustment measures and the belated rollout of a Social Impact Amelioration Programme that provided some relief to especially disadvantaged populations. Studies of poverty that emphasised monetary measures showed a decrease in extreme and moderate poverty between 1993 and 1999 (with the decline stalling after this period), although saying little about how poverty was actually experienced. Disaggregating these figures also reveals a far more uneven landscape; there is regional variation, for instance, with three regions actually seeing an increase in poverty between 1992 and 2006. Henry argues instead for a multidimensional (human capabilities) approach to poverty that pays attention to the wider contexts in which households are situated, finding significant concerns on questions of societal, political, environmental, and health security.

The human security survey that Henry draws on did not include education, a sector that, in fact, has been one of the prime targets of state disinvestment – what Diana Abraham refers to in her chapter as the 'unfreeing' of education – following the adoption of a structural adjustment programme. Though in the 1970s free education from nursery to university was guaranteed, by the 1990s tertiary fees were reinstituted as part of a cost recovery programme, while a creeping return to private schools at all levels would eventually find protection through the constitutional reform process. Article 149H, which provides that '[e]very child is guaranteed free primary and secondary education in schools owned or funded by the State,' is followed by Article 149I which stipulates that 'no person shall be hindered in the enjoyment of the right to establish a private school which shall be under regulation by the State.' Notwithstanding official reassurances, in fact, the opening up of the education sector to for-profit schools has drastically undermined the *aim* of free education – to ensure that all children have equal access to quality education across geography, class, race, gender, and other markers. Focusing specifically on the impact on the teaching profession, Abraham describes a situation in which poor salaries, decrepit conditions, and deteriorating infrastructure in the public system lead to unsustainably high levels of attrition as teachers migrate overseas or (for those who remain in the country) seek employment in private schools. Others move between sectors, which includes finding work that represents a professional demotion but an increase in salary. Several supplement their inadequate salaries through private classes, giving rise to a pervasive 'lessons culture' that starts early in the morning before school and continues long after the end of the school day. In a context in which teaching is no longer seen as a viable or highly respected career, attracting suitably trained candidates has also become a challenge, compromising the quality of public educational delivery. The selective reprivatisation also has an uneven distributional effect, with more devastating effects in economically marginalised communities where families cannot afford extra lessons and where there is an absence of well-connected alumni organisations to subsidise the drastic reduction of state spending on educational infrastructure.

Ironically, while public disinvestment seems to be fast creating a two-tier system for teachers and pupils alike, emphasising Guyana as home to an educated workforce has been one of the ways in which the state has sought to court foreign investment. Trotz, Mirchandani and Khan turn their attention to transnational customer mediated service work as a site that reveals what the authors describe as the sovereignty of global capital. Advertised by the government as a country that is open for business, Guyana's locational advantage is sold to would-be investors not just as a nearshore site with proximity to and within the same time zone as North America, but crucially as home to a literate population that speaks relatively unaccented English, able to communicate easily with customers, thus eliminating the need for extensive language training as takes place in other countries in the Global South. Domestically, call centre work is officially promoted as providing white-collar jobs for educated youth. These official win-win narratives are belied by employee accounts; they describe their jobs as dead end and temporary and see themselves not as a professionalised service class in a fulfilling career with prospects for social mobility, but rather as a contingent and disposable workforce facing few choices in the local economy. Call centres are heavily feminised, both in terms of being dominated by women (due to gendered stereotypes about who is most suited for the emotional labour that customer service work requires) as well as in relation to the poorly paid and demeaning conditions that face all workers. Far from being a transformative solution to high rates of youth unemployment and the attrition of the population through out-migration, these 'problems' are, in fact, the very conditions of possibility that enable the state to deliver a captive (reserve army) labour force where call centres have the upper hand in setting the terms of engagement.

But today it is not so much Guyana's coast as the interior of the country – heralded as a contemporary El Dorado – that is seen as a prime site for foreign investment. Clement Henry points to unacceptably high levels of environmental insecurity among the population, particularly in hinterland regions that are home to the vast majority of Amerindian peoples. Some contexts for such anxieties are elaborated in Janette Bulkan's discussion of the management of state forests and lands during the PPP's tenure in office, as they pertain specifically to the forestry sector and logging concessions. She argues that the capture of the sector by a small elite was facilitated by deepening executive control over natural resources inherited from the previous PNC administration. Lack of oversight in relation to laws and policies, secrecy, and discretionary allocation of state lands have resulted in the unprecedented privatisation of forest resources with little public benefit. While communal land title awards were increased during the PPP's time in office, Amerindians have no inherent rights to territory and resources, ensuring that in the current dispensation indigenous stewardship of the land comes second to extractive industry sponsored by foreign capital. There has been no significant employment of Guyanese; little to no value added; and indiscriminate logging for export which has hastened the degradation of forest resources and endangered several commercially valuable tree species. Remarkably, this unsustainable extractive-oriented approach existed simultaneously with the government's pursuit of a Low-Carbon Development Strategy under then President Bharratt Jagdeo, through which the international community was courted to compensate Guyana for maintaining its forest cover. This strategy enabled the government to secure additional payments from overseas donors (primarily the Norwegian government), while – in the absence of proper oversight and enforcement – business as usual continued apace in mining and logging sectors in the country.

The Politics of Gender and Sexuality

The ravages of neoliberalism have been unevenly distributed. In particular, much of the burden of social reproduction – as the state has retreated from what were already limited forms of social provision prior to the imposition of structural adjustment programmes – has fallen on women. The chapters in this section consider the processes of gendered differentiation that work to secure female subordination, despite constitutional and other legislative acts that guarantee women's equality. Savitri Persaud considers the constitutive work of violence in producing gendered subjects/subjection. Reflecting upon the murder of a disabled Indian-Guyanese woman, Radika Singh, at the hands of residents of a neighbouring, predominantly African-Guyanese community which she had wandered into, she explores the discursive conditions of possibility through which violence against women in Guyana materialises and is made intelligible. Singh's death was explained as a necessary and *foretold* response to the fact that she was an Ole Higue. A mythical figure of Guyanese folklore, the Ole Higue is a woman who shapeshifts between human form and a ball of fire, who feeds off the blood of children, and who must be killed after an elaborate ritual of capture. The Ole Higue's alleged vampiric propensity to feed on children symbolises her threat to potentiality; these are the non-reproductive women whose threat to the future of the nation must be extinguished. In effect, her presence foreshadows her death. Directing our attention to the discursive mechanisms through which othering is produced, Persaud considers how Singh's psychiatric disability was so easily misrecognised as 'madness' and spirit possession, removing her agency and rendering her a necessary target for violence. Media reports (stories, editorials, letters) converge in displacing responsibility for the killing – either the residents' fears were understandable, or they were trapped by superstition into taking a woman's life. In none of these narratives is the issue of the wider enabling environment that produces women – unevenly – as violable, foregrounded. Drawing on the Ole Higue section of a Mashramani parade in 2014 (a national celebration that marks the country's becoming a republic), Persaud asks us to consider how we are implicated in a national patrimony which differentiates some women as parasitic and predatory, underlining how intervening in these narratives is crucial to interrupting their deadly effects.

Ironically, the Mashramani float that incorporated the Ole Higue was sponsored by the female minster within the ministry of labour, human services and security at the time, underlining the need for a national conversation on gender, and raising important questions about how this might be accomplished within the formal political arena. This is the subject of Natalie Persadie's chapter, which notes that Guyanese women have had a long history of involvement in politics in Guyana and were centrally involved in early political party formation in the anti-colonial period. For example, Janet Jagan, one of the founders of the PPP, was among the first women elected to Parliament in 1953 and, following the death of her husband Cheddi Jagan, would go on to serve as president of Guyana from 1997–99. For the most part, however, such activism did not translate into leadership levels in formal political institutions, except within the women's arms of the two major political parties that enjoyed little autonomy to carve out space to work across hardened lines in a deeply polarising context. Against this backdrop, Persadie assesses the deeply ambitious post-1992 initiatives to incorporate gender into the formal political sphere. Those entailed the establishment of the Women and Gender Equality Commission as well as the adoption of a quota system – the first of its kind in the Caribbean – to ensure that a minimum of one-third of the electoral lists comprised women. The results, she argues, have been disappointing on both numerical and substantive grounds. Women's presence on electoral lists did not translate into parliamentary representation, as selection was entirely at the discretion of the party leader. It is only since 2006 that the minimum standard of one third women parliamentarians has been met. Gender equality is now routinely included in political party manifestos, but in the absence of specific commitments and targets, such promises are little more than a *pro forma* gesture, raising the question of the effectiveness of women's arms if they fail to even broaden access within the political parties with which they are affiliated. On the question of whether female presence might lead to the enactment of policies that tackle deep-seated gender inequalities, Persadie points to the debilitating effects of winner-take-all tribalism, which demands party loyalty as a first order priority, thus inhibiting cross-party caucusing on key issues. With the rare exception, party identity trumps gender affiliation. Significantly, change seems most likely and long-lasting when female parliamentarians work with, or are consistently pressured to act from, the outside – as clearly demonstrated in the passage into law of the Sexual Offences Act of 2010. This initiative was led and developed by women activists across several organisations in consultation with the government, and found an advocate at the time in Priya Manickchand, then minister of human services and social security. (Implementation and enforcement remain significant obstacles.) While not underestimating the significance of making women more visible in parliamentary politics – through quotas or other measures – this example suggests an expanded sense of the political; one that simultaneously attends to class, race, sexuality, ability, and other social relations that render women a complex category to begin with, lest we end up privileging a strategy in which a politics of recognition takes precedence over a politics of transformation. Is the struggle one to access normative decision-making structures in what Arif Bulkan has argued is a deeply deformed, unaccountable and authoritarian system, or fundamentally to transform them?

The limit of recognition is also the subject of Shanya Cordis's discussion of what is described as the 'unthought position' of Amerindians that informs how the state arbitrates indigenous relations to the land (even as it appeared to put those relationships on a new footing with the establishment of a ministry of Amerindian – now Indigenous People's – affairs in 1993). Rather than a pathway to securing livelihoods and autonomies, Cordis argues that in fact statutory recognition of indigenous land titles in Guyana reproduces conditions of coloniality in the service of neoliberal extractive regimes. Post-independence governments extend a colonial logic of protectionism and intervention, which limits the rights and property of Amerindians through an uncritical re-inscription of inherited ideas about the hinterland and its communities. Far from inhabiting an inherently neutral and objective domain, legal and spatial techniques of power – contested demarcation and titling processes that sideline local knowledges; the separation of indigenous territory into 'titled' and 'untitled' lands – extend state control over indigenous space, which in the current moment has meant opening up the interior to the penetration of foreign capital in mining and logging and increasing environmental and social vulnerability. Cordis reads such techniques as the materialisation of a deeply racialised and sexualised territorialising logic that positions the hinterland and the people who dwell there as backward and in need of development. The chapter details how Amerindian women are represented in the coastlander imagination as either suited for sex work in mining camps or requiring paternalistic protection as victims of trafficking and sexual exploitation. Cordis also argues that the racialisation of Amerindian women is part of the process through which hierarchical social orders are re-inscribed in relation to place and territory. Standing in metonymic relation to the land, both are considered violable and exploitable.

Alternative Engagements with the State

Shanya Cordis's chapter asks us to envision different ways of being, by centring indigenous epistemologies, collective memory and sense of place – a challenge Hollis France takes up through her discussion of the Wowetta Women's Agro-processing Cassava Enterprise, a women's group in the North Rupununi involved in a cooperative cassava production business. Farine, cassava bread and cassareep (the staple ingredient in the popular dish, pepperpot) are marketed primarily in hinterland regions, as well as occasionally at regional and national food fairs. France is careful not to downplay what the cassava enterprise is up against: logistical and infrastructural challenges that are made more difficult to resolve by an international funding environment that privileges a neoliberal microenterprise-driven approach to relatively small-scale groupings like Wowetta; the politics of state patronage and paternalism which dispenses resources in the interior to gain and maintain loyalty to the ruling party; and the dominance of an extractive, low value added approach to interior 'development,' driven by large scale foreign investment and in which mining and logging are prioritised. What is remarkable is the enterprise's seemingly stubborn insistence on not being in thrall to a purely profit-oriented and individualised approach, engaging instead in a ground to market process that France describes as serving as an opportunity for the women to collectively explore how 'markets will work for them instead of solely acting on them'. Indigenous knowledge regarding land use and inputs is a necessary point of departure, in which stewardship, rather than possession and exploitation of nature, is emphasised, offering a model of sustainable relationships to land that is not territorialising but based upon an ethic of care. This informs women's decision-making practices as well as the development of their production strategies and networks, such as labour arrangements based on a rotating basis; explicit attention to social reproduction and unwaged work; the development of a two-tier pricing system to ensure farine remains affordable and locally sourced; and other market arrangements that prioritise collectivist norms and community welfare. By interrupting neoliberal approaches to economic development with their privileged emphasis on the profit-seeking, rational individual economic actor, the Wowetta women offer a hopeful example of indigenous resilience in the face of sustained intrusion into Amerindian communities and lives by the state.

Back on the coast, Sarah Vaughn examines possibilities for reimagining affiliation and citizenship beyond the scripted (and seemingly predictable) politics of racialisation, through an exploration of the environmental dimensions of disaster capitalism. Walter Rodney's opening account in the *History of the Guyanese Working People*, of what George Lamming has described as the humanisation of Guyana's coast through the labour of enslaved and indentured peoples, offers a stark reminder that recovering a narrow strip of land six feet below sea level is an arduous, massive, and continuous undertaking (as the chapter by Wazir Mohammed suggests, the scale of coastal management in Guyana has also been a primary mechanism through which efforts at local autonomy have been thwarted by the state), a precarity that is only intensified in the face of new threats from climate change. The disastrous flood of 2005 that affected over 60 per cent of the coastal population becomes a point of departure to consider what challenges are presented under neoliberalism when it comes to creating and maintaining coastal systems of drainage and irrigation. If floods provided the condition of possibility for the state to embark on an ambitious infrastructure adaptation project that involved partnerships with the private sector and infusions of funds from international development organisations, what unfolds is not a straightforward or coherent process in which a catastrophic event simply becomes a space-clearing gesture for the entrenchment of market fundamentalism and the private sector. Instead, disaster management seems to be a process characterised more by disjointedness than by coherence, where, against a backdrop of uncertainty and unpredictability about the specific effects of climate change on the landscape, knowledge about what to do and what kind of infrastructure is required is produced and debated by a range of actors – engineers, the private sector, farmers living in affected areas. Cautioning against premature analytical closure that assumes a 'hollowed-out public sector', Vaughn draws attention to the reconfiguration of relations between citizens and state actors over how to understand and respond to the floods in a neoliberal context. We might well ask, what new horizons of possibility and affinity might emerge in the face of a shared – if unevenly so – vulnerability to inundation?

Finally, Vidyaratha Kissoon reflects on the shifting landscape of LGBTIQ+ rights in Guyana, taking the 2015 political party manifesto promises to tackle sexual orientation discrimination as a point of departure. Earlier courageous work to provide support for and decrease stigmatisation of Guyanese living with HIV/AIDS has been extended to include tackling post-independence laws that are holdovers from colonialism and that render LGBTIQ+ persons second class citizens; engaging the constitutional reform process; and shifting the terms of public debate on same-sex desire and intimacy. As previous chapters note, recognition does not necessarily lead to justice. Pressured by sections of the Christian community, President Jagdeo refused to assent to a bill that would prohibit discrimination based on sexual orientation that had earlier been unanimously approved by Parliament. By the time the bill was presented again to a new Parliament in 2003, members were lobbied strongly from the same quarter and ultimately it was never even put to a vote. In 2012, a motion to consider the issue of decriminalisation of adult, consensual same sex activity could not get off the ground. And while there remain immense challenges in tackling homophobia and transphobia in ways that ensure the most marginalised members of LGBTIQ+ communities are heard, there are a few reasons for hope. The first is the visibility and increasing leadership of young people on this issue, best exemplified by University of Guyana students establishing Students against Sexual Orientation Discrimination (SASOD) in 2003; and older groups like Guybow and more recent ones like Guyana Trans

United, which have since emerged. Secondly, as Kissoon notes, regional and international networks have been a significant part of local organising efforts. One important example was SASOD's effort to join a case initiated by the University of the West Indies Rights Action Project (U-RAP) that launched a constitutional challenge to the laws under which several working-class persons were charged with cross-dressing for an improper purpose. Both the High Court and Court of Appeal of Guyana held that while permissible as an expression of one's sexual orientation or gender identity, cross-dressing is nonetheless a crime if done for an improper purpose. The litigants appealed to Guyana's apex court – the Caribbean Court of Justice, which heard oral arguments at the end of June 2018 and has since struck down the law. Building connections with others – indigenous persons, persons with disabilities, women, and domestic violence survivors – demonstrates recognition of the need to work on several fronts. Such an intersectional approach can undercut popular understandings that sexual orientation discrimination is a single issue, while meaningful collaboration might potentially make it more difficult for activists to see their work coopted by the mainstream international funding environment and reduced to the language of individual rights in which the social and economic ravages of neoliberalism remain unchallenged. Crucially, then, LGBTIQ+ activism in Guyana offers a tentative glimpse of something different. It is not an easy road. As SASOD founding member Joel Simpson notes, 'In a society which is marred by conflict and the abuses of power, it is not easy to try alternative ways of engagement which are not meant to destroy or humiliate.' Its promise is that it widens the scope and space of the political, beyond party loyalty in which any criticism is seen as demonstrating not independence but allegiance to 'the other side,' beyond tired and reductive conversations on race that as Percy Hintzen argues, work in the interests of global capital.

Conclusion: Plus Ça Change, Plus C'est la Même Chose?

The reductive analyses that understand and consistently explain Guyana's history and politics through the lens of race might now seem to be in need of revision given the outcomes of the 2011 and 2015 national elections. For the first time in 2011 the PPP (in its current incarnation as PPP/C) failed to win a parliamentary majority, and for the next three years until 2015 when the Party actually lost political power altogether it governed as a minority in Parliament. This could only happen under Guyana's unique electoral system where a mere plurality of votes is needed to capture the presidency. This the PPP/C managed to secure in 2011, allowing Donald Ramotar, their presidential candidate, to assume office. But two opposition parties – A Partnership for National Unity (APNU), which was a coalition consisting of the PNC and several other parties formed specifically to contest the 2011 elections, and relative newcomer, the Alliance For Change, which was formed in 2005 by defectors from the PNC, PPP, and WPA – obtained more votes than the PPP/C, and together they outnumbered the PPP/C in Parliament. By 2015, such was the discontent that the PPP/C failed even to win a plurality in the presidential election, and were finally, after 23 years of uninterrupted rule, voted out of office altogether in a free and fair election.

Many observers and commentators at the time interpreted this as an historic shift in the tribalism that has dogged Guyanese politics since the 1950s. However, a closer look at the 2015 electoral results might not support such a sanguine view. In particular, the actual numbers are telling: APNU, which joined with the Alliance for Change (AFC) this time around, won by a mere 4,506 votes. This slim margin suggests that the base of the two main parties – Indo and Afro Guyanese voting blocs – still overwhelmingly supported the PPP/C and PNC respectively. The historic outcome, then, might simply have been largely the result of changing demographics – namely, a diminishing percentage of Indo Guyanese due to steady migration and a corresponding rise in the numbers of mixed race and Indigenous Guyanese (as well as disillusioned PPP/C supporters who chose to stay home on polling day rather than cast their vote for the alternative slate). Nonetheless, despite the restraint with which a narrow PPP election defeat must be viewed, for the first time in Guyana's post-colonial history, the 2015 electoral outcome offered a glimmer of light suggesting a break from a past held captive to a rigidly racialised political identity.

Belying its moniker, however, and having seemingly ridden the wave of widespread discontent into office, the current administration has failed thus far to implement policies or usher in any semblance of national unity. Quite the contrary, like the PPP/C before it, APNU quickly rejected constitutional directives for inclusivity and accountability. A few troubling features signal that the cycle of authoritarianism continues.

Possibly the most ominous portent is the obvious disinterest in constitutional reform. This was one of the most prominent talking points of the opposition electoral campaign, borne perhaps of its marginalisation at the instance of a constitutional framework that reposed executive authority in the president and simultaneously subordinated all other arms of the government and institutions of state. Three years into its term of office, however, and enjoying the benefits of that framework, only the most tentative and desultory steps towards reform have been taken. A six-member steering committee headed by AFC chairman and prominent attorney-at-law, Nigel Hughes, was established almost immediately in August 2015 with a mandate to submit a preliminary report by December 2015. This deadline was duly met and then followed up by a final report at the end of April 2016, which was only slightly delayed due to the death of one member of the committee. Since then, however, the report – itself confidential and not released to the public – seems to be languishing somewhere as nothing else of consequence has taken place. The inaction has prompted RISE Guyana (Rise Organise and Rebuild Guyana), a self-described collection of 'free-thinking, post-racial individuals who have decided to put Guyana and Guyanese first' to lament its concern in a letter to the press that 'the impetus for constitutional reform has been lost, [and] that the coalition government, now in power, has no desire to proceed with the reforms they acknowledged were vital to promoting greater consultative democracy.'[10]

Even as it has abandoned any pretence of interest in constitutional reform, the APNU administration has seamlessly adopted the authoritarian style of its predecessor. The most disturbing manifestation of this has occurred in the treatment of electoral-related issues. Upon the resignation of Steve Surujbally as chairman of the Guyana Elections Commission (GECOM) on February 28, 2017, the vacancy at the top of this sensitive entity unleashed a period of prolonged non-cooperation, revealing an obdurate determination by the incumbent government to install only a candidate of its choice. Under the formula instituted in 2000, which represented one of the key aspects of the exhaustive constitutional reform process, the chairman is to be chosen by the president from a list of six persons, not unacceptable to him, submitted by the leader of the opposition.[11] A proviso to this section stipulated, however, that if the leader of the opposition 'fails to submit a list as provided for', the president could proceed to appoint a judge or former judge as chairman. In the aftermath of Surujbally's resignation, and having rejected two lists of names submitted by Mr Jagdeo, President Granger claimed that only a judge could be appointed chairman – a patently unsustainable interpretation of the constitutional provision that was rejected by the acting chief justice, Roxane George SC. In an action brought by a private citizen seeking an interpretation of the relevant provision, the acting chief justice ruled in July 2017 that the GECOM chairman does not necessarily have to be a judge or former judge, nor did he or she have to be qualified as such. She added that it was up to the president to determine if the persons on the list were 'fit and proper,' though she also held that in the spirit of the provision the president was required to give reasons for the rejection of any person as not being 'fit and proper'.

Following the court ruling, the leader of the opposition (LO) duly submitted a third list of names. These were all rejected once again, and on October 19, 2017, an 84-year-old former judge, James Patterson, was unilaterally appointed by President Granger as chairman of GECOM. In so doing, the President indicated that he found the third list of nominees to be unacceptable and, purporting to act under the proviso to the section, he made the appointment. Despite the ruling of acting Chief Justice George, no reasons were provided for rejecting the further six names submitted by the LO.

A constitutional challenge to this unilateral appointment brought by executive member of the PPP, Zulfikar Mustapha, was dismissed by the acting chief justice in June 2018, who ruled this time around that based on the proviso to Article 161(2) of the Constitution, the president is entitled to reject the list of names provided by the leader of the opposition and appoint a former judge as chairman of GECOM.[12] An appeal filed immediately by the PPP against this ruling is currently pending. However, the result of the president's interpretation – thus far judicially accepted – is that the elaborate processes of the Constitution, designed to secure inclusive and broad-based governance structures, can simply be avoided by the president to implement his will.

Similar uncertainty continues to plague the top judicial positions. The longstanding acting chancellor, Justice Carl Singh, as well as the acting Chief Justice Ian Chang, both retired after the accession of APNU into government. To date, however, no consensus can be achieved as to their replacements. In a further twist, the president even rejected the current holders of the posts, despite widespread support for both from the Bar Association as well as from wider civil society, nominating instead the current chief justice of Belize, Kenneth Benjamin, for chancellor.[13] Once again, the predominant impression conveyed by the continuing inability to compromise by the respective office holders is that of profound division and entrenched partisanship. It speaks as much as to the inadequate constitutional arrangements as it does to political immaturity and poor governance.

That the cycle of authoritarianism will be actively maintained has also been signalled by the termination of two prominent columnists at the *Chronicle*, the state-owned newspaper. Academic and WPA activist David Hinds and trade unionist Lincoln Lewis, both of whom consistently criticised the policies of the APNU government in their columns, were summarily terminated in March 2018 without explanation. As Arif Bulkan describes in his chapter, intolerance of criticism was a hallmark of both Burnham and Jagdeo's years in office, as each actively stifled dissent from every quarter in order to consolidate power. The muzzling of Hinds and Lewis is in keeping with such authoritarianism, indicating that notwithstanding free and fair elections, substantive democracy continues to elude Guyana.

Significantly, too, the APNU-AFC administration has signalled firm adherence to the neoliberal agenda of its predecessors – with all of the latter's attendant dislocation and inequality. Nowhere is this clearer than in the massive offshore discovery of oil, hundreds of kilometres off of Guyana's coast by ExxonMobil, which secured a generous prospecting licence under a petroleum agreement signed with the PPP government in 1999. The appointment of the incoming APNU-AFC administration coincided with the announcement by Exxon that exploratory work had yielded the largest discovery in 2015.[14] Further drilling has since confirmed the vast economic, strategic, and geopolitical value of Guyana's offshore wells. Today, Guyanese face a deepening of the neoliberal state (at the same time that in crucial ways, decision-making is being ceded to external forces); compounded by a refusal to consider a government of national unity based upon the constitutional promise enshrined in Article 13 of the Constitution, which declares the establishment of an inclusionary democracy as the principal objective of the state.

Percy Hintzen argues in this collection that in the Guyanese context, political democracy (via electoral reform) is not accompanied by sovereignty. In fact, the conditions of its eventual return – a return that as we have briefly outlined above, is threatened by a continuation of deeply authoritarian practices of rule – have 'tied the country even more firmly to global capital while elevating foreign decision makers in international financial agencies to positions of de facto governance, supported by Western and regional governments.'[15] If the last section of this book tentatively traces other modalities of engagement and value, the challenge lies in multiplying and connecting these possibilities so as to transcend a continuing present that leaves most Guyanese hopelessly at the margins.

Notes

1. Hari Ramkarran, 'Seeking a Democratic Path: Constitutional Reform in Guyana.' *Georgia Journal of International & Comparative Law* 32 (2004): 585, 594.
2. Quoted in M. Shahabuddeen, *Constitutional Development in Guyana 1621–1978* (Georgetown: Guyana Printers, 1978), 527.
3. Tracy Robinson, Arif Bulkan and Adrian Saunders, *Fundamentals of Caribbean Constitutional Law* (London: Sweet and Maxwell 2015) paras. 1-030 to 1-031.
4. Percy C. Hintzen, 'Creoleness and Nationalism in Guyanese Anticolonialism and Postcolonial Formation,' *Small Axe* 8, no. 1(2004): 106, 118.
5. There are several works which document this period; one relatively contemporary account is that of Andrew Morrison, *Justice: The Struggle for Democracy in Guyana, 1952–1992* (Georgetown: Red Thread Women's Press, 1998).
6. For a recent collection that engages this argument, see Leela Fernandes (ed.), *Feminists Rethink the Neoliberal State* (NY: NYU Press, 2018).
7. On this point, see Rupert Lewis's discussion of perspectives on the Grenadian Revolution by WPA activists like Andaiye, C.Y. Thomas and Walter Rodney (Lewis 1998).
8. Civic members were not PPP members, and the narrower alliance came out of a broad-based struggle for free and fair elections that included political parties forming themselves into the Patriotic Coalition for Democracy. In the early 1990s, members of civil society founded Guyanese Action for Reform and Democracy (GUARD). Initially declaring its independence from any political parties, GUARD threw its hat into the political ring, but failure to reach agreement on transforming itself into a viable electoral coalition would see several members joining forces with the PPP to form the PPP-Civic, which was formally approved in 1991 at the PPP Congress, with a slate of candidates fielded at the 1992 elections.
9. See, for instance, Percy Hintzen, *The Costs of Regime Survival: Racial Mobilization, Elite Domination and Control of the State in Guyana and Trinidad* (Cambridge: Cambridge University Press, 1989); Tyrone Ferguson, *To Survive Sensibly or to Court Heroic Death: Management of Guyana's Political Economy, 1965–85* (Georgetown, Guyana: Public Affairs Consulting Enterprise, 1999);

Steve Garner, *Guyana 1838–1985: Ethnicity, Class and Gender* (Kingston, Jamaica: Ian Randle Publishers, 2008); Rahul Bhattacharya, *The Sly Company of People Who Care* (NY: Farrar, Strauss and Giroux, 2011).
10. 'Constitutional Reform is still to be a reality' *Kaieteur News*, February 5, 2018, accessed July 1, 2018, https://www.kaieteurnewsonline.com/2018/02/05/constitutional-reform-is-still-to-be-a-reality.
11. Article 161 of the Constitution.
12. 'Chief Justice dismisses PPP challenge to GECOM Chairman appointment' *Kaieteur News*, June 9, 2018, accessed July 1, 2018, https://www.kaieteurnewsonline.com/2018/06/09/chief-justice-dismisses-ppp-challenge-to-gecom-chairman-appointment.
13. 'President sticking with Justice Benjamin as nominee for Chancellor' *Stabroek News*, June 7, 2018, online at https://www.stabroeknews.com/2018/news/guyana/06/07/president-sticking-with-justice-benjamin-as-nominee-for-chancellor/ (accessed July 1, 2018).
14. Helman, C. 'With Second Big Oil Discovery, Exxon Puts Guyana on the Map.' *Forbes*, June 30, 2016, accessed July 3, 2018, https://www.forbes.com/sites/christopherhelman/2016/06/30/with-second-big-oil-discovery-exxon-puts-guyana-on-the-map/#7836b7f247cd.
15. For a discussion that engages the regional context, see Linden Lewis (ed.), *Caribbean Sovereignty, Development and Democracy in an Age of Globalization* (London: Routledge, 2012).

References

Bhattacharya, Rahul. 2011. *The Sly Company of People Who Care*. NY: Farrar, Strauss.
Ferguson, Tyrone. 1999. *To Survive Sensibly or to Court Heroic Death: Management of Guyana's Political Economy, 1965–85*. Georgetown, Guyana: Public Affairs Consulting Enterprise.
Fernandes, Leela, ed. 2018. *Feminists Rethink the Neoliberal State*. NY: NYU Press.
Garner, Steve. 2008. *Guyana 1838–1985: Ethnicity, Class and Gender*. Kingston, Jamaica: Ian Randle Publishers.
Girvan, Norman. 'Fifty Years of In-Dependence in Jamaica: Reflections.' Keynote lecture delivered at the SALISES 50-50 Conference, 'Critical Reflections in a Time of Uncertainty.' Kingston, Jamaica, August 22, 2012. https://www.alainet.org/images/girvan-jamaica-in-dependence.pdf (accessed May 30, 2018).
Government of the Co-operative Republic of Guyana and Esso Exploration and Production Guyana Limited. 1999. *Petroleum Prospecting License*. https://s1.stabroeknews.com/images/2017/06/PETROLEUM-PROSPECTING-LICENCE.pdf (accessed July 3, 2018).
Helman, C. 2016. 'With Second Big Oil Discovery, Exxon Puts Guyana on the Map,' *Forbes*, June 30. https://www.forbes.com/sites/christopherhelman/2016/06/30/with-second-big-oil-discovery-exxon-puts-guyana-on-the-map/#7836b7f247cd (accessed July 3, 2018).

Hintzen, Percy C. 1989. *The Costs of Regime Survival: Racial Mobilization, Elite Domination and Control of the State in Guyana and Trinidad.* Cambridge: Cambridge University Press.

———. 2004. 'Creoleness and Nationalism in Guyanese Anticolonialism and Postcolonial Formation' *Small Axe* 8, no.1: 106, 118.

Jagan, Cheddi. 1992. Address by his Excellency Dr Cheddi Jagan at the Ceremonial Opening of the First Session of the Sixth Parliament of Guyana, December 17. http://jagan.org/CJ%20Articles/President/Images/4106a.pdf (accessed May 28, 2018).

Lewis, Rupert. 1998. *Walter Rodney's Intellectual and Political Thought.* Detroit: Wayne State University Press.

Lewis, Linden, ed. 2012. *Caribbean Sovereignty, Development and Democracy in an Age of Globalization.* London: Routledge.

Morrison, Andrew. 1998. *Justice: The Struggle for Democracy in Guyana, 1952–1992.* Georgetown: Red Thread Women's Press.

Ramkarran, Hari. 2004. 'Seeking a Democratic Path: Constitutional Reform in Guyana,' Georgia *Journal of International & Comparative* Law 32: 585, 594.

Robinson, Tracy, Arif Bulkan and Adrian Saunders. 2015. *Fundamentals of Caribbean Constitutional Law.* London: Sweet and Maxwell.

Shahabuddeen, Mohammed. 1978 *Constitutional Development in Guyana 1621–1978.* Georgetown: Guyana Printers.

Trotz, D. Alissa. 2014. 'Lest We Forget: Terror and the Politics of Commemoration in Guyana.' In *In a Far Country: Women of Colour and the War on Terror*, ed. Sherene Razack and Suvendrini Perera. Toronto: University of Toronto Press.

Constitutionalism, Democracy & Governance

1.
Constitutional Architecture and the Production of Authoritarianism
Arif Bulkan

Introduction

In October 1992, the People's Progressive Party (PPP) was elected along with a so-called Civic component (PPP/C), after more than half a decade's worth of incremental reforms to the political and social landscape in Guyana. The abolition of overseas voting, the institutionalisation of counting at the place of polls, and the appointment of an independent elections commissioner were some of the tangible measures which preceded the vote and which were accompanied by increasing press freedom, a renewed growth in civic consciousness, and the liberalisation of the economy (Benjamin 2007, 65–77). With former US President Jimmy Carter leading a team of international and regional observers, the election was widely touted as Guyana's 'return to democracy'. Excitement about entering into a new era of accountable and participatory governance, which would replace decades of authoritarian rule, was met with the hitherto unprecedented phenomenon of 're-migrants', namely overseas-based Guyanese returning home to resettle.

Almost immediately, however, prospects of deep-seated change to the political culture dimmed as the victorious PPP/C reneged on its pre-election promises of rejecting a 'winner-take-all' approach. The Working People's Alliance (WPA), so central to the country's struggle against dictatorship, faded into oblivion; also troubling was that constituencies other than those belonging to the PPP were not represented anywhere in government. The death of the venerated Cheddi Jagan before the end of the government's first term revealed the fault lines in the PPP's internal structure, as first his widow, Janet Jagan, and then Bharrat Jagdeo, both hand-picked successors, were installed as replacements, bypassing transparent processes and thereby nourishing the anti-democratic culture of both party and, by extension, the government.

As the PPP/C monopoly on power was maintained over the next decade, expectations of participatory, transparent, and neutral governance processes remained unfulfilled. It seemed that the PPP/C increasingly embraced the repressive and partisan style of governance favoured by their predecessors. This meant that endemic crime and corruption, cronyism, and the pervasive disregard for human rights (especially political freedoms of expression and assembly) did not abate, but possibly deepened. State-sponsored terrorism, which had emerged first during the Burnham years with the dreaded 'black-clothes' police and organised gangs of thugs, also continued, though in different guises. Thus, for example, under the People's National Congress (PNC) regime, members of a quasi-religious group, the House of Israel, notoriously terrorised WPA rallies in the late 1970s[1] and were responsible for the murder of prominent opposition figures such as the Jesuit Priest Father Bernard Darke.[2] Under the PPP/C, it was rogue elements in the police force, complemented by a so-called 'Phantom Squad' led by one Roger Khan, a drug kingpin on the run from American law enforcement, which fulfilled the same shadowy role.

Nepotism and corruption were facilitated by the systematic criminalisation of the state, with one study estimating that between 2001 and 2008, illegal activities – namely the narcotics trade, money laundering and trafficking in persons – contributed more than half of the national economy (Thomas, Jourdain and Pasha 2011). Tacit state involvement in underground criminal activity became increasingly evident, confirmed by revelations of the government's support of Roger Khan,[3] its appointment of a commissioner of police in spite of US intelligence as to his facilitation of the narco-trade, and Bharrat Jagdeo's own ties to a succession of criminals. None of this information was uncovered locally, becoming public solely through prosecutions in the US, the revocation of visas (including those of sitting government ministers) by the American embassy, and the Wikileaks website, which in turn underscored the failure of local institutions.

As early as 1999, Trinidadian political scientist Selwyn Ryan commented that 'Guyana...is in a state of economic and political pre-collapse' (329); a decade later, economist Clive Thomas would describe the country as a 'state for itself'.[4] Elaborating, Thomas explained that such an entity has no 'higher altruistic purpose' of national development or national advancement, but is concerned instead with obtaining benefits for those who control it. By May 2015, when the PPP/C was finally voted out of office after 23 years of uninterrupted rule, one could fairly comment that the country did not enjoy any reprieve from the excesses and violations that had first emerged in the Burnham era. Protestations of a 'return to democracy' notwithstanding, the country remained at the bottom of the Anglophone Caribbean on every international indicator of economic and human development, governance, and transparency.[5] Successive postcolonial administrations had thus fallen into the same traps of incompetence, corruption, and repression.

It would be rash to attribute serial dysfunction in governance to one cause, though the trademark postcolonial bequest of economic dependence, compounded in Guyana's case by the pervasive racialised dimension, are two of the more significant factors that come readily to mind. Equally important however, and certainly less considered in the literature, is the constitutional structure of the state, which enabled and ultimately cemented the negative legacies of colonial rule. This chapter proposes to explore this constitutional framework in greater detail, so as to demonstrate the integral role of law in producing and sustaining successive cycles of authoritarian and, inevitably, failed governance.

The Westminster Inheritance

By the time of independence in 1966, the habits of authoritarianism were well-inscribed in local structures and processes of government in Guyana. One study of constitutionalism in eastern and southern Africa identifies the weakening of local participatory governance systems in place of authoritarian processes that privileged colonial officials, concluding that postcolonial dysfunction was a predictable effect of autocratic colonial rule: 'Colonial rule was philosophically and organisationally elitist, centralist and absolute and left no room for either constitutions or representative institutions' (Hatchard, Ndulo and Slinn 2004, 14). A similar history exists in the Anglophone Caribbean. Decades, even centuries, of Crown colony government meant rule from the centre, which inhibited the development of democratic practices and constitutionalism within the colonies themselves. By the time of decolonisation in the mid-twentieth century, the overriding concern of both the departing colonials (Mawby 2012, 24; Robinson et al. 2015, 1-043) and their elite successors (Girvan 2015) was for order and continuity, which left an indelible imprint on the design of the newly inaugurated political and legal systems. Where anything was omitted, 'history and tradition' (Robinson et al. 2015, 3-007–08) became a compelling normative standard to which resort could be had for the missing details.[6]

This history and tradition led to the adoption across the Caribbean of an electoral system for single member constituencies based on 'first past the post' (FPTP), whereby the candidate receiving the most – and not necessarily a majority of – votes wins the election (O'Brien 2014). In turn, the government would be formed by the party securing the majority of seats in Parliament, with the leader of that party being appointed as prime minister (1966 Const, s 34(3)). A key feature of this system was the interlocking nature of the legislative and executive branches. Cabinet is drawn from the elected members of the Assembly, resulting in a *de facto* fusion of these branches, at least in terms of personnel. Other, more insidious, features retained included the primacy accorded to the prime minister, in whom was vested substantial control over ministers and thus ultimately the entire executive (1966 Const, s 34(4)). And although the government would be required to maintain the confidence of the legislature to remain in office, this apparent safeguard was neutralised by two factors: first, the dominance enjoyed by the executive in Parliament, and second, the power of the prime minister to prorogue or dissolve Parliament without notice.

The full import of these features would be painfully lived over time, not just in Guyana but across the Anglophone Caribbean. Their naturally authoritarian bent was possibly blunted in Britain by centuries of practice, unwritten conventions, and a flourishing civil society with multiple avenues of accountability, including a vibrant press. In the absence of equally moderating influences in small Caribbean polities, one early outcome was the ascendancy of the prime minister over other ministers and other arms and institutions of government (Sutton 2013). As head of the Cabinet with powers to appoint and terminate ministers at will, loyalty, even subservience, to this office was guaranteed. Combined with the power to appoint other functionaries in the bureaucracy, service commissions and indirectly even the judiciary, the prime minister's influence became all-encompassing, extending across the key branches of government. The result was to produce strongly authoritarian leaders, invariably a charismatic personality who attracted fierce loyalty.

The centrality of the state in small economies also enabled governments, and more particularly the executive, to wield tremendous influence in society. As the largest employer and the source of lucrative contracts for goods and services, the government possesses outsized ability to favour and disfavour (O'Brien 2014, 72). Political patronage, or victimisation as the case might be, rapidly became such a disfiguring trait of these societies that Bruce Golding, a former Caribbean prime minister, could freely admit: 'There is no joy in being in opposition, you know. When you are in opposition, you control nothing!' (Ryan 1999, 277).

Completing the dysfunctional situation was the FPTP electoral system, which consistently produced skewed majorities. Since a mere plurality was sufficient to win a seat in single-member constituencies, one result could be representation in Parliament that did not match the proportion of votes cast. The real losers would be third parties, who could secure a substantial percentage of the popular vote and yet not win a single seat in the elected House (Midgett 2003). Over time, this would make support for third parties an exercise in futility, thus indirectly strengthening the two main parties between whom power would tend to fluctuate. The danger of this pattern is that where political allegiance is, in turn, rooted in polarised notions of identity, entrenchment of the parties exacerbates the underlying pathologies, whether they are social or colour based as in Belize and Jamaica (Ryan 1999, 277), or race-based as in Trinidad and Tobago and Guyana (J. Bulkan 2014).

Although the Anglophone Caribbean has enjoyed a large measure of stability in its political affairs as compared to its Latin American neighbours (Payne and Sutton 1993, 18–20), this often masks debilitating problems such as fragile economies accompanied by world-record rates of homicide, suicide, and outward migration (Girvan 2015). The extent to which these pathologies might be produced by or even linked to inadequate governance is curiously overlooked, given that our constitutional structures and institutions are consistently held up as exemplary (Dale 1993, 80). It is naïve, however, to discount the role played by this strongly centralist model of government – with executive power concentrated in a prime minister and fluctuating between two monolithic blocs – in producing and sustaining weak processes and unaccountable leaders, and thereby incompetent and corrupt governance.

The Socialist Constitution

In the case of Guyana, the FPTP electoral system was replaced early on by proportional representation (O'Brien 2014, 73), while the Westminster-based arrangements formalised at independence were eventually modified to make way for a hybrid constitutional system. As the accompanying political events unfolded over the ensuing decades, it would be impossible to deny the links between the constitutional framework and societal decay. The rationale for the shift from the Westminster model was never concealed from the nation, manifested openly in the public pronouncements of Forbes Burnham (head of government from 1964 until his death in 1985) and the systematic miniaturisation of the state over which he presided. A coalition between Burnham's Peoples National Congress (PNC) and the United Force (UF) allowed them to form the government in 1964 (Gafar 41); thereafter all the general elections in 1968, 1973, 1980, and 1985 were rigged (Hintzen 2004, 118) enabling the PNC to remain in power despite the widely acknowledged racialised patterns of voting that would have more likely resulted in PPP victory at the polls. Meanwhile, the principle of 'paramountcy of the party' was adopted in 1973, by virtue of which the ruling party was accorded ascendancy over every branch of government (Ryan 1999, 149). Following a rigged referendum in 1980 (Ramcharan 2002, 67–71; DeMerieux 1992, 17–18), a constitution embodying this philosophy was imposed on the nation. Proclaiming the state to be in transition from capitalism to socialism (1980 Const Art 1), it created the framework for unfettered, authoritarian rule.

The most notable feature of the 1980 Constitution was its embrace of a semi-presidential system, which is widely regarded as the most problematic form of government because of its tendency to degenerate into authoritarianism (Elgie 2005, 99). Research has indicated that labels are of limited help in describing constitutional systems since there is no dependable homogeneity within each category (Cheibub, Elkins and Ginsburg 2014, 25–26). Nonetheless, one could generally describe parliamentary systems as those with strong overlaps between the legislative and executive branches and a split executive, while presidential systems tend to have a clear separation of powers between each branch of government (Stepan and Skach 1993, 3). In between these extremes are constrained parliamentarianism and semi-presidentialism, which can fall at different points on this spectrum depending on the degree of separation of powers that obtains, the respective position of each branch vis-à-vis the others, and the extent of judicial review available (Fix-Fierro and Salazar-Ugarte 2012, 631).

In Guyana, the defining feature of the 1980 Constitution was the centrality accorded to the executive branch, at the apex of which was positioned an executive president in whom the positions of head of state and head of government were merged (Art 89). In the ways described below, prime ministerial powers of the Westminster model were amplified, while safeguards were neutralised to create what legal scholar Rudy James has summed up as 'power without responsibility' (2006, 15). Thus, formal executive authority was vested in the president (Art 99(1)), who was empowered, in turn, to appoint both the prime minister and all ministers of the cabinet (Art 103(2)) from among the elected members of the national assembly. Cementing the absolute control of the president over the cabinet was his sole discretionary power to terminate the office of any minister (Art 183(3)(b)). Meanwhile, cabinet was reduced to a secondary role of merely aiding and advising the president 'in the general direction and control of the Government' (Art 106(2)).

Crucially, the president's reach was not limited to the political executive, which by itself is possibly defensible, but extended over the entire civil service by virtue of the president's role in appointing members of the constitutional commissions regulating the Public Service (Art 200(1)), Teaching Service (Art 207(2)), and the Police Force (Art 210(1)), along with vital and strategic functionaries including the director of public prosecutions (Art 203), auditor general (Art 204), solicitor general, permanent secretaries, ambassadors and other principal foreign representatives (Art 205). The combination of these provisions meant that appointments to all of the most senior and influential public offices, not confined to the political executive but encompassing the civilian bureaucracy as well, were entrusted directly or indirectly to the president.

Complementing this influence over the executive was the president's position in relation to the legislative branch. Parliament comprised the president and the national assembly (Art 51), but these were by no means equal partners, for the president could both summon (Art 69(1)) and prorogue and dissolve Parliament 'at any time' within his or her sole discretion (Art 70). There was no reciprocity in this relationship because the procedures for removal of the president by the assembly were so onerous (Arts 179 and 180) that there was no realistic prospect of constraining an unfit president in the same way that a president could 'check' the assembly. Even the work of the assembly was subjected to the president's overriding authority, for in practice the presidential power to withhold assent and return bills for re-consideration by members amounted to a de facto veto power over legislation. This was so because where returned to the assembly, the president was thereafter required to assent only if the bill was then supported by a two-thirds majority (Art 170), an unlikely occurrence since that would require the open defiance of the president's own ministers/ MPs. The subordination of the legislative branch was decisively completed by its lack of administrative independence, which made it subject to the executive for funding.

Already extensive on paper, executive presidential authority was made even more absolute by the removal of standard mechanisms of accountability. The president was under no obligation to attend sittings of the national assembly, though if s/he so deigned s/he could at any time attend and address it (Art 67). This alone represented a drastic break with the Westminster tradition of accountable government, by which those with the power are required to attend Parliament and, in the normal course, answer questions, disclose policies and defend action and inaction. This constitution thus created an anomalous state of affairs in which the functionary in whom ultimate power was vested, that is, the president, was nowhere obliged to act in accordance with cabinet's advice. Yet, despite its supporting role, it was cabinet and not the president which was made collectively responsible to Parliament (Art 106(2)).

In other areas the president's powers were similarly unfettered. The powers of appointment to the plethora of constitutional, executive, and administrative offices were constrained if at all by only weak 'consultation' requirements. Even where some obligation to consult or to act on advice existed, the president's conformity therewith was insulated from judicial scrutiny by a blanket ouster clause (Art 231), the effect of which was to oust the jurisdiction of the courts – that is to say, preclude judicial inquiry into how the power or discretion was exercised (Robinson et al. 2015, 5-017–20). The icing was provided by the conferral of extensive immunities, one type of which attached to the president at all times (both in and out of office) in relation to acts done in the performance of functions (Art 182). This could not be compared to the position of the British monarchy, as Forbes Burnham actually sought to do (James and Lutchman 1984, 105), because the former is a ceremonial institution without substantive functions. By contrast, the post-1980 executive president in Guyana was entrusted with ultimate control over all areas of governance.

In sum, the 1980 Constitution embraced the most potent aspects of the parliamentary and presidential models of government, while jettisoning their respective safeguards. While executive authority was reposed in a directly elected executive president in keeping with a presidential system, unlike in the latter, no separation was maintained between the executive and legislative branches as the executive government was chosen from among the elected representatives in Parliament. The other significant change implemented in 1980 was the abolition of the split executive, a feature of parliamentary systems (Albert 2010) whereby executive authority is vested in the head of state but effectively exercised by the head of government. Although this dichotomy may appear to be inconsequential, it can be useful to the extent that it diffuses executive power between two functionaries – a ceremonial president or governor general and a prime minister. Such a division provides openings for a head of state to moderate a prime minister's excesses, both in the normal course of things and during moments of crisis (Ghany 2000; Ryan 2000, 41–46). Considered in their totality, then, presidential powers in this hybrid model were not diluted or diffused in any direction – neither upward to a head of state, down to cabinet ministers and the civilian bureaucracy, nor sideways to other branches of government. Such untrammelled power is not characteristic of pure presidential or parliamentary systems, and it laid the foundation for a strongly authoritarian one.

Embracing Authoritarianism: The Mild Reforms of 2000–03

Historically, presidential systems have displayed a tendency to degenerate into authoritarianism, depending upon how power is distributed (Fix-Fierro and Salazar-Ugarte 2012, 647). Semi-presidential systems are potentially more vulnerable because of the lack of separation between the executive and legislative branches, for this means that there is no autonomous organ which can operate as a check on the executive (Elgie 2005). Guyana's experience did not deviate from this known trajectory, and in Robert Elgie's euphemistic assessment its 'very difficult political situations...were exacerbated by the highly presidentialised nature of its semi-presidential system' (103). Yet, although the 1980 Constitution was widely reviled, both for its content and the fact of its imposition by way of a rigged process, once elected in 1992, the PPP/C administration evinced no inclination to implement meaningful reforms or otherwise curb the extravagant powers of the executive presidency. It was only when the capital city Georgetown erupted in violence and looting following the declaration of the PPP/C as the winner of the second consecutive general election in December 1997 that constitutional reform was finally undertaken, this being one of the conditions demanded by the PNC for calling their supporters off the streets (Ramkarran 2004). In keeping with this forced commitment, the recommendations eventually made by the Constitution Reform Commission and enacted into law from 2000 to 2003 only tinkered at the margins, leaving untouched the structural deficiencies of the 1980 Constitution. Worse still, the limited outcomes of this process were effectively neutralised over the following decade, as Bharrat Jagdeo – Janet Jagan's handpicked successor – set about consolidating his own authority and power.

The single most unproductive aspect of the costly reform process conducted pursuant to the Herdmanston Accord of 1997 was its retention of the highly presidentialised nature of Guyana's hybrid constitutional system. Power remained concentrated in an executive president, whose control over cabinet with powers to appoint and terminate ministers in his absolute discretion was left undiminished. Cabinet's secondary role of merely having to 'aid and advise' the president remained (1980 Const, Art 106(2)), yet the president was kept above accountability mechanisms and still was not required to act on cabinet's advice, or to attend and answer for his actions in Parliament, all the while protected by continued and inappropriate immunities (Art 182). Parliament remained subordinate to the presidency in crucial respects: it was still subject to dissolution and prorogation by the president, the president could still frustrate its legislative agenda by returning bills for re-consideration, and the manner of election remained predicated on the 'List' system, which entrusted to the party leader the power to handpick MPs based on the proportion of the vote won. In other words, the ultimate say regarding who from the list of candidates would be rewarded with a seat in Parliament lay with the party, not the electorate.

Where reforms were attempted, for the most part they did not go far enough. For instance, one of the most undemocratic features of the 1980 Constitution was the extensive powers it conferred on the president over the entire executive because of his ability to influence its composition, either by way of direct appointments or indirectly because of his control over appointments to the relevant Service Commissions. Instead of diluting these powers, a cosmetic alteration was made obliging the president to 'meaningfully' consult with the leader of the opposition and/or to act on the nomination of the national assembly before making the relevant appointments. Appointed in this way would be five of the six members of the Public Service Commission, with the sixth member appointed by the president acting in his 'deliberate judgment' (Art 200); three of the six members of the Teaching Service Commission, with a further two nominated by the minister assigned responsibility for local government (that is, another member of Cabinet) (Art 207); five of the six members of the Police Service Commission (Art 210); and at least three of the six members of the Judicial Services Commission (Art 198), whose functions extend beyond the judicial branch and include the appointment of the director of public prosecutions (Art 203). The appointment to some offices, such as solicitor general, permanent secretaries, and ambassadors, all remained firmly within the president's discretion (Art 205). This modification was thus wholly insufficient, for 'meaningful consultation' imposes only a perfunctory and subjectively variable obligation to afford the person consulted 'a reasonable opportunity to express an opinion on the subject of the consultation' (Art 232), while still leaving the final decision up to the president. As for the role given to the national assembly, this too was superficial because of its domination by the ruling party. Ultimately, then, the president's inordinate influence over the composition of the entire executive was left intact.

Given that the highly centralised nature of the presidential system emerged unscathed from this reform process, arguably the most meaningful change introduced was presidential term limits. An ambiguously worded insertion declared that a 'person elected as President after the year 2000 is eligible for re-election only once' (Art 90(2)). Taken at face value this suggests that a person can serve only two terms as president, but poor drafting has opened up space for arguing, however tenuously, that the provision only restricts more than two *consecutive* terms. In other words, the question that remains open is whether a fresh election for a third term, after an intervening period in which someone else is president, could be described as 're-election'. Syntactic complexities aside, the amendment has since been held to be unconstitutional on the dubious basis that it restricts the pre-existing democratic rights of the electorate to elect as president a person of their own choice,⁷ contrary to the Constitution's affirmation in Article 1 that Guyana is a 'democratic' state and its conferral of sovereignty on the People in Article 9. Since Articles 1 and 9 require a referendum for any alteration, which was not conducted to bring the amending Act into law, the term limit enacted in this way was accordingly declared to be invalid.

Another two amendments were made which had the potential to strengthen the role of the legislature in monitoring the executive, but their impact has been negligible precisely because the skewed system of ultimate executive dominance was left intact. The first was the restoration of the no-confidence procedure, which had been removed from the 1980 Constitution, and the second was the establishment of four sectoral committees in Parliament.

Regarding the first, the no-confidence procedure is a lynchpin of the Westminster system of responsible government, by which the executive must maintain the confidence of the elected members of the House in order to govern (Bradley and Pinelli 2012; Barnett 2011). As reinserted in 2000, the provision stipulated that the entire Cabinet must resign if defeated on a vote of no-confidence (Art 106(6)), unless a general election is held within three months in order to elect a new government (Art 106(7)). However, this no-confidence procedure can be thwarted by the earlier prorogation of Parliament, which the president is empowered to bring about in his sole, unfettered discretion (Art 70(2)). If Parliament is sent on enforced recess then it cannot meet and vote on anything, in which case the government can prolong its life, six months at a time. This is precisely what happened on November 10, 2014 when former president, Donald Ramotar, unilaterally prorogued Parliament to forestall a planned no-confidence vote against the entire government, which the Alliance for Change (AFC) had tabled because of the continued spending by the minister of finance without parliamentary approval.⁸ Thus, what ought to have been a positive reform which would facilitate at least one avenue of accountability, was neutralised by the retention of the president's superordinate position over Parliament.

The four parliamentary sectoral committees established are responsible for scrutinising 'all areas of Government policy and administration', including natural resources, economic services, foreign relations, and social services (1980 Const Art 119(b)). These committees were meant to provide opportunities for the opposition to oversee the work of the government, theoretically facilitating more participatory and broad-based governance. To date they have been of minimal value – rarely meeting, spurned by ministers who refuse to attend and answer questions, and ultimately failing to monitor government administration as envisaged (James 2006, 39–40). Since no consequences attach to non-cooperation these committees have faded into insignificance, unable to penetrate the culture of unaccountability.

Finally, the reforms included a conspicuous attempt to strengthen the protection of fundamental rights, both in terms of substance and process. A number of 'new' rights were added to the regime of rights and freedoms contained in Title 1, covering specific areas of equality along with rights to work, pension, education, the environment and even to participate in the decision-making processes of the state (Arts 149A–149J). Innovatively, seven core international human rights treaties were directly incorporated (Art 154A), binding upon all organs of government and private individuals where applicable, enforceable through a newly established Human Rights Commission (Art 212G(1)(a)). An additional three Rights Commissions were established, with mandates governing women and gender equality (Art 212G(1)(b)), indigenous peoples (Art 212G(1)(c)) and children (Art 212G(1)(d)). Rounding off this ambitious network was an Ethnic Relations Commission, established with a gargantuan mandate to promote equality and help eliminate discrimination on the basis of ethnicity (Art 212A). The enacting provision itemises no less than 24 responsibilities, covering every conceivable activity including public education, training, arbitration, investigation, research, monitoring, analysis, and 'all other things as may be necessary to facilitate the efficient discharge' of the Commission's functions (Art 212D(a)–212D(x)).

As laudable as all these innovations to the human rights' framework may seem, in reality they amount to little more than rhetoric (A. Bulkan 2004). Many of the rights are simply repetitive, since with a general guarantee of equality there is arguably no need to list specific areas of non-discrimination. On the other hand, an eviscerating savings law clause which saves all pre-1980 laws from challenge under any of the Title 1 provisions was left intact (Art 152), so that despite the appearance of a commitment to promoting human rights, the scope of protection actually afforded remains in substance quite limited. The direct incorporation of international treaties was also an illusory development, as the rights covered this way were expressly limited to those not already guaranteed in Title 1 (Art 154A(2)). Since Title 1 already guarantees the standard list of rights and freedoms recognised under international human rights law, not much (if anything) is left over from the exclusion. Crucially, the PPP/C government never bothered to actually set up the Human Rights Commission (McCormack 2002, 261–65) although it had another 14 years in office to do so, bringing into question its true position on enforcement. As for the other Rights Commissions, they were simply too extravagantly conceptualised to have any realistic prospect of fulfilling their mandates, reflected ultimately in their desultory reporting to the National Assembly in violation of the constitutional requirement of submitting annual reports for each year of existence.

Irrespective of the flaws of this enhanced fundamental rights regime, however, its impact can at most be palliative since it merely addresses the symptoms of poor governance. Ultimately, where the reform process failed was by not correcting the systemic problems created by the country's constitutional structure, which gave rise to abuses of power in the first place. In order to transcend rhetoric, rights and accompanying processes require an informed citizenry as well as supporting institutions willing and able to confront and remedy executive abuses. As the following section shows, the consolidation of executive authority and gradual collapse of other institutions of government doomed these elaborate processes from the start.

Descent Into Autocracy

Armed with extensive powers, and unaccountable to party, cabinet, Parliament and even the electorate, Bharrat Jagdeo – the president who served for almost 13 of the 23 years of PPP/C rule – decisively set about consolidating his dominance over every other institution of state. Throughout his tenure as president, from 1999 to 2011, and even thereafter until the party's loss of power in May 2015, Jagdeo presided over what appeared to be a concerted, multi-faceted strategy targeting coordinate branches of government and constitutional offices and processes. Other organs of state were sidelined, accountability mechanisms neutralised or simply ignored, and fundamental rights – particularly those crucial to sustaining democracy – were systematically repressed. In this way, Jagdeo's tenure quickly degenerated into thinly disguised autocracy.[9]

Presidential dominance was achieved by the destabilisation of the three main organs of government, a stratagem first adopted by Burnham early on in his tenure (Morrison 1998). The executive – the most sprawling of all the branches and the one in most direct contact with the citizenry – was subordinated to the ruling party, with one of the most significant casualties being the civil service. The bedrock of government in the Westminster/Whitehall tradition consists of a professional civil service expected to function neutrally, carrying on the business of government without political bias (Barnett 2011). While the political executive changes at regular intervals, the civil service is a permanent establishment, its officers expected to provide stability and to function as the repositories of institutional knowledge as politicians come and go. At independence these attributes of continuity and neutrality were sought through the establishment of various Service Commissions, entrusted with control over hiring, promotion, discipline, and termination in the public service, the teaching profession, and the police force. Since then, the Privy Council has consistently reinforced the necessity of having a civilian bureaucracy,[10] in one case robustly asserting that the 'preservation of the impartiality and neutrality of civil servants has long been recognised in democratic societies as of importance in the preservation of public confidence in the conduct of public affairs.'[11] This tradition was explicitly acknowledged during the constitution reform process, out of which a provision was inserted guaranteeing the 'integrity' of the public service (1980 Const, Art 38G).

However, cynically belying this ethos was the post-1999 continuity with processes inaugurated during Burnham's tenure. As pointed out above, under the 1980 Constitution the president was accorded control over the composition of these Service Commissions, as well as power to make appointments directly to some of the most senior positions in the civil service. This power was not substantially diluted by the 2001 'reforms,' and in fact was utilised by Jagdeo's PPP/C to ensure a compliant executive across all levels. It translated first of all into a policy of outright racial preference in appointments, presumably on the assumption that racial solidarity was a precondition for unswerving allegiance, just as had obtained prior to 1992 under PNC rule. This produced the conditions for deepening racialised ties to political parties. Notwithstanding token appointees in senior cabinet positions, elsewhere across the public sector Guyanese of East Indian descent dominated by 2011, heading every major state entity, corporation, commission, and agency. This bias was so blatantly practised that the Head of the Presidential Secretariat (HPS) Roger Luncheon unapologetically testified in 2011, during the libel trial brought by President Jagdeo against Freddie Kissoon, a popular newspaper columnist and former lecturer at the University of Guyana, that there were no Afro-Guyanese qualified to be posted overseas as ambassadors.[12]

The politicisation of the public service was also pursued in more direct ways, one of which was the appointment of party members as permanent secretaries in government ministries. Defying convention, permanent secretaries campaigned for the ruling PPP/C and even contested general elections as candidates, with several moving on to become government ministers.[13] Permanent secretaries are the most senior functionaries in government ministries, in control of administration and finances, so with loyal party members leapfrogging into this top post the ruling party was given substantial control over the entire public service. In a conversion of Damascene proportions, Hydar Ally, a post-1992 long-serving permanent secretary who was also a senior member of the PPP, acknowledged the impropriety of this practice only *after* the PPP/C's loss of power in 2015. Testifying before a Commission of Inquiry into the public service in October 2015, Ally insisted that the public service should be depoliticised, belatedly regretting his own high profile in the party even as he simultaneously functioned as a permanent secretary.[14]

Another tactic was employing persons in the public service on contract. This practice, which proliferated to unprecedented levels by 2013, circumvented the Public Service Commission and so enabled the ruling party to handpick persons for jobs. It facilitated hiring on the basis of qualities other than education and experience, privileging factors such as ethnicity and family connections that should ideally be overlooked in a neutral process.[15] Because it occurred outside of public service regulations, attendant salaries and benefits of contractors were significantly higher. Employment on contract was also a means by which retired ministers, senior party members, and their relatives could be offered sinecures.[16] The danger of this practice was that the beneficiaries of these positions would be unswervingly loyal to the ruling party,[17] a practice that became so widespread that by 2013 as many as one-fifth of government employees were hired on contract,[18] while expenditure for contract employees doubled between 2010 and 2014, reaching the astronomical sum in 2014 of GY$9.4 billion.[19]

Political control was completed through the formal privatisation of certain public entities. Divestment of state control has been pursued by governments in a bid to make the delivery of services more efficient and less costly. In neighbouring Trinidad and Tobago, a constitutional challenge to the government's privatisation of the postal service failed for this very reason, with the Privy Council distinguishing between 'core' and 'non-core' functions of government.[20] But while collecting and delivering letters could hardly be intrinsically governmental, the same cannot be said for the collection of taxes and customs duties. In spite of legitimate concerns (Fraser 2001, 103), both the Inland Revenue Department and the Customs and Excise Department in Guyana were privatised and merged into one entity called the Guyana Revenue Authority (GRA). Tax assessment and duty collection are quintessential manifestations of state power, involving the (albeit legitimate) expropriation of private property and backed by a potent arsenal of coercive powers. Where entrusted to persons not subject to the traditional safeguards of the public service, lacking in security of tenure and potentially loyal to the ruling party, the potential for misuse is acute. This is precisely what came to pass with the GRA, which during the PPP/C administration was known to target and harass members of the opposition and critics of the government.[21]

The combined effect of these practices was the capture of the (lower) executive branch by the ruling party. With permanent secretaries as card-carrying members of the PPP/C and a loyal cadre of contract employees, the constitutional separation between the *political* executive and the independent civil service was blurred, if not erased altogether. It meant, ultimately, that the influence of the party and president extended across the breadth of civilian life, with enormous ability to reward and to punish. Indeed, by the PPP's last term even the pretence of an independent bureaucracy was abandoned, perhaps most clearly articulated by Head of the Presidential Secretariat Roger Luncheon, who at a post-cabinet press conference justified the unlawful award of a radio licence frequency by saying that he or the government could unilaterally instruct the relevant state entity what to do, and it would have no option but to comply.[22]

As the executive became ascendant, the legislature shrank downward with brutal symmetry. This facilitated executive dominance, since in the Westminster system, which Guyana follows in part, the executive is answerable to the legislature in the ways outlined above. Yet even though the 1980 constitutional provisions already relegate the legislative branch to a subordinate role, the government set about completing its dominance by undermining even those minimal processes as well as the actual work of the assembly. A constitutional amendment was enacted in 2007 providing for the removal of a member of parliament (MP) where s/he declares support for a different party or simply where the representative of the list indicates in writing on behalf of the party that they have 'lost confidence' in the MP.[23] Recall of an MP can be justified in a list system where that parliamentarian defects to another party, since votes are cast for the entire list and the choice of representatives lies solely with the representative of the list (in effect, the president or leader of the opposition). But extending the grounds for removal to cover loss of confidence in the MP annihilates any chance of independent representation in Parliament. Members are thereby compelled to toe the party line since incurring the displeasure of the leader could result in summary recall, with no legal recourse. This draconian law thus made it clear that members are accountable to their respective parties and not the electorate or the nation. It acted as a clear disincentive for MPs to freely vote based on principle or to scrutinise the actions and policies of their own colleagues.

This being the climate as regards independence within the government benches, it was natural that an even lower tolerance existed for criticism emanating from elsewhere. The Speaker of the House, traditionally a neutral office in the Westminster system (Ghany 1997, 114), was captured by the PPP/C at the outset, with Cheddi Jagan appointing his brother Derek to this position in 1992, a position the latter retained until his death in 2000 (Narain 2009, 99). Following general elections in March 2001, the next Speaker appointed was Hari (Ralph) Ramkarran, who also served for two terms until the PPP/C failed to win a parliamentary majority in the 2011 general election and the nominee of the combined opposition succeeded him. Ramkarran, whose father was a founding member of the PPP, came from the elite hierarchy of the party. While Speaker, his loyalty to the party was most noticeable when he refused to allow a debate in Parliament on the government's connections to drug kingpin Roger Khan.[24] Roger Khan was the alleged leader of an organised gang of vigilantes, which flourished for a period in the mid-2000s during which the country was engulfed by a series of brutal killings that predominantly targeted Indo-Guyanese. Triggered by a catastrophic jailbreak on Republic Day in 2002, the escapees touted themselves as an African liberation army, sparking terror particularly along the villages of the lower East Coast of Demerara corridor. Casualties piled up in a hitherto unprecedented scale, with one investigation by researchers on behalf of a newly formed pressure group, the Guyana Indian Heritage Association (GIHA), estimating as many as 155 murders in the year following the jailbreak (Thakur 2008–2009, 81). As the situation spiralled out of control and the army refused to intervene, the government turned to Khan to coordinate a response, allegedly providing him with lists of persons to be eliminated.[25] Murders and reprisals proliferated, though soon the line between politically motivated killings and gang/drug warfare became indistinguishable. Eventually, it was only through foreign intervention that Khan was arrested by American authorities in Suriname, extradited to the US and brought before the courts where he pleaded guilty to trafficking in cocaine, witness tampering, and weapons smuggling.[26] During Khan's trial, explosive disclosures of his ties to the government followed, hence the opposition's anxiety to seek explanations within a national setting. The refusal of the Speaker to allow any such debate was a low point in the life of Parliament as a forum for accountability and democracy, providing an instructive insight into the country's democratic culture.

Ultimately, and despite the plethora of sectoral committees introduced by the constitutional reforms, the legislative branch was unable to realise its democratic potential. The opposition was completely marginalised for the entire period in which the PPP enjoyed a parliamentary majority, evidenced by their almost non-existent success in effecting changes to proposed legislation or in introducing any laws (James 2006, 61–62). Further, such was the disregard of both Jagdeo and his successor for the work of the assembly that large numbers of bills successfully passed never received presidential assent. Under the constitution the president has no power to veto legislation, and at most can send bills back to the assembly for re-consideration. Jagdeo, however, never bothered with the niceties of those constitutional requirements, and each Parliament over which he presided came to an end with bills languishing for want of presidential assent.[27] According to Sir Michael Davies, senior parliamentary staff advisor of the Commonwealth Secretariat, who in 2005 authored a report on Guyana's parliamentary system, this refusal of assent represented the very 'negation of parliamentary government' (James 2006, 64).

The remaining branch of government is the judiciary, which in a parliamentary system where the executive and legislature are closely intertwined is of vital importance in promoting accountable government through its power to review (and invalidate) executive and legislative action.[28] Guyana's hybrid system which features an outsized executive is especially reliant on an independent judiciary for restoring balance and accountability. This was recognised early on by the PNC, which assiduously pursued a policy of emasculating the judicial branch by a sustained policy of covert manipulation and outright interference (A. Bulkan 2013; Ramcharan 2002, 16). As the following account demonstrates, the approach of the PPP/C would be no different.

As with the executive branch, the default approach towards achieving a compliant judiciary was to reserve the most senior positions for loyalists. The most prominent illustration of this practice occurred with the appointment of a relatively junior judge as chief justice in 2001, bypassing more senior members of the bench. No justification was ever proffered for departing from the norm of promotions based on seniority. However, invalidation of the 1997 general election by the bypassed judge sealed her reputation as fearless and independent,[29] whereas the judge favoured by the executive had plainly signalled his sympathies by upholding the constitutionality of the controversial GRA.[30] The next time a vacancy arose in the top judicial position, that of chancellor, loyalty prevailed once more over professional experience. This time around, however, the consent of the opposition was needed because of a key constitutional amendment in 2001 (Art 127(1)), and since the leader of the opposition favoured the previously bypassed judge, no agreement could be had. For the remainder of the PPP/C administration this impasse was not broken, and since 2005 there has been no confirmed occupant of this position (A. Bulkan 2013, 205–08).

The extent to which political partisanship was prioritised was strongly reinforced by the appointment of a foreign-based lawyer, Rabi Sukul, directly to the Court of Appeal in 2013, when at the time of his appointment he had been disbarred by the Bar of England and Wales. Compounding the irregularities surrounding this appointment was the fact that the Judicial Services Commission (JSC) was not fully constituted at the time it was made.[31] Missing were those members of the JSC appointed after consultation with the leader of the opposition and from the recommendations of the national assembly,[32] leaving the commission constituted only by three *ex officio* members. Thus not only was the appointment itself questionable, but more fundamentally it involved a process that had bypassed the constitutionally required input of the opposition and the national assembly.

These machinations were not isolated incidents and the integrity of the judicial branch came under attack in other ways during the PPP/C administration. Several other judges were appointed without a properly constituted JSC,[33] while on occasion binding recommendations of the JSC were ignored by the president, exercising a power he does not have. There were allegations of executive pressure being exerted upon members of the judiciary, with one former judge publicly complaining that his remuneration was withheld because of his rulings against the government,[34] while another condemned pervasive executive neglect of the needs of the judiciary, describing the criminal justice system from the Bench as 'broken'.[35] Such was the state of affairs that at one point, the registrar became engaged in a very public battle with the then acting chancellor over allegations of financial impropriety. Her complaint was that the chancellor, administering a grant aimed at reducing the backlog of cases, assigned himself a majority of them (which were also abandoned and did not require a trial) and so monopolised one-half of the $41.2 million obtained for the project.[36] These allegations came on the heels of a charge of forgery brought against the said registrar,[37] who was eventually acquitted and then immediately re-employed as solicitor general. This drama unfolded publicly in the press, causing incalculable damage to the reputation not just of the judiciary but the entire state apparatus. Ultimately, the extent of executive interference with and disregard for the judicial branch would lead a number of senior members of the bar to form an organisation called the 'Committee for the Defence of the Constitution', which in turn challenged the constitutionality of some of the more blatant constitutional violations in relation to the judiciary. However, this Committee did not sustain its activism, and for much of its tenure the PPP/C was able to circumvent and even violate various constitutional safeguards, in the process calling into question the independence and efficiency of the judiciary.

Presidential and executive dominance would not have been possible, however, simply by weakening other branches of government, as modern democracies have multiple mechanisms of accountability. Already weakened after the long period of repressive PNC rule (Morrison), those other mechanisms were not invigorated during the tenure of the PPP/C, particularly during the years 1999 and 2015, thus explaining how autocratic rule was able to persist for such an extended period.

A major governance issue concerns the management of public finances, which the government was able to manipulate in order to bankroll its agenda by bypassing the constitutional safeguards. Constitutionally, all public revenues must be paid into what is called a 'Consolidated Fund' (1980 Const, Art 216). The Constitution strictly regulates the conditions under which withdrawals may be made, all of which involve parliamentary approval (Art 217). An independent auditor general is tasked with scrutinising spending through audits of public accounts and reporting to the national assembly (Art 223). These processes are designed to ensure prudent and transparent management of the country's finances under the watchful eye of the legislature.

In Guyana, however, these mechanisms were circumvented through a company that had been set up in 1990 called National Industrial and Commercial Investments Ltd (NICIL) to acquire, hold and manage all of the government's shareholdings.[38] NICIL was run by a board of directors consisting of the minister of finance, the HPS, the CEO of Go-Invest (another state entity), an executive director (appointed by cabinet) and one lone representative of the opposition. NICIL is required by law to submit an annual report of its finances to the minister of finance, but the absurdity of this process is that the same minister of finance is the chair of the board of directors, so that he/she is required to report to him/herself. Even with non-existent oversight, for more than a decade after 2002 NICIL did not file any annual returns nor did it lay any report or accounts in the national assembly, in clear breach of the law.[39]

It was only after the PPP's loss of power in 2015 that a financial audit of NICIL was finally conducted, which revealed significant irregularities, if not outright criminal conduct. From 2002 onwards, pursuant to a Management Cooperation Agreement signed in December 2001, revenues earned by NICIL were retained in breach of the law instead of paid into the Consolidated Fund. Over the following 12 years, as very lucrative assets were vested in NICIL and then liquidated, more than $26.8 billion was intercepted from the national treasury and thereafter disposed of at the discretion of NICIL's controlling players and in a context in which audited statements of NICIL's accounts were never publicly released. Thus shielded from constitutional controls, parliamentary and public oversight, and with no scrutiny from a compromised audit office, NICIL presided over a litany of questionable deals, some of which ended up benefiting those in the highest echelons of the PPP/C and their associates. Among these were the sale of the government's shares in Guyana Telephone and Telegraph (GT&T), by which the state lost over US$7.6 million in just two years (from 2012 to 2014), the public financing of the Marriot Hotel, and the disposal of valuable state properties apparently without any form of competitive bidding and thus at severely undervalued prices. Sometimes, astronomical sums were expended with no apparent aim of promoting development or equitable distribution of resources, such as with the diversion of funds in 2007 to finance the Cricket World Cup, or facilitating the removal of a transmission tower in one community (Sparendaam) at a cost of over GY$185,000,000, so as to develop the area as an exclusive residential one. Known as Pradoville 2, this area was then carved into oversized house lots and sold at uncompetitive prices primarily to loyalists of the ruling party, including President Jagdeo and several Cabinet members.[40] Ultimately, according to the audit report, NICIL operated as a conduit for unaccountable spending, functioning as a 'parallel treasury' and exhibiting what one financial analyst described as a 'posture ... of indiscipline and contempt for public opinion.'[41]

Another safeguard, the office of the auditor general, which is designed to provide 'an additional layer of ex post facto scrutiny of government expenditure' (O'Brien 2014, 185), was also undermined in critical respects, in particular by targeting its capacity and compromising its independence. Long-serving Auditor-General Anand Goolsarran resigned in January 2005 following an audit by him which revealed a potential $50-million fraud involving a high-profile presidential adviser. This sparked a public confrontation with the Office of the President, after which Goolsarran claimed to be fearful for his life and secretly fled to the US.[42] For another seven years, the person appointed to act in this position was not a certified accountant, which ironically made him ineligible under the law for employment as an auditor in a private company. Nonetheless, he was confirmed in 2012, despite concerns that his lack of qualifications, to say nothing of his compromised independence after seven years of acting, made him unsuitable for this position with its wide, complex and technical portfolio. Completing the irregularities in this sensitive constitutional office is that its only professionally qualified accountant, who was appointed audit director in 2012, was the wife of the minister of finance. Thus, oversight of the work of the minister of finance in managing public finances was entrusted to his wife, a clear conflict of interest. Irrespective of the personal integrity of these officials, their intimate relationship legitimately called into question the objectivity and value of the entire oversight process.

Hand in hand with the diminution of the office of the auditor general was a corresponding policy of undermining the efficacy of other constitutional offices designed to provide oversight of public administration. The Office of the Ombudsman, which serves as a watchdog of public officers and processes, was invisible for a long period and then unoccupied from 2005 until 2014. Similarly, an Integrity Commission, first set up in 1999 to monitor the assets and financial standing of public officials, their spouses and children, never functioned effectively while compliance with its requirements was minimal. After the resignation of its chairman in 2006, the body was never properly re-constituted for the remainder of the PPP/C's tenure in office. Thus, for almost the entirety of the PPP/C's tenure, essential constitutional offices designed to improve public accountability and good governance were mostly non-functioning.

Completing autocratic rule from the centre was the fact that for its entire 23-year reign, the PPP/C held local government elections only once, in 1994 (McIntosh, this volume). In the place of elections when they became constitutionally due the government set up 'Interim Management Councils' to which party loyalists were appointed. This extended the government's reach into the far recesses of the country through handpicked councillors, who were backed up with subventions from the Consolidated Fund to dispense in their discretion. Unsurprisingly, there existed 'overwhelming evidence of a lack of accountability in respect of these councils'.[43]

These varied manoeuvres that served to cement executive and presidential authority would not have been as successful if imposed on a vibrant civil society, a fact that the ruling party obviously appreciated. As a countervailing strategy it embraced a militant posture towards dissent, in whatever form this was manifested, adopting the example set from the Burnham era in which free expression and public dissent were curtailed in multiple ways. Margaret DeMerieux observed in relation to Caribbean politicians that defamation suits were misused as a 'tool' to 'punish critical discussion of public issues' (1992, 217); in this area, the PPP/C displayed a rare ingenuity, deploying an arsenal of weapons well beyond litigation to intimidate and silence opponents. Time and again, individuals critical of the government were harassed, vilified, and victimised. Employing the full range of coercive powers at the state's disposal, some critics were imprisoned on sedition charges[44] while many more were targeted economically, by threatening or removing their source of income. Economic victimisation was visited not only upon those in government employ, who were summarily terminated,[45] but critics in the private sector were also subjected to retaliation in whatever form it could be dispensed. Examples abound of privately employed individuals whose employers or business associates were lobbied by the government to secure their dismissal on account of their public stance against the government.[46] Self-employed professionals or businessmen critical of the state were discriminatorily targeted by state agencies, most graphically illustrated in the campaign against *Kaieteur News* and its publisher by the GRA, which included the release of private tax information to unauthorised persons. Such became the PPP/C's intolerance of dissent, to say nothing of its distance from the society, that shortly before the 2011 general election a water cannon was bought, at a previously declared cost of GY$37 million, for crowd control.[47] It would be less than a year later that a peaceful protest in the mining town of Linden was broken up by the police, in the course of which live ammunition was fired into the crowd causing the deaths of three persons.[48]

Complementing these individual attacks, and again following the precedent set by the PNC in the 1980s,[49] the PPP/C administration methodically sought to control various modes of expression at their source – whether print, radio, or television. For close to two decades the government exercised an unlawful monopoly of the radio spectrum, which was only relaxed on the eve of national elections in 2011. Unknown to the public, radio licences were unilaterally issued by outgoing President Jagdeo, even though a broadcasting authority had by then been set up by law. The lion's share of radio licences was gifted to PPP members of government, their friends and supporters, while applicants with an established track record in journalism and broadcasting were passed over.[50]

The print media presented a greater challenge, since this had already been freed up by President Hoyte in 1986 (Benjamin 2007, 95). Here, the strategy adopted was to sideline dissenting private media through uncompetitive practices. In 2006, all taxpayer-funded state advertising was withdrawn from a leading independent daily, the *Stabroek News*, for 17 months; and again from August 2010, both *Stabroek News* and *Kaieteur News*, the other independent newspaper, were denied state advertisements. This move was complemented by the issue of a raft of illegal concessions to a close friend of then President Jagdeo (the Ramroop group of companies) which established the *Guyana Times*, a competing newspaper. Other tactics used to cripple freedom and democracy in the media included the marginalising of independent journalists, suspending the licences of independent TV stations, and the frequent resort to criminal charges, including treason, against journalists.[51] After describing the tense and difficult relationship between the *Stabroek News* and the Hoyte government in the late 1980s, former editor Anna Benjamin lamented: 'One might have thought that after the PPP/C government came to office in 1992, the situation would have been very different, but in fact there were problems of a similar order' (2007, 137).

Concurrently, the state media was hijacked into a vehicle for PPP/C propaganda. Stories critical of the government or favourable to the opposition were rarely if ever carried in the *Chronicle*; state radio was banned from playing calypsos critical of the government; and when during the budget debates in 2014 an employee of the state agency broadcast the speech of an opposition parliamentarian during prime time, he was terminated from his position. Meanwhile, phantom bloggers were employed at taxpayers' expense, seemingly with no function other than to disparage critics of the government in online fora.[52] More ominously, critics of the government were relentlessly pursued and publicly subjected to a barrage of personal attacks, including allegations of being unpatriotic, immoral, criminal, and even non-human. This was taken to such extremes that it prompted Amnesty International, as far back as 2002, to caution the government that its inflammatory rhetoric against the opposition could 'undermine the right of freedom of expression and lead to further human rights violations', and that its intolerance risked 'debasing legitimate public debate and encouraging violence against certain individuals'.[53] This was a prophetic warning. Four years later, mere months before a general election, gunmen stormed the premises of the *Kaieteur News* offices, shooting five staffers to death in an incident described as 'one of the most violent in Latin America.'[54] Even if there were no connection between the government's rhetoric against the media and the attack on *Kaieteur News* officers, at the very least the Nandlall recording, described below, demonstrates the callous disregard for press safety at the highest echelons of the party.

The government's nadir in relation to free expression and democratic values was revealed in their unguarded moments, made publicly available because of the ease of recording in modern times. The first, and shocking, disclosure was the (surreptitiously taped) conversation between the attorney general and a senior journalist at the *Kaieteur News*, in which the former graphically attacked the newspaper's operations. In the recording, which the attorney general admitted was that of his voice, violence against the newspaper was casually contemplated and discussed:

> when you continue to attack people like that and they have no way of responding they gun just walk with their weapon into that same (expletive) Saffon street office and wha come suh do and innocent Peter gun gah pay fuh (expletive) paul in deh one day, me ah tell you innocent, me a tell you honestly man to man that will happen soon.[55]

Despite boasts of access to far more effective measures than the media or the law in a conversation littered with references to weapons, war, and his alleged warrior status, the attorney general never faced any censure for his statements. In an ignominious first, the Inter-American Commission on Human Rights – a regional human rights body – granted Precautionary Measures in favour of the newspaper, noting:

> the commission considers that the requirement of seriousness is met, in light of the alleged threat expressed against the lives and personal integrity of the Kaieteur News personnel, within the framework of their right to freedom of expression. In particular, the information presented suggests that the purported threat was oriented toward preventing the members of Kaieteur News from freely exercising their role as journalists, related to a series of reports on corruption cases, among other issues, which allegedly affected high ranking officials within the government.[56]

In a similar vein was the reaction of the minister of health when confronted by a prominent social activist. As she was attempting to question him about his stewardship of the health sector, the minister was recorded telling her to 'F- off', calling her a 'little piece of shit' and threatening to have her slapped and stripped 'just for the fun'.[57] That an elected official would react in this manner to a question from a voter demonstrates how the combined electoral and constitutional system fosters poor governance. Continually re-elected on the basis of ethnic loyalty, enjoying constitutional dominance over other organs of government, and operating in the context of weak institutions and a weaker civil society, the PPP/C eventually came to function as if it were completely unaccountable.

Conclusion

The failures of governance described above did not originate with the PPP/C in 1992. They repeated and sometimes even deepened what had prevailed under the PNC, particularly during the Burnham years. That such continuity occurred seamlessly across successive administrations is partly a product of a strongly authoritarian constitutional framework in which executive power is concentrated in one person while other institutions of state are correspondingly neutralised or emasculated. Guyana's unique constitutional structure adopts the most potent elements of pure parliamentary and presidential systems, while jettisoning their respective safeguards. Given the president's control over the cabinet, the civil service, a majority of the parliamentarians, and ultimately his own party, no individual or entity possesses the legal backing to contradict or otherwise check him or her. An already imbalanced power structure was reinforced by Jagdeo as president through further miniaturisation and outright disregard of the few constitutional mechanisms and processes that promote neutrality and transparency. This left him with enormous, unchecked powers, accountable to none, inexorably leading to rampant corruption, nepotism, and mismanagement.

Reforms must therefore tackle the country's hybrid constitutional structure, which is at the root of its dysfunctional governance. The solution lies not only in restoring each branch to a position of equality vis-à-vis the others, but the manner of selecting each one must be reformed to increase democratic participation and remove the disproportionate executive and presidential influence. This would require changes not only to the existing electoral system, but also to the processes for selection of the wider bureaucracy and perhaps even the judiciary. Remaining state institutions and constitutional mechanisms of accountability must be strengthened, which would provide a check on those who exercise power and means to hold defaulters accountable.

Constitutional theorists have long warned of the dangers of concentrating too much power in one organ of government or one individual. Consequences such as the loss of individual liberty, arbitrariness in public affairs and tyranny have proved to be, in Guyana's experience, not academic speculations but a lived reality. The solution clearly lies in moderating those sources of untrammelled power and creating the space for civil society to flourish.

Notes

1. See, for example, the facts as recounted *Ramson v Barker* (1982) 33 WIR 183 (CA Guy) for an insight into how political rallies were actively discouraged by agents of the state.
2. A first-hand account of this chilling period can be gleaned from veteran journalist and Jesuit priest, Fr. Andrew Morrison. See *Justice: The Struggle for Democracy in Guyana, 1952–1992* (Georgetown: Red Thread Women's Press, 1998).
3. Roger Khan himself claimed an association with the government, and there were events that tend to support this claim such as the written permission given to him to purchase high-tech spy equipment, allegedly signed by then Minister of Health Leslie Ramsammy. When this letter surfaced at Khan's trial, the minister claimed that his signature was forged: *Stabroek News*, 'Links between Roger Khan, Leslie Ramsammy were strong – US Chargé d'Affaires in cable,' September 9, 2011. https://www.stabroeknews.com/2011/news/stories/09/09/links-between-roger-khan-leslie-ramsammy-were-strong/ (accessed April 5, 2017).
4. Public Forum, Georgetown, August 2009.
5. The renamed Fragile States Index, whose scores are based on a comprehensive set of political, social and economic indicators, placed Guyana at No. 106 in 2014, higher than every other country in the Anglophone Caribbean surveyed: http://library.fundforpeace.org/library/cfsir1423-fragilestatesindex2014-06d.pdf (accessed June 30, 2016).
6. *Hinds v R* (1975) 24 WIR 326 (PC Jam).
7. *Richardson v AG of Guyana*, unreported, 2015 HC-DEM-CIV-CM-10 (July 9, 2015), affirmed by the Court of Appeal, Cummings-Edwards JA dissenting, see: *AG of Guyana v Richardson*, civil appeal 45/2015 (Jan. 13, 2017). Since the time of writing, a further appeal by the Attorney General succeeded in the Caribbean Court of Justice and the amendment has been held to be constitutional: *Attorney General v Richardson* [2018] 4 LRC 488 (CCJ Guy).
8. BBC News, 'Guyana President Suspends Parliament to Avoid No-confidence Vote,' November 11, 2014. http://www.bbc.com/news/world-latin-america-29996877 (accessed June 30, 2016).
9. Popular newspaper columnist Freddie Kissoon frequently described the Jagdeo Presidency as an 'elected dictatorship'. See 'Elected Dictatorship: Applying Zakaria to Guyana,' *Kaieteur News*, March 5, 2010. http://www.kaieteurnewsonline.com/2010/03/05/elected-dictatorship-applying-zakaria-to-guyana/ (accessed June 30, 2016).
10. *Thomas v AG of T&T* (1981) 32 WIR 375, 382; *Cooper v AG of T&T* (2006) 68 WIR 477, para. [28].
11. *de Freitas v Permanent Secretary* (1998) 53 WIR 131, 138.
12. *Kaieteur News*, 'Luncheon's Court Admissions on Non-Afro Ambassadorial Postings Shocking – APNU.' August 26, 2011. http://www.kaieteurnewsonline.com/2011/08/26/luncheon%E2%80%99s-court-admissions-on-non-afro-ambassadorial-postings-shocking-apnu/ (accessed June 1, 2016).

13. *Stabroek News*, 'Few new faces in Ramotar Cabinet,' December 5, 2011. http://www.stabroeknews.com/2011/news/stories/12/05/bishop-edghill-to-be-minister-in-ministry-of-finance/ (accessed June 30, 2016).
14. *Stabroek News*, 'Politically Neutral Public Service is an Ideal, Hydar Ally Tells Inquiry,' Oct. 10, 2015. http://www.stabroeknews.com/2015/news/stories/10/10/politically-neutral-public-service-is-an-ideal-hydar-ally-tells-inquiry/ (accessed June 1, 2016).
15. For evidence of the extensive nepotism practised, see *Stabroek News*, 'The PPP's Theory of Relativity, as Einstein Never Imagined It,' May 8, 2015. http://www.stabroeknews.com/2015/features/05/08/the-ppps-theory-of-relativity-as-einstein-never-imagined-it/ (accessed June 1, 2016).
16. *Kaieteur News*, 'Retirees Getting "Fat Cat" Salaries,' January 17, 2016. http://www.kaieteurnewsonline.com/2016/01/17/retirees-getting-fat-cat-salaries/ (accessed June 30, 2016).
17. One astute letter writer insightfully linked the lack of impartiality to the lack of security enjoyed by contract employees who, unlike workers on the permanent establishment, serve at the pleasure of the minister: Sasenarine Singh. 'Contract Workers become Political Stooges,' *Kaieteur News*, April 22, 2012. http://www.kaieteurnewsonline.com/2012/04/22/contract-workers-become-political-stooges-to-survive-the-life-term-of-their-contracts/ (accessed June 1, 2016).
18. Based on figures compiled by Transparency Institute Guyana Inc and presented to the OAS: *Stabroek News*, 'Serious Conflict of Interest around Ashni Singh, Wife,' October 10, 2013. http://www.stabroeknews.com/2013/news/stories/10/10/serious-conflict-of-interest-around-ashni-singh-wife/ (accessed June 1, 2016).
19. Figures based on comparison of national budgets by chartered accountant Chris Ram. Inews, 'Stop the Abuse,' February 9, 2016. http://www.inewsguyana.com/stop-the-abuse-ram-mcrae-urges-president-regarding-employment-of-contract-workers/ (accessed June 1, 2016).
20. *Perch v AG* (2003) 62 WIR 461 (PC TT).
21. *Stabroek News*, 'GRA and its Analysis of Media Houses,' October 6, 2014. http://www.stabroeknews.com/2014/opinion/editorial/10/06/gra-analysis-media-houses/ (accessed June 1, 2016).
22. *Stabroek News*, 'Luncheon Admits Government Broke Law in CCTV Licensing,' February 16, 2013. http://www.stabroeknews.com/2013/news/stories/02/16/luncheon-admits-govt-broke-law-in-cctv-licensing-nascimento/ (accessed June 1, 2016).
23. Constitution of Guyana 1980, Article 156(b) and (c), inserted in 2007. Courts around the Commonwealth have ruled on the importance of security of tenure for the independence of Parliamentarians and constitutional democracy: *Tumukunde v AG* [2009] 4 LRC 154 (SC Uganda); *Williams v Holness* [2015] JMCA Civ 21 (CA Jam).
24. *Stabroek News*, 'Opposition Quits Parliament over US Court Evidence,' July 31, 2009. http://www.stabroeknews.com/2009/archives/07/31/opposition-quits-parliament-over-us-court-evidence/ (accessed June 1, 2016).

25. Interview with Michael McCormack, 5–6. May 8, 2009. Innovations for Successful Societies, Oral History Project. Princeton University.
26. *Stabroek News*, 'Shaheed "Roger" Khan: Drugs, Dirty Money and the Death Squad.' August 20, 2009. http://www.stabroeknews.com/2009/guyana-review/08/20/shaheed-%E2%80%98roger%E2%80%99-khan-drugs-dirty-money-and-the-death-squad/ (accessed June 30, 2016).
27. *Stabroek News*, 'Lack of Expedition in Presidential Assent of Bills Questioned,' January 24, 2010. http://www.stabroeknews.com/2010/archives/01/24/lack-of-expedition-in-presidential-assent-of-bills-questioned/ accessed Jun 30, 2016; *Stabroek News*, 'Greenidge Motion Seeking to Have President's Non-signing of Some Bills Declared as Unconstitutional,' November 12, 2014. http://www.stabroeknews.com/2014/news/stories/11/12/greenidge-motion-seeking-presidents-non-signing-bills-declared-unconstitutional/(accessed June 30, 2016).
28. *State v Khoyratty* [2007] 1 AC 80 (PC Mauritius).
29. *Esther Perreira v Chief Election Officer* (unrep) Jan 15, 2001, No. 36-P/1998 (HC Guy).
30. *Chue v Attorney General* (unrep) Jan 27, 2000, No. 66-M/1998 (HC Guy).
31. *Stabroek News*, 'Judiciary Problems Mounting with Absence of JSC,' April 25, 2014. http://www.stabroeknews.com/2014/news/stories/04/25/judiciary-problems-mounting-absence-jsc/ (accessed June 1, 2016).
32. *Stabroek News*, 'Justice Sukul and the JSC,' February 24, 2014. http://www.stabroeknews.com/2014/opinion/editorial/02/24/justice-sukul-jsc-2/ (accessed Jun 1, 2016).
33. *Stabroek News*, 'Hughes: Judges Being Appointed even though JSC not Properly Constituted,' November 12, 2012. http://www.stabroeknews.com/2012/news/stories/11/12/hughes-judges-being-appointed-even-though-jsc-not-properly-constituted/ (accessed Jun 1, 2016).
34. *Stabroek News*, 'Benefits Delay Forces Judge out of Retirement,' September 30, 2009. http://www.stabroeknews.com/2009/archives/09/30/benefits-delay-forces-judge-out-of-retirement/ (accessed June 1, 2016).
35. *Stabroek News*, 'Broken Criminal Justice System Denying Prisoners Their Rights – Justice George,' May 28, 2010. http://www.stabroeknews.com/2010/archives/05/28/%E2%80%98broken%E2%80%99-criminal-justice-system-denying-prisoners-their-rights-%E2%80%93justice-george/(accessed Jun 1, 2016).
36. *Stabroek* News, 'High Court Registrar Complains to HPS about Chancellor,' May 1, 2009. http://www.stabroeknews.com/2009/archives/05/01/high-court-registrar-complains-to-hps-about-chancellor/ (accessed June 1, 2016).
37. *Stabroek News*, 'Ramlall, McLean Charged in Alleged Adoption Fraud,' April 28, 2009. http://www.stabroeknews.com/2009/archives/04/28/ramlal-mclean-charged-in-alleged-adoption-fraud/ (accessed June 1, 2016).
38. Companies Act 1998, Chapter 89:01, and continued under Act No. 29 of 1991, Laws of Guyana.
39. Chris Ram, 'NICIL is in Violation of the Law.' http://www.chrisram.net/?paged=5&tag=nicil (accessed June 30, 2016).

40. *Stabroek News*, 'Audit Report on NICIL Calls for Firm Action,' December 9, 2015. http://www.stabroeknews.com/2015/news/stories/12/09/audit-report-nicil-calls-firm-action/ (June 30, 2016).
41. Rawle Lucas, 'NICIL Examined,' *Stabroek News*, April 5, 2015. http://www.stabroeknews.com/2015/features/04/05/nicil-examined/ (accessed June 30, 2016).
42. *Stabroek News*, 'Anand Goolsarran Says Left Guyana Fearing for his Life, Sees Role in Improving Accounting Practices,' March 25, 2012. http://www.stabroeknews.com/2012/news/stories/03/25/anand-goolsarran-sees-role-in-improving-accounting-practices/ (accessed June 30, 2016).
43. Anand Goolsarran, '2014 an Annus Horribilis for Governance, Transparency and Accountability,' *Stabroek News*, January 12, 2015. http://www.stabroeknews.com/2015/features/01/12/2014-annus-horribilis-governance-transparency-accountability/ (accessed June 30, 2016).
44. *Stabroek News*, 'PPP/C Used Sedition Law against Me, Waddell and Hinckson,' May 1, 2018. https://www.stabroeknews.com/2018/opinion/letters/05/01/ppp-c-used-sedition-law-against-me-waddell-and-hinckson/ (accessed June 7, 2018).
45. No one was too big (as in prominent newspaper columnist and UG lecturer Freddie Kissoon) or too small (a mere officer in the Guyana Tourism Authority and a 'young technical producer' at the state-owned National Telecommunications Network, NCN) to be fired for criticising the government. See Bulkan et al., 'Freddie Kissoon's Dismissal: The Dictatorial Actions of an Insecure Political Elite,' *Stabroek News*, January 30, 2012. https://www.stabroeknews.com/2012/features/in-the-diaspora/01/30/freddie-kissoon%E2%80%99s-dismissal-the-dictatorial-actions-of-an-insecure-political-elite/ (accessed April 15, 2018); and 'Tourism Officer Suspended for Criticising Dynamic Airways,' *Kaieteur News*, July 31, 2014. https://www.kaieteurnewsonline.com/2014/07/31/tourism-officer-suspended-for-criticising-dynamic-airways/ (accessed Apr 15, 2018); 'NCN Producer Suspended – after Cathy Hughes Clip Mistakenly Aired,' *Kaieteur News*, April 5, 2014. https://www.kaieteurnewsonline.com/2014/04/05/mccoy-allegedly-orders-ncn-producer-suspended/ (accessed April 15, 2018) – these being only three of many instances.
46. A long list of critics in the private sector were targeted economically, such as by protesting their employment in intergovernmental (Carl Greenidge, Janette Bulkan) and even private (David Hinds, Ruel Johnson) organisations, or by opposing offers of employment locally (Gino Persaud), to list only a few of many examples publicised in the press.
47. *Stabroek News*, 'Rohee Dismisses Fears about Water Cannon,' November 17, 2011. http://www.stabroeknews.com/2011/archives/11/17/rohee-dismisses-fears-about-water-cannon/ (accessed June 1, 2016).
48. *Stabroek News*, 'Three Die during Linden Power Protest,' July 18, 2012. http://www.stabroeknews.com/2012/news/stories/07/18/three-die-during-linden-power-protest/ (accessed June 30, 2016).
49. *Hope and AG v New Guyana Company Ltd* (1979) 26 WIR 233 (CA Guy).

50. Arif Bulkan, 'A Perfect Storm – the Radio Broadcast Licences,' *Stabroek News*, April 15, 2013. http://www.stabroeknews.com/2013/features/in-the-diaspora/04/15/a-perfect-storm/ (accessed June 30, 2016).
51. US Department of State, *Guyana Country Report*, March 4, 2002, section 2(a). More than a decade later the situation remained unchanged: 'US Envoy Challenges Government over Censorship, Intimidation of Media,' *Stabroek News*, May 4, 2014. https://www.stabroeknews.com/2014/news/stories/05/04/us-envoy-challenges-govt-censorship-intimidation-media/ (accessed June 30, 2016).
52. The evidence of these attacks on freedom of expression is voluminous, available online with the most cursory of searches. For a broad overview see Ruel Johnson, 'The PPP Has no Moral Currency to Condemn the Attacks on the Freedom of Expression of Writers and Artists,' *Stabroek News*, January 10, 2015. http://www.stabroeknews.com/2015/opinion/letters/01/10/ppp-no-moral-currency-condemn-attacks-freedom-expression-writers-artists/ (accessed Jun 30, 2016).
53. Amnesty International, 'Guyana: Legitimate Debate around Human Rights Issues Must not be Stifled,' April 19, 2002. AMR 35/001/2002. Prefiguring the name-calling so favoured by current US President Donald Trump, former President Jagdeo – also at political rallies like Trump – launched an attack on the independent media, calling them 'vultures' and 'carrion crow': 'Jagdeo's statements designed to endanger lives of media practitioners – ACM'. *Kaieteur News*, October 14, 2011. https://www.kaieteurnewsonline.com/2011/10/14/jagdeo%E2%80%99s-statements-designed-to-endanger-lives-of-media-practitioners-acm/ accessed (April 15, 2018).
54. International Federation of Journalists, 'Journalism Put to the Sword in 2006,' 17–18.
55. *Stabroek News*, 'Pressure Mounts on Nandlall,' October 30, 2014. http://www.stabroeknews.com/2014/news/stories/10/30/pressure-mounts-nandlall/ (accessed June 30, 2016). Translated, without the expletives: 'When you continue to attack people like that and they have no way of responding, they will simply walk with their weapon into that same Saffron street office [where the newspaper is located] and whatever happens, happens, and innocent Peter will pay for Paul in there one day; I tell you innocently, I tell you honestly man to man, that will happen soon.'
56. Inter-American Commission on Human Rights, Resolution 35/2014. Precautionary Measure 458–14, para. 6. November 18, 2014.
57. *Stabroek News*, 'I apologise – Health Minister Sorry after Verbally Abusing Rights Activist,' April 22, 2015 http://www.stabroeknews.com/2015/news/stories/04/22/i-apologise/ (accessed June 30, 2016).

References

Albert, Richard. 2010. Presidential values in parliamentary democracies. *International Journal of Constitutional Law* 8, no. 2 (April): 207–36.
Barnett, Hilaire. 2011. *Constitutional and Administrative Law*. 9th ed. London: Routledge.

Benjamin, Anna. 2007. *Freedom of Expression and the Birth of Stabroek News*. Georgetown: Guyana Publications Incorporated.

Bradley, Anthony, and Cesare Pinelli. 2012. Parliamentarism. In the *Oxford Handbook of Comparative Constitutional Law*, ed. Michel Rosenfeld and András Sajó, 650–70. Oxford: Oxford University Press.

Bulkan, Arif. 2004. Democracy in Disguise: Assessing the Reforms to the Fundamental Rights Provisions in Guyana. *Georgia Journal of International and Comparative Law* 32, no. 3 (Summer): 613–55.

———. 2013. Judicial Independence as an Indispensable feature of the Rule of Law and democracy: implications for the Commonwealth Caribbean. In *Transitions in Caribbean Law: Law-making, Constitutionalism and the Convergence of National and International Law*, edited by David Berry and Tracy Robinson, 199–224. Kingston: Ian Randle Publishers.

Bulkan, Janette. 2014. REDD Letter Days: Entrenching Political Racialization and State Patronage through the Norway-Guyana REDD-plus Agreement. *Social and Economic Studies* 63, nos. 3 and 4:249–79.

Cheibub, José, Zachary Elkins and Tom Ginsburg. 2014. Beyond Presidentialism and Parliamentarism. *British Journal of Political Science* (Nov.): 1–30.

Dale, William. 1993. The Making and Remaking of Commonwealth Constitutions. *International and Comparative Law Quarterly* 42 (Jan.): 67–83.

DeMerieux, Margaret. 1992. *Fundamental Rights in Commonwealth Caribbean Constitutions*. Bridgetown: Faculty of Law Library, University of the West Indies.

Elgie, Robert. 2005. A Fresh Look at Semipresidentialism. *Journal of Democracy* 16, no. 3 (July): 98–112.

Fix-Fierro, Héctor and Pedro Salazar-Ugarte. 2012. Presidentialism. In *The Oxford Handbook of Comparative Constitutional Law*, ed. Michel Rosenfeld and András Sajó, 628–49. Oxford: Oxford University Press.

Fraser, Stephen.2001. The Evolution of Constitutional Protection of Fundamental Rights in Guyana. *Caribbean Law Review* 11:89.

Ghany, Hamid. 1997. Parliamentary Crisis and the Removal of the Speaker: The Case of Trinidad and Tobago. *The Journal of Legislative Studies* 3, no. 3 (Summer): 112–38.

———. 2000. Constitutional Interpretation and Presidential Powers: The Case of Trinidad and Tobago. *Caribbean Dialogue* 6, no. 3/4:23–40.

Girvan, Norman. 2015. Assessing Westminster in the Caribbean: Then and Now. *Commonwealth and Comparative Politics* 53, no. 1:95–107.

Hatchard, John, Muna Ndulo and Peter Slinn. 2004. *Comparative Constitutionalism and Good Governance in the Commonwealth: An Eastern and Southern African Perspective*. Cambridge: Cambridge University Press.

Hinds, David. 2008. Beyond Formal Democracy: The Discourse on Democracy and Governance in the Anglophone Caribbean. *Commonwealth and Comparative Politics* 46, no. 3 (July): 387–406.

Hintzen, Percy. 2004. Creoleness and Nationalism in Guyanese Anticolonialism and Postcolonial Formation. *Small Axe* 8:106–22.

International Federation of Journalists. 2007. *Journalism Put to the Sword in 2006*. Brussels: International Federation of Journalists.
James, Rudolph. 2006. The Constitution of Guyana: A Study of its Dysfunctional Application. *Transition* 35, no. 6:1–178.
James, Rudolph and Harold Lutchman. 1984. *Law and the Political Environment in Guyana*. Turkeyen: Institute of Development Studies, University of Guyana.
McCormack, Michael. 2002. Human Rights Commission: An Elaborate Façade. *Guyana Law Review* 3, no. 2 (Dec): 261–65.
McIntosh, Esther. 2019. Uncontested Democratic Spaces: The Politics and Practice of Local Government in Post-Independence Guyana, 1992–2015 (this volume).
Mawby, Spencer. 2012. *Ordering Independence: The End of Empire in the Anglophone Caribbean, 1947–1969*. London: Palgrave Macmillan.
Midgett, Douglas. 2003. Democracy and Electoral Reform in the Anglophone Eastern Caribbean. In *Living at the Borderlines: Caribbean Sovereignty and Development*, ed. Cynthia Barrow-Giles and Don Marshall, 397–413. Kingston: Ian Randle Publishers.
Morrison, Fr. Andrew. 1998. *Justice: The Struggle for Democracy in Guyana, 1952–1992*. Georgetown: Red Thread Women's Press.
Narain, Frank. 2009. *Historical Information, Events and Dates on the Parliament of Guyana from 1718 to 2006*. Georgetown: Parliament Office.
O'Brien, Derek. 2014. *The Constitutional Systems of the Commonwealth Caribbean*. Oxford: Hart Publishing.
Payne, Anthony, and Paul Sutton. 1993. *Modern Caribbean Politics*. Baltimore: Johns Hopkins University Press.
Ramcharan, Bertrand. 2002. *The Guyana Court of Appeal: The Challenges of the Rule of Law in a Developing Country*. London: Cavendish Publishing.
Ramkarran, Hari. 2004. Seeking a Democratic Path: Constitutional Reform in Guyana. *Georgia Journal of International and Comparative Law* 32, no. 3 (Summer): 585–611.
Robinson, Tracy, Arif Bulkan and Adrian Saunders. 2015. *Fundamentals of Caribbean Constitutional Law*. London: Sweet and Maxwell.
Ryan, Selwyn. 1999. *Winner Takes All: The Westminster Experience in the Caribbean*. St Augustine: Institute of Social and Economic Research.
———. 2000. The President vs the Prime Minister: Testing the Limits of the Constitution. *Caribbean Dialogue* 6, nos. 3 and 4:41–46.
Stepan, Alfred, and Cindy Skach. 1993. Constitutional Frameworks and Democratic Consolidation: Parliamentarianism and Presidentialism. *World Politics* 46:1–22.
Sutton, Paul K. 2013. Westminster Challenged, Westminster Confirmed: Which Way Caribbean Constitutional Reform? *Journal of Eastern Caribbean Studies* 38, nos. 1 and 2:63–79.
Thakur, Rishee S. 2008–2009. Crime, Ethnicity and the Political Impasse in Guyana. *Transition* 38–39:78–105.

Thomas, Clive, N. Jourdain and S. Pasha. 2011. Revisiting the Underground Economy in Guyana 2001–2008. *Transition* 40:60–86.

US Department of State. 2002. *Guyana Country Report*. Mar 4. http://www.state.gov/j/drl/rls/hrrpt/2001/wha/8337.htm.

2.
Guyana's Public Financial Management Systems in the Post-Independence Period

Anand Goolsarran

Introduction

Guyana has had a poor record of public financial management since it gained independence from Britain. A progressive deterioration at all levels of government led to a standstill in public accountability by 1981. Although the Hoyte government made genuine efforts to address this decline, its efforts were short-lived because of a change in administration in 1992.

The decline in public accountability was arrested in 1992, and in addition other reform initiatives were undertaken. This chapter discusses each of these and assesses the extent to which they have achieved their desired impacts and outcomes.

Historical Background

Guyana attained independence from Britain in 1966. It inherited a booming economy due mainly to the high prices it obtained on the export market for its sugar. But with the collapse of sugar prices in 1975 and a weakening demand for bauxite, the economy began to deteriorate rapidly. Reduced export earnings led to a shortage of foreign exchange. As a result, Guyana began to experience difficulties in servicing its external debts, which stood at 187 per cent of total exports in 1980. By 1989, that figure rose to the astronomical figure of 668 per cent. With the devaluation of the Guyana dollar in 1989, total debt exceeded 600 per cent of GDP.[1]

By the mid-1980s, Guyana was unable to meet its debt servicing obligations and ceased making payments to most bilateral and multilateral lenders.[2] As a result, the International Monetary Fund (IMF) declared it ineligible for further credit, making Guyana the first member country to be denied such access.[3] The country was technically bankrupt.

Real gross domestic product declined by an average of 2.8 per cent during the period 1980-88; output in 1986 was only 68 per cent of 1976 levels; and inflation averaged 20 per cent, resulting in a widening of the public sector deficit.[4] More significantly, Guyana's per capita income in 1991 was only US$290, one of the lowest in the southern hemisphere and the lowest in the western hemisphere. Correspondingly, the value of the Guyana dollar depreciated dramatically from GY$2.55 = US$1 in 1975, to GY$10 = US$1 in 1988, then GY$122 = US$1 at the end of 1991.[5]

Following the death of President Burnham in 1985, it was left to the Hoyte administration to initiate efforts aimed at reversing the economic decline. By mid-1986, the government had entered into negotiations with the World Bank and the IMF for a rescue package to overhaul the economy and free it up to market forces. The formulation of the Economic Recovery Programme (ERP) was completed in 1988 and involved, among other actions, the implementation of various austerity measures.

In the area of financial management, the 1966 audited public accounts were produced 19 months after the deadline, compared with an average of seven months delay in the pre-independence period from 1954 to 1964. For 1971, the deadline was missed by over nine years, and in order to correct the situation, the government took an unconventional approach. From 1972 to 1981 it combined several years, and sought to produce accounts for 1972-73, 1974-76, 1977-79 and 1980-81 – with an average of seven years' delay planned for each period.[6] However, these deadlines were not met, and the progressive slippages inevitably led to a halt in public accountability by the end of 1981. By the time the PPP/C was elected in 1992, audited public accounts were ten years in arrears.

The Hoyte administration had inherited seven years of backlogged accounts covering the period from 1977 to 1983. To its credit, it was able to produce audited public accounts for the first five of these years (1977-81) in 1987, albeit in combined form.[7] Further efforts were stymied by computerisation problems involving first the IBM System 3/15 mainframe computer acquired in 1967, followed by an IBM System 34, which ceased to function in 1987, except for the payroll application.[8]

Early Struggle to Restore Public Accountability

In 1990, the auditor general retired, having served 21 years in the position. His successor immediately drew to the attention of the minister of finance, the accountant general, and accounting officers, the legal requirements relating to government's financial reporting and the fact that these had not been honoured for eight years. The accountant general was adamant that computer problems had prevented him from finalising the public accounts for not only the backlogged years, 1982–89, but also for the year in question – 1990. He could not give an indication of how soon these statements would be submitted. On the other hand, accounting officers contended that it was the responsibility of the Ministry of Finance to process transactions and to submit periodic print-outs for reconciliation with the records of all ministries and departments. Because of the absence of such printouts, these officers claimed that they could not carry out the necessary reconciliations and therefore could not prepare their appropriation accounts for submission to the auditor general.[9] The auditor general, however, asserted that:

> Accounting officers and principal receivers of revenue have the responsibility of ensuring that proper records are maintained to account for the receipts and utilisation of the funds under their control. These records must be maintained in such a manner as to facilitate the timely extraction of balances for the purpose of periodic financial reporting.

While it is true that the Ministry of Finance was required to maintain an independent record of transactions relating to ministries and departments for the purpose of updating the public accounts of the country, it should not be relied upon to serve as the bookkeeper of accounting officers. The independent record maintained by the Ministry of Finance would reconcile the records of the accounting officers. However, the fact that the Ministry of Finance was unable to produce printouts of balances relating to ministries and departments does not remove from the accounting officers the responsibility for producing financial statements and is no justification for failure to do so.[10]

Prior to 1992, the audit office had conducted preliminary audits of ministries and departments and had held its findings in abeyance pending the submission of financial statements. The new auditor general proposed that in the absence of financial statements, the results of the preliminary audits should be presented to the legislature, as existing legislation permitted the auditor general to issue a special report on any matter incidental to his powers and duties, if he considered it desirable.[11] The government vigorously opposed this view, prompting the auditor general to seek a legal opinion from the attorney general on the matter. The opinion supported the auditor general's view, resulting in preliminary reports being presented to the national assembly for the years 1982–85.[12]

In October 1991, the auditor general wrote to the minister of finance outlining the problems associated with the government's financial management and making a number of recommendations, including a proposal for a two-pronged approach to restart the process of financial reporting with 1991 as the cut-off year. The key recommendations were:

a. the closure of all government bank accounts and the opening of new ones with effect from 1992 to avoid any contamination from the backlogged years;

b. instituting proper systems and procedures to ensure accurate recordkeeping and reconciliation, and to facilitate timely, reliable, and accurate financial reporting for the future, commencing 1992; and

c. the setting up of a task force to deal with the backlogged accounts covering the period 1982–91.[13]

Although the minister accepted these recommendations, they were not implemented despite strenuous efforts by the audit office to influence the ministry of finance to do so.[14]

Renewed Struggle for the Restoration of Public Accountability

Following the October 1992 national elections, the auditor general renewed his representations to the new minister of finance and met with the head of the presidential secretariat and the accountant general to present his arguments in favour of a resumption of annual financial reporting based on the two-pronged approach he had advocated. The accountant general was not in favour of this approach. He insisted that the level of accuracy in financial reporting would be in considerable doubt, and that it was unprecedented to have financial reporting for later years without completing the earlier years since opening balances were needed. While the auditor general acknowledged that it would take approximately six months to finalise each backlogged year of accounts by way of reconstruction, by the time the exercise would have been completed the 1992 accounts would have been in arrears by five years, hence his recommendation for the adoption of the two-pronged approach.

In February 1993, the government issued instructions to the accountant general and accounting officers to comply with the requirements of the law relating to annual financial reporting of the public accounts.[15] As a result, financial statements for the fiscal year 1992 were submitted for audit. However, submissions were not made without their fair share of resistance and lack of cooperation from those responsible for preparing them.

As was expected, they were somewhat incomplete, in that of the 12 consolidated statements which comprised the public accounts, two were not submitted.[16] However, individual statements of revenues and expenditures of all 200 ministries and departments were presented. The auditor general completed the audit of these statements and accounts, and gave his report to the minister on September 14, 1993 for laying in the assembly, thereby bringing to an end, ten years of absence in financial reporting at the national level. It was a hard-fought victory for public accountability. Since then, there have been annual financial reporting and audits, and laying of the related reports in the assembly.

In relation to the backlogged accounts for the years 1982–91, a task force was set up to compile the financial statements. However, little progress was made and the effort had to be abandoned, resulting in a significant blemish on the history of public accountability in Guyana.

The restoration of public accountability was not without its criticisms. Because the auditor general was extremely critical of the government's management of the country's finances, the Public Accounts Committee (PAC) vigorously challenged the legality and validity of the 1992 audited accounts on the grounds that: (a) they had to be presented as a whole and that the omission of two important statements rendered them invalid; and (b), it was unprecedented to have financial reporting for a later year without the reports of earlier years.

The chairmanship of the PAC was held by a senior minister of the Hoyte administration. The reality was that he was chairing a committee that was examining the auditor general's report covering a substantial part of the fiscal year (namely, 1992) during which his party was in government. Political expediency took precedence over the broader interest in that the opposition members took an extremely defensive position and vigorously sought to discredit the auditor general's report. Instead of the accountant general and accounting officers being asked to explain the deficiencies identified, they were encouraged and prodded to disagree with the findings of the auditor general. Paragraph 7 of the 1992 PAC report captures the essence of what transpired:

> However, because of the apparent inadequacy of the statements provided him by the Accountant General and the Debt Management Unit, the Auditor General was unable to determine the true nature of the Public Debt of Guyana. Indeed, the Accountant General fiercely challenges the amount presented in the report which was tabled in Parliament. In addition, the Auditor General was unable to verify the statement of outstanding loans or credits that had been guaranteed by the government, and the statement of outstanding loans and advances that had been made from the Consolidated Fund. On top of all of this, the Auditor General could not determine also what balances on deposit, at the end of 1992, were held by the Accountant General and what outstanding advances had been made. He could not even certify the current assets and liabilities of the Government.[17]

Despite these criticisms of the auditor general, the effort was a landmark achievement, ushering a new era in public accountability in Guyana. The auditor general's report for the fiscal years 1993 and 1994 were also presented to the minister within the statutory deadline. In terms of content, they were as critical as that of 1992, especially with regard to the failure of the government to submit the two important statements. The 1993 PAC report, which was also finalised in the same month as that for 1992, took a dramatic change in tone. Paragraph 21 reads as follows:

> The Committee commends the Auditor General and his staff for preparing a report on the several statements and accounts submitted to their office. The Committee notes with approval that, because of the omission of two statements, the Auditor General has properly qualified the accounts and statements which the Minister of Finance has laid in Parliament. The Committee emphasizes most strongly that it does not wish to discourage the Auditor General from presenting and commenting on the reports that are made available to him. It urges, however, that it be always made clear that the reports do not represent the public accounts in their entirety, and that those accounts and reports are of crucial importance.[18]

With a change in chairmanship of the PAC, the committee appeared to have set aside partisan political interests, and was genuinely seen to be functioning in the national interest. At the conclusion of the PAC examination, the auditor general was requested to draft the PAC report for 1994 which was laid in the national assembly in March 2000. Through the continuous efforts of the audit office to influence the accountant general's department to prepare and submit the two outstanding statements, it was not until 1996 and 1999 respectively that they were eventually included in the public accounts. Complete and full financial reporting was therefore not achieved until seven years after the restoration of public accountability in 1992.

However, the timeliness of the PAC examination and reporting on the public accounts declined progressively in relation to the fiscal years of 1994 and after. While such examinations can be regarded as relatively timely for the years 1992 and 1993, the same cannot be said for subsequent years, when the initial momentum appeared to have waned. At the time of writing, the PAC's reports for 2012–15 remained outstanding. In addition, a number of years were reported on together: 1995–98 in October 2000; 2000–2001 in February 2006; 2007–08 in March 2014; and 2010–11 in December 2016.[19] This declining trend and combined reporting are disappointing, given the earlier struggles, indeed battles, to restore public accountability.

Once the PAC issues its report on the public accounts, it is expected that a serious effort would be made to inform legislators and the public at large of the actions the government took or intended to take in relation to the findings and recommendations. This is done through the issue of a Treasury Memorandum. However, there was none for the first seven years in the post-1992 period, that is, from 1992 to 1998, and it was not until July 2005 that the first was issued on the 1999 public accounts.[20]

With the resumption of annual financial reporting, one would have also expected to observe gradual improvements in government's financial management. The fact that no Treasury Memorandum was issued for the first seven years would suggest that little or no attention had been paid to the deficiencies identified in the auditor general's reports. It is not surprising therefore that a comparison of those of 1992, with those of 2015, revealed that most of the deficiencies highlighted remained uncorrected.

Financial Administration and Audit (Amendment) Act 1993

The Financial Administration and Audit (FAA) Act was amended in 1993 to clarify the extent of the auditor general's mandate. Should 'the public accounts of Guyana' and 'authorities of the Government' in Article 223(1) of the constitution include public corporations and other entities in which controlling interest vests in the state? Attempts to address this issue date back to 1970 when the auditor general sought a legal opinion on the matter. The response was that the relevant section of the constitution did not directly bring within the authority of the auditor general, the audit of the accounts of those entities, and that provision existed in the law where the minister of finance might require the auditor general to audit such accounts.[21] Despite this provision, most of the public corporations were audited by a private auditing firm without the involvement of the auditor general.

In 1991, another attempt was made to clarify the mandate of the auditor general. This was at a time when several public corporations were experiencing severe financial difficulties, yet the auditors were issuing unqualified opinions on the financial statements of these entities. It was also at a time when the government had embarked on a massive privatisation programme, and there were calls from the political opposition and the media for the auditor general to review the privatisation deals.[22]

What precisely led to the amendment of the FAA Act is beyond the scope of this chapter. Suffice it to state that section 33 was amended to provide the auditor general with the legal mandate to audit all entities in which controlling interest was vested with the state. Provision was made for the auditor general to engage the services of chartered accountants in public practice to audit on his behalf, and under his supervision, any of these entities, if he considered it desirable. The selection of the contracted auditors was based on public advertisement and assessment by a committee comprising the secretary to the treasury, the governor of the central bank, the commissioner of the inland revenue department, the head of department of management at the University of Guyana, and a member of the institute of chartered accountants who was not in public practice. Once appointed, the chartered accountants were prohibited from undertaking accounting, consulting, or taxation services for the entities for which they were appointed auditors, and they could not render auditing services for a particular entity for more than four consecutive years (later increased to six years). Under this arrangement, at least ten chartered accounting firms are now undertaking audits on behalf of the auditor general. It is relevant to note that 11 years later, following the Enron and WorldCom accounting scandals, the Sarbanes-Oxley Act of 2004 was passed in the US to, among other things, provide for similar prohibition of auditors of publicly listed companies.

Integrity Commission Act 1997

Guyana is a signatory to the Inter-American Convention against Corruption (IACAC) which it also ratified in December 2000.[23] Guyana also acceded to the United Nations Convention against Corruption (UNCAC) in April 2008.[24] Both conventions require state parties to take concrete measures to minimise the extent to which corruption is perceived to exist among politicians and senior bureaucrats. This is done through several procedures, including annual declarations of assets and liabilities to an independent body comprising technically and professionally competent persons. Article III (4) of the IACAC refers to 'systems for disclosing the income, assets and liabilities of persons who perform public functions in certain posts as specified by law and, where appropriate, for making such disclosures public.' On the other hand, UNCAC requires state parties to endeavour 'to establish measures and systems requiring public officials to make declarations to appropriate authorities regarding, inter alia, their outside activities, employment, investments, assets and substantial gifts or benefits from which a conflict of interest may result with respect to their functions as public officials.'[25]

The independent body scrutinises the declarations and probes any inconsistencies with observable lifestyles as well as any unexplained increase in wealth. In Guyana, such scrutiny is required to be undertaken by the integrity commission, whose responsibility is to monitor and review annual declarations of assets and liabilities of senior government officials and politicians, and to promulgate a code of ethics to which these officials and politicians are required to adhere.

The Integrity Commission Act 1997 provides for the appointment of a chairman and not less than two or more than four other persons appointed by the president after consultation with the leader of the opposition. Appointment is for such period, not less than a year, as may be specified by the president. Members are also eligible for re-appointment. Three members of the commission constitute a quorum. The commission may also employ a secretary and such other persons required for the proper discharge of its functions, including the retention of the services of professional persons.

Before June 30 of each year, every person in public life is required to make a declaration to the commission, giving full, true and complete particulars of assets and liabilities as at the end of the preceding year, and income for that year, including that of their spouses and children. Schedule I of the Act specifies the list of persons who are required to make a declaration under this act. This includes ministers of the government, members of the national assembly, and senior public servants. Notably absent from the list are officials who are involved in public procurement, especially members of the various tender committees. The Procurement Act of 2003 nevertheless provides for members of the national, regional, and departmental tender boards as well as the secretariat of the national procurement and tender administration board to declare their assets with the commission.

The commission may make such inquiries to verify or determine the accuracy of the submissions, and may request further particulars. Where an eligible person fails to make a declaration or provide additional information as requested, that fact shall be published in the official Gazette and in a daily newspaper. On summary conviction, the penalties for the failure to do this are a fine of GY$25,000 and imprisonment of not less than six months and not more than one year.

Within three months of the close of the year, the commission is required to submit to the president a report containing an account of its activities for that year and difficulties, if any, experienced in the performance of its functions. The report is also to be laid before the national assembly within 60 days of its issue.

It was, however, not until 1999 that the first commissioners were appointed, and these were exclusively from the religious community. Arguably, they would have lacked the relevant skills to properly evaluate the declarations made and therefore it would have been necessary for the commission to engage the services of professional persons. The commissioners were re-appointed after their tenure of office expired but without consultation with the opposition leader. This prompted the latter to institute legal proceedings in May 2005 to nullify their appointments. In April 2006, the chairman of the commission resigned and was not replaced for the remainder of the PPP/C's tenure in office. It was not until February 2018, after a change in administration, that the Integrity Commission was re-constituted.

Successive US Department of State Country Report(s) on Human Rights Practices continued to highlight the lack of effectiveness of the integrity commission as a key anti-corruption mechanism. The 2015 report stated that although there was general implementation of the law relating to criminal penalties for corruption by officials and that the current administration had responded to isolated reports of government corruption, there remained a widespread public perception of corruption involving officials at all levels, including the police and the judiciary. In addition, although the law required public officials to declare their assets to the integrity commission, this has not been constituted despite a statement by the then prime minister in 2012 that its members would soon be appointed.[26] Guyana continues to be rated poorly on the Corruption Perceptions Index (CPI) with a ranking in 2016 of 108 out of 168 countries surveyed, and a score of 34 out of 100,[27] despite a five-point improvement over 2015.

Introduction of Programme Budgeting

Prior to 1998, the government's budget focused mainly on accountability for inputs. This was particularly so in relation to current expenditure. Legislators were therefore approving funding for government departments with little or no knowledge of the intended outputs, outcomes, and impacts. This practice also had the effect of restricting the legislative audit's ex post facto evaluation to one of regularity and compliance, and the evaluation of performance was rendered difficult.

In 1998, the Guyana government attempted to shift the focus from accountability for inputs to accountability for results, through a system of programme-based budgeting. This involved the allocation of resources based on functions and objectives, and results and outputs. Within each entity, a number of programmes were identified, and these were to be supported by sub-programmes and activities. Initially, budgeting was introduced at the programme level and there was to be a gradual phasing in of sub-programmes and activities.

This writer's review of the budget documents since the introduction of this system indicates that although resources were allocated on a programme basis, there were no sub-programmes and activities identified. In addition, although Programme Performance Statements by ministries and departments were presented to the national assembly at the time of the national budget, they were only brief bullet-point statements of objectives, strategies, impacts, and indicators. Given the absence of the quantification of indicators of achievement as well as a report of actual performance, it was not surprising that the auditor general's reports did not include any evaluation of the performance of government departments vis-à-vis their programme budgets. As a result, legislators and the public at large had no way of knowing to what extent these departments had achieved their stated objectives, and what were the actual outputs, outcomes, and impacts.

At the time of writing, the government had committed itself to enhancing its programme budgeting framework with effect from 2018, through the adoption of a Budget Transparency Action Plan in 2015.[28]

Guyana Revenue Authority Act 2000

In 1993, the government took several measures to improve revenue collection, especially at the Customs and Excise department where, with the assistance of a consultant, systems and procedures were overhauled. This has resulted in an average annual increase of 14.4 per cent.[29] In a further attempt at strengthening, the Guyana Revenue Authority (GRA) was established in January 2000 as a replacement to the former government departments of Customs and Excise, and Inland Revenue. This initiative saw a significant increase in the emoluments of the staff in order to attract and retain the much-needed skills; the creation of the position of commissioner-general to manage the day-to-day operations of the re-designated customs and trade administration and the internal revenue; and the establishment of a governing board to provide oversight responsibilities.[30] With these measures in place, revenue collections increased by an average of 9.2 per cent annually between 2000 and 2005.[31]

In January 2007, the government introduced a value added tax (VAT) at a rate of 16 per cent,[32] resulting in a substantial increase in revenue collections. It had indicated that the implementation of the VAT was a revenue neutral measure since a number of other taxes were being abolished. However, several interest groups, including the then political opposition, claimed that the VAT caused a significant increase in the cost of living and argued for a lowering of the rate. According to the audited public accounts for 2007, the amount budgeted to be collected from the VAT was GY$12.111 billion while actual collections totalled $21.384 billion, an increase of 76.7 per cent.[33]

The Value Added Tax Act was amended in 2017[34] to provide for a reduction of the rate from 16 per cent to 14 per cent, while the threshold for VAT registration was increased from GY$10 million to GY$15 million.

However, previously not subject to this form of taxation, the VAT was now imposed on water and electricity, where monthly consumption levels exceeded GY$1,500 and GY$10,000 respectively. In addition, the list of exempted items was expanded and all zero-rated items eliminated, except for those pertaining to exports and manufacturing inputs.[35]

Constitutional Amendments in 2001

One of the main constitutional amendments undertaken in 2001 was the provision for the establishment of a Public Procurement Commission. This amendment was in response to the persistent criticisms by the auditor general of the ministries and departments which failed to adhere to the requirements of the Tender Board Regulations. Contract-splitting to avoid open and transparent competition among potential bidders and adjudication by the relevant tender committees was a common practice. Other issues of concern included defective work performed; inferior quality of goods supplied; and overpayments to contractors and suppliers.[36]

There was public pressure to reform the government's tendering procedures, since many stakeholders, especially suppliers and contractors, held the view that the arrangements in place did not engender confidence in the fairness and transparency of the process. In particular, the various tender committees, including the then Central Tender Board, were appointed by the minister of finance, and the cabinet was responsible for offering 'no objection' to the award of contacts which exceeded GY$15 million. Many contractors also believed that they were not fairly treated during the tender process and there was no mechanism in place to address their concerns. Furthermore, the existing tender regulations were outdated and did not have the force of law.

It is against this background that, during the constitutional review process in 2001, Parliament decided on implementing several procedures, including an independent and impartial public procurement commission with reporting relations not to the executive, but to the legislature.[37] Under this new arrangement, the cabinet would no longer have any involvement in public procurement. Its role would either be progressively phased out, or would cease entirely.[38] The commission of five members who have expertise and experience in procurement, legal, financial, and administrative matters, was to be appointed by the president after persons had been nominated by the PAC, and approved by no less than two-thirds of the elected members of the assembly. In addition, a member could not be removed from office except as provided for in the constitution. An important safeguard is that none of the functions of the commission could be removed or varied except by the votes of not less than two-thirds of the elected members of the assembly. However, any addition required the votes of a majority of elected members.[39]

Despite this important amendment to the constitution aimed at securing public confidence in the public procurement process, it took 15 years for the commission to become a reality, which only happened in 2016 under a new government. The delay was mainly due to the cabinet's reluctance to surrender its role in the procurement process, a role the current cabinet continues to retain at the time of writing.[40] In addition, the responsibility for the appointment of members of the National Procurement and Tender Administration Board (NPTAB), established under the Public Procurement Act 2003 to replace the Central Tender Board, continues to be vested with the minister who also appoints three of the five members of the tender boards of government departments.[41] Suffice it to state that a year after the establishment of the commission, the impact of its work was yet to be felt.

Included in the 2001 constitutional amendments was the requirement for the auditor general to submit his reports to the speaker of the assembly rather than to the minister. In addition, the public accounts of Guyana were defined to include the accounts of (i) all central and local government bodies and entities; (ii) bodies and entities in which controlling interest vested with the state; and (iii) all projects funded by way of loans or grants by a foreign state or organisation. The audit office was also given financial and operational autonomy with oversight responsibility by the PAC.[42]

The Fiscal Management and Accountability Act 2003

The Fiscal Management and Accountability (FMA) Act 2003[43] replaced the administration section of the Financial Administration and Audit Act. Its key features are:

a. the establishment of a timeframe for the commencement of the preparation of the government's budget;
b. the approval of budget submissions, accompanied by programme performance statements by the concerned minister of each budget agency. These statements are to be presented to the assembly together with the national budget;

c. the variation of appropriations permitted across programmes within a budget agency. The maximum variation is ten per cent of the appropriation of the relevant programme;
d. permission for the transfer of appropriations for current expenditures to capital expenditure, though not for the reverse;
e. approval for not more than five supplementary appropriations except in cases of grave national emergency;
f. reporting by the minister at the next sitting of the assembly on all advances made from the contingencies fund since the previous report;
g. repayment of all overdrafts before the end of the fiscal year in which they were incurred;
h. promulgation by the minister of appropriate accounting standards for the maintenance of accounts and records;
i. establishment by the minister of regulations for, among other things, provision for electronic authorisations and certifications as well as digital signatures;
j. maintenance of effective internal audit systems by heads of budget agencies;
k. presentation by the minister to the assembly within 60 days of the end of the first half year, a mid-year report on the annual budget and prospects for the remainder of the year;
l. assumption of responsibility by the minister of finance for preparation of the consolidated financial statements of the government;
m. inclusion in the consolidated statements of an end-of-year budget outcome and reconciliation report, and a statement of contingent liabilities; and
n. presentation by the minister to the assembly, budgetary proposals of all statutory bodies not later than the time of submission of the national budget. In addition, the concerned minister is required to present the annual report of a statutory body to the assembly within two months of its receipt.

As regards the incurrence of overdraft, the two consolidated fund bank accounts were overdrawn by amounts totalling GY$89.455 billion as at December 31, 2015.[44] In addition, standards for the accounting and recording of transactions are yet to be promulgated, and the government continues to use the cash basis of accounting. In recognition of the significant shortcomings in this method, particularly in relation to asset accounting and inventory management, several countries as well as international organisations have migrated to International Public Sector Accounting Standards (IPSAS) or are in the process of doing so.[45] As of May 2017, based on a recent survey carried out by the International Federation of Accountants (IFAC) and the Institute of Chartered Accountants of the Caribbean (ICAC), nearly 60 per cent of Caribbean countries have already adopted IPSAS.[46] While Guyana is committed to its implementation, little progress has so far been made at the time of writing.

Since the passing of the Act, little or no attempt has been made to establish an organised system of internal audit at ministries and departments. Larger ministries continue the old practice of having field auditors whose responsibilities are mainly related to conducting inventory counts and reporting discrepancies. The ministry of finance has nevertheless introduced a centralised internal audit system with a staffing of about 16 persons. However, this is inadequate to provide internal audit coverage of all government departments and therefore there is a need for larger ministries and departments to have their own dedicated internal audit units.

Regarding the presentation to the national assembly of a mid-year report on the annual budget and prospects for the remainder of the year, the first such report to be presented was in respect of the first half of 2007. Although due at the end of August 2007, it was not presented until November 2007. There were also delays in meeting the deadline for some of the subsequent years. However, for 2016 and 2017, the mid-year report was presented in the assembly on August 8, 2016 and August 4, 2017 respectively, well within the statutory deadline.[47]

Procurement Act 2003

The Procurement Act was passed in July 2003 and came into effect in January 2004.[48] It provided for the regulation of the procurement of goods and services, and the execution of works in order to promote competition among suppliers and contractors, as well as fairness and transparency in the procurement process. It replaced the Tender Board Regulations which had become outdated and did not have the effect of law. It was therefore a step in the right direction towards a comprehensive and modern set of rules governing procurement, codified in the form of legislation. Key elements in the new legislation included:

a. prequalification of suppliers and contractors to ensure that the requisite criteria in terms of, inter alia, technical competence and financial standing are met;
b. recording of procurement proceedings leading to the award of contracts;
c. publication of contract awards;
d. prohibition of the splitting of contracts to avoid review by higher authority levels;
e. creation and membership of the national procurement and tender administration board;
f. creation and membership of regional, departmental, and district tender boards;
g. public corporations and other bodies in which controlling interest vests with the state to have their own procurements rules. However, where this is an inconsistency, the requirements of this act prevail;
h. methods of procurement, whether by open tendering, restricted tendering, requests for quotations, single-source procurement, and procurement through community participation; and
i. procedures for dealing with complaints in relation to the award of a contract.

The Act acknowledged the non-establishment of the public procurement commission. It accordingly vested the key responsibilities of the commission with the NPTAB until such time as the commission was established. In addition, by section 54(1) of the Act, the cabinet was given the right to review all procurements exceeding GY$15 million in value with the proviso that, upon the establishment of the commission, this threshold would be revised upward over time so as to promote the goal of progressively phasing out the cabinet's involvement and decentralising the procurement process. In keeping with section 54(6), the cabinet's role would cease upon the establishment of the commission. At the time of writing, the cabinet continued to retain its 'no objection' role.

Audit Act 2004

At a meeting of the constitutional review committee established in 1999, the auditor general met with the committee on possible amendments to the constitution for a strengthened audit office, free of political interference and with adequate resources to discharge its responsibility to the legislature. The results are reflected in the constitutional amendment of 2001 to which reference has already been made.

The Audit Act 2004 was passed on April 13, 2004 and assented to on April 28, 2004,[49] but was not made operational until April 27, 2005. The key changes were as follows:

- The auditor general is mandated to undertake performance or value-for-money audits.
- The government may cause an additional audit to be conducted by an auditor other than the auditor general, where this is dictated by an agreement with an international financial institution.
- The minister of finance may request the PAC to cause an additional audit to be conducted by an auditor other than the auditor general.
- The auditor general is to make regulations for the administration of the act, duly approved by the PAC. The regulations are to include a rules, policies and procedures manual as well as the standards to be used in the conduct of audits.
- The auditor general is vested with the responsibility for the human resources management of the Audit Office, including the development of job specifications and descriptions. However, appointment and discipline of senior officers are subject to ratification by the PAC.
- The auditor general is to include responses to draft audit reports in his report to the legislature. The act reiterates the constitutional provision dealing with financial autonomy of the Audit Office. The budget is to be supported by work plans and programmes, duly approved by the PAC.
- Within four months of the close of the fiscal year, the auditor general is to submit to the PAC an Annual Performance and Financial Audit Report duly audited by an independent auditor.

Included in the draft Audit Act were: (i) the qualification requirements for appointment as auditor general; and (ii) the requirement for the auditor general to be deemed a principal for the purpose of eligible officers to obtain practice certificates from the Institute of Chartered Accountants of Guyana. Unfortunately, these did not find favour with the government and were left out of the final legislation.

Introduction of IFMAS

The Integrated Financial Management and Accounting System (IFMAS) is an IT-based budgeting, accounting and reporting system that manages spending, payment processing, budgeting and reporting for governments and other entities. It incorporates essential financial management functions into one software suite that can be either an off-the-shelf or a custom-made system, depending on the size and needs of the organisation using it.[50]

Prior to 2004, the government's financial management systems operated mainly manually. A Canadian-based software company was contracted to undertake the introduction of IFMAS with the objective of implementing a robust integrated budgeting and accounting system and to further the modernisation of public financial management. This was not only timely, but also a step in the right direction, to take advantage of advances in information technology and to lessen the burden of paperwork associated with manual systems.

IFMAS has seven modules, namely, Appropriation, Expenditure, General Ledger, Budgeting Preparation and Reporting System (BPRS), Purchasing, Revenue and Asset and Inventory. An integral component of the programme involved training of staff to provide them with the skills needed to operate the system. This task was completed by October 2003 in preparation for the roll-out in January 2004 of the first three modules. In 2006, two additional modules – BPRS and Revenue – were introduced, leaving the remaining two – Purchasing and Asset and Inventory – unimplemented to date. Considering the extent of public procurement of materials and services, and works, it is rather disappointing that procurement and accountability for assets and inventory continue to be operated on a manual basis.

AML/CFT Act 2009 and Related Amendments

In 2002, Guyana became a member of the Caribbean Financial Action Task Force (CFATF) which is the regional body of the Financial Action Task Force (FATF), an inter-governmental body established in 1989 to set standards and promote effective implementation of legal, regulatory, and operational measures for combatting money laundering, terrorist financing and other related threats to the integrity of the international financial system. FATF has developed a series of recommendations that are recognised as international standards for combatting money laundering, terrorist financing, and proliferation of weapons of mass destruction.

CFATF's first evaluation report issued in October 2006[51] highlighted the absence of legislation on money laundering. In response, the government tabled draft legislation in the national assembly in January 2007. The assembly referred it to the select committee, and it took more than two years for it to be approved in the form of the Anti-Money Laundering and Countering the Financing of Terrorism (AML/CFT) Act 2009.

The third evaluation report dated July 25, 2011 was very critical of the Act. The main conclusion was that Guyana's legislation needed to be overhauled to conform to the standard recommendations used to evaluate countries' efforts to combat money laundering and terrorist financing. CFATF informed Guyana that the steps it had taken were minimal and that it remained in 'expedited follow-up'. In particular, there was concern that the Financial Intelligence Unit (FIU) had only the director, whereas it was to be staffed also with a lawyer, an accountant and other officials trained in investigative work.[52]

On May 7, 2013, the government tabled amendments to the Act based on the deficiencies identified by the CFATF. The national assembly referred them to a select committee for detailed scrutiny. The government was, however, unhappy with this course, wanting an urgent passage of the amendments as presented, contending that: (a) they addressed all the concerns that the CFATF had raised; (b) the latter had dictated the contents of the amendment bill; and (c) if the amendments were not approved by the May 27, 2013 deadline, Guyana would be blacklisted. However, the then opposition felt that the opportunity should be taken to carry out a more rigorous and comprehensive review of the legislation in view of the following:

 a. Guyana is a transhipment point for cocaine destined for North America, Europe and the Caribbean;
 b. Money laundering is linked to trafficking in drugs, firearms, and persons as well as corruption and fraud;
 c. Money laundering appears to prop up the economy;

d. The proceeds from trafficking in cocaine, estimated to be at least 20 per cent of Guyana's GDP, are used mainly for money laundering purposes;
e. The estimated the size of the informal economy was 40–60 per cent of the of the formal economy;
f. A significant degree of unexplained wealth was being flaunted in front of the eyes of Guyanese with impunity; and
g. There had been no significant arrests and/or prosecutions since the FIU was established.[53]

The government was, however, unwilling to extend the select committee's work to other aspects of the legislation and was concerned only with the deficiencies identified by CFATF. The opposition's position was that it would not be rushed into passing the amendments to the Act. If the deadline was not met, it would be the government's fault since it had had adequate time since July 2011 to prepare the amendments. The opposition stated that it would not support the bill because the government had withheld information it had been requested to share with them. That information was contained in a letter dated April 10, 2013 from the CFATF addressed to the president. The letter referred to several warnings and references to earlier notifications of the precarious position to which Guyana was exposed since November 2012, as well as to assurances given by the attorney general, the minister of finance and the head of the presidential secretariat that the issues raised were being dealt with expeditiously.

The government suggested that in order to meet the deadline, whatever amendments agreed upon so far should be passed in the assembly, and that the other proposed amendments could be dealt with later. This did not, however, find favour with the opposition on the grounds that, based on past experience, the government could not be trusted to keep its word. Fuelled by the thought that doomsday had arrived, the business community, through their elected representatives, went full gear into a panic-stricken mode in support of the government's position, which caused quite a hysteria among the populace. Before any further action could have been taken, Parliament was prorogued, followed by its dissolution and the holding of fresh elections on May 11, 2015.

One of the first tasks of the new administration, based on the position it had taken while in opposition, was the tabling of the proposed amendments to the Act. The opposition chose to boycott the event and therefore the bill gained unanimous support from those legislators who were present. The amendments, which were assented to by the president on July 10, 2015,[54] covered three main areas, namely: (a) the expansion and tightening of certain definitions, and the inclusion of new ones in the interpretation section of the Act; (b) the creation of an AML/CFT authority which would act as a kind of board to provide oversight of the operations of the FIU; and (c) new procedures for the appointment of the director and the deputy director of the FIU.

The entire subsection 2(1) was replaced, essentially to remove the role of the attorney general in recommending to the minister of finance, appropriate action in respect of any person or entity suspected of being involved in anti-money laundering activities and of violating the Act. The amendments now vested that responsibility in the director of the FIU. In addition, the creation of an AML/CFT Authority removed ministerial control over the functioning of the FIU and placed oversight responsibility in the hands of the AML/CFT Authority, comprising ten members appointed by the national assembly by simple majority on the recommendation of the parliamentary committee on appointments.

The minister had been responsible for appointing the director of the FIU. The relevant section was now amended to provide the assembly with the authority to appoint the director and the deputy director by simple majority, based on a recommendation of the parliamentary committee on appointments.

The second amendment to the Act[55] provides for, among other measures, a new definition for beneficial ownership; procedures for the freezing of property of a terrorist or terrorist organisation; and amendments of three other Acts referred to in the schedule.

The latest amendment to the Act in early May 2016[56] provides for: (a) the tightening of the language in the Principal Act; (b) the requirement for all financial institutions to adopt effective risk-based procedures relating to wire transfers; (c) additional responsibilities of the FIU director as regards funds or assets of persons or entities suspected to have met the criteria set out in the United Nations Security Council Resolution 1267 and its successor resolutions, and the procedures to be followed for the freezing of those funds or assets; and (d) amendments to four other Acts contained in the schedule.

Conclusion

There is no doubt that the post-1992 period has been a turning point in the history of public financial management in Guyana, particularly 1993, which saw the restoration of public accountability after a ten-year gap. That gap would remain a significant blemish for the country, and an indictment against the decision-makers and those responsible for maintaining the public accounts.

With the restoration of public accountability, the work of the PAC has been facilitated. Unfortunately, for the fiscal years 1992 and 1993, the PAC allowed political expediency to take precedence over the national interest, but in subsequent years, it settled down and discharged its responsibility in an objective manner. However, there have been slippages in the timeliness of its work and in the preparation of its reports since, at the time of writing, the PAC was still to finalise its reports for the fiscal years 2012 to 2015.

The passing of the Integrity Commission Act, the creation of the Guyana Revenue Authority and the passing of the Public Procurement Act and the FMA Act should be viewed in a positive light. However, the Integrity Commission has not been functioning effectively since 2006. In addition, though the Public Procurement Commission has become a reality after 16 years, the impact of its work is yet to be felt. Indeed, Guyana's fight against corruption over the years has been inadequate, as confirmed by successive US Department of State Country Report(s) on Human Rights Practices.

Several of the requirements of the FMA Act are still unfulfilled. These include quantifying not only indicators of achievement by ministries and departments in the national budget but also indicators of the programme impacts achieved during the current fiscal year; liquidation overdrafts incurred prior to the passing of the FMA Act; promulgating accounting standards for the accounting and recording of transactions; establishing an organised system of internal audit at larger ministries and departments; and reconciling planned execution of the annual budget with the out-turn of that budget, including detailed explanations of any significant variances and their related impact.

The reform initiatives relating to the audit office to insulate it from political influence and to provide it with autonomy and flexibility to discharge its mandate are a welcome development, as is the introduction of IFMAS. However, two important modules of IFMAS remain unimplemented. Finally, the enactment of effective anti-money laundering legislation is commendable, considering the stalemate that had existed prior to 2015.

Notes

1. World Bank, *Guyana: From Economic Recovery to Sustained Growth* (Washington, DC: World Bank, 1993), 3.
2. Ibid.
3. James M. Boughton, *Silent Revolution: The IMF 1979–1989* (Washington, DC: IMF 2001), 763.
4. World Bank, *Guyana: From Economic Recovery*, 3.
5. Ibid., iv.
6. S.A. Goolsarran, *Improving Public Accountability: The Guyana Experience 1985–2007* (Denver: Outskirts Press, 2010), 68.
7. Ibid.
8. Ibid., 75.
9. Government of Guyana, *Report of the Auditor General on the Public Accounts of Guyana and the Accounts of Ministries, Departments and Regions for the Fiscal Year Ended 31 December 1993* (Georgetown: Government of Guyana), 5.
10. Ibid.
11. Financial Administration and Audit Act, Chapter 73:01, Revised Laws of Guyana, s. 32.
12. Ibid., 6.
13. Ibid.
14. Ibid.
15. Ibid.
16. Ibid., 7.
17. S.A. Goolsarran, *Improving Public Accountability*, 91.
18. Ibid., 93.
19. Source: Parliament Office and Audit Office websites.
20. Source: Parliament Office.
21. S.A. Goolsarran, *Improving Public Accountability*, 131.
22. Ibid., 129–32.
23. The Inter-American Convention against Corruption was adopted by Member States on March 29, 1996 in Caracas, Venezuela. It was brought into force at a signing ceremony in Mexico on December 9, 2003.
24. The United Nations Convention against Corruption was approved by General Assembly Resolution 58/4 of October 31, 2003.
25. United Nations Convention against Corruption (UNCAC) 2003, Article 8(5).
26. US Department of State 2015 Country Report on Human Rights Practices, 9.
27. https://www.transparency.org/news/feature/corruption_perceptions_index_2016
28. http://finance.gov.gy/wp-content/uploads/2017/06/budget_transparency_action_plan.pdf
29. Based on author's analysis of the reports of the Auditor general for the years 1992–99.
30. Revenue Authority Act No. 13 of 1996.
31. Based on the author's analysis of the reports of the Auditor general for the years 2000–05.

32. Act No. 10 of 2005, Value Added Tax Act 2005.
33. Government of Guyana, *Report of the Auditor General 2007*, 2/1.
34. Value Added Tax (Amendment) Act 2017, Act No. 3 of 2017.
35. Minister of Finance 2017 Budget Speech, page 81.
36. Based on the author's review of the reports of the auditor general for the years 1992–99.
37. Articles 212W to 212EE of the Constitution of the Cooperative Republic of Guyana.
38. The Public Procurement Act, sections 54(1) and 54(6).
39. Articles 212W to 212EE of the Constitution of the Cooperative Republic of Guyana.
40. Cabinet still exercises its role of offering 'no objections' to contracts in excess of GY$15 million, though it is supposed to surrender that role to a decentralised structure. What that structure should be is to be determined by the Commission, and until that happens, it is likely that Cabinet will continue to be involved in procurement.
41. Sections 16, 19, 21, and 22 of the Procurement Act 2003.
42. Article 223 of the Constitution of the Cooperative Republic of Guyana.
43. Act No. 20 of 2003.
44. Government of Guyana, *Report of the Auditor General 2016*, 14.
45. http://www.ifac.org/system/files/publications/files/IPSAS_Adoption_Governments.pdf.
46. http://www.ifac.org/news-events/2017-03/most-caribbean-countries-have-adopted-or-are-process-implementing-ipsas.
47. http://finance.gov.gy/wp-content/uploads/2017/06/mid-year-report-2016-final-2.pdf.
48. Act No. 8 of 2003.
49. Act No. 5 of 2004.
50. https://www.techopedia.com/definition/981/integrated-financial-management-system-ifms
51. Mutual Evaluation Report: Anti Money Laundering and Combating the Financing of Terrorism (Guyana) dated July 25, 2011, 26.
52. Ibid., 27–109.
53. https://www.stabroeknews.com/2016/features/05/16/guyanas-anti-money-laundering-efforts/
54. Anti-Money Laundering and Countering the Financing of Terrorism (1st Amendment) Act 2015, Act No. 1 of 2015.
55. Anti-Money Laundering and Countering the Financing of Terrorism (2nd Amendment) Act 2015, Act No. 10 of 2015.
56. Anti-Money Laundering and Countering the Financing of Terrorism (3rd Amendment) Act 2015, Act No. 15 of 2016.

3.
Uncontested Democratic Spaces: The Politics and Practice of Local Government in Post-Independence Guyana: 1992–2015

Esther M. McIntosh

> *Democracy is by definition an egalitarian, majority and Unitarian system. It avoids any splitting up of the governing (and at the same time governed) body, any atomisation, any appearance of intermediaries between the whole and the individual.*
>
> P.G Langrod 1953, 'Local Government and Democracy'

The 1990s is an instructive decade for examining the genesis of a seminal and persistent contradiction in the evolution of representative democracy in post-independence Guyana. In 1992, after a 28-year period of autocratic rule, democracy was restored through a democratic electoral process (Carter Center 1992). Since then, the practice of periodically electing officials by popular vote has largely been institutionalised, respected and valued by the state, citizens, and political parties. From this perspective, the Guyana experience reflects normative democratic values for collective decision-making with elections as an accepted pre-condition for representative democracy (Heywood 1997, 196–221). However, the same sustained practice of conducting periodic elections did not hold for the only other representative institution outside of the Parliament: local government. By the time of its 49th year as an independent nation, the Guyanese state had provided only two opportunities for its citizens to elect their local representatives.[1] The first was in 1970 under an undemocratic electoral system (1968–92),[2] and the second in 1994 under a democratic one (1992–2015).

In both cases local elections were held within the first five years of a major transition (colonisation to independence, un-democratic to democratic), and then discontinued. In both instances decentralisation was followed by a greater tendency to centralise, or recentralise, power by the governing parties. Both regime types produced similar results –

namely a 'skeletal', 'inefficient and fragmented' local government system (NDI 1995), in which citizens were disempowered and from which they became disengaged (Skocpol 2003). This chapter uses political economy analysis[3] to examine the political dimensions of Guyana's decentralisation experience. Specifically, it examines the interests and motivations of political actors and of citizens, in order to understand the protracted reform process and the absence of elected representatives for more than two decades. The chapter focuses primarily on the period from 1992 to 2015,[4] but begins with an examination of the post-independence context that shaped local state formation. The Guyana case transcends immediate domestic relevance, providing insights for examining the complex political and institutional dimensions of local government reform, as well as the role of local government in the development of a democratic system of government.

Background

The background section of this chapter seeks to outline the initial national and local government context leading up to the 1992 general election and the reforms to local government that commenced thereafter, to identify key actors and the trajectory of the local government reform process.

Guyana gained independence from Britain in 1966[5] and held general elections in 1968. The first post-independence election is significant because it established several key socio-political characteristics that are contextually relevant to the study of local government. Firstly, it marked the beginning of undemocratic electoral government (up until 1992), and the introduction and practice of a politically centralised system of rule under the supremacy of a single party. Secondly, it showed the continuation from the pre-independence period of the practice of ethnic mobilisation and bloc voting (Premdas 1972; Mars 1995; Hintzen 1989; Danns 2014) by the two main parties: the People's National Congress (PNC) and the Peoples Progressive Party (PPP),[6] which still persists. Under that model, political parties ensured their survival by appealing to and being sustained by their ethnic bases, patronage, and control. In his seminal work on regime survival in Guyana, Percy Hintzen identifies three conditions: '(i) the need to satisfy or neutralize powerful local and international actors (ii) the need to demobilize or co-opt the organized opposition; and (iii) the need to retain mass support and to prevent outbidding' (1989, 57).

Local government elections were held in 1970 for the first time in the post-independence era, the same year the country became a Co-operative Republic.[7] The 1970 election was preceded by a number of laws – the Local Authorities (Elections) Act, Act No. 23 of 1969; the Municipal and District Councils Act, Act No. 24 of 1969 and the Local Authorities (Validation of Appointment and Acts of Members) Act, Act No. 25 of 1969 – which moved the country away from the village level administration.[8] Elections were held in five registration districts, including the major towns of Greater Georgetown and New Amsterdam. Ishmael argues that the 'main objective of the PNC government in holding the local government elections was to try to convince the international community that it was winning support from Guyanese' – as evidenced by its 'victory' in December 1968 – and that it was making inroads into the strongholds of the opposition PPP (2012, 82). Although the elections were mandated to be held every two years, the PNC administration never held local government elections again for the remainder of its time in government.

Marilyn Silverman[9] has documented how the PNC-controlled state perceived and integrated local government and citizens (1979, 466–90). Silverman states that this was done through a policy of 'incorporation', which consisted of controlling 'the workings of the local government organs within the village…the creation of political middlemen or brokers who were historically tied to local factional competition,' noting that 'the incorporation policy exploited existing political, economic, and religious schisms in the village' (Silverman 1976, 480). Using ethnographic research she was able to document the tendency of the state to use coercion, as a result of which citizen support could be obtained through an 'influx of patronage resources' and the 'upward mobility' of citizens achieved through political affiliation with the party in power. Similarly, Grant describes a rural local government context in Guyana in which country district councils were nominated by the Local Government Board, which, like the village councils, were 'subject to the same degree of central control' (1967, 61). He goes on to argue that the main functions of the local government bodies that have 'an obvious significance to the lives of the villages and the future development of their communities have been removed or withheld…by the central government' (73).

In 1973 the government declared its Doctrine of Paramountcy (also known as the Declaration of Sophia), as part of a series of policy reforms in pursuit of the *socialist transformation* of the country. This policy allowed the party to consolidate and centralise its power by bringing all organs of the state under the party. However, under Article 50 of the 1980 Constitution, the regime included the National Congress on Local Government Organs as one of five 'supreme organs of democratic power'. In theory, this was meant to deepen the democratic organisation of the state and to involve citizens in 'managing and developing the communities in which they live' (Chandisingh 1982). These provisions echoed democratic theory, which viewed local government as the basis for strong democracy, capable of moulding future leaders, and a mechanism for popular participation (Lisk 1985). The structures created under the constitution were regional democratic councils (RDCs), municipalities, neighbourhood democratic councils (NDCs), and village and community councils. The representatives of the people were to be elected. The Local Democratic Organ Act of 1980 resulted in the creation of ten RDCs, 65 NDCs and six municipal councils. That year also witnessed the creation of an executive presidency for the country and the installation of its first office holder.

After the PPP/CIVIC's victory at the general elections in 1992, the re-introduction of local government elections was viewed as part of the broader transition to democracy and the provision of greater autonomy at the local level (International Foundation for Electoral Systems (IFES) Report 1994). There was also heavy international involvement and support through agencies such as the National Democratic Institute (NDI) and IFES, which remained engaged in the country and supported the local election.[10] Though there was no strongly stated policy at the time, the incumbent government of Cheddi Jagan showed an interest in community governance and subsequently established Community Development Councils. And given the sweeping electoral victory in 1992, it was highly probable that the elections would return a result that was favourable to the ruling party. In the 1994 election, 1,238 officials were elected to govern six municipalities and 65 Neighbourhood Democratic Councils. The Local Government Commission also ended its term in the same year. The PPP gained control over 49 of 71 localities.

The elections were held amidst criticism from the opposition that there was insufficient legislation. Apart from the legislative framework, there was indication that the new local government bodies required significant investment, streamlining, and development in order to effectively assume the role as representative bodies or service providers. For example, in the post-election period the NDI made a number of recommendations which reflected the lack of capacity, both human and institutional. The recommendations included developing a local government association, convening of a national local government summit to cover topics such as the role and function of local government, parliamentary procedure, and financial management (NDI 1995). The aim was also to begin a dialogue on local government with a view to contributing to the debate on constitutional reform. NDI also identified the need for institutional strengthening and supporting the focal ministry to enhance local government, supporting the central government on local government structures, and on strengthening training institutions for providing adult education training for counsellors.

Provisions around local government were inserted in the 1980 Constitution, and later revised in 2001, which specified – among other things – the need for a new electoral system, the establishment of a local government commission, and a system for fiscal transfer and greater autonomy for local government.[11] Local government elections were mandated to take place every three years, but the one due after 1994 coincided with general elections and the two main parties agreed that it should be postponed. This would again be the case in 2001.

Meanwhile, the 1997 general elections were followed by heightened ethnic tension and violence, which reflected the political fragility of the time and increased tension and distrust among political actors. The situation was ultimately mediated by the Caribbean Community (CARICOM) resulting in the Herdmanston Accord (1998), which recommended the establishment of a Constitutional Reform Commission with a 'wide mandate and a broad-based membership'. The resulting Constitution Reform Act 1999 required the Commission to consider the 'functioning of the local government system and measures to improve its capacity and effectiveness' (1999, 6). A year later, the constitutional reform of 2000 abolished the Supreme Congress and the National Congress of Local Organs.

In 2001, a Joint Task Force on Local Government was established with representation[12] and agreement of the two main political parties – the Peoples Progressive Party/Civic (PPP/C) and the People's National Congress/Reform (PNC/R). The Task Force was mandated[13] to recommend constitutional reforms to local government, which would give local democratic authorities greater autonomy, and to draft and implement legislation. The Task Force held a number of public consultations[14] across the country, numbering 31 altogether, although one key informant reported that these meetings were poorly attended. These recommendations formed the basis of a report that was submitted in 2003, which advocated the following key reforms:

- having members of a lower council sit on a higher council;
- expanding the revenue base of local authorities through a container tax, environmental meters and like measures, and developing an objective criteria for resource allocation;
- the exercise of 'control' by the Local Government Commission which should have substantial powers;
- allowing local authorities the ability to 'influence' programmes and projects in their area;
- a mixed system (simple majority voting and proportional representation) for elections of NDCs and municipalities.

There were inconclusive discussions on creating a single act to govern local government (including the Amerindian Act). The stated intention was to have the next elections governed by a revised system, which would be put in place beforehand and which the Task Force would continue to oversee. The working relationship among members of the Task Force was characterised by intermittent periods of collaboration and periods of discord,[15] and was eventually disbanded in 2009 at the instigation of the government's representative. By 2008, the negotiations between the political parties centred on the five legislative reforms, which were actualised over a seven-year period. This paved the way for local government elections, which were eventually held 22 years later after a regime change in 2016. The suite of legislation and the enactment dates are as follows: (a) Local Authorities (Elections) (Amendment) (No.2) Act, #26 of 2009;[16] (b) Municipal and District Councils (Amendment) Act, #15 of 2013; (c) Fiscal Transfers Act, #16 of 2013; (d) Local Government Commission Act, #18 of 2013, and (e) Local Government (Amendment) Act, #5 of 2015.[17] The last of these was enacted following the 2015 general election.

The Politics of Institutionalising Guyana's Third Tier of Government

Party Politics and Ethnic Voting

Guyana's political system and its broader governance arrangements are central to understanding non-cooperation among political actors in local government reform. The political system places significant power in the hands of the executive (president, cabinet, and government departments). Ivan Bynoe and Talia Choy (2007) point out that the ability of the Constitution to limit the power of government, as well as the independence of the National Assembly, are questionable. Another important variable is the existing inter-party dynamics. Guyana's partisan politics, and the polarisation that resulted from the country's ethnic politics, meant that decision-making during much of the reform process was dominated by the two main political parties. The interactions between them were often marked by discord, acts of non-cooperation, and political stalemate on a range of issues. These factors are significant because they suggest that perceived threats to the governing regime's survival and the consolidation of its power, or in the case of the opposition, of regime domination in a biased political system, would influence the choices and behaviour of political actors.

Public Choice Theorists James Buchanan and Tullock (1962) argue that political actors are largely self-interested agents who pursue their own agendas, which may conflict with the needs or priorities of the public. During the reform process the two political parties were often locked in a prisoner's dilemma, resulting in non-cooperation attributed in part to the perceived future electoral fortunes. At any one time there were other immediate, and often broader political issues, which influenced decentralisation reform and elections. For example, in 2014, the then president candidly remarked that,

> I campaigned [in 2011] and promised people that once we win the next elections, we will have local government elections very, very quickly. That is true, but I did not anticipate that we would have a one-seat minority in the Parliament. That created political uncertainty in the situation and in the body politics of the country.[18]

The 'political uncertainty' referred to was the potential dissolution of Parliament based on a no confidence motion brought by the opposition in Parliament. In addition, the opposition was at the time effectively using the lack of local government elections to rally the public and international community's support 'in defence of democracy'. However, even when such destabilising factors were not present and when the government had a majority in Parliament, it did not hold elections, nor seemed to have had a strong motivation to do so.

The support of the reform process was not constant among parties, and showed signs of shifting over time. There were periods of greater cooperation that advanced reform, and other times when there was a serious breakdown in cooperation and a weakened incentive for change. Importantly, the initiation of the local government reform process was largely the result of a socio-political crisis that engulfed the country in 1997 and generated a sense of urgency, which was not sustained. As time passed both government and opposition evinced decreasing urgency towards advancing local government reform. In fact, both parties agreed to postpone local government elections on many occasions, with the required legislative amendment to facilitate this legally being consensually passed in Parliament.

Nonetheless, both political parties, at various points in time, demonstrated some degree of political will for local government reform and holding elections. Both endorsed the need for *de jure* changes to the legal framework to support the requisite legislation. The PNC and the PPP agreed to the Herdmanston Accord, and were willing to adopt an institutionalised dialogue process to resolve the issue of local government reform. Both supported the establishment of the Special Task Force and participated in advancing its work. Both continued to acknowledge generally the importance of local government and the importance of holding elections, including in their 2011 manifestos. The PPP/C promised to hold elections within a year of the general elections and to reinvigorate local government, while the PNC/APNU pledged to reintroduce village councils, retain the NDCs and RDCs, and introduce constituent elections at the level of the RDC. But political will is in itself inadequate in understanding the behaviour of political actors.

The temporal dimensions are also significant. Each time local government elections occurred after a democratic transition, when a new government was in power after several decades in opposition. The 1992 government inherited an institutional legacy of control and domination by the centre, and its response was to consolidate its power and establish the legitimacy of the new government. As explored in the next section of this chapter, that consolidation included the use of informal mechanisms such as coercion and patronage, which could explain a propensity to limit reform. The unrest of 1997 brought to a head the issue of constitutional reform and linked to that, local government reform, which had previously not been a priority of the new government. For example, the 1994 elections were held under the old system and without a strong legislative basis. Constitutional reform presented not just a choice of whether or not to have local government elections, but also of holding local government under a new dispensation that significantly empowered local actors and potentially took power away from, and competed with, the centre.

The proposed reforms had different implications for the three aspects of decentralisation: administrative, fiscal, and political. The suite of reforms required all the legislation to be put in place at once, which meant that political parties were locked into a zero sum game in which they had to agree on what collectively represented significant changes, as opposed, for example, to sequencing reform.[19] One reason for this is that the reform package was seen as interdependent and reinforcing. Tulia Falleti argues that there are preferences among national stakeholders for some types of reform over others; administrative reform is preferred over fiscal decentralisation and fiscal over political decentralisation (2005, 330). The roll out of the five proposed reforms suggests that the government was more motivated to support some reforms rather than others, which in reality resulted in a gradual approach. The government and opposition were able to advance the Local Authorities (Elections) (Amendment) Act, which was assented to in 2009 relatively quickly. The government thereafter assented to three out of four remaining bills four years later when it was at the time a minority government. The final piece of legislation (the Local Government (Amendment) Act) was never enacted during the PPP/C's administration and was only assented to in 2015 after an opposition coalition took office.

The inter-party dynamics of the main opposition parties were a key driver of non-cooperation. The relationship between the two political parties was tense at various times throughout the reform process, and there were periods of political strain and discord, with the political opposition refusing to participate in Parliament and staging a series of 'walkouts' from the national assembly on a range of issues apart from local government. For example, the opposition staged a walk out in 2003 on the basis of a

Customs Duties (Amendment) Bill, which was lodged with the clerk of Parliament beyond the time prescribed by the Customs Act. Similarly, in 2013 the then minority government of the PPP also practised this form of resistance against the tabling of a motion to establish a National Heritage Commission. In 2014 the leader of the opposition issued an ultimatum to the PPP government demanding that local government elections be held by a particular date.[20] There were high levels of non-cooperation as each side accused the other of 'obstructionist tactics' and 'theatrics'.

The accusations and counter-accusations among political parties were often played out under the eye of a watchful international donor community, which on occasion publicly advocated for local government elections to be held and reforms realised. Several international donors had invested over the years in local government capacity development. The ability of international actors to influence local government reform in the country was considerably weaker, and less effective than its role in general elections. However, the international community showed a propensity to work together and adopt a common position vis-á-vis local government elections when it engaged the state.[21] The advocacy of international actors at times resulted in tensions with the ruling administration.[22]

Reform Process Design

The *design* of the reform process itself is also central to understanding the issue of local government. One decision, agreed upon at the time of the Herdmanston Accord, was that reform should precede local government elections. The result was that a reform process meant to empower citizens ultimately became politicised and produced outcomes that were arguably not in the public's interest. The realisation and efficiency of the reform process was tied to the workings and practice of the Task Force, which itself was generally unable to deliver agreed outputs in a timely manner and to reach consensus. Apart from this, despite the passage of time and key developments in local government approaches and in the local context, 'reform' centred on areas of agreement initiated in 2001. In addition, even with the presence of various mechanisms (the Task Force, Special Select Committees) to ensure dialogue and consensus, these proved inadequate. For example, in response to the decision of the government not to endorse the fifth and final piece of legislation, President Ramotar accused the opposition of reneging on changes previously agreed to, saying that it was unconstitutional: 'They [the opposition] have tried to take the authority of the minister and invest it into a commission. That goes against the Constitution, that's why I didn't assent to it.'[23]

Both sides regularly accused the other of derailing the reform process by acts of non-cooperation, including non-attendance at meetings. The government accused the opposition of 'dancing'[24] about the issues and holding the process to 'ransom'.[25] At other times there was agreement that dialogue had to be parked because consensus could not be reached, as happened with the composition of the Elections Commission and the formula to be used for the transfer of monies to the local government organs.

The introductory section of the 2003 Task Force report alludes to these challenges, disclosing that the task force had 'weathered the storms' to produce the report and listing several key areas where they were unable to arrive at consensus, referred to as minority positions. Despite the difficulties with collaboration, the task force continued to function in support of drafting the legislation. This drafting required extensive dialogue, the production of a bill and submission to the Select Committee, all of which suffered numerous delays. Ultimately, after a situation of impasse the Special Task Force was dissolved in 2009. Following the 2011 general election and the emergence of a minority government, the PPP often shifted the blame for not having the election to the 'people with the one seat majority'.[26]

Crook (2003) argues that in practice, decentralisation is often used as a tool by national level actors in order to exert control, and of both mobilising and maintaining regional power bases. Put differently, local government is a means to advance the interests of those in power, which runs counter to actions which seek to devolve power away to the centre. G. Filkin et al. (2000) argue that centre-local relations are very top down and the government sees 'local government primarily as a means to deliver its own policies, as its agent.' Until 2011 when it became a minority government, the ruling party had recorded successive victories at the general elections and maintained a majority in Parliament, but even while outnumbered in Parliament the government was still able to continue to consolidate its power. Through the power vested in the executive, it was also able to exert control over key organs of the state. During this time the government also adopted an increasingly centralised approach to decision-making with power vested in political elites, including the president and ministers of government, which ran counter to the proposed reforms that sought to limit the power of functionaries such as the minister with responsibility for local government.

The local government reform process, and the changed institutional rules that it proposed, would have significantly altered the design of state institutions and the power and authority that the state previously enjoyed. For example, the reforms reduced the power of the minister of local government. It vested power in a shared body (the Local Government Commission), created opportunities for greater and more egalitarian distribution of resources, and reduced the control of the state over resources, the latter being crucial to sustain political patronage and coercion. Undoubtedly, the reform process would limit the power and authority of the ruling party. Local government could have strengthened the government's base or it could have provided an opportunity for the opposition to consolidate its own base of support. It could also have empowered alternative blocs to rival the state. An example of this is the tension between city and national government in 1994 brought about because of the dissolving of the City Council and its replacement with a presidentially appointed interim committee. Further, the victory of a small, independent party of the country's largest and most politically significant municipality (Georgetown) in 1994 posed a potential challenge to the PPP regime. Similarly, the opposition could also have perceived that local government could potentially have helped the government to further strengthen its base of supporters and make inroads into opposition strongholds.

The decision of whether local government elections should be held or not, and what priorities the reforms should take, remained issues which were controlled by political parties and political elites. One implication was that reform options were tied to party interests. For example, the proposal to ban political parties from contesting local government elections was ruled out as being unconstitutional, but it also served the interest of both parties for the process to include political parties. Despite the growing strength and presence of civil society actors at the national level, there was no representation of civil society organs on the task force. And citizen participation was largely through consultation (31 meetings were held across the country by the task force) or other tokenistic (Arnstein 1969) forms of inclusion. Gordon Tullock (1965) argues that the 'rational ignorance of the voter' is a key contributing factor to the dominance of political actors. And in the Guyana case, both citizens and civil society representatives were largely excluded from the decision-making table, leaving political actors to make decisions in their best interest. Even though political parties would profess a commitment and willingness to decentralise, in keeping with constitutional dictates for inclusivity and citizen participation, this was not followed by action. Moreover, neither citizens nor civil society exerted sustained pressure on the government to implement the reforms or hold local government elections. The motivations and incentives of citizens and civil society in this regard are examined separately in the following section.

Popular Participation and Voice

Elections are a central feature of a representative democracy (Dahl 1971), and are the primary – though not the sole – mechanism that allows citizens to influence the state apparatus. In this regard two important dynamics in Guyana warrant closer attention, those of electoral incentives, as well as citizen motivation and demand for participation and representation. It is recognised that as Heywood (1997, 211) argues, 'elections may not in themselves be a sufficient condition for political representation', but they are 'a necessary condition'. G. Cheema and A. Rondinelli (2007) and R.C. Crook and J. Manor (1998, 1–31) have all discussed the participation in local governance as a precondition for consolidating democracy. It can be argued that in the period of transition that was initiated in the 1992 national elections, by extension, local elections were an equally important mechanism for deepening and embedding a culture of democratic rule. Guyana's 1980 Constitution specifically elaborated that the authority exercised by local government was to be legitimised through a democratic process.

A democratic local government system allows citizens to vote for their representatives, who in turn represent their interests and make decisions and act on their behalf. And citizens are able to hold them to account through the process of election. By extension, local government would allow citizens to express preferences – to influence larger processes and institutions at the national level. In a country with high poverty levels as existed in Guyana in the 1980s and 1990s, and a history of centralisation, the opportunity for greater localised control could arguably have been empowering for citizens, particularly marginalised groups. However, throughout the post-1992 period under examination, there was no significant or sustained demand (in the form of demonstrations and petitions) from citizens or civil society organisations for local government elections, and calls for elections were led mainly by political opposition parties.[27] The relationship between the Guyanese state and its citizens, as well as the experience and perceived utility of local government by citizens, are central to understanding the levels of apathy that characterised citizen participation and the low value that they ascribed to local government.

There is a substantial body of literature on local government that advances a Tocquevillian[28] view of citizen participation[29] and 'voice' (Hirschman 1970) in local government processes. Guyana's constitution is consistent with the argument that attributes an important role for participatory democracy. Local government by freely elected representatives of the people is an integral part of the democratic organisation of the state. Article 13 of the Constitution notably provides:

> The principal objective of the political system of the State is to establish an inclusionary democracy by providing increasing opportunities for the participation of citizens, and their organisations in the management and decision-making processes of the State, with particular emphasis on those areas of decision-making that directly affect their well-being.

This is reinforced by specific provisions in the Constitution, such as for the organisation of local government to involve as many people as possible in the task of managing and developing the communities in which they live;[30] and the organisation by local democratic organs of popular co-operation in respect of the political, economic, cultural, and social life of local areas and cooperation with the social organisations of the working people.[31]

The failure to hold regular LGEs in the post-independence period, after the sole one in 1970, meant there was a generational gap in experience of local representative democracy. Citizens did not in recent times have a culture of electing local representatives to occupy NDCs and municipal authorities, which possibly accounts for the low levels of voter turnout at the 1994 election (47.91 per cent), even in key urban centres such as the capital where the turnout was especially low (33.37 per cent). These low levels contrast starkly with participation in the national election of 1992, in which more than 80 per cent of eligible voters exercised their franchise.

There is a paucity of research in Guyana on citizen participation, especially at the local level. However, there is some research that gives insight into perceptions and actual experiences of citizens with local government. Mark Pelling (1998) examined community level participation and social capital in relation to climate vulnerability in two communities four years after the 1994 election. The study highlights a number of important features that existed at the local level. For example, citizen participation was practically understood through the notion of self-help and contributing labour and resources to community development projects, what Sherry Arnstein (1969) refers to as manipulation or tokenism with little power to affect process and development outcomes.

In 1998, Pelling's qualitative research showed that the system was non-representative, top-down and politicised. It was found that 'government positions [were] being appointed by political parties rather than directly elected by the community'. The leadership of the local authorities was largely male and from persons within the community who held power such as businessmen. In addition there was overlap in the leadership of community based, non-governmental bodies and the local government authorities (NDI 1995; Pelling 1998). As a result, 'When local residents were asked who their representatives were and what works had been done most were unable to make a distinction between the roles of the elected local authority and the unelected community group leaders.' The system was highly politicised, as resource distribution was biased 'in favour of community groups associated with local authorities that supported the party in power' (Pelling 1998, 479). The community's leadership as well as the community itself became an 'external construct' with command coming from higher authorities under the direction of national parties and funding agencies to whom they were more responsive. In practice, low levels of accountability to citizens by leaders and elected officials affected the public value that local government was able to realise and this resulted in non-participation and withdrawal as reflected in the significant absence of citizens in public meetings.

Less than a decade later, a national quantitative study conducted by Vanderbilt University[32] examined the phenomenon of citizen perceptions of local government and found striking parallels to the Pelling study. This suggests that the local political culture remained largely ingrained and revealed declining civic participation (measured by participation in meetings), a sense of alienation, and low levels of awareness and value ascribed to local as opposed to central government.

The LAPOP study, authored by Bynoe and Choy (2007)[33] found that a slightly greater margin (12.3 per cent) of persons reported that they would seek assistance from local government as opposed to central government. However, the overall engagement with either state actor was low (11.2 per cent), and a significant number (33.4 per cent) contributed (money or materials) to community development initiatives or services in their community. The study also found a correlation between citizens who were politically affiliated and those more likely to seek assistance. Overall there was the implication that 'party paramountcy takes precedence over the operations of democratic organs'. In response to a question to gauge participation – 'Have you attended an open town meeting or a municipal or district session during the last twelve months?' – the vast majority (86 per cent) had not.[34]

The presence of civil society organisations – community based organisations and non-governmental organisations – also meant that there were other opportunities for citizens to participate and address their needs outside of the state structure. Whereas women's participation in such groups tended to be high, female participation in local government was low (Myers 2002, 1–16).[35] 'A number of unsatisfactory interactions with local officials may erode confidence in the democratic institutions of governance and cause persons to seek redress by either forming their own social groups, or taking matters into their own hands' (LAPOP 2007). The study found that 'nearly 33 per cent of respondents who attended meetings were of the view that very little attention was paid to their issues,' and 61.7 per cent felt that 'some attention' was paid.

Contrary to viewing their local authorities as allowing for, among other things, direct representation of their interests and an opportunity for more efficient service delivery as the literature suggests, the perception of citizens was that it had little value, and 38 per cent of citizen respondents reported that 'the national government should assume greater responsibility of the six (6) municipalities in the country'. This finding suggests that citizens have a better view of the ability of the state to manage their local services and a poor view of the abilities of their local authorities, several of whom were being reported to have high levels of corruption and poor performance. Linked to this was an unwillingness (75 per cent) to pay increased taxes to support the work of the local authorities. Citizens generally held a poor perception of the usefulness and capabilities of local government in part because they generally could not influence the decisions of their local governments, nor did they perceive that they stood to receive any significant benefit. After several decades of dysfunction, local government was largely undermined especially with regard to its role as a democratic institution.

Prevalence of Alternative Mechanisms

A notable feature of the Guyanese political context was the tendency of the formal state structure to create alternative or 'shadow' institutions that ensured that power rested with the centre (Briscoe 2008) and supported greater flexibility in allocating resources. It is, however, important to note that alternatives were not just features of state practice but also an indication of the views of citizens.

The return to democracy in 1992 resulted in an exponential increase in the number of civil society organisations throughout the country, covering a spectrum that ranged from community based organisations to national level non-governmental organisations (NGOs) and to special interest groups.[36] These provided citizens with an opportunity to get involved directly with issues that affected them and thereby obtain services and benefits that either replaced or complemented the provisions that could be made by local government. These groups were also supported by funding that was specific to non-governmental bodies, mainly from international non-governmental organisations (NGOs) and donors.

At the local level, poverty and the absence of services in some areas increased the demand for such formations. The 2008 LAPOP study found that almost half of the respondents (47 per cent) indicated that they sought to establish some social grouping to address issues affecting their community. These were potentially more responsive to citizens and afforded them greater control than they had over their local authorities. In addition, the interaction between local governments and civil society is clearly very substantial, not only in sharing common leadership (Pelling 1998) but also in the form of collaboration and the possibilities for influencing each other.

At the national level these structures took two forms. Some were specifically linked to the local government structures (Interim Management

Committees) while others, such as the CDCs, allowed the government to channel support to areas and communities which they prioritised, or which were potentially more politically aligned to them. The presence of these mechanisms can also be seen in light of the depleted capacity and legitimacy of local government institutions to perform their duties, and in fact the justification was usually the non-performance of the NDCs. Pelling (1998) observed these two structures working side by side, recording that resource management decision-making in rural areas was being done by elected organs (NDCs) and non-elected groups, specifically Community Development Committees.

The introduction and use of the Interim Management Committees (IMCs) was by far the most contentious. The Local Government Act allows for the dissolution[37] through a process in which a request is made by registered voters, which then triggers an inquiry to be commissioned by the minister who would in turn dissolve and appoint new officers. For example, in 2012 there were concerns about the level of accountability and efficiency of the NDC that governed Port Kaituma, Arakaka and Matthews Ridge, which was dissolved and an IMC formed. This comprised 13 persons who were sworn in under the auspices of the Regional Chairman's office. This then allowed for the identification of the governance body (chairman, vice chairman, and councillors) but it did not affect its staff. The IMCs allowed the governing party to select persons who were politically aligned to its interests. As a result, as the example of the IMC installed in Bartica in 2012 demonstrates, these bodies were not recognised by the opposition and were branded as illegitimate. Despite the legal basis for the dissolution of a local authority, the frequency[38] with which it was exercised made it seem less as a measure for exceptional circumstances, and more as a means of exerting control and influence in local affairs by the centre.

Conclusion

Guyana's historical legacy and its institutional framework are two important factors that have contributed to centre-local relations in post-independence state formation. Other factors such as the ethnic divide are also significant. However, the Guyana case highlights the primacy of politics and the influence of politicians and political parties on local government reform. Although there was a broad commitment to reform, contested local democratic spaces remained unrealised for more than 20 years. The

Guyana local government reform process suggests that there is likely to be little cooperation among political actors, and a likelihood of stalemate for protracted periods of time. The way that the reform process was structured had a direct bearing on the introduction of regular and sustained local government elections. In such a context, political considerations of political parties and governments will likely supersede the interests of ordinary citizens and impede the development of local democracy. The more than two-decade reform process resulted in very specific reforms, but with hardly any ongoing dialogue on further development or on integrating innovative practices (such as participatory budgeting).

Despite the fact that the ruling party showed an interest in having local government reform in the immediate aftermath of entering office, that interest was not sustained beyond one election in 1994. The national government had a greater proclivity to rule from the centre, maintaining central government control and reducing the risk of potential competition from localities and the strengthening of opposition groups. In this way, the Guyana experience runs counter to the literature that suggests that decentralisation can be used as a means by central political parties and governments to exert control by mobilising and maintaining local power bases (Crook 2003). One explanation for this could be the patronage and control that the ruling party was able to exert directly from the centre or through alternative mechanisms that were favourable to it. The interest in and prioritisation of local government reform and elections were hardly consistent from the opposition, and at many critical junctures they agreed with the government to defer elections.

Ultimately, local democracy in Guyana was retarded significantly by the absence of elections. This led to the weakening of the local democratic bodies to the point where they became dysfunctional and held little utility in the eyes of citizens. It can be argued that had citizens been provided an opportunity to elect and govern their own localities with less political interference, greater power and resources, this perception could have been very different. The global trend to move from a narrow understanding of local government and its functions to a broader and more dynamic approach to community or participatory *governance* resonates well with the local experience in communities. The absence of strong local government authorities has enhanced the importance of non-state actors (including community-based organisations and non-governmental organisations) to respond to local needs and represent local interests. The capacity and skills developed among individuals within the non-state actors can produce a cadre of future leaders who can transition from functioning within non-state structures to being local government representatives and contest local elections. However, in the short term, the partisan nature of the political system will likely be replicated at the local level to ensure the survival of political actors. The Guyana experience highlights the challenges and fragility of local government within a complex socio-political context. At any given time the interests of key individuals and collectives who hold national power will determine and shape the presence and quality of local democracy in Guyana.

Notes

1. Local government here refers specifically to neighbourhood democratic councils and municipalities since village council elections in indigenous areas are governed under the Amerindian Act 2006, and elections for regional democratic councils are held at the same time as general elections.
2. There is an emerging body of research that examines local government in autocratic states mainly written as an examination of individual country experiences, including China.
3. Political Economy Analysis (PEA) examines how interests, incentives, and institutions shape and explain how agents behave and the political processes and practices that affect development outcomes (Hudson and Leftwich 2013).
4. The period under examination is from 1992 up to the regime change in 2015; during this period, the country was consistently governed by a single political party.
5. For a review of the local government system during the colonial period, see Allan Young, *Approaches to Local Self-Government in British Guiana* (London: Longmans Green, 1958). At the time of independence, the country had inherited the 1945 Local Government Act Chapter 150 (now Chap 28:02 of the Revised Laws of Guyana), the Municipal District Councils Act (Chapter 28:01), and another act establishing a fund for local authorities, now Chap. 28:05.
6. See Ralph Premdas for a detailed analysis of how in the pre-independence period ethnic bloc voting between Afro- and Indo-Guyanese became ingrained over the 1957, 1961, and 1964 elections.
7. A key feature of socio-political organisation at the time was the introduction of co-operative bodies (see Lutchman 1970) that were formed across the country with local authorities serving as co-ordinating agencies at the district level. It is noteworthy that at the time of the 1970 election Prime Minister LFS Burnham had responsibility for local government as well as for the following portfolios: external affairs, economic development, public service, and community development. By 1972, the responsibility for local government

had been passed to W. Haynes. Source: John Paxton, *The Statesman's Year-Book 1970–71: The One-volume Encyclopedia of all Nations* (Basingstoke: Palgrave Macmillan Ltd.).
8. Paul Singh's *Problems of Institutional Transplantation: The Case of the Commonwealth Caribbean Local Government System* argues that in Guyana both the 'uneconomic size' and inadequate resources were a factor in the weakness of local government systems. As early as 1960, the thrust towards larger geographic centres was discussed, through the creation of larger all-purpose authorities that would include small village units and sugar estates. The latter were outside of the local government system.
9. Marilyn Silverman's research in *Dependency, Mediation, and Class Formation in Rural Guyana* is based on qualitative research in a community renamed Rajghar.
10. IFES supported voting infrastructure and educating citizens and polling officials, producing a guide *The ABC for Local Government Elections, 1994* to equip polling stations. In total, more than 3,800 persons were trained to conduct the elections at 929 polling places. The IFES report acknowledged that 'many citizens do not yet understand the important role government, national and local, play in their daily lives or the responsibilities of citizens in a democratic society. Confidence is still lacking in the government and the democratic process. Coupled with building confidence in the government, the programme should also instil a sense of pride of being a citizen of Guyana' (1994, 31).
11. Guyana Constitution 1980, amended in 2001, articles 71–78.
12. There were four members from the government, three members from the opposition, a resource person, and a scribe. Both sides had a legal expert and persons with recognised expertise in local government. The report also acknowledges the technical assistance provided by the American government which overall suggests that there was adequate capacity to support the reform process.
13. Specifically, the task force was supposed to (1) generally ensure the conclusion of the constitutional reform process and give effect to the new constitutional provisions regarding local democracy; (2) specifically monitor and guide the drafting, passing and implementation of legislation to give greater autonomy to local government bodies, including: (a) the establishment of the local government commission and (b) the formulation and implementation of objective criteria for the purpose of the allocation of resources to, and the garnering of resources by local government organs; (3) recommend measures for continuous education programmes on the new local government system, and; (4) recommend to the Local Government Commission mechanisms to monitor the work and functions of all established local government institutions and bodies.
14. The consultations covered topics such as what is a pertinent system, the autonomy of local government bodies, the electoral system of local government and the operation of local government bodies.

15. In 2009, a local newspaper, the *Guyana Chronicle*, reported on a statement by the co-chair of the Local Government Task Force, Mr Clinton Collymore, in which he cited a range of issues, including the lack of a quorum at meetings to more fundamental discord among task force members – in particular he referenced the opposition's unwillingness to discuss the Local Government (Amendment) Bill and to instead focus on the Local Government Commission Bill that was less of a priority for the PPP/C members of the task force (*Guyana Chronicle*, Terminated, April 9, 2009).
16. The Local Authorities (Elections) (Amendment) Act No. 26 of 2009 provides for local government elections to be held in all of the existing local authority areas in Guyana using a mixed electoral system of proportional representation and first-past-the-post. Fifty per cent or half of the number of councillors of each local authority area would be elected through the proportional representation component and the other 50 per cent through the first-past-the-post or constituency component. It also allowed voluntary groups, political parties, and individual candidates to contest for seats in the municipalities and NDCs.
17. The final piece of legislation was especially contentious since it removed the power of the minister of local government to dissolve local authorities and place those powers in the hands of a local government commission.
18. *Kaieteur News*, 'Pick One, it's Either Local Government or General Elections – Says Ramotar in New York,' September 23, 2014.
19. In 2007, the parliamentary opposition (PNCR-1G, AFC and GAP-ROAR) issued a press release which stated that 'the Reform of the Local Government System, as recommended by the Joint Task Force on Local Government Reform, including the reform of the Local Government Electoral System, the institution of the new system for Fiscal Transfers and the establishment of the Local Government Commission, should be fully implemented prior to the holding of Local Government Elections' and that the task force should be 'responsible for overseeing the drafting of the new Local Government Act to ensure that its provisions accurately reflect their recommendations' (source: www.guyanapnc.org).
20. *Kaieteur News*, 'Local Govt. Elections...Granger Gives Ramotar Sept. 15 Ultimatum,' September 10, 2014.
21. The donor community (comprising mainly the UK, US, Canadian governments and the EU) have consistently advocated for local government elections mainly through issuing joint statements, raising the issue in meetings and at public events. In January 2013, the ambassadors and high commissioners of the US, UK, Canada, and the European Union stated, jointly, 'Given the important and pressing need for effective local governance, we believe that 2013 should be a watershed moment for the people of Guyana – the year they can once again democratically elect their local government...the institutions and practice of local governance have withered on the vine.' *Stabroek News*, January 10, 2013, 'Western Envoys Urge Local Government Polls.' In 2014, the UK High Commissioner described the lack of local government elections as a 'stain on

Guyana's international standing,' *Stabroek News*, June 11, 2014. Similarly, the US Ambassador reiterated the support of the US government for local elections, *Stabroek News*, October 6, 2015.
22. For example, in response to the public call by the UK High Commissioner the then Prime Minister Sam Hinds stated on the government's behalf that elections should be kept a 'local issue', i.e., outside of the purview of international scrutiny, *Stabroek News*, 'A Stain on Guyana' – UK Envoy Says about Withholding of Local Gov't Polls,' June 11, 2014).
23. *Guyana Chronicle*, 'Local Government (Amendment) Bill Unconstitutional – President Ramotar,' November 11, 2013.
24. Comment attributed to Local Government Minister Ganga Persaud, in *Weekend Mirror*, June 1, 2013, 'PPP exposes opposition's historic efforts to delay local government elections to the detriment of all Guyanese.'
25. Comment made by Clinton Collymore, adviser to the minister of local government and regional development, in the *Guyana Chronicle*, 'Local Government Elections Issue...,' June 23, 2012.
26. Ibid.
27. In the run up to the elections some civil society groups such as the Blue Caps and the media did advocate for local elections.
28. Alexis de Tocqueville focused on the importance of local government and civil society in relation to the development of democratic institutions in a country. He argued that local government is a necessary element of democracy.
29. Anwar and Shaw argue that the literature is still weak on how participation could be achieved in local governments (2002).
30. Constitution of Guyana, 1980, Article 71(1).
31. Ibid., Article 74(2).
32. Latin American Public Opinion Poll is a scientifically rigorous comparative survey of public opinion in the Americas and produces reports on individual attitudes, evaluations and experiences.
33. See Mark Bynoe and Talia Choy, *The Political Culture of Democracy in Guyana: 2006*, part of the research conducted by the Institute of Development Studies (IDS) and coordinated by the Vanderbilt University Latin American Public Opinion Project (LAPOP).
34. Based on the comparative findings, this response is comparable to those in other Caribbean countries.
35. In *Local Government, Decentralization and Gender*, Roxanne Myers cited the low levels of female representation in Guyana arguing that 'the current status of women in local government will reveal that female representation is at best minimal.' She found that of the current 1,125 councillors in 65 NDCs, only two chairs, eight deputy chairs, and 132 councillors were women. In the ten RDCs, there were no female chairs and only one female deputy chair. Similarly, in the six municipalities there were no women mayors and only one woman deputy mayor.
36. There is little data on the number of non-governmental organisations (NGOs) operating in the country, but for example the president in 2008 reported to

the Organization of American States the convening of approximately 100 organisations from civil society representing political parties, religious bodies, women's groups, and NGOs.
37. Section 30, (1) of the Local Government Act, Chapter 28:02 provides that 'Where twelve registered voters of a village district represent to the Minister that the further continuance in office of the village council is prejudicial to the welfare of the inhabitants of the village district, the Minister may direct an inquiry to be made by a person appointed by him, at which inquiry opportunity shall be given to the counsellors and to the inhabitants to be heard in the matter of the representation, and the Minister may after such inquiry, by order, declare the village council to be dissolved.'
38. In 2013, 29 out of 65 (44.6 per cent) established NDCs were reported to have IMCs in place.

References

Arnstein, Sherry R. 1969. A Ladder of Citizen Participation. *JAIP* 35, no. 4 (July): 216–24.
Brisco, Ivan. 2008. The Proliferation of the 'Parallel State'. FRIDE Working Paper 71, October.
Buchanan, James M., and Gordon Tullock. 1962. *The Calculus of Consent: The Logical Foundations of Constitutional Democracy*. Ann Arbor, MI: University of Michigan Press.
Bynoe, Mark, and Talia Choy. 2007. *Latin American Public Opinion Poll (LAPOP)*. Nashville: Vanderbilt University.
———. 2007. *The Political Culture of Democracy in Guyana 2006*. Nashville: Vanderbilt University.
Carter Center. 1992. *Observing Guyana's Electoral Processes 1990–1992: Report of the Council of Freely Elected Heads of Government*. Atlanta: Carter Center of Emory University.
Chandisingh, Rajendra. 1982. Guyana's new Constitution and the Elections of 1980: A Case of People's Power? *Law and Politics in Africa, Asia and Latin America* Vol. 15, No. 2, 145–161.
Cheema, G., and A. Rondinelli. 2007. From Government Decentralisation to Decentralised Government. In *Decentralising Governance: Emerging Concepts and Practices*, ed. G. Shabbir Cheema and Dennis A. Rondenelli, 1–20. Washington, DC: Brookings Institute Press.
Corral, Margarita, Brian Faughnan, Lawrence Lachmansingh, Diana Orces, Elizabeth Zechmeister and Dominique Zephyr. 2009. *The Political Culture of Democracy in Guyana, 2009: The Impact of Governance*. Nashville: Vanderbilt University.
https://www.vanderbilt.edu/lapop/guyana/2009-Guyana-Report-v6-7dic11.pdf.
Crook, R. C. 2003. Decentralisation and Poverty Reduction in Africa: The Politics of Local–Central Relations. *Public Administration and Development* 23, no. 1:77–88. doi:10.1002/pad.261.

Crook, R.C., and A.S. Sverrisson. 2001. Decentralisation and Poverty Alleviation in Developing Countries: A Comparative Analysis or, Is West Bengal Unique? Working Paper 130, Institute of Development Studies, University of Sussex, Brighton.

Crook, R.C., and J. Manor. 1998. *Democracy and Decentralisation in South Asia and West Africa: Participation, Accountability and Performance.* New York: Cambridge University Press.

Dahl, Robert A. 1971. *Polyarchy: Participation and Opposition.* New Haven: Yale University Press.

Danns, George K. 2014. The Impact of Identity, Ethnicity and Class on Guyana's Strategic Culture. *American International Journal of Contemporary Research* 4, no. 11(November): 65–77.

Faletti, Tulia. G. 2005. A Sequential Theory of Decentralization: Latin American Case in Comparative Perspective. *American Political Science Review* 99, no. 3 (August): 327–46.

Filkin, G., G. Stoker, G. Wilkinson and J. Williams. 2000. Towards a New Localism: A Discussion Paper, New Local Government Network (NLGN), London.

Grant, C. H. 1967. Rural Local Government in Guyana and British Honduras. *Social and Economic Studies* 16, no. 1, (March): 57–76.

Heywood, A. 1997. *Politics.* 4th ed. London: Palgrave Macmillan.

Hinds, David. 2010. *Ethno-Politics and Power Sharing in Guyana: History and Discourse.* Washington, DC: New Academia Publishing.

Hintzen, Percy C. 1989. *The Costs of Regime Survival: Racial Mobilization, Elite Domination and Control of the State in Guyana and Trinidad.* New York: Cambridge University Press.

Hirschman, Albert. O. 1970. *Exit, Voice and Loyalty: Responses to Decline in Firms, Organizations and States.* London: Harvard University Press.

International Foundation for Electoral Systems (IFES). 1994. *Guyana Election Technical Assessment Report: 1994 Local Government and Municipal Elections.* Arlington: International Foundation for Electoral Systems.

Ishmael, Odeen. 2012. *From Autocracy to Democracy in Guyana: Aspects Of Post-Independence Guyanese History (1966–1992).* Georgetown: GNI Publications.

Kempe R., Hope, and Maurice St. Pierre. 1983. Ethnic Political Participation and Cooperative Socialism in Guyana: A Critical Assessment. *Ethnic and Racial Studies*, 6, no. 4: 505–16.

Kwayana, Eusi. 2007. *Victoria's historic Model of Village Governance.* Excerpt from a new book on the Guyana Villages. https://guyaneseonline.files.wordpress.com/2010/09/victoria-the-first-village.pdf.

Langrod, Georges. 1953. Local Government and Democracy. *Public Administration* 31, no. 1 (March): 25–34.

Lisk, F. 1985. The Role of Popular Participation in Basic Needs-Oriented Development Planning. In *Popular Participation in Planning for Basic Needs: Concepts, Methods and Practices*, ed. F. Lisk, Hampshire, UK: Gower.

Lutchman, Harold A. 1970. The Cooperative Republic of Guyana. *Caribbean Studies* 10, no. 3 (October): 97–115.

Manor, James. 2011. Perspectives on Decentralization. Working Paper No. 3, Swedish International Centre for Local Democracy (ICLD, Visby, Sweden. https://icld.se/static/files/forskningspublikationer/icld-wp3-printerfriendly.pdf.

Mars, Joan. 2011. *Countries at the Crossroads 2011: Guyana*. Washington, DC: Freedom House.

Mars, Perry. 1995. State Intervention and Ethnic Conflict Resolution: Guyana and the Caribbean Experience. *Comparative Politics* 27, no. 2:167–86.

Merrill, Tim. 1992. *Guyana and Belize Country Studies*. Washington: Federal Research Division, Library of Congress.

Myers, Roxanne. 2002. Local Government, Decentralization and Gender. Paper presented at the Caribbean Conference on Local Government Decentralization, June 25–28.

National Democratic Institute (NDI). 1995. *Local Democracy in Guyana*. Georgetown: NDI.

Pelling, Mark. 1998. Participation, Social Capital and Vulnerability to Urban Flooding in Guyana. *Journal of International Development* 10, no. 4: 469–86.

Premdas, Ralph. 1972. Elections and Political Campaigns in a Racially Bifurcated State: The Case of Guyana. *Journal of Inter-American Studies and World Affairs* 14, no. 3 (August): 271–96.

Putnam, R. 1993. *Making Democracy Work: Civic Transitions in Modern Italy*. Princeton: Princeton University Press.

Ramkarran, Hari N. 2014. Seeking a Democratic Path: Constitutional Reform in Guyana. *Georgia Journal of International and Comparative Law* 32, no. 3:585–611.

Rose, James G. 1992. British Colonial Policy and the Transfer of Power in British Guiana, 1945–1964. PhD Thesis, King›s College, London.

Shah, Anwar and Matthew Andrews. 2002. *Voice and Local Governance in the Developing World: What is Done, to What Effect, and Why?* Washington, DC: World Bank.

Singh, Paul. 1970. Problems of Institutional Transplantation: The Case of the Commonwealth Caribbean Local Government System. *Caribbean Studies* 10, no. 1 (April): 22–33.

Silverman, Marilyn. 1976. The Role of Factionalism in Political Encapsulation: East Indian Villagers in Guyana. In *Ethnicity in the Americas: Proceedings of the IXth International Congress of Anthropological and Ethnographical Sciences*, ed. F. Henry. The Hague: Mouton.

———. 1979. Dependency, Mediation and Class Formation in Rural Guyana. *American Ethnologist* 6, no. 3 (1979): 466–90.

Skocpol, Theda. 2003. *Diminished Democracy: From Membership to Management in American Civic Life*. Norman, Oakland: University of Oakland Press.

Smith, R. 1995. 'Living in the Gun Mouth': Race, Class, and Political Violence in Guyana. *New West Indian Guide/ Nieuwe West-Indische Gids* 69, nos 3 and 4:223–52.

Teague, Randal Cornell Sr., and Ronald A. Gould. 1991. *Guyana Pre-Election Technical Assessment Report, October 1990*. Arlington: International Foundation for Electoral Systems.

Tullock, Gordon. 1965. Entry Barriers in Politics. *American Economic Review* 55, nos. 1 and 2:458–66.

Young, Allan. 1958. *Approaches to Local Self-Government in British Guiana*. London: Longmans, Green.

———. 2000. Decentralization, Local Governance and Community Participation: A Caribbean Perspective. Paper presented at the Caribbean Sub-Regional Forum on Effective Local Governance: Innovative Approaches to Improving Municipal Management, Montego Bay, Jamaica, May 16–17.

Legacies of Racial Dysfunction

4.
Politics and Underdevelopment: The Case of Guyana

Tarron Khemraj

Introduction

The main patronage system evolving in the post-1992 period is known as Elected Oligarchy (EO), a system under which the Peoples Progressive Party/Civic (PPP/C) sought to mould a supportive business class. EO depended on the ethnic masses of PPP supporters to turn out and vote strategically for their elites on the day of election. This form of governance, however, was bound to result in opposition and conflict given the bi-communal and fractured nature of the society. Immediately after losing the 1992 election, the Peoples National Congress/Reform (PNC/R) – which is now the major partner in the governing Alliance, A Partnership for National Unity (APNU) – assumed the responsibility of explicit representation of the African Guyanese population. It accused the PPP/C very early on of 'ethnic cleansing' (Hinds 2010, 95). The PPP/C's system of patronage had a more free-market flair, while the pre-1992 system of patronage under the PNC,[1] Party Paramountcy (PP), took the form of Co-operative Socialism.[2]

Pro-ethnic voting by the two dominant groups – East Indian and African masses – is endogenous or is jointly determined by external factors rooted in history, geography, production structure, and foreign price shocks. The African masses cannot know for certain how the Indian masses will vote on the day of secret ballot. They might be willing to vote for an independent political party, but they cannot have perfect information regarding how East Indian masses will vote on the day of election. On the other hand, the largest number of East Indian masses might also be willing to vote for a third party, but they also cannot know for certain that most Afro-Guyanese will do the same. The respective masses (the overall majority) also perceive – rightly or wrongly – that their economic interests would be harmed if the other side were to win the election. In other words, if one group splits its votes, while the other does not, then that group expects a loss of income because of perceived discrimination.³ In this classic strategic game setup, the safe strategy is to vote for one's ethnic elites. This distrust results in a non-co-operative equilibrium in which the long-term income is lower than what would prevail if the two groups had an institutional mechanism for cooperation. For the majority, the unwillingness to split the votes is also incentivised by the present constitution which permits only pre-election alliances instead of post-election alliances. This constitutional system allows one group of leaders to explicitly or implicitly blame the independent third party for colluding with the other side against the interests of their masses.

This does not imply that independent voters or a vibrant civil society does not exist in Guyana. Independent voters since 1992 voted for the Working People's Alliance (WPA), Rise, Organise and Rebuild (ROAR), and other smaller parties, with the Alliance for Change (AFC), being the most successful of the third parties in the post-1992 period. Whether it can maintain the five to seven seats is not assured, largely because of the continuation of the pro-ethnic strategic vote. In the coming years, we should have a better feel for the size and persistence of the independent swing voters. The upcoming 2020 general election would test whether the nascent independent class of voters is, indeed, independent. Furthermore, civil society stepped up participation from the time of the 2006 general election in order to facilitate conflict resolution between the two dominant sides (Myers and Calder 2011).

The primary aim of this chapter is to demonstrate the transmission channel through which the post-1992 politics of patronage under democracy perpetuates the colonial underdevelopment trap, which has two reinforcing features that emerged from history and geography (Khemraj 2015A).⁴ First, there is the added cost of continual drainage and irrigation that government and farmers have to bear. Since the dominant coastal region is below sea level during high tide, a mechanical pumping system also has to be utilised in modern times, as was the case during the colonial period when steam-driven engines were used by the larger farmers who could afford the extra cost (Rodney 1981; Adamson 1972). The pumping system and the continual need for desilting and draining the coastal region add an extra layer to production cost.⁵ Second, the small and dispersed Guyanese population is not large enough to spread the unit cost of drainage, pumping, irrigation, and desilting. Furthermore, the dispersed population adds yet another layer of cost of business and infrastructure. The small dispersed population means an added unit transportation cost – relative to market size – is incurred when transporting bulky agricultural produce from farm to market. In addition, the per capita cost of infrastructure would be higher compared with a geographically smaller and densely populated region. For example, it would take an enormous amount of finance to connect dispersed hinterland (and rural coastal) villages via a network of roads, communication cables, and electrical grid system.

The underdevelopment trap has colonial roots or is path-dependent because it is associated with decisions made in the mid-1700s by Dutch settlers to move from hinterland locations along riverbanks to coastal settlements.[6] The latter required using slave labour to dig canals and drain the coastal region for polder agriculture, hence the colonial origin of coastal dominance in agriculture and the reinforcing structure of extra layers of cost associated with drainage, desilting, mechanical pumping, and transport. An obvious policy conclusion is to move to the relatively more favourable savannah lands in the hinterland for agriculture and manufacturing. However, this requires vast amounts of financial capital to establish new production systems and infrastructure to transport the bulk products to the coast for exports to the Caribbean and northern markets. The financial capital does not exist given that the underdevelopment trap has reinforced income stagnation and low savings for over three centuries. The situation is often made worse by the volatile export commodity prices and the price-taker status of Guyana in the world markets. Therefore, it should be no surprise that there is a long-term structural stagnation of economic growth over the period for which national account statistics are available. For example, Gampat (2015) calculates the long-term average growth rate from 1960 to 2014 to be 1.2 per cent.

The rest of this chapter is organised as follows: section two presents stylised facts comparing Guyana's development outcomes with several peer economies; section 3 outlines the colonial underdevelopment trap; section 4 explores the post-1992 tit-for-tat political economy; section five derives the post-1992 equilibrium of economic underperformance; section six explains the transmission channel through which the post-1992 political economy perpetuates the colonial underdevelopment trap; and section seven concludes.

Broad Trends

The data compare selected measures of comparative development given that the concept of development (or underdevelopment) could include several different indicators from human rights to per capita income (Nafziger 2006). Table 4.1 indicates three broad measures of economic development, two of which are included in the Human Development Index (HDI) for Guyana and ten other peer economies – The Bahamas, Barbados, Botswana, Fiji, Jamaica, Mauritius, Singapore, Sri Lanka, Suriname, and Trinidad and Tobago. These can all be considered as small open economies susceptible to the same external shocks. They all gained political independence around the same period. Except for Suriname, they are former British colonies. Several of the countries – The Bahamas, Barbados, Guyana, Jamaica, Trinidad and Tobago, and Suriname – are part of the CARICOM common market.

For the first indicator – per capita income – Botswana, Fiji, Mauritius, and Sri Lanka had a lower level compared to Guyana's in 1965. This single indicator shows that Guyana did not start off in a position of strength, partly due to its geography and ethnic polarisation after 1838 (Khemraj 2015A). The data further expose a recurring myth that Guyana was at the same level of average income as Barbados or Singapore by 1965. By 2013, all the countries in the sample had a higher average income than Guyana, except Sri Lanka that has a per capita income just below Guyana's. Sri Lanka experienced a severe civil war that led to the death of thousands and significant economic damage, yet its per capita income is not far behind that of Guyana. Two of the potential explanatory variables for this relative performance could be geography and differences in policy. For example, Singapore or Barbados's relative success can be attributed to smart policies and favourable geography.

The second indicator shows the amount of money in the economy relative to the size of GDP. It is often taken as a measure of financial development, which is seen as a crucial aspect of the development experience. In 1965, Botswana, Jamaica, Suriname, and Trinidad and Tobago showed less financial development compared with Guyana. By 2013, the money stock to GDP ratio for Guyana is higher than that of Botswana, Jamaica, Sri Lanka, Suriname, and Trinidad and Tobago. However, it appears as if this indicator does not correlate well with the development of financial products of Jamaica, and Trinidad and Tobago, both of which have a much more vibrant stock exchange and larger bond markets.

Table 4.1: Broad Indicators of Relative Economic Development

	Per Capita Income Current US$		Broad Money % of GDP		Life Expectancy	
	1965	2013	1965	2013	1960	2013
The Bahamas	1,900	21,570	35.0	74.8	63	75
Barbados	530	15,220	42.4	123	61	75
Botswana	90	7,770	26.6	40.9	51	47
Fiji	290	4,370	32.6	80.6	60	70
Guyana	320	3,750	28.0	65.2	58	66
Jamaica	510	5,220	24.6	50.3	64	73
Mauritius	198	9,290	45.3	100	59	74
Singapore	540	54,040	55.3	133	66	82
Sri Lanka	130	3,170	28.6	40.0	60	74
Suriname	630	9,370	23.8	51.5	60	71
Trinidad and Tobago	760	15,760	20.9	60.7	63	70

Source: World Development Indicators

The final measure compares life expectancy across the countries for 1960 and 2013. Only Botswana had a lower life expectancy than Guyana's in 1960. The same pattern continued until 2013 with life expectancy in Botswana below that of Guyana. Guyana's life expectancy increased from 58 years to 66 years as did all the other countries, except Botswana that shows a decline to 47 years.

Table 4.2 presents the aggregative measure of economic development known as the HDI. The Gini coefficient measures income inequality and the table also reports a measure of ethnic polarisation using the methodology of Jose Montalvo and Marta Reynal-Querol (2005). The numbers are for the same countries as given in table 4.1. For the HDI, each country's score is given along with the relative ranking out of 187 countries for the year 2013. The highest score of development is obtained by Singapore, placing it at number 9 out of 187 countries. This is followed by the Bahamas which ranks 51 out of 187 and Barbados 59 out of 187. Guyana has the lowest overall measure of development among the peer economies with a ranking of 121 out of 187. Even Sri Lanka with its long and deadly civil war does better with a ranking of 73 out of 187. The Gini coefficient suggests that Botswana and Suriname have the most unequal distribution of income in the sample. In a sense, Guyana has a mid-level of inequality, with a number (45) just below that of Jamaica and Singapore. It is important to note, however, that some of the inequality data are dated since recent calculations are not available.

Table 4.2: Broad Measures of Development, Inequality and Polarization

	Gini Coefficient	Polarization index	HDI
	Various years	2014	2013
The Bahamas	Na	0.3012 *	0.789 (51/187)
Barbados	40	0.3116 *	0.776 (59/187)
Botswana	63	0.605 **	0.683 (109/187)
Fiji	43	0.9298 **	0.724 (88/187)
Guyana	45	0.8144 *	0.638 (121/187)
Jamaica	46	0.6002 **	0.715 (96/187)
Mauritius	39	0.8031 **	0.771 (63/187)
Singapore	46	0.6663 **	0.901 (9/187)
Sri Lanka	36	0.7493 **	0.750 (73/187)
Suriname	53	0.6132 *	0.705 (100/187)
Trinidad & Tobago	39	0.8417 **	0.766 (64/187)

Source: World Development Indicators, Gören (2014), Human Development Report (2013) and author's calculation.

Notes:

* Author's calculation using polarization equation of Montalvo and Reynal-Querol (2005).

** Taken from Gören (2014).

Gini coefficient for Singapore (2013), Guyana (2007), Mauritius (2006), and Trinidad and Tobago (2005) taken from CIA estimates. Otherwise obtained from HDI.

HDI = Human Development Index (0 to 1 where 1 implies highest development)

Guyana is an example of a classic bi-communal society (Milne 1988; Premdas 1992). Bi-communal societies would tend to have a high polarisation index and therefore they are more susceptible to conflict of various forms. Donald Horowitz (1985) observes that conflict is less likely to occur in highly heterogeneous and homogenous societies. The problem, according to Horowitz, is more likely to result in the middle cases; for example, when there are two dominant groups vying for economic and political control. Therefore, the polarisation equation measures how close the country's ethnic or religious composition brings it to middle distribution. An index value closer to 1 shows a higher degree of polarisation. The index is indeed highest for Fiji, Guyana, Trinidad and Tobago, and Sri Lanka, the typical examples of bi-communal societies. The Bahamas and Barbados have much lower measures of polarisation given their relatively more homogenous societies. Suriname scores relatively lower, reflecting the fact that there are five ethnic groups with none having an absolute majority.

Mauritius also has a fairly high index reflecting its bi-communal structure; however, one group has a clear majority possibly explaining why the number is lower than that of Guyana, Fiji, or Trinidad and Tobago. Polarisation could engender inequality as the groups are less willing to share, caring mainly for their own ethnic or religious group (Dincer and Lambert 2012). Ethnic and religious polarisation could increase the probability of corruption (Nissan and Naghshpour 2013). Polarisation could also be negatively related to economic development because of its adverse effect on private investment and tendency to increase in wasteful government consumption (Montalvo and Reynal-Querol 2005).

Colonial Underdevelopment Trap

One of the patterns emerging from a reading of Guyanese historical political economy is the tendency of writers to observe the difficult nature of the country's geography and the hindrance it places on human development. The theme of adverse geography can be seen in the works of Alan Adamson (1972), Walter Rodney (1981), Clem Seecharan (1997) and others. In general, these authors thought the polder system made it difficult for independent peasants and medium-scale farmers to succeed. However, Rodney and Adamson in particular tend to cast greater blame on the global capitalist system for the dismal state of farmers and workers in the colonial period, instead of on the geographical constraint. No doubt labourers in the formative new country, British Guiana, were exploited under a global system of capitalism. However, this work attributes a greater weight to geography as a hindrance to human development. Geography and topography of Guyana retard competitiveness and productivity gains by adding several layers of costs that would otherwise not be available to a non-polder system, as for example the vast agricultural lands of US, Argentina, Chile, and others.

Eric Williams, the first prime minister of Trinidad and Tobago, was much more explicit in recognising how the manmade polder system impedes the competitiveness of the sugar industry. He argued that the high cost of maintaining coastal agriculture made British Guiana sugar less competitive relative to sugar coming from Mauritius, Puerto Rico, Cuba, and Brazil. The cost of production on Guyana's coastal strip takes away the competitive advantage in a free trading arrangement. Williams noted that not only were Guyana's yields lower, but also the country could not compete with those benefiting from more favourable conditions (Williams 1945). Irene Taeuber observes:

> the failure of extended economic development is related to the difficulty of topography, the deficiencies of soil and the general overabundance of water.... The area back of the coastal ribbon tends to be swampy and the soils are often sterile.... There are four great rivers and numerous tributaries and lesser streams, but the falls and rapids prevent navigation from the coast to the interior (Taeuber 1952, 4).

She went on to imply that the proposed Jewish and Assyrian settlements in the interior of British Guiana did not materialise because of the high cost of settling the interior and the difficulty of reaching the Atlantic with a cheap source of transportation out from the hinterland.

Another important fact of Guyanese historical political economy is the suppression of worker wages for a very long period of time (see Rodney 1981; Adamson 1972). Since the planters were price takers, they supressed wages to maintain a target profit after the collapse of world sugar price in the late nineteenth century. The planters brought immigrants of different ethnic backgrounds to undermine the labour market bargaining power of free African slaves who just after 1838 demanded better wages and working conditions (Rodney 1981). By the 1870s East Indians would become the largest immigrant group, thus transforming the population into its bi-communal structure of two dominant ethnic groups (Mandel

1973). Immigration was meant to increase the elasticity of supply of labour and drive the wage rate towards the subsistence rate (Khemraj 2015A). This implies that about one century of subsistence production resulted in limited opportunities for the accumulation of savings. The savings rate is often seen as an important source of economic growth in several growth models.

Dutch settlers initially went up river in Essequibo, Demerara, and Berbice to live and grow various crops. However, they eventually found the land to be less fertile and so entered into an elaborate scheme to create a coastal polder system of agriculture just after 1750 (Farley 1954). African slave labour was used to drain the coastal plain to create the estates that are typically rectangular in shape. There is a front dam keeping out the sea water and a back dam keeping out the waters flowing from the highlands of the interior. Each estate has two sideline dams preventing the water of the neighbouring estate from interfering with farming of the adjoining planter. Running along the dams are trenches that serve as store of water and provide transportation of sugarcane to the factories. This pattern exists up to today, thus the path dependency of the decision to drain and settle the coastal plain.[7]

The key point to note, however, is this system of farming and village settlement requires significant costs of maintenance and desilting. It adds fixed and variable costs to the production process, thus possibly accounting for the high cost of production for sugar and other crops. Meanwhile, the small and dispersed Guyanese population does not create a large enough internal market for spreading out the high costs. In other words, Guyanese farmers cannot achieve the economies of scale necessary for being globally competitive, while also rewarding labour a larger share of income. If non-labour cost of production is high and the planters had no control over the world market price, then maintaining the profit margin required supressing wages through various means such as immigration and control of the colonial legislature. It also involved playing off one ethnic group against the other, particularly in the labour market.

From this survey of historical political economy, a theory of underdevelopment trap is presented by figure 4.1, which was first proposed in Khemraj (2015A). The first point to observe is that the colonial settlement pattern is determined by the geography of the country. Dutch settlers realised early that inland farming was not realistic given the limited soil fertility and other factors. Polder agriculture, in spite of its higher costs, was seen as a better option.

Figure 4.1: The Colonial Underdevelopment Trap

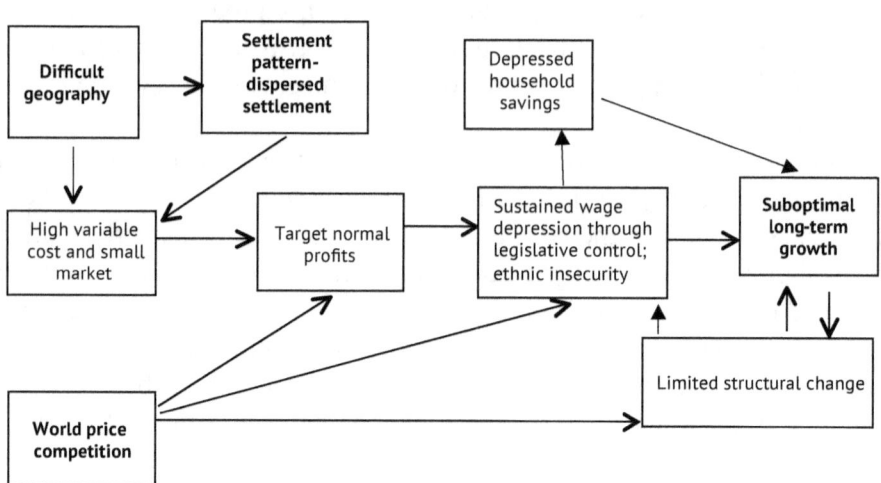

They therefore moved to the coast in the second half of the 1700s, thus locking Guyana into its present dispersed settlement pattern and coastal polder system. The settlement on the coast implies that the small population is spread over a wide geographical space, necessitating high per capita fixed cost to establish infrastructure and drainage, and subsequent high non-wage average variable cost to keep the drainage canals unblocked. The small internal market was/is often not enough to allow peasants to grow into large-scale producers. Hence, there is the conspiracy of high average cost and a small dispersed market over the relatively large coastal space. The second exogenous variable was/is the world market competition that producers of agricultural products faced since the beginning of settlement. Cotton and coffee failed because Guyana's plantations could not compete globally (Adamson 1972).

Sugar, the dominant crop, faced severe global competition from new producers after the elimination of colonial preferences and from beet sugar by the middle of the twentieth century (Bulmer-Thomas 2012). For the sugar industry to survive – in the face of polder agriculture – normal profit rates (or perhaps just above normal profits) were targeted and wages suppressed by political force. In addition, estates survived through merger for gaining economies of scale. The term normal profit is used to express the idea that British Guiana planters were price takers instead of global price makers given the emergence of serious competition in the world sugar market (Guyana is still a price taker in all commodity markets).[8] Normal profit implies margins are slim given the inability to influence world prices; therefore, for the planters to make money wages were suppressed through political mechanisms and playing off one ethnic group against the other in the labour market. Policies such as immigration were explicitly promoted to drive the wage rate as close as possible to subsistence. A perfectly elastic supply curve, which indicates a labour surplus, implies the planters could attract as many labourers at a low subsistence wage rate, similar to the model outlined by W. Arthur Lewis (1954). The labour force, however, by the 1870s was bifurcated, implying a choice between two dominant ethnic groups of Indian and African masses.[9] The long-term wage depression further implies low savings accumulation.

Global competition also made it necessary to target normal profits and suppress wages (as the arrows indicate). The global competition, moreover, made it necessary to prevent alternative industries from emerging through political control. For example, the rice industry in part was allowed to develop because the planters wanted to keep labourers tied to the sugar industry and at the same time avoid paying the high cost of repatriation of Indians to India (Mandle 1970). But this lack of structural change would also eventually hinder economic growth in the long run by preventing the emergence of higher productivity sectors such as manufacturing.

The importance of economic structure and structural change as a fundamental cause of economic development has been recognised for some time in the literature (Kaldor 1967; Thirlwall 2007; Reinert 2008). Earlier Sir Arthur Lewis emphasised the importance of structural change in terms of the emergence of a high marginal productivity sector that eventually pulls up wages in the subsistence sector (Lewis 1954). C.A. Hidalgo et al. (2007) proffer a reinterpretation of long-run economic performance that relates to structure of production. They look at the interrelatedness of products in a product space as a predictor of economic performance. Countries producing products that are at the centre of the space would be able to develop technologies which are more complex. The complexity will generate positive spill overs to other sectors as well as innovation through learning by doing. Countries that make products on the periphery of the product space would find less of these benefits and therefore there is little room for production linkages and technological interrelatedness. These countries would likely be more susceptible to external shocks and foreign exchange problems. More recently, Constantine (2017) adds another dimension to the literature by explaining how structural change determines the institutions necessary for production and exchange. It should be noted that mainstream development economics focuses mainly on institutions of exchange (property rights and legal systems). However, institutions of production (developmental state, tariffs, subsidies, and so on) are at the heart of structural change. According to Constantine, both institutions are shaped by the structure of production, technological change and learning by doing, and not the other way around.

Figure 4.2: Inner Vicious Endogenous Cycle of Underdevelopment

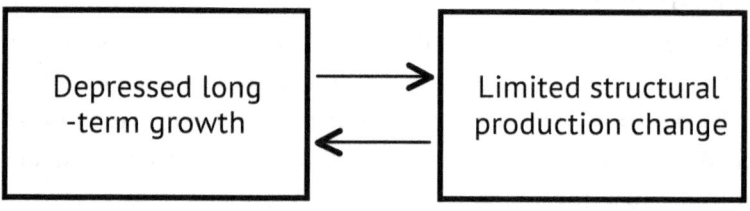

Figure 4.3: Outer Vicious Endogenous Cycle of Underdevelopment

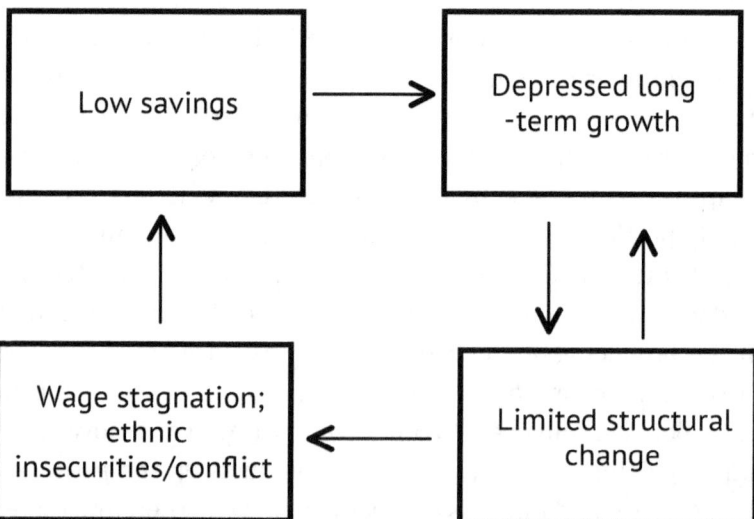

The sustained wage stagnation also implies lower savings and long-term economic growth. Therefore, the economy is trapped in a vicious cycle in which global conditions precipitate limited structural change, which, in turn, results in wage stagnation that causes low long-term economic growth and circle back to limited structural change. Furthermore, the depressed household savings and normal profit impact negatively on economic growth, which again engenders another vicious cycle. Therefore, the two exogenous factors – adverse geography and world price competition – engender the vicious cycle through two endogenous channels; first through profit targeting (wage stagnation) and second through limited structural production change.

Figure 4.2 indicates two vicious cycles in action that are still active in modern Guyana (Khemraj 2015A). There is an inner cycle and an outer cycle. They are both sparked by exogenous history and exogenous external price competition. Figure 4.2 gives the inner cycle while figure 4.3 the outer cycle. The inner cycle has depressed long-term economic growth causing limited structural change, which in turn reinforces unsustainable long-term growth. The outer cycle shows the endogenous variables reinforcing underdevelopment. These variables continue to reinforce each other today, but they were set in motion by the forces of history and nature. Long-term wage depression results from low growth and limited structural production change.

The Struggle for Political and Economic Power

This section examines the post-1992 political economy in which the leaders of the PPP and PNC competed for control of the state and the economic patronage that flows from this control. Over this period, we can see evidence of several tit-for-tat actions between the PPP and PNC. The ethnic masses in general stayed with their respective elites and voted strategically (more on this in the next section). Controlling the government allows the respective political elites to not only enrich themselves through favoured access to government jobs, land rights, gold mining concessions and scholarships, but also to buy token loyalties from the other side. Moreover, each political party operates as a unified bloc once in government. The constitutional party list system forces ministers and members of parliament to fall in line with a party programme, which may not coincide with the requirements of good policies for national development. The Constitution also enables ethnic mobilisation and entrenches the party leader at the expense of political independents inside and outside the ruling party (Harripaul 2017).

The constitution of the PPP declares it to be a Marxist-Leninist political party. Democratic centralism is the core decision-making tool of that party. Before the 2011 general election, there were heated debates within and outside the PPP regarding how the presidential candidate should be selected. Some members preferred secret ballot while others wanted show-of-hands. Show-of-hands was the method preferred by the subgroup that controlled party. The method allowed for intimidating those members of the central and executive committees who might not agree with the hand-picked candidate. This was crucial for capturing the political party and facilitating special outside interests (Khemraj 2011). Command of the party would determine the distribution of economic resources and opportunities. This scenario, however, would almost always result in limited transparency and accountability, corruption perceptions and actual corruption – or at least the permission for corruption to fester as explained by *Stabroek News* (2007).

The regime of Elected Oligarchy under the PPP involved the following stages. First, democratic centralism is used by an entrenched group of PPP leaders to select a presidential candidate who is then presented to the party mass supporters and the nation as a whole. Second, given the persistent ethnic voting patterns, the candidate is likely to win the national election and therefore enjoy the immunities of the mildly reformed 1980 Burnham Constitution. Third, this candidate then surrounds himself with chosen like-minded individuals. Fourth, generous government-sponsored incentives are then offered to chosen members of the business class. This allows a few powerful leaders to direct the economic space in Guyana. (Some members of the oligarchy eventually reached the point of buying out media assets to further dominate the society and public views).

Political mobilisation after 1992 took on an explicit ethnic face by both main parties. A most comprehensive review of the events surrounding the post-1992 political conflicts is documented by Myers and Calder (2011). An early example of ethno-political mobilisation in the post-1992 period is the careless use of the term 'ethnic cleansing' by leaders of the PNC just two years into the Jagan government. This term was also popularly used by local TV talk show hosts. Former President Hoyte used the term in a letter to *Stabroek News* in 1996; just four years after the PPP came to power (Hinds 2010). From 1992 to 1997, the PNC leadership expressed a fear that their supporters in the leadership of the public service were being systematically displaced by Indian PPP supporters. The PNC was not too bothered by the fact that by 1992 East Indians were virtually non-existent in the senior echelons of the public service and prestigious semi-autonomous agencies such as the Bank of Guyana. The PPP went about reversing this pattern by replacing senior public servants – many of whom they perceived to be pro-PNC – with their trusted supporters. The new APNU+AFC coalition government also recently came in for criticisms from the public, including the Guyana Human Rights Association, over the ethnic and gender composition of the candidates it appointed to various state boards (*Stabroek News* 2015).

The PNC consistently challenged the elections it lost in 1992, 1997, and 2001. The party used these challenges as a means of destabilising the incumbent administration and extracting concessions from the PPP. These concessions were meant to secure the economic and political interests of its base. The demands included de-politicisation of the public service, African land rights and extra-judicial killings by the police. The destabilisation and rigged elections prior to 1992 have to be seen in the context of ethnic politics in which the slight numerical majority of East Indians, prior to 2015, guaranteed a PPP victory (*Stabroek News* 2001). Considering that the support of the winning party comes mainly from one ethnic group, we can expect a significant percentage of economic resources to be skewed in the direction of the supporters of that party, resulting in, at best, unwitting marginalisation or at worst complicit marginalisation.

The fear of marginalisation by African supporters of the PNC was perhaps best expressed by the calypsonian, Mighty Rebel, who sang a calypso 'Desi yuh wrong' (Danns 1997). The Mighty Rebel was expressing the viewpoint that President Desmond Hoyte should not have acquiesced to free and fair elections. The Mighty Rebel was basically implying the patronage system that was controlled by African elites in the pre-1992 period should be maintained even if it meant rigging the national elections. Widespread resentments in the African community emerged by the mid-1990s as the PPP started to bring its supporters into the civil service. Africans felt they were being pushed out from prestigious government jobs and taxpayers monies were not being spent on African villages (Danns 1997). As noted by

Danns, President Cheddi Jagan's comment in Canada that '...black people are generally at the lowest scale of the social ladder' faced an immediate and harsh reaction from African Guyanese.

Certain elements in the PNC tacitly supported violent extremists camping out in Buxton after the 2001 general election, which the PNC lost (Kissoon 2007). In 2002 several prisoners escaped and also encamped in Buxton. They declared themselves freedom fighters for the African cause. The events were believed to be engineered by political activists, media personalities, and former military officers (Myers and Calder 2011, 17). Several East Indian businessmen were killed while others had their properties destroyed during riots in Georgetown. Several perceived supporters of the PPP and police officers were also executed. Meanwhile, several East Indians were beaten while minibuses were on a few occasions stopped and robbed on the East Coast. Frederick Kissoon (2007) argues that this extremism was in response to the PPP's heavy-handed manner of governance, its perceived corruption, and its perceived economic marginalisation of African Guyanese. Since the police were powerless during the period of civil conflict, the East Indian business community established its own phantom squad that resulted in the extra-judicial execution of a number of young men of African origin (*Stabroek News* 2008).

From the 2011 election campaign to the one in 2015, the PPP became most aggressive and explicit in its ethnic mobilisation. This strategy involves stoking the fears of East Indians by reminding them of perceived wrongs committed by the African-dominated PNC when that party was in power from 1964 to 1992. Implied in the ethnic mobilisation strategy is the notion that African Guyanese are the aggressors and Indian Guyanese are the victims. Senior leaders in the PPP led the campaign of terrifying rural East Indians into voting solidly for PPP. Rural supporters of the party, on one occasion, were told at a public meeting that ex-army supporters of APNU would be kicking down their doors (Ramkarran 2015; Khemraj 2015B). This was in reference to the sordid period of kick-down-the-door banditry during the late 1970s and early 1980s when mainly rural East Indians were at the receiving end. Meanwhile, proxy groups writing in the *Guyana Times* and *Guyana Chronicle* were responsible for promoting a strategy of fear, insecurity and crass racist stereotyping of Africans. A point to note, however, is that the Hoyte government of 1985–92 is often credited with ending the period of kick-down-the door banditry.

The pro-ethnic electoral strategy of the PPP is strange because that party attracts a substantial percentage of mixed voters and a relatively smaller percentage of African voters (see table 3 in the next section). It has a fairly multi-ethnic list of parliamentarians, perhaps more so than the present list of the APNU+AFC administration. Elsewhere, I have underscored that the PPP wants it both ways – it wants to 'suck cane and blow whistle' (Khemraj 2015B), meaning the party wants to keep its mixed voters and retain the small percentage of Afro-Guyanese voters as well as pursue a scheme of scaring Indian Guyanese and stereotyping Africans. This strategy of ethnic mobilisation by the PPP could backfire by turning off the independent voters.

Strategic Pro-Ethnic Voting

As noted above, ethnic mobilisation for controlling economic resources is at the centre of Guyanese politics. This section connects the dots by demonstrating how ethno-political mobilisation is harmful to economic progress. The illustration requires using an economic model to analyse cause and effect. In this regard, the canonical prisoners' dilemma game is used to derive the Nash equilibrium of sub-optimal lifetime income for all voters regardless of ethnicity. The prisoners' dilemma game outlined below helps us to understand how the masses of African Guyanese (AGMs) and East Indian masses (EIMs) inadvertently vote to perpetuate the colonial underdevelopment trap, which involves long-term wage, income, and savings stagnation (see figures 4.1, 4.2, and 4.3).

The aggregative group of African voters (hereafter AGM) has two options or strategies when voting on the day of secret ballot: vote for AGE (African Guyanese elites) or vote for an independent third party, which could be multi-ethnic or otherwise. The African voters – in the aggregate – have the option of voting for the party of East Indian elites (EIEs). However, historically this is a dominated strategy with little likelihood of it changing the electoral outcomes (see the data in table 4.3). Similarly, East Indian masses (hereafter EIM) as a group have two strategies: vote for East Indian elites (EIEs) or the multi-ethnic independent third party. The historical voting patterns suggest that that EIMs will not vote for AGEs to significantly alter the election result, thus giving a dominated strategy.

Some may question whether data are available showing a strong enough overlap between ethnicity and voting patterns. Data presented in table 4.3

come from the Latin American Public Opinion Project (LAPOP) surveys of 2006, 2009, and 2014. The LAPOP surveys typically involve a sample of approximately 1,400 Guyanese taking into consideration geographical, ethnic, and other stratifications. One of the key questions tracked by the survey is choice of party by voter's ethnicity. One of the consistent features of the data is the strong overlap between ethnic identification and voting pattern (or support), consistent with the thesis of strategic voting that is proposed in this paper.

As expected, the majority of East Indians vote for the PPP while the majority of African Guyanese vote for PNC. In 2006, 85.7 per cent of East Indians identified as having voted for the PPP in the previous election, while 76.1 per cent of Africans identified they voted for the PNC.

Table 4.3: Source of Votes and Party Identification by Ethnicity

2014 Survey	Ethnic identification with parties - %		
	PPP	PNC	AFC
Mixed	22.0	54.1	18.9
Amerindian	66.7	11.1	22.2
Black	7.1	**89.3**	3.6
Indian	**83.5**	1.2	15.3

2009 Survey	Source of votes by ethnicity - %		
	PPP	PNC	AFC
Mixed	11.3	22.7	39.6
Amerindian	16.3	4.0	11.5
Black	3.7	**71.5**	31.7
Indian	**68.7**	1.7	17.3

2006 Survey	Ethnic identification with parties - %		
	PPP	PNC	AFC
Mixed	21.7	48.7	23.9
Amerindian	42.1	31.6	21.1
Black	6.5	**76.1**	14.1
Indian	**85.7**	3.1	3.1

Source: LAPOP 2006, 2009 and 2014

For the 2009 survey, 68.7 per cent of East Indians indicated they voted for the PPP, while 71.5 per cent of African Guyanese said they did same for the PNC. By 2014, 83.5 per cent of East Indians said they voted for the PPP in 2011, while 89.3 per cent of Africans said they did the same for their party. East Indian support for the AFC increased from 3.1 per cent in 2006 to 15.3 per cent by 2014. The AFC's support from African Guyanese has declined significantly from 31.7 per cent in 2009 to 3.6 per cent in the 2014 survey. The surveys indicate a higher percentage of Amerindians tends to support the PPP. The mixed voters tend to randomise their votes among the three main political parties.

The application of any strategic game, prisoners' dilemma or otherwise, requires a specification of the strategies (given above) and the payoffs associated with each strategy. The payoffs are expressed in the present value of income. Each payoff can be calculated by using the equation presented by Collier (2000). This equation allows us to make the payoffs endogenous, instead of taking them arbitrarily as given.

$$\max PY_{j1} = \max \{(1 - \tau)y_{j1} + [(1 + g(\tau))(1 - \tau)y_{j1}] / (1 + d_j)\}$$

The equation indicates that each group maximizes their present value of income (max PY_{j1}), where $j = (EIM, AGM)$. The symbol y_{j1} indicates the first period income of each group. The present value of each of the two ethnic masses depends on the subjective discount factor (d_j), which is a function of perceived political risk and fear that the other side could win the election and therefore skew resources in favour of its ethnic base.[10] This discount rate, therefore, explains the origin of the payoffs in this setup. In other words, we do not have to take them as given. If one elite group loses political power the masses of that group expect a loss of income owing to perceived discrimination that would come if the other side wins. Therefore, they attach a steeper discount rate to future flows of income when the other side wins (higher discount rate implies lower present income). The discount rate, moreover, embodies the ethnic economic security dilemmas.

The model depends on a simplifying assumption. That is, we assume that both EIMs and AGMs have the same fear of losing income if the other side wins the election; hence they both have identical discount rates. In other words, both dominant groups face an economic ethnic security dilemma that causes them to discount expected income if their party loses the election. A standard assumption of this literature is that the growth rate of income is a negative function of the tax rate, $g'(\tau) < 0$, where $\tau =$ the tax rate on income.

If EIMs are uncertain how AGMs will vote on the day of secret ballot they will attach a high discount rate to the event in which AGEs win the election. The same principle holds when AGMs are uncertain how EIMs will vote on the day of secret ballot; they will also attach a high discount rate to the event of EIEs winning the election. The Nash equilibrium results when each side assumes the other will not want to split their votes; hence the dominant strategy is not to split the votes. The discount rate is associated with assuming that the worst is higher – hence lower lifetime income – than the rate that would prevail if both groups worked together in some co-operative democratic arrangement (as would occur if the Constitution were rewritten to incentivise co-operation instead of patronage competition).

Table 4.4 presents the hypothetical permanent income or net present value of income (PY) for the African and East Indian masses. On the surface, it would appear that the best outcome for both AGM and EIM is for them to ignore ethnic allegiance and vote for the multi-ethnic political party. This would allow a genuine multi-ethnic group of leaders to emerge, backed by cross-ethnic support, greater legitimacy and multi-ethnic social networks. The multi-ethnic government would be better positioned, with greater legitimacy, to allocate resources more equitably across groups as social networking processes would more likely draw on people from diverse backgrounds. In this optimal situation, let us assume the payoff of PY is (10, 10).

However, uncertainty and suspicion in secret ballot brings distrust, which is worsened by the pro-ethnic campaigns – subliminal messages of 'don't split the votes' – of the respective elites. The representative EIM cannot be certain that the representative AGM will vote for the third party. If EIMs vote for the independent multi-ethnic party and AGMs do not, then the payoff is (($PY_{EIM} = 2$; $PY_{AGM} = 15$)) since EIMs are the ones splitting their votes. In this case EIMs are likely to attach a higher discount rate given the uncertainty how the other side will vote. They assume that if the AGEs win the election, distribution of resources will be skewed in favour AGM. This perception, right or wrong, causes them to attach a high discount rate to their future flow of incomes.

On the other hand, AGMs do not have certain knowledge of how the EIMs will vote in secret ballot. Indeed, they have historical evidence that suggests EIMs will largely vote for their own political party dominated by their elites. AGMs know that the best opportunity they have for winning the government and therefore the distribution of economic resources in their favour is to stay with the political party of their elites. They understand that if they vote in large enough numbers for the independent multi-ethnic party, and EIMs do not, then the PPP wins the election. Therefore, AGMs will attach a high discount rate to future income flows because if they split their votes, and EIMs do not, then EIEs will win the election. Their perception, right or wrong, causes AGM to attach a high discount rate to their future flow of incomes. The payoff structure is as follows (PY_{EIM} = 15; PY_{AGM} = 2).

Table 4.4: Hypothetical Lifetime Income Payoff from Bi-Communal Voting

		African Guyanese Masses	
		Vote AGE	Vote multi-ethnic party
E.I. masses	Vote EIE	PY_{EIM} = 3; PY_{AGM} = 3	PY_{EIM} = 15; PY_{AGM} = 2
	Vote multi-ethnic party	PY_{EIM} = 2; PY_{AGM} = 15	PY_{EIM} = 10; PY_{AGM} = 10

In the classic prisoners' dilemma game, each group assumes the worst about the competitor's action. In other words, each group votes strategically for its political party (or votes to keep the other side from power) regardless of how a member of the other group votes. The outcome is driven by the inherent uncertainty in the political process. This is expressed as a non-co-operative equilibrium in the prisoners' dilemma game. One can argue that the non-co-operation is promoted or incentivised by the winner-take-all constitution that does not permit post-election coalitions. There is no information of how the other side will vote on the day of secret ballot. The Nash equilibrium – Vote EIE, Vote AGE – results in sub-optimal payoff (3, 3) as each group plays it safe since it cannot trust how the other group will vote on the day of election. This sub-optimal income payoff comes on the heels of a prolonged period of income stagnation associated with the colonial underdevelopment trap.

On the other hand, if the masses can co-operate within the specifications of some constitutional arrangement, the best equilibrium of (10, 10) would be a possibility, but this is highly unlikely under present constitutional and institutional arrangements that reinforce suspicion and competition to share limited resources. The sub-optimal payoff (3, 3) is the Nash equilibrium that is consistent with the perpetuation of the colonial underdevelopment trap.

How Ethnic Competition Sustains the Underdevelopment Trap

The Nash equilibrium is essentially a perpetuation of the colonial underdevelopment trap, which was outlined earlier. Figure 4.4 illustrates the connection between strategic pro-ethnic voting and the development trap with colonial origins. It illustrates another vicious cycle in which contemporary politics perpetuate the colonial trap and long-term economic stagnation. This long-term stagnation should not be confused with short-term cyclical growth spurts as would result from a global commodity price boom. Moving in a clockwise direction, we can observe the starting point of post-independence stagnation. First, voters of one dominant ethnic group place a high subjective discount rate on their expected future incomes if the elites of the other group win the election.[11] They perceive that the other side would discriminate against their economic interests, hence the higher discount of the future if their people do not win. There is, indeed, a substantial literature on this perceived fear in the Guyanese context, as for example the work of Danns (1997), Hinds (2010), and Wilson (2012) indicate.

The higher discount rate necessitates the second outcome of pro-ethnic strategic voting, which involves voting to keep the other side out of power. The results – as illustrated by the third box – are the lack of economic cohesion, national economic vision, and sabotage from the side losing the election. Even if the incumbent government has sound policy proposals, it would not be in the interest of the losing party to have the policies succeed. In addition, patronage formations and rewarding of loyalties tend to become important considerations in economic policymaking, instead of a coherent development agenda that would need to account for the constraint of the ethnic dilemmas. Perhaps one of the most important proposals of development policy came from Ravi Dev who argues for each important policy decision to be subjected to an 'ethnic impact statement' (Dev 2011). Such a proposal could create an enabling environment that addresses the steep subjective discount rate of private investors and individuals desiring to accumulate human capital inside Guyana.

Figure 4.4: Reinforcement of Colonial Underdevelopment Trap

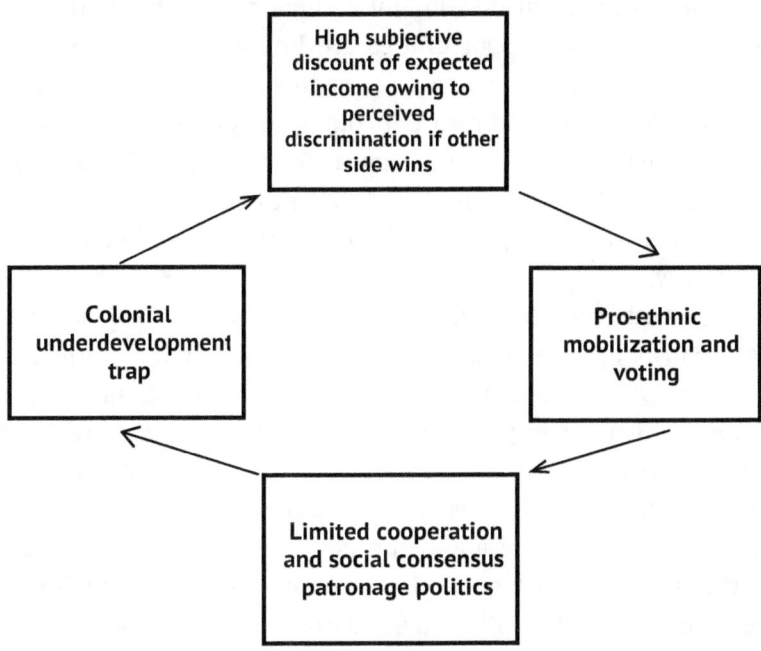

In addition, it would force the winning party to think about how policies determine social cohesion and subjective discount. A severe shortcoming of the APNU + AFC economic policy agenda, in spite of its well-intentioned statements about social cohesion, is a lack of consistency between economic policy and subjective discount. The Ministry of Finance and the Ministry of the Presidency have no mechanisms in place that connect the rhetoric of social cohesion and economic policy legitimacy. The government's economic agenda would achieve greater legitimacy, thereby reducing the subjective discount of the losing group, if it can make the connection between policy and legitimacy. Earlier, much of the PPP's economic agenda faced exactly this constraint. The seeming illegitimacy of the roles of National Industrial and Commercial Investments Limited (NICIL), the office of the president and other government agencies stemmed from the inability of the Jagdeo and Ramotar administrations to spell out clearly how their industrial policies were consistent with a national development agenda. In other words, they failed to shape the subjective discount rate of those who lost the election and also a small percentage of some of their supporters.

This results in the continuation of the colonial trap that brings about decades of income stagnation and limited financial capital. In the colonial underdevelopment trap opportunities are limited, thus competition for this limited space is fierce. The masses express their economic insecurity by discounting the expected future incomes and opportunities that could possibly result if the other side wins. Hence, the colonial underdevelopment trap determines the subjective discount rate as much as the latter perpetuates the trap through pro-ethnic politics and limited cooperation and legitimacy.

The arguments contained in this chapter do not imply it is impossible to develop Guyana. Instead, the point is being made that historical factors of geography and contemporary political conflicts will make the task much more difficult than peer economies which are blessed with a more favourable geography and greater social consensus. The recent discovery of about 2.5 billion barrels of recoverable sweet crude by ExxonMobil has captivated the imagination about the developmental possibilities. A lot of uncertainties exist that could derail the developmental aspirations of Guyanese and curtail the optimum utilisation of the oil revenues.

These include the border dispute between Guyana and Venezuela, global energy demand and supply trends, and domestic factors. The extent to which ExxonMobil will use the border dispute as leverage in revenue sharing is unknown. The Guyanese civil service and government would have a greater responsibility in resource allocation and economic planning. History suggests that the civil service is a far way off the mark of a developmental state, as defined by Peter Evans. Careful planning would be necessary for overcoming the constraints geography imposes. The Constitution is not appropriate for solving the tit-for-tat politics and institutionalising cooperation. The price of oil could remain depressed for the foreseeable future given the efficiency gains in vehicles, the growing prevalence of renewable sources, and the technologies enabling fracking. Finally, a percentage of the revenues would be replacing the export decline of sugar, rice, and bauxite industries.

Conclusion

This chapter has examined the ethno-political mobilisation and the pro-ethnic voting of the two dominant ethnic masses, and the implication of these for economic development. The fundamental argument is that the post-1992 political conflict – which at its core involves voting to express one's economic insecurity – serves to reinforce the endogenous cycles that perpetuate the colonial underdevelopment trap, and which were put in motion by two exogenous variables: adverse geography and world price competition. In particular, the chapter used the canonical prisoners' dilemma game to illustrate how ethno-political mobilisation perpetuates the underdevelopment trap.

At the root of the propagation mechanism – as illustrated by the prisoners' dilemma game – is the uncertainty associated with how the other side will vote on the day of secret ballot. Although most people might prefer to co-operate and vote for a multi-ethnic third party, they cannot be certain the other side would do the same. Therefore, this is a major coordination failure which a system of free and fair elections cannot solve in a polarised bi-communal society such as Guyana. Legal and constitutional arrangements would be necessary to promote a system of competitive cooperation within a democratic structure.

Many have argued over the years for some kind of power sharing mechanism ranging from federalism to sharing of ministries. Any power sharing formula would require a suitable constitution to make it possible. The political elites will not jettison the present constitution for a new one, which would be the ideal policy outcome. In the interim, a more incremental form of constitutional reform might be needed to break the political uncertainty inherent in the present system as the prisoners' dilemma game illustrates. Incremental constitutional reform that promotes a greater degree of randomness in the electoral outcomes might do the trick. For example, the rule should change from pre-election to post-election alliances to allow for independent voters to have a greater say in the political process. Post-election alliance also makes it more difficult to accuse the third party of colluding against the interests of the incumbent ethnic group.

Even without any constitutional reform, civil society can do more to mould a higher percentage of swing voters so that ethnic elites cannot be assured of election victory. A larger percentage of independent swing voters will add a greater degree of randomness to the election outcome. If leaders are not certain they will win the election, they are more likely to shift the discussion towards important issues and policies. Finally, from an economic modelling standpoint, the emergence of a more vibrant class of swing voters would require a more complicated game theory, set up with independent voters playing mixed strategies instead of pure strategies, as this paper has assumed.

Notes

1. Then the party was just Peoples' National Congress (PNC). Before 1992, the PPP also did not have the civic term in its name. Hereafter, I use PNC and PPP.
2. This work will focus mainly on political economy issues from 1992. However, detailed analyses of the PNC's system of Party Paramountcy can be found in the works of Percy Hintzen (1989), Chaitram Singh (1988) and George K. Danns (1982). Hintzen, in particular, explains how Party Paramountcy was not only a form of coercion, but also an elaborate system of patronage. David Hinds (2010) notes the early pre-independence PPP government favoured Indian production interests over African interests. Ralph Premdas (1992) observes, among other things, how the PNC used the state as an instrument of its own middle-class interests. Jayan Jose Thomas (1988) explores reasons for underdevelopment. This chapter looks at a fundamentally different transmission channel of underdevelopment.
3. From a technical standpoint, this perceived discrimination results in a high subjective discount rate attached to the event of the other side winning the election. This idea is developed formally later in the chapter.
4. Several studies have examined the ethnic conflict of Guyana. However, the first explicit systematic attempt to examine the relationship between ethnic conflict and development in the Guyanese context is that of Premdas (1992). Premdas proposes several predisposing and triggering factors determining the relationship between ethnic conflict and development. This chapter extends Premdas's analysis by adding to the literature in the following ways: (i) it shows how ethnic mobilisation under free and fair elections could still engender underdevelopment; (ii) it proposes a clear transmission channel that explains within the context of a model how a sub-optimal growth equilibrium is possible with strategic voting in a democracy; (iii) relating to the latter, the chapter endogenises the payoff structure within the prisoners' dilemma model; and (iv) it suggests the difficult situation in which independent third parties operate. Ethnic conflict and development are, however, endogenous. Therefore, the chapter introduces a causal mechanism from geography, colonial history, and external prices to subjective discount and ethno-political conflict.
5. Most of the flat lands of the US are either easy to develop or moderately difficult to develop, and the US possesses the longest naturally navigable river and numerous natural ports (Zeihan 2014). Guyana's location on Zeihan's world map of agricultural lands is mainly in the region he classifies as lands that are more difficult to develop.
6. See Rawle Farley (1954) for a discussion of these events.
7. Numerous outcomes in economic development have to do with path dependency. One example is the state of industrial development in the Indian state of Kerala (Thomas 2005).

8. In microeconomics, normal profit means the business is just covering its opportunity costs associated with an alternative activity. There is no exit from the industry and the profit rate is not high enough to attract new entrants into the industry.
9. The population data for that period can be found in Jay Mandle (1973). In 1851, the population of British Guiana was 127, 695. Indians made up six per cent of the population, Africans 86 per cent, Portuguese six per cent, and other Europeans two per cent. By 1921, the population increased to 288, 451. Indians accounted for 43 per cent, Africans 41 per cent, mixed race 11 per cent, Chinese one per cent, Portuguese three per cent, and other Europeans one per cent.
10. The discount rate is at the core of the theory of investment in economics (whether physical or human capital). If the investor is pessimistic about the future he or she assigns a high subjective rate of discount to future cash flows that will curtail investments. Optimism results in a low discount rate and therefore the investor would be motivated to invest in physical or human capital. This discount rate could be highly subjective relying on gut feelings or objectives based on mathematical calculations of expectation.
11. See endnote 10 for an explanation of the role of the discount rate in investment decisions relating to physical and human capital.

References

Adamson, Alan. 1972. *Sugar without Slaves: The Political Economy of British Guiana, 1838–1904*. New Haven and London: Yale University Press.

Bulmer-Thomas, Victor. 2012. *The Economic History of the Caribbean since the Napoleonic Wars*. Cambridge and New York: Cambridge University Press.

Constantine, Collin. 2017. Economic Structures, Institutions and Economic Performance. *Journal of Economic Structures* 6, no. 2:1–18.

Collier, Paul. 2000. Ethnicity, Politics and Economic Performance. *Economics and Politics* 12, no. 3:225–45.

Danns, George K. 1997. Race and Development in Plural Societies: The Case of Guyana. *Caribbean Dialogue* 3, no. 2:32–41.

———. 1982. *Domination and Power in Guyana: A Study of the Police in a Third World Context*. New Brunswick and London: Transaction Books.

Dev, Ravi. 2011. Ethnic Impact Statement. *Kaieteur News*, Features, July 17.

Dincer, Oguzhan, and Peter Lambert. 2012. Taking Care of Your Own: Ethnic and Religious Heterogeneity and Income Inequality. *Journal of Economic Studies* 39, no. 3:290–313.

Evans, Peter. 1995. *Embedded Autonomy: States and Industrial Transformation*. Princeton, NJ: Princeton University Press.

Farley, Rawle. 1954. The Rise of the Peasantry in British Guiana. *Social and Economic Studies* 2, no. 4:87–103.

Gampat, Ramesh. 2015. The Developmental Prospects for Guyana are Dim. *Stabroek News*, Letter Column, August 18.

Gören, Erkan. 2014. How Ethnic Diversity Affects Economic Growth. *World Development* 59 (July): 275–97.

Harripaul, Malcolm. 2017. The List System Has Contributed to Racial Mobilisation and Party Dictatorship. *Kaieteur News*, Letter Column, March 31.

Hidalgo, C. A., B. Klinger, A.L. Barabasi and R. Hausmann. 2007. The Product Space Conditions the Development of Nations. *Science* 317:482–87.

Hinds, David. 2010. *Ethno-Politics and Power Sharing in Guyana: History and Discourse*. Washington, DC: New Academia Publishing.

Hintzen, Percy. 1989. *The Cost of Regime Survival: Racial Mobilization, Elite Domination and the Control of the State in Guyana and Trinidad*. Cambridge: Cambridge University Press.

Horowitz, Donald. 1985. *Ethnic Groups in Conflict*. Berkeley: University of California Press.

Kaldor, Nicholas. 1967. *Strategic Factors in Economic Development*. New York: New York State School of Industrial and Labor Relations, Cornell University.

Khemraj, Tarron. 2011. Show-of-hands, Secret Ballot and the Making of an Elected Oligarchy. *Stabroek News*, Development Watch, February 9.

———. 2015A. The Colonial Origins of Guyana's Underdevelopment. *Social and Economic Studies* 64, nos. 3 and 4:49–83.

———. 2015B. Can the PPP Suck Cane and Blow Whistle? *Stabroek News*, Development Watch, May 6.

Kissoon, Fredrick. 2002. Part III: Tired Men in Black. *Guyana Chronicle*, republished online, 2013, Failure of Buxton Conspiracy. http://guyanachronicle.com/2013/01/14/the-failure-of-the-buxton-conspiracy-2.

———. 2007. African Extremism in the Age of Political Decay: The Case of Guyana. In *Governance, Conflict Analysis and Conflict Resolution*, ed. C.H.Grant and R. Mark Kirton. Kingston: Ian Randle Publishers.

Lewis, W. Arthur. 1954. Economic Development with Unlimited Supplies of Labour. *Manchester School* 22, no.2: 139–91.

Mandle, Jay. 1970. Population and Economic Change: The Emergence of the Rice Industry in Guyana, 1895–1915. *Journal of Economic History* 30 no. 4:785–801.

———. 1973. *The Plantation Economy: Population and Economic Change in Guyana, 1838–1960*. Philadelphia, PA: Temple University Press.

Milne, R.S. 1988. Bi-communal Systems: Guyana, Malaysia and Fiji. *Publius: The Journal of Federalism* 18, no. 2:101–13.

Montalvo, Jose and Marta Reynal-Querol. 2005. *Journal of Development Economics* 76, no. 2 (April): 293–323.

Myers, Roxanne, and Jason Calder. 2011. Toward Ethnic Conflict Transformation: A Case Study of Citizen Peacebuilding Initiatives on the 2006 General Elections. Occasional Paper: Peace Building Series No. 4, Future Generations Graduate School.

Nafziger, E.W. 2006. From Seers to Sen: The Meaning of Economic Development. Research Paper No. 2006/20, United Nations University.

Nissan, Edward and Shahdad Naghshpour. 2013. Connecting Corruption to Ethnic Polarization and Religious Fractionalization. *Journal of Economic Studies* 40, no. 6:763–74.

Premdas, Ralph. 1992. Ethnic Conflict and Development: The Case of Guyana. Discussion Paper 30, Geneva, United Nations Institute for Social Development.
Ramkarran, Ralph. 2015. Pit Bull Politics. *Stabroek News*, Conversation Tree, April 26.
Reinert, Erik. 2008. *How Rich Countries Got Rich...and Why Poor Countries Stay Poor.* New York: Carroll and Graf Publishers.
Rodney, Walter. 1981. *A History of the Guyanese Working People, 1881–1905.* Baltimore: Johns Hopkins University Press.
Seecharan, Clem. 1997. *Tiger in the Stars: The Anatomy of Indian Achievement in British Guiana, 1919–29.* London: Macmillan Education.
Singh, Chaitram. 1988. *Guyana: Politics in a Plantation Society.* New York and London: Praeger.
Stabroek News. 2001. Whither the Dialogue Process. Editorial, November 14.
———. 2007. A Dialogue on Corruption. Editorial, December 17.
———. 2008. Is the Phantom Squad Still Lurking in Guyana? October 5.
———. 2015. Criticisms Grow over Imbalance of State Boards. August 1.
Taeuber, Irene. 1952. British Guiana: Some Demographic Aspects of Economic Development. *Population Index* 18, no. 1:3–19.
Thirlwall, A. P. 2007. The Least Developed Country Report, 2006: Developing Productive Capacities. *Journal of Development Studies* 43, no. 4:766–78.
Thomas, Clive. 1988. *The Poor and the Powerless: Economic Policy and Change in the Caribbean.* New York: Monthly Review Press.
Thomas, Jayan Jose. 2005. Kerala's Industrial Backwardness: A Case of Path Dependence in Industrialization? *World Development* 33, no. 5:763–83.
Williams, Eric. 1945. The Historical Background of British Guiana's Problems. *Journal of Negro History* 30, no.4:357–81.
Wilson, Stacey-Ann. 2012. *Politics of Identity in Small Plural Societies: Guyana, the Fiji Islands, and Trinidad and Tobago.* New York: Palgrave Macmillan.
Zeihan, Peter. 2014. *The Accidental Superpower: The Next Generation of American Prominence and the Coming Global Disorder.* New York and Boston: Twelve, The Hachette Book Group.

5.
Crime, Ethnicity and the Political Impasse in Guyana

Rishee S. Thakur

Abstract changes in moral concepts are always embodied in real particular events.... There ought not to be two histories, one of political and moral action and one of political and moral theorizing, because there were not two pasts, one populated only by actions, the other only by theories. Every action is the bearer and expression of more or less theory-laden beliefs and concepts; every piece of theorising and every expression of belief is a political and moral action.

Alister McIntyre

This I have learnt:
today a speck
tomorrow a hero
hero or monster
you are consumed!
Like a jig
shakes the loom;
like a web
is spun the pattern
all are involved!
all are consumed!
   Martin Carter

Introduction[1]

The details are as shocking as they are grim. Anyone living through the carnage could not but be stunned and rendered helpless by its mind-numbing repetition. Only Professor Ralph Premdas in his most pessimistic and cynical mood could have guessed or predicted the outcome, but in ways that even he could not have imagined or anticipated.[2]

"Crime, Ethnicity and the Political Impasse in Guyana," by Rishee S. Thakur was originally published in *Transition: Journal of the Institute of Development Studies,* Special Issue on Consociationalism and Governance in Guyana, edited by Rishee S. Thakur, No. 38–39, pp. 78–105. © University of Guyana 2008–2009.

For the better part of two years, between February 2002 and early 2004, Guyana was caught in an orgy of violence and criminality that threatened to rend the country apart. It began in February 2002 after the spectacular escape of five high-profile African-Guyanese prisoners from the main prison, cum 'holding' facility, in the capital city of Georgetown and ended around the first quarter of 2004 when it appeared that more than a common criminality fed by inter-ethnic rivalry was involved and other, larger, forces were at work.[3]

There was, however, nothing really new in any of this. Indeed, one could make out a reasonably good case that most of Guyana's post-war history is a narrative of violence and racial strife that has sapped energy, exhausted passions and driven the best and brightest from the land.

A cursory review would indicate that Guyana's entry into the nationalist/post-war world was a grim portent.[4] It greeted the post-war settlement with the continuing struggle of workers that resulted in the death of five of their colleagues in 1948, at the hands of the colonial police, on the east coast of Demerara – the story was now famously enshrined in the nationalist mythology as the Enmore Martyrs. This was followed five years later by the suspension of the constitution and the removal of the government on charges of communist subversion, when the People's Progressive Party (PPP) won the country's first post-war elections held under universal adult suffrage. Unfortunately, suspension also involved the landing of British troops under the protective cover of gunboats and the permanent occupation of the country for the next ten years. In the midst of the occupation even British troops could not contain the violence and between 1961 and 1964 the country exploded in a rage of inter-ethnic rivalry and racial one-upmanship that was nothing short of a civil war. By then, of course, it had already become obvious that whatever once held the country together was no longer there or had come unstuck, and the only game in town was played with a toxic, ethnic deck.

Even the subsequent political settlement, engineered by the British to remove the 'communists', turned out to be worse than the problem it was intended to resolve. On the shoulders of the Central Intelligence Agency (CIA) and with the connivance of the Colonial Office, a new electoral system was put in place, designed to remove the communists. That it did. Unfortunately, in doing so it also put in place a strongman and kleptocrat that unleashed a period of 'civilian' violence that satisfied neither his American sponsors nor the local opposition. By the time he passed away in office, 20 years later, Guyana had become a pariah state in the international community, while the nation and its hapless citizens hit rock-bottom and were, now unfavourably, compared to Haiti.

Finally, at the end of the Cold War when the 'communists' had shelved some of their more strident claims, the Americans, with no more use for anti-communist strongmen, sponsored and supported free and fair elections. That came in 1992 and with it a great deal of hope and goodwill. Unfortunately, by then the inspiring leader of the 'communists', for the better part of half a century, had seen better days. He was less than sensitive and agile to pick up on the need for healing and a more consensual/accommodating politics. Instead, he fell in with his more hard line colleagues and opted for the Westminster prize of 'winner take all'. Not unexpectedly, good will and hope evaporated, while the ugly racial fears emerged to take their place – once more. Subsequently, like a well-planned and orchestrated simulation, Guyanese played out their ritualistic urges – each election conducted in fear and apprehension followed by racial strife. Guyana now occupies pride of place in David Horowitz's *The Deadly Ethnic Riot* with at least 20 references.[5]

In what follows I: (a) review a brief moment of the latest episode in Guyana's recurring racial conflict; (b) place it in the larger context of Guyana's post-war history; (c) attempt to interrogate some of the circumstances and forces that seem to have initiated and sustained it; and (d) ask some questions of where all of this leaves Guyana and its beleaguered citizens.

Uzis and Cell Phones

A brief survey of *Stabroek News,* Guyana's only independent daily, of events for a brief period between October and November 2002 indicates that there were at least 57 front page stories of violence consisting of 23 headlined pieces and 34 secondary stories.

On the October 24, 2002, *Stabroek News* reported that popular Georgetown businessman, Brama Nandalall, owner of Keishar's, a fashionable gift shop on Regent Street, was kidnapped in broad daylight in the early hours of the morning.[6] According to the report, the businessman was abducted by heavily armed gunmen in bullet proof vests 'following a running gun battle in central Georgetown'. In the view of *Stabroek*, the 'abduction sent shockwaves through the city which has been in the grips of a ferocious eight-month long crime wave.'[7]

Three days later, October 27, 2002, all hell broke loose when it was announced, in bold headline: 'Seven Die in Shoot out: Two Mash Day Escapees: Large Arms Cache Found in Rented House: Keishar's Owner Escapes from Captors.' The story indicated that there were at least six separate incidents of shooting the previous evening, with a clear undercurrent. The first and most important was the shooting of Dale Moore (a Mash escapee) and a companion who were gunned down at a 'safe' house in Lamaha Gardens (an upscale neighbourhood in the northern half of the city), three doors from the residence of the minister of home affairs. The second was a lone body in a bulletproof vest found in the popular La Repentir Cemetery in the middle of the city. The third incident involved Mark Fraser (another Mash escapee) and Lancelot Roach, the owner of an electronic stall (Lance Electronics) in Bourda Market, son of a senior police officer in the communications division of the force, who were shot by unknown gunmen on the east coast of Demerara near Annandale, about four miles from the capital city. Fourth, Frank Solomon, an ex-police officer, was shot, and later died in hospital while his companion, a female teenager, was in police custody. It is believed that Solomon was shot by the same persons who shot Roach and Fraser. And finally, a seventh person was killed by the police in Section 'M', Campbellville, when the police, in a 'sweep' of the area, encountered a lone resister in a house whom they easily flushed out.[8]

In addition, it was found that the safe house in Lamaha Gardens, where Moore and his companion were holed-up, contained 13 high powered firearms, including four assault rifles with telescopic sights, an Uzi machine gun and a number of semi-automatic pistols. Also found on the premises were one flare, one suitcase containing 'channa' bombs, a salt bag of channa, along with 45 magazines for the semiautomatic pistols and 3,097 rounds of other live ammunition. The bandits also appeared to have acquired a large quantity of 'sophisticated communications devices' since the police claimed to have removed a quantity of radio sets and cell phones from the safe house.

One week later, November 5, 2002, another headline in *Stabroek News* read 'Six shot dead in City'. This time it was reported six men were shot in two separate incidents, one involving five men, shot 'execution style' on the corner of Robb and Light Streets, and a lone 'would-be bandit' was shot in another part of the city, La Penitence. According to *Stabroek News* the incident brought the total number of violent deaths to 18 within eight days.⁹

One estimate suggests that for the one-year period, between February 2002 (Mash jail break) and February 2003, there were at least 155 murders – a significant increase from 52 in 1997–1998 and 79 in 2001. Most of these occurred between the months of September 2002 and January 2003. It is estimated that no less than 100 persons were killed in the five-month period at a rate of 20 per month.¹⁰

Other violent crimes for the same period included ten kidnappings, involving 18 victims. Of these three were females, including a 14 year-old. Of the 18 that were kidnapped two were murdered, six escaped while nine were released after the payment of ransom estimated at GY$85 million, while the fate of one is still unknown.

The report also indicated that, while in the past the choice of weapons was the ordinary hand gun, today it was more likely to be the popular AK47. And not all of these, the report noted, were obtained through theft, which suggests a brisk traffic in and out of Guyana of high-powered small arms.

Another estimate, in the same report, suggested that there were, for the same one year period between February 2002 and February 2003, at least 438 instances of violent crimes – most of them with an ethnic flavour.¹¹

There was nothing new in the violence itself. Guyana had already experienced some of this in the early '60s. What was new was the sustained intensity and the high powered weapons that appeared readily available. The surprising part of all of this, however, despite some clear provocations, is that the society did not degenerate into an ethnic civil war. Instead, there was a resounding call on 'both' sides for immediate and earnest dialogue not only to end the escalating and uncontrolled crime wave but to begin the process of healing and reconstruction. Whether the call for sanity was an act of desperation or longing, remains uncertain, since many of those writing were a part of Guyana's large diaspora living in the US, Canada, and the UK – with very little immediate intent to return – keenly aware that the society offered little hope for a safe or sane future.

Elections and Violence

In order to appreciate the context and the internal nuances of the violence it is important to rehearse the debate in which it emerged and the various political currents that fed it.

In the run-up to the elections of 1997 several independent forums were held to explore the possibilities of a more creative political future for Guyana given what appeared to be the twin monsters of an entrenched racial-political divide and a Westminster electoral/constitutional arrangement of 'winner take all'.[12] Two of the models that were widely debated and hotly contested were the federalism of Rise, Organise and Rebuild (ROAR)[13] and a more immediately recognisable power sharing scheme drawn from Arend Lipjhart's consociational model of democracy. In fact, the two positions have much in common and ROAR's leader Ravi Dev is a convert and firmly convinced of the utility of Lipjhart's model for Guyana. What prevented convergence it seems, was/is ROAR's 'federalist' initiative. This would see Guyana divided into four states, the traditional three counties (Essequibo, Demerara and Berbice) and a fourth division, Rupununi, to accommodate the indigenous Amerindian communities in the interior of the country. ROAR's proposals were seen as a welcome addition, especially its call for greater autonomy to local communities. Critics felt, however, that it sought, too quickly perhaps, to foreclose the debate and the emergence of other political possibilities by locking it in a federal scheme. They argued that federalism in itself and especially the US version, given Dev's frequent reference to the latter, provided few guarantees that racial minorities would or could not be marginalised and put upon in such states, as indeed happened in the US, especially in the Jim Crow south – well into the 1960s.

Unfortunately, the debate did not get far. And, while a small but vocal group within the Peoples' National Congress (PNC) made strident claims for its inclusion in a national debate, the leadership would have nothing of it. The PPP, on the other hand, scoffed at the idea and saw little benefit in it. And not averse to chiding the PNC, whenever the opportunity arose, it shot back by accusing the latter of trying to get back into power 'through the back door' – the very charge that the PNC had made about similar proposals from the PPP, while the latter was in opposition.[14]

And there was the rub. It had already become clear that electoral outcomes in Guyana were a foregone conclusion – given the ethnic divisions and the entrenched racial animosity, the results were nothing more than 'ethnic censuses'. If this was not up for debate, then the prospects for African Guyanese to participate in any future government were slim at best. With an East Indian majority and ethnic voting at a premium, Africans were fast becoming a permanent, excluded minority.

With this unresolved issue simmering in the background, the elections became a testing ground and a portent for future contests. Even before it was announced and began in earnest, the PPP's prospective presidential candidate had become a matter of controversy. When the aged leader of the PPP, Dr Cheddi Jagan passed away in March 1997 without a clear successor, his wife and lifelong political partner, Janet Jagan, claimed, without confirming evidence, that 'Cheddi wanted' her to lead the party after he passed on. This did not go down well with many inside the PNC, some of whom accused her of being a racist while others suggested that her American birth did not entitle her to such high office in Guyana. And while others inside the PPP privately grumbled about a dynasty, they stayed clear of any public opposition.

Indeed, a little over a year before he passed away the old communist had, himself become the subject of public controversy. Part manufactured and part propaganda, an innocuous statement in Toronto about Africans occupying 'the lowest rung of the social ladder' was transformed into 'insulting' and 'degrading' by local spin doctors. Expectedly it found ready reception in sections of the African community and after a protracted and rancorous debate and name calling Jagan was forced to offer a public apology. Importantly though, while the statement itself was never in doubt and did make for considerable verbal mud-slinging, it was not far from what African scholars and politicians had been saying for a long time: that social and institutional racism had reduced Africans to the 'lowest rung....' In the end, however, the story was not really about what the president may or may not have said but another opportunity to raise fears about African marginalisation and exclusion and the continuing racial fears in which Guyanese politics was written. And while the 'apology' was enough to appease and provide a moment of temporary satisfaction – not a little of it received as 'our pound of flesh' – it did nothing to resolve the underlying tension and political dilemma to which it spoke. The point then was not just about the president's statement but how it was seen and read: entwined and imbricated in the underlying dilemma where constitutional/institutional arrangements are stacked against Africans in a Westminster system of 'winner take all' and a zero-sum contest of tribal voting where they are the minority.[15] And it is, I believe, this underlying dilemma that constitutes the discursive space from which Africans speak to power and politics. But we are getting ahead of ourselves.

By most accounts, including local (Elections Assistance Bureau) and international observers (Organisation of American States, the Carter Center, and the International Foundation for Electoral Systems) and despite a few hiccups and organisational lapses the elections (1997) were deemed to be 'free and fair'. But not, they readily admit, free from fear, as most of the campaigning stirred the traditional anxieties and apprehensions, provoked by the expected outcome and ritual fall-out – PPP victory followed by violence.

But even as ballots were counted it appeared that something was dreadfully wrong – whether due to organisational incompetence, calculated attempt at deception, or care to ensure accuracy, was anyone's guess. Three days after the elections, the Guyana Elections Commission (GECOM) could not pronounce on the outcome while the ruling party appeared headed for another victory. At this point the PNC withdrew from the verification process.[16]

On the fourth day, December 19, 1997, things began to unravel. With 61,000 votes still to be counted the Chairman of GECOM announced that the ruling party had won while the new president, Mrs. Jagan, was sworn in at a private/secret ceremony by the chancellor of the judiciary in the office of the elections commission.

Expectedly, as news of the latter filtered through the streets of the city, supporters of the PNC, estimated at between 300 and 500, laid siege to the offices of GECOM and headquarters of the PPP at Freedom House. In the meantime, counting and verification continued at GECOM after the latter agreed to the PNC's conditions for its continued participation in the process.

The PNC, in the meantime, had already gone to court and sought an injunction to: (a) restrain the chairman of GECOM from pronouncing on the outcome of the elections; (b) prohibit the chancellor of the judiciary from conferring the oath of office on Mrs Jagan; and (c) prevent Mrs. Jagan from assuming, entering, and performing the duties of president. This writ was granted on December 20, 1997, and served the same day scheduled for the official swearing-in ceremony at State House. In the meantime, word had spread throughout the city that the latter had already occurred the day before under covert circumstances. It did not help much when it was also learnt that the marshall, in his attempt to serve the writ, was physically restrained by supporters of the ruling party, who had gone to State House to witness and participate in the swearing-in ceremony. And even when he was able to eventually do so, Mrs Jagan treated both the marshall and the writ with undue disregard. It was reported, and captured on television, on receipt of the writ Mrs Jagan turned a pirouette and tossed it over her shoulder.[17]

By then the die was cast and the parties and their more strident supporters had locked horns, bent on a battle of moral outrage and political correctness. The crescendo of voices began to build when PNC supporters gathered every morning at the Square of the Revolution and then made their way into the city through the main (East Indian) business districts on bicycles, mopeds, and on foot. They ended at the High Court where the PNC's petition was being heard. At one meeting, estimated at near 25,000 at the Square of the Revolution, December 22, 1997, leader of the opposition, Desmond Hoyte, promised to 'shut down the country' and called for massive protest action. Later that evening two bombs were found in one upscale neighbourhood, Bel Air, in the city.

On the December 24, 1997, another march of 10,000 invaded both the business district and government offices, forcibly shutting down many in the process, while the PNC pulled out of the counting/verification process – again.

On the December 31, 1997, the final election results were announced giving the PPP a 15-point victory over the PNC.

On January 6, 1998, a local television station (NTN, Channel 19) was bombed and an East Indian security guard critically injured and died a few days later in hospital.

In the next few days protests and demonstrations escalated to involve not only businesses and government offices but were now extended to include schools in the city. On January 7, 1998, a bomb was thrown at the main hotel in the city, Le Meriden Pegasus, that served as a popular 'night spot' for expatriates, the Guyanese business and professional community and employees of the multilateral financial institutions and international organisations.

Expectedly, the escalating violence raised the climate of fear and apprehension in the city. And since most of the marchers were Afro-Guyanese and most of the businesses were East Indian it also gave it a deadly ethnic edge. Georgetown was soon transformed into a city under siege – businesses spent millions in new security systems, using almost anything – from large steel reinforced containers to impregnable steel doors and windows to block potential 'rioters' from damaging or entering their premises.

On the January 11, 1997 CARICOM Chairman Keith Mitchell announced that a team headed by Sir Henry Forde and including Sir Shridath Ramphal and Sir Alister McIntyre would visit Guyana to intervene in the continuing violence.

On January 12, 1998, the Chief Justice delivered her verdict on the elections petition brought by the PNC. In a 21-page statement she ruled that the courts did not have the competence to enquire into the validity of the election of the president as announced by the chairman of the elections commission. In her view:

> Article 177 (6) [of the Constitution of Guyana] precluded any direct challenge to the election of the person named as President in the instrument executed under the hand of the Chairman of the Election Commission. The draftsmen and crafters of our existing constitution intended in 1980 that the persons elected in the high office of the President of Guyana should be insulated and shielded from inquiry into his/her election and that the validity of the election should not be the subject of direct judicial scrutiny.[18]

Predictably, even before the chief justice had completed reading her judgment marauding bands of PNC supporters had already taken to the streets and, as one report noted, '...armed with guns, knives, cutlasses, clubs, sticks and bricks, in short whatever could be used as a weapon, carefully and systematically selected Indians robbing, molesting and beating them.'[19]

Next morning, January 13, 1998, the *Stabroek News* headline read in bold black type 'Terror in the City'. The government then declared a state of emergency and banned demonstrations in the city.

CARICOM, in the meantime, was already on its way and on January 17, 1998, prevailed on the parties to sign a peace agreement, The *Herdmanston Accord*, to bring the situation under control. And while the *Accord* did bring an end to street protests and the accompanying apprehension and violence – the PNC honoured the 'moratorium on public demonstrations' – it did not do much else. Instead, the usual grandstanding, recriminations and finger pointing ensured that neither the promised dialogue nor the 'agreed commitment to...(a) dispute settlement' would be honoured. In fact, another CARICOM intervention six months later, July 1998, was required to kick-start the process – the *St Lucia Agreement*.

Eventually, after much teeth gnashing and the usual bickering, CARICOM intervention did produce two results. First, the requested audit of the electoral process revealed that it was free and fair and the PPP had won without connivance of either its government prerogative or collusion with GECOM. Second, the parties agreed to constitutional reform and appointed a commission to investigate and recommend on its findings. Unfortunately, the only significant outcome was the Elections Amendment Act of 2000 which altered the electoral process by eliminating the ten regional seats and the two reserved for the local democratic organs. In its stead, the 65 seats were retained but now redistributed differently. The more important, substantive changes included:

i. Retention of a regional allocation, 25 seats, that would be wholly elective and allocated on the basis of, though not strict, proportionality, while the rest, 40 would be drawn from the national count and be known as the 'top-up list'.

ii. The electoral formula – the Israeli single list system – for both geographic and national constituencies would be guided by the Largest Remainder – Hare Quota.

iii. Each elector is allocated one vote that serves to indicate intent to vote for the same party at both the regional and national levels.

iv. Each party must contest in at least six geographic regions to qualify.

v. Each party list must contain at least one-third female candidates.[20]

Substantively the new geographic/regional distribution was allocated in the following manner:

Table 5.1: Population Distribution and Allocation of Regional Seats

Region	Population	Percent	Seats
1	24,375	3.2	2
2	49,253	6.6	2
3	103,061	13.7	3
4	310,320	41.3	7
5	52,428	7.0	2
6	123,695	16.5	3
7	17,597	2.3	2
8	10,095	1.3	1
9	19,387	2.6	1
10	41,112	5.5	2

Source: GECOM website and the Population and Housing Census 2002/2003, National Census Report, (Georgetown: Government of Guyana/Bureau of Statistics, 2002).

While it is generally conceded that the new formula attempted to accommodate regional 'differences' that favoured the geographic concentration of ethnic communities it provided little improvement on what was already there and, ultimately, little variance in outcomes, as we will see.

Finally, after a lengthy and testy court case initiated by the PNC that lasted near three years, beginning in February 1999 and concluding in January 2001, the 1997 elections were declared null and void ('vitiated' was the popular legal expression chosen to name it). In the view of the court, Justice Claudette Singh, the conduct of the elections was unlawful on two counts:

> (i) That the Elections Law (Amendment) act No. 22 of 1997 is *ultra vires* Articles 59 and 159 of the Guyana Constitution, and as a consequence the said act is null and void; and ii) That the aforesaid Elections were not conducted in accordance with the provisions of the Representation of the People's Act Chapter 1:03 and the said articles 59 and 159 of the Constitution of Guyana and are, therefore, unlawful.[21]

In the perverse logic of Guyanese politics the court's decision was seen to have given moral succour to the PNC, while it was heralded by the PPP as vindication of its position, i.e., that the elections were a fair contest that it won, and only 'vitiated' by procedural and legal questions over which it had no control.

After considerable mudslinging on both sides and without much either in the way of dialogue or political rapprochement, new elections were held in 2001. Not unexpectedly and close to the racial arithmetic (elections in Guyana having long become racial censuses) the PPP with 'youth man' Bharat Jagdeo at its head won both the presidential and legislative elections giving it control of both the executive and legislative branches of government.

While there was little surprise in the outcome it was not very encouraging to either the PNC or its supporters. Indeed, it was becoming a matter of serious internal discussion and debate and a younger, clearly more impatient second generation leadership was beginning to snap back at the old guard, who appeared cornered and vulnerable. It was now publicly rumoured in African communities that the PNC had sold out 'black people' for a mess of pottage, since none of the agreements that the leader had signed with the president amounted to anything, while the former appeared completely helpless in the face of an intractable and immovable government.

In addition, there were few prospects elsewhere. After the 1997 elections and subsequent disturbances, the little foreign investment that came into the country was beginning to dry up; while the government showed few signs of moving off the course set by the PNC in 1989 with its Economic Recovery Programme (ERP) and the IMF/World Bank structural adjustment conditionalities.

Moreover, it was now clear that African communities were the real losers in the ERP. In addition to the lost jobs, due to public sector reform where Africans constituted about 80 per cent of employees, privatisation was now taking a new toll on both survival and dignity.[22] The privatisation of such basic and important utilities as electricity and now water (management contract) with demands for 'cost recovery' meant not only an increase in individual privation but also the inability of communities to physically reproduce themselves at a decent and acceptable standard of human habitation. In comparison, the sectors where East Indians traditionally dominated employment expanded, particularly in rice and sugar, the former by 165 per cent and the latter by 65 per cent.[23]

The 2001 elections were conducted without incident, and while there were a few procedural and administrative glitches on the day of voting they were seen to be of little consequence for the outcome. In addition, unlike 1997, GECOM appeared up to the task. Three days after the elections, March 22, 2001, preliminary results were announced, predictably, giving the PPP a clear victory with 52 per cent of the vote while the local observer group, the Elections Assistance Bureau (EAB) gave the process a clean bill of health. International observers were not far behind and, while noting the few hiccups, were in fulsome praise of both the process and outcome and had no doubt that the elections represented the will of the Guyanese people.

Despite outward appearances, however, sections of the press reported a 'sense of apprehension and fear'. The day of the results, March 22, 2001, *Stabroek News* reported that an 'eerie calm continues to pervade the city'. Indeed, as the result of the elections were announced a large section of the East Coast of Demerara 'was turned into a battle zone...as police and villagers clashed following a mid-morning incident involving Guyana Elections Commission staff at Buxton.' According to the report, nearly a dozen civilians and at least two men were injured in the mêlée which continued for most of the day and was still on as night fell. The incident began when persons identified as employees of GECOM arrived in Buxton and began removing statements of poll posted outside polling stations. Simmering suspicion, fear and anger then took over.[24]

On March 24, 2001, Joseph Hamilton, a PNC candidate repeated the PNC writ of 1997 and asked the courts to: a) prevent the Chairman of the Elections Commission from declaring the PPP's presidential candidate Bharat Jagdeo, president; (b) Prohibit the Chief Elections Officer from ascertaining the results of the elections; and (c) forbid the chancellor of the judiciary from swearing-in the PPP's candidate as president.

The same afternoon PNC member of the elections commission, Haslyn Parris, 'was brutally attacked and his car severely damaged' in the PNC Compound. It was believed that Parris was attacked because he sat in at the briefing the previous afternoon when the election results were announced and was seen as a 'traitor' to the PNC and Africans for first, observing the event and then, seemingly and willingly acknowledging it.

By the second day of the trial, large crowds began to assemble in front of the court house where a steady stream of chants, heckles and a macabre soap opera was played out. One 'radical' TV host, described by *Stabroek News* as a 'preacher of hate', served as the live wire for the crowd and had come to play both host and messianic leader. At lunch break on March 27, 2001, he led the crowd in a hysteric frenzy around the court and, by the time the afternoon was done the police had to be called in, but unable to manage the unruly crowd, the Army had to intervene, resulting in a tense face-off. At the end of the day shots were fired to break up the crowd in which at least seven persons were injured.

In the meantime, individual and 'guerrilla' skirmishes continued to create havoc as private homes and public buildings were targeted and razed in 'mystery fires' – an East Indian home in Annandale was burnt leaving a single mother and two young daughters homeless; the ministry of works building in Kingston, the northern section of the city, was targeted and razed to the ground. Similarly, the Mahaica/Mahaicony (rice) project building on the east coast of Demerara was set afire and destroyed.

The situation began to deteriorate further when on April 1, 2001, Chief Justice Desiree Bernard dismissed Hamilton's injunction and ruled that both the letter and spirit of the law had been observed in the announcement of the election results and the declaration of the PPP candidate as president.[25] Subsequently, as in 1998, daily demonstrations took over the streets of Georgetown, raising both tension and fear. Matters worsened when on April 7, 2001, the PNC rejected the appointment of Dr Roger Luncheon, head of the presidential secretariat and secretary to the cabinet, as head of the civil service as well. The PNC argued that the latter position should not be politicised and should have been offered, instead, to a neutral civil servant.

Two days later the city was consumed. On April 9, 2001, fires were started in the main business district of Regent and Robb Streets following several clashes between police and protesters during the day. Tempers flared when a woman was shot outside the PPP headquarters later in the afternoon. By the time the fires were brought under control 10–12 buildings were razed, consuming nearly half a city block in one of the more popular business districts.

By then the violence returned to the East Coast involving several villages along a 12–15 mile stretch. Anti-government protesters using old tyres, tree trunks, old vehicles and just about anything they could get their hands on to set ablaze, blocked commuters and engaged the police. The police reported that some 40 obstructions were erected along the East Coast highway. Not unexpectedly, the violence also took on a decidedly racial twist and East Indian commuters and citizens were targeted. On May 4, 2001, a father and his ten-year-old son were murdered in the backlands of Enterprise where they had gone fishing; while not far away, in Non Pariel, a third Indian body was found.

Since early April it had become clear that the situation was unravelling out of control and required urgent attention. President Jagdeo made the first move, and contrary to his earlier claims that he would not be intimidated by violence issued an open invitation on April, 7, 2001, to Opposition Leader Desmond Hoyte. On April 8, 2001, amidst teeth gnashing and some reservations, Hoyte announced to the PNC that dialogue with the PPP was on and he would accept the president's invitation.

The first meeting on April 24, 2001, was held at the Presidential Secretariat and was seen as both productive and hopeful. It produced a menu of measures that included:
- recognition of the neutrality of the public service that would involve a review of the office of the Head of the Presidential Secretariat to ensure that the principle was not breached;
- no extension on the outgoing Chancellor of the Judiciary's term of office;

- the PNC's recognition of the government without prejudice to any outstanding elections petition;
- pending consultation, the passing of legislation within one month of the convening of Parliament to advance constitutional reform;
- the promise to end violence and street protests; and
- agreement on an agenda, including the 17-Point Programme raised by the PNC.[26]

However, while a temporary truce was secured, the dialogue was going nowhere. One year later in a five-page letter to the president dated April 23, 2002, the leader of the opposition provided a long list of issues upon which they had agreed but on which the government refused to act, engaged in foot-dragging, grandstanding, or wilful manipulation. These included, according to the letter, the report on the border and national security; report on the committee on radio monopoly and non-partisan boards; de-politicisation of the public service; national policy on the distribution of house lots; the depressed community needs' committee; ethnic relations commission; state boards commissions and committees; parliamentary management committee; the sectoral committees; the appointments committee and the constitutional reform committee.[27] In the end the letter concluded that the central executive of the PNC:

> ...has noted that, after nearly one year of the process and several decisions taken, you have failed, for whatever reasons, to ensure that those decisions were implemented fully or at all. Consequently, the CEC has determined that the dialogue should be halted until they are implemented. For the avoidance of doubts, I wish to state that I concur entirely.

And so it remained.

In the meantime, new and more menacing signs began to appear on the horizon. By all estimates Guyana had now become a major conduit and transhipment point for drug running and a host of other high profile crimes. Indeed, according to Professor Clive Thomas of the Institute of Development Studies, University of Guyana, the parallel economy of the seventies and eighties was not transformed after liberalisation was introduced in the early '90s, as was generally believed. He noted, with remarkable prescience,

> ...[The] clandestine economy was not dismantled as...[it] became progressively liberalised. Instead it was transformed and is now

focused on six major areas: (i) Narco-economy i.e. the production and trafficking in narcotics; (ii) Money laundering; (iii) "Back-tracking," or body smuggling; (iv) Commodity smuggling; (v) Gold smuggling (this being reduced as Gold Board Regulations are being liberalised); and (vi) makeshift construction firms and operators, designed to exploit public sector infrastructural project contracts.[28]

What made all of this troubling is not just its appearance in a small, poor, fragmented third world country, but its presence in a situation that was quickly deteriorating and ripe for manipulation. Under the circumstances, the security forces were pressed beyond their meagre and limited capacity while their moral and political willingness were tested to the limit. Indeed, as *Stabroek News* observed in an editorial, we now appear to have 'a criminal state within a state'[29] after the dubious manner in which Keishar's boss 'escaped' from his captors. It was publicly rumoured, far from what appeared in the press, that the police/security forces had little to do with his release. In fact, the police was simply called in to pick-up the bodies after the fact, or so it was suggested. In other words, according to *Stabroek News,* the political battle was gradually being hauled into the drug war for turf, in which the state appeared outwitted and helpless.

Africans and East Indians

In the midst of the conundrum a new Indian organisation, Guyana Indian Heritage Association (GIHA) emerged to speak for, in its view, the rights of Indians who were being wantonly slaughtered by African 'thugs'. In its view, what was happening, the violence of 1997/98, 2001, and now again in 2002, was nothing short of a race war in which Indians were singled out for elimination, while spreading fear and apocalyptic visions of the 'final solution' in the Indian communities generally. The problem, in its view, was 'the intolerance and violence of the Black Community towards Indians ...' It was 'distressed by the race hate and bullyism that have been numbered within ... [the African] community,' and was now thoroughly disappointed that African Guyanese were less than forthright in condemning the bullyism and the spate of violence directed against Indians.[30]

The argument took on an entirely different spin when one letter asked the GIHA and Indians generally to 'indulge in self-examination'. The letter suggested that GIHA itself may be contributing to the violence by trying to create an 'offensive generalisation' of an inclusive, guilty black community.

This, it suggested, should not be allowed to innocently slip by.[31] Thereafter the argument descended into vitriol and became increasingly shrill and pointless.

Most of the GIHA's thunder was effectively neutralised when three prominent African WPA members, Kwayana, Andaiye, and David Hinds wrote a long letter condemning the attack on Indians. The letter readily admitted that up to that time 'most of those assaulted were Indian Guyanese.' It then went on to suggest that 'In the past, each of us has made statements condemning African Guyanese atrocities against Indian Guyanese and we condemn them even more strongly now, as the violence becomes more brutal.' Moreover, it added that the 'inter-ethnic violence' was counterproductive since it did not and would not bring the government to its knees nor create the conditions for trust and confidence between and among communities that was required at the moment to heal the breach. The letter went further and argued that while 'Buxton is a terror camp in which villagers are held prisoners,' the responsibility for this must fall squarely on the shoulders of both the PPP and PNC. In the view of the authors the 'zero sum political behaviour' of the parties 'paved the way for the boldness of the criminals and other extreme elements who now run things there'. Indeed, the letter took the extraordinary step of singling out the PNC for its political reticence on the matter and suggested that:

> The PNC by not publicly breaking with those who have been pushing Black supremacy and violence and excusing murder, rape and mayhem as revolution, has contributed in no small way to the crisis.
>
> This is no longer simply about politics and "marginalisation," it is about the destruction of the nation in the name of saving the nation or under the guise of seeking power for African Guyanese.[32]

While there is much to reflect on in the letter and perhaps criticise, including the 'equal blame' theory, the recognition of both the source and target of the violence is unmistakable. In the end, it seemed that GIHA was hard-pressed, in both authority and skill, to match the eloquence and moral presence of the statement.[33]

A week later, one of the authors, Hinds, argued while responding to critics, both Africans and Indians, that the present problem in black communities was not the result of Indian connivance and collusion, as some would like to believe, but the result of a historic and systematic process in which both Indians and Africans had been marginalised and oppressed. And, even now, with independence, while the rulers had changed, the 'system' had not and continued to oppress both Africans and Indians. In the process he recognised that the statement made by the late president, Dr Jagan, some six years before in Toronto about Africans being 'at the bottom of the social ladder' was precisely what he was talking about and which required correction. He concluded by noting that while there was a certain bravado among some Africans with guns in hand, killing Indians would not change much. 'Don't fight Indians' he cautioned; 'fight injustice....'[34]

In the mounting crescendo of voices, while the GIHA was quickly marginalised, its intervention did make room for another, more pointed and critical 'Indian' view to emerge. Partly emboldened by the statement from Kwayana, Andaiye, and Hinds, a number of Indians began to publicly ask why the government appeared so helpless in the face of criminals. In the view of one expatriate from Toronto, 'At the present time Guyanese of every racial background are fed up with the present PPP government which has proved itself incompetent when it comes to addressing matters of security of person and property.'[35] Another called for villages to organise their own security since the government appeared completely helpless and incapable.[36] Others were less polite. Rajesh Singh called Guyana 'a land of death and despair'. He continued:

> Just as nauseating is the freak show, called "public consultation on crime" sponsored by officious groups trying vainly to cover their incompetence. I will acknowledge the legitimacy of the PPP/C, a fact being reinforced by the PPP public relations gladiators. Yes sirs! You won the election fair and square you deserve to be in government if even for that reason only, but your governance, enforcement of the rule of law and protection of your constituents stinks![37]

Another critic found that the PPP/C had always had a difficulty in facing crises and much of its leadership was seriously wanting. In the end he warned that:

> The Indians of Guyana must come to the realisation that the PPP has rendered them naked and defenseless and must begin the process of search for alternative leadership, which takes them away from confrontation, into the possibility of Africans and Indians becoming Guyanese.[38]

Whether the government accepts any of this as legitimate criticism is an open question, but now that some of it is coming from one of its stronger constituencies, Region 11,[39] it may want to think twice.

Hopes and Aspirations

Even before the emergence of the 'Mash escapees', it had become clear that the PPP's tenure in office was less than encouraging and it was now presiding over a society that was deeply, if not irreparably, divided. In August–September 2000, the St Augustine Research Associates of the Trinidad Campus of the University of the West Indies conducted a wide ranging survey of 'Political Attitudes and Party Choices in Contemporary Guyana' funded and sponsored by 'The Initiative' a 'grouping of Guyanese Civil Society' organisations.[40] What the survey revealed was a society that was internally fractured in which Africans and East Indians rarely agreed on any of the major issues of the day other than the racial divide and state of insecurity in the country.

The survey interviewed 1,000 persons over a three-day period, August 29–31, 2000, in seven of the ten regions of Guyana – 2, 3, 4, 5, 6, 7, and 10.[41] The respondents consisted of: (a) ethnic background: 52.2 per cent Indians, 32.9 per cent Africans, 12 per cent mixed (including dougla) and 2.9 per cent other; (b) gender: 50.7 per cent female and 48.9 per cent male; (c) age: 18–24: 24.1 per cent; 25–34: 28.3 per cent; 35–40: 24.0 per cent; 45 and over: 23.3 per cent; and (d) religious background: Hindu 27.7 per cent; Muslim 11.6 per cent; Catholic 9.6 per cent; Anglican 7.8 per cent; Baptist 2.8 per cent; Methodist 2.4 per cent; Presbyterian 2.3 per cent; other Christian 12.4 per cent; other non-Christian 1.7 per cent and no stated religious background 6.0 per cent.[42]

The findings are instructive. At the national level, the poll found that no less than 56 per cent of Guyanese were dissatisfied with 'the way that "democracy" works' in the country, while only 37 per cent expressed satisfaction (33 per cent satisfied and four per cent very satisfied). What is probably more interesting is the ethnic breakdown of the respondents: 16 per cent of Afro-Guyanese were satisfied (2 per cent were very and 14 per cent satisfied); 31 per cent of the mixed group were similarly satisfied; while 53 per cent of East Indians expressed satisfaction with the way that democracy worked in the country. On the other hand, no less than 79 per cent of Africans were dissatisfied, 55 per cent of the mixed group was of a similar view, while only 37 per cent of East Indians were so inclined.

Generally and not unexpectedly, both major ethnic groups were apprehensive about the upcoming elections in 2001. Nationally, 48 per cent expected violence while 30 per cent did not. The ethnic breakdown indicated that 30 per cent of East Indians did not expect violence, 33 per cent of Africans were of the same view; while the mixed group were far more apprehensive, and only 18 per cent did not believe violence would accompany the elections. The groups were similarly matched in their expectation of violence with 44 per cent of East Indians expecting some violence; 46 per cent of Africans doing the same; while more than half, 53 per cent of the mixed group believed that violence would occur.

Similarly, all groups were pessimistic about race relations and only 34 per cent of those surveyed believed that race relations would improve; while 51 per cent believed that it would either stay the same or get worse. Expectedly, 40 per cent of East Indians believed that it would improve, 29 per cent Africans believed that it would while 36 per cent of the mixed group were of a similar view. On the other hand, 46 per cent of East Indians believed that it would either stay the same or get worse. Africans were considerably more apprehensive and more than half, 56 per cent, were of the view that race relations would either stay the same or get worse, while the mixed group were closer to their East Indian cohorts and 47 per cent believed that race relations would either stay the same or get worse.

On the whole, East Indians expressed more 'civic competence' and commitment to the political process than their African counterparts. Predictably East Indians were more inclined to view the electoral process with favour and believed that their participation (voting) was of some consequence. No less than 61 per cent believed that voting mattered and could or would lead to improvement. For Africans, less than half, 47 per cent, was of that view, matched by the mixed group, among whom only 45 per cent believed that voting mattered. On the other hand, while 38 per cent of East Indians were either sceptical or convinced that voting would not lead to improvement, no less than 52 per cent of Africans were so inclined and matched the mixed group, of whom 53 per cent were of a similar view.

The coincidence of the Economic Recovery Programme (ERP, IMF/World Bank Structural Adjustment/conditionalities/privatisation) of the late 1980s and the election of the PPP in 1992 was expected to bring relief to the economy and hope to beleaguered citizens. However, despite a brief period of 'honeymoon', relief turned into a trickle, while hopes were eventually dashed. No less than 60 per cent of respondents believed that poverty had increased a little (16 per cent) or a lot (44 per cent). A breakdown of the ethnic groups was even more revealing. No less than 74 per cent of Africans were of the view that poverty had increased, 52 per cent of East Indians were similarly inclined, while 65 per cent of the mixed group concurred. On the other hand, only 23 per cent of the national sample was of the view that poverty had decreased.

Not unexpectedly East Indians also believed that opportunities for economic improvement had increased considerably while their African counterparts were less sanguine. More than half of East Indians, 52 per cent, believed that economic opportunities had increased while only 26 per cent of Africans were of that view. Correspondingly, 17 per cent of Africans believed that economic conditions had remained the same while 56 per cent believed that it had got worse. Of their East Indian cohorts on the other hand, only 15 per cent believed that conditions had remained the same while 22 per cent believed that things had got worse.

On the issue of governance and satisfaction with the existing management of the economy respondents tended to reflect the same ethnic divide. Expectedly a full 66 per cent of East Indians expressed satisfaction with the PPP administration while only 18 per cent of Africans were so inclined. East Indians also tended to support the view that the government was fair to all groups, 61 per cent, and that the performance of the president was good or very good, 67 per cent. Africans, of course, thought differently and only 16 per cent believed that the government was 'fair to all groups', while only 29 per cent gave the president a positive rating in the performance of his job. Similarly, the majority of East Indians, 57 per cent, gave the PPP a satisfactory rating in the management of the economy while only 14 per cent of Africans did so, while 63 per cent of the latter thought that the PPP did a poor job in managing the economy.

Trust and confidence in the government and the political system as a whole was seen as a major issue. The survey indicated that while 51 per cent of those polled had some trust in the government there was significant variance among the two major ethnic groups. East Indians, for example, appeared very trusting and 69 per cent said that they either had some or great trust in the government. A majority of the mixed group, 54 per cent, were of the same view while only 28 per cent of Africans trusted the government. Similarly, while 46 per cent of respondents trusted the president there was significant variation between and among ethnic groups. A full 72 per cent of Africans expressed grave doubts about the president, 47 per cent of the mixed group had similar views, while only 29 per cent of East Indians had reservations about the president.

The judicial system received a very poor review. No less than 53 per cent of respondents expressed doubts about its honesty and fairness. But again there was considerable variation between ethnic groups. Among Africans, for example, 66 per cent expressed some degree of mistrust in the Judiciary while 53 per cent of the mixed group did likewise. Among East Indians, on the other hand, the degree of mistrust had fallen to 42 per cent.

Expectedly the desire to leave was quite high and 45 per cent of those surveyed indicated they were willing to do so – given the opportunity. But here there was little difference between and among ethnic groups – 48 per cent of Africans were so inclined, while 42 per cent of East Indians and 51 per cent of the mixed group felt the same way.[43]

The Way Forward

However, and despite what appeared to be an entirely hopeless situation, the society did not degenerate into warring ethnic factions. Indeed, quite the contrary. In one month, August 2002, there were no less than 20 letters, from both Indians and Africans, and at least two editorials in the *Stabroek News* suggesting ways of ending the political impasse. Most of these offered variations of Lipjhart's consociational formula of ethnic bargaining in which parties are accorded shares of various statutory positions, including ministerial ones, based on their respective strengths in Parliament.[44] Some suggested specific formulae by which such positions would be allocated based on the number of seats in the existing or any new parliament after elections. Some called it 'shared governance', others called it 'inclusive governance' while others still proffered 'power sharing'. Whatever nomenclature was chosen for the proposals or models on offer, most contributors were convinced that the present Westminster system of 'winner take all' not only did not work but, in fact, was the source of much of our present troubles.

Most critics were convinced that the country 'badly needs respite, a period of calm, conviviality, and political partnership,' in order to begin the process of healing and reconstruction. They were of the view that whatever name was chosen to call the experiment, it should be seen as an 'interim measure' with a specific time table after which it could be reviewed and be subject to a referendum for renewal. In addition, it was suggested, proposals should be directed towards the creation of a collective and agreed upon agenda with a time frame for each item to ensure commitment and the willingness to act. Most of this, unfortunately, appears to have fallen on deaf ears, while the government continues to behave as if it's business as usual.

In addition, a new grouping under the general name of 'social partners' consisting of the Trades Union Congress, the Guyana Bar Association and the Private Sector Commission emerged, and crafted a proposal for the parties to consider as means of breaking the impasse. However, while both parties publicly indicated interest in the process, no one held out much hope for its success.

The situation is, to say the least, bleak and dismal and, for some, entirely hopeless. The only question now is: Can the contending claimants be convinced that a way forward can be found as happened with the CARICOM intervention in the post-1997 elections and the dialogue after 2001?

The PNC is, I believe, aware that under present circumstances its options are limited if it is to retake the initiative and, at least, stay at the head of its constituency. Under the circumstances, it can be convinced that some formula for 'power sharing' can be worked out that will provide the incentive to return to Parliament, restart the dialogue and work with the other parliamentary parties to start the process of healing and national reconstruction.

The PNC, I think, must confront and resolve its view of some version of the consociational model. First, public protests and demonstrations in Georgetown have shown to be particularly worrisome to both the government and some of its supporters, while its strategic political value has been temporarily exhausted. Second, its flirtations with the 'Buxton resistance' has not been particularly rewarding and it is keenly aware that much of what was there, either real or perceived, has reached the end of its political tether and had unravelled out of control to its detriment. Third, respect for the opposition as a real partner in stability and development, with a matching constituency, is not a priority for the governing party at the moment and thus leaves the PNC out in the cold. And, as the 'Dialogue' has shown, continued belief and participation in such a process has become a decided liability. Fourth, the electoral demographics are stacked against it and there is little prospect that it can win an election under the present electoral system in the near future. Fifth, the reform arm of the party has not distinguished itself in any particular manner and is seen as lacklustre, at best, and without any creative impulses of its own. Finally, with the emergence of a younger generation of leaders, the party can use the occasion and opportunity to rethink its strategic vision and craft a new direction, while seeking to win over some of the PPP/C's disgruntled supporters and reclaim erstwhile civic converts. It is worth extending the latter point. Hoyte's letter to the president at the time of the stalled dialogue in April 2002, whatever his political intentions, indicates that the issue is not just about African marginalisation and their attempt to get back in government through the back door, but a studied effort in real democratic reforms. Indeed, a cursory review of the government's performance in managing public institutions and agencies leaves much to be desired and those who have had the cause and opportunity to look at them close-up are not sanguine about the prospects. An effort, therefore, to bring those reforms to fruition can go a long way in convincing many that the PNC/R is not just interested in African marginalisation but, in addition, in fair, just and transparent management for the public good of all citizens.

On the other hand, the governing PPP/C must admit, whatever it may have believed or imagined that after four elections and corresponding terms in office the society is at the brink, if it is not there already. It must act and do so quickly not only to bring the situation under control but to demonstrate that it can govern the country in peace and security with some sense of hope of a meaningful future for all its frightened citizens. It must begin to show that it can do more than just win elections, which, in the view of some, it does nothing to merit since that particular largesse is given not out of an enthusiastic commitment to its programmes, policies or astute leadership, but rather out of fear of a PNC that is still mistrusted in large sections of the Indian community. In addition, as our addiction to the Westminster model of 'winner take all' has demonstrated, elections maybe a necessary condition for democracy; it is not, however, sufficient.

An experiment in power sharing need not be to its detriment as it so firmly believes. While some of its fears, insecurities, and sense of siege are understandable, given its history and background, these should not be impediments in accommodating the opposition as real stakeholders in the country with a matching constituency whom it must seek to represent in a real and meaningful way. Refusal to do so is what has us here at the moment. Such admission and accommodation leads neither to 'bullyism' nor a surrender. Its hold on the East Indian electorate will see to that.

None of this involves extensive preparation and/or negotiation. Much of it, as indicated in the text, has already been publicly discussed and subject to searching comments well within the political grasp of the leadership of the parliamentary parties, many of whom were, and have been party to such discussions. The only thing that seems missing is the political will.[45]

Conclusion

Since then, while much has changed, the fundamental problems remain – up front and just as intractable. The PNC, for its part, has dropped its opposition to and now embraces the consociational principle under the name of 'Shared Governance'. In the meantime, however, it has lost its elder statesman and the party has been embroiled in a leadership contest that it seems unable to resolve. The 2006 elections came with the same depressing results and while a new party, the Alliance for Change, appeared on the horizon it was incapable of breaking the PPP's stranglehold on its East Indian constituency. But it did manage to secure five seats, a remarkable feat in Guyana for a third party the first time around. Whether it can use its youthful leadership and novelty for a more serious challenge to the old parties will be the litmus test of it survival and success. So far, unfortunately, it has not shown that it can bring the required organisational skills and robust leadership needed for the task.

In the meantime, a low intensity violence continues to dash hopes and undermine expectations while few with prospects elsewhere are likely to remain for long. Moreover, the spectre of violence continues to haunt East Indian communities and its occasional/unexpected eruption has ensured that they will remain committed to the PPP, if only negatively. As long as the PPP remains hostile and continues to treat the opposition, and the PNC in particular, as an unwanted nuisance, its supporters will continue to pay the price for its political unwillingness at serious dialogue. This is not because the PNC, or anyone else for that matter, wants it that way. The fact is that large segments of the African population remain marginal to both the political process and the formal economy. If, on every public occasion, their party is humiliated and chastised for 20 years of wrong while corruption goes unheeded, the drug trade eats into both economy and society and East Indians are seen as the major beneficiaries of government largesse, their anger and frustration will find an obvious and available target.

We would be mistaken if we believe that that the violence of Africans towards East Indians is a matter of mere banditry or rogue elements bent on spreading mayhem. Cursory reflection will suggest that when a community – and I want to emphasise community as a collective identity embedded in feelings and the knowing posture of a common experience – believes that its leaders are seen as less than adequate and treated as pariahs; when its members are routinely left out in consideration for contracts and job opportunities; when its youths drop out of schools and unemployment is the only meaningful figure in which they matter; and when, on the other side, they see success attached to official encouragement and support, they are rightly frustrated and angry. This, then, is not 'Buxton bandits' on the rampage, but the anger and frustration that circulate in African communities and come to find expression in a young African with an AK-47. He needs not be encouraged nor supported. In fact, he seldom is. He finds enough hardened courage in the lacerating experience of his community and a ready target in an Indian village, far too frightened to demand a way out.

On the other hand, the ruling party/government has always been publicly oblivious to the issue of race and has steadfastly refused to address it. There is no African marginalisation. There are enough statistics around to tell a different story and enough visible black faces in public places to give a lie to the claim – and, no need, therefore, for African discontent; but not always. Its 'case for compromise' in the '60s, the 'national front government' of the '70s and its 'civic component' in the '90s tell quite a different story. And while it has often explained these 'compromises' as the historic divisions of the working class based on an elitist assumption of *divide et imperia,* it has been forced to recognise the division if only as a matter of strategic necessity. But these moments of *realpolitik*, as the New World Group suggested in the sixties, maybe nothing more than the 'ideological fig leaf' the party was forced to administer to cover its own 'sins' as racially based, while its supporters know better, are securely fastened and knowingly act on it. However, it is argued and whatever rules are used to play it out in its latest avatar, the 'civic' has not been particularly exceptional or outstanding. For the most part it has been rendered transparent and helpless, a singular failure in its response to the 'Buxton resistance'.

But, there is also the 'private script' which tells another story retailed and delivered at crucial moments – elections – to secure and bind the fold, increasingly conscious of the fact that after 1957 its strategic *volte face* was as much an ideological as an organisational one – the moment that the nationalist movement was transformed into an electioneering machine under a decidedly Indian leadership. And, it is the imprint of that moment that continues to haunt it. These are hushed and private conversations at 'bottom house' meetings where the converted are reminded of the need for communal solidarity and ethnic unity, conveyed in apocalyptic visions of an African triumph. And here the demonisation is not just of Africans but of 'turn coat' Indians as well, who are singled out with uncommon venom for their betrayal of the communal cause and seen as the 'fifth column' that would deliver the faithful up to the enemy.

Not unexpectedly, then, the ruling party sees the PNC not as the representative of Africans, but its historical nemesis who must be subdued and wrestled to the ground. In this, the PNC has been less than adroit and sensitive to the game that was being played out. Its record and continued denials that elections were not rigged or that it did not really lose, as in 1997 and again in 2001, have only served to undermine its own position and claims. From where does it speak and for whom if not the African community? And, if that is its constituency, it must face up to the fact of both its limitations and possibilities. Skirmishes on the streets of Georgetown may prevent the ruling party from getting its way, but it is not likely to provide much for its beleaguered supporters or the country at large.

Notes

1. This is an extended and updated version of a paper read at the second Diaspora Conference, *Clark-Atlanta/University of Guyana, Conflict and Analysis and Conflict Resolution Project,* Ralph Bunche International Centre, Howard University, Washington, DC, December 2002.
2. At a conference at the University of the West Indies, St Augustine, Trinidad, in June 1998, commenting on the situation in Guyana, Ralph Premdas suggested that the country had reached its political limits and was in the process of disintegration, *Trinidad Guardian*, March 6, 1998. The Report from Gillian Caliste was headlined 'Guyana Finished Says professor.' According to the story,

Premdas is reported to have said 'Guyana is finished. A pragmatic solution cannot resolve it. The only alternative is the Bosnian solution of forced intervention by a third party. If not there will be genocide or partition.' The same story was repeated in the *Trinidad Independent*, March 6, 1998. Two years later, 2000, nothing had happened to change his mind. Writing then he noted that 'Guyana probably fits more closely to countries outside the Caribbean such as Northern Ireland, Bosnia, and Sri Lanka because the politics of ethnic hate has left that place pathetically prostrated and poor.' See 'Diversity and Liberation in the Caribbean: The Decentralist Policy Challenge in the New Millennium,' in *Contending with Destiny: The Caribbean in the 21st Century*, ed. Kenneth Hall and Dennis Benn, 161 (Kingston: Ian Randle Publishers, 2000).
3. The escape occurred on February 26, 2002, the nation's birthday, and a time for national celebrations around the Amerindian festival of Mashramani. The escapees were subsequently named the 'Mash Escapees'.
4. See among others Philip Reno, The *Ordeal of British Guiana* (New York: Monthly Review Press, 1964); Cheddi Jagan, *The West on Trial: My Fight for Guyana's Freedom* (London: Hansib, 1999); Leo Despres, *Cultural Pluralism and Nationalist Politics in British Guiana* (Chicago: Rand McNally, 1967); and Reynold Burrowes, *The Wild Coast: An Account of Politics in Guyana* (Cambridge, Mass: Schenkman Publishing, 1984).
5. David Horowitz, *The Deadly Ethnic Riot* (Berkeley: University of California Press, 2001).
6. Regent Street is a major shopping district in the city owned primarily by East Indians.
7. 'Keishar's Proprietor Kidnapped: Snatched after running Gun Battle,' *Stabroek News*, October 25, 2002.
8. 'Seven Die in Shootouts: Two Mash Day Escapees: Large Arms Cache Found in Rented House: Keishar's Owner Escapes from Captors,' *Stabroek News*, October 29, 2002.
9. 'Six Shot Dead in City,' *Stabroek News*, November 5, 2002.
10. These and the following figures and estimates are taken from Ramesh Gampat and Somdat Mahabir's Cross Sectional Study of Crime and Criminal Transfer of Wealth in Guyana in Guyana Indian Heritage Association (GIHA), *GIHA Crime Report: Indians Betrayed*, 9–11 (Georgetown: GIHA, 2003).
11. Ibid., 120–48.
12. These were organised by the Guyana Human Rights Association (GHRA), which has come to occupy a prominent and signal place in Guyanese politics, particularly after its decades-long struggle for free and fair elections in the 1980s.
13. ROAR is the acronym for Rise, Organise and Rebuild, and is the political offshoot of the Jaguar Committee for Democracy, the brainchild of Ravi Dev, its leader, and some of his colleagues in New York, now headquartered in Lenora, an East Indian community on the west coast of Demerara. ROAR has made it very clear and very public that the organisation is Indian based and the leader,

Dev, proudly declares that he is an 'Indian rights' activist'. ROAR also produces an occasional paper called *Gurkha*.
14. See my 'Pluralism, Ethnicity and Governance in the Southern Caribbean,' in *Governance, Conflict and Conflict Resolution*, ed. Cedric Grant and Mark Kirton, 126–27 (Kingston: Ian Randle Publishers, 2007).
15. Some of this is rehearsed in my 'The Occasion for the War, not the Cause of it,' *Stabroek News*, January 14, 1996. The brouhaha was initiated by popular spin doctor, Kit Nascimento, later to become spokesman for the very ruling party/government that he had done so much to castigate and undermine since the 1960s.
16. Verification, independent of counting, was necessary because not all the statements of polls were signed by scrutineers.
17. *Stabroek News*, December 21, 1997.
18. *Stabroek News*, January 13, 1998. Section 177, subsection 6 to which the chief justice referred in her judgment reads 'Subject to the provision of Paragraph (4), an instrument which (a) is executed under the hand of the Chairman of the Elections Commission; and (b) states that a person named in the instrument and declared elected as President at an election held pursuant to the provisions of Article 60 (2) shall be conclusive evidence that the person so named was so elected and no question as to the validity of the election as the President of the so named shall be enquired into in any court,' *Constitution of the Co-operative Republic of Guyana,* Act No. 2 of 1980, 90 (Georgetown: Government of Guyana, 1980).
19. Guyanese Indian Foundation Trust, 'Civil Disorder', 30 (paper presented at symposium, Georgetown: GIFT, 1998).
20. *The Elections (Amendment) Act*, No. 15 of 2000 (Georgetown: Government of Guyana, 2002); and Guyana Elections Commission website, under Constitutional Reform.
21. Court documents reveal that a formal petition was filed, February 25, 1998, by Esther Perreira, petitioner, against the chief elections officer, Doodnauth Singh, chairman of the Elections Commission, and the leaders of the ten political parties that contested the elections of December 15, 1997. The petition asked the court to set aside the election results on grounds that they were unconstitutional and at variance with normal electoral practices. The petition raised 37 complaints, among them: i) That the elections were not held in conformity with the laws as to elections particularly the constitution and representation of the People's Act; ii) That the requirement of the voters' ID card as a qualification to be an elector at the elections as provided for under the Election Laws (Amendment) Act 1997 is *ultra vires* Article 159 of the Constitution of Guyana; and iii) That the unlawful acts and omissions set out herein affected the results of the said elections which would otherwise have lawfully resulted in different placing of the respective list of candidates. After the ruling, the Judge issued a series of injunctions restricting the activities of the government and advised that 'fresh National and Regional elections...[be]

held on or before the 31st day of March, 2001,...' See the judgment by Justice Claudette Singh, in *The High Court of the Supreme Court of Judicature, Petition Questioning an Election to the National Assembly Validity of the Elections Act Chapter 1:04* (Georgetown: High Court, January 2001), 3–4.

22. Some estimates suggest that nearly 40,000 jobs were lost in the public service due to the IMF/World Bank structural adjustment programmes initiated in 1988 through the PNC's Economic Recovery Programme. Overall, it is estimated that the percentage of jobs fell in the public sector from 15 per cent of total employment in 1980 to about seven per cent in 1992. See chapter six, 'Structural Adjustment and the Reform of the Public Service,' in *Structural Adjustment and Good Governance: The Case of Guyana*, ed. Tyrone Ferguson, 170–203 (Georgetown: Public Consulting Enterprise, 1995).
23. See C.Y. Thomas 'The Situation of African Guyanese in the Economy,' in *Themes in African Guyanese History*, ed. Winston Mc Gowan, James Rose and David Granger (Georgetown: Free Press, 1998); and Ferguson chapter three,'The Social Impact of Structural Adjustment,' 93–122 in *Structural Adjustment*.
24. *Stabroek News*, March 23, 2001.
25. *Stabroek News*, April 2, 2001.
26. *Stabroek News*, April 25, 2001. The PNC's 17-point programme included public sector reforms: all-party management of Parliament; end to the government monopoly of radio frequency; independent management of the government owned media; inquiry into charges of police brutality; end to discrimination in housing and acquisition of land; end to the politicisation of the public service; local government reform; check-off for the public service union; guaranteed subvention to Critchlow Labour College; tender board reforms; bring forward the agenda on constitutional reform; and economic stimulus: improve infrastructure in poor communities, reorganise the bauxite industry to resuscitate the bauxite town of Linden, recapitalise the army; etc.
27. Letter to President Bharat Jagdeo from Hugh Desmond Hoyte, leader of the opposition, dated April 23, 2002, Mimeo. See also *Stabroek News*, 26 April, 2002.
28. See Clive Y. Thomas, 'The Situation of African Guyanese in the Economy,' in *Themes in African-Guyanese History*, eds. Winston McGowan, James G. Rose and David A. Granger, 411 (Georgetown: Free Press, 1998).
29. *Stabroek News*, November 24, 2002.
30. 'The Indian Voice is Valid and Must be Respected,' *Stabroek News*, Letter to the Editor, August 29, 2002. The letter was signed by Ryhann Shaw, president of the GIHA.
31. Abu Bakr, 'The Indians Must Also Indulge in Self-examination,' *Stabroek News*, Letter to the Editor, September 4, 2002.
32. 'Buxton is a Terror Camp in Which Villagers Have Become Prisoners...' *Stabroek News*, Letter to the Editor, September 1, 2002.
33. To clarify, while we do agree that both parties in their differing ways have contributed to the 'zero sum' politics of Guyana we are of the view, as were many in the seventies and eighties in the struggle for 'fair and free elections,'

that the party in government holds the initiative since it has at its disposal both resources and space in which to manoeuvre. The latter have always been denied the opposition as it is today. We are, therefore, not entirely convinced by the 'equal blame' theory.
34. 'Don't Fight Indians, Fight Injustice...,' *Stabroek News*, letter to the editor, September 8, 2002.
35. 'Guyanese Feel Threatened by Crime,' *Stabroek News*, August 28, 2002. The letter is signed by Roop Misir (PhD), Toronto.
36. 'Indian Villages Must Organise Their Own Security,' *Stabroek News*, letter to the editor, September 5, 2002.
37. 'The Impunity with Which the Criminals Operate is Revolting,' *Stabroek News*, letter to the editor, September 7, 2002.
38. 'PPP Government Has Left Indians Defenceless,' *Stabroek News*, letter to the editor, August 7, 2002. See also for similar sentiments 'Indians are being left defenceless,' *Stabroek News*, August 8, 2002.
39. Editors' note: Region 11 is a colloquial, tongue in cheek reference to the vast number of Guyanese living in the diaspora.
40. St Augustine Research Associates, *Hopes and Aspirations: Political Attitudes and Party Choices in Contemporary Guyana* (Trinidad: St Augustine Research Associates, 2000). While we readily agree that the survey is dated and needs updating, we are taking it as a measure and indicative of 'popular' opinion. In fact, given the recent past, especially after the introduction of a value added tax in January 2007 and the continuous low intensity violence, sometimes breaking out in spectacular outbursts (see the introduction), opinion may be far more depressing on hopes for a better future.
41. There appears to be a mistake in the compilation of the data. In the 'Note on the Sample and Survey Methodology' (27) it suggests that 'The interviews were conducted in 7 of the 10 regions in districts chosen to ensure that the sample would be ethnically representative as well as reflect the geographical, sociological and political realities of Guyana as indicated in the 1991 census and available election reports. See Appendix 1 for the matrix of interviews conducted.' An examination of Appendix 1, i and ii, where the figures are given, indicates, however, that there are figures for only six regions. The names and figures under the designation "Region Five" are actually for Region Six, with 208 respondents and not 75 as indicated under the caption 'Region 5, Interviews 75.' I suspect that the designation and the numbers were confused, as the names of the districts/areas in which the interviews were conducted and the numbers given are actually for Region Six without the appropriate designation. When the numbers are cumulatively computed, including the 75 for Region 5 and the 208 for Region Six, they do amount to the 1000 given as the total number of respondents.
42. While I am aware that the survey is dated (the original essay was completed in 2002), it would not be at much variance with more recent/contemporary views. In fact, given current events (see the introduction), around the drug trade,

corruption, violence, and the general sense of the lawlessness that seems to prevail, opinion is likely to be less divisive among ethnic communities about the problems that afflict the society and considerably less sanguine about the possibilities of resolution. In fact, as we go to press an unknown group of armed men from the African village of Buxton invaded the Indian village of Lusignan on the East Coast of Demerara and in organised/military formation entered homes, shooting everyone in sight, including women and children. When the massacre was over in the early morning of Saturday January 25, 2008, 11 persons lay dead, including five children. The epitaph was written on the bodies of the slain – race/politics. Earlier, late Friday evening, and as a prelude to what was to come, heavily armed gunmen stormed the police headquarters in Georgetown. Two days earlier, Wednesday, January 22, 2008, gunmen in Buxton engaged the army in a firefight in which one soldier was killed. The previous week the army had been publicly accused of torture in its attempt to locate missing weapons.

43. This makes for interesting comparison with national statistics which reveals that it is the East Indian population that is more likely to pull up stakes and leave. I argue in the introduction that it is the heavily East Indian population of Region Six that has shown the most readiness and willingness to leave. The 2002 census indicates that the population of Region Six/East Berbice, near 70 per cent East Indian, declined from some 152,000 in 1991 to 123,695 in 2002 – a decline of near 30,000 and a drop in the overall population from 19 per cent to a little over 16 per cent.

44. Much of what follows is a summary of some of the more elaborate pieces taken from *Stabroek News* and include H. Case, August 10, 2002; D. Hinds, August 12, 2002; G. Peters, August 16, 2002; R. Dev, August 20, 2002; Marcus, August 23, 2002; K. Persaud, August 24, 2002; and S. Bavikatte, August 31, 2002.

45. 'The Way Forward' was originally written for the conclusion to the 2002 essay. I allow it to stand for two reasons. First, it speaks to some of the sentiments that informed my thinking then and which continue to linger. Second, it is also a reminder of the panel I shared with the late Deryck Bernard at Howard University where parts of the paper were read, followed by an hour of discussion in which he was more interested in my view of the PNC than he was in my paper.

References

Burrowes, Reynold. 1984. *The Wild Coast: An Account of Politics in Guyana*. Cambridge, MA: Schenkman Publishing.

Despres, Leo. 1967. *Cultural Pluralism and Nationalist Politics in British Guiana*. Chicago: Rand McNally.

Ferguson, Tyrone.1995. *Structural Adjustment and Good Governance: The Case of Guyana*. Georgetown: Public Consulting Enterprise.

Gampat, Ramesh, and Somdat Mahabir. 2003. Cross Sectional Study of Crime and Criminal Transfer of Wealth in Guyana. In *GIHA Crime Report: Indians Betrayed*, 9–11. Georgetown: Guyana Indian Heritage Association.

Government of Guyana. 1980. *Constitution of the Co-operative Republic of Guyana, Act No. 2 of 1980*. Georgetown: Government of Guyana.

——. 2002. *The Elections (Amendment) Act, No. 15 of 2000*. Georgetown: Government of Guyana.

Guyanese Indian Foundation Trust. 1998. Civil Disorder, 30. Paper presented at a symposium. Georgetown: GIFT.

Horowitz, David. 2001. *The Deadly Ethnic Riot*. Berkeley: University of California Press.

Hubbard, Jocelyn. 1969. *Race and Guyana*. Georgetown: self-published.

Jagan, C.B. 1965. *The West on Trial: The Fight for Guyana's Freedom*. London: Michael Joseph.

Premdas, Ralph. 2000. Diversity and Liberation in the Caribbean: The Decentralist Policy Challenge in the New Millennium. In *Contending with Destiny: The Caribbean in the 21st Century*, ed. Kenneth Hall and Dennis Benn, 161–78. Kingston: Ian Randle Publishers.

Reno, Philip. 1964. *The Ordeal of British Guiana*. New York: Monthly Review Press.

St Augustine Research Associates. YEAR. *Hopes and Aspirations: Political Attitudes and Party Choices in Contemporary Guyana*. St Augustine, Trinidad: St Augustine Research Associates.

Thakur, Rishee. 2007. Pluralism, Ethnicity and Governance in the Southern Caribbean. In *Governance, Conflict and Conflict Resolution*, ed. Cedric Grant and Mark Kirton, 126–27. Kingston: Ian Randle Publishers.

Thomas, C.Y. 1998. The Situation of African Guyanese in the Economy. In *Themes in African Guyanese History*, ed. Winston McGowan et al. Georgetown: Free Press.

6.
Between Despair and Hope: Towards an Analysis of Women and Violence in Contemporary Guyana[1]

D. Alissa Trotz

Introduction

The immediate aftermath of the 1997 and 2001 elections in Guyana was marked by violence, most of which targeted members of the Indo-Guyanese community. While far more men than women were *directly* assaulted in the recent waves of political violence, this essay specifically addresses the violence that women experience as members of racially marked communities to ask three questions: How is gender implicated in racialised electoral violence and community responses to such assaults? How can we account for women's different responses to violence? How might we begin to realistically construct a viable opposition against all forms of violence against women?

I begin by outlining some gendered after effects of the 1997 and 2001 elections. As a way of making sense of these events, I raise some questions about colonial inheritances and contemporary inequalities, in an effort to suggest linkages between pasts and presents, private and public domains. This chapter then explores how women come to symbolise racialised difference, and the investments women themselves may have in such self-other notions, as racialised subjects who are female. The final section draws on the work of Red Thread, a women's organisation in Guyana, in an effort to stimulate discussion of anti-racist and anti-violence work that centrally acknowledges differences among women. The example is used here, not as a final word on the subject, but rather as a provisional gesture towards inclusion and conversation.

"Between Despair and Hope: Women and Violence in Contemporary Guyana," by D. Alissa Trotz was originally published in *Small Axe* 15, Vol. 8:1, pp. 1–20. © 2004, *Small Axe*, Inc. All rights reserved. Republished by permission of the rightsholder and the present publisher, Duke University Press. www.dukeupress.edu.

Gendered Political Violence in Contemporary Guyana: A Synopsis

In 1992 Cheddi Jagan came to power as leader of the People's Progressive Party (PPP/Civic) in an election hailed internationally as being free and fair, ending 24 years of authoritarian rule and rigged elections under the People's National Congress (PNC).[2] That election and the following two in 1997 and 2001 have made it patently clear that the electoral process remains a site of racialisation and racial reproduction.

This stalemate can be traced to the collapse of the broad-based, nationalist, Marxist-led movement (the PPP) in the 1950s. After winning elections in 1953, the PPP was removed from office following the suspension of the Constitution by the British. In 1955 internal power struggles occasioned a split in the PPP and later the formation of the People's National Congress led by Afro-Guyanese Forbes Burnham. The split, originally along ideological lines, soon solidified into racialised polarities. Today, the divide between Afro-Guyanese/PNC supporters and Indo-Guyanese/PPP supporters is deeply embedded in Guyana's coastal fabric. In a country where 'stubborn racial arithmetic'[3] determines electoral outcome (Indo-Guyanese currently account for some 52 per cent of the population), the widespread marginalisation that has resulted from economic crisis and, since the late 1980s, neoliberal policies, is accompanied by increasingly polarised camps among these two dominant groups. As Rupert Roopnaraine, co-leader of the opposition Working People's Alliance Party wryly commented, 'the perversity and paradox of Guyana is that the better the elections, the deeper the racial crisis' (2001A).[4] This deadlock also ensures the marginalisation of other racial-ethnic groups (Amerindians are the most disadvantaged in Guyanese society) as well as 'others' within Afro-Guyanese and Indo-Guyanese constituencies (such as women and children).

At the December 15, 1997 polls, the PPP took 55.3 per cent of the votes (36 of 65 parliamentary seats), with 40.5 per cent (25 seats) going to the PNC. Simmering unrest erupted into various forms of violence amidst opposition claims of electoral irregularity, a PNC call for civil disobedience and the filing of an injunction against the inauguration of President Janet Jagan (who was nevertheless hastily installed).[5] Events came to a head on January 12, 1998, dubbed 'A Day of Terror' by the *Stabroek Daily News*. The trigger was the dismissal of the PNC injunction as unconstitutional by Chief Justice Desiree Bernard, a decision that immediately prompted widespread looting and acts of brutality against Indo-Guyanese businesses, women, and men on the streets of the capital city Georgetown. The disenchantment felt among sections of the Afro-Guyanese community over what they saw as their political and economic marginalisation under the PPP was directed against 'Indians tekkin' over'. The rioting led to the deployment of the police and army, and resulted in the dispatch of a Caribbean Community (CARICOM) mission in mid-January 1998. The Mission finally reached a compromise agreement between the PNC/R and PPP/Civic, the Herdmanston Accord, which included political dialogue, constitutional reform, and a CARICOM electoral audit. The PPP/Civic government also agreed to hold elections prematurely (within three instead of the constitutionally mandated five years) by 2001.[6]

The Guyana Indian Foundation Trust (GIFT) was formed in 1998 as a direct consequence of the violence unleashed against Indo-Guyanese.[7] The welcoming address to launch GIFT singled out an incident in which a young Indian woman had been stripped by mobs in Georgetown, as a catalyzing factor behind the decision to break the silence on the violence affecting the Indian community. GIFT placed advertisements in the media in March 1998 inviting people to bear witness to the events that had transpired. Some 228 testimonies were obtained (224 from self-identified 'Indian Guyanese'). It was estimated that over 1,000 persons had experienced physical violence, with over 10,000 experiencing some curtailment of their freedom of movement in Georgetown. Some 37 per cent of those attacked were women, over half of whom indicated that they were 'both physically and sexually abused' (no men reported sexual abuse of any kind). The GIFT report states, 'In this regard then women were twice victims. As Indians they were victims and as women they were victims.' All of the 228 testimonies pointed to Afro-Guyanese perpetrators; in 40 per cent of the cases, it was alleged that Afro-Guyanese women were involved in verbal and physical assaults against women and men.[8]

The failure of the Herdmanston Accord to resolve the political deadlock was evident by 2001, when the PPP Civic victory at the polls (with some 53.1 per cent of the vote, compared with 41.7 per cent for the PNC Reform), once again led to anti-Indian violence in Georgetown and outlying areas. While there is no systematic documentation of the effects on women, newspaper reports carried scattered stories in which Indo-Guyanese women were assaulted.[9] Afro-Guyanese women were prominent in street protests; in one demonstration outside the party headquarters of the PPP, one woman was shot and killed, and sections of the Afro-Guyanese community (women and men) were also assaulted in the police response to the post-electoral unrest.

Sporadic violence continued to punctuate the coastal landscape, escalating in 2002 following the violent escape from prison of five men, one of whom later appeared in a taped broadcast on television in which he alluded to himself as a freedom fighter.[10] Although the violence would later become far more generalised (and included the targeted assassinations of policemen, most of whom were Afro-Guyanese), most of the initial attacks specifically terrorised Indo-Guyanese businesses, homes and in some cases entire villages.[11] In one case an Indo-Guyanese woman was assaulted, racial taunts were made and her hair was cut off by her attackers, an act that led to the Guyana Indian Heritage Association launching a campaign ('For Anita's Pride'), aimed at providing support for 'victims of ethnic violence'.[12]

Violence and the Production of Difference: Tracing Difficult Connections

How do we situate and understand these events? I would suggest that such expressions of political violence come from somewhere; that is to say, they are not exceptional but are generated out of broader structural and ideological co-ordinates that position women as subordinate citizens and – in the Guyanese as in other cases – as markers of ethnic group identity.[13] In contemporary Guyana, a relatively progressive constitutional and legal framework coexists with pervasive gender inequalities within the family and the workforce. The economic crisis of the 1970s – the combined result of a hostile international climate, state mismanagement, and the PNC's lack of legitimacy – led to disinvestment in social services and physical infrastructure, the gendered consequences of which affected women in a number of ways: high levels of female out-migration as a survival strategy; growing rates of maternal malnutrition and infant mortality; high rates of female unemployment; the exponential growth of the informal sector and women's occupation of the most marginal jobs within this sector.

That the burden of coping with economic/structural violence has fallen most heavily on women's shoulders has to do with the definition of women as mothers and household managers. Under PNC rule the co-operative socialist exhortation to 'Feed, Clothe and House the Nation' never made explicit just whose labour would be required, without compensation or recognition. The deterioration in women's situation that this invisibility produced has been reinforced further following the implementation of neoliberal measures at the end of the 1980s.[14] Increasing incidents and reports of domestic violence are another clear indicator of the power relations that secure women's secondary status. A recently conducted survey of Georgetown found that 80 per cent of the women interviewed believed that domestic violence was endemic to Guyanese society, with over 30 per cent experiencing some form of violence as adults.[15]

If women's positioning as secondary citizens renders them susceptible to expressions of violence – economic, domestic, political – we also need to think about the multiple ways in which women are located by and experience different forms of violence. For example, we might consider how structural adjustment measures have affected public sector workers, most of whom have been Afro-Guyanese. We could explore how historically variable living arrangements among Afro-Guyanese and Indo-Guyanese women impinge on experiences/understandings of and responses to domestic violence. Or we might ask how a focus on hinterland issues foregrounds the particular forms of violence that Amerindian women face in their everyday lives.

Discussions of the differential effects of particular manifestations of violence, especially as they relate to women, have not been at the forefront of Caribbean debates.[16] In relation to Guyana, existing commentaries give us little scope for understanding the politically motivated, sexualised violence against Indo-Guyanese women described in the previous section. Analysts have been fairly quick off the mark in pointing to historical continuities in racial confrontations in Guyana: 'As in the 1950s with the hopes of a united nationalist movement; as in the 1960s on the verge of independence; as in the early 1990s with great expectations of a new beginning; so it is today our ethnic past comes back to haunt us with murderous rage.'[17] Yet nationalist representations of Guyana as a 'land of six races'[18] beg the question of how such purportedly stable differences are reproduced, through whose bodies and at whose expense. There has been virtually no scholarly attention paid to the gendered effects of the 1960s 'race riots' that dramatised most tragically the post–1953 collapse of the anti-colonial movement and the turn to race-based politics as a means of voter mobilisation. Part of the task is to specify how gender and sexuality emerge as central in the creation of racialised Guyanese identities, such that assaulting particular constituencies of women can be seen as an attack on the viability of the community with which they are identified.

Revisiting this history in the current moment is a politically imperative line of inquiry. For example, an official Commission of Inquiry into the Wismar disturbances of May 1964 (in which the Indo-Guyanese community was attacked and expelled from the area), cites numerous cases of the sexual assault of Indo-Guyanese women by Afro-Guyanese men, sometimes in the presence of Afro-Guyanese women. And in a 1962 publication, Eusi Kwayana documents several instances of the sexual humiliation and abuse of Afro-Guyanese women by Indo-Guyanese men.[19]

How does an initially unified nationalist struggle degenerate into communal warfare, one that gets partly fought on and over the bodies of women? Feminist scholarship has drawn our attention to the centrality of 'woman' to the establishment of racial/ethnic/national demarcations. Of particular relevance is the observation that women's ascribed familial responsibilities (as managers of households, bearers, and rearers of children and keepers of traditions to hand down through generations), become pivotal in reproducing the limits of racialised groups.[20] As those who embody the boundaries of group identity and respectability, women are vulnerable to sanctions both from within and without: while the regulation of women's behaviour (particularly in relation to questions of sexuality) may become of central concern to the group, assaulting women is also one way of attacking the community and calling into question its ability to reproduce itself.

Ania Loomba points out that colonial hierarchies tended to be expressed in familial terms that invoked gendered and racialised inferiority.[21] Anti-colonial struggles and narratives opposed the terms of their subordination, but frequently deployed reconstructed kinship imaginaries to project possible futures. Such efforts to reclaim private spaces free from colonial inscription and to use them as the basis for public assertions of community and nationhood did not necessarily challenge, and in some instances even reinforced indigenous forms of patriarchy and clearly delimited roles and responsibilities for women.

In the case of Guyana, colonial productions of racial difference between Africans and Indians – productions that hinged on the culturalisation of a racialised division of labour in the colonial plantation economy – would come to depend critically on representations of women in the closing years of indentureship. A changing labour regime was accompanied by the circulation of ideas of the submissive and chaste Indian housewife compared with the independent and emasculating African matriarch, both evaluated in relation to Eurocentric ideals of the family.[22] We have yet to tell how struggles for selfhood and self-definition drew on and contributed to the reification of the relationship between women and the family as well as the idea of women as representative of group/community/national identity. How do these discursive deployments of 'woman' combine with the legal and social production of second-class female citizens, to create spaces wherein masculinised violence against women becomes sanctioned (within communities, as a way of keeping women in their respective places, and between communities, as a way of attacking a racialised group identity)? How is such violence implicated in the creation of Indian and African male identities?

The ongoing centrality of gender to contemporary racialised constructions of community is illustrated not only by the violence that occurred against Indo-Guyanese women as discussed in the previous section, but also by the frequency with which 'women' became the basis upon which competing claims for racial justice were framed in letters to the local newspapers after the 2001 elections and in 2002, as violence escalated and widened:

> When shamelessness is greater than decency, and strength is measured by an insatiable appetite to prey upon women, children and the innocent; the notoriety of Georgetown and some ignominious villages on the East Coast, will be indelibly stamped upon the body and minds of the victims. Georgetown, the raped capital, bleeds...(*Stabroek News*, May 8, 2001).
>
> Just how many Indian women have to be humiliated before they are granted what they've been requesting for years, government – sponsored programmes to train and equip communities with the resources for self-defense? (*Stabroek News*, May 10, 2001).
>
> How is it that so much is being said by so many about violence against certain specific people, when already, the glaring violent snuffing out of [an Afro-Guyanese woman's] vibrant life seems so quietly and conveniently forgotten? (*Stabroek News*, May 14, 2001).[23]
>
> So these stone hearted criminals are spreading their activities in villages predominantly occupied by Indians...They are not only robbing people, but burning the sick and raping defenceless young women...The Indian

communities must now undertake their own security as a general neighbourhood watch. All those who do not live in your community must feel the force of the community...(*Stabroek News*, September 5, 2002).

Here we see how tensions across 'race' divides get played out in gendered terms and with women's bodies becoming the site on which group loyalties are inscribed and enacted.[24] When communities – or sections therewith – go public in their opposition to inter-group violence against women, they may rely on ideas of absolute difference to evoke communal loyalty and close ranks, while at the same time decrying the way in which 'our' women have been attacked by outsiders because they are different. In this schema, 'outsiders' are made into absolute others, inherently ('racially') predisposed to particular forms of violence against innocent insiders. Women, projected here as victims, are simultaneously required and silenced by such narratives. They become the basis of community indignation, but in the process they are objectified.

That there has been little public outcry over the growing incidence of domestic and other forms of violence against women (with the exception of some women's organisations), only underlines the point that the expressed outrage is less with the 'real' effects of violence against women, and more with the ways in which specifically marked acts symbolically stand in for the dishonouring of a racialised group identity and therefore the need to reiterate masculinist narratives of community and protection. Bracketing off some forms of violence (the domestic abuse that women experience at the hands of – largely – men they know) from the apparently spectacular assaults that predominantly Indo-Guyanese women have recently faced, makes it difficult for us to see how 'women' get produced as subordinate in ways that create all kinds of possibilities for the infliction of violence on female bodies.[25] Gendered community rhetorics of protection, by representing 'our women' as vulnerable and violable, also help to create the spaces wherein intra-community violence against women – as inferior members – can take place.[26] In both cases (domestic and political assaults) embodied women, and the pain of violence they experience, disappear into the shadows.

Complicating Responses

So far we have looked at what gets said about 'women' and at what gets done to different constituencies of women – in a sense arguing for a complexly gendered account of the socio-economic and political crisis in Guyana. What we also need to address is how women themselves take up various positions defined by difference. Such an analysis cannot proceed by privileging gender as if it is the only or primary aspect of women's identities that matters; recent feminist discussions of nationalism and the state suggest a risk producing ahistorical images of women as universal victims. We may also inadvertently reinforce gendered assumptions about women's inherent opposition to violence.[27] As a move away from such reductive associations, Lata Mani draws our attention to the complexities of agency in the constitution of female subjectivities, as a way of signalling how women are never simply women outside of other – such as class, sexual, racial, religious – identifications and associations.[28]

In the Guyanese context, it appears that while women are responding to the crisis, their solidarity is more frequently along the lines of communal identification. In a letter to the daily *Stabroek* newspaper, written shortly after the 2001 elections, Andaiye, member of the women's group Red Thread, stated:

> A note to other women: these silences in defence of race are against women…it is simply and sadly not true that we are one big happy family in between elections. It has always struck me that those who tell the histories of each side speak with particular bitterness of what was done to the women of their side. There are no ethnic conflicts anywhere in the world in which women are not targeted, often for sexual violence…It says something shameful about us as women if we allow our responses to violence against women to be determined by race and party loyalty. And is this not what we are doing by loudly condemning such violence when one of "ours" is attacked and staying silent when one of "theirs" is?[29]

This statement is significant for its recognition that while *all* women are potentially vulnerable to violence, this shared positioning does not lead to an unmediated disposition against such assaults. Women – in this context, racialised subjects who are gendered female – actively participate in the production of difference and the infliction of verbal and physical wounds on other women. Both the 1964 Wismar Inquiry and the 1998 GIFT Report, for instance, speak of Afro-Guyanese women assaulting Indo-Guyanese women, and in the aftermath of the 2001 elections there were scattered reports of attacks on Indo-Guyanese by Afro-Guyanese women and men.[30]

Moreover, silence does not necessarily bespeak opposition; in the letter above it is made equivalent to complicity. Nor is the apparent inability or refusal to speak out only in relation to the violence (predominantly Indo-Guyanese) women directly experienced, because male relatives and friends (increasingly including many Afro-Guyanese) have been among the majority of the casualties. Yet the potential connections among women as female relatives of dead men and children are so far not being created.

We are also reminded that organising on 'women's' issues is not at all free from the racialisms that have infected the post-1953 Guyanese political landscape. Patterns of women's mobilisation have been predominantly characterised by the cultivation of partisan allegiances along dominant party lines, leaving little breathing space for autonomous organising. This has been especially obvious in the reluctance of both the PNC affiliated Women's Revolutionary Socialist Movement (WRSM, renamed the National Congress of Women in 1994) and the women's arm of the PPP (Women's Political Organization, WPO) to speak comprehensively and critically while their parties were in power, on the social and economic consequences for women of adjustment measures that were put in place under both PNC and PPP-led administrations.[31]

It is analytically and politically important to address women's involvement in the oppression of other groups of women, to unravel it in all its complexity. While there has been some recognition in the Caribbean of class divisions amongst women, epitomised most acutely in the profoundly unequal relationships between domestic workers and their female employers, there has been little on the question of racialised barriers, both across and within classes.[32] If we accept the argument about making visible women's contribution to the forging of Caribbean cultures,[33] and if we agree that culture is often announced as the making of racial difference, then it follows that women bear some culpability for culture's various exclusions.

This involves paying attention to the varied investments that Caribbean women have had in (re)building communities in the colonial and postcolonial moments. In the case of Guyana, we need to look not only at shifting representations of racial differences among women in the post-emancipation/post-indentureship periods, but the ways in which women occupied subject –positions defined by such difference, and how this (constrained) choice was partly a condition of their belonging to communities defined in relation and often in opposition to each other. It is worth remembering that notwithstanding feminist insight into its –

historically specific – oppressive dynamics, 'family' was both a class and racial privilege under slavery and indentureship, a site around which assertions of community and racial kinship would coalesce, and something that both women and men who were excluded from its terms fought (and continue to fight) for.[34]

What is striking is the extent to which colonial stereotypes of dominant Afro-Guyanese women and submissive Indo-Guyanese women in relation to the family are recirculated amongst men and women today.[35] For example, in an urban community I worked in during the early 1990s, both groups of women saw themselves and each other in ways that were often mutually incompatible, notwithstanding the fact that they shared similar conditions of material deprivation and their practices (sometimes co-operative) defied any easy 'ethnic' compartmentalisation. Specifically, Indian women were portrayed as docile and dependent on their men, while African women were described as aggressive and independent in relation to men. Such stereotypes may help to regulate the behaviour of women, so that one is not seen to be acting inconsistently with one's ethnic identity. When individuals feel under siege as members of racialised communities, families become even more symbolically important as the boundaries of communalised difference. Under these circumstances, representations of different women in different families solidify, superseding possible linkages among women across racial lines, and creating possible spaces for the violence and the silences surrounding it to occur.

Anti-Violence Activism and the Work of Red Thread

Recently Stuart Hall noted that 'It is...tempting to fall into the trap of assuming that, because essentialism has been deconstructed *theoretically*, therefore, it has been displaced *politically*.'[36] This chapter ends with the work of Red Thread, a women's NGO, because I believe that it provides us with one possible example – on the ground so to speak – of a political effort to address violence outside of the stultifying frames of gender and race. Red Thread was formed in 1986, its founders, a small group of middle-class, racially diverse women who had come to believe that confronting the varied inequalities women faced was best done outside the political party system. Running through its work is a constant theme: to intervene in the terms of a debate whose parameters appear to be so rigidly set, by openly and self-critically questioning divisions and hierarchies among women along party, race and class lines.[37]

Much of the anti-violence work to date in Guyana has focused on domestic abuse, and here awareness (however halting) of domestic violence as a violation of human rights – most frequently women and children's – is almost entirely due to the work of women. For instance, the Domestic Violence Act of 1996 was primarily the work of the National Women's Rights Campaign, consisting of women lawyers and other activists and interested women. Women's initiatives also helped launch Help and Shelter in 1994, a counselling service and shelter for women who have experienced domestic abuse, and groups like Red Thread, Men Against Violence Against Women, Help and Shelter and Mothers in Black have occasionally worked together to address questions of violence against women.[38]

Red Thread has also been involved in anti-violence public education and advocacy over the years, including the launch of a radio series and community-based workshops on domestic violence, intervention on women's behalf with criminal justice, health, and social agencies, organising and participating in various demonstrations and producing and distributing a household guide to the 1996 Domestic Violence Act. Members recently conducted a large-scale survey and published a report on domestic violence and women's reproductive and sexual health, which includes a series of recommendations for institutional and cultural transformation.

Given Red Thread's partial origins in disillusion with party politics, it was perhaps not surprising that members would publicly oppose the recent wave of electoral violence without losing sight of either the connections across other forms of violence women experience or the ways in which women were differently implicated in the events that transpired in the post-electoral period. Such disillusion is perhaps understandable when we consider that women representatives of political parties came together days before the 2001 general elections to publicly appeal for peace and justice before and after polling. In a press release, they described Guyana as 'a country with serious conflict between the two largest race groups – conflict that becomes sharper and more visible during electoral periods… in this rising conflict women can play three roles: contribute to it; turn a blind eye; or speak out against it.' While they clearly located themselves in the third category, they called especially upon women who decided to engage in protest action not to encourage or even permit sexual or other abuse of other women, including women of other races. This broad-based appeal did not prevent either racialised voting, or racialised violence after the elections.

The statement from Red Thread below addressed itself publicly to women as a *diverse* collectivity:

> Individually and together we have said this before: in every war, the usual kind of abuse and violence, often sexual in nature, that is used against women is multiplied. In Guyana, right now, Indo-Guyanese women are being targeted for that kind of violence. Whoever we are, of whatever race, we have to stop turning a blind eye to this. The issue now is not whether or not there is justice in the cause of the war. The issue is that there is no justice in how it is being executed.[39]

The refusal to be silent or silenced invites women to envisage anti-violence work as struggles for social, political and economic justice that base 'the identities on politics rather than the politics on identity.'[40] It involves challenging boundaries and making connections between public and private spaces, between domestic/intra-community and inter-community and state violence, between the violence of structural adjustment and the invisibility of women's labour.

Along these lines, Red Thread is currently imagining into existence an anti-racist approach to counting women's work that will initially involve some one hundred Amerindian, Indian, African, and mixed women from a number of coastal and hinterland communities. Counting women's work campaigns are not new; in more than 70 countries women go on strike on international women's day (March 8) to draw attention to the labour that is officially invisible yet essential for the running of the global economy.[41] Making women's work visible is a critical point of departure for a transnational campaign that takes aim at the human costs of neo-liberalism, while remaining respectful of differences within and across national borders.

The relevance of this vision to Guyana and to anti-violence efforts, as well as the specific shape such located conversations and practices will take, have perhaps not been adequately understood by some feminist and women activists inside and outside of the region, who see counting women's work as having outlived its particular context and time, a relic of Euro-centrically defined second wave feminism that is concerned to make women's work visible even as it threatens to further entrench women's relationship to domesticity.[42] However, Red Thread is not concerned with being judged out of context, nor with being made the subject of academic debate and argument.⁴³ Their focus is the violence of poverty and the poverty of violence that affect and divide women, and poor women in particular.

In Guyana, this means understanding and counting work in its fullest sense to include the work that racism makes necessary. It requires, arguably for the first time, the identification and political recognition of the emotional labour that women expend, much of which is invisible but much of which is also no cause for celebration (such as the process through which, for example, one comes to rationalise voting for a particular political party because one is a black woman and fears 'Indians *tekkin* over'). As Red Thread member Karen de Souza notes,

> I think internationally (even here) there's a paper acknowledgement or intent to acknowledge the physical [dimension of unpaid] labour. It's the mental and emotional dimension that this work should add – in the voices and words of the grassroots women rather than the statisticians and economists.⁴⁴

Surveys, daily journals (some of the first stages have been completed) and workshops are part of the process. It is not a short or painless journey (made more complicated by the reality that in structurally adjusted countries like Guyana, time is the one thing that women especially have least to spare), and its vision is individual and collective, enabling women to move beyond the mutual misrecognition that informs the current conjuncture to '...see themselves and each other.'⁴⁵

To mark International Women's Day 2002, Red Thread organised a group of about 150 – predominantly – women on a militant walk through Linden, an urban Afro-Guyanese mining town whose livelihood has been severely eroded in the wake of structural adjustment programmes. Significantly, one of the reasons that Linden was chosen had to do with the fact that the community had historically been home to a number of Indo-Guyanese who had been brutally assaulted, murdered, and expelled during the riots of the 1960s. The handbill distributed by the participants said: '[Ours] is a struggle of women of all races for women of all races. Because Wismar was a symbol of the terrible racial violence of the 1960s, we, the women, send out this call – Let us make Linden a symbol of how women can cross race divides and fight for a world which values all women's work and all women's lives!' Bringing a multi-racial group (that included Amerindian and Mixed women) symbolised an insistence on remembering these collective pasts (that included other communities in which Afro-Guyanese and Indo-

Guyanese had been terrorised, and Amerindian communities that suffer the violence of non-recognition), in order to challenge their repetition in the current moment, through a focus on the hidden labours of love, sorrow, and violence that women shared in their daily lives – and here I believe that Red Thread would argue that even the work it takes to racialise others is shared, in that all women take part in such acts of violence against each other as members of their 'communities'.

In 2003 some 500 women marched in Georgetown, the capital city, in response to Red Thread's call to mark the Global Women's Strike. The violence that had engulfed the country since early 2002 was the focus and once again the strike called on people, and women in particular, to make difficult connections across entrenched divisions:

> It is not OK to accept that any mother's son be murdered by police *because* he is African-Guyanese … It is not OK to accept that any mother's 18-year-old son be murdered *because* he is a policeman (where else was he to work?). It is not OK to accept that any mother's daughter or son be abused, or raped, or robbed or killed *because* she/he is Indian-Guyanese…It is not OK to continue this war, and to use this war to continue ignoring the desperate needs and demands of Amerindian people. (emphasis added)

The specific and apparent address to women as *mothers* could perhaps be mistaken for a generalizable appeal based on assumptions of an undifferentiated identity. I would suggest that what is, in fact, being staged here is three-fold: a recognition of the work and investment (bodily, emotional) that motherhood demands of different groups of Guyanese women; a challenge to the inequalities that devalue such work and constitute it as 'women's business'; and an explicit acknowledgement that mothering, as currently organised in the post-colonial Guyanese context, comes with its fair share of costs and exclusions (as symbolised by the caveat *'because'* repeated through the statement above that consistently serves an exculpatory function for forms of violence against 'others').

Addressing difference in this way is crucial, for it asks us to construct a politics of solidarity and not sameness. Nor should recognition – 'seeing each other' – be mistaken for the revelation of some true or authentic gendered self, which has been hidden or manipulated by false consciousness (misrecognition). What is being suggested instead is the constant striving towards a 'politics without guarantees', building viable nodes of connection that do not assume *a priori* differences (of race, class, or gender) as an unfixed point of departure.

Nor does naming difference up front mean overlooking the existence of sparks of intimate connection and empathy. In one largely working-class multi-racial urban community during the 1990s, for example, exchanges of services, goods, money and information were usual practices across all households. In the local markets and in churches, box hand and penny banks (informal savings mechanisms) among vendors and parishioners are commonplace. In the midst of the economic crisis of the 1970s, it was women who, alongside and often ahead of men, formed the breadlines, travelled overseas to bring scarce goods to Guyanese sidewalks, and migrated in order to maintain remaining kin. We have yet to tell the story of the supportive inter-racial networks these women formed to save and share acquired knowledge about how to negotiate the borders of variously hostile Caribbean states. One challenge for anti-racist, anti-violence work, I believe, lies in multiplying these relationships into a field of fluid possibilities that does not gloss over differences, as well as in ensuring that confronting difference does not lead down the well-worn path to division and exclusion.

From Despair to Hope?

> *In despair there is hope, but there is none in death.*
> *Now I repeat it here, feeling a waste of life, in a market-place of doom,*
> *Watching the human face!* (Martin Carter, Black Friday, 1962)

> *Some women wait for themselves around the next corner and call the empty spot peace. But the opposite of living is only not living and the stars do not care. Some women wait for something to change and nothing does change so they change themselves.* Audre Lorde, 'Stations', 1986

This article has attempted to examine how attacking Indo-Guyanese women in the aftermath of the recent Guyanese elections can become an imaginable and even justifiable assault on racialised communities, and how the defence of women can be the basis of appeals to racialised solidarities. I have suggested that we need to make historical connections, as a way of understanding the terms upon which differences came to be produced in the colonial context, and continue to be enabled today through the differential incorporation of racialised women into the Guyanese nation. Part of this process requires us to broaden feminist analysis of the family beyond gender and generational hierarchies, in order to consider how various rhetorics of kinship (as domestic, as community, as nation) are racialised, rely on women's bodies as boundary markers, and help shape and constrain the everyday realities of Guyanese women. Moreover, making these connections among women seems easier said than done. As the discussion and example of Red Thread show, there are no innocent positions among women. A politics of solidarity is not a point of departure, but rather something to be struggled towards.

'Barred: Trinidad 1987' is a tentative and hopeful/hope filled short story by Ramabai Espinet that speaks to the experiences and buried memories of displaced Indo-Trinidadian female subjectivities, and it resonates powerfully with the current moment in Guyana. Male violence against women, the violence of poverty and displacement and the burden of history are all implicated.[46] Racism is also central – Espinet names prevailing stereotypes of the rich Indian class 'controlling ninety-five percent of the business in this country.' In the final paragraphs of the story, such popular understandings come up against the embodied experiences of women. We learn how the narrator, with children to care for and a male partner whose meagre earnings end up at the rum shop, starts selling cigarettes from her window, and ends up eventually with a 'bottom house' shop. Equally important is the assistance she receives from 'a Creole woman down the road [who] showed [her] how to make sugar-cakes and tamarind balls.'[47] This piece is wonderfully evocative for undermining racist stereotypes about 'acquisitive Indians' via emphasising female agency in the midst of exclusion. Additionally it suggests a point of reference – in this case a shared materiality – for both the Indian and Creole women, and also (and perhaps more importantly?) dares to name a possible identification among women through and beyond difference. This helps enable survival – as the narrator says, 'I have lived through the long night,' but it is not just or even about the necessity of making it intact to a set of unchanging tomorrows. Espinet's short story, by acknowledging history without being doomed by it, signals for her female protagonist/s the hope that Martin Carter senses lurking beneath the despair, and the transformation which Audre Lorde dreams into words. What does it mean to self-consciously acknowledge, as Jacqui Alexander says in another context, that 'we have been neighbours, living in the raucous seams of deprivation?'[48] The current wave of violence that is engulfing Guyana, and which seems *at least* partly bent on instilling fear of 'the other' in racialised communities, will both test the strength of such neighbourly connections amongst women and underscore the imperative for finding a collective voice that resists this vicious impulse before it spirals completely out of control.

Postscript

In January 2003, a small group of Guyanese women that included some Red Thread members called on all women to gather in the capital to begin a committed struggle to end the widespread violence. In a press release the organisers explained the group's purpose:

> It is no longer a choice...between violence and non-violence. It is either non-violence or non-existence – Dr Martin Luther King Jnr., in his last sermon.
>
> On Tuesday, January 28, more than 130 women of all races, classes, and ages met at the Tower Hotel and decided to work to build a non-party movement of Guyanese women. We affirmed that what unites us is that as care givers, we refuse to accept abstract notions of justice which destroy children. We welcome the support of men who are in solidarity with our determination to organise autonomously against violence.
>
> We are organizing against all violence – and in this spirit, we have named ourselves simply Women against Violence Everywhere (WAVE).
>
> Our work will be of different kinds. We want to work on the causes of violence and the effects of violence. We will use the media and public demonstrations to fight against the growing numbness to violence, including our own. We will be present and active not only in Georgetown, but everywhere. We will be in touch with families who are victims of violence of all kinds, and will try to respond to their requests for support, both emotional and practical. Whatever capacity we lack now, we will build. (WAVE Press Release, Wednesday January 29, 2003)

According to one newspaper, some 400 women turned out at the first vigil held in Georgetown on January 24, and some 600 signatures were collected calling for an end to the killings, addressed to the political leadership, law enforcement and the criminals. The international community – Guyanese from all walks of life, Caribbean academics, and artistes – also signed the petition. In March and April, WAVE meetings produced a consensus to form a political committee, build networks across the country, gather information on violence in Guyana, and meet with other groups to discuss areas of mutual interest and co-operation. It is not clear if any of this work has begun. We have yet to see where WAVE will take us and whether it can withstand, confront, and surmount the bitter and as yet enduring legacy of Guyana's past.

Acknowledgments

Thanks to Linzi Manicom for her detailed and hugely insightful comments. My ongoing indebtedness to Red Thread Women's Development Organisation is surely reflected in the analysis that guides this chapter. I say this also as a way of disclosing my own positionality, and the fact that I do not write as a 'disinterested' observer or academic, but as a Guyanese woman living overseas who shares the vision of Red Thread and whose relationship to the group can perhaps best be described as distanced but not detached. Much respect to Andaiye, whose conversations – and interview – with me in Toronto in the summer of 2002 when she was very unwell have shaped much of what is written here, particularly the last section of this essay, and whose e-mail exchanges remind me always to constantly sharpen my focus and to work on being readable. This one's for you.

Notes

1. This essay first appeared in *Small Axe: A Journal of Criticism* 15 (2004): 1–20.
2. Both the PPP and the PNC, in an effort to go outside their traditional bases of support, now include civic components (Reform in the case of the PNC) which do not require political party membership.
3. Rupert Roopnaraine, 'Some Internal Dynamics of Insecurity: The Case of Guyana,' unpublished paper, 9.
4. Rupert Roopnaraine, Plenary Presentation (Caribbean Studies Association Conference, St Maarten, May 28, 2001).
5. Janet Jagan took over the leadership of the PPP when Cheddi Jagan died in 1997. In 1999, she stepped down from the presidency, citing failing health, and was replaced by Bharrat Jagdeo who successfully contested the 2001 elections.
6. See Percy C. Hintzen, 'Democracy on Trial: The December 1997 Elections in Guyana and its Aftermath.' *Caribbean Studies Newsletter* 25, no. 3 (1998): 13–16.
7. See Rishee Thakur, 'Writing the History of the East Indian Diaspora: Race and Politics in Post-Colonial Guyana. Conjunctures and Debates' (Occasional Paper Series, No. 1, Berbice Campus, University of Guyana, August 2003).
8. Civil Disorder (symposium, GIFT, Georgetown, 1998).
9. See, for example, *Stabroek News*, April 20, 2001.
10. Reported in *Stabroek News*, May 10, 23, and June 8, 2002. Leaflets were also apparently printed and distributed expressing support for Afro-Guyanese freedom fighters (see Andaiye, 'Not in my name,' *Stabroek News*, May 14, 2002).
11. The anti-Indian violence following the most recent 2001 elections has since spread to affect a broad cross section of the country, although it is impossible at this stage to disentangle underlying motives – political, racial, opportunistic, drugs. Police brutality (and retaliatory attacks on and assassinations of police

officers) has also contributed in no small way to the spiral of violence, with the targets predominantly young black men. Over 100 people were murdered in 2002, 15 of whom were policemen, and in the first three weeks of 2003 alone there were over two dozen murders, including five policemen. The figures have so far not been disaggregated by gender and race, but it is clear that the vast majority of those killed have been men. This chapter – focusing on the violence that women experienced in the post-election period – does not fully address these more recent developments, although in the postscript I mention a recent initiative to address all levels of violence in society.

12. *Stabroek News*, August 26, 2002.
13. For an elaboration of this argument see Vesna Kesic, 'From Reverence to Rape: An Anthropology of Ethnic and Genderized Violence,' in *Frontline Feminisms: Women, War and Resistance*, ed. Marguerite Waller and Jennifer Rycenga, 23–36 (New York: Garland Publishing, 2000). Answering the second part of this question comprehensively (the uses to which the discursive categories of 'woman' and 'women' are put in the post-colonial Guyanese context) requires an extensive study of representations of women by the state, media, civic, and religious organisations.
14. For a discussion of its affects of differently racialised women, see D. Alissa Trotz and Linda Peake, 'Work, Family and Organizing: An Overview of the Contemporary Economic, Social and Political Roles of Women in Guyana,' *Social and Economic Studies* 50, no. 2 (2001): 67–101.
15. In 1996, a Domestic Violence Law was finally passed, but there remains little in the way of NGO and state resources to give this law much effect. See Red Thread Women's Development Programme in conjunction with Linda Peake, *Women Researching Women: Case Studies by Red Thread Women's Development Programme on Domestic Violence and Women's Reproductive and Sexual Health in Guyana* (Georgetown, Guyana: IDRC, 2000) 4.
16. In the Caribbean feminist literature, while violence has been on the activist and scholarly agenda for some time, the bulk of the work continues to focus on domestic violence against women and children. Moreover, there is relatively little that looks at how different forms of violence are racialised, or at how differently racialised women experience violence. For an excellent article that takes up some of these questions in relation to narratives of nation and community, see Shalini Puri, 'Race, Rape, and Representation: Indo-Caribbean Women and Cultural Nationalism,' *Cultural Critique* (1997): 119–63.
17. Rishee Thakur, 'Writing the History of the East Indian Diaspora,' 4.
18. Amerindians, Europeans, African, East Indian, Chinese, Portuguese.
19. Eusi Kwayana, *Next Witness* (Guyana: Labour Advocate Press, 1962).
20. See Floya Anthias and Nira Yuval-Davis, *Woman-Nation-State* (London: Macmillan, 1989).
21. Ania Loomba, *Colonialism/Postcolonialism* (London: Routledge, 1988), 217.
22. D. Alissa Trotz, 'Behind the Banner of Culture: Gender, Race and the Family in Guyana,' *NWIG* 77, nos. 1 and 2 (2003): 5–29.

23. This letter referred to a protest that was held outside the party headquarters of the PPP, in which an Afro-Guyanese woman was shot and killed by an unknown assailant who fired into the crowd. To date, there have been no arrests.
24. Letters decrying the murders of men often tended to refer to widows, mothers and other grieving female family members left behind to carry on the work of maintaining the family.
25. This does not mean that racial, sexual, domestic, economic/structural violence are commensurable; what I am arguing is for connections to be made across different modalities of power that target women in varied ways.
26. Vesna Kesic has pointed out that tropes of women as victims all too easily slide into constructions of violated and therefore violable women, such that all women (not just racial others but 'ours' as well) become othered by extreme patriarchal stereotypes of virgin (in need of protection but having the potential to be weak and dishonoured) or whore (absolute others). 'From Reverence to Rape, 33.
27. For example, see Sita Ranchod-Nilsson and Mary Ann Tétreault, eds. *Women, States and Nationalism: At Home in the Nation?* (London: Routledge, 2000), 1–17.
28. Lata Mani, 'Multiple mediations: Feminist Scholarship in the Age of Multinational Reception,' *Inscriptions* 5 (1989).
29. Letter to the editor, *Stabroek News*, Tuesday April 24, 2001.
30. For example, the *Stabroek News* (April 20, 2001) carried a story of an Indo-Guyanese woman (described as a mother) who was beaten and stripped by a gang of two men and three women.
31. Linda Peake, The Development and Role of Women's Political Organizations in Guyana,' in *Women and Change in the Caribbean*, ed. Janet Momsen (London: James Currey, 1993); and Peake and Trotz, *Gender, Ethnicity and Place: Women and Identities in Guyana* (London: Routledge, 1999), chapters 3, 4, and 9.
32. For a critique, see Andaiye, 'The Angle You Look from Determines What You See: Towards a Critique of Feminist Politics in the Caribbean, (The Lucille Mathurin Mair Lecture (Centre for Gender and Development Studies, Kingston, 2002), 10–11.
33. Jean Besson, 'Reputation and Respectability Reconsidered: A New Perspective on Afro-Caribbean Peasant Women,' in *Women and Change in the Caribbean*, ed. J.H. Momsen, (Bloomington: Indiana University Press, 1993).
34. Patricia Mohammed, *A Social History of Post-Migrant Indians in Trinidad from 1917 to 1947: A Gender Perspective* (PhD thesis, Institute of Social Studies, The Hague, 1994); and Bridget Brereton, 'Family Strategies, Gender and the Shift to Wage Labour in the British Caribbean,' in *The Colonial Caribbean in Transition: Essays on Postemancipation Social and Cultural History*, ed. Bridget Brereton and Kevin Yelvington (Kingston, Jamaica: UWI Press, 1999).
35. Academic discourses on the Caribbean family need also to be carefully and critically scrutinised for their role in reproducing culturalist notions of difference. See D. Alissa Trotz, 'Beyond the Banner of Culture,' 7–11.

36. Stuart Hall 'When Was the "Post-Colonial"? Thinking at the Limit', in *The Post-Colonial Question: Common Skies, Divided Horizons*, ed. Iain Chambers and Lidia Curti, 249 (London: Routledge, 1996).
37. Andaiye 'The Red Thread Story,' in *Spitting in the Wind: Lessons in Empowerment from the Caribbean*, ed. Francis Brown (Kingston: Ian Randle Publishers, 2000).
38. In early January 2003, Help and Shelter was on the verge of closing due to lack of resources; a late intervention by the government and a private sector donor has kept it temporarily open. Mothers in Black was intended to raise public awareness of road safety and demand that those causing death by dangerous driving were adequately and successfully prosecuted.
39. 'When we look at the terror of those of us who are Indo-Guyanese women we know there is a war,' Red Thread's letter to the editor, *Stabroek News*, July 8, 2002. This letter was prompted by a series of events that started when a group of protesters entered and temporarily occupied the Office of the President in Georgetown. In the fray that followed, two protesters were killed by the police. Sporadic violence broke out, mainly along the East Coast, that can be characterised as both anti-police and anti-Indian, and that included roadblocks, burning vehicles and assaulting and robbing Indo-Guyanese women, men, and children.
40. Angela Davis, 'Reflections on Race, Class and Gender in the United States: Interview with Lisa Lowe,' in *The Politics of Culture in the Shadow of Capital*, ed. Lisa Lowe and David Lloyd, 318 (North Carolina: Duke University Press, 1997).
41. For information on the Global Women's Strike, see http://womenstrike8m.server101.com/.
42. Interview with Andaiye, November 5, 2002.
43. As Andaiye puts it 'Yes, some see it [counting women's work] as second-wave, or early second-wave, or part of some fucking wave.....I have no idea what they are talking about. I for one never waved yet.'
44. Personal correspondence with Karen de Souza, September 5, 2003.
45. The quote is from Ramabai Espinet, in conversation with Andaiye, who notes that it was the first time that someone not involved in the work at hand immediately understood what it was about.
46. For an excellent discussion, see Shalini Puri, 'Race, Rape, and Representation,' 144–56.
47. R. Espinet, 'Barred: Trinidad 1987,' in *Green Cane and Juicy Flotsam: Short Stories by Caribbean Women*, ed. C. Esteves and L. Paravisini-Gebert, 85 (Brunswick, NJ: Rutgers University Press).
48. M. Jacqui Alexander, 'Remembering This Bridge, Remembering Ourselves: Yearning, Memory, and Desire,' in *This Bridge We Call Home: Radical Visions for Transformation*, ed. Gloria E. Anzaldúa and Analouise Keating, 93 (New York and London: Routledge).

References

Alexander, M. Jacqui. 2002. Remembering This Bridge, Remembering Ourselves: Yearning, Memory, and Desire. In *This Bridge We Call Home: Radical Visions for Transformation*, ed. Gloria E. Anzaldúa and Analouise Keating. New York and London: Routledge.

Andaiye. 2000. The Red Thread Story. In *Spitting in the Wind: Lessons in Empowerment from the Caribbean*, ed. Francis Brown. Kingston: Ian Randle Publishers.

———. 2002. The Angle You Look from Determines What You See: Towards a Critique of Feminist Politics in the Caribbean. The Lucille Mathurin Mair Lecture. Centre for Gender and Development Studies, Kingston.

Anthias, Floya and Nira Yuval-Davis. 1989. *Woman-Nation-State*. London: Macmillan.

Besson, Jean. 1993. Reputation and Respectability reconsidered: A New Perspective on AfroCaribbean Peasant Women. In *Women and Change in the Caribbean*, ed. J.H. Momsen. Bloomington: Indiana University Press.

Brereton, Bridget. 1999. Family Strategies, Gender and the Shift to Wage Labour in the British Caribbean. In *The Colonial Caribbean in Transition: Essays on Postemancipation Social and Cultural History*, ed. Bridget Brereton and Kevin Yelvington. Kingston, Jamaica: UWI Press.

Davis, Angela. 1997. Reflections on Race, Class and Gender in the United States: Interview with Lisa Lowe. In *The Politics of Culture in the Shadow of Capital*, ed. Lisa Lowe and David Lloyd, 318. North Carolina: Duke University Press.

Espinet, R. 1991. Barred: Trinidad 1987. In *Green Cane and Juicy Flotsam: Short Stories by Caribbean Women*, ed. C. Esteves and L. Paravisini-Gebert, 85. New Jersey: Rutgers University Press.

Hall, Stuart. 1996. When Was the 'Post-Colonial'? Thinking at the Limit. In *The Post-Colonial Question: Common Skies, Divided Horizons*, ed. Iain Chambers and Lidia Curti, 249. London: Routledge.

Hintzen, Percy C. 1998. Democracy on Trial: The December 1997 Elections in Guyana and its Aftermath. *Caribbean Studies Newsletter* 25, no. 3:13–16.

Kesic, Vesna. 2000. From Reverence to Rape: An Anthropology of Ethnic and Genderized Violence. In *Frontline Feminisms: Women, War and Resistance*, ed. Marguerite Waller and Jennifer Rycenga, 23–36. New York: Garland Publishing.

Kwayana, Eusi. 1962. *Next Witness*. Guyana: Labour Advocate Press.

Loomba, Ania. 1988. *Colonialism/Postcolonialism*. London: Routledge, 217.

Mani, Lata. 1989. Multiple mediations: Feminist Scholarship in the Age of Multinational Reception. *Inscriptions* 5.

Mohammed, Patricia. 1994. *A Social History of Post-Migrant Indians in Trinidad from 1917 to 1947: A Gender Perspective*. PhD thesis, Institute of Social Studies, The Hague.

Peake, Linda. 1993. The Development and Role of Women's Political Organizations in Guyana. In *Women and Change in the Caribbean*, ed. Janet Momsen. London: James Currey.

Peake, Linda, and D. Alissa Trotz. 1999. *Gender, Ethnicity and Place: Women and Identities in Guyana.* London: Routledge.
Puri, Shalini. 1997. Race, Rape, and Representation: Indo-Caribbean Women and Cultural
Nationalism. *Cultural Critique,* no. 36:119–63.
Ranchod-Nilsson, Sita, and Mary Ann Tétreault, eds. 2000. *Women, States and Nationalism: At Home in the Nation?* London: Routledge, 1–17.
Red Thread Women's Development Programme in conjunction with Linda Peake. 2000.
Women Researching Women: Case Studies by Red Thread Women's Development Programme on Domestic Violence and Women's Reproductive and Sexual Health in Guyana. Georgetown, Guyana: IDRC, 4.
Roopnaraine, Rupert. 2001A. Plenary presentation. Caribbean Studies Association Conference, St. Maarten, May 28.
———. 2001B. The Internal Dynamics of Insecurity: The Case of Guyana. Research and Education in Defense and Security Studies (REDES). Panel on Caribbean Security, Center for Hemispheric Defense Studies, Washington, DC, May 22–25, unpublished paper, 9.
Thakur, Rishee. 2003. Writing the History of the East Indian Diaspora: Race and Politics in Post-Colonial Guyana. Conjunctures and Debates in *Occasional Paper Series, No. 1.* August, Berbice Campus, University of Guyana.
Trotz, D. Alissa. 2003. Behind the Banner of Culture: Gender, Race and the Family in Guyana. *NWIG* 77, nos. 1 and 2:5–29.
Trotz, D. Alissa, and Linda Peake. 2001. Work, Family and Organizing: An Overview of the Contemporary Economic, Social and Political Roles of Women in Guyana. *Social and Economic Studies* 50, no. 2:67–101.

7.
Race, Ideology, and International Relations: Sovereignty and the Disciplining of Guyana's Working Class

Percy C. Hintzen

Nationalism and Neocolonial Accommodation

As an ideology, nationalism has proven to be quite amenable to the interests of global capital. As a construct, it easily accommodates the changing technical and social conditions of economic capital without losing its power as a symbol of national sovereignty and self-determination. In the post-war era, new forms of capitalist organisation began to emerge, creating conditions for the demise of colonialism and the emergence of new neocolonial forms of dependency. Colonialism was rapidly becoming an impediment to the development of more intensive forms of exploitation in the peripheral economies. By challenging colonial domination, nationalism began to lay the groundwork for the accommodation of these new forms of neocolonial exploitation in the political economies of the European colonies. As colonialism was giving way to the new nationalist movements these new forms of economic organisation began laying the groundwork for postcolonial formation.

Embedded in notions of nationalist self-determination were the ideas of sovereignty and the autonomy of the state.[1] These have acted to hide a reality of the postcolonial condition where global capital has maintained and intensified its active presence. Either this, or its agents have increased their capacities for retaliation against those who choose to resist. The ex-colonies of Britain in the West Indies provide typical examples of these new forms of interventionism that hide behind nationalist ideologies of self-determination and sovereignty. These ideologies, rather than presaging

"Race, Ideology and International Relations: Sovereignty and the Disciplining of Guyana's Working Class," by Percy C. Hintzen was originally published in *Living at the Borderlines: Issues in Caribbean Sovereignty and Development* edited by Cynthia Barrow-Giles and Don D. Marshall, 414–37. Kingston: Ian Randle Publishers, 2003.

a break with colonial patterns of dependency, effected a transfer of their positions of economic, political, and social subordination from Britain to the US. The anticolonial agenda of the West Indian nationalists fit well with decisions to establish closer relations with the US. There was an inherent contradiction between the quest for sovereignty and continuation of the exclusive pattern of economic relations with Britain. Absolute dependence upon the former colonial power was inconsistent with ideas of national self-determination as a critical component of sovereignty. West Indian nationalist leaders had to seek alternatives to economic relationships with the British colonial metropole. But given the absolute dependence of their economies on commodity exports, they were trapped in conditions of economic dependence on the industrialised North. The emergence of the US as the dominant global economic power led the way out of this dilemma. A shift in the focus of economic and political relations away from Britain and to the US had both symbolic and practical value. It was consistent with nationalist assertions of sovereignty while allowing the newly independent countries to retain relations of economic dependency in the global capitalist economy. These new relations did not come with the taint of colonial domination. The establishment and intensification of economic and political ties with North America were justified, also, by the quest for developmental transformation, another of the pillars of nationalism. As the dominant, richest, and most technologically advanced economic power, the US became the ideal partner in such a quest.

Thus, anticolonialism in the West Indies became rapidly transformed into an instrumentality for the penetration of neocolonial forms of global capital in the region. The latter came with the need for significant changes in the political economies of the former colonies. The emergence of the US as the financial and technological superpower of the industrialised capitalist world and as the world's major market was the force driving these transformations. Anticolonialism, by attacking relations of empire between the European colonial powers and their non-European colonies, acted to accommodate new patterns of international relations centred upon the US. The discourse of sovereignty freed the new postcolonial leadership from obligations imposed and maintained by colonial power. It facilitated the reorientation of economic relations toward the US. This came with the tremendous benefits derived from closer relations with the world's newly dominant economic, financial, and military power.

The reorientation began during the '50s, even before independence was granted. West Indian nationalist leaders began to employ their increasing autonomy, derived from reform of colonial political organisation, to effect a gradual shift in their economic and political relations toward the US. A potent signal of the shift was the development of plans to introduce a 'Puerto Rican' type economic model into the region. This was patterned after forms of 'industrialization by invitation' through which the bootstrap policies of the US were being implemented in Puerto Rico.[2] This predictable outcome of the deepening of ties of dependence with the US was intensified even further by a developing tourist industry based on North American visitors that was becoming indispensable to the economic well-being of islands such as Barbados and Jamaica. Additionally, the US was beginning to absorb a growing number of West Indian immigrants under conditions of escalating unemployment and underemployment in the region. North American migration was becoming critical to the region's efforts at poverty alleviation. Remittances from these migrants were proving important as additional sources of income, revenue, and economic support.[3]

Nationalism and the Cold War Agenda[4]

The US began to provide significant support to West Indian nationalist political leaders sympathetic to its economic, political, and strategic interests. This shored up its anticolonial image and convinced many of the region's radicals to shift their ideological position (see Fraser 1994). At the same time, there was a high price to be paid for challenging US hegemony in the region. Soon after the end of the Second World War, the US became consumed by a virulent anti-communism, fed by the dogma of McCarthyism sweeping the country. Combating domestic and international communism became the primary concern in its corridors of power. This produced an absolute intolerance for nationalist movements overseas even mildly critical of the West.

The nationalist movement in British Guiana was formalised in the crucible of the two imperatives of economic dependency upon the US and commitment to its ideology. Unlike the rest of the region, the class dynamics of the country were dictating an alternative path that challenged the tenets not only of colonialism but also of neocolonial dependence upon the US. By 1950, the colony's anticolonial movement had formalised itself into a radical class-based nationalist party called the People's Progressive

Party (PPP). It was organised and led by a group of anti-capitalist radicals who were strongly supported by the colony's black and Asian Indian working class, the two ethno-racial groups that together comprised over 90 per cent of the country's population. From the very beginning, the stated goal of the party, contained in its manifesto, was the establishment of an independent socialist state:

> Recognising that the final abolition of exploitation and oppression, of economic crises and unemployment and war will be achieved only by the socialist reorganisation of society, (the party) pledges itself to the task of winning a free and independent Guiana, of building a just socialist society, in which the industries of the country shall be socially and democratically owned and managed for the common good, a society in which security, plenty, peace and freedom shall be the heritage of all.[5]

While the socialist populism of the party generated tremendous support among the colony's working classes, it placed its leadership on an inevitable collision course with Britain. The party was formed at a time when archconservative Winston Churchill, as prime minister, was reviving Britain's colonial appetite. His Conservative Party was using executive authority to wage a campaign against the thrust toward decolonisation of its progressive Labour Party predecessor. The interests of British capital rested as much in the preservation and prolonging of colonial dominion as in the containment of communism. And Britain's political leadership viewed the PPP's strident advocacy of self-government and socialism as a considerable and direct threat to its political, economic, and strategic interests.

A PPP victory in 1953 in the first national elections to be held under universal suffrage was interpreted as a threat to Britain's colonial interests. The British Colonial Office wasted little time before embarking on efforts to secure the PPP's ouster. Cold war definitions became superimposed upon nationalist politics and inserted into popular interpretations of political and labour organisation. Even before the elections, cold war slogans and images were deployed in a vicious assault against the People's Progressive Party. This shift to cold war terminology was important because it brought the US into the picture. Concerns were raised that events in British Guiana foretold the direction of the emerging nationalist anticolonial movements in the region.[6]

Britain managed to use the PPP's election to office to convince the US of the need for collaboration in shaping the conditions and terms of

West Indian nationalism. Its entreaties fell on fertile ground. It provoked considerable alarm as a harbinger of the future of Britain's other West Indian colonies. The Eisenhower administration was more than willing to be convinced of the danger to American interests posed by British Guiana's nationalist movement to American interests. In October 1953, the American Consul General cabled the Department of State over concerns about the consolidation of a 'communist bridgehead in the area'. He advocated that this 'menace' be 'firmly met.' With the groundwork laid and with the approval if not active support of the US, Britain intervened militarily on October 9, 1953, suspended the colony's constitution, and ousted the PPP from office. The party had lasted only 133 days in office. With the PPP's ouster, British Guiana took its place with Iran and Guatemala as the first of the political economies of the global south to have cold war categories imposed upon their domestic politics. In all three instances, the indictment of communism was used against a legitimate elected government to justify direct foreign intervention. In the wake of the suspension of the new constitution, the US increased its involvement in the region significantly. This presaged a new globalisation that compromised significantly any possibility for the exercise of sovereignty and self-determination in the region.

With colonialism under attack, Britain sought to justify its intervention by claiming to act on behalf of domestic representatives of the population to forestall a 'communist takeover'. This claim of intervention in response to domestic appeals is consistent with discourses of sovereignty. Intervention serves to protect the domestic political economy from 'subversive' 'foreign' ideologies. The pragmatics of a nationalist discourse that accommodated a new dependency upon the US act to normalise this form of intervention in the region. It produced a pro-capitalist agenda that placed severe limits and imposed strict conditionalities upon domestic and international policy. West Indian nationalist leaders began to line up behind the US across the Cold War divide. Once their countries became inserted into the arena of cold war contestations, they were quick to impose the litmus test of anti-communism as a legitimising principle of political participation at any level. In the process, the neocolonial forms of global capitalism came to be cast as the national will. And nationalist leaders became its active agents.

Without exception, the anti-Communist leaders led the governments of the region to independence during the '60s and '70s. They were able to count on the covert, and sometimes overt, support by the US for their claims to power. Supported by persistent and pervasive efforts of destabilisation directed at radical movements, these leaders acted to keep the region free from radical expression. The radical nationalist leadership found itself isolated and abandoned as the new anti-Communist agenda began to unfold. Those who attempted to break out of the ambit of the regional superpower and of the strictures of anti-communism found themselves under attack.

Creole Nationalism and Regional Interventionism

The PPP's ouster ushered in an era where interventionism was deployed to discipline and punish nationalist aspirations for sovereignty and self-determination. The party came to be perceived not merely as anti-capitalist, but anti nationalist. To be West Indian is to occupy the hierarchical, hybridised 'Creole' space between two racial poles. These serve as markers for civilisation and savagery. It is to be constituted of various degrees of cultural and racial mixing. At the apex is the white Creole as the historical product of cultural hybridisation. The Afro-Creole is located at the other end of the Creole continuum. The 'creolisation' of the latter derives from the contingencies of separation from Africa and the civilising influences of transformative contact with Europeans. Creoleness is central to the social construction of nationalist belonging and 'peoplehood' in the West Indies. It does not accommodate the indigenous groups of the region and the diasporic communities with cultural and racial origins outside of Africa and Europe. In representation and practice, they remain marginal to Creole reality unless amalgamated through individual practices of cultural and sexual immersion. As such, these groups were excluded from the new imageries of nationalist belonging.[7] Soon, these Creole definitions of national belonging began to dictate the terms of alliance between political leaders in British Guiana and the West Indian nationalists.

Unlike the rest of the English-speaking Caribbean, valorised Creole cultural forms were less important than institutional solidarity in representations of national belonging in British Guiana. The historical absence of white Creoles in the colour class order of Guyanese social construction lessened significantly the need for idioms of belonging that bridged the divide between white coloniser and the colonised. Thus, class solidarity became much more potent a force in the organisation of the nationalist movement. While no racial grouping in Guyana enjoyed a numerical majority, Asian Indians, by virtue of their numbers, comprised the largest of the ethno-racial groupings. Africans, mixed Creoles and considerably smaller groupings of Amerindians (indigenous native groups), Portuguese, and Chinese followed them.

Sovereignty, Interventionism, and Racialised Politics

Ideological fissures within the PPP after its ouster from power, instigated by Britain with the promise of support to the more moderate leaders, produced competing claims to the party's leadership. Unable to resolve these claims, the nationalist movement split into two factions, one led by the more radical and the other by the more moderate of its co-leaders. The former, an Asian Indian dentist, Cheddi Jagan, had a support base in the rural predominantly Asian Indian plantation proletariat and peasantry. The support base of the latter, an Afro-Guyanese Attorney named Forbes Burnham, rested in the black urban proletariat. The radical faction of the PPP headed by Cheddi Jagan was elected to power in 1957. Britain agreed to the new elections with the hope of a victory by the moderates. Taking no chances, however, it restricted even further the exercise of executive authority enjoyed by the elected executive in 1953. While the working class continued to provide its overwhelming support to the nationalist leaders, such support began to rupture along racial lines.

With the victory of the radical faction of the nationalist movement, racial political alliances began forming across ideological and class lines, rendering invisible the hand of North Atlantic international capital. In 1959, Burnham's more moderate faction joined with a vehemently anti-Communist party representing the petite bourgeois Afro-Creole to form the Peoples National Congress (PNC). Around the same time, the United Force (UF) was founded as a right wing minority party. It received the bulk of its support from the country's Portuguese, Chinese, and lighter-skinned coloured population. The party relied for its survival upon the active backing of the country's business elite, international investors, and Western governments. Finding themselves on the other side of the racial divide, most of the East Indian middle strata, including its business, professional, and educated elite, threw their support behind Jagan's PPP, irrespective of the party's communist label.

By 1960, the country was politically divided into highly racialised camps. This was notwithstanding efforts by United Force to present itself as a multi-racial flag bearer of anti-communism. But ideology took a back seat to the issue of race. Burnham's PNC began feeding the fires of anti-Indianism by exploiting the fears harboured by the predominantly black and coloured urban middle and working class of an East Indian take-over of the urban sector. Racial politics assumed a new urgency as the PPP won elections held in 1960 and went on to lead a government under a new constitution of expanded self-government. The PPP's victory was on the strength of its almost exclusively Asian Indian support base.

By providing the mass base of support for the competing racialised parties, the working classes and peasantry became deployed against itself in support of a system of global capital that dictated their continuing exploitation. Britain's explicit promise, made before the elections, that the country would be granted independence, intensified the racial struggle. Caribbean nationalist leaders began to impose their own understanding of nationalist belonging on the terms for the country's independence. From the inception, West Indian nationalist discourse acted to legitimise a pattern of regional interventionism in the country in the interests of Western capital. In pursuit of their ideological and Creole nationalist agendas, the leaders of the West Indies were prepared to violate the very principles of sovereignty and self-determination for which they had fought in their anticolonial campaign. With the split in the nationalist movement, notions of West Indian belonging predisposed this political leadership to support the moderate faction of the Guyanese nationalist movement. Initially, their support seemed to be provided on ideological grounds as they rejected the PPP's radical challenge to global capital. So, in the early '60s, they rallied around an anti-communist coalition of the Peoples' National Congress (PNC) and the United Force (UF) notwithstanding the fair and free elections that brought the PPP to power and the campaign of violence unleashed by these two opposition parties to secure its ouster. In the process, they provided legitimacy to the campaign of intervention conducted and orchestrated by the US and Great Britain against the party. This contributed significantly to the success of the campaign. Both governments justified their intervention by charges of communism. Reeling from a combination of covert activity, constitutional fiat and violent confrontation, Cheddi Jagan, the colony's premier, was forced to yield to demands for an imposed constitutional settlement that guaranteed the ouster of his party from power. Under the terms of the settlement authored by Britain's colonial office, the Westminster-style constituency system for allocating seats in the colony's Legislative Assembly was to be replaced by an electoral system of proportional representation. This was guaranteed to give the combined opposition, supported by all of the racialised voting blocs except the Asian Indians, a legislative majority and the right to form the government. Elections were held in 1964 and a coalition government of the PNC and the UF was elected to executive office.[8]

The support base of the PNC rested firmly in the country's black and mixed proletarian working class and in the group's salaried and professional middle classes who dominated the state sector, worked as functionaries in the private sector, or provided their professional services to both. The ideology of the former had been fashioned out of the radical nationalism of the '50s. This was reflected in the Fabianism of the party leader, Forbes Burnham. The party's middle-class support was much more conservative and apprehensive. Its commitment to nationalism stemmed from the clear expectation of power, authority, status and socio-economic position to be inherited from the white coloniser. The interest of the United Force rested squarely in the continuation of relations of dependency with the global North, a policy highly favoured by its supporters in the commercial and productive sectors whose interests were inextricably linked to international capital. It used its strategic position in the coalition to impose its conservative pro-Western ideological agenda upon the government. Between 1964 and 1968, state policy explicitly favoured the domestic and international private sector. This demonstrated the considerable influence of the United Force in the coalition. Its leader, a businessman named Peter D'Aguiar assumed the powerful portfolio of minister of finance. This gave him control over the state budget and the sole authority for authorship of fiscal policy. Commerce, industry, and the private professions became the primary beneficiaries of this policy. In 1966, with the coalition in power, Britain agreed to grant the colony its independence.

With the change in government in power, popular interests took a back seat to those of international capital. During its term of office, the PPP implemented policies that, even though far from socialist, were directed at ameliorating the conditions of the country's lower strata. Operating under the considerable political restrictions of colonialism between 1957 and 1964, the party nonetheless managed an impressive array of domestic accomplishments. Its policies were focused on agriculture, health delivery, education, and social welfare. Development planning was introduced. Extensive and comprehensive surveys of the country's resources were made for the first time in its history. The country's electricity generating capacity was upgraded and expanded with state takeover of the Canadian-owned electric company. Agricultural production, particularly rice and vegetables, was expanded considerably. Malaria was eradicated and successful campaigns were introduced to control polio, typhoid and other forms of diseases. Numerous health centres, cottage hospitals, and maternity and child welfare clinics were built, particularly in the rural areas. And free medical care was introduced. There was considerable expansion and upgrading of housing throughout the country and rent control ordinances were enacted to protect the rights of tenants. There was also considerable expansion of primary and secondary education with the state assuming full control and management of all primary schools in the colony. Technical education and teacher training were expanded and a University of Guyana was established.

In the intensely political climate of the '60s, the political opposition labelled these policies as racially biased. The party's effort at rural development was represented as favouring its rural Asian Indian supporters concentrated in the agricultural sector. As a result, the middle- and working-class supporters of the opposition opposed them. The prism of race through which everything was interpreted rendered irrelevant the considerable improvements that these policies brought to the life conditions of the working and middle classes. By 1967 when the PNC managed to gain full control of the government after enticing elected Members of Parliament from the United Force to 'cross the floor', its policies were firmly locked into a racial agenda. This imposed upon the party an almost exclusive focus on the overwhelmingly black urban sector and foreclosed a rural agricultural emphasis that offered the best prospects for the country's development.[9] The politics of race imposed conditions upon the PNC that vitiated the democratic terms of legitimate governance. Without the support of the United Force, the PNC could not hope to win a national election. And by 1968, it had become increasingly the case that the PPP's support base was large enough to guarantee the party a majority even under the existing terms of proportional representation. In 1970, the black and mixed groups comprised 42 per cent of the country's population. With the exception of 'near whites', the mixed population comprising mostly descendants of black-white (coloured) and black-East Indian unions identified politically, socially, and culturally with the blacks, East Indians comprised slightly over 51 per cent, whites (including Portuguese) and Chinese less than two per cent respectively, and Amerindians around four per cent (see Population Census of the Commonwealth Caribbean 1970).

To maintain its hold on power the PNC was forced to rig the elections. Fraudulent electoral victories were secured in 1968, 1973, 1980, and 1985. A fraudulent referendum in 1978 paved the way for the establishment of an executive presidency in 1980. Beginning in the late '70s, coercive violence was deployed against the regime's opponents.[10] The PNC employed this combination of violence and electoral fraud to remain in power until 1992.[11]

Sovereignty, Democracy, and Interventionism

The issue of sovereignty cannot be divorced from terms of legitimacy. Nationalist discourse in the region was rooted in the idea of the free exercise of the will of the people. This was the very essence of the demand for self-determination by the anticolonial movement. It was to be guaranteed through the practice of formalised democracy. When external political actors intervene to thwart democratic practice, then sovereignty is compromised.

Nationalist constructs of belonging in the rest of the English-speaking West Indies imposed particular definitions of legitimacy upon the institutions of governance in postcolonial British Guiana (now called Guyana). This supported forms of regional interventionism that undermined democratic practice. West Indian nationalism could not accommodate any claims to national belonging made by Asian Indians. In Guyana, however, the party supported by the latter was guaranteed to win any election that was freely and fairly conducted. The contradiction was resolved by replacing the requirements of majoritarian democracy with legitimacy constructs of belonging cast in racial terms of inclusion and exclusion.[12] Under these terms, regional governments refused to acknowledge the right of the PPP to rule, despite its majority support. The PNC, by virtue of its claim to represent the Creole population of

Guyana, had, in the worldview of West Indian leaders, sole and legitimate claims to governance. They continued to recognise the party despite its resort to undemocratic practice and its deployment of coercion to stay in power. This bolstered efforts by Western governments in support of global capital, to keep the PPP out of power because of its left wing radicalism. The resolve to do so intensified considerably after party leaders openly committed the PPP to the ideology of Marxism/Leninism and developed formalised relations with the communist parties of the Soviet Union and Eastern Europe.[13]

Thus, by the end of the '60s, three types of external impositions were acting upon the country's political economy to undermine its sovereignty. First was the conservative orthodox ideology of pro-Western capitalism imposed by the industrialised North Atlantic. Second was nationalist ideology of Creole belonging imposed by West Indian national actors. And third was the radical Marxism-Leninism of pro-Soviet communism imposed by Eastern European political actors upon the party that enjoyed the support of the majority of the country's population. The first two of these impositions combined to keep the PPP out of power. The third became a condition of its continued viability as it turned to Eastern Europe, its allies and its international sympathisers for support.

Isolation and Punishment as Instrumentalities of Interventionism

Soon the class dictates of the PNC's support base forced a confrontation with foreign international capital. The interests of the party's black lower-class and black and coloured middle-class supporters were inconsistent with the terms of continued participation of international capital in the country's political economy. The party's racial legitimacy rested with policies that improved the life conditions of these supporters. And these groups were certainly not the beneficiaries of a continuation of the policies inherited from the period of the coalition. This became quite evident during the early '70s as segments of the black working class began to mobilise against the ruling party. The visible benefits of party policy for the East Indian, white, and near-white elite produced a cleavage among the party's racial supporters. It led to the forced departure of leading Black Nationalist, Eusi Kwayana, who enjoyed considerable support among the younger members of the black middle class and a significant segment of the black lower class. In leaving, Kwayana pulled his African Society for

Cultural Relations with Independent Africa (ASCRIA) out of the PNC. He accused the party of being 'a unity of the black political leaders with the Portuguese and Indian exploiting classes.'[14] The loss was quite significant since ASCRIA was a major recruiting and organising arm of the PNC.[15] Many blacks, reflecting ASCRIA's position, were no longer prepared to accept as legitimate the claims of the PNC to be the party representing the black population.

The PNC leadership responded with a series of policy initiatives. First, it attempted to wean the country away from the need for foreign imports by embarking on a campaign of national economic self-sufficiency in a Feed, Clothes, and House Ourselves programme (FCH).[16] The programme was an attempt to deploy domestic productive resources to meet domestic consumer needs. The second strategy rested with an attempt to harness the savings of the black population through cooperative organisation. A programme of cooperative development was initiated to catapult blacks into agriculture, fishing, and small and mid-scale industry. Most importantly, however, the ruling party began to undertake efforts, through equity participation in the foreign-owned sectors of the economy, to gain access to the economic surplus generated by these industries for domestic redistribution. This began with an effort to enter negotiations with a subsidiary of an Aluminium Company in Canada for equity participation. Western capital was willing to brook no challenge to its right to untrammelled operation in the country. At their petitioning, the negotiations precipitated a campaign of economic retaliation, organised by Western governments led by the US that became so extraordinarily punitive that it destroyed the country's economic viability and produced a crisis of poverty and despoliation.

With economic retaliation against the regime mounting, a decision was made in 1973 to forge a protective alliance with the eastern bloc and with socialist countries internationally. The ruling party began making ideological declarations in support of Marxism/Leninism and began to identify with radical causes internationally. Burnham made the decision to cast his lot with the radical anti-capitalist regimes of the global south. By 1976, most of the major holdings of foreign capital were nationalised placing the state in control of over 80 per cent of the economic assets of the country. The radical turn led, naturally, to efforts at restoring cross-racial class alliances. In 1973, attempts were made by the ruling party to recruit

East Indians into its ranks. Between 1975 and 1976, the PPP provided the ruling party with 'critical support' after it made an unambiguous commitment to socialism.[17]

The problem for the country was its profound economic dependency and its inextricable ties to Western capital. This made its economy vulnerable to punitive retaliation. And these came with a vengeance in the form of economic destabilisation efforts that, combined with spiralling oil prices and a recession following the 1973 Middle East war, wreaked havoc on the Guyanese economy. By 1978 an escalating economic crisis began to force the regime to cutback drastically on its capital projects, to curtail state spending, to retrench state employees, and to reduce the importation of essential commodities. A second oil shock in 1979 and an international recession during the early '80s contributed further to the country's rapid downward economic spiral. During the entire period of the eighties Guyana's economy was in a persistent state of near total economic collapse. Much more strident interventionist policies by the US and Great Britain, in the wake of the election of Ronald Reagan and Margaret Thatcher, led to further deterioration in the relations between these two countries and the PNC government. Their campaign of retaliation intensified, deepening an already severe economic crisis. The unemployment rate skyrocketed to 30 per cent and the country began to experience a severe health crisis leading to dramatic increases in mortality rates, particularly among children and pregnant women (Hintzen 1989, 183–92). Its foreign debt ballooned dramatically.

The government dealt with the crisis in two ways. First, it intensified its relationship with the Soviet Union, Eastern Europe, Cuba, and China in efforts to develop alternative sources of economic support. This produced intensified retaliatory action by Western governments. In 1983, Burnham strongly condemned the US administration for its invasion of Grenada. In 1985, the US suspended all economic assistance programmes to the government, closed the office of its Agency for International Development in the capital city, and began actively to bloc economic assistance from multilateral donors to the country. Second, the regime resorted to coercive measures and constitutional fiat to maintain its control of the state. These were added to its arsenal of electoral fraud. As the crisis escalated, the regime's effort at cross-racial alliance collapsed, and its own racial support began to erode. The PPP withdrew its offer of critical support in 1976 and in 1977 began a campaign of 'non-cooperation and civil resistance' accompanied by strikes and demonstrations.[18]

The anti-Western and anti-capitalist turn of the PNC regime exposed the racial agenda of the West Indian nationalist leaders in their relations with Guyana. They continued to reject claims by the PPP to governance and to accept the legitimacy of the PNC regime. This was notwithstanding the new policy of state socialism and the regime's international alliances with the Communist bloc. The recognition of the PNC's legitimacy by the West Indian leadership resolved a dilemma faced by Western governments. The alternative to the PNC was the even more radical PPP with considerably stronger ties to the USSR. The best strategy was therefore one of isolation rather than regime change. This freed the ruling party to make economic policy and to reorganise the political system without the impositions of foreign international actors. At the same time, Western governments actively intervened to ensure the destruction of the country's economy. From the perspective of Western capitalist actors, economic retaliation without the prospect of regime change was the ideal solution to the imbroglio of Guyana. Both of the major parties were declared Marxist-Leninist and supporters of the Soviet Union and its socialist allies internationally. The deployment of the economic instrumentalities of punishment demonstrated the consequences of challenges to the hegemony of Western capital. In the process, as an economic basket case and as a cauldron of political coercion, crisis, and conflict, Guyana could serve as a lesson in the consequences of challenging Western capitalism. It became a symbol of socialist degradation in the region. The fact that it seemed to be left to its own devices was all the more telling. This rendered invisible the pervasive interventionism that drove the political and economic crisis as its government appeared free to choose the direction of its policy.

Globalism and New Instrumentalities of Control

By the latter half of the '80s, the deepening economic crisis in Guyana began to dictate an imperative of massive external assistance. The was at a time when the Soviet-led Eastern bloc countries and their allies were less able and less willing to provide economic and political support to sympathetic regimes. The PNC found itself with little option but to seek economic assistance from the West at the very time when the terms of access to external financing were becoming subjected, increasingly, to the dictates of international financial institutions. The latter were under the absolute control of powerful capitalist Western governments, particularly the US. Countries seeking external financing were being forced to transfer authority over national economic policy to these institutions on terms authored by their international boards of directors acting on behalf of Western governments. These were implemented by economic technocrats. This rendered ideology of little consequence in policy formulation.[19] Progressive and radical leaders found themselves with little option but to accept the dictates of international public policy informed by a resurgent liberal orthodoxy fashioned by increasingly conservative Western governments. Robbed of their autonomy, they posed little threat to capitalist interests. The need for surveillance and intervention against radical governments and movements in the global South diminished as regimes were forced to give up autonomy in their economic affairs in exchange for access to external funding. The image of democratic governance could be preserved under conditions where the protected interests of global capital sought to increase its penetration of their respective political economies.

In 1988, after two years of negotiations, the World Bank and the International Monetary Fund (IMF) approved a policy framework paper for economic stabilisation for Guyana. At the time, the country's foreign debt was US$1.9 billion, an extraordinarily high figure relative to the country's GDP. Payment arrears on this debt had ballooned to US$1.1 billion. The policy framework laid the foundation for access to external funding.[20] It set the groundwork for a three-year Enhanced Structural Adjustment facility programme that led, in 1990, to a Structural Adjustment Loan. This has become the basis for the formulation of economic policy ever since.[21] Any government coming to power in Guyana has been forced to abide by its terms. Continued access to external financing has become contingent upon their full satisfaction.

Guyana was typical of countries of the Global south, overcome with heavy debt burdens. Without access to external financing, economic integrity, and political stability would be seriously imperiled. Increasing dependence upon multilateral financial institutions provided the opportunity for imposing, controlling, and regulating public policy in these countries. Policy formulation became sharply constrained by the dictates of the International Monetary Fund, the World Bank and other bilateral and multilateral funding agencies. Under these conditions, the ideology of the ruling regime was rendered irrelevant.

As the relationship between ideology and policy began to erode, Western governments found a new cause in the popular movements of protest that began sweeping Eastern Europe. These were mounted in the name of democratic governance and civil and political rights. Western governments strongly supported these movements using as justification the claim of the moral right of any populace to mount challenges against undemocratic regimes. As a result, democratic rule and the practice of civil rights became the new litmus tests of Western support for a regime and new justifications for intervention.

The interest of global capital can be shrouded by practices of democratic governance because it can give the appearance of popular will at a time when international actors dictate national policy. Popular support for a government reduces the possibility of domestic opposition to its policies. A democratically elected or popular government can sell to its supporters the outcomes of international negotiations as being best for the country and for their interests.

Democracy and Civil Rights: New Instruments of Intervention

The changing international climate in favour of civil and political rights in the Global South fostered by the US and its Western allies in the wake of popular movements in Eastern Europe enhanced considerably the moral and ethical claim of the PPP to power. It combined with the new instrumentalities of economic control located in multilateral and bilateral financial institutions to impose new terms of political and economic organisation upon Guyana. Support for a PPP government in Guyana would underscore the commitment of the US and Western Europe to democracy under conditions where the party could pose little threat to western and capitalist interests. For the first time, the persistent calls by the party's leaders for democracy began to get a sympathetic hearing by Western and West Indian governments. The collapse of Euro-communism at the end of the 1980s reduced considerably the anxieties, stemming from geo-strategic concerns. These centred on the threat posed to the West by ideological alliances between Eastern Europe and the Global South. The PPP was no longer an international pariah of the western world.

In the new technologies of interventionism, overt and covert use of violence and subversion by international actors has given way to dictates by and impositions of those in charge of making and implementing international public policy. They are deployed by those in control of foreign funding. Failure to satisfy the stipulated conditions under which these funds are delivered can prove economically and politically devastating for a government. Powerful western governments dictate these conditions in support of the interests of international capital. In 1985, the Guyana government's refusal to abide by these conditions was met by the suspension of economic assistance from the US. Under the influence of the latter, Guyana became the first country in the history of the IMF to be declared ineligible for funding.[22] One year later, the regime was forced to enter into negotiations with the IMF and World Bank out of which emerged a 'Policy Framework' for economic stabilisation. Under its terms, the ruling party agreed to reorganise the country's economy and dismantle most of the institutions of state socialism.[23] International financial agencies and aid donors began to demand a significant shift of economic control away from the public sector and an expanded role for a viable private sector as the mainstay of the economy. They insisted upon deep cutbacks in the state bureaucratic sector and upon the hiring of a British consulting firm to advise on restructuring the country's ministries to reduce the size of the state bureaucracy. The 18 ministries existing at the time were eventually reduced to 11.[24]

As has been the case since the first nationalist government came to power in 1953, local bases of organisation were employed to impose the dictates of Western governments over the terms of governance. A Patriotic Coalition for Democracy (PCD), formed in 1986 by five opposition parties, including the PPP, began acquiring a new international legitimacy. At their instigation, the restoration of democracy and civil and human rights soon became the basis for international political and economic support for the regime. By 1989, this unified, multi-party political opposition was able to demonstrate, unequivocally, that its cooperation was indispensable if the government's efforts to gain access to external funding were to succeed. In 1989 it used its control of the country's most powerful unions, representing workers in the country's major industries (sugar and bauxite) to call a series of crippling strikes at a pivotal point in negotiations between the regime and potential international aid donors and lenders, causing economic disruption.[25] The strikes proved critical in preventing the government from meeting the conditions stipulated by the IMF and World Bank in order to qualify for an enhanced structural adjustment facility and for other foreign exchange assistance that it desperately needed.²⁶ The opposition also called a successful boycott of local government elections in October 1989 and mounted a campaign petitioning for the intervention of Western and Caribbean governments, particularly the 13-member English-speaking Caribbean Community.

The organised political opposition was joined by a civic coalition launched in 1990 as the Guyanese Action for Reform and Democracy (GUARD) as a 'reform movement'. It added its voice of stridency to the PCD in demanding the restoration of democracy and human rights in the country. Organised by a Guyanese elite of trade union leaders, businessmen, religious leaders, public officials, and professionals, the movement was patterned directly after the protest movements of Eastern Europe.²⁷

Whatever their ideological and racial divisions, the opposition parties and civic organisations remained united in their calls for fair and free elections. Their campaigns to bring this about were well coordinated, particularly in their overseas efforts. The latter crystallised with the formation of a 'World Union of Guyanese' by a former PPP attorney general, Dr Fenton Ramsahoye, who resided 'in exile' in the Caribbean. The Union made plans to approach the United Nations, the Organization of American States and the governments of the Caribbean, North America, and Western Europe.²⁸ It also began to mobilise the vast Guyanese migrant population overseas in support of its calls for the restoration of democracy. In March 1990, representatives of 10 Guyanese organisations in the US met to organise a US chapter. Similar efforts were undertaken in Great Britain and the Caribbean where the bulk of this migrant population resides.²⁹

The opposition's overseas campaign began to pay early dividends. The US administration began to make forceful and unequivocal calls for electoral reform. As early as February, 1990, President George Bush, using the occasion of a republic anniversary message to Guyana, openly called upon the Hoyte government to respect democratic values. This was quickly followed by a visit to the country, in March, of US State Department official, Sally Cowall. She emphasised, in no uncertain terms, her government's expectation that the Hoyte regime would be 'working towards…having an open, free and fair election.' She also made clear her administration's commitment to supporting an international observer team to monitor the country's electoral processes.

The US backed up its words with a steep cut in foreign aid allocation. It provided the country with only US$1 million of an expected US$10–13 million promised as part of a package of assistance from a multi-country support group. The group was formed to bail the country out of its economic woes.[30]

The US Congress also got into the act. On March 19, Senator Edward Kennedy issued a statement urging the government to ensure fair and free elections, guarantee civil and political rights, and to restructure the party-controlled Elections Commission.[31] By August, members of both the US Senate and House of Representatives, including most democrats, began to call on the secretary of state to 'seek to ensure that US taxpayer dollars do not support and entrench a regime that holds power only through electoral fraud'.[32] It was a call for conditioning economic assistance to the willingness of the regime to agree to free and fair elections. In September, The Hon. Stephen J. Solarz cited Guyana in the US House of Representatives as one of the countries 'whose governments do not yet permit fundamental political freedoms.'[33] Finally, in October, the US Congress managed to put a hold on US$600,000 in economic assistance to the country until 'the government has agreed to certain ground rules' for elections.[34] The calls for free and fair elections were also being pressed in other countries. In March, the Canadian Council of Churches called upon Prime Minister Brian Mulroney 'to use Canada's influence in support of democratic elections.'[35] There were similar appeals throughout the British Commonwealth, including the English-speaking Caribbean. The Washington-based Council for Hemispheric Affairs also joined in appeals for free and fair elections.[36]

In September, international pressures forced the Hoyte government to concede, after staunch resistance, to the monitoring of the elections by international observers. Finally, the government permitted visits by representatives of Americas Watch, the National Democratic Institute, and the International Foundation for Electoral Systems, among other international human and political rights organisations, to assess the country's electoral system. It also extended an invitation to the Secretary General of the Commonwealth and to former US President Jimmy Carter's Council of Freely Elected Heads of Governments.[37] President Carter made the decision, in October, to visit Guyana for a meeting with the Hoyte government. He succeeded, during his talks with the government, in convincing the regime to agree to a number of electoral reform measures. These included the compilation of a fresh voters' list by house-to-house enumerations, the presence of party scrutinisers at these enumerations, and the preliminary counting of ballots at polling stations. The Elections Laws (Amendment) Bill and the Representation of the People (Amendment)

Bill containing these provisions were tabled and passed in the country's Parliament in December.[38]

The decision to demand fair and free elections by the international community was in keeping with the new morality of international support that rested with democracy and civil rights. So it was made despite the pointed efforts by the new party leader, Desmond Hoyte who had succeed Forbes Burnham after his death in 1986, at compliance with the demands of the international funding agencies. This produced a political rapprochement with the US. Party policies began a significant shift. By 1990, the PNC began wide-scale divestment of state holdings in both the export sector and in state-owned utilities and undertook a major effort to attract foreign private investments and to pursue export-led economic development. It began to make severe cuts in the state expenditure and in spending on state subsidies. It also implemented a series of massive devaluations. All these were in keeping with the demands of the IMF and World Bank. They resulted in significant improvements in the country's relationship with the US.

The fly in the ointment for the Hoyte government was its continued unwillingness to guarantee fair and free elections.[39] In 1990, this became a major obstacle in the country's international relations. The administration and Congress of the US became much more critical of the government's human rights record. As both bodies began to call pointedly for fair and free elections,[40] the ruling party was forced to accept a formula for electoral reform worked out by former US president, Jimmy Carter. He had intervened in the face of growing international pressure. The terms of reform were almost identical to those demanded by the opposition in the country.[41] Elections under the terms of the new agreement were set for March 1991 but later postponed, against strong protests from the opposition. The regime's actions were met with strong US retaliation. The US Senate quickly announced that it would appropriate no aid to the country without guarantees of a free and fair vote. Senators also added their voices to the calls by the opposition for the establishment of an independent electoral commission to prepare an accurate voter registration list and guarantee against ballot tampering and fraud when counting the votes. In addition, the senate called upon the Organization of American States and the United Nations to monitor the elections.[42] In the end, the ruling party was forced to accept a formula for electoral reform, worked out by former US President Jimmy Carter, who had intervened in the face of growing international pressure upon the government. This paved the way for elections on October 6, 1992. Despite evidence of continued fraud, the PPP secured the majority of the vote and Cheddi Jagan went on to form the new government while assuming the position of executive president. It was, certifiably, the first 'free and fair' election to be held in the country since 1968 and the first to be conducted with a PNC government in power.

Even though enjoying support from the majority of the country's population, the leadership of the PPP fully recognised the new reality where political power rested squarely in the hands of international political and economic actors. Before the elections, the party's leader, Cheddi Jagan embarked on several trips to the US to engage in a concerted lobbying effort, meeting with Bush administration officials, members of the US Congress, and ex-President Jimmy Carter. In acts of appeasement, he declared in 1990 that 'the building of a so-called Communist state in Guyana is not on the agenda of the PPP and we have even dropped our insistence on a socialist-orientated (sic) programme.' He began publicly to support private enterprise, to welcome foreign capital to the country, and to divest publicly owned corporations in favour of foreign private investment.[43] These were the very terms stipulated by the IMF and World Bank for guarantees of continued access to foreign exchange support.

Democracy without Sovereignty: Race and Discipline

After the PPP was elected to power, the Carter Center organised and run by former President Jimmy Carter began playing a central role in the country's international affairs and in its domestic policy. It had been instrumental in organising and overseeing the 1992 elections that brought the party to power and had intervened with the US Embassy in Georgetown and the International Foundation for Electoral Systems when the PNC began to show reluctance in handing over power. After the elections, the center was directly inserted into the country's decision-making process. It was instrumental in the fashioning of a National Development Strategy and began to serve as a conduit between the Guyanese government, international actors and multilateral aid donors. Its intervention was particularly important in relations with the US. In effect, it became an international bargaining agent for the government.[44]

The idiom of race disciplines and regulates party-political support in Guyana. This explains the ability of the PPP and the PNC to retain popular support despite deteriorating social, political, and economic conditions in the face of intensive penetration of global capital. Legitimacy rests with racial control of the governing institutions of the state rather than with popular interests. In the 1992 elections, the PPP received massive victories in areas of the country where the East Indian population was in the majority. The PNC's regional victories came in areas of black majorities. Between them, the two parties received 95.8 per cent of the votes with the PPP receiving 53.5 per cent and the PNC 42.3 per cent.[45] The electoral results demonstrated a continued salience of idiomatically defined racial identity. This allowed the PPP to retain support from the majority of the electorate.

On March 19, the electorate of Guyana again went to the polls. By the unanimous account of all neutral observers, including official foreign delegations, the elections could have served as the 'poster child' for fairness and transparency. Former US President, Jimmy Carter, who led an observer mission for the Carter Center in Atlanta, declared that the elections were 'almost perfect'. With a full 88 per cent of the electorate voting, the ruling party received 54 per cent of the vote to 42 per cent received by its nearest rival, the People's National Congress. With 34 seats in the country's National Assembly, the leader of the PPP became, once again, the country's executive president.

It was the third electoral victory for the PPP since 1992. In elections held in December 1997 the party won with 55.3 per cent of the votes and in 1992 with 53.4 per cent. Yet, despite the unanimous opinion of all electoral observers that the 2001 elections were fair, free, and devoid of fraud, the results were immediately contested by the PNC, the country's major opposition party. This was despite the strong endorsement by its own appointed members to the Guyana Elections Commission as to its fairness and transparency. The Commission was charged with running the election under a chairman who was considered, universally, to be neutral and impartial. Charges by the PNC that the elections were fraudulent were accompanied by an orchestrated campaign of violence. The campaign began even before the elections were contested, and escalated into mass mobilisation in the capital city. It was accompanied by politically motivated beatings and murder. On April 9, an area of the capital city of Georgetown was torched. Perceived supporters of the governing party owned many of the businesses that were burnt.

It was not the first time that the opposition employed tactics of protest and violence to contest the results of elections that were unquestionably free, fair, and 'transparent'. There was similar campaign after the 1997 elections. While demands by the People's National Congress for a 'national front' government comprising itself and other opposition parties went unheeded, the campaign of violence and protest forced the ruling regime into making compromises that included agreements to consider establishment of joint committees of governance and joint management of parliamentary business and the working out of constitutional reform aimed particularly at reducing the power of the executive president.

The 2001 elections served as a stark reconfirmation of a racially polarised electorate. This has been the most pervasive feature of Guyanese politics since the racial splintering of the progressive nationalist Peoples Progressive Party in 1956.

The three electoral victories by the PPP beginning in 1992 came with solid support of the Indo-Guyanese majority, comprising over 51 per cent of the country's population. The PNC, backed by the country's black and mixed racial group comprising around 39 per cent of the country's population, gained 42 per cent of the popular vote. Of the 11 parties contesting the elections, only three managed enough support to gain parliamentary seats. One, the Guyana Action Party/Working People's Alliance is distinguished by its comprehensively and genuinely multi-racial character. It secured two of the 65 seats in the country's National Assembly. The other was the United Force (TUF) with its pro-Western and pro-business ideology and a support base in the country's Portuguese, Chinese, and Amerindian population. It managed to secure one parliamentary seat. The third, Rise Organize and Rebuild Guyana movement (ROAR) with a predominantly East Indian appeal, managed to gain one seat. The PPP ended up with 34 seats and the PNC with 27.

What is important in an analysis of the Guyana elections of 1997 and 2001 and their aftermath is the light it throws upon conditions of power in postcolonial political economies. Such an analysis raises the question of the relationship of effective power to the ideals of representative democracy. An increase in its percentage of the popular support, from 53.4 per cent in 1992 to 55.2 per cent in 1997, was not enough to guarantee the PPP's hold on political power. This had to be secured through international intervention. And despite such intervention, and an election outcome that was clearly incontestable, the post-election crisis in 2001 was much more violent and destructive. In the post-1997 political environment, the PPP's ability to maintain control of the state was underwritten by international intervention and demonstrations of international support. These served to counter the effective control by the PNC of the strategic domestic instruments of power. There were a number of ways in which international intervention negated the strategic power of the PNC in the domestic arena. In the highly racialised environment, PNC control of the judiciary was the first hurdle that the PPP had to overcome. It did so with the help of pressure and surveillance by the official body of Caribbean jurists. Efforts to neutralise the judiciary were accompanied by the formalisation of international intervention by Western and regional governments in support of the PPP's majoritarian claim to executive office.

One may surmise that the possibility of regional and international military intervention must have loomed large in the decision of the military and police to maintain political neutrality given the overwhelming support enjoyed by the PNC among their ranks. This was particularly true in the immediate post-1997 election environment. By the 2001 elections, the depoliticisation of the military and police was clearly evident. The ruling party was confident enough to agree to the appointment of the former head of the Guyana Defence Force, Major General Joe Singh, to the position of chair of the Elections Commission charged with the conduct of the elections. By 2001, the principle of neutrality had emerged in the military with clear and unambiguous certainty. Nonetheless, the opposition PNC continued to demonstrate its ability to disrupt the social, political, and economic order, forcing the PPP into negotiated compromise.

In the strategic equation, the PPP could count on the absolute support of the predominantly East Indian private sector. The influence of this sector rested heavily on the relations it established with its powerful international allies, particularly international business, international aid donors, and Western governments. In both 1997 and 2001, the influential East Indian dominated Private Sector Commission mounted a campaign pointing out the need for a 'stable economic environment' and the destabilising consequences for the country's political economy of a campaign of protest and violence. This, undoubtedly, struck a resonant chord among the international actors concerned with the potential effects of political upheaval on the country's economy. These were the actors involved in efforts directed at economic liberalisation and privatisation aimed at guaranteeing repayment of the country's foreign debt of over US$2 billion. In the post-elections environment of 1997, the Private Sector Commission put its weight behind proposals for an international audit of the contested election returns, correctly anticipating that such an audit would confirm the PPP's victory. It also supported a negotiated political settlement as a basis for a return to political and social order. This, as it turned out, was precisely the solution imposed by the international community. Included was the decision for new elections in 2001. Through international mediation, the Caribbean Community (CARICOM, a common market comprising primarily English-speaking countries of the Caribbean) was given the official role of establishing binding terms for resolving the ongoing political crisis. In 1997, in the face of escalating violence and a refusal of the PNC to observe a ban on demonstrations and protest, the prime ministers of CARICOM countries negotiated the Herdmanston Accord, signed by members of the ruling party and the opposition. The accord formalised an official role for CARICOM. It committed both political parties to a process of negotiations and to the establishment of a Constitution Reform Commission under mutually acceptable terms. It also formalised the agreement to hold the general elections of 2001 under a new constitution.

In exchange for political order and stability, the ruling party made concessions to the PNC by agreeing to hold new elections in three years, rather than the constitutionally defined five years. It agreed also to renegotiate a new constitution that came with the possibility of reducing its hold on power, despite its clear and growing majority in popular support. These were the terms under which elections were held in 2001.

Clearly, it was the demonstration by the PNC of its ability to mobilise strategic sectors of power in the political economy that forced the PPP into making political concessions in exchange for political stability. The PNC continued this demonstration of strategic power in a campaign of protest and non-cooperation with the government even after signing the Herdmanston Accord. There was considerable pressure placed upon the PNC for a return to normalcy given international authentication of the official results of the 1997 elections. After some hesitation and resistance, the party's leadership decided, finally, to assume its place in Parliament in exchange for the new concessions by the ruling party to hold the 2001 elections under terms determined by the CARICOM accord.

The issue of legitimacy in Guyana rests with effective representation of the competing communal groupings in the process of decision-making about resource allocation. The more politicised or exclusive this process is, the more intense the demands for communal representation. The consequences have been devastating. The dependence upon international intervention by racialised political parties has intensified the penetration of global capital and has eviscerated any semblance of sovereignty. Efforts at racial accommodation have been stymied by international intervention, first in 1953, then in the 1960s, and later in the first half of the 1970s. Since then, economic decline and new technologies of intervention have tied the country even more firmly to international capital while elevating international decision makers in international financial agencies to positions of de facto governance. While conditions continue to deteriorate, the popular segments of the Guyanese population continue to focus on racial control of the state under the disciplinary regimes of racially organised political parties.

Notes

1. See Oswaldo de Rivero, *The Myth of Development* (London and New York: Zed Books, 2001), 11–31.
2. See Mandle 1996, 57–71.
3. See Cary Fraser, *Ambivalent Anti-Colonialism* (Westport, CT and London: Greenwood, 1994), 123–68.
4. This section is informed by a number of sources, including Percy C. Hintzen, *The Costs of Regime Survival* (Cambridge and New York: New York University Press, 1989); Thomas J. Spinner, *A Political and Social History of Guyana, 1945–1983* (Boulder, CO: Westview 1984); Robert H. Manley, *Guyana Emergent* (Boston, G.K. Hall, and Cambridge, MA: Schenkman, 1979).
5. People's Progressive Party 1971, 5.
6. Fraser, *Ambivalent Anti-Colonialism*.
7. For a fuller discussion see Percy C. Hintzen, 'Racial and Ethnic Identity in the Caribbean,' in *The Blackwell Companion to Racial and Ethnic Studies*, ed. John Solomos and David Goldberg (Oxford: Blackwell, 2001); and Percy C. Hintzen, 'Race and Creole Ethnicity in the Caribbean,' in *Questioning Creole: Creolisation Discourses in Caribbean Culture*, ed. Verene A. Shepherd and Glen L. Richards, 92–110. (Kingston: Ian Randle Publishers; London: James Currey, 2002).
8. This and the following discussions are covered in Hintzen 1989, Spinner 1994; Manley 1979, and Fraser 1994, 123–68.
9. Hintzen, *Costs of Regime Survival*, 175–193.
10. Ibid., 52–56; Sheehan 1967; Pearson 1964; Lens 1965; Schlesinger 1965, 779.

11. See Hintzen, *Costs of Regime Survival*; Hintzen and Premdas, 'Coercion and Control in Political Change.' *Journal of Inter-American Studies and World Affairs* 24, no. 3 (August): 337–54.
12. See Hintzen, 'Race and Creole Ethnicity in the Caribbean.'
13. Hintzen, *Costs of Regime Survival*, 63–70.
14. ASCRIA 1974.
15. See Hintzen 1975, 113–128.
16. Hintzen, *Costs of Regime Survival*, 184.
17. Ibid., 170.
18. See Central Committee Document, Peoples Progressive Party 1977.
19. See Hintzen, *Structural Adjustment and Good Governance: The Case of Guyana*. Georgetown Guyana: Public Affairs Consulting Enterprise, 1975.
20. International Monetary Fund 1990, 1.
21. See Ferguson, *Structural Adjustment and Good Governance*, 50–55.
22. Ibid., 1.
23. Hintzen, *Structural Adjustment and Good Governance*.
24. *Latin American Regional Report: Caribbean*, January 24, 1991, 2.
25. See Ferguson, *Structural Adjustment and Good Governance: The Case of Guyana*. (Georgetown Guyana: Public Affairs Consulting Enterprise, 1995), 50.
26. Hintzen, *Costs of Regime Survival*.
27. *Catholic Standard*, January 21, 1990, 1–2.
28. *Trinidad Guardian*, April 12, 1990, 7.
29. *Miami Herald*, March 26, 1990.
30. *Caribbean Contact*, April 1990, 6; *Catholic Standard*, March 11, 1990, 2.
31. *Catholic Standard*, March 25, 1990, 1.
32. Latin American Regional Reports: Caribbean, August 30, 1990.
33. US House of Representatives, Sept 11, 1990.
34. *Miami Herald*, October 8, 1990.
35. *Catholic Standard*, March 25, 1990.
36. *Catholic Standard*, April 29, 1990, 1–8.
37. *Miami Herald*, October 8, 1990.
38. *Guyana Chronicle*, January 4, 1991, 4–5.
39. Hintzen 1989b.
40. Congressional Record 1990, 1.
41. *Trinidad Guardian*, Nov. 28, 1990, 11; *Guyana Chronicle*, January 27, 1990, 15.
42. *Stabroek News*, January 15, 1991, 1–2; Latin American Regional Report: Caribbean, February 28, 1991, 6–8.
43. D. Bohning, 'Ex-enemy Seeks US Help to Gain Fair Guyana Vote,' *Miami Herald*, December 8, 1990; *Catholic Standard*, May 13, 1990, 5.
44. See Lynette Harvey, 'Guyana's Democracy, America's Policy,' *Guyana Review* 42 (July): 10–11.
45. See Report of the Council of Freely Elected Heads of Government.

References

Bohning, D. 1990. Ex-enemy Seeks US Help to Gain Fair Guyana Vote. *Miami Herald*, December 8.
Catholic Standard, 1990. May 13, 5.
Despres, L. 1967. *Cultural Pluralism and Nationalist Politics in British Guiana*. Chicago: Rand, McNally.
Economist Intelligence Unit. 1990. Country Report, No 1, 1990.
Ferguson, T. 1995. *Structural Adjustment and Good Governance: The Case of Guyana*. Georgetown Guyana: Public Affairs Consulting Enterprise.
Fraser, C. 1994. *Ambivalent Anticolonialism*. Westport: Greenwood Press.
Harvey, L. 1996. Guyana's Democracy, America's Policy. *Guyana Review* 42 (July): 10–11.
Hintzen, P. 1989. *The Costs of Regime Survival*. Cambridge and New York: Cambridge University Press.
———. 1993. Democracy and Middle Class Domination in the West Indies. In *Democracy in the West Indies*, ed. C. Edie. Boulder: Westview.
———. 1995. Structural Adjustment and the New International Middle Class. *Transition* 24 (February): 52–74.
———. 1997. Reproducing Domination: Identity and Legitimacy Constructs in the West Indies. *Social Identities* 3, no. 1:47–75.
———. 1999. Creole Construction and Nationalist Ideology. In *The Blackwell Companion to Racial and Ethnic Studies*, ed. David T.Goldberg, and John Soplomos. Oxford: Blackwell.
Hintzen, P.C. and R. Premdas. 1982. Coercion and Control in Political Change. *Journal of Inter-American Studies and World Affairs* 24, no. 3 (August): 337–54.
Huberman, L., and P.M. Sweezy. 1968. *Cuba: Anatomy of a Revolution*. New York: Monthly Review Press.
International Monetary Fund. 1990. Guyana: Enhanced Structural Adjustment Facility Economic and Financial Policy Framework 1990–92 June 20: 1.
Jagan. C. 1980. *The West on Trial*. Berlin: Seven Seas.
———. 1996. President Cheddi B. Jagan on Independence. *Guyana Review* 41 (June): 4–7.
Latin American Regional Reports: Caribbean. 1990. April 5: 4–5.
Lens, S. 1965. American Labor Abroad. *The Nation*, July 5.
Meeker-Lowry, S. 1995. Guyana Takes on the IMF. *Context* 41:33–5.
Pearson, D. 1964. US Faces Line Holding Decision. *Washington Post*, May 31.
People's Progressive Party. 1971. *People's Progressive Party: 21 Years*. Georgetown: New Guiana Co.
Schlesinger, A. Jr. 1965. *A Thousand Days*. New York: Houghton Mifflin.
Sheehan, N. 1967. C.I.A. Men and Strikers in Guiana against Dr Jagan. *New York Times*, February 22.
US State Department. 1963. Decimal File, Telegram Maddox to Secretary of State, September 11. R.G. 59, Box 3542.
Weiner, T. 1994. Ghost of a Kennedy-C.I.A. Plot Has Come Back to Haunt Clinton. *New York Times*, September 30, 1994, 1, 4.

Insecurities of Neoliberalism

8.
Local Impact of Global Change: Rice and Sugar in the History and Memory of Africans and East Indians in Guyana

Wazir Mohamed

Introduction

Two food crops – sugar and rice – have been integral to the vitality, political economy, culture, and food security of the Guyanese population since the nineteenth century. This chapter discusses crucial phases in the history and evolution of these two crops, the interrelationships that evolved and through which the cultural landscape of rural Guyana, the coastal villages on the outskirts of the major city (Georgetown) and the sugar belt towns – New Amsterdam, Corriverton, and Rosehall – are integrated with rice and sugar. This is not an attempt to downplay the presence of other crops in Guyana's history and memory; rather it seeks to explain the organic historical relationship between these crops and the two dominant ethnic groups on the coast, Afro- and Indo-Guyanese.

This chapter is divided into four main sections. The first focuses on the ways in which the lifeways of Africans and East Indians in rural Guyana became interwoven with the mono-crop sugar industry. The second addresses the historical connection between land laws and labour control, and the third section traces the connection between Africans and East Indians and rice. Against the backdrop of Guyana's slavish attachment to the International Monetary Fund's (IMF) prescription of economic liberalisation, the concluding section examines the impact of structural adjustment and its linkages to the ongoing crisis of the rice and sugar industries, primarily marked by the recent redundancy of thousands of sugar workers and small rice farmers.

Sugar Monoculture and the Structure of Life in Rural Guyana

The undulating fortunes of the working class cannot be understood without reference to the fact that the local economy, or production, evolved historically as an appendage of the global capitalist economy; in Guyana's case, primarily the nineteenth century sugar revolution.[1]

The guiding historical narrative that Africans were first brought to Guyana to work on the sugar plantations is not strictly accurate. From initial Dutch occupation in the seventeenth century until British rule from 1802, the colony boasted a multi-crop economy. Coffee, cotton and sugar were exported to Europe, and the enslaved grew a multiplicity of food crops in plantation gardens and provision grounds. In the shadow of the abolition of the trade in enslaved Africans (1806), the death of mercantilism, and the rise of free trade, Guyana lost its competitive advantage in coffee production to Brazil and cotton to the US.[2] Within this global economic cauldron, sugar became king in colonial Guyana. Although Cuba had become the premier Caribbean sugar producer by the mid-nineteenth century, colonial sugar production in Guyana survived owing to natural advantages – fertility of soil and favourable topography.

The contribution of working people of African descent to the sugar industry and the formation of the coastal landscape is captured in the seminal works of Walter Rodney (1981) and Emilia Viotti Da Costa (1994). Rodney noted that the construction of Guyana's coastal drainage and irrigation system must have entailed the moving, by enslaved people, of at least '100 million tons of heavy, waterlogged clay with shovel in hand, while enduring conditions of perpetual mud and water.'[3]

While Rodney brings to life the role of African labour in creating habitable space – towns and villages on the banks of the main rivers and the Atlantic coast – Viotti da Costa details how super exploitation of African labour between 1806 and 1838 accounted for the rise, growth and survival of sugar monoculture, and captures the draconian regimentation of African labour in the formative phases of the sugar industry:

> From the time Demerara was integrated into the British Empire, the slaves' condition of living and perceptions have been changing in significant ways...massive capital investment transformed the landscape and altered both the nature of plantation life and the slaves' experience. With British capital came new machinery, a more intense pace of work, new ideas, and a new style of living...for the slaves all these changes meant longer hours of work, a faster pace of labor, less time to cultivate their own gardens and provision grounds or to go to church and the market, diminishing supplies of food and clothing, more rigorous supervision and punishment, and more frequent separation from family and kin (Viotti da Costa 1994, 39–40).

In Guyana, colonial capital employed every coercive tactic already in use in Europe, and plantations mimicked the rise of new management approaches to labour control. Where workers in industrialising Europe were dispossessed of their connections to the land, the enslaved in Guyana were forcibly disconnected through the labour process from their provision grounds, that 'space of accommodation' (Mintz 2013) that enabled some relative independence within slave society. Regimentation and loss of independence were primary factors that produced the 1823 slave rebellion, one of the 'greatest slave uprisings in the history of the New World' (Viotti da Costa 1994), which was brutally repressed.[4]

Guyana's history is replete with accounts of the struggles of slaves, indentured labourers and workers for rights within the confines of the plantation. Many wonder why Guyana progressed to sugar monoculture while territories such as Jamaica diversified their economies away from sugar. Guyana's unique ecological circumstances favoured the adoption of industrial era technologies. Despite the acknowledged paucity of labour, on account of the country's geographical expanse, the steam engine and the vacuum pan and other innovations were successfully deployed for sugar production. The vacuum pan, invented in 1813, was installed at Richmond and Land of Plenty on the Essequibo and at Vreed-en-Hoop on the West Demerara by 1832. By 1862, as a result of the technical improvements driven by the vacuum pan, the now famed Demerara sugar 'established a reputation for having the best grain' (Beachey 1957, 74) and the trade-name 'Demerara Crystals' emerged.[5]

The high quality of Guyana's sugar products raised the stakes for investment capital and this circumstance predetermined the fate of enslaved Africans emerging from bondage in the late 1830s. The freedom and independence which the African population eked out for themselves in the first ten years after Emancipation were stymied, in many instances, as capital engaged in its quest for the cheapest possible labour. This quest predated emancipation but quickened as the ex-slave population asserted their rights to equality.

Beginning in the 1840s, new but important markers shaped the relations between labour and capital. The imposition of competing groups within the plantation workforce altered and circumscribed the formerly enslaved population's quest for equal rights. It also altered and affected the right to work, to a living wage and decent work conditions, the right to independent thought and action, the right to own land and to develop autonomous economic activities, and the right to own and conduct business. The economic stagnation of many villages dominated by people of African descent in the immediate post-emancipation period is directly related to the way their rights became circumscribed by the servile relationship between capital and indentureship. And it was because of the circumscription of the rights of the ex-enslaved population, that the sugar industry became synonymous with East Indian labour.

Historical discourses on Guyana persistently link East Indians to sugar. Admittedly, this segment of the population emerged as the labouring majority in that industry after 1848. Nevertheless, East Indians did not found the industry, nor did they save it. The more accurate premise is that East Indian indentured labourers supplanted the majority African labourers in field and factory, and by accepting abysmally low wages, compromised the struggle for equality and helped consolidate the pernicious structure of inequality between labour and the sugar plantocracy. The importation of East Indians, Portuguese, and Chinese was not related to the so-called 'flight' of African labour from the plantation in Guyana. Rather, the movement of Africans away from plantation housing, first, and later from plantation work, is connected to the ferment of their struggle for independent thought and action, especially in the first ten years after emancipation (Rodney 1981; Rose 1990). Here, it is necessary to examine some of the more pertinent external factors that helped structure Guyana's social, economic, political, and cultural relationships during that period and beyond.

A significant global factor that directly impacted Guyana's history was the imposition of the Sugar Duties Act 1846, which equalized duties on home-grown sugar produced in the British colonies with those on slave grown sugar entering the British market. This opened the way for sugar produced by the enslaved in Cuba and Brazil, mainly, to compete with sugar from British colonies where emancipation had occurred and which had opted to expand sugar production. Up to that time, Guyanese and other British colonial sugar producers enjoyed preferential access to the British market. But the passage of the Act in 1846 prompted the termination of lines of credit for the planting interests in the British colonies and forced Guyanese planters to match the lower costs associated with sugar produced via enslaved labour. This turn of events proved disastrous for the emerging working class in the British sugar colonies as workers strove to compete in a global market artificially boosted by the enslaved.

The Sugar Duties Act reduced the profitability of plantations and caused financial upheaval within the banking and finance industry that catered to the Caribbean. Many estates lost support for their payroll obligations and, in this cesspool, the formerly enslaved were not only forced to go for long periods without pay but were asked to accept a wage cut of 25 per cent.[6] This put an end to their efforts at collective bargaining for better wages and led to the famous sugar strike of 1847–48. Although the bulk of the African workforce answered the call, the strike ended as a failure, as the combined presence of East Indian and Portuguese contract labourers served as replacements for them. The majority of those who had remained living on the plantations up to the time of the strike opted to leave. From June 1847 to December 1848, 15,443 labourers left the estates to reside in villages and the sparsely populated hinterland of Guyana (Adamson 1970; 1972, 36–37). After 1848, the free villages were overcrowded with workers who had rejected low wages, and who abandoned plantation housing and work in the sugar industry altogether. The villages mostly affected were in Demerara, the locus of expanding sugar production. Abandonment of plantation housing by the majority of the formerly enslaved population opened these spaces for occupation by East Indian contract labourers, importation of whom expanded. This was a major turning point in the sugar industry, as East Indians emerged as the ethnic majority within the workforce of the sugar industry, the only employer outside of the local colonial administration. In this climate, Africans became the minority within the labouring workforce. They competed for employment on plantations which were without their full complement of contract labour for tasks at which they were most skilled – shovel work.[7] Indentured East Indians did not just supplant Africans in the workforce; their acceptance of low wages effectively blunted the capacity of African workers to struggle for a basic living wage in the society (Rodney 1981, 42–44).

After 1850 a new dispensation surfaced. The bulk of the African population subsisted on whatever they produced in the overcrowded villages, while the majority of East Indian workers enjoyed the circumscribed privileges of regular employment in the sugar industry. Both groups were at the mercy of the Portuguese shopkeepers who seized control of the retail trade in the 1840s following the recognition by the ruling planter class of the need for a buffer group between the dark-skinned workers and themselves. In any situation, as Karl Marx points out, low wages can only be kept low if there is an army of unemployed ready and willing to work.[8] Sugar's survival depended in large measure on the construction, maintenance, and evolution of the African labour force as a perpetual army of unemployed people.

Sugar monoculture could not have been sustained without the decay that consumed the villages after 1850. Effectually, one segment of the population was sacrificed in order for sugar to survive. Governments and states have always engaged in social engineering and, invariably, this serves the ruling class. In 1848, African sugar workers were also defeated by the paramountcy of the market and by land laws – another mechanism adopted to keep them in check during the period 1836–98 – and both contrivances were deployed to address the labour question in colonial Guyana.

The Land Market and Labour – The Ancestral Rights Conundrum

Two sets of land laws emerged in the post-emancipation period. The first of these locked the formerly enslaved within the plantation zone. The second, which emerged in the early 1850s, was specifically designed to address the problem of title and ownership. The 1848 exodus from the sugar plantations caused the areas close by to became overcrowded, and these laws heightened the fragmentation from which the villages and the African community are yet to recover.[9]

The Land Ordinance of 1836 (expanded in 1839) limited the sale of 'Crown Lands' (state owned lands beyond the Crown Dam) to parcels of 100 acres at one British pound per acre.[10] This law was further amended in 1851 and again in 1861, when the purchase price was raised to five and ten dollars per acre respectively. Even before emancipation, the planter-run government was thinking about land control. The land laws first enacted in 1836 served to regulate the labour market through domination over all un-alienated Crown Lands in the colony. This policy made it almost impossible for the African population to acquire Crown Lands.[11] These laws were prohibitive in the sense that they served to debar the African population from venturing outside the poldered coastal region. This stifled significant movement of Africans away from the plantation zone, which may have allowed for the growth of a more diversified economy and the establishment of new industries like those established in Jamaica by the formerly enslaved. Added to this prohibition was the unwritten addendum which permitted planters to extend their cultivations beyond the boundary of the Crown Dam, a respite not afforded villagers in that time period. This law was further amended in 1898, reducing the price for the Crown Lands to 15 and 25 cents per acre, to accommodate the exodus of East Indian labour from the crisis-ridden sugar plantations.[12]

A second tranche of land laws was enacted over the years 1851, 1852 and 1856 which further constricted the African people in their quest for new found independence. These laws prevented groups of more than 20 from joining together to purchase lands, and required that all lands purchased by more than 10 persons be partitioned (Ramsahoye 1966).[13] These new measures prevented the growth of cooperative styled entities. Notably, in the 1840s, the first villagers in the post-emancipation period pooled their resources to purchase abandoned estates, intending to mimic the plantation layout by establishing them as joint enterprises. The new laws did not only stymie the dreams of the village founders, but also fragmented the villages by effectively converting the plots into small, unworkable parcels. The economic intent of the land laws was clear. Whereas the first set of laws dealing with Crown Lands sought to bind free Africans to the plantation zone, the second set met the planters' demands for ready access to cheap labour. The laws ultimately curtailed the progress of the village movement by constraining the development of communal villages and by curbing the expansion of existing villages.

Any commitment to righting historical wrongs in Guyana must revisit the village problem. Factors such as ecology and topography which informed the original planation layout must be taken into account. A primary historical problem is that the villages of the formerly enslaved were established and superimposed on infrastructural spaces designed and constructed to mitigate the effects of flooding of the cultivable coastal lands. Thereafter, superimposition of the village footprint on plantation space was compounded by colonial land laws which subdivided village plots into smaller parcels. These subdivisions created enormous hardships for the villagers and presented serious impediments to progress. Villagers could not mimic plantation organisation to work the land cooperatively, or as corporate entities. Subdivision made it impossible for the African villages to thrive economically owing to distance between land parcels, and more importantly, the problems which fragmented lands posed to the organisation and maintenance of effective drainage. The varying quality of soils and the topography of each village plot compounded the problems after sub-division was effected, primarily with upkeep of dams, and clearance of outfalls to allow free drainage of excess water to the sea. Cecil Clementi's 1848 *Constitutional History of British Guiana* captures the essence of the structural problem which rendered the villages unworkable agricultural and settlement units, as they were situated 'in the plantation'.

No individual villager could cultivate his plot with success unless the whole system of main drainage throughout the estate was kept in order. So long, therefore, as the drainage system with which the plantation was provided at the time of purchase remained in good order, it was not impossible that the new village situated in the plantation should prosper (281–82).

Figure 8.1 shows the layout of two post-emancipation proprietary villages, overlaid by a rendering of the original plantation layout.

Figure 8.1: Plan number 16852 dated March 31, 1973

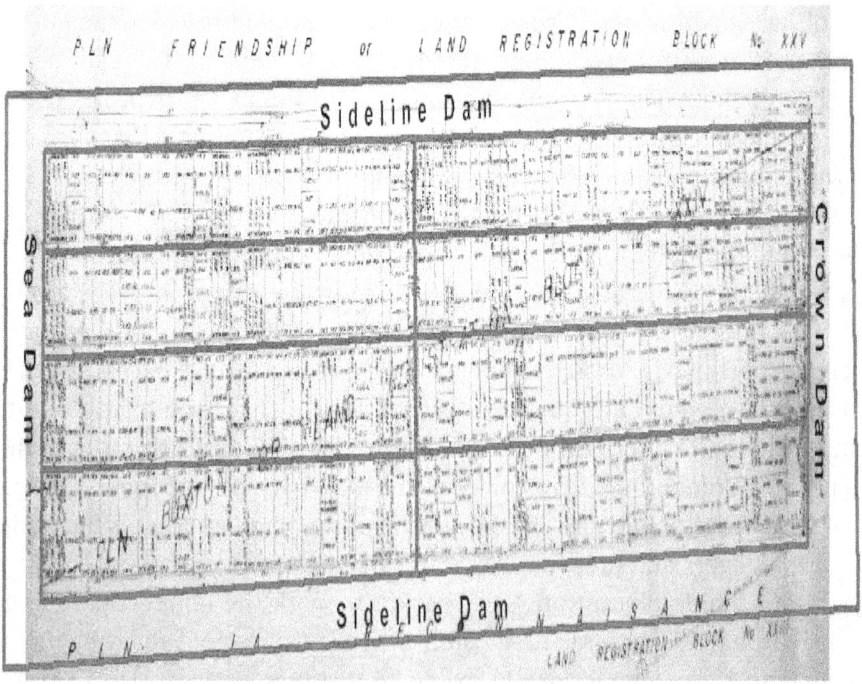

Source: Registry of the Guyana Lands and Surveys Department.

This rendering presents a graphic demonstration of the level of village fragmentation. The plan outlines parcels 1,335 to 2,138 of Plantation Buxton, a proprietary village which was bought in 1841 by 128 Africans and sub-divided into 2,138 parcels. In every village, lands are sub-divided according to topographic quality and fertility of soil. Partitioning arrangements ensured that each shareholder of the original purchase received equal amounts of 'good' and 'bad' land. This, in its turn, produced a high level of fragmentation in the villages, from which they are yet to recover after more than 150 years. While the size of the plots presented problems of its own, it was the distance between them and the issue of water control which presented bigger hurdles. Moreover, figure 1 does not show the subsequent sub-divisions of the already fragmented plots on account of inheritance, by which plots were passed down to children and grandchildren of the original purchasers. It also does not account for sub-divisions based on individual sale to subsequent buyers after the passage of the land laws of 1852 and 1856.

The foregoing is a brief expose of how land was co-opted as a means of labour control, which kept wages low, and which was essential to ensure sugar's survival. Prosperity within the African villages would have been viewed by the sugar barons as detrimental to the control which they needed to maintain over the captive indentured labour force. Without doubt, this is the reason that no alternative crop or export industry to rival sugar was permitted until the global sugar crisis intervened towards the end of the nineteenth century. The Afro-Guyanese population suffered the most from sugar's dominance over land and the economy. However, to fully show sugar's dominance over alternative crops, it is necessary to examine the undulating history of rice, especially during the course of the nineteenth century.

Africans and East Indians and Rice

Owing to Guyana's focus on sugar and its stranglehold on the economy in the nineteenth century, the enslaved and formerly enslaved populations were not only prevented from planting rice officially, but were also restrained by force of arms from doing so unofficially.[14] Unlike other areas of the Caribbean, in Guyana, the planter class neither permitted nor sanctioned agricultural diversification. It curtailed the growth of provision grounds and by the 1820s had smashed efforts by the enslaved to establish maroon communities in the interior. The records show that in many of these communities in the far reaches of the Abary, Mahaica, and Mahaicony rivers, the enslaved had organized their lives around the production of rice. British Militia Captain Charles Edmonstone, who stumbled on a maroon community in the Abary-Mahaicony district during an escapade to capture runaway slaves, found well-cultivated rice fields and 14 houses filled with rice, which he estimated could have fed 700 men for an entire year (Thompson 1987, 143).

Rice is a staple of Africa's 'Rice Coast' and was among the crops around which resistance and accommodation centred in the Americas during the long colonial period. It was one of many food crops that crisscrossed the Atlantic in the Columbian Exchange (Carney 2001A, 377–96). The proliferation of rice as a crop of the poor and those marginalized by the colonial economy meant that it became integral to the life and survival of the enslaved, free people, the indentured and their descendants, and the Indigenous people throughout the region. For several centuries it was produced primarily on minuscule patches of land by small-scale farmers (variously described as 'proto-peasants', 'paddy proletariat', and small-scale farmers – who comprise approximately 75 per cent of rice producers in the region).[15]

In her excavations Judith Carney establishes that rice came to the Americas with the enslaved.[16] Knowledge of the history of rice in Central and Latin America, especially among the indigenous communities, can deepen our understanding of its role in shaping indigenous development trajectories. It is now confirmed that indigenous and African crops were exchanged during the slave trade and that rice slowly became a staple of much of the region of the Americas outside of the US and Canada. This is especially true with respect to the cultural connection reflected in the fusion between rice and beans in the region into the dietary cuisine of the Black and Indigenous communities. A resistance crop that survived sugar monoculture, today, rice is the food of choice and, in many cases, of necessity for surviving Afro and Indigenous (Amerindian) communities across Central America, Brazil, Latin America, and Mexico.

In Guyana, rice did not survive as an African crop. Every effort by Africans in Guyana to grow rice even after emancipation was met with planter resistance: first, owing to the clash with the harvest times with sugar; and second because of the problems of drainage and irrigation in the villages and the inhospitable atmosphere that existed between sugar and rice husbandry. Sketchy reports suggest that in the decade after slavery ended, some attempts by small groups of ex-slaves to produce rice came to an abrupt end because of the clash of reaping times between rice and sugar (Russell 1886, 102–3).

The predominance of East Indians in the rice industry today is more a result of the local impact of global change than a representation of cultural identity.[17] Africans trafficked to the Americas, including Guyana, were as familiar with rice cultivation and rice culture as were the East Indians and Chinese recruited from India and China as indentured (contract) labourers.[18] The differences reside within the practices of enslavement. In the formative period of freedom, when the ex-slaves created personal spaces in the form of free villages, they were denied the freedom of engaging in rice production because of the demands of sugar. The intersection of the global sugar trade and the continuance of slavery in the new sugar colonies (Cuba, Brazil, the US, and Puerto Rico) were the catalysts that kept African people (enslaved and free) in Guyana, from meaningful involvement with rice during the nineteenth century, before and after emancipation. In contrast, indentured East Indians were grudgingly allowed to plant rice on the margins of the sugar plantations (1865–97) as a means of subsidising and reducing the cost of their food imports. The discrepancies with regard to access to land as described earlier characterized the racialisation of Guyanese society. The inequity surrounding the growth and development of the rice industry illustrates a central problem of Guyanese history.

From Subsistence to Small-farming Rice Peasantry

Reasons for East Indian dominance in the rice industry cannot therefore be restricted to cultural awareness and agency. Issues such as cost of and manipulation of labour, adaptability of land, and tacit administrative policies that supported cultivation must be considered. The rice industry did not just emerge because it was part of the Indian culture; it emerged to serve the interests of the sugar dominated economy. Its emergence, rise, and growth were connected to sugar's interest, as well as to the growing acceptance by the planter class of its compatibility with plantation space and the long-term economic plans.

Although rice was being planted by East Indians from as early as 1865, it was not until the sugar crisis began to take its toll on the economy in the 1880s and 1890s that East Indians were allowed to commence large scale production of the crop. As Potter (1992, 3) observed, acceptability of rice's compatibility with sugar within the plantation space evolved over a 30-year period (1865–94). The first part of this evolution had to do with planter support, though limited over the first 30 years, which came from prominent planters such as William Russell and later A. R. Gilzean (Ruhomon 1989, 170). The second related to the role of rice in subsidising the overall sugar economy. The third relates to depressed wages in the sugar industry and the need for subsistence enterprise on the part of the labourer, who was able, through access to minuscule parcels of land on the margins of the sugar zone, to supplement his household budget. Finally this evolution had to do with the adaptability of marginal, unused land for rice cultivation; this is a complex undertaking and a main reason that subsistence rice cultivation, where permitted by estate owners, was carried out only on marginal lands with some access to water (Potter 1992, 2).

The shift in the planters' attitude to rice marked a transformative turn in Guyana's history. Earlier, sugar planters had discouraged rice production because it was felt to be incompatible with sugar cultivation (Whitfield 1872, 9). Despite the shift in planter mindset, cultivation was constrained by the way coastal plantations were structured and by the draconian control planters exercised over land ownership and land use. Although the psychological barrier to rice cultivation was being lowered, resident indentured labourers who wanted to engage in rice cultivation between 1865 and 1894 had to contend with similar constraints experienced by the African workforce with regards to where and how much land they could access. Like their African counterparts, they could not expand, nor think about expanding rice cultivation beyond subsistence production. From this standpoint, permissible rice cultivation within the sugar plantation zone between 1865 and 1894 in many ways mimicked ground provision cultivation in the pre-emancipation period, and village subsistence activities carried out by the African population of the villages after 1838.

Rice emerged out of economic necessity, first as a subsistence crop. Subsistence activity occurred in four phases. First, the planter class relaxed its psychological objections to rice but did not promote its cultivation. In the second phase from 1884 to 1894, when faced with the possibility of total collapse of the sugar industry, the planters began to promote rice cultivation through the release of 'estate front lands' (Potter 1992, 2). In that period, approximately 2,500 acres of rice was being cultivated (Nath

1950, 260). As the sugar crisis deepened, more land was gradually released within the plantation zone for rice cultivation. The change was dramatic. By 1897, 15,500 acres of rice was being cultivated, four fifths of which were either on front lands of existing plantations or on abandoned plantations (Potter 1992, 3). In the third phase, in areas such as the Essequibo coast from which the sugar industry had begun to retreat, abandoned estates were converted to rice. This process coincided with the fourth phase of expansion that occurred between 1898 and 1920. Rice cultivation increased from 15,500 acres in 1897 to 47,037 acres by 1914, and 61,200 acres by 1919 (Nath 1950, 110–11; Potter 1992).

To understand the expansion of rice cultivation one must take note of the push factor, that is the release of 'excess' labour and 'excess' land from the sugar industry, a direct result of the global sugar crisis which began to take effect in the mid-1880s. The exodus of labour and land from the stranglehold of the sugar barons provided the impetus for the growth the rice industry, especially in 1897 and beyond. This crisis impelled the colonial-inspired plan to entice the East Indian immigrants to remain in the colony, and thus land was either given in lieu of return passages, or made available at concessionary rates. As Lesley Potter (1992) points out, the sharp rise in production after 1894 was related to the sugar crisis and the decision to open up the bottlenecks which had prevented diversification of the economy. Ordinary East Indian rice farmers became the beneficiaries of concessions to promote an export crop. Undoubtedly, this changed the economic dynamic between the two groups of labourers in Guyana.

In the fourth phase also, it became legally permissible for agricultural activity to extend beyond the plantation zone, which is beyond the lands which were encumbered by sugar, and which were empoldered. Colonial Ordinance 10 of 1898 released Crown Lands which had been the preserve of the planter class since slavery ended. Under the terms of this ordinance, the price for grants of Crown Lands by purchase of up to 100 acres was reduced to 15 cents per acre, and homestead plots (25-acre maximum) were priced at 10 cents per acre (Potter 1992). This ordinance was further amended in 1903 reducing the maximum plot size to 25 acres and homestead grants to five acres. The East Indian population took full advantage of this windfall. Those who had completed their indentured contracts accepted land grants from the colonial authorities in lieu of return passages; and those with additional savings cashed in as land became cheap and readily available as the sugar crisis worsened, and as pressure mounted for Crown Lands to be made accessible to other segments of the population. East Indians who had completed their periods of indenture seized the opportunity to move away from the empoldered coastal area into fertile, outlying coastal districts in Mahaica, Mahaicony, and the riverain areas of the Corentyne (Potter 1992, 2–13).

The relaxation of the land laws was a landmark occurrence. It altered settlement patterns by opening up lands on the Atlantic Coast which had been legally inaccessible to Africans for 60 years. East Indians who had completed their period of indenture but were marooned on the sugar plantations and on the margins of the plantations were now free to relocate and acquire lands adjacent to existing plantations, and also in former plantation zones from which sugar had receded. Others became tenant cultivators on rice estates in remote districts. Based on evidence that many formerly indentured East Indians had either engaged in cultivation while working as labourers on sugar estates, or as tenants on rice estates, scholars such as Potter (1992) contended that the bulk of rice cultivators between 1884 and 1920 were not merely 'peasants.' Rather, they comprised an emerging 'paddy proletariat'.

Between 1920 and 1970 the rice industry was owned, managed, and maintained by rural based small farmers. In Guyana, a peasantry came into being for the first time after 1920 with the rise of the East Indian rice industry, which the planter class in its self-interest, permitted to develop. There is some confusion as to when East Indian rice growers were able to constitute themselves into a peasantry. Prior to 1920 the majority of rice growers consisted of the 'paddy proletariat'. It was only after 1920 that some separation developed between work on estates and rice production. In this regard, it is easy to establish parallels between the African population and early indentured labourers. The reconstitution of the African population into 'a reserve army of labor' (Mohamed 2008, 214–54) after 1850, and the construction of the paddy proletariat between 1865 and 1920 to reduce the cost of food imports, were directly related to the demand for the cheapest possible labour.

Emergence of Small-farming Rice Industry in Rural Indo- and Afro-Guyanese Villages

By the 1950s, the rice industry became the largest user of land in the country. The paddy proletariat had graduated and a fully formed rice peasantry was in place. Except for pockets of tenant farmers in various parts of the country, the number of rice farmers more than doubled from approximately 10,000 in 1921 (Potter 1992, 9) to 22,156 in 1955 (O'Loughlin 1958, 121). While not enough statistical evidence exists to quantify the number of large and small land holders involved in rice production in 1921, C. O'Loughlin (1958, 121) provides ample evidence to confirm that out of the total number of rice farmers in 1955 (spring crop-small crop), a very small number – 900 – was cultivating plots in excess of 16 acres, while the majority was cultivating plots of less than 15 acres each. In fact, approximately 15,000 farmers were cultivating between two and eight acres and an approximate 5,000 farmers were cultivating less than two acres.[19]

The phenomenal rise in the number of rice farmers after 1950 had a direct link to the processes of democratisation of decision-making in the industry and the struggle for representative democracy at the national level. The birth of the Rice Producers Association in 1946 and the election of the first national government in 1953 were important factors in the expansion of agriculture. During this period, drainage and irrigation matters which had been the preserve of the planter class became national priorities. It is safe to assume that the growth in the industry after 1950 was attributable to the emphasis placed by the national government on drainage and irrigation schemes and on agriculture. The record confirms that after 1950 the number of rice farmers grew steadily and by 1970 had reached its zenith of approximately 40,000. Thereafter, the number has declined steadily, and by the spring crop of 2009 the total stood at 5,324 farmers.[20]

Throughout the twentieth century, the pattern of growth of rice in the Indo-Guyanese villages was matched by growth in many of the rural Afro-Guyanese villages, that is, except for those in close proximity to Georgetown. Six important factors were responsible for the rise of the industry among Indo- and Afro-Guyanese small farmers. First among these was the camaraderie that existed among the villagers. This rapport included, but was not limited to, knowledge sharing. Cooperation between small farmers across racial lines was part and parcel of rural culture. In many villages communal labour exchanges had existed for a long time. Also prominent in this culture of sharing was borrowing and paying back of animals (oxen) used in the production process. The second factor was access to adequate drainage and irrigation, as this slowly emerged as the responsibility of the state.[21] Third was the birth and evolution of extension services, which in 1952 became the responsibility of the ministry of agriculture. Allied to extension services was the birth of the British Guiana Rice Development Company (BGRDC) in 1952, which became the Rice Development Company (RDC) in 1966 and Guyana Rice Corporation in 1969. This governmental entity was responsible for research, production and extension. It aided the rise of the small farmers through its services, chief among which was the provision of such inputs as machinery for field preparation, harvesting, and transport, at concessionary rental rates, which meant that they were free from the encumbrance of massive loans to purchase machinery and equipment which were only necessary during crop time. The fourth factor was the establishment of the Guyana Credit Corporation (GCC) with offices in each district, which enabled small farmers to escape the trap of the unscrupulous moneylenders, who became increasingly active as the rice industry expanded. The Guyana Cooperative Agricultural and Industrial Development Bank (GAIBANK) was established in 1973, giving small farmers access to loans at concessionary rates for the purchase of machinery and related inputs. The fifth factor was the recognition of the importance of cooperatives as a way forward for rural development. Rural cooperatives flowered between 1960 and 1975. The sixth factor was the rise of Land Settlement Schemes (LSS), which initially arose to address the issue of rural unemployment brought about chiefly by the continued consolidation of the sugar industry. The Black Bush Polder LSS, for instance, was intended to lessen the impact of the closure of the Port Mourant sugar factory in the early 1950s (Greenidge 2010, 93–97).

Such potent development-era objectives were thrown out the window in the decade of the 1980s, as Guyana's economy became an appendage to the global capitalist system. As the country accepted and employed the tactics of management of its economy supervised by the International Monetary Fund and the World Bank, these pro-small farmer agencies were either abolished or privatized. Effectually Guyana's small farmers were engulfed by local and global market forces. The haemorrhaging of small rice farmers from the rice industry represents the impact of liberalisation of the economy, a local dimension of global change. The following section gives some insight into the impact of neoliberalism on Guyana's small rice farmers and sugar workers in the midst of what David Harvey (2003) describes as 'accumulation by dispossession', a process that enables the consolidation of corporate style agriculture through privatisation of public supports.

Neoliberalism: Uncertain Futures

As Guyana continues its slavish adherence to the dictates of neoliberal economic policies, working people in rice and sugar are being impoverished. The possibility of achievement of full employment by working people in the sugar industry, and rights to ownership of land for rice production are eroding steadily.

For almost 100 years, between 1897 and 1980, rice cultivation was predominantly small-farmer based. However, the slow transition from small- to large-farmer holdings that started in the 1980s became a deluge as small farmers were expelled due to the exigencies of globally driven market conditions. While many former colonies are in the throes of land grabbing projects sustained by foreign capital (Borras et al. 2011), the Guyana rice industry is enduring a less visible but no less insidious land grab.[22] Lands formerly owned and cultivated by small landholders are being acquired or cultivated by larger farmers either through purchase, prescriptive rights acquisition, outright theft, or land rental.[23] While there is no reliable current census with regard to land ownership and tenure, in some cases the agricultural lands of entire villages are occupied and or cultivated by a clique of capital-endowed farmers.[24] These 'large' farmers, who now occupy most of the rice lands in Guyana, secure leverage through loose rental arrangements, which have opened the proverbial floodgates for illegal transfers and outright theft of lands.[25] Such transfers are not new. The phenomenon is rooted in the aftermath of the global economic crisis of the 1980s, accelerating in the period of economic liberalisation beginning in 1989. Hence while liberalisation has accelerated the process of the demise of the small farmer and of the small farming rural rice culture, these developments had already begun in the 1980s. From the mid-1980s, in the throes of the economic crisis, production, marketing, price, access and availability of rice came under the control of political operatives who wreaked havoc over the rights of farmers to their crops. This is partly reflected in the production figures which nosedived during the Burnham years, 1964–85. The statistics of that period are bleak; the acreage under production fell from 270,000 in 1970 to a low of 126,000 by 1990.

A significant transformation occurred during the 1990–96 period. Rice lands which had been idle for several years were brought back into cultivation, and buoyancy returned to the rice farming areas. This period of relative boom was due to two important factors. First, the easing of political tensions during the Hoyte years (1985–92) engendered sentiments of freedom as social and political forces were now free to speak, mobilize, and contest power. Second was the impetus to satisfy growing demand for Guyana's rice in Europe and the Caribbean. Intra-regionally, Guyana's rice enjoyed immunity from the 20 per cent Common External Tariff (CET), which was imposed on imports originating outside the Caribbean region. And, more especially, the rice boom was driven by the presence of the Other Countries and Territories Route (OCT), through which the greater proportion of Guyana's rice exports entered the European Market unrestricted by the European Union (EU) rice quota and free of duty.[26] Under the OCT arrangement, cargo rice was shipped from Guyana for processing to EU protectorate territories, namely: Curaçao, Bonaire, Aruba, Montserrat, and the Turks and Caicos Islands for partial milling in preparation for shipment to Europe.

Unfortunately, the boom period ended in 1996 and since then the rice industry has been in relative crisis. By the end of 1996–97 all preferential arrangements ended. The EU closed off the OCT loophole, while simultaneously Guyana's preferential access to its regional CARICOM markets was also restricted. In the face of the free trade in agriculture clause of the World Trade Organization (WTO), after 1996 Guyana was forced to scramble for new rice and sugar markets globally. Its main competitors continue to be highly subsidized rice from the US, cheaper rice from Southeast Asia, and higher quality rice from other regional competitors such as Argentina and Uruguay. These visceral shocks sent the industry into a tailspin from 1997, alleviated to some extent by the Petro Caribe arrangement (oil for rice) entered into between the Venezuelan and Guyanese governments in 2005. Despite the reprieve, by the time this preferential access arrangement began, the impact of liberalisation had already taken a heavy toll on the industry, altering the structure of land occupation, and the culture of rural communities, where small farming families had organized their lives around rice production since the opening decades of the twentieth century.

Liberalisation brought catastrophic results for small-scale farmers in Guyana. The calamity for small rice farmers was explained by Fazal Ally –

former general secretary of the Guyana Rice Producers Association (GRPA) – who noted that the number of rice farming families had declined from 45,000 in 1970 to between 15,000 and 20,000 by 1999. Ally clarified that the economic picture was more dismal when consideration was given to the fact that upwards of 70 per cent of the approximately 200,000 acres under cultivation was under the control of 'fewer than five large companies' (*Guyana Review*, August 1999). The drastic reduction in the number of small farmers and the marked rise of large farmers reflect the extent to which the global economy drives changes at the local and community levels. In an interview with an OXFAM Canada team in 2001, Dharamkumar Seeraj, general secretary of the GRPA, noted that with the impact of global change, we are seeing 'the break-up of farming families, because farmers have to leave home to go in search of employment...We see the migration of young potential farmers and qualified people.' Seeraj noted further that this disruption of rural life affected not only the farmer, but the younger members within small farming households who make up the bulk of the rural population:

> We see children called out of school because farming families can no longer afford the cost of transportation, uniforms, and school books. We see cases of suicides, farmers literally dying from the pressures of not being able to pay the banks – heart attacks on the increase, high blood pressure...there are fallouts at all levels. [27]

Since 1996/97, the number of rice farmers has continued to decline. It may be argued that Petro Caribe – started in 2005 – brought some stability to the industry as production grew exponentially. However, the plight of small farmers remained unchanged and the industry continued to lose this critical demographic.[28] Based on the analysis of the 2009 Farmer's Register of the Guyana Rice Development Board (GRDB) for the first crop, the number of farmers declined to 5,324.[29] These figures correspond with a changing pattern of land concentration within the rice industry. In the absence of reliable statistics for the 1970s, if land holding patterns between 1954 and 1955 (or the period before the LSS) and 2009 are compared, the average farm size in the former is revealed as six acres per rice farming family, whereas in 2009 this had risen to 29 acres per family. What is more revealing is that when the statistics provided by O'Loughlin (1958, 121) are compared with the Guyana Development Board's Register for 2009, where in 1954 there was a maximum of 274 rice landholders planting acreages in excess of 32 acres, in 2009 there were 1,160 rice landholders (farmers) who planted acreages between 31 and in excess of 1,000 acres. Further, when compared with 1954/55, the number of farmers cultivating between one and 31 acres in 2009 declined from an approximate 26,709 (1954) to 4,164 (2009).

These figures are representative of the growing problem in which the number of rice farmers cultivating larger acreages and the total acreage under cultivation increases as the number of small farmers decreases. Since 1999, the acreage under cultivation has more than doubled.[30] Where have the small farmers gone? The short answer is migration. A more complete explanation rests with the transfer of rights to occupation through sale, prescriptive rights acquisition, land theft, and rentals. The issue of land theft is currently under investigation by the Guyana Lands Commission of Inquiry of 2017–18, and here it is pertinent to point out a factual concern regarding the impact of this shift on ethnic disparity with regards to land occupation. While the changes that occurred between 1955 and 1980 helped create a more equitable arrangement that enabled small farmers from historical African and East Indian villages – notably No. 51, Vergenoegen, Seafield, Lichfield, Bushlot, Queenstown, Dartmouth, Ledestein, and Greenwich Park – to access machinery and support, current changes have opened the gate for takeovers. In this climate, small rice farmers in many villages are being obliterated.[31]

The reduction in the number of small farmers is related to the hefty unit costs of production, lack of access to affordable credit, machinery, and inputs. These structural impediments are directly connected to economic liberalisation policies that have resulted in the privatisation of the public support system for rice. Hence, many small farmers – those still residing in the rice-growing communities and those who have migrated – have resorted to renting out their plots to big farmers who have access to capital, machinery, and other support. In areas such as the Essequibo coast where small rice farmers are still in the majority, many now rely on the established millers for financial support, becoming increasingly tied to them in a kind of loose contractual and/or semi-feudal relationship. The past has returned in that working people who were born into sugar now face new vulnerabilities.[32]

Sugar has been in a recurring crisis since the 1880s. The current crisis in sugar is not new and, in many ways, is similar to the crisis with rice. The problem faced by both industries is the cost of production. So long as preferential access existed for rice and sugar to the EU market, successive national governments ignored the need for long-term planning and diversification. Hence, the structure of the rice and sugar industries remained as colonial appendages with all the trappings and management style of that period. According to the Report of the Commission of Inquiry for the Guyana Sugar Corporation (2015), a characteristic problem centres on market volatility, compounded and enlarged by loss of preferential access which, in turn, demands reductions in production and associated operating costs. Here, the discussion will expound on the neoliberal structure of management which emerges as a foil for corrupt practices at many levels. The report fails, for example, to consider the existing system of procurement involving contracting and subcontracting out of essential industry services, which leaves the industry open to corrupt practices that could drain its scarce resources. The problems in rice and sugar cannot be blamed only on loss of markets and geophysical constraints. All the issues cited in the report started and worsened in the era of liberalisation, yet there is no mention of the changes in management approaches that have impacted the industry negatively since 1990.

The changes in the rice and sugar industries will continue to impact both the national economy and households in every village. Evidently, Guyana is not tackling the challenge in the best possible ways. In real time, the sugar industry is being downsized, and thousands of sugar working families are being made redundant. This is not the first time since 1980 that workers have been relegated to the breadlines en masse. There was the redeployment of public servants after the IMF deals of the early 1980s, which helped to produce the informal economy of street vendors. There was also the retrenchment of bauxite workers in the early 1980s, and the downsising which followed divestment of many state companies after the Economic Recovery Programme budget of 1989 that cemented the neoliberal structure in the management of the country.

Selling sugar lands to private speculators can only precipitate an even greater imbalance in the ownership of resources. Such approaches extend inequality gaps and increase food insecurity among vulnerable sections of the population. Global institutions and organisations such as the Food and Agricultural Organization (FAO) point to efficacy of small landholders over large-scale agricultural enterprises. Both rice and sugar are global crops that emerged in the colonial period and which sustained the livelihoods of workers as well as entire communities. Both crops gave rise to the dependent relationship between the colonial power and the colony. Hence, in the dying days of colonialism, the colonial powers acting in concert with former colonies established multilateral trading agreements, such as the Lomé Convention, which served to guarantee preferential access to these products.[33] While these agreements presented the framework for continued economic sustenance of countries like Guyana, they maintained the neocolonial structure of production relations in the country. This presented a false sense of security and, as sugar's fortune began to wane as Lomé was coming to an end, the WTO came into being during the tenure of the Hoyte administration. It was President Hoyte who first alerted the nation to the fact that sugar faced an impending crisis, and that tough decisions were required. But because of Guyana's ethnic politics, tough decisions eluded and continue to elude the political directorates. Clearly, Guyana has no need for a new class of big landowners as seen in the rice industry. Fifty years after independence, Guyana finds itself at the crossroads, seemingly adrift in a sea of unrelenting change and crisis.

Guyana needs boldness. It can produce managed development of a diversified agriculture for the new global market through involvement of its people (Afro- and Indo-Guyanese). Guyana can be innovative. Divestment is the way of the international bankers, but it should not be Guyana's way. The sugar lands could be leased in a managed manner for small-farm production. If sugar is diversified by bringing the people into the process in a well-organized and managed way, the macro and microeconomies can be protected, food security increased for the bulk of the population, and the food sovereignty of the people safeguarded. The current approach of handing over the resources of the abandoned sugar estates to the government butcher, National Industrial and Commercial Investments Limited (NICIL), can only lead to further disaster. Privatisation of public resources and of public supports is not the answer.

What is needed is greater participatory decision-making. The top down market oriented system, wherein the belief is that the centre of progress is private investment and privatisation of the commons, must end. Guyana is faced with crises in every major industry. The people did not produce these crises; private capital did, but it is only by putting the people first can these crises be solved.

Notes

1. The sugar revolution was characterised by monoculture and the immiseration of labour and loss of crop diversity. See Mohamed 2016 in *New Frontiers of Slavery*.
2. With the expansion of slavery in Brazil and the US south, they emerged as the world's primary producer and supplier of coffee and cotton respectively.
3. Walter Rodney, *A History of the Guianese Working People, 1881–1905* (Baltimore: Johns Hopkins University Press, 1981), 2–3.
4. The uprisings began at Success and eventually spread and consumed 60 sugar estates on the narrow East Demerara coastal plain.
5. This history, memory, and patent no longer resides in Guyana. 'Demerara Crystals' is available in supermarkets worldwide, but Guyana does not benefit from the deserved royalty. It is to be expected that a truly independent government would emerge to struggle for this patent to be returned to the country.
6. See correspondence from Governor Light to Lord Grey, January 18, 1848-C.O. 111/249.
7. See Rodney (1981) on the workings of the independent task gangs.
8. See Francis Green, 'The Reserve Army Hypothesis: A Survey of Empirical Applications,' in *Quantitative Marxism*, ed. Paul Dunne, 123–40 (Cambridge: Polity Press, 1991).
9. My submission to the Guyana Land Commission of Inquiry (November 23, 2017) was an attempt to articulate this history, and to affirm that the resolution to the African (ancestral) lands issue lies in acknowledgement of the problems of history, and in empowering discourses that can lead to equity with regards to land occupation and ownership.
10. Alan Adamson, 'Monoculture and Village Decay in British Guiana: 1854–1872,' *Journal of Social History* 111, no. 4 (1970): 386–405.
11. Alan Young, *The Approaches to Local Self-Government in British Guiana* (London: Longman, Green, 1958), 10. Gibbon Wakefield was a British Colonial official who first implemented land policies in Australia and New Zealand as a means of labour control.
12. Incidentally, the exodus became the impetus for the rice industry.
13. Land ordinance number 4 of 1851, number 1 of 1852, and number 33 of 1856 were enacted with the clear intent of restricting any further communal purchases.
14. This work addresses what happens with Africans and rice during the period of the sugar revolution, when Africans did not have support and opportunity to plant rice. It does not cover the history before 1800, a period when the enslaved had some opportunity to plant rice within the plantations to meet subsistence needs. See articles by Winston McGowan published in *Stabroek News*, November 18, 2008.
15. See in particular Sidney Mintz's (2013) discourse on the question of 'Caribbean Peasantries.' Also see Lesley Potter, 'The Paddy Proletariat and the Dependent Peasantry,' *History Gazette* 47. Further, thanks to the excavations of Judith

Carney 2001 and 2004, it is widely acknowledged that rice came to the Americas with the enslaved. In 'Grains in Her Hair,' she explained that 'rice cultivation provides a signature of the black (non-white) Atlantic,' and that rice links the Upper Guinea Coast to the Americas. Africans, Amerindians, and their respective knowledge systems in the production of rice shaped the early development of the rice industry both as a plantation and subsistence crop. Such new evidence indicates some fusion of African and Amerindian knowledge systems in the production and proliferation of subsistence crops, including rice in the highlands of Central and Latin America (parts of Spanish America). The history of rice in Central and Latin America, especially among the indigenous communities can deepen our understanding of its role in shaping indigenous development trajectories. It is now confirmed that that Amerindian and African crops were exchanged during the period of the slave trade and, from this exchange, rice slowly became a staple of much of the region of the Americas outside of the US and Canada. This is especially true with respect to the cultural connection reflected in the fusion between rice and beans in the region into the dietary cuisine of the black and indigenous communities. Today, rice is the produce of choice and in many cases of necessity for surviving indigenous Afro and Amerindian communities across Central America, Brazil, Latin America, and Mexico.

16. In 'Grains in Her Hair,' Carney explained that 'rice cultivation provides a signature of the black (non-white) Atlantic,' and that rice links the Upper Guinea Coast to the Americas (Carney 2004, 22). Africans, Amerindians, and their respective knowledge systems in the production of rice shaped the early development of the rice industry both as a plantation and subsistence crop.
17. It has been argued by some scholars, especially Dwarka Nath (1950, 110) that the reason Africans are not involved as they should in the rice industry is because of what he describes as lack of knowledge of rice culture.
18. The best example that brings out the relationship between the enslaved and rice culture is the construction of rice plantations in the Low Country of South Carolina in the seventeenth century. This is extensively discussed by Judith Carney in 'Black Rice,' 2001B.
19. There is always a differential in the number of farmers cultivating the spring and autumn crops. Hence, according to the figures presented by O'Loughlin (1958), the number of farmers engaged in cultivation of the spring crop of 1955 was lower than that which had cultivated the autumn crop of 1954. For the autumn crop of 1954, there were 4,827 more producers than had been engaged in spring 1955.
20. Guyana Rice Development Board's Farmers Register for 2009.
21. This was a prominent theme that was addressed by the Moyne Commission. The Moyne Commission of inquiry (1934–39) was established by the Imperial British Empire to examine the factors that lead to labour unrest and make recommendations on the future of the British Colonies of the Anglophone Caribbean.

22. The issue of global land grabs is widely examined in the literature. See summaries of this problem in reports published by Grain.org. For instance, at https://www.grain.org/article/entries/5492-the-global-farmland-grab-in-2016-how-big-how-bad.
23. Although rice lands formerly owned and occupied by small farmers in Regions, 3, 4, 5, and 6 are now occupied by large farmers, because of loose rental arrangements, records at local authority Neighbourhood Democratic Council (NDC) offices continue to show owners, rather than occupiers. In many cases the land tax to the local authority is paid by the occupiers for the original owners, many of whom live outside of Guyana. Further, acquisition of other peoples titled land through prescriptive titles application to the courts became a more common practice over the last 20 years. But because of the charges of corruption within the system, inclusive of collusion between moneyed people, people in the legal fraternity and in the judicial system; prescriptive rights application is now not as prevalent as three to four years ago.
24. The takeover or occupation by the few of lands of the many is prevalent across the Regions, but is more pronounced in Regions 3, 4, 5, and 6. While it exists in Region 2, this is the only region to retain the bulk of its small farmers.
25. I am being deliberately general here. This is because the Land Commission of Inquiry currently in session has received information on these matters and is expected to investigate and report to the government.
26. *Guyana Review* 79 (August 1999): 15–17.
27. See excerpt of this interview in Challenging the Rice Industry – https://www.oxfam.ca/sites/default/files/oxfam-canada-annual-report-2001.pdf.
28. Millers reaped the harvest from the Petro Caribe deal. In most parts of the country, the benefits were not transferred to small farmers, many of whom suffered from lack of payment for paddy supplied.
29. This latter figure represents the number of farmers who cultivated the spring crop of 2009. This number, though somewhat higher when the number of cultivators for autumn 2009 is considered, does not alter the downward trajectory. It represents a reduction since 1999 of approximately 10,500 farmers, and since 1970, approximately 39,500. Another point of note here is that the number of total farmers fluctuates from crop to crop.
30. See presentations at the GRDB National Rice Conference of 2015 - http://grdb.gy/national-rice-industry-conference-2015.
31. This is an issue that should receive national attention, because the culture of the rural community is being reshaped. There is need for a comprehensive census to bring out the major disparity that exists between land ownership and land occupation.
32. In my recent research visit to the rice communities on the Essequibo coast, preliminarily I have been able to surmise that a form of neo-feudal relationship is emerging. This is not uncommon in this new global age. Formal and informal contracts that tie small farmers to big operators and Agri-business companies abound in Africa and Asia, especially in India. On the Essequibo coast, there is

an emerging contract relationship that binds some small farmers to particular millers, who provide machinery and other inputs.
33. This Convention is a trade and aid agreement between the European Economic Community (EEC) and 71 African, Caribbean, and Pacific (ACP) countries, signed in February 1975 in Lomé, Togo.

References

Adamson, Alan. 1970. Monoculture and Village Decay in British Guiana: 1854–1872. *Journal of Social History* 3, no. 4.
———. 1972. *Sugar Without Slaves*. New Haven: Yale University Press.
Beachey, R.W. 1957. *The British West Indies Sugar Industry in the Late 19th Century*. Westport: Greenwood Press.
Borras, Saturnino M., Ruth Hall, Ian Scoones, Ben White, and Wendy Woolford. 2011. Towards a Better Understanding of Global Land Grabbing: An Editorial Introduction, *Journal of Peasant Studies* 38, no. 2:209–16.
Carney, Judith. 2001A. African Rice in the Columbian Exchange. *Journal of African History* 42, no. 3:377–96.
———. 2001B. *Black Rice: The African Origins of Rice Cultivation in the Americas*. Cambridge: Harvard University Press.
———. 2004. With Grains in Her Hair: Rice in Colonial Brazil. *Slavery and Abolition* 25, no. 1: 1–27.
———. 2005. Rice in the Memory in the Age of Enslavement: Atlantic Passages to Suriname. *Slavery and Abolition* 26, no. 3:325–47.
Clementi, Cecil. 1937. *A Constitutional History of British Guiana*. New York: McMillan.
Green, Francis. 1991. The Reserve Army Hypothesis: A Survey of Empirical Applications. In *Quantitative Marxism*, ed. Paul Dunne, 123–40. Cambridge: Polity Press.
Greenidge, Carl. 2010. Empowering a Peasantry in a Caribbean Context: The Case of Land Settlement Schemes in Guyana, 1865–1985.
Harvey, David. 2003. *The New Imperialism*. Oxford: Oxford University Press.
McGowan, Winston. 2008. The Beginnings of Rice Cultivation in Guyana, Parts 1–3. *Stabroek News*, November 18, 19, and 20.
Mintz, Sidney. 1974. *Caribbean Transformations*. New York: Columbia University Press.
———. 2013. Slavery and the Rise of the Peasantries. In *Roots and Branches*, ed. Michael Craton, 213–42. Oxford: Pergamon Press.
Mohamed, Wazir. 2008. *Frustrated Peasant, Marginalized Workers: Freed African Villages of Guyana, 1838-1885*. PhD diss. Retrieved from proquest.com (3320171).
———. 2009. Guyana's Rice Industry: A Historical Perspective. *Guyana Journal*. Accessed June 1, 2018. http://www.guyanajournal.com/Wazir_Mohamed_Guyana_Rice_Industry.html.
———. 2016. African Labor in Guyana and the Expansion of the Second Slavery. In

New Frontiers of Slavery, ed. Dale W. Tomich. Albany: SUNY Press.

———. 2017. Guyana Land Tenure Problems: Historical roots. Unpublished Submission to the Guyana Lands Commission of Inquiry.

———. Forthcoming. Race and Class Marginalization through Globalization of the Rice Industry. In *Race and Rurality in the Global Economy*, ed. Michaeline Crichlow. Albany: SUNY Press.

Nath, Dwarka. 1950. *A History of Indians in Guyana*. London: Butler and Tanner.

O'Loughlin, C. 1958. The Rice Sector in the Economy of British Guiana. *Social and Economic Studies* 7, no. 2:115–43.

Potter, Lesley. 1992. The Paddy Proletariat and the Dependent Peasantry. *History Gazette* 47.

Ramsahoye, Fenton. 1966. *The Development of Land Law in British Guiana*. New York: Oceana Publications.

Rodney, Walter. 1981. *A History of the Guianese Working People, 1881–1905*. Baltimore: Johns Hopkins University Press.

Rose, James. 1990. The Sugar Strike of 1848. *History Gazette* 23.

Ruhomon, Peter. 1989. *Centenary History of the East Indians of British Guiana, 1838–1938*. Georgetown: Guyana National Printers.

Russell, William. 1886. Rice. *Timehri V* (June): 101–20.

Thompson, Alvin O. 1987. *Colonialism & Underdevelopment in Guyana, 1580–1803*. Bridgetown: Carib Research & Publications Inc.

Viotti da Costa, Emilia. 1994. *Crowns of Glory, Tears of Blood: The Demerara Slave Rebellion of 1823*. New York: Oxford University Press.

Whitfield, R. H. 1872. *Hints on Villages, Villagers; on Drainage, Cultivation, Roads, Taxation, and on other matters of vital importance to the colony generally*. Georgetown: Colonial era pamphlet vol. xxix.

Young, Alan. 1958. *The Approaches to Local Self-Government in British Guiana*. London: Longman, Green.

9.
Poverty and Human Security in Guyana

Clement Henry

> Poverty is not really a discrete condition. One does not immediately acquire or shed the afflictions we associate with the notion of poverty by crossing any particular income line.
>
> Watts 1968, 325

Introduction

Watts's observation is a convenient starting point for this discussion, since the hardships and miseries associated with the social phenomenon referred to as 'poverty' are not instantaneously jettisoned as one crosses the poverty threshold. This chapter, therefore, challenges the classic view of poverty as a unidimensional measure – a shortage of income – and argues for a multidimensional view as the only way of capturing the multiple disadvantages associated with poverty. Moreover, numerous miseries and adverse situations that are part of the daily experiences of the poor deny them and their children the opportunity to flourish and escape the unrelenting clutches of poverty.

The importance of looking beyond income-based poverty statistics is heightened in circumstances such as those in Guyana where these figures can give policymakers the impression that poverty is being eradicated. Worse, they can encourage quick-fix approaches in addressing the issue, based on the assumption that as individuals secure liveable incomes, they will be free from the conditions associated with poverty. But current realities show that escaping poverty's tenacious grasp is more complicated.

Take, for instance, the results of national poverty studies in 1993 and 2006 which show that moderate poverty, defined as living on US$2 per day (2005 prices), fell considerably from 43.2 per cent in 1993 to 36.1 per cent in 2006; and extreme poverty, defined as living on less than US$1.25 per day (2005 prices), declined significantly from 28.7 per cent in 1993 to 18.6 per cent in 2006 (Government of Guyana 2011, 6–7). No doubt these figures show encouraging prospects for eliminating poverty. However, another reality must be considered. John Renshaw (2006) in a qualitative study on access to social services paints a bleak picture of the experiences of individuals living in poor communities that included: crippling social and economic exclusion; incessant humiliation and discrimination from private and public actors; increasing vulnerability; high levels of crime and violence; HIV/AIDS prevalence rates that are higher than the national average; deficient and/or declining standards of service provision and basic infrastructure; and environmental challenges such as flooding. Additionally, an Inter-American Development Bank's assessment revealed that the 20 communities with the highest prevalence of crime and violence had an economic participation rate – namely, persons over 15 years old reported as working – of 31.1 per cent, far below the national average of 48.8 per cent.[1] These same communities in 2013 accounted for 19.5 per cent of the robberies, 19.4 per cent of the burglaries, and 13.9 per cent of the domestic violence in the country.[2]

Instinctively, it is believed that education is the path out of poverty. But even achieving educational goals are challenging for individuals living in poor households and in economically depressed communities. In the 20 communities referred to above, 73.9 per cent of persons over 15 years old lacked formal qualification.[3] Additionally, analysis of data from the 2014 Multiple Indicator Cluster Survey showed that among 12–15 year olds, 11.9 per cent from the poorest quintile had dropped out of school compared to only 1.2 per cent from the richest quintile.[4] Thus, in Guyana, like elsewhere, economic disadvantage and numerous other risk factors – such as elevated levels of crime and violence, limited access to health and other public services, low educational attainment, intolerable discrimination and exclusion, heightened fear driven by an overwhelming perception of insecurity, and hopelessness and helplessness – all converge in the poverty experience. As Jethro Pettit points out, the day-to-day experiences of the poor involve a complex interaction of forces and barriers that define the options that are available to them, constrain their agency, and shape what they feel they can do to secure their needs and rights (Pettit 2016, 91).

This chapter examines the various dimensions of poverty through the human security lens. It suggests that current assessments should be supplemented with multidimensional approaches since poverty is a multifaceted phenomenon. It covers the period from 1988 to 2013 for three reasons: one, because of the availability of data; two, it captures poverty experiences of citizens brought on by the state's embrace of stabilisation and structural adjustment policies as it sought to emerge from a deep economic trough; and three, it assesses the outcomes of poverty alleviation strategies such as the Social Impact Amelioration Programme (SIMAP) and the Poverty Reduction Strategy Paper (PRSP).

The chapter comprises six subdivisions. Following this introduction, I outline the key studies undertaken on poverty in Guyana. I then briefly review conventional approaches to poverty measurement, here making the argument that these are insufficient to analyse the poverty condition and contending for the inclusion of multidimensional measures of human well-being. The fourth section outlines the study design. The penultimate section outlines the analytical steps undertaken, key results of the study, and discusses the findings. Here, I also present the human security scores for the seven human security dimensions, disaggregating by region for each of the human security dimensions presented. The final section presents my conclusions.

Previous Poverty Studies Conducted in Guyana

A 1992 World Bank Report lamented the absence of consistent and reliable methodology for poverty assessment in Guyana and consequently the lack of reliable poverty estimates (World Bank 1992, 80). Clive Thomas (1993) acknowledges the situation highlighted by the World Bank, opining that even in the absence of robust poverty estimates, declining economic indicators in the late 1980s could only suggest worsening of poverty across the country. Thomas was referring to challenges faced by Guyanese, particularly between 1988 and 1990, brought on in part by the failure of the country's experiment with a planned economy along with poor performance of the three key export sectors (bauxite, sugar, and rice).

In order to improve the country's macroeconomics, the Economic Recovery Programme (ERP) was launched in mid-1988. The overarching objective of this programme was to achieve macroeconomic stabilisation and far-reaching structural reforms to restore sustainable output and employment growth in the context of a market-based economy. The ERP was able to remedy some of the major economic pathologies that engendered the recession and consequently was effective in halting the economic downturn and generating a 6.1 per cent growth in 1991 (Henry 2012, 96). But although successful, the reforms resulted in serious economic difficulties and diminished standard of living for individuals and families. Thomas, in discussing the impact of the economic reforms on the poor, relates that the spike in exchange rates associated with liberalisation policies, wage restraint, sharp increases in commodity prices, reduction in food subsidies, and cuts in government's social expenditure, all converged, and drove increasing numbers into poverty (Thomas 1993, 134).

The SIMAP, implemented from 1992, was an institutionalised response to target the poor and vulnerable groups in the population. Designed to cushion the effects of the Structural Adjustment Programme on citizens, there were two constraints on its implementation: one, there were not enough resources to fund the programme; and two, the absence of data made it difficult to have a profile of the poor. SIMAP, however, targeted the urban unemployed, small farmers, pregnant and lactating mothers, children under five years old, and pensioners.

Subsequently, three studies on poverty were conducted in Guyana, viz.: the 1993 and 2006 Household Income and Expenditure Surveys and the 1999 Guyana Living Conditions Survey. The poor in these surveys were defined as those who lived in households that were unable to muster the required resources to meet their basic consumption needs, including food and non-food items (Government of Guyana 2011, 6–7). Results of these three national poverty studies showed significant gains in combating poverty from 1993 to 1999 (figure 9.1). However, the data reveal that progress in reducing poverty stalled after 1999. In fact, the data show that moderate poverty and extreme poverty fell by 8.2 per cent and 9.7 per cent, respectively from 1993 to 1999; comparatively, from 2000 to 2006, moderate poverty increased marginally by 1.1 per cent and extreme poverty decreased slightly by 0.4 per cent. The appreciable improvement in poverty estimates from 1993 to 1999 was, in part, due to the successful implementation of the SIMAP and effective execution of macroeconomic reforms. A number of intersecting forces may have contributed to stalled progress in reducing poverty after 1999, including erratic performance of the national economy from 1998 to 2005; adverse weather conditions leading to flooding; political instability; and a debilitating crime wave during the period 2002–06.

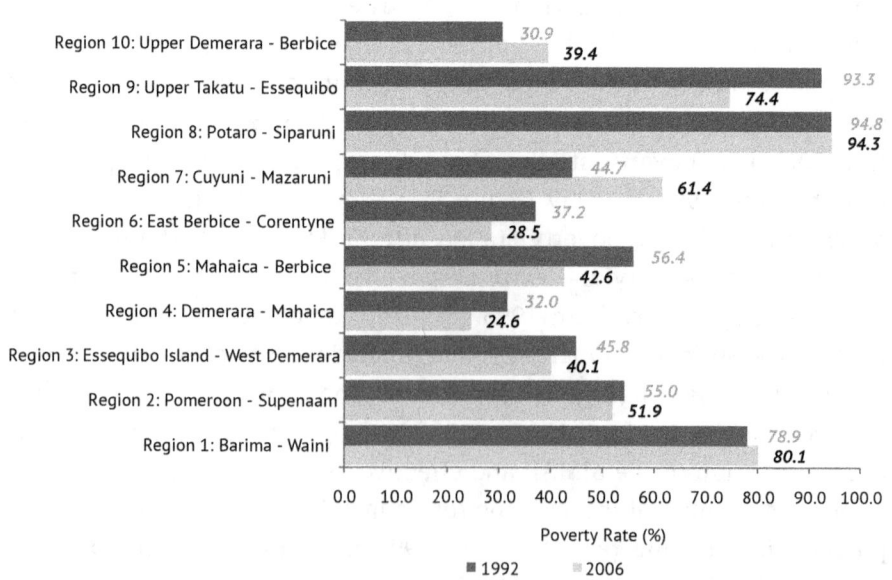

Figure 9.1: Results of Three Poverty Studies in Guyana

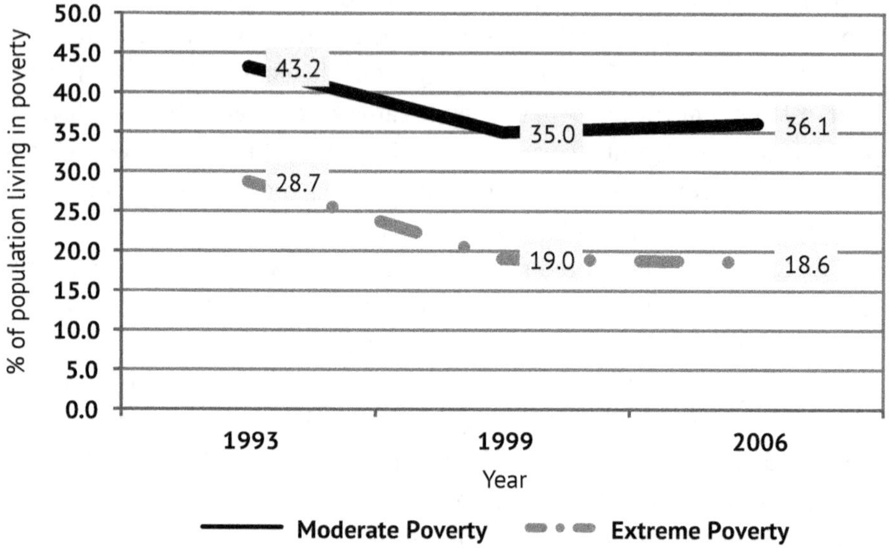

Figure 9.2: Poverty Rates by Region, 1993 and 2006

(Source: Guyana Poverty Reduction Strategy Paper 2011)

It is also interesting to observe the regional disparities in poverty levels. Both in 1993 and in 2006 moderate poverty rates in hinterland regions were very high. For instance, in 2006, the moderate poverty rate for Region 1 was 80.6 per cent, in Region 7 it was 61.4 per cent, in Region 8 it was 94.3 per cent, and in Region 9 it was 74.4 per cent. In three regions, these rates were worse than they had been in 1992. In Region 7, it rose from 44.2 per cent to 61.4 per cent; in Region 10 from 30.9 to 39.4 per cent; and in Region 1 it increased marginally by 1.2 per cent. On the positive side, Regions 5 and 9 had substantial gains in reducing poverty by 13.8 per cent and 18.9 per cent respectively during the period 1993 to 2006. In Regions 2, 3, 4 and 6 poverty rates improved by 3.1 per cent, 5.7 per cent, 7.4 per cent, and 8.8 per cent, respectively. Region 8 had a marginal reduction in poverty rate of less than one per cent (figure 9.2).

During the period 1997–2002, governmental and non-governmental institutions along with the private sector collaborated in the design of a Poverty Reduction Strategy Paper aimed at reducing poverty by 2005. This new strategy comprised seven elements: broad-based job generating economic growth; stronger institutional and governance framework; investment in human capital, emphasising basic education and health; infrastructure investments to support services in water, sanitation, and housing; investments in growth-supporting infrastructure; improved safety nets; and special intervention programmes addressing regional disparities in poverty incidence. It is evident from the foregoing statistics that the poverty reduction strategy was not a resounding success.

Aldrie Henry-Lee and Elsie Le Franc (2002), using data from the 1993 Household Income and Expenditure Survey, found that the main predictors of poverty in Guyana were years of schooling, household size, and rural living. However, their results must be interpreted with some caution, since cross-sectional data analysis only establishes empirical association at the time of the data collection.

The Deficiency of Monetary Measures of Poverty

So far, poverty studies in Guyana have adopted monetary -poverty measures. Monetary measures of poverty have quite an extensive pedigree in the social sciences. As early as 1902, Benjamin Seebohm Rowntree's publication *Poverty: A Study of Town Life* adopted a poverty line based on the monetary value of a basket of products considered essential goods and services required to meet the minimum sustenance requirements of households. Poverty in this context is traditionally understood as command over resources, typically annual income (Orshansky 1965, 4). In this tradition, the poor are those families that fall below a prescribed threshold based on household income. Individuals, families, and groups in the population are said to be in poverty when the resources they command are below the level required for them to access the types of diet, participate in the activities, and have the living conditions and amenities which are customary, or are at least widely encouraged or approved, in the societies to which they belong (Townsend 1979, 31). Computing poverty rates using this approach requires accurate definitions of both available economic resources and the minimum level of economic needs (Haveman 2009, 81).

There are differences in opinions among adherents of income-based poverty measures regarding which is the best measure of two types: absolute and relative. The absolute poverty line, according to Paul Spicker et al. (2007, 7), is prescribed based on experts' conclusion on the level of income that meets people's minimum needs. This manner of counting the poor is popularly referred to as the head count poverty index which gives the proportion of the population whose household income falls below the poverty line. However, others in the monetary poverty measures school of orthodoxy suggest that poverty should be defined relative to standards of living in the society. The poverty line in relative terms is computed as 50 per cent of the median family income (Williamson and Hyer 1975, 654). The attractiveness and enduring nature of monetary based measures of poverty are linked to their simplicity. Monetary-based poverty measures are now trending more towards assessing consumption rather than income for the reason that consumption is believed to be a more accurate measure of long-term welfare when compared to income, which often fluctuates over short periods.

Despite the popularity of monetary measures of well-being, these approaches have been consistently challenged. A number of problems have been highlighted with statistics originating from monetary-based poverty measures. In particular, these fail to differentiate poverty experiences among households classed as poor, and rest on a weak core assumption that there are qualitative differences in life experiences between families with income just below the poverty line, and those with income just above the poverty line, which assumption is not matched by reality.

Additionally, monetary-based approaches omit many non-economic considerations, such as living in unsafe surroundings, being socially isolated, or experiencing adverse health, all of which impact on individual opportunities for achieving well-being. Because of these shortcomings, the approach of measuring poverty based on the command over resources may overlook important dimensions of poverty (Haverman 2009, 81).

Among scholars who challenge the traditional approach to poverty assessment, Buhong Zheng (1997, 125–27) expresses concern over the use of income as a single indicator of poverty. Zheng argues that emphasis should be placed on the multidimensional nature of poverty because the concept encompasses cumulative deprivation in relation to income, housing, education, and health care. Sabina Alkire et al. (2014, 1) see poverty as 'a condition in which people are exposed to multiple disadvantages – actual and potential.' Sudhir Anand (1977, 2) posits that income is not necessarily a good indicator of poverty. Amartya Sen (1985) challenges the adequacy of income-based measures in reflecting the complex nature of poverty. He condemns the income approach as being too crude to account for differences in individuals' capacities to use economic resources. Duncan Green (2012, 7) argues for a multidimensional notion of poverty covering health, physical safety, meaningful work, connection to community, and other non-monetary factors.

The recognition of the various limitations of monetary based assessment of poverty has resulted in heightened interest in non-monetary indicators and a fundamental shift towards a multidimensional approach in assessing human deprivation and poverty (Nolan and Whelan 2011). One such approach is Amartya Sen's capability approach, which offers a way to integrate both the narrow conceptualisation of poverty which favours command of resources, and broader multidimensional notions of poverty.[5] It is an evaluative framework that focuses on the extent of freedom individuals have to promote or achieve 'functionings' they value (Alkire 2015). As Sen argues in *The Idea of Justice* (2009), this represents a fundamental change in poverty assessment by shifting focus from the means of living to the actual opportunities that people have (253). Sen contends that the focal space for analysis should be human lives and not just the resources they command. Poverty evaluation, therefore, should be based on the opportunities that individuals have, that is, their capabilities and functionings (Sen 2009, 253).

An important challenge in operationalising this approach is determining which dimensions are relevant, as Sen does not specify these. A multi-dimensional concept referred to as human security offers much promise as this is linked to the capability approach, and it considers all the major constraints and threats to humans achieving well-being. Human security boldly specifies the evaluative space in assessing human well-being. The concept proposes that human well-being should be evaluated in a broad informational space – covering economic, food and health security; personal security from physical violence; environmental, societal, and political security. This broad analytical space facilitates a better depiction of the many ways in which human lives are blighted, and therefore offers a promising informational space for poverty analysis. Human security analysis, despite criticism in some circles (Khong 2001, 231–36; Paris 2001, 92–96), has received widespread support internationally as a way of evaluating individual well-being (UNDP 1994; Hampson et al. 2002; Commission on Human Security 2003; Owen 2004, 373–87; Tadjbakhsh and Chenoy 2007; Reveron and Mahoney-Norris 2011).

To operationalise human security, we must define the concept and determine the appropriate indicators. Definition has proven difficult in the past mainly because there is little agreement on the meaning and content of its root concept – security. This is probably so because the word security is used in many different contexts without any precise meaning. For example, Richard Post and Arthur Kingsbury (1991, 1) point out that:

> Security is often used loosely and in different contexts. For example, national security, international security, internal security, private security, retail security, physical security, and industrial security are all used in daily conversations. The definitions of these terms are not often clear and are often used interchangeably.

Arnold Wolfers (1952, 483) argues that the term security when used without specification leads to more confusion than scientific usage can afford. Paul Williams (2013) offers a method for specifying security by delineating four key elements associated with the word: (i) a referent object (ii) the asset/value related to the referent object that is worth protecting; (iii) threats/risks/dangers to the asset/value; and (iv) agency offering protection. Based on the preceding a function (f) can be deduced for security:

$S = f\{R, V, T, P\}$

Where S is security, R is object being secured or security referent, V is the value worth protecting, T is the threat, danger, and/or risk, and P is the actor involved in protection and/or mitigation. Based on the functional relationship human security is defined as preservation and protection (P) of individuals (R) from threats and dangers (T) to their survival and functioning (V).

A concise overview of key elements of the definition is necessitated. Human security makes humans the referent object of security as apart from nation-states. Current and past global realities dictate that the security of a nation-state and of its citizens must be analysed and addressed as two distinct albeit related phenomena. This is so because of the numerous examples across the globe where people have suffered and died as a result of hunger, disease, criminal violence, and environmental disasters even as state structures remain intact. Threats are the undesirable or adverse events or occurrences that are likely to cause harm, damage, or pose danger. The threats referred to here are not those to all aspects of human lives or else the concept would be without analytical utility. The human security threats are those that constrain human survival and functioning. The critical dimensions for human survival and functioning or the values worth protecting are: economic security, food security, health security, societal security, political security, physical safety, and a healthy environment. These value dimensions have their legitimacy enshrined in a time-proven and internationally accepted list of norms and values.[6]

Finally, preservation of human security requires agency. In the current context, agency comprises: state agency, non-state agency, and individual agency. The next step is to identify and validate the indicators of human security.

Study Design

A 17-item instrument each structured on a 5-point Likert-type scale ranging from 1 for low ratings to 5 for higher ratings was designed (table 1 and appendix A for questionnaire items). Higher scores represented higher human security and conversely lower values represented lower human security. The instrument comprised seven subscales based on the seven dimensions of human security. Pre-survey evaluation of the instrument included: focus group discussions, intensive individual interviews, and field pretesting. These approaches have been deemed effective in improving the reliability and validity of survey instruments (Fowler 1995, 104).

Table 9.1: Summary Table on the 17-Indicator Instrument

Indicator Variables	Corresponding Factor	Indicators
X_1	Economic Security	Access to resources/income
X_2	Economic Security	Income adequacy
X_3	Food Security	Capability to access/purchase food
X_4	Food Security	Adequacy of Food Resources
X_5	Food Security	Worry over access to food
X_6	Health Security	Access to Health Care
X_7	Health Security	Satisfaction with health care services
X_8	Health Security	Satisfaction with communicable diseases prevention
X_9	Personal Security	Experience with crime/violence victimization
X_{10}	Personal Security	Fear of crime and violence
X_{11}	Environmental Security	Perception on the severity of environmental problems
X_{12}	Environmental Security	Fear of impact of future environmental disasters
X_{13}	Societal Security	Perception on citizens' access to fair justice
X_{14}	Societal Security	Perception on the level of respect for citizens' rights in the country
X_{15}	Political Security	Freedom of expression
X_{16}	Political Security	Trust in State Institutions
X_{17}	Political Security	Freedom to exercise political choices

To garner data on human security a quantitative study was conducted. A multi-stage proportional probability sampling design was utilised. In multi-stage sampling, the selected clusters are sampled at each stage (Crano and Brewer 2002, 179). Multi-stage sampling is used when it is almost impractical to compile an exhaustive list of members comprising the target population owing to the size of the population under study (Babbie 2010, 219; Bryman and Bell 2007, 188). In this type of sampling, the natural segments/clusters of the population are utilised (Crano and Brewer 2002, 179). The variations in population size are accounted for by using proportional sampling, since in this technique the probability of selection into the survey sample for each sample unit is directly proportional to the number of elements in the unit (Lohr 210, 266). The application of proportionality was done only at the regional level. At the village/ward level, 20 interviews were conducted in each village/ward randomly selected. All ten administrative regions are sampled. One respondent from each household was randomly selected through the last birthday method. Face-to-face interviews were conducted using the pre-designed questionnaire. Data collection covered four months, September 15, 2013–January 15, 2014. Cochran's formula (appendix B) was used to compute sample size. Data collected were coded and entered into EPIDATA before being exported to Mplus and statistical package for the social sciences (SPSS) for analysis. There were two stages to the analysis. In stage one, Mplus was used to validate the human security indicators. Once this was successful, at stage two, the paper evaluated the distribution of the indicators of the various dimensions of human security in SPSS.

Confirmatory factor analysis technique was adopted for the multivariate analysis. The aim of this analysis was to validate the indicators of human security. This approach is preferred because it offers four distinct advantages:

i. it is a commonly used method to assess construct validity by adding a level of statistical precision and confirmation of the sub-domains of a concept (Boelen, van den Hout, and van den Bout 2008; Atkinson et al. 2011, 559);

ii. it incorporates the theoretical framework on which the latent construct is based (Khine 2013, 3);

iii. while other statistical methods such as analysis of variance, simple regression analysis, and multiple regression analysis ignore potential measurement error of variables in the model, confirmatory factor analysis provides a mechanism for taking into account measurement errors in indicator variables, since variables in the social sciences are generally known to contain sizable measurement errors. Measurement errors if disregarded can result in biased parameter estimates and incorrect conclusions (Wang and Wang 2012, 1); and

iv. unlike other techniques that can only utilise observed variables and measurements, it is able to model both observed and latent variables (Byrne 2010, 3–4).

The latter property is extremely important in the current context due to the fact that the dimensions of human security are all latent variables (Byrne 2010, 3-4; Wang and Wang 2012, 1).

Below is the seven-factor confirmatory factor analysis (CFA) model in the format of 17 structural equation model (SEM) basic equations. In the SEM basic equations, each observed indicator ($X_1, X_2, X_3...X_{17}$) is presented as a linear function of one of the latent factor (ξ) and a random error (δ). The various factor loads are represented by λ. The subscript of a factor load refers to the indicator number and its corresponding factor number.

$X_1 = \xi_1 + \delta_1$	$X_2 = \lambda_{21}\xi_1 + \delta_2$	
$X_3 = \xi_2 + \delta_3$	$X_4 = \lambda_{42}\xi_2 + \delta_4$	$X_5 = \lambda_{52}\xi_2 + \delta_5$
$X_6 = \xi_3 + \delta_6$	$X_7 = \lambda_{73}\xi_3 + \delta_7$	$X_8 = \lambda_{83}\xi_3 + \delta_8$
$X_9 = \xi_4 + \delta_9$	$X_{10} = \lambda_{104}\xi_4 + \delta_{10}$	
$X_{11} = \xi_5 + \delta_{11}$	$X_{12} = \lambda_{125}\xi_5 + \delta_{12}$	
$X_{13} = \xi_6 + \delta_{13}$	$X_{14} = \lambda_{146}\xi_6 + \delta_{14}$	
$X_{15} = \xi_7 + \delta_{15}$	$X_{16} = \lambda_{167}\xi_7 + \delta_{16}$	$X_{17} = \lambda_{177}\xi_7 + \delta_{17}$

Table 9.2: Indicator Variables and Corresponding Factors

Indicator Variables (X)	Corresponding Factors (ξ)	Indicator Variables (X)	Corresponding Factors (ξ)
X_{1-2}	Economic Security	X_{11-12}	Environmental Security
X_{3-5}	Food Security	X_{13-14}	Societal Security
X_{6-8}	Health Security	X_{15-17}	Political Security
X_{9-10}	Personal Security		

Analysis, Findings, and Discussion

The modelling was completed with 20 iterations using the Mean-Adjusted Maximum Likelihood (MLM) method. During the analysis the researcher parcelled two of the indicators on health (X_7 and X_8) to improve estimation. All the main fit indices indicate a good fit between the model and the data. The $\chi 2$ to degrees of freedom ratio in the estimation equals 180.823/82 which gives a ratio of 2.205 to 1. The Root Mean Square Error of Approximation (RMSEA) value in the current estimation is 0.038 with 90 per cent confidence interval (CI) ranging from 0.031 to 0.046. The probability value of 0.996 for the RMSEA indicates that there is a high likelihood of getting a population RMSEA that is no greater than .05. The Standardised Root Mean Square Residual (SRMR) is 0.034. The Comparative Fit Index (CFI) and the Tucker Lewis Index (TLI) for the estimated model are 0.967 and 0.952, respectively (appendix C).

The validation of the various dimensions of human security through confirmatory factor analysis indicates that all seven dimensions are interlinked. The indicators of goodness of fit of the specified model are supportive of a conceptualisation of human security comprising seven dimensions. The good fit suggests that the data support the relationship among the variables. It can be inferred from the preceding that a true picture of the multiple disadvantages associated with poverty and deprivation must encompass these seven interconnected dimensions. Validation of the seven human security dimensions along with the 16 indicator variables offers a simple human security evaluative tool. The strength of the tool is that it captures individuals' perceptions and experiences in assessing human security.

As validated in the confirmatory factor analysis each dimension had two or three indicator variables. Values for all the indicator variables were transformed to a new scale of zero to 100. The seven value-dimensions of human security were computed using the SPSS syntax as presented in table 9.3. The values for all of the dimensions are calculated first. These values are then aggregated and the mean score is used as the value for human security.

The results from computing the human security scale yielded 825 data points. The mean value was 56.1 and the median value was 55.9 on a scale of 0–100. Both measures of central tendencies were not particularly strong but fell within the moderate range. As the box plot indicates the

75th percentile was approximately 63 and the 25th percentile score was approximately 49 (figure 3). There were not many outliers in the data and most of the data hover around the middle range of the scale.

Table 9.3: Syntax for Computing Human Security

Latent Variable	SPSS Syntax
Economic Security	COMPUTE ECONOMIC_SECURITY = $(X_1 + X_2)/2$.
Food Security	COMPUTE FOOD_SECURITY = $(X_3 + X_4 + X_5)/3$
Health Security	COMPUTE HEALTH_SECURITY = $(X_6 + X_{7,8}{}^*)/2$.
Personal Security	COMPUTE PERSONAL_SECURITY = $(X_9 + X_{10})/2$.
Environmental Security	COMPUTE ENVIRONMENTAL_SECURITY = $(X_{11} + X_{12})/2$.
Societal Security	COMPUTE SOCIETAL_SECURITY = $(X_{13} + X_{14})/2$.
Political Security	COMPUTE POLITICAL_SECURITY = $(X_{15} + X_{16} + X_{17})/3$.
Human Security	COMPUTE HUMAN_SECURITY = (ECONOMIC_SECURITY + FOOD_SECURITY + HEALTH_SECURITY + PERSONAL_SECURITY + ENVIRONMENTAL_SECURITY + + SOCIETAL_SECURITY + POLITICAL_SECURITY)/7.

• *New variable resulting from the parcelling of X_7 and X_8*

Figure 9.3: Box Plot for Human Security Scores

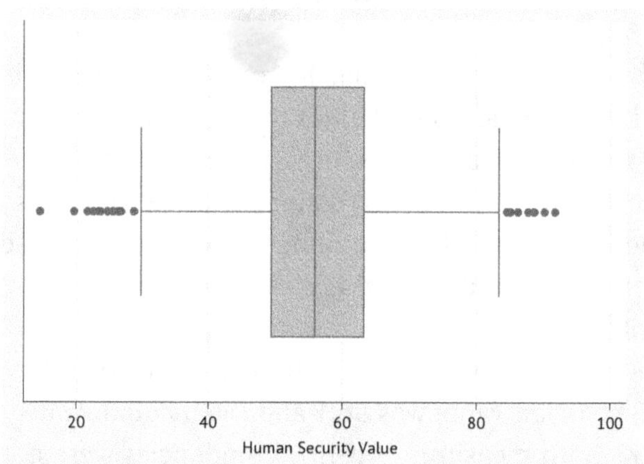

The analysis further examined values of the different dimensions. The results show that the value for economic security was 73.1, food security 71.7, personal security 63.4, health security 51.8, political security 47.9, environmental security 43.5, and societal security 41.4 (figure 9.4).

When variables have multiple values it is common to group them for analytical purposes. The original Likert scale offers some natural cut-off points for group classification. The value 50 (3 on the Likert scale) is the midpoint. The two upper responses in the Likert scale that are coded 4 and 5 were valued 75 and 100, respectively. Therefore, values 75 and over indicate favourable human security conditions. Consistent with the preceding, three classifications are derived as depicted in the table 9.4 below.

Figure 9.4: Graph Depicting Levels of Human Security for Guyana

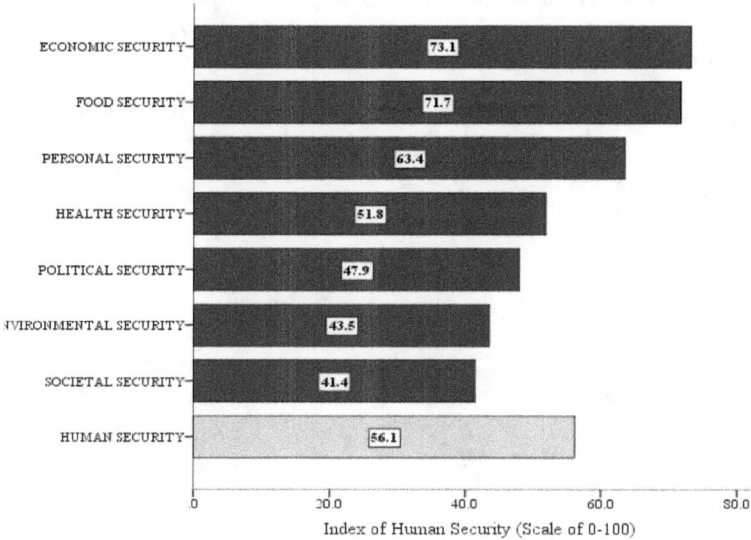

Table 9.4: Human Security Classifications

Range	Classification	Assessment
0 – 49	Unacceptable Level	Problematic; needs urgent attention
50 – 74	Moderate Level	Somewhat problematic; needs attention
75 – 100	Acceptable Level	Satisfactory

252 Unmasking The State

Using the classification above, it is enlightening to compare findings on economic security with statistics from the 2006 poverty study. As figure 9.5 indicates, there is little difference between the percentage of people considered outside of poverty in the 2006 poverty study (63.9 per cent) and those with acceptable economic security in the current analysis (66.3 per cent). Economic security in this study measured individuals' access to financial resources/income and their perception on the adequacy of household income. The similarity in figures from the 2006 poverty study and the economic security dimension is probably indicative that these two measures parallel each other.

In broadening the analysis, an examination of the regional averages for all the dimensions of human security is undertaken. As depicted in table 9.5, mean economic security scores were at acceptable levels only in Regions 3 and 4. In the remaining regions, mean economic security scores were at moderate levels. Region 3 had the highest mean economic security score and Region 2 had the lowest mean economic security score.

Figure 9.5: Comparison between the Findings of the 2006 Poverty Study and 2013 Human Security Study

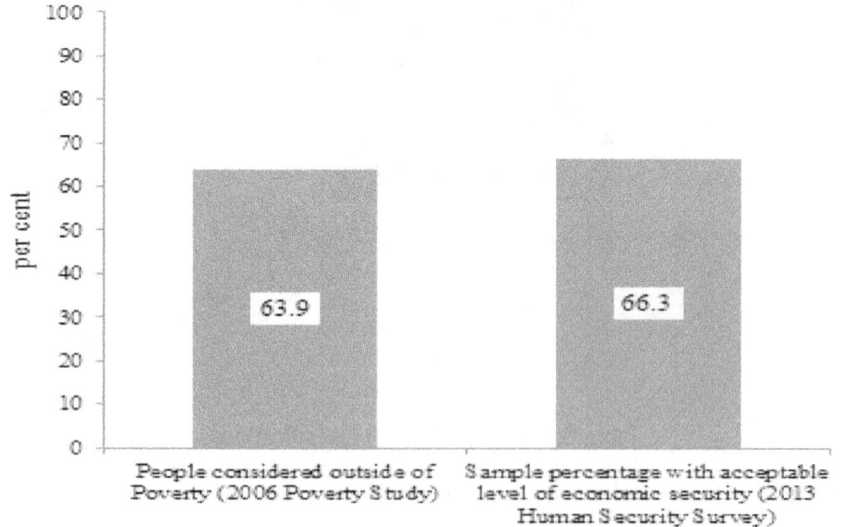

Table 9.5: Mean Economic Security Scores by Region

Region	Mean Economic Security Score	Classification	Assessment
Regions 1,7,8,9 (Hinterland Regions)	69.8	Moderate	Somewhat problematic; needs attention
Region 2	62.3	Moderate	Somewhat problematic; needs attention
Region 3	77.3	Acceptable	Satisfactory
Region 4	75.2	Acceptable	Satisfactory
Region 5	72.3	Moderate	Somewhat problematic; needs attention
Region 6	72.8	Moderate	Somewhat problematic; needs attention
Region 10	71.7	Moderate	Somewhat problematic; needs attention

Table 9.6 shows that based on people's experiences and perception the mean food security scores were at moderate levels in all the regions. Regions 3 and 4 had the highest mean food security score (72.8), and Region 10 had the lowest mean food security score (65.4).

Table 9.6: Mean Food Security Scores by Region

Region	Mean Food Security Score	Classification	Assessment
Hinterland Regions	71.6	Moderate	Somewhat problematic; needs attention
Region 2	71.6	Moderate	Somewhat problematic; needs attention
Region 3	72.8	Moderate	Somewhat problematic; needs attention
Region 4	72.8	Moderate	Somewhat problematic; needs attention
Region 5	70.4	Moderate	Somewhat problematic; needs attention
Region 6	72.1	Moderate	Somewhat problematic; needs attention
Region 10	65.4	Moderate	Somewhat problematic; needs attention

As illustrated in table 9.7, mean health security scores were at moderate levels in Regions 3, 4, 5, and 6. In Regions 2 and 10 and the Hinterland Regions, the mean health security scores were at unacceptable levels. The data also show that Region 3 had the highest mean health security score (60.1), and the Hinterland Regions had the lowest mean health security score (42.3).

Table 9.7: Mean Health Security Scores by Region

Region	Mean Health Security Score	Classification	Assessment
Hinterland Regions	42.3	Unacceptable	Problematic; needs urgent attention
Region 2	49.4	Unacceptable	Problematic; needs urgent attention
Region 3	60.1	Moderate	Somewhat problematic; needs attention
Region 4	51.5	Moderate	Somewhat problematic; needs attention
Region 5	58.0	Moderate	Somewhat problematic; needs attention
Region 6	53.2	Moderate	Somewhat problematic; needs attention
Region 10	45.6	Unacceptable	Problematic; needs urgent attention

Table 9.8: Mean Personal Security Scores by Region

Region	Mean Personal Security Score	Classification	Assessment
Hinterland Regions	67.3	Moderate	Somewhat problematic; needs attention
Region 2	77.5	Acceptable	Satisfactory
Region 3	70.0	Moderate	Somewhat problematic; needs attention
Region 4	56.0	Moderate	Somewhat problematic; needs attention
Region 5	70.4	Moderate	Somewhat problematic; needs attention
Region 6	64.7	Moderate	Somewhat problematic; needs attention
Region 10	63.1	Moderate	Somewhat problematic; needs attention

With regard to personal security only in one region – Region 2 (77.5) – was the mean personal security score at an acceptable level (table 9.8). In the remaining regions, the mean personal security scores were at moderate levels. Region 4 had the lowest mean personal security score (56.0).

Turning to environmental security, in all the regions with the exception of Region 3, mean environmental security scores were at unacceptable levels (table 9.9). In Region 3, the mean environmental security score was at a moderate level (51.8). The Hinterland Regions had the lowest mean environmental security score (35.6).

Table 9.9: Mean Environmental Security Scores by Region

Region	Mean Environmental Security Score	Classification	Assessment
Hinterland Regions	35.6	Unacceptable	Problematic; needs urgent attention
Region 2	47.4	Unacceptable	Problematic; needs urgent attention
Region 3	51.8	Moderate	Somewhat problematic; needs attention
Region 4	40.8	Unacceptable	Problematic; needs urgent attention
Region 5	41.5	Unacceptable	Problematic; needs urgent attention
Region 6	46.7	Unacceptable	Problematic; needs urgent attention
Region 10	48.5	Unacceptable	Problematic; needs urgent attention

As observed in table 9.10, the mean societal security scores were at unacceptable levels in all the regions. According to the data, Region 3 had the highest mean societal security score (47.6), and Region 10 had the lowest mean societal security score (34.5).

With regard to political security, the data indicate that the mean political security scores in all the regions, with the exception of Region 3 (51.1) and Region 6 (52.0), were at unacceptable levels (table 9.11). Region 10 had the lowest mean political security score (42.4).

Table 9.10: Mean Societal Security Scores by Region

Region	Mean Societal Security Score	Classification	Assessment
Hinterland Regions	43.0	Unacceptable	Problematic; needs urgent attention
Region 2	39.1	Unacceptable	Problematic; needs urgent attention
Region 3	47.6	Unacceptable	Problematic; needs urgent attention
Region 4	37.2	Unacceptable	Problematic; needs urgent attention
Region 5	40.0	Unacceptable	Problematic; needs urgent attention
Region 6	36.3	Unacceptable	Problematic; needs urgent attention
Region 10	34.5	Unacceptable	Problematic; needs urgent attention

Table 9.11: Mean Political Security Scores by Region

Region	Mean Political Security Score	Classification	Assessment
Hinterland Regions	45.6	Unacceptable	Problematic; needs urgent attention
Region 2	45.8	Unacceptable	Problematic; needs urgent attention
Region 3	51.1	Moderate	Somewhat problematic; needs attention
Region 4	45.7	Unacceptable	Problematic; needs urgent attention
Region 5	48.9	Unacceptable	Problematic; needs urgent attention
Region 6	52.0	Moderate	Somewhat problematic; needs attention
Region 10	42.4	Unacceptable	Problematic; needs urgent attention

From the foregoing analysis societal security was the most problematic dimension in all the regions in Guyana. In the study, societal security encompassed perception on equality and respect for citizen rights. Inequalities and discriminatory practices negatively impact people's ability to effectively participate in all aspects of public life in a fair and equal way and therefore can both cause poverty and be a significant obstacle in alleviating poverty. In fact, the importance of equality and non-discrimination in addressing poverty should be instinctively recognised and not require instrumental justifications. Inequalities and discrimination limit individuals' agency in protecting and enhancing their security and overcoming poverty, which means that remedies to a large extent will have to come from sources external to the individuals. From this standpoint, proactive measures are required by governmental and private actors to identify and address entrenched inequitable and discriminatory practices, both direct and structural.

A closely related issue in the analysis is the level of political security, which comprises individual perception of freedom to exercise political choices, the freedom to express oneself without fear of reprisals, and trust in institutions of the state. Political security, which was problematic in all the regions with the exception of two (where it was somewhat problematic), is another significant barrier to individual agency in addressing poverty. Pettit (2016) explains that poor people do not engage because their survival and access to income and services are dependent on patronage relationships which they sensibly are reluctant to challenge for fear of losing what little they have.

Health security and environmental security were also problematic dimensions in almost all the regions. Health and environmental insecurities are both causes and barriers to overcoming poverty. Poor health and environmental challenges trap individuals and communities in poverty. In Regions 1, 7, and 8 malaria infection rates in 2010 were 25.6 per cent, 43.3 per cent, and 55.6 per cent, respectively (Government of Guyana 2011, 12). Such alarming rates do have intolerable consequences on family expenses, individual capacity to engage in remunerative work, and attendance at institutions of learning. While flooding has been a persistent environmental challenge, information on the impact of the 2005 flood is most instructive. A 2005 Report from the Economic Commission for Latin America and the Caribbean assessed the damages and costs of the 2005 flood and reported that:

- 70,000 households were affected;
- 34 lives were lost;
- 10.9 billion dollars were lost in the agriculture sector, and
- the estimated total cost of the flood was pegged at $93 billion.

Personal security, not surprisingly, was only satisfactory in Region 2. In the remaining regions it was somewhat problematic, requiring attention. Comparatively, the statistics for economic security, food security, and personal security were not as challenging as the other human security dimensions.

The cross-cutting nature of the dimensions of human security makes it difficult to assess government expenditure on the individual dimensions. Even if these figures were available, experience has shown that there is no guarantee that they would be evenly distributed. Notwithstanding, government is the main actor in advancing the different dimensions of human security mainly through its budget prescriptions. Several states, international and regional organisations, private sector and non-governmental organisations, address different facets of human security.

A few clarifications are relevant. While the use of a cross-sectional data collection method is a limitation of the study, the simplicity of the instrument can allow for low-budget annual replications leading to reliable time series. Traditional poverty studies carry hefty costs, which are a disincentive for frequent repetition. Further, the current tool can serve as a simple early warning mechanism to identify and react to challenges to any of the value dimensions.

Conclusion and Recommendations

The chapter aimed to assess poverty in Guyana. In doing so I reviewed secondary poverty data for Guyana during the period 1992–2006 along with primary data garnered from a human security survey conducted in 2013. Combining these approaches to poverty assessment facilitated an analysis on poverty and insecurity, which often go hand-in-hand. The analysis showed that income-based poverty declined steadily during the period 1993–1999 and stalled during the period 2000–2006. The analysis also revealed that the three most problematic dimensions for Guyanese citizens were environmental security, societal security, and political security. Health security was also a troubling dimension.

Based on the foregoing, the following measures are recommended: one – the institutional response to tackling poverty should recognise its multidimensionality, and the evidence used in designing poverty reduction strategies should cover a broader range of indicators than income; two – priority should be given to addressing societal security, environmental security, political security, and health security issues; and three – multidimensional and multidisciplinary approaches are required as research on poverty remains as critical today as it was two and half decades ago.

Notes

1. Inter-American Development Bank, *Citizen Security Strengthening Programme Loan Proposal*, 2, http://idbdocs.iadb.org/wsdocs/getdocument.aspx?docnum=39241069, 2014.
2. *Guyana Chronicle*, $3B for Citizen Security, January 23, 2016, 3.
3. Inter-American Development Bank, *Citizen Security Strengthening Programme Loan Proposal*, 3.
4. Researcher's analysis of the 2014 Guyana Multiple Indicator Cluster Survey (MICS). The 2014 Guyana MICS is a household survey conducted nationally during the period April to July 2014 capturing a representative sample of 5,077 households. Overall, data was collected for 22,637 household members (10,901 males and 11,736 females). The Guyana Bureau of Statistics with technical support from the United Nations Children's Fund (UNICEF) did data collection.
5. Amartya Sen, *The Idea of Justice* (Cambridge: Belknap Press, 2009), 223–52. 'Functionings' is the various things a person may value and have reasons to value. 'Capabilities' are various combinations of functionings (beings and doings) that a person can achieve. 'Freedom' in the capability approach refers to the real opportunities people have to achieve valued functionings.
   Rod Hick, *The Capability Approach: Insights for a New Poverty Focus*, 1–3, http://eprints.lse.ac. uk/39745/1/ The_capability_approach_Insights_for_a_new_poverty_focus_%28lsero%29.pdf, 2012. Poverty is conceptualised as capability deprivation.
6. UN General Assembly, Universal Declaration of Human Rights, *Resolution 217 A (III)*, http://www.refworld.org/docid/3ae6b3712c.html, 1948.
   UN General Assembly, International Covenant on Economic, Social and Cultural Rights, *United Nations, Treaty Series* 993, 3, http://www.refworld.org/docid/3ae6b36c0.html, 1966b.
   UN General Assembly, International Covenant on Civil and Political Rights, *United Nations, Treaty Series* 999, 171, http://www.refworld.org/docid/3ae6b3aa0.html, 1966a.

References

Alkire, Sabina. 2015. Introduction to the Capability Approach. *You Tube Video*, 1:20:02,. Moin Ahmed. February 28, 2015. Accessed February 16, 2016. https://www.youtube.com/watch?v=Hz6kUnoS7MM.
Alkire, Sabina, James Foster, Suman Seth, Maria Santos, Jose Roche, and Paola Ballon. 2014. Multidimensional Poverty Measurement and Analysis. *Oxford*

Poverty & Human Development Initiative. Accessed February 23, 2016. http://www.ophi.org.uk/wp-content/uploads/OPHIWP082_Ch1.pdf.
Anand, Sudhir. 1977. Aspects of Poverty in Malaysia. *Review of Income & Wealth* 23, no. 1:1–16.
Atkinson, Thomas, Barry Rosenfeld, Laura Sit, Tito Mendoza, Mike Fruscione, Dawn Lavene, Mary Shaw, Yuelin Li, Jennifer Hay, Charles Cleeland, Howard Scher, William Breitbart, and Ethan Basch. 2011. Using Confirmatory Factor Analysis to Evaluate Construct Validity of the Brief Pain Inventory (BPI). *Journal of Pain and Symptom Management* 41, no. 3:558–65.
Babbie, Earl. 2010. *The Practice of Social Research*. Belmont: Wadsworth.
Boelen, Paul, Marcel van den Hout, and Jan van den Bout. 2008. The Factor Structure of Posttraumatic Stress Disorder Symptoms among Bereaved Individuals: A Confirmatory Factor Analysis Study. *Journal of Anxiety Disorder* 22, no. 8:1,377–83.
Bryman, Alan, and Emma Bell. 2007. *Business Research Methods*. Oxford: Oxford University Press.
Byrne, Barbara. 2010. *Structural Equation Modelling with Amos: Basic Concepts, Applications, and Programming*. New York: Routledge.
Commission on Human Security (CHS). 2003. *Human Security Now: Final Report of the Commission on Human Security*. New York: United Nations Publishing.
Crano, William, and Marilynn Brewer. 2002. *Principles and Methods of Social Research*. Mahwah: Lawrence Erlbaum Associates.
Fowler, Floyd. 1995. *Improving Survey Questions: Design and Evaluation*. London: Sage.
Government of Guyana. 2002. *Poverty Reduction Strategy Paper*. Georgetown: Government of Guyana.
———. 2011. *Guyana Poverty Reduction Strategy Paper 2011–2015*. Georgetown: Government of Guyana.
Green, Duncan. 2012. *From Poverty to Power: How Active Citizens and Effective States can Change the World*. 2nd ed. Rugby: Practical Action Publishing and Oxfam International.
Guyana Chronicle. 2016. *$3B for Citizen Security*. January 23, 3.
Hampson, Fen, Jean Daudelin, John Hay, Todd Martin, and Holly Reid. 2002. *Madness in the Multitude: Human Security and World Disorder*. Toronto: Oxford University Press.
Haveman, Robert. 2009. What Does it Mean to be Poor in a Rich Society. *Focus* 26, no. 2: 1–86.
Henry, Clement. 2012. An Analysis of the Effectiveness of Foreign Aid Flows to Guyana. In *Selected Essays on Contemporary Caribbean Issues*, ed. Marlon Anatol and Mark Kirton, 90–134. Newton: Total Printing Systems.
Henry-Lee, Aldrie, and Elsie Le Franc. 2002. Private Poverty and Gender in Guyana and Barbados. *Social and Economic Studies* 51, no. 4:1–30.
Hick, Rod. 2012. The Capability Approach: Insights for a New Poverty Focus. *LSE Research* Accessed January 15, 2016. http://eprints.lse.ac.uk/39745/1/The_capability_approach_Insights_for_a_new_ poverty_focus_%28lsero%29.pdf.

Inter-American Development Bank. 2014. Citizen Security Strengthening Programme (GY-L1042) Loan Proposal. Accessed June 6, 2016. http://idbdocs.iadb.org/wsdocs/getdocument.aspx? docnum=39241069.
Khine, Myint Swe. 2013. *Application of Structural Equation Modelling in Educational Research and Practice*. Rotterdam: Sense Publishers.
Khong, Yuen Foong. 2001. Human Security: A Shotgun Approach to Alleviating Human Misery? *Global Governance* 7, no. 3: 231–36.
Lohr, Sharon. 2010. *Sampling: Design and Analysis*. Boston: Brooks/Cole Cengage Learning.
Nolan, Brian, and Christopher Whelan. 2011. *Poverty and Deprivation in Europe*. Oxford: Oxford University Press.
Orshansky, Mollie. 1965. Counting the Poor: Another Look at the Poverty Profile. *Bulletin*: 3–29.
Owen, Taylor. 2004. Human Security – Conflict, Critique and Consensus: Colloquium Remarks and a Proposal for a Threshold-Based Definition. *Security Dialogue* 35, no. 3:373–87.
Paris, Roland. 2001. Human Security: Paradigm Shift or Hot Air? *International Security* 26, no. 2:87–102.
Pettit, Jethro. 2016. Why Citizens Don't Engage – Power, Poverty and Civic Habitus. *Institute of Development Studies* 47, no. 5. doi:http://dx.doi.org/10.19088/1968-2016.169.
Post, Richard, and Arthur Kingsbury. 1991. *Security Administration: An Introduction to the Protective Services*. Stoneham: Butterworth-Heinemann.
Renshaw, John. 2006. Access to Social Services in Guyana. A Report Commissioned by the Inter-American Development Bank under Technical Cooperation GY-T1010, Georgetown.
Reveron, Derek, and Kathleen Mahoney-Norris. 2011. *Human Security in A Borderless World*. Colorado: West View Press.
Rowntree, Benjamin. 1902. *Poverty: A Study of Town Life*. New York: The Macmillan Company.
Sen, Amartya. 1985. *Commodities and Capabilities*, vol. 7. New York: Elsevier.
——. 2009. *The Idea of Justice*. Cambridge: The Belknap Press.
——. 2012. Foreword. In *From Poverty to Power: How Active Citizens and Effective States Can Change the World*, ed. Duncan Green. Rugby: Practical Action Publishing and Oxfam International.
Spicker, Paul, Sonia Alvarez Leguizamón, and David Gordon. 2007. *Poverty: An International Glossary*. New York: Zed Books.
Tadjbaksh, Shahrbanou, and Anuradha Chenoy. 2007. *Human Security: Concepts and Implications*. New York: Routledge.
Thomas, Clive. 1993. Lesson from Experience: Structural Adjustment and Poverty in Guyana. *Social and Econmic Studies* 42, no. 4:133–84.
Townsend, Peter. 1979. *Poverty in the United Kingdom*. London: Penguin.
UN General Assembly. 1948. Universal Declaration of Human Rights. *Resolution 217 A (III)*. Accessed June 13, 2016. http://www.refworld.org/docid/3ae6b3712c.html.

———. 1966a. International Covenant on Civil and Political Rights. *United Nations Treaty Series* 999. Accessed June 13, 2016. http://www.refworld.org/docid/3ae6b3aa0.html.
———. 1966b. International Covenant on Economic, Social and Cultural Rights. *United Nations, Treaty Series* 993. Accessed June 13, 2016. http://www.refworld.org/docid/3ae6b36c0.html.
United Nations Development Programme (UNDP). 1994. *Human Development Report 1994: New Dimensions of Human Security*. New York: United Nations Development Programme.
Wang, Jichuan and Xiaoqian Wang. 2012. *Structural Equation Modelling: Applications Using Mplus*. Sussex: John Wiley & Sons.
Watts, Harold. 1968. An Economic Definition of Poverty. In *On Understanding Poverty*, ed. Daniel Moynihan. New York: Basic Books.
Williams, Paul. 2013. *Security Studies: An Introduction*. 2nd ed. New York: Routledge.
Williamson, John, and Kathryn Hyer. 1975. The Measurement and Meaning of Poverty. *Social Problems* 22, no. 5:652–63.
Wolfers, Arnold. 1952. 'National Security' as an Ambiguous Symbol. *Political Science Quarterly* 67, no. 4:481–502.
World Bank. 1992. Guyana from Economic Recovery to Sustained Growth. Report No. 10307–GUY, Washington.
Zheng, Buhong. 1997. Aggregate Poverty Measures. *Journal of Economic Surveys* 11, no. 2:123–62.

Appendix 9A: Questionnaire

Item	Summary Variable	Indicator Name	Questionnaire Statement
X_1	Economic Security	Access to financial resources/income	In the past 12 months, how many months have you gone without a cash income? 1 Often (10 or more times) 2 Fairly Often (5-9 times) 3 Sometimes (3-4 times) 4 Rarely (1-2 times) 5 Never
X_2	Economic Security	Perception on household income adequacy	Considering food, shelter, clothing and medicine: how often in the past 12 months, because of your household income level, was your family unable to cover any of these basic necessities? 1 Often (10 or more times) 2 Fairly Often (5-9 times) 3 Sometimes (3-4 times) 4 Rarely (1-2 times) 5 Never
X_3	Food Security	Access to food produce/resources to purchase food	In the past four weeks, how often did the food that you bought/grew just didn't last, and you didn't have money to get more? 1 Often (10 or more times) 2 Fairly Often (5-9 times) 3 Sometimes (3-4 times) 4 Rarely (1-2 times) 5 Never
X_4	Food Security	Adequacy of Food Resources	Sometimes people eat less, miss meals or go hungry because there are not enough resources to get food. In the past four weeks, how often did this happen to you or to a household member? 1 Often (10 or more times) 2 Fairly Often (5-9 times) 3 Sometimes (3-4 times) 4 Rarely (1-2 times) 5 Never
X_5	Food Security	Worry associated with food access and availability	In the past four weeks, how often did you worry that your household would not have enough food? 1 Often (10 or more times) 2 Fairly Often (5-9 times) 3 Sometimes (3-4 times) 4 Rarely (1-2 times) 5 Never

Item	Summary Variable	Indicator Name	Questionnaire Statement
X_6	Health Security	Perception on access to Health Care	How difficult would you say it is to get good health care and medicine at an affordable cost when someone in your household is sick or in an emergency? 1 Very Difficult 2 Difficult 3 Not too difficult 4 Easy 5 Very easy
X_7	Health Security	Level of satisfaction with health care services	Thinking about the last time you or someone you know were in need of medical attention and visited a public or private health care facility, how satisfied were/was you/he/she with the quality of health care you/he/she received? 1 very dissatisfied 2 fairly dissatisfied 3 neither satisfied nor dissatisfied 4 fairly satisfied 5 Very satisfied
X_8	Health Security	Level of satisfaction with communicable disease prevention	In general, would you say that you are very satisfied, fairly satisfied, neither satisfied nor dissatisfied, fairly dissatisfied or very dissatisfied with the quality of public services available to prevent communicable diseases. 1 very dissatisfied 2 fairly dissatisfied 3 neither satisfied nor dissatisfied 4 fairly satisfied 5 Very satisfied
X_9	Personal Security	Experience with crime/ violence victimization	In the past 12 months, how often have you or anyone in your household been the victim of a violent crime such as murder, assault, robbery, kidnapping or rape? 1 Often (6 or more times) 2 Fairly Often (4-5 times) 3 Sometimes (2-3 times) 4 Rarely (once) 5 Never
X_{10}	Personal Security	Fear of crime and violence	In general, how safe from crime and violence do you feel when you are walking on the streets of your community at nights? 1 Not safe at all 2 Slightly safe 3 Moderately Safe 4 Safe 5 Completely safe

Item	Summary Variable	Indicator Name	Questionnaire Statement
X_{11}	Environmental Security	Where people live and the nature of environmental challenges	Please rate how these problems [environmental] have affected your household over the past 5 years using a five-point scale corresponding to very severe, severe, slightly severe, not severe, and not at all affected. 1 Very Severe 2 Severe 3 Slightly Severe 4 Not Severe 5 Not affected at all
X_{12}	Environmental Security	People's susceptibility to environmental threats	How worried are you about environmental/natural disasters taking your life and livelihood? 1 Extremely worried 2 Worried 3 Moderately worried 4 Not worried 5 Not at all worried
X_{13}	Societal Security	Perception of whether there is equality before the law	In relation to police matters and justice, is every group in society (including different ethnic groups) treated equally? 1 Completely disagree 2 disagree 3 Neither agree nor disagree 4 Agree 5 Completely Agree
X_{14}	Societal Security	Perception on the level of respect for citizens' rights	Kindly indicate your view on the level of respect for citizens' rights in the country. Consider rights such as protection from inhumane treatment & torture, protection against arbitrary search or entry, protection against forced labour or slavery, freedom of association and movement and equality of persons before the law. Would you say that there is _____ for citizens' rights nowadays in this country? 1 No respect at all 2 Not much respect 3 Neutral 4 Fairly much respect 5 A great deal of respect
X_{15}	Political Security	Perception of individual freedom to express oneself on political matters	How free do you think you are to express yourself without fear of government reprisal? 1 Not free at all 2 Not free 3 Slightly free 4 free 5 Completely free

Item	Summary Variable	Indicator Name	Questionnaire Statement
X_{16}	Political Security	Level of trust in state institutions	Using a 5-point scale with each point indicating a score that goes from 1 meaning NOT AT ALL to 5, meaning A LOT, kindly state how much you trust the following state institutions. A) The Guyana Defence Force 1 Not at all 2 3 4 5 A lot B) The Guyana Police Force 1 Not at all 2 3 4 5 A lot
X_{17}	Political Security	Perception of individual freedom to exercise political choices	A) Freedom of voting is secured in this country. 1 Completely disagree 2 disagree 3 Neither agree nor disagree 4 Agree 5 Completely Agree B) Votes are counted fairly in this country. 1 Completely disagree 2 disagree 3 Neither agree nor disagree 4 Agree 5 Completely Agree C) Voters are threatened with violence at the polls. 1 Completely Agree 2 Agree 3 Neither agree nor disagree 4 disagree 5 Completely disagree

Appendix 9B: Sample Size Selection

In determining the size of the sample Cochran's (1963, 75) formula for computing sample size was applied. This method is ideally suited for categorical data collection (Bartlett, Kotrlik and Higgins 2001, 47). Cochran's formula is presented below:

$$N_0 = \frac{Z^2 * pq}{E^2} \qquad \text{Equation 1}$$

Where N_0 is the sample size, Z^2 is the value for the selected alpha level based on the confidence level (e.g. 1.96 for 95% confidence level), E is the desired level of precision or the amount of error the researcher is willing to accept, p is the estimated proportion of an attribute that is present in the population, and q is 1-p.

Since there was no knowledge of the variability in the proportion of human insecurities, it is customary, in similar instances, to adopt the maximum variability option of p =0.5. The research aims for 95% confidence and ±3% precision. Taking these figures into consideration, the sample size was computed as:

$$N_0 = \frac{(1.96)^2 * .05 * .05}{(03)^2} \qquad \text{Equation 2}$$

From equation 2 the sample size equals 1,067.

Appendix 9.C: Model Fit Information

Number of Free Parameters	70
Loglikelihood H_0 Value H_1 Value	-17,782.577 -17,685.138
Information Criteria Akaike (AIC) Bayesian (BIC) Sample-Size Adjusted BIC $n^* = (n + 2) / 24)$	35,705.155 36,035.231 35,812.937
Chi-Square Test of Model Fit Value Degrees of freedom P-Value Scaling Correction Factor for MLM	180.823 82 0.00001 1.0777
RMSEA (Root Mean Square Error of Approximation) Estimate 90 Per cent C.I Probability RMSEA <= 0.5	0.038 0.031 0.046 0.996
CFI/TLI CFI TLI	0.967 0.952
SRMR (Standardised Root Mean Square Residual) Value	0.034

10.
The Myth of Free Education
Diana Abraham

This chapter examines the travails of Guyana's public education system, when reductions in state funding and promotion of private sector substitutions unhinged the post-independence commitment to free and equal access to education. My analysis incorporates a selection of findings from a qualitative interpretative phenomenological analysis (IPA) research project, which explored issues surrounding the transnational and intersectoral migration of qualified teachers and their consequences for primary and secondary public education. It draws on data gathered in reviews of government policies, local print media, and other relevant publications. Field activities were restricted to qualified teachers and administrative personnel associated with two sixth form secondary schools, one public primary school, and one private school in Georgetown, Guyana. It also draws on interviews with senior-level individuals associated with Guyana's Ministry of Education (MoEd) and civil society activists engaged in educational projects.[1]

The chapter begins with a brief historical review of the Guyana government's commitment to equity in education and a consideration of the circumstances compelling the reversal of this promise. In this context, attention is paid to how neoliberal conditionalities governing the Structural Adjustment Program (SAP) of the International Monetary Fund (IMF) demanded the application of austerity measures to public-sector salaries and infrastructural supports, and encouraged the entrenchment of private education as a fundamental right in 2003 (Guyana Constitution, Article 149I). I then examine the impact of the austerity measures on the socio-economic infrastructure and consequent delivery of public education, and conclude with an analysis of the effect of the 'un-freeing' of public education on the most vulnerable members of Guyana's school-age population.

Historical Background

Formal schooling in the era of slavery was intended for the offspring of the plantocracy to support the reproduction of the social structure in the colony (Samaroo 1989, 6). This historical context influenced the vision for Guyana's system of free public education in the post-independence era. In their immediate pre- and post-independence governments, Cheddi Jagan and Forbes Burnham began the process of 'freeing' public education in Guyana.[2] Their dreams were grounded in lofty visions of an independent state unshackled from the oppressive edicts of Christian, colonial ideologies, and the establishment of a path to economic development where public education recognised multi-denominational voices and the new political realities.

In 1963, during a period of intense political unrest, the People's Progressive Party (PPP) administration led by Cheddi Jagan published a memorandum of public education and broadcast a policy which sought to 'ensure that educational opportunities are available on an equal basis to all sections of the population whatever their economic and social position' (PPP Memorandum on Education cited in Bacchus 1980, 246). The elections of 1964 snatched away the Jagan government's ability to realise the dream. Forbes Burnham's new administration published their own policy memorandum on education in 1968, with an explicit commitment to a system of public, secular education embedded in the adoption of principles dedicated to eradicating the old colonial and capitalist values and introducing new and relevant ones (Benjamin 2009, 1; Burnham 1974, cited in Jennings 1999, 3). The minister of education proclaimed the new system vital since, 'the colonial political economy and the associated education system were simply not concerned with development' (cited in Benjamin 2009, 2).

The structural changes undergirding adoption of these principles included:

1. centralisation and imposition of state control of schools so that close to 696 schools – most of which were privately financed or owned by church organisations – were brought under the control of the state (Benjamin 2009, 2).

2. abolition of fees in 1976;
3. universal access to primary schools across the land;
4. expansion of the curriculum beyond the traditional grammar school model; and
5. specialist teacher training centres.

These measures increased enrolment and state expenditure on a number of educational institutions, so that:

> Between 1970 and 1979 the number of educational institutions in Guyana expanded from 432 to 1,214 (primary school and primary tops were 758). This increase was equally matched by increases in enrolment numbers and participation rates from a total of 162,076 to 182,682 (Benjamin 2009, 3).

The system makeover was enshrined in the proclamation of the right to a free education, which stated: 'Every citizen has the right to a free education from nursery to university as well as at non-formal places where opportunities are provided for education and training' (Art 27(1), Constitution of Guyana 1980). This was additionally underwritten by high levels of public spending:

> Increases in educational expenditures as a percentage of Gross Domestic Product between 1970 and 1980 averaged in excess of 5.3 per cent as compared to 4.6 per cent between 1966 and 1969. Similarly, educational expenditures as a percentage of total government expenditures also increased during the same period from 13.7 per cent in 1970 to 18.1 per cent in 1978 and by 1980 it was almost 16 per cent (Tyrone Ferguson, cited in Benjamin 2009, 3).

Indeed, this public outlay on education was facilitated by the economic growth Guyana experienced between 1970 and 1975. 'Driven largely by favourable global commodity prices and increased production in the country's major export commodities such as rice, sugar and bauxite, Guyana experienced consistently rapid economic growth rates averaging 3.9 per cent between 1970 and 1975' (Benjamin 2009, 4).

In addition, the policy and economic transformations were grounded in state control of the economy and nationalisation of all major production and distribution enterprises, including the large bauxite and sugar industries in 1971 and 1973 respectively. These actions increased the size of the public sector to about two-thirds of the economy (MacCuish 2005, 4) and were responsible for the rise in public employment to over ten per cent of the population (Egoumé-Bossogo et al. 2003, 2).

The upward economic trajectory was, however, shattered, by the 1980 global recession and oil crisis, falling world prices for the country's commodity exports of sugar and bauxite (a collapse which also revealed structural vulnerabilities of the government's co-operative socialist experiment), high government spending and an increase in emigration especially of skilled people (MacCuish 2005, 4). Guyana's economy was severely constrained by a crippling debt burden, the inability to generate adequate foreign exchange to service the debt, and the near impossibility of acquiring external financing (Ifill 2002, 1).

The devastated economy impelled Burnham's successor, Desmond Hoyte's 1985 decision to steer the country toward the market system, and with a verbal commitment to economic liberalism, the government was able to re-establish relations with the IMF and the World Bank in 1986 (Ifill 2002, 1). Directed by the neoliberal practices of these bodies, in 1989 the government launched an Economic Recovery Program (ERP) and made a stronger shift to market policies that continued through the 1990s (MacCuish 2005, 4). The two principal objectives of the ERP were to source external funding and to implement specific economic strategies as a condition for this funding to be continuously secured. The policy and operational measures most relevant to the present discourse were 'wage control in the public sector' and 'privatisation' (Ifill 2002, 2). Following the return to free and fair elections in 1992, the newly elected PPP administration led by President Bharrat Jagdeo continued the path of a largely externally dictated economic liberalisation programme.

Impact of Austerity Measures

In their analyses of the effects of the neoliberal interventions embedded in the SAP conditionalities, Martin Carnoy and Carlos Torres (1992, preface), Cornelia Staritz, Judith Gold and Ruben Atoyan (2007, 4) and the International Labour Organization (ILO) (ILO 1996) identified reductions in public expenditures in social services, and the adoption of austerity measures as instruments that compromised the quality of education. Furthermore, reforms aimed at the development of a market-based economy, entailed significant privatisation (Staritz, Gold and Atoyan 2007, 4), and reductions in public service salaries and infrastructural disbursements. In a 1996 press release, the ILO singled out Guyana as one of the economies with negative to zero-to-negative relative public expenditure growth, which translated into decreases in educational expenditure of 7.6 per cent per annum.

This slowdown was acknowledged in several government publications during the last decade and a half. For example, the following citation in the 2001–10 Guyana National Development Strategy (NDS) has appeared in varying iterations in the May 2000 NDS, the 2004 National Report of Guyana's MoEd, and the 2014–18 Guyana Education Sector Work Plan:

> The Government...found it difficult to meet growing public expectations for full access to education of a high quality...The inability to maintain standards...[and] declining financial allocations from the State ... have adversely affected both the quality of education in Guyana, and citizens' access to it (Guyana National Development Strategy 2001–10, Annex 18).

Enmeshed in meeting the demands of the monetary debt crises and the conditionalities imposed by the SAP investors, Guyana was and continues to be unable to meet the post-independence dream of full access to wholly subsidised high quality education.[3]

The 2001–10 NDS and other government publications cite the erosion of the population's access to primary schools as significant; a diagnosis illustrated with citations related to the rising 'repetition' and 'drop-out' rates, along with the 'alarmingly high levels of functional illiteracy among school-leavers and the adult population' (Guyana National Development Strategy 2001–10, chapter 18). This is substantiated in Jennings' documentation of the functional illiteracy among 'Out of School' youth in Guyana (Jennings 2000, 385).

Like Reimers's elaboration on the consequences of SAP conditionalities (cited in Carnoy and Torres 1992, 28), decreased education expenditures in Guyana have brought about restrictions on teachers' salaries and benefits, on infrastructural spending – such as for building maintenance, and on the provision of school supplies and laboratory and other equipment essential to the educational process.[4]

All these factors have contributed to the depreciation of state-supported education and consequent teacher attrition. The sector has lost teachers to migration and to a newly emerged private primary and secondary education sector. Additionally, a loss of prestige has meant that qualified candidates are choosing to enter other professions to the detriment of teaching, creating further deficits in the public education system.

Push Factor for Teacher Attrition Rates
Poor Salaries

Several Research Participants (RPs) provided vivid examples of how salary restrictions contributed to the loss of qualified teachers, the impact of their departure on the professional and classroom practice of those left behind, and the consequences for the children in public primary and secondary schools. In the words of a former minister of education, 'We can't pay them. That's why they're going...You are paying the average teacher C$300 [per month]. That's the reality' (Personal Interview MoEdP1).

A senior administrator with the MoEd indicated that while there was no substantiating research, anecdotal evidence suggested that dissatisfaction with salaries was also a major impetus for teachers' migration. This view was forcefully expressed by the chair of the board of governors of a sixth form secondary school (BoGP1), who described public sector teachers' salaries as 'disgracefully poor' (Personal Interview BoGP1).

Another chair offered the following details of teachers' compensation in 2009:

> A head teacher would get about G$130,000 (C$650) [per month]. A very well-paid teacher gets about a G$100,000 [per month]. Before that teacher puts his hand on the money the first G$40,000 is tax free, so on the next $60,000 he is paying 33.3 per cent. So that means that $20,000 gone off the $100,000 in addition to which he has the contribution to NIS which is another chunk. So he is going to end up getting about $75,000 out of the $100,000 – well the $100,000 is already low cause it's C$500. When he comes down to $75,000 it means he is getting C$375 [per month] (Personal Interview BoGP2).

Teacher Research Participants (TRPs) described the effects of the 'disgracefully poor' salaries, on their living conditions, which made it 'hard to acquire the necessities that would allow for a comfortable family life.' They compared their situations to those of colleagues in other Caribbean countries who had parking lots in their school. 'If I look out my school all I would see is tree (three) motorcycles (sic). Teachers want to have a better living standard, they want to drive to work and own a home.' As a result, many were forced to depend on supplementary sources of income. One TRP described depending on two additional jobs and a partner's salary to support their family:

> As we speak I am doing three jobs to pay the bills. [In addition to teaching I am a] Chef Junior...at...Hotel three times a week and on weekends; and

tutoring after school – going to homes. My wife works, and that's how we manage to make it from pay cheque to pay cheque.

Another source of supplementary income was the provision of after school extra lessons in situations where there were no subject teachers in the schools.[5] Two TRPs reported:

> There is a shortage of Physics teachers. I recognised it and filled that gap. Parents were prepared to pay. Students were [that is, came] from three sixth form secondary schools.

> (2) The children had no teacher to teach them language...The first time I did it as a volunteer. After they had done really well I decided I wasn't going to continue. But then the next batch approached me. "Sir we heard you were really good." That's how I started and now I charge them.

Other supplemental sources of income included the family's reliance on the spouse's seasonal income: facilitation of adult evening classes sponsored by a private school; provision of extra classes in the August holidays; part-time contracts with the Guyana Elections Commission; and teaching in the University of Guyana's Distance Education programme or in a private school started by a return migrant teacher. Indeed, to quote one TRP, 'Any outside job I would try, to facilitate to make ends meet' (sic).

Poor Infrastructure and Working Conditions

Alongside teachers' dissatisfaction with their salaries, the research revealed examples of the working conditions 'which definitely contribute[d] to somebody wanting to migrate' (Personal Interview TRP9). One TRP described the demands made on teachers who had to compensate for dysfunctional conditions which existed in the homes of students:

> As a teacher you have to be everything. You have to be a counsellor because some of them coming with their own problems from home; and you have to be sometimes, the cleaner for the children because of different situations, and so on' (Personal Interview TRP12).

These conditions are aggravated by the confidence-sapping results teachers would experience when addressing indiscipline in the classroom. As reported in April 2013:

> Teachers have been known to complain about what they say is their own diminished authority in the face of what they regard as a serious upsurge of indiscipline in schools. ...These developments have sapped their confidence and diminished their authority (*Stabroek News* 2013A).

One TRP described having to meet the curriculum demands of 'practically-oriented subjects' in a secondary school without basic teaching tools:

> If you think of the more practically oriented subjects, [there is a] lack of resources. [The] physics lab, for example, does not have adequate instruments or devices to conduct the experiments. We have the same problem with [the] chemistry lab – lack of chemicals and also the various [pieces of] apparatus. [It is impossible] to conduct experiments to the [required] standards if they are not adequate or they malfunction or they aren't working properly. You have the same problem with the technology department. You don't have a lab per se (Personal Interview TRP15).

Among the endogenous factors pushing the exodus of teachers was the stress of functioning in overcrowded, poorly furnished classes. One TRP recalled teaching in a public secondary school where 'There were about 60 students in a class...Imagine one teacher to 60 students where you are supposed to have 35 students. You [should] have two students on a bench [but it's] sometimes three and four students on a bench (Personal Interview TRP11).[6]

Another TRP referred to the 'pressures' in the classroom and their effects on a teacher's family life. 'The pressures in a classroom [with] 30–40-something students, half of them slow learners...when you get home you don't want to hear anything from your [own] children (Personal Interview TRP8).

Migration

Poor salaries, infrastructure, and working conditions were not the only reasons cited for dissatisfaction which led to migration. Research participants described how the open-space arrangements and inadequate toilet facilities in the public primary schools contributed to teachers' decisions to 'seek greener pastures'.[7]

> Open spaces, no classrooms. Some of the schools they don't have proper facilities for the teachers and the children and so on...In some of the schools...the toilet situation for the children, sometimes it could be smelling not too pleasant at all, and then you as a teacher you have to be everything (Personal Interview TRP12).

These conditions were substantiated by an inspection of 50 schools in Georgetown by the City Public Health Department (*Stabroek News* 2012) and by teachers who staged a 'sit-out on the deplorable conditions' on June 10, 2016 (*Stabroek News* 2016).

Teacher dissatisfaction was aggravated by the lack of appreciation for their efforts by both head teachers and decision-makers at the MoEd. One TRP described the expectations of teachers who had to perform with limited resources. 'They expect you to do so much and sometimes it's not possible for you to do anymore, because of the limited resources that you might have to help these children' (Personal Interview TRP12).

Another TRP identified the futility of demanding improvements in classroom hardware. 'If you complain about anything about your classroom, or chairs, it's the same thing – "we can't do anything about it." That's what the Ministry sends' (Personal Interview TRP 6).

The ministry's failure to appreciate the realities of the classroom was illustrated with the description of a composition writing workshop with a MoEd contracted facilitator.

> Somebody who came from the US or Canada stressed that the children "must feel comfortable" for learning to take place. "If they feel like going on the floor and write, if they feel like going under the table" they must feel comfortable.

The TRP mused on the facilitator's lack of awareness of the conditions in the local schools. 'But how can we apply that to our schools? The floor is not even clean enough for the children to go on…We don't have the resources; we don't have the space to do it (Personal Interview TRP12).

The 'loss of respect for the profession' was a recurring theme throughout the research and a contributing factor in the dissatisfaction of teachers who migrate. TRP12 suggested that the children's disrespect may emanate from their parents' attitudes and behaviours towards the teachers. Another TRP spoke of disrespect in the MoEd's dealings with senior teachers which impacted their relationships with the rest of the teaching staff, and ultimately affected their morale:

> The attitude of MoEd, how they deal with the senior teachers in the schools, how you treat them; there is not a sense of respect; and I think that contributes to the morale of the school, because if it's not there at the level of the principal it could filter down (Personal Interview TRP15).

A summation of the motivations for the international migration of teachers is succinctly captured in the following statement by one chair of a board of governors:

> The situation here, the salaries, the decline in comfortable living, the corruption and violence, all of that cause people to leave. It's not only the salaries. If they have children they want their children to have better opportunities (Personal Interview BoGP1).

The data provided by a broad spectrum of research participants confirmed that it is impossible to 'get a numerical handle' on the exodus of qualified teachers from Guyana between 2000 and 2010. As per a personal communiqué from a MoEdP, 'teachers rarely state when they resign that they are migrating [so] the ministry does not have migration data' although it may have some idea on the numbers who are teaching abroad from the requests received 'for records of service from foreign institutions. But it is not comprehensive.' The lack of specific data was noted in a July 2013 news item where representatives of the MoEd and the Guyana Teachers Union were unable to provide data to substantiate their boasts on the 'slow down' in teacher migration. This report noted that 'no figures were available to compare the impact of migration over the last ten years' (*Demerara News* 2014).

Privatisation of the Sector: The Pull of Better Salaries and Infrastructure

Other than the information gathered from the research and in the local media, it is difficult to locate any substantive data on the numbers of teachers who transfer to private sector schools. As evident in the information provided above by the research participant affiliated with the MoEd (MoEdP2), the government is unable to systematically track the rates and reasons for teacher attrition at the primary and secondary levels – a practice deemed to be central to the strategic planning for fulfilling teacher requirements in state-sponsored schools (UNESCO 2010).

One TRP recalled teachers' 'migration' to the private schools when they came into existence in the early 1990s. 'Of course they were paying better salaries, [had better] working conditions, better labs and better facilities and so.' TRPs who relocated to the private sector described the salary differential as motivating their decisions.[8] TRP7 deemed the *pull* factors to be better compensation, smaller classes, lighter workloads, and less burdensome class preparation:

> In the public school, you have a class of 36; in the private school you are working with a class of 15 and sometimes 12. And so they see it

less demanding. And the other thing, the teachers, when they go to the private school there is no burden...to prepare these laborious notes of lessons and...your own scheme of work and...your own teaching aids. There it's a package to work with. In the public system there is no package...everything you have to prepare (Personal Interview).

The local media described the initiative of one retired teacher and captured some of the essence of the competition the private sector schools pose for the public system:

> Latchmin Gopal is passionate about teaching, and about helping children to tap into their potential. A teacher for over 37 years, she is poised to open her private school at Cornelia Ida, the Academy of Excellence, on September 5 ... The newly built school is spacious. Classrooms are large, and students access them along a corridor that has two wide staircases. The school also has a canteen and male and female washrooms built far apart from each other. It is expected to hold 250 students from grade one to level six (*Stabroek News* 2011A).

The effects of the privatisation of primary and secondary schools in Guyana are summarised by UNESCO:

> First, private schools are attracting the better-qualified teachers from the public system with the result that an already ailing public system is being further depleted of its scarce human resources, including school principals. Second, private schools are excelling at the SSEE (Secondary School Entrance Examination), putting out the top students.[9] They seem to be offering a better quality of education, not only on account of their broader and more balanced curriculum, but also because of their physical conditions, supply of textbooks and smaller classes (UNESCO 2006, 26).[10]

The departure of experienced teachers to the private sector severely undercut the quality of state-subsidised primary and secondary education. This loss and the trend towards private schools are manifestations of the SAP directed 'un-freeing' of education in Guyana.[11]

Another manifestation became evident when in 2005 the ministry of education created volunteer boards of governors to manage sixth form secondary schools (History of St Stanislaus College 2009). The chair of one of the boards linked this development to the SAP conditionalities:

> I believe they were forced or encouraged by the IDB to get the community involved by the establishment of school boards...they had no choice, but to have school boards and expect them to do what they are expecting us to do (Personal Interview BoGP2).[12]

Indeed, the data provided by the two chairs suggest that the creation of these boards was a move by the government of Guyana to engineer a 'low cost' download of obligations for the administration of these schools, to groups of individuals who were prepared to undertake the responsibilities on a volunteer basis. With the exception of Queen's College[13] which does receive an annual allowance, the boards resemble other MoEd SAP cost-cutting enterprises. Operational descriptions provided by the BoGPs indicate that they include alumni from the respective schools, and along with the participation of overseas and local alumni associations, and service organisations like Rotary International, they are frequently engaged in fund-raising for various infrastructural needs in their home schools. In some situations, they also cover the costs of recreation and other appreciation events for the faculties. In effect the private sector subsidises the operation of 'public schools'.

Members of various international non-government organisations such as the American-based Volunteer Services Organisation (VSO) and Youth Challenge Guyana (YCG) volunteer teachers' programme are also sometimes substituted for salaried teachers (*Kaieteur News* 2016A). And while the commitment of volunteers – especially in schools in the interior of Guyana – is admirable, these interventions are another money saving 'quick fix' which ultimately deprives the students of the benefits of the experience gained when there is continuity in a teaching faculty.

Other Deficits

The 'unfreeing' of the system also has other deleterious effects. A perspective shared by participants in this study was that another level of problems had to do with the academic qualifications of the individuals who applied for and were accepted into the teacher training programme. Indeed, they revealed that students from the *'high flying'* Level A, sixth form secondary schools, with 11 or more CSEC credits, *do not enter the profession*. They reject teaching as being at the 'bottom of the respect scale' with salaries paying 'less than planting rice,' and instead seek prestigious, higher paying occupations which 'bring in' the money (Personal Interview BoGP2). The days when to be a teacher carried a certain amount of status have gone. Another participant suggested:

> I think people are now looking at higher paid jobs. People want to get in the engineering field, become a businessman or woman, become a

doctor; and people are looking in another direction. Long ago teaching was a prestigious job. [Now] people want to go into another direction (Personal Interview TP1).

These observations were substantiated in the press:

> The nation's best and brightest are not clamouring for admission to the Cyril Potter College of Education immediately having received their CSEC results that include good grades in English and Mathematics. They are looking elsewhere (*Stabroek News* 2014A).

The picture which emerges is of a vicious circle, as those who enter teacher training programmes begin with questionable qualifications, and serious issues arise regarding the competence of replacements for departing teachers.

Despite a number of international government-funded projects for teacher education[14] and the former minister of education's frequent boasts about the numbers of trained teachers, the research revealed serious flaws in the capabilities of individuals graduating from the teacher education programmes at the Cyril Potter College of Education and the University of Guyana. In the view of one participant, 'Now it's not so much [the] teachers we are producing being exported. It is that the quality of intake into the training college is so poor that the quality of output cannot be good' (Personal Interview BoGP2).

One civil society research participant ruminated on the situation where 'We are sending students to the university who can't spell; can't write a sentence,'[15] and drolly recounted the following experience, with a primary schoolteacher:

> Probably the most comical encounter we had with one of the schools was the teacher asking us if we could take her whole class because they could not read. This would have been a couple years before common entrance (the NGSA); the kids would have been 9 or 10 [years old] (Personal Interview, CSRP2).

Thus, the challenge to replace qualified teachers lost within the public education system begins with the shortage of competent personnel. This issue was captured in a 2012 press release from the Teaching Services Commission:

> In 2012, the (Teaching Services) Commission received 1,016 applications from Secondary School Graduates for employment at the Junior Level. Only 347 of them were employed. There were many applicants with ten or more CSEC or CXC passes with Grades I to IV but who had lower

than Grade III in English Language and Mathematics. A pass grade II and higher in English Language and Mathematics is compulsory for appointment as a Temporary Qualified Master/Mistress.

In the case of junior appointments, some vacancies were unfilled because applicants with passes in technical fields were deficient in English Language and to a lesser extent Mathematics (*Stabroek News* 2013B).

Where vacancies have been filled, the following are snapshots of participants' experiences with trained graduate teachers:

Inability to impart lessons, or cope with the requirements of the syllabus:

- They come into the system. They cannot handle form one students – the content. Sometimes the children (students) complain they cannot comprehend the teacher because sometimes they (the teachers) cannot express themselves in a way that the children can learn whatever concept they are trying to put forward (Personal Interview TRP1).

  I am not satisfied with the level of knowledge the teachers who are coming from the training college come with into the system. I think it's far below what the syllabus and the curriculum require for sure. Many of them cannot cope with the level of work that is required for the technology syllabus (Personal Interview TRP15).

- Difficulties reading and conjugating verbs:

  I don't want to be too critical but some of them, in terms of expressing themselves, reading in a way that you understand what they are saying is sometimes difficult. You wonder how 'how did you get the degree?' Because getting a degree you have to be fluent, you have to make presentations, especially in sociology class. I often wonder how they deliver (Personal Interview TRP4).

  An (English) teacher said to me 'I don't know how you form the past tense of verbs. It's something that I have been trying to research.' She tried to teach the children that you form the past tense of verbs by adding 'ed' so the children had irregular verbs an (sic) they added 'ed'. So for 'tell' they put 'telled' – that's what she had taught them. Why would you do this? "Well remember I don't really know English. I taught dis (thought this) is what you could do,"' and things like that. She graduated from CPC this year. (Personal Interview TRP19).

- In one job interview, a graduate teacher was unable to identify one Caribbean author:

  In an interview for an English teacher, I asked her to name her favourite West Indian author and she said Shakespeare. I reformulated the question. Who do you like best of all the authors in the Caribbean? She repeated, Shakespeare. I indicated that Shakespeare was an English writer and asked, do you know any writers from the Caribbean? I gave examples, Naipaul, Selvon, etc. 'No Miss,' she said. This is an example of someone applying to our schools to teach English (Personal Interview BoGP1).

- Levels of literacy were 'sometimes not good' and many had 'difficulty grasping the concepts addressed in the programme' (Personal Interview TRP2).

- In-service trainee-teacher's inability to impart the concepts of a lesson:[16]

  Simple, simple things – yet they were going to College at the In-Service level – these teachers really didn't understand; really, really didn't understand. And so I find it really hard to believe that, yes, you are going to classes in the afternoon, and then when you are placed in the class room there are simple basic things you can't 'put over' to these children. It was sad (Personal Interview TRP7).

- Unpreparedness to address behavioural problems:

  Two graduate teachers sought assistance to address difficulties with a student's behaviour. When asked if the degree in Sociology they had completed had not prepared them for these classroom situations their response was 'what we did is not for this situation.' [The TRP concluded that] whatever the graduate teachers had learned 'they couldn't use back that knowledge to deal with this very simple child who was having difficulties settling in class' (Personal Interview TRP4).

The difficulties the graduate teachers were experiencing led participants to conclude that the problems had been there 'long before they [the students] reached UG' (Personal Interview TRP2). Another corroborated this view:

> It is like a chicken and egg. They come out of the primary schools bad. When I say 'bad' I mean schools...haven't done what they are

supposed to do...They go to the secondary school system which again is substandard, and they enter the [college] – by the time they come out of their four years at the teachers training college – you get an 'end product' that is substandard according to my criteria (Personal Interview BoGP1).

TRP7 described how government policies contributed to the 'long before' failures in the public education system, and why the teachers applying to training college were the products of that system. 'The system we now have with the 'automatic promotion – no child left behind' – it is failing our children miserably. Another TRP described how the automatic promotion directive affected learners:[17]

> I am teaching children in grade five who can't write their names...pupils from a number of schools. They are so accustomed to not writing [that] even when you try to help them, they then miss classes...I know of two children in secondary school who can't form letters properly, don't know to distinguish a b from a d...(Personal Interview TRP9).

Effects on the Teaching Profession and on Students

The professional practice of those who remain in the public education system is undermined by the presence of incompetent replacements for teachers who have left and by vacancies. There is also the expectation that those competent teachers who have endured will voluntarily assume additional classroom responsibilities, either through the merging of classes in the primary schools, or by simultaneously teaching two subject areas at the secondary level.[18] The demands embedded in these double and at times triple responsibilities contribute to both the lowering of morale and the intensification of mental health stresses, which in turn impact the quality of classroom lessons and the quotidian lives of teachers and students.

In the primary schools when a teacher is absent from work, the other teachers and students are *juggled* between classes. In some situations, classes are merged within grades and/or the teacher is moved between classes.[19] Whether the absence is for one day or a permanent move, and whatever configuration is used, whether grade classes were merged or split, the upshot for the teachers 'left behind' is an increased workload, defined in terms of the numbers of children they are responsible for and the consequent administrative responsibilities:

> It's more work, we have more work to do, you know. We have more books to mark, we got to enforce more disciplinary measures cause the classes

are larger and children get out of hand. Most times we split classes, cause you can't manoeuvre from one class to the next. So we split the classes and one is without the teacher. So [perhaps] we have ten extra. You have 25 or 30 children already and we have to get 10 extra. It's a large class and workload increases (Personal Interview TRP 13).

Another TRP noted that prior knowledge of departures was sometimes not communicated by administrators: 'All the times when I heard, even if they leave midterm, the administration would have known. But sometimes too they don't tell' (Personal Interview TRP10). One participant with responsibility for setting the timetable at a sixth form secondary school described the adjustments that had to be made when subject specialists leave or disappear without notice at the midterm:

> The person (teacher) might just disappear. When that happens you gotta (sic) be jostling around. In the case of the Science teachers you just don't have [them]. It always puts you under tremendous pressure because you have to adjust the timetable. When the loss is to the quota of language teachers, if there are three [teachers] and one leaves, or one of two leaves, you have to go back to the timetable and see how you can fit them in to teach the classes the [absent] teacher was teaching. and so that is a real helluva job. If you have three or four cases like that it will be real stressful (Personal Interview TRP 15).

In worst case scenarios children are transferred to another school.

> When there are real emergency departures, and the teaching complement at the home school is unable to accommodate additional children they may be transferred to a nearby school where there may be vacancies in classrooms. If there is a real emergency and this school hasn't got the teacher... and there is a school nearby with the teacher to teach these children, the children will have to go over to join that class (Personal Interview TRP10).

Excerpts from interviews with participants illustrate the concerns for the effects of teachers' demoralisation on the children in their schools. One TRP was distressed by how the accommodation of additional numbers of children affected the scope and quality of lessons delivered to the class. This last double-edged sword saw the teachers being demoralised by the at times futile attempts to impart the full curriculum, and their awareness that the children were suffering because of this inability:

> Many times the teacher, when she had been committed to her set of children, she has to [now] concentrate on these extra pupils. Most times she sits. What can I say? It's not that she would just sit there. I mean if she is doing six subjects a day she would end up doing three, cause she

has more books to mark, she has more work to do, so she can't do it all (Personal Interview TRP13).

The next statement reflects the speaker's anxieties that teachers' 'resistance' to filling-in for a missing teacher impacts the quality of classroom lessons:

> We got some teachers who say 'I ain't going teach nobody (sic) class.'... Some agree to put work on the black board...*putting work on the black board is not it*...It's ensuring that the children understand the concepts... some teachers saying 'I ain't getting nothing extra' *and that's where the children suffer*...this affects the children's results...some will be ahead others will be back. At the end of it all they have to do the one exam (Personal Interview TRP8).

TRP's offered a number of perspectives on the consequences of the loss of qualified personnel on their working lives and in particular on their mental health. One described the frustration experienced when required to expand well-organised pre-planned lessons to accommodate an additional 17 students at the beginning of the school year. The level of stress was such that this teacher would 'at times just give up.'

> They come in at this time and you have so many to look after. By the time you are finished setting the books up and you ready (sic) to do one thing maybe you have made place cards for your 19 now you have to share. And what you wanted to bring in at the first place, that went out the window because you have the other 17 in your class. At times you just give up. And not do anything (Personal Interview TRP5).

The foregoing reflections were analogous to those articulated in personal interviews with several TRPs. Both primary and secondary schoolteachers described variations of frustration and stress associated with juggling schedules, delivering lessons well enough to keep their students engaged, and fulfil the expectations of the parents, while gaining professional satisfaction from the lessons they imparted. Guyana's desperate shortage of teachers in Science, Technology, Engineering and Mathematics (STEM) meant that the head of department had no option but to take responsibility for the instruction of all the secondary school classes in this area. 'I have been teaching from the first right up to the fifth [years], all the classes, because I don't have anybody else,' he said, postulating that surviving the management of the emotional interference embedded in the intense schedules teachers were asked to maintain was 'miraculous'.

> Is a miracle. I am so stressed and tired when I get home, yes, because I am just going. Between classroom contact time and administration [I

am] going non-stop. Maybe I just have one day I think, in the afternoon when I have two periods [in which] I am free. Sometimes you are in a class and you are being called to a meeting. So that adds to the whole thing. Very stressful. *Very* stressful (Personal Interview TRP15).

The psychological pressure experienced by secondary school subject teachers – who 'have the extra workload because in some cases you are the only teacher there,' and who have to be prepared to go 'back and forth' between classes from first to fifth forms, running and planning lessons – is aggravated by the awareness, that 'at the end of the day it's the students who move on without knowing what it is they are supposed to know' (Personal Interview TRP19). TRP1's observations of the '*edgy*' behaviours of colleagues in a secondary school, led to the conclusion that the burden of assuming additional responsibilities without adequate preparation,

> impacted significantly on those teachers who are left behind; and then you find that this can make people become very edgy and people can snap at little things because they are so taxed, they are so burdened with so many things, that some people do not really cope well with having to do all of this within a short period of time (Personal Interview TRP1).

One primary schoolteacher argued that the MoEd's directives instructing school administrators to ensure the adherence to and documentation of the use of the pre-set curriculum, became especially '*fatiguing*' in situations where teachers were suddenly called on to replace a teacher who hadn't '*turned up*'.

> So if the teacher doesn't turn up, any teacher who is assigned to the class can pick up the book and say, 'Okay, this is what Miss is doing,' and they can teach the class to enable continuity. But if teachers have been in the system for so long, I don't see the need actually for this. It's fatiguing, and the teachers should be allowed to be creative, you know. But even that they want you to document. The notes get to me sometimes (Personal Interview TRP11).

Conclusion: Poverty and the Myth of Free Education

The interviews with research participants revealed that the lacuna caused by the loss of qualified teachers impacts the delivery of classroom instruction, outcomes, professional relations among teaching faculty, and the morale of those charged with sustaining the quality of the state sanctioned curriculum. These findings also revealed a serious flaw in the MoEd's failure to acknowledge the damaging effects which its policies have on the quality of schooling to which it is committed.[20]

The reduction in teacher's salaries and infrastructure expenditures has in effect meant that the schools and students most affected by the SAP demands to reduce educational spending, are often located in areas of Guyana where the landscapes of the surrounding communities are fractured by poverty and a loss of hope in the value of education. The following excerpt from Jennings describes conditions encountered in one of the villages where field assistants were attempting to recruit research participants:

> In the back streets of this community persons were more concerned about living from day to day with little or no interest in pursuing formal education. Only about ten homes in the back streets had all their school age members attending school. The others had either dropped out or attended school occasionally. The number of members in these homes who are unable to read/write never attended school is terrifying (Jennings 2000, 399).

A participant who was a head teacher affiliated with an 'inner city' public primary school in Georgetown, recounted the home life situations of many students, and the consequences these had for their school attendance:

> They don't live in homes that are really comfortable and things like that. They don't have enough meals to eat, they don't have enough parental guidance I would say. There are lots of single parent homes, or let's say matrifocal homes, where the mother is the head of the home, right, and so children come here with a whole lot of issues. Some children come to school hungry and all kinds of things (Personal Interview HTP1).

These findings question the quality of schooling in a neoliberal context, and belie the official assurance that privatisation will not compromise the provision of a level playing field for all school age children in Guyana: 'Although private schools will be encouraged to operate, the ministry is committed to providing free and compulsory education from the pre-primary to secondary levels' (Ministry of Education 2014–2018 Volume One, v). This chapter has demonstrated that SAP related and other financial cutbacks in government support for education and the privatisation of the sector have had destructive consequences for educational opportunities for disadvantaged members of Guyana's school-age population. In spite of the valiant efforts and dedication of teachers who remain in the public school system, the quality and scope of state subsidised primary and secondary schools are plagued by teacher shortages and substandard infrastructure, where the only recourse is private fee-paying schools which demand that parents have the means to cover the relevant costs.[21] As UNESCO noted in 2006/07:

> The high fees that these institutions charge (while they allow some amount of cost sharing of education with the government) effectively debar the poor, yet academically talented, from benefitting from a quality of education not available in the public system. This, in the final analysis, will make the realisation of the goal of equality of educational opportunity all the more elusive (UNESCO 2006, 26).[22]

In these circumstances it is not surprising that 'children from families in the top income quintile completed school at a 94 per cent rate compared to children in the lowest income quintile at a 47 percent rate' (Inter-American Development Bank 2015, 17)[23] and those in the latter group are in the words of one of the research participants 'left to wallow in whatever the system is giving' (Personal Interview BoGP2).

All may not be lost. Following the 2015 elections which brought a coalition government led by A Partnership for National Unity and the Alliance for Change (APNU-AFC), former Minister of Education Dr Rupert Roopnarine announced the establishment of a Commission of Inquiry to examine 'the way in which our children are actually educated and whether the education they are receiving is really preparing them for a future in Guyana' (*Kaieteur News* 2016B). Along with the commission there was also reason for cautious optimism in the percentage of the national budget allocated to the sector. The 2016 budget tabled by the finance minister on January 29 has allocated a total of $40.3 billion to education, or 17.5 per cent of the $230 billion 2016 budget.

Overriding the laundry list of initiatives included in the estimates is a commitment that the interventions will be allocated to determine equity and quality across regions,[24] with special attention given to the hinterland where both the deployment of manpower and the monitoring of education delivery require urgent attention (*Kaieteur News* 2016C). At the same time, it is important to remember that the economy of Guyana remains mired in the clutches of the World Bank and the accompanying conditionalities discussed at the beginning of this chapter. This has remained consistent since 1985, across all elected governments, including the present one. In effect, the country has not moved to demonstrate 'ownership' of economic policies, but continues to depend on the financial support of donors (both bilateral and multilateral), with a substantial amount of policy direction determined by the international financial institutions (MacCuish 2005, 25).

To counter the 'power' wielded by those managing the SAPs and to demonstrate its commitment to transparency, the government of Guyana might seek the engagement of civil society and particularly those most affected by the commitment to equity in education, in the policy decision-making processes (MacCuish 2005, 26). A good beginning would be their active participation in the Commission of Inquiry and a demonstrated commitment to implement its recommendations.

Notes

1. Research Participants are designated Teacher Research Participant (TRP); Board of Governor Participant (BoGP); Ministry of Education Participant (MoEdP) or Civil Society Research Participant (CSRP). Demographically the average number of years of professional practice of teacher participants was 14 years. Their locations in the hierarchy of the schools included head teachers and heads of departments.
2. In 196,1 Guyana achieved full internal self-government, and the People's Progressive Party (PPP), under the leadership of Jagan, gained a majority in the legislative assembly.
3. A review of economic policy in Guyana shows that the country continues to be dependent on the financial support of donors (both bilateral and multilateral) with a substantial amount of policy direction dictated by the international financial institutions (MacCuish 2005, 25).
4. In 2012, Guyana expended three per cent of its GDP on education (Inter-American Development Bank 2015).
5. The issue of 'extra lessons' has been the subject of much public discourse. A common argument is that teacher's short circuit their class room curriculum and make attendance at their 'after school' lessons as a condition for students who want to successfully complete the end of year examinations. The research participants offered a number of explanations for the phenomenon of extra lessons and while in agreement that there may be some instances of 'rogue teachers' exhibiting the abovementioned behaviours, this is not substantiated in an examination of the situations where extra lessons are provided. The cohort of teachers I interviewed identified of a number of situations which created the demand for extra lessons. Examples included the need to compensate for inadequate classroom time to accommodate the syllabus in Agri Science: '... and when you look at the time that is allotted, normally we work at three 35-minute periods and the syllabus is asking for eight 40-minute periods a week' (TRP3). To fill shortage '...I taught Upgrading or Physics in the afternoon to students from Saint Stanislaus College and elsewhere. There is a shortage of Physics teachers. I recognised it and filled that gap' (TRP15).
6. The consequences of these situations are also described in the local media. 'Inside classrooms, a lack of adequate quantities of furniture and overcrowding

impose their own hazards, not least of which are limitations of space, the risk of the spread of communicable infections resulting from proximity among children and the attendant discomfort for students and teachers which, of course, impacts directly on both the delivery and receipt of education (*Stabroek News* 2011B).

7. In the public primary schools, it is common for several classes to be set up in large open halls.
8.

Public School Salary	Private Sector Salary
In 2004 when I left (Name of Public Primary School) my take home salary was about $30 something thousand I think; nearly 40. I can't remember (Personal Interview TRP2).	(Seven years ago) I went to (Name of Private School) my salary was take home about $50-something thousand (Personal Interview TRP2).
Fifteen years ago, at (Name of Public Primary School) I was taking home $17,000 net; it was about 25,000 gross (Personal Interview TRP4).	Current gross salary $140,000.00. No pension plan at the Private sector school (Personal Interview TRP4).
In 2000-2007 a trained teacher was $25,000.00 and some odd change (Personal Interview TRP 5).	Current Salary is $70,000. No Pension Plan (Personal Interview TRP5).

9. Replaced by the National Grade Six Assessment (NGSA) Secondary School Entrance Examination.
10. Of the 12,600 students in Guyana who wrote the 2015 CSEC examinations, 47 students passed with 11 grade ones or more, and of that number, 23 per cent were students of the Hindu Saraswati Vidya Niketan (SVN) Secondary School, founded by Swami Aksharananda of Guyana in 2002. The Principal noted that in addition to the benefits outlined by UNESCO, the teachers had to be commended for their hard work with students, some of whom had entered the school with average marks at the National Grade Six Assessment (NGSA). Fourteen students with marks in the low 400s at the NGSA graduated with 12 subjects or more at CSEC at the institution (*Guyana Times* 2015).
11. The dream of creating state subsidised education for development was premised on the 1976 rejection of the structures in place in the pre-independence era and the secularisation of schools administered by various religious bodies. This move was viewed by many as retrograde to the quality of education provided by religious organisations (See Jennings 2000, 398).
12. There is no reference to the IDB, in the *Manual for Governance of Schools by Boards* Published by the MoEd in 2013.
13. 1According to the *Guyana Budget Estimates, Current and Capital Revenue and Expenditure* 1 (2013): 397, the Board of Governors of Queen's College received an Annual Subvention $96,589. Information verified in the Minister of Educations' response to a question posed in the Tenth Parliament of Guyana – First Session (2012) National Assembly Notice Paper No. 160.

14. These are described in:
    1. World Bank. 1975. World Bank Report *Appraisal of a Second Education Project*. Guyana April 3, 1975, January 1999–December 2003 Guyana Education Access Project GEAP Project Region 6 Background;
    2. World Bank 2010 For an Improving Teacher Education: *Project Appraisal Document* on a Proposed Credit in the Amount of Sdr 2.8 Million (US$4.2 Million Equivalent) Report No: 53927-Gy Including Sdr 1.2 Million in Pilot CRW Resources (US$1.8 Million Equivalent) to the Cooperative Republic of Guyana.
15. The staff at the Red Thread Women's Centre, which provides after school lessons for underprivileged children.
16. 1Individuals employed as teachers attend this in-service teacher-training programme at the Cyril Potter Training College. They are allowed time off to attend classes which may be offered during the school day. This is another source of contention for the teachers who have to fill-in for them.
17. Like many other poorly conceptualised policies, this one was perceived as a way of saving the embarrassment of handling the potential 'drop out' of students who fail to meet the expected grade at the end of the term and have to repeat the class (*Stabroek News* 2010).
18. Involves the preparation and delivery of lessons, the grading of tests and all the accompanying bureaucratic demands.
19. Along with the permanent loss of teachers to migration, the private sector or retirement, teacher absence – short or long term – may be also be due to attendance at UG during class time or illness.
20. A situation illustrated when the then Minister of Education Priya Manickchand was questioned, following the announcement of the results of the 2014 National Grade Six Assessment (NGSA) when Private Schools had cupped the ten top spots. When asked whether her ministry was concerned about the possibility of parents neglecting the public education system, Minister Manickchand – seemingly oblivious to the numerous issues discussed in this chapter sought to excuse underperforming in the public schools on the basis that there were things that private institutions were allowed to do that the public system could not, hence their ability to outperform the public system. 'Private schools get to screen students. We don't; we take all children. Also, if a student doesn't perform, private schools ask them to leave; we persevere with all children… underperforming teachers are booted [from] the private system. We can't do that with the same efficiency in public school' (*Inewsguyana* 2014).
21. It is well known that many elected officials opt to send their children to private sector schools. When called upon to explain her daughter's attendance at a private school, for instance, the former Education Minister Manickchand said that while she could not speak for others, the law provided for parents to make choices on their children's education. The Constitution of Guyana allowed for private schools, which allowed parents from across the country to make choices for their children. 'Most parents I know do what they believe would be best for their children' (*Stabroek News* 2014B).

22. Interviews in the local press with private-school students who successfully complete the NGSA and CSEC examinations frequently attribute their success to the 'extra-lessons' for which their parents had covered the costs.
23. This year, 12 private schools account for 95 of the 166 students (57 per cent) who make up the top one per cent. The remaining 71 students (43 per cent) hail from 36 schools in the public school system (*Stabroek News* 2015).
24. Budget Detailed by the Minister of Education, http://educationgy.org/web/index.php/mediacenter/budget-speech-2016.

References

Government of Guyana Documents

Constitution of the Co-operative Republic of Guyana 1980. Accessed February 6, 2018. https://www.constituteproject.org/constitution/Guyana_2009.pdf.

Ministry of Education. 2013. Manual for Governance of Schools by Boards.

———. 2014. Guyana Education Sector Work Plan 2014–2018. Accessed April 3, 2016. http://educationgy.org/web/index.php/education-sector-plan-2014-2018.

National Assembly. 2012. The Minister of Educations' Response to a Question Posed in the Tenth Parliament of Guyana – First Session (2012) Notice Paper No. 160. Accessed June 26, 2016. https://educationgy.org/web/index.php/answers-to-parliamentary-questions/item/689-subvention-for-senior-secondary-board-managed-high-schools-in-guyana.

National Development Strategy. 2001–2010. Chapter 18 Education. Accessed March 26, 2016. www.guyana.org/NDS/NDS.htm.

Local Publications

History of Saint Stanislaus College. Accessed February 6, 2018. https://www.st-stanislaus-gy.com/History/SSC-History-2009.pdf.

Media

Benjamin, Dwayne. 2009. Education Policy Changes and Economic Crisis in Guyana 1970–1985. *Stabroek News*, November 12. Accessed April 5, 2016. http://www.stabroeknews.com/2009/features/11/12/education-policy-changes-and-economic-crisis-in-guyana-1970-1985.

Demerara News. 2014 Teacher Migration Slows. Accessed February 6, 2018. July 8, 2013. https://demerarawaves.com.

Guyana Times. 2015. President Awards Top CSEC Student. October 13. Accessed February 6, 2018. https://issuu.com/gytimes/docs/binder1_45a229a4287e27.

Ifill, Melissa. 2002. Structural Adjustment and Political Reform in Guyana. *Stabroek News*, November 28. Accessed August 17, 2016. Monday, August 20, 18http://www.stabroeknews.com/2009/features/09/17/history-this-week-43.

Inewsguyana. 2014. Private Schools across Guyana Have Dominated the Top Ten Spots of the 2014 National Grade Six Assessment (NGSA) for which Results were RToday. June 12. Accessed 20 August 18. https://www.inewsguyana.com/ngsa-results-private-schools-dominate-top-10.

Kaieteur News. 2016A. Volunteer Teachers Playing Major Role in Hinterland Schools January 7. Accessed June 13, 2016. NEWS www.kaieteurnewsonline.com/2016/01/07/volunteer-teachers-playing.

———. 2016B. Education Ministry Seeking Public Support to Conduct COI. April 6. Accessed April 6, 2016. http://www.kaieteurnewsonline.com/2016/04/06/education-ministry-seeking-public-support-to-conduct-coi.

———. 2016C. 2016 National budget...Improving Education Equity and Quality Attracts $40.3B January 31. Accessed January 31, 2016. www.kaieteurnewsonline.com/2016/01/31/2016-national-budget.

———. 2010. Automatic Promotion Seeks to Stem High Dropout Rate – Baksh. December 4. http://www.stabroeknews.com/2010/archives/12/04/automatic-promotion-seeks-to-stem-high-dropout-rate---baksh.

———. 2011A. Retired Teacher Opening School at Cornelia Ida. August 15. http://www.stabroeknews.com 2011/archives/08/15/retired-teacher-opening-school-at-cornelia-ida.

———. 2011B. Editorial: Crumbling Schools and Effective Education Delivery. February 8. Accessed February 8, 2011. http://www.stabroeknews.com/2011/opinion/editorial/02/08/crumbling-schools-and-effective-education-delivery.

———. 2012. Inspection of 50 Schools in Georgetown by the City Public Health Department. April 28. Accessed June 24, 2016. http://www.stabroeknews.com/2012/news/stories/04/28/inspection-of-50-city.

———. 2013A. Guyana Review 2013: Is Official Indifference Fuelling Violence in Schools? April 10. Accessed June 24, 2016. http://www.stabroeknews.com/2013/guyana-review/04/10/is-official.

———. 2013B. 659 Junior Teachers Appointed in 2012 – TSC. February 21. Accessed August 17, 2016. http://www.stabroeknews.com/2013/news/stories/02/21/659-junior-teachers-appointed-in-2012-tsc.

———. 2014A 'Editorial: Teachers and the State School System. February 25. Accessed August 17, 2016. http://www.stabroeknews.com/2014/opinion/editorial/02/25/teachers-state-school-system.

———. 2014B. Manickchand Says Private School Education in Her Child's best Interest. December 13. Accessed August 17, 2016. http://www.stabroeknews.com/2014/news/stories/12/13/manickchand-says-private-school-education-childs-best-interest.

———. 2015. Private Schools Continue to Outstrip Public at Grade Six Assessment. June 13. Accessed February 6, 2018. http://www.stabroeknews.com/2015/news/stories/06/13/private-schools-continue-to-outstrip-public-at-grade-six-assessment.

———. 2016. Teachers Stage Sit out over Deplorable Conditions at Brickdam Secondary. June 11. Accessed June 11, 2016. http://www.stabroeknews.com/2016/news/stories/06/11/teachers-stage-sit-deplorable-conditions-brickdam-secondary.

Academic Publications

Bacchus, M.K. 1980. *Education for Development or Underdevelopment? Guyana's Educational System and its Implications for the Third World.* Waterloo: Wilfrid Laurier University Press.

Hamilton, Donald B. 2014. Appraisal of the Cooperative Republic of Guyana Education Sector Plan 2014–2018. A Report Submitted to the Local Education Group. Accessed April 15, 2016. http://webcache.googleusercontent.com/search?q=cache:uPqeIyy5atEJ:www.globalpartnership.org/fr/download/file/fid/46711+&cd=1&hl=en&ct=clnk&gl=ca.

Jennings, Zellynne. 1999. Educational Reform in Guyana in the Post-War Period. *Educational Reform in the Commonwealth Caribbean.* www.educoas.org/Portal/bdigital/contenido/.../mil_jen.htm.

———. 2000. Adult Literacy in the Commonwealth Caribbean with Special Reference to a Study of the Functional Literacy of Young Guyanese Adults. *International Journal of Lifelong Education* 19, no. 5 (September–October): 385–406.

MacCuish, Derek. 2005. Guyana: Experience of Economic Reform under World Bank and IMF Direction. *Social Justice Committee on Behalf of the Halifax Initiative Coalition.* Accessed March 29, 2016. http://www.halifaxinitiative.org/updir/Guyana.pdf.

Samaroo, Noel K. 1989. Education and Human Rights Violation in Guyana. Texas Papers on Latin America: Pre-publication Working Papers of the Institute of Latin American Studies, University of Texas at Austin. Paper No. 90-03. Accessed December 11, 2015. http://www.researchgate.net/publication/234693021_Education_and_Human_Rights_Violation_inGuyana_Texas_Papers_on_Latin_America_Prepublication_Working_Papers_of_the_Institute_of_Latin_American_Studies_University_of_Texas_at_Austin_Paper_No_90-03.

International Publications

Carnoy, Martin and Carlos Torres. 1992. Educational Change and Structural Adjustment: A Case Study of Costa Rica. Paris: UNESCO-ILO. Accessed June 1, 2016. http://unesdoc.unesco.org/images/0009/000934/093466eo.pdf.

Inter-American Development Bank. 2015. *Caribbean Region Quarterly Bulletin* 4, no. 2 (July). Accessed February 6, 2018. http://documents.caribseek.com/sites/default/files/files/2015/pdfs/caribseek-documents/united-states-america/2015-0731-csd-us-idb-caribbean-region-quarterly-bulletin-volume-4-issue-2-july-2015.pdf.

Egoumé-Bossogo, Phillipe, Ebrina Faal, Raj Nallari and Ethan Weisman. 2003. *Guyana Experience with Macroeconomic Stabilisation, Structural Adjustment and Poverty Reduction.* Washington, DC: International Monetary Fund

ILO. 1996. Teachers' Salaries, Class Sizes at Risk under Structural Adjustment Policies, ILO Says ILO/96/12. Accessed August 17, 2016. http://www.ilo.org/global/about-the-ilo/newsroom/news/WCMS_008052/lang--en/index.htm.

Staritz, Cornelia, Judith Gold, and Ruben Atoyan. 2007. Guyana: Why Has Growth Stopped? An Empirical Study on the Stagnation of Economic Growth. IMF Working Paper, April 2007. Accessed March 6, 2016. https://www.researchgate.net/publication/5125391_Guyana_Why_Has_Growth_Stopped_An_Empirical_Study_on_the_Stagnation_of_Economic_Growth.

UNESCO. 2006. World Data on Education. 6th ed., 2006/07 Updated version, August 2006. *Compiled by UNESCO-IBE*. Accessed March 26, 2016. http://www.ibe.unesco.org.

———. 2010. Teacher Attrition in Sub-Saharan Africa The Neglected Dimension of the Teacher Supply Challenge: A Review of the Literature. International Taskforce on Teachers for Education for All. Aidan Mulkeen with the Assistance of Ms. Nuala Crowe-Taft. Accessed September 2, 2010. http://www.unesco.org/new/en/media-services/single-view/news/teacher.

VSO. 2011. Making Teachers Count: Voices and Views from the Classroom. VSO Guyana Valuing Teachers. Last updated September 2011. Accessed June 16, 2016. https://www.google.ca/?gws_rd=ssl#q=Making+Teachers+Count:+Voices+and+views+from+the+classroom+VSO+Guyana+Valuing+Teacher.

World Bank. 1975. World Bank Report Appraisal of a Second Education Project. Guyana, April 3, 1975; January 1999–December 2003 Guyana Education Access Project GEAP Project Region 6 Background Webpage. Accessed February 3, 2013. http://www.sdnp.org.gy/geap/info/index.html.

———. 2010. For an Improving Teacher Education: Project Appraisal Document on a Proposed Credit in the Amount of Sdr 2.8 Million (US$4.2 Million Equivalent) Report No: 53927-Gy Including Sdr 1.2 Million in Pilot CRW Resources (US$1.8 Million Equivalent) to the Cooperative Republic of Guyana.

11.
Growing Downhill? Contestations of Sovereignty and the Creation of Itinerant Workers in Guyanese Call Centres

Alissa Trotz, Kiran Mirchandani, and Iman Khan

Introduction

In the global clamour to attract foreign capital, Guyana is a small player with high stakes. As in many other countries that house transnational call centres, the enticement of foreign capital has been an important part of state economic policy for the past three decades. Alongside its attempt to generate capital flows into the country, however, Guyana is unique in the scale of its simultaneous outflow of educated citizens in response to few local employment prospects and an ambivalent state policy that has both lamented outmigration and fostered the reliance on remittances from overseas Guyanese. This was the backdrop and condition of possibility for the entry of the transnational call centre sector to Guyana less than a decade ago. Explicitly constructed as a shift away from the routine factory work that global manufacturing firms provide, telemediated customer service work is frequently promoted as creating white-collar jobs for educated youth. Such official optimism is belied by the wry observation of Ray, a young man whom we interviewed for this project, who noted that 'the call centre seems to be a growing factor in Guyana, even though its growing seems to be going on a downhill.' In this chapter we trace the practices through which Guyana's transnational call centres are constructed as sites of hope and progress by state, organisational, and media actors. We explore three forms of sovereignty that are continually being enacted and expressed within Guyanese call centres – state sovereignty, customer sovereignty, and the sovereignty of global capital. We draw on interviews

"Growing Downhill? Contestations of Sovereignty and the Creation of Itinerant Workers in Guyanese Call Centers," by Alissa Trotz, Kiran Mirchandani and Iman Khan was previously published in *Borders in Service: Enactments of Nationhood in Transnational Call Centres*, edited by Kiran Mirchandani and Winifred Poster © University of Toronto Press 2016 (pp. 58–85).

with 17 call centre workers to explore their experiences in the sector, as well as two key informants who reflect on state and organisational policies relating to the emergence of the call centre industry in Guyana. Our findings reveal that, despite the promise of high-paying, stable jobs, call centres are highly itinerant spaces, with employees bearing the brunt of firm closures and contractions. Instead of providing sustainable careers for educated youth, jobs are designed to be low paid and extractive. With striking uniformity, the workers we interviewed noted that call centre jobs cast Guyana as a nation with a young, captive workforce ripe for exploitation by foreign actors.

Contested Sovereignty and Guyanese National Identity

The contested nature of the sovereignty of modern states is now well established. Traditional constructions of states as holding unilateral, complete, and final decision-making authority (referred to broadly as the Westphalian international order) over their territories and citizens have been overtaken by the recognition that states are one of multiple actors that exercise sovereignty within national spaces, with varying degrees of success and coherence (for an excellent overview see Trouillot 2001). While some theorists argue that the capacity of nation states to influence local and international policy has been eclipsed by the reach of global capital (see Hardt and Negri 2000), others suggest that state sovereignty has not so much declined as it has been transformed, taking, as Aihwa Ong notes, a 'graduated' form (Ong 2007; also see Brown 2010; Sassen 1996). State practices collude with global capital and have differing effects on various groups of citizens depending on their deemed 'usefulness' to processes of capital accumulation. In this context, states play a key role in mediating the tensions between global and national interests in relation to market ideologies (Brown 2010). The project of constructing the wall along the US southern border, for example, is a state strategy to negotiate the tensions between the needs of North American businesses for the cheap labour of illegal migrants, and the demands of workers on the US side who are affected by the downward pressure on wages and working conditions brought about by easy access to this labour (Brown 2010).

At the same time, the sovereignty of states and of global capital is continually contested through elaborating what Lisa Lowe refers to as a transnational counterpolitics (Lowe 2008), as well as through emerging global cosmopolitan norms (Benhabib 2007) that universalise rather than segment access to livelihoods and rights. These sovereignties are exercised in conjunction with another extremely significant actor having sovereign power in the call-centre setting – the customer. D.T. Goldberg (2009) has observed that the customers' exercise of power is privatised as an expression of 'preference' that can supersede state or global actors in the context of neoliberal, market-oriented global capitalism. In service encounters, for example, customers are made to feel sovereign in two ways – first, by being positioned as 'relationally superior' to the server on the other end of the call and, second, through constructing service exchanges as ones in which customers are 'in charge' (Korczynski 2007, 78). Although this power may be far from complete, customers' real or imagined preferences play an important role in the ways in which states exercise their sovereignty. As discussed in the sections to follow, the transnational call centre in Guyana is one site where these varied sovereignties materialise and overlap and are visibly in contest.

Methodology

The analysis in this chapter is based on reviews of local newspapers, company descriptions, promotional materials, and websites that refer to Guyana's call centre industries. These include several YouTube video recordings of site visits and interviews with company officials. In addition, 17 call centre workers (none in a managerial position) and two key informants were anonymously interviewed, based on contacts made through sources that were unconnected to call centre administrators. Interviews were held in a home space after working hours, and workers were invited to share their job experiences without employer involvement or knowledge. Pseudonyms have been used, and specific information, particularly about employers and work situations that might identify individuals have been omitted to protect worker identities.

Companies solicit applications in a variety of ways, placing advertisements in newspapers and on television as well as using social media tools like Facebook to advertise recruitment drives and provide information to prospective applicants. Responses on social media represented a significant way to gauge someone's comfort level with using computers and the Internet, all important attributes for a job in the industry. A survey of advertisements, websites, and Facebook pages reveals an emphasis on attracting applications from those with educational qualifications (in several cases, evidence of the successful completion of secondary-school-leaving examinations) and communication skills. In return, potential recruits are promised excellent remuneration and a highly professional and transnational work environment that entails handling overseas clients (one can interact with the outside while remaining in the country). The Facebook page of one company carries an image of a cheque with the payee section reading 'Pay yourself GyD$250,000 (USD$1,207).' This is no small amount in a country where the minimum monthly wage is GY$35,000 (US$169). Facebook pages also regularly feature company promotions for employees, like competitions for trips to Kaieteur Falls (a local tourist destination in Guyana's hinterland) and to neighbouring islands like Trinidad and Tobago. Pictures of company-sponsored outings – picnics, sports days – for employees and their families are also posted, and team loyalty is encouraged through participation in tournaments (dominoes, basketball, and cricket) that pit company employees against other teams around the city and country. The larger companies in particular are also involved in various activities that confirm their narratives of being good corporate citizens. Employees volunteer in several company-sponsored initiatives that range from donating food and other goods to orphanages and senior citizens' homes, to participating in clean-up activities in the capital city, Georgetown.

Of the 17 people interviewed, 12 were currently employed in a call centre, and the remaining 5 had recently left call centre jobs. Of the respondents, 15 were women, and the average age of the interviewees was 22 years, reflecting the official emphasis on providing employment for youth. All the people interviewed had completed secondary education, and 13 had gone on to further studies, with two people also receiving some of their tertiary education in other Caribbean countries before returning to Guyana. Such educational diversity raises important questions about job opportunities as well as the possibilities for career fulfilment within the call service sector.

Exercising State Sovereignty By Selling Guyana

In the mid-1980s, Guyana began a process of economic and political liberalisation, after a decade and a half of a failed co-operative socialist experiment in the immediate post-independence era, embarking upon a home-grown version of structural adjustment in 1985 and ushering in democratic elections in 1992, the first since 1964.[1] Under the Economic Recovery Programme (as it is locally referred to, and which has been continued or intensified by the administration that has been in power since 1992), this process has included aggressively courting private capital in such areas as logging, ecotourism, mining, and oil exploration; pursuing public-private partnerships; and putting mechanisms in place to attract and facilitate foreign investment, like GO-Invest, a governmental organisation that offers tax breaks, duty-free concessions, and other perks to would-be investors. Such initiatives signalled a shift towards the 'graduated sovereignty' of the Guyanese state whereby 'corporations [hold] an indirect power over the political conditions of citizens in zones that are differently articulated to global production and financial circuits' (Ong 2007, 78).

While the bulk of the investment opportunities so far have been in the country's hinterland (home to most of Guyana's indigenous peoples, and the site of diamonds and other precious metals and one of the largest remaining rainforests), one of the key demonstrations of interest in investing on the coast (where some 90 per cent of Guyana's population resides) has come from call centres and business-processing outsourcing firms (BPOs). Emerging on the local scene over the past ten or so years, this is still a relatively incipient market, providing employment to about 3,000 people, most of them young women between the ages of 17 and 25. With about a dozen call centres in operation, the sector is dominated by one large firm that has locations also in Southeast Asia and Latin America, and which grew from a workforce of less than 100 people a decade ago to being reportedly the largest private employer in the country today with over 1,000 employees. There are a few medium-sized enterprises with over 100 workers (these appear mainly to be companies that have established themselves only in Guyana), and some much smaller and struggling firms. Most of the companies are located in or near the main urban centre and capital city of Georgetown. According to one media report, they 'perform such services as outbound sales/telemarketing; inbound customer support; voicemail transcription; medical records transcription; and data warehousing for clients in the United Kingdom, the United States, Canada and Mexico' (*Guyana Chronicle* July 3, 2012).[2]

Effusive predictions by state and industry officials that 'Guyana's future as an outsourcing destination is brightening by the day'

(Ammachchi n.d.) are accompanied by news reports of expansion, such as an announcement that a global call centre organisation is currently in the process of building what is described as one of the world's largest call centres in Guyana, a multi-purpose site that will include educational, interfaith, and other facilities for the six thousand additional employees whom it hopes to attract (*Guyana Chronicle*, September 5, 2013). In addition, Teleperformance USA is reported to have invested US$2 billion to set up a 1,500-seat call centre that is anticipated to be operational by 2016 (*Stabroek News*, 2015). Call service investment is described by the government of Guyana not only as essential to economic diversification but specifically as creating high-value jobs in information and communications technology,[3] with official efforts to improve infrastructure and put in place regulatory frameworks to support increased investment in this sector.[4]

This emphasis on creating highly skilled service-sector jobs and specific assurances that call centres offer what one company describes as the 'ultimate dream career' assumes particular urgency in a country from which some 43 per cent of secondary-educated citizens and 89 per cent of tertiary-educated citizens migrate to OECD countries, the highest rates in the world (Mishra 2006; Thomas 2014B). Although the migration rates appear to have slowed over the last two decades, they remain comparatively high (Vezzoli 2014). Guyana is one of the few countries in the world that has been experiencing a negative net-population-growth rate since the 1980s. Preliminary results from the 2012 Population and Housing Census suggest that the downward trend continues, with a recorded drop in the population from 751,223 in 2002 to 747,884 at the 2012 count, which analysts attribute to the continuing and unsustainable external migration (Guyana Population and Housing Census 2012; Thomas 2014A, 2014B). The scale of the outflow was precipitated by the economic crisis facing the country in the 1970s, and the continuing attrition suggests that the majority of educated Guyanese still see their future as lying outside of the country, which is perhaps not surprising given some official estimates that youth unemployment was as high as 42 per cent in 2012.[5] In accounting for Guyana's emergence in the last decade as a desirable destination, it is not insignificant that this demographic is targeted by the call centre industry and constructed by the state as providing a key national edge in the global competition for jobs. As our interviews with workers revealed,

Guyana's comparative advantage appears to lie in the supply of a low-waged, professional, and captive workforce.

Moreover, the global geography of the contemporary outsourced call centre industry is significantly structured by histories of colonialism. Not coincidentally, the countries colonised by Britain and the US (such as India and the Philippines), currently dominate the industry. Guyana's stated 'promise' as a potential site for such work is situated similarly in its colonial past, and histories of exploitation, destruction, and extraction are celebrated in glossy promotional material as a 'heritage' that lends itself perfectly to the needs of a burgeoning new industry, with the accompanying and essential benefit of a widespread use of standard English.

In fact, it is 'location, location, location' (in the words of one company) that is singled out as Guyana's strategic advantage. In a highly competitive global environment, state and industry officials promote Guyana, a relative newcomer to the call centre scene, as an 'alternative India' and a 'complement to the Philippines'.[6] Location here has multiple meanings. First, to the North American market in particular, the country is represented as one that offers physical proximity. A mere six-hour flight away from the US and Canada and in the same time zone (an hour ahead during daylight saving time in North America), Guyana is sold in some advertisements as an ideal 'nearshore' site, especially for companies thinking of venturing into outsourcing for the first time. As one local website boasts, 'operating nearshore enables [X] to offer world-class service and quality at a fraction of the cost, compared to US call centers.'

In addition, Guyana is home to a highly literate and educated English-speaking population that is located on the northwestern shoulder of South America, bordered by Venezuela, Brazil, and Suriname. The country was colonised first by the Dutch, and then by the British, who took control in the late-nineteenth century, unifying the three Dutch colonies of Demerara, Berbice, and Essequibo into British Guiana in 1831. The only English-speaking country in South America, Guyana has historically been seen – and sees itself – as fundamentally Caribbean. At the level of interstate relations, Guyana is a founding member of the Caribbean Community and Common Market, CARICOM. In more popular terms, the country has consistently supplied team members to the West

Indies cricket team, for years a symbol of Caribbean unity and resistance. However, in recent years there has been increasing interest in pursuing bilateral relations with neighbouring Latin American countries as well as regional initiatives with South America. Extra-regional migration from the country has been historically to the United Kingdom (UK) and since the early 1960s to the US and Canada; within the region it is primarily to the anglophone Caribbean, although there is also regular movement across the country's borders to Suriname, French Guiana, Brazil, and Venezuela. Against this backdrop, location is meant to signal cultural and linguistic overlap and proximity with the predominantly North American client base of the companies, therefore promising an excellent return on investment. In one promotional video, scenes from around the country are accompanied by a voiceover that describes Guyana as 'an excellent opportunity for the world outsourcing market, because [of] English, native language English, high scalability and the cost structure, so at the end of the day, it is that alternative to India, it is that complement to the Philippines.'[7] As the chief executive officer of one company remarked, '[our] largest market is serving customers in the US, and Guyana understands Americans. They speak the same native-English language and watch the same TV' (*Stabroek Daily News* September 3, 2013).

Cost competitiveness includes the fact that there seems to be relatively little outlay on the intensive accent training that takes place in other locations (see Mirchandani 2012). We came across only one company that mentioned training on 'speech and diction, Americanisation, accent training,' unlike call centres in India, in which language and accent training are universal. In fact, the people to whom we spoke seemed surprised to learn that such emphasis was devoted in other countries to inculcating a certain way of speaking English, and they surmised that – in addition to familiarity with North America via migratory histories (remittances constitute one of the major sources of the country's foreign exchange earnings), saturation via television programming, the Internet, and the circulation of commodities (in this regard the country is similar to other call centre locations) – Guyanese spoke English with what was described as a flatter, more internationally comprehensible accent. Several workers whom we interviewed stated that they believed Guyana to be an ideal location for outsourced customer service work because of its linguistic advantage.[8] Stephanie reports that customer compliments are often based on perceptions of her superior accent compared to that of call-centre workers from other countries. She elaborates on this principle of distinction:

> The person speaking to you may not be able to assist you ... they have other persons from Spanish-speaking countries, so their English wouldn't be as good as mine ... so they would be like, "I was talking to someone and I couldn't understand them...your English is so much clearer," ...As much as we are in South America...we don't speak Spanish, so that's a good thing for us.

Similarly Troy reports: 'A lot of my customers would be like, "Where are you from?" I say, Guyana. That's in South America. And they say, "Wow. Your English is perfect. Your English is better than mine!"' We were told in one interview that pass rates for call centre English tests ranged regularly in the eightieth percentile and higher, as opposed to pass rates in Latin American countries of between ten and 25 per cent. Moreover, respondents not only attempted to distinguish themselves from workers in non-English-speaking countries but also compared the Guyanese accent favourably with the accent of more popular offshore call centre sites like India and the Philippines, as well as other English-speaking Caribbean countries like Jamaica and Barbados that have a far longer history of continuous and direct interaction with 'foreigners' through investment and highly developed tourism industries. Interviewees distinguished the Guyanese accent as being far less heavy and much easier to understand; in fact, Belize was the only other country that was singled out as having a relatively neutral English accent. As we shall see later, however, workers report that while some customers compliment them on their accents, others do not believe that Guyanese English is 'superior' to the English spoken in other call centres.

In the context of Guyana, the call centre sector not only occupies a unique economic niche in so far as it promises to provide accessible, prestigious, and professional jobs for the segment of the population that is most prone to migration from the country, but it is also an important symbol of Guyana's future prospects for social and economic wealth, as well as a marker of the country's proximity to the West. To pursue its neoliberal agenda, and much like other Caribbean countries over the last two decades, the Guyanese state has developed incentives, institutional sites, and promotional material to clearly send the signal to foreign investors that it is open for business (Klak and Myers 1998), while also engaging locally in a comprehensive branding campaign to promote the idea that the infusion of global capital is in the country's national interest. Do employee narratives resonate with the anticipated convergence of foreign capital and local development promised by these official representations? Odessa, a young woman in her mid–twenties, stated that Guyana as a nation benefits from the industry: 'not only are they gaining some sort of revenue for the country, they are also providing jobs for persons who need the jobs, and they are also giving you skill in [the] customer service line.' Her optimism, however, was tempered by the sense that the benefits from the call centre industry are unevenly distributed within the country, a sentiment shared by all the young people we interviewed for this study.

Such scepticism reflects a wider suspicion about government policy that seems unable to stem the persistently high emigration of educated citizens. According to one of our key informants, the distrust is also fuelled by a lack of transparency: agreements made between foreign investors and the government are not public knowledge. Shantie noted that she would like to stay in Guyana because she likes living close to family but knows that she might have to leave if she is unable to find suitable employment related to her interests and education. She explained:

> A lot of Guyanese have less faith in the government for providing jobs for them. Everybody is trying to do their own thing – open a shop here, open sewing, try to do nails. You lose hope in your government…I think people in high places are more concerned about their welfare and the welfare of their families. The government body is not making decisions to benefit the citizens as a whole.

Drawing extensively on our interviews with present and past call centre employees, the remainder of this chapter attempts to make sense of this significant discrepancy between the highly optimistic tone represented by the state and the call centre industry and the over-whelming frustration expressed by those who have been named as local beneficiaries.

The 'Guyanese Wage' and the Sovereignty of Global Capital

A prominent transnational call centre in Guyana recently announced plans to set up a new centre that would be 'amongst the largest contact centers in the world'. Officials of the company provide several reasons for its decision to make 'its largest investment to date' in Guyana, including the country's location, English proficiency, and state support. The announcement was also welcomed by Guyana's president, who noted, 'The Government of Guyana recognises and appreciates the work being done by [the company] in providing jobs for hundreds of our people.'[9] A company video also highlighted the contributions that it would make to the local economy through the provision of over 6,000 jobs and the construction of an energy-efficient building that would include water harvesting, solar energy, and state-of-the-art facilities for workers.[10]

Despite this rhetoric about the possible benefits accruing to Guyana, such as potential revenue, employment, and customer service training, all the respondents noted that Guyana's primary competitive advantage lay in the unavailability of jobs for young, educated people, which was reflected in the staggering emigration levels of those with secondary schooling and beyond, precisely the group interviewed for this project. The workers we interviewed had all sought call centre jobs after having completed their post-secondary education in such subjects as communications, social work, business management, computer studies, industrial relations, accounting, and tourism. Ray, who had recently left his job as a call centre operator in the hope of finding something more suitable to his training, had sent out more than 50 job applications to no avail and was on the verge of losing his apartment; he observed:

Job opportunity is lacking. You know, there isn't much for young people to do in Guyana

> ...I now see why it is young people turn to guns, young people turn to drugs, young people sell their bodies to make money. Because you have no other choice. People have qualifications [but] are being paid next to nothing.

This sense of having little to no choice (a situation that leaves one vulnerable to exploitation, with one interviewee using terms like *guinea pigs*, *test rabbits*, and *lab rats* to convey her sense that Guyanese employees have little negotiating power) overwhelmingly framed workers' descriptions of a highly unequal playing field tilted in favour of companies. Despite recruitment advertisements claiming that call centre jobs provided wages comparable to those of professional jobs (such as accountants or mid-level managers) in Guyana, no one whom we interviewed indicated that the job was well paid or a match for the training they had received, with most describing call centre work as something they turned to because they were unable to find employment in their areas, and as 'better than no job'.

Marlia, who had a diploma in business management, as well as secretarial qualifications said that she felt overqualified for her position at the call centre, but 'I wanted a job. I didn't want to be home doing nothing, and you're waiting and waiting.'

This bleak employment scenario translates into a context in which having few competitors, employers can set low wage levels and minimal benefits and yet ensure a continuous supply of prospective workers. Cynthia, who worked for a call centre for more than five years, stated that even if they provided the best service, they could not earn more than what was deemed appropriate for a 'third-world worker,' what she called 'a Guyanese wage'.

L. Salzinger (2003), in her ethnography of workers in Mexican maquiladoras, argues that firms create rather than simply find the workers whom they hire. Like the women who produce televisions on assembly lines in Mexico, Guyanese call centre workers are subject to hyper-surveillance and poor wages. Paying a 'Guyanese wage' to workers with few other employment options fosters a sense of both entrapment and docility because their jobs are unsustainable and simultaneously play a key role in maintaining the precarious balance of inputs that workers receive from a variety of sources to piece together their livelihoods. The greatest challenge mentioned by most respondents was the fact that, despite having professional, full-time jobs, they were unable to make enough to cover their rent and food bills. As Marisa noted, 'the main challenge for me is the money. [We] just go and work there because [we] are not getting anything else. But that's a huge problem.' Respondents observed that their jobs seemed to call for a well-educated workforce, but the levels of remuneration and the working conditions were established not in the light of living costs but in terms of the lowest possible wage that would ensure a continuous supply of labour. In the context of a nation in which educated youth have severely limited work options, this wage is extremely depressed. About half of the respondents had worked in at least two call centres, and the monthly take-home pay ranged from a low of GY$30,000 (US$144) to a high of GY$50,000 (US$241), with over two-thirds earning between GY$40,000 and GY$45,000 (US$193–US$217). Three people indicated that they had been promised much higher monthly salaries at one company (roughly GY$70,000, or US$338), but these had not materialised, and two of the interviewees recalled one company that had for a short while only offered a significantly higher salary than had the other centres.

The average monthly earnings of those employed at the time of the interviews was GY$44,000 (US$212), not significantly higher (especially given the educational qualifications of our respondents) than the current legal minimum wage of GY$35,000 (US$169). They do not begin to cover the daily expenses of running a household, given the recommended basket of goods for a family of four (two adults and two children), estimated at GY$59,972 (US$289) in December 2013; notably, the basket was restricted to food items and did not include housing, health care, transportation, and utilities (*Stabroek Daily News*, March 30, 2014). Shantie, who had received approximately GY$40,000 (US$193) per month, but had been laid off from her job, said, 'Who can live on 40,000 when the month come...because my rent alone is 40,000 and you have to pay transportation and food.' Indeed, even local managers seemed to recognise the disconnect between wages and the cost of living; a company video that focused on efforts being undertaken to reduce absenteeism among its workforce identified the provision of coffee and crackers as important incentives for employees to come to work regularly and on time.[11]

To make ends meet, workers must rely on a combination of wages, performance incentives, and company handouts, as well as income from other sources. Base salaries are complemented by incentives that workers can receive for meeting or exceeding their targets. Agents in Guyana are more likely to receive supermarket vouchers than the leisure-related luxury items that many call centre organisations provide as incentives.[12] Workers said that they preferred vouchers because vouchers were untaxed, and they depended on them to meet their basic needs. Companies offer extremely low wages in conjunction with corporate 'perks,' which include things like competitions for teamwork or milk programmes for women with children, but many of these handouts are 'earned' through performance and are not automatically given. While organisations construct these incentives in order to motivate employees and to transform 'productivity pursuits into an exercise of "fun"' (Alferoff and Knights 2003, 76), as in the case of interviewees who reported to us that their employer sometimes held competitions for things like 'best hair day' and 'best dressed day', workers report that they rely on bonuses to meet their food needs and to make ends meet. As one woman pointedly told us, 'I am sure most persons would forego the incentives for more money on their pay cheques.'

Therefore, despite having full-time jobs, many workers were frequently forced to turn to family or friends at home and abroad for help or to seek supplemental self-employment incomes. Marlia pointed out that 'they have some people who have more than one job...when they come off, they go and do a receptionist job or part-time work somewhere...The money couldn't do.'

Cindy said, 'The salary that I am working for can't even look after me and my daughter. If it wasn't for my child's father, I don't know what would happen.' Lisa described the salary she received as 'harsh', but noted that her company provided some flexibility to its employees and had schedules that allowed them to attend school if needed, 'especially if you don't have responsibilities and you're still living with mom and dad, it's nice.' Sherry commented similarly: 'it's kind of like a temporary place when you're done school. It's not something you can support your family on. It's not something you can have two kids and pay your rent with. Or actually support a household.'

Call centres in Guyana are predominantly staffed by women workers. P. Korvajärvi (2009), in her ethnography in Finland, traces three ways in which call centre work is feminised. First, work is numerically dominated by women. Second, interactive service work is seen to be closely related to the traditionally feminised roles of serving and caring. Finally, the structural conditions of work such as the low pay and the limited possibility of career advantage are seen to be appropriate for women (Korvajärvi 2009, 132). For Guyanese women, however, as elsewhere in the Caribbean, there is also a strong relationship between motherhood and waged work, which makes them more reliable employees and more likely to seek call centre jobs. As Lisa explained, 'Women are coming forward, women are coming forward, men in Guyana...I call [Guyanese men] "not working millionaires". But women, when you see you have responsibilities, you wanna earn a dollar.'

Workers therefore confront the contradictions of being involved in feminised work that is 'professional', yet poorly paid and demeaning. In their research on call centres in India, P. D'Cruz and E. Noronha (2006) trace the ways in which professionalism is 'at the heart of organizational control' in customer service work (344). While traditional notions of professionalism relate to employee control and discretion over work, a call centre worker is:

> defined as a person who has the desire to satisfy customers, puts aside personal problems and concentrates on service; accepts stringent monitoring and self-timings; is able to withstand strains and pressures

of work; and is receptive to the idea of taking on another identity in the interest of the organisation and the customer (346).

Indeed, employees report little control and discretion over their timings and scripts. Marlia noted, 'you don't get a break. You are only allowed a half-hour lunch. You might get a chance to go [to the] washroom, but as soon as you come off a call, there is another one waiting for you.'

D. Van den Broek (2002) describes surveillance systems typical of call centre work environments around the world, and the centres in Guyana clearly follow these geographical blueprints. Work environments consist of open-plan offices; large display boards on which the productivity statistics for each employee are prominently visible and continuously updated; daily reports on average handling times and numbers of calls; and automated telephone dialling systems that minimise wait times between calls (49 and 50). Methods of public shaming for unmet quotas are also common. Shantie described a 'big board' at her call centre that was updated every 15 minutes and could be seen by all agents and supervisors; she felt embarrassed by the publicly displayed low scores that she sometimes received, which had her 'depressed'. Shannon shared her experience of a call in which the customer had been abusive, and her supervisors had felt that she had been rude. She was asked to write 'lines'. Clearly angry and humiliated by this disciplinary strategy, Shannon noted:

> I will never forget this thing – a yellow paper saying "I will not interrupt the customer or speak rudely to the customer." I had to do back and front. And I told them. "I am getting paid for this? I am not writing lines! I am not in school! I never write lines in school and I'm not going to write it now." So then I got disciplinary action. I didn't get suspended, but I got a warning letter.

Employees are also exposed to industry instability. According to the workers interviewed, hiring and firing occurs continuously at call centres. There was a strong sense among interviewees that one 'got through right away' with a job there because of the 'high turnover,' even though one manager to whom we spoke insisted that there was a very low turnover rate of employees. Ray pointed out, 'In my opinion it's one of the easiest jobs to get…so because of that a lot of people are going into call centre work… [it] has been turning over employment all the time…you see someone, "Oh, you're working at a call centre," and next couple of mornings you're no longer there.' Despite the stressful nature of their work and the low pay they receive, workers report being treated as easily replaceable. Sherry recounted a situation in which her manager called her in to the office to inform her that she was being fired. She was told that one of her calls had been randomly surveyed and found to be unacceptable and that she had also been absent from work for one day. Sherry informed the manager that she had called the supervisor because she was sick, and she wanted more information on the unacceptable call, but she received no further details. Ria had a similar experience:

> I was given extra work to do that I was not paid for, so I spoke up about that, and it was a problem...I stood up and said, "It's unfair for you guys to give me extra work and I'm not being paid for it." So that was a big issue, and they made an excuse that I was rude to a customer, which I was not. And that was my reason for being fired.

Workers' experiences reveal the significant volatility built into outsourced customer service work, particularly in some of the smaller firms that rely heavily on outgoing calls in which agents make sales pitches for various products and services, and are promised incentives depending on the number of 'leads' they score per shift.[13] 'Campaigns,' sometimes only months long, are held by companies that then hire workers to complete the task. Companies may downsize drastically and rapidly with the loss of contracts, and workers bear the brunt of these shifts. One company, for example, offered jobs to workers but, after several months, revealed that it was not able to pay wages. Shantie was an extremely successful employee who earned three times her base wage in performance incentives one month. She received an award for being the best agent. However, with the loss of the contract, she and her colleagues were fired without being paid for completed months of work. To no avail, she made several telephone calls, asking to be paid for the work she had completed. Instead, she received an email from a manager who accused her of being disrespectful, even as the company admitted it was simply unable to find monies to pay employees. Shantie noted the futility of making a complaint to the state, pointing to her sense that the sovereignty of the state had been eclipsed by the sovereignty of global capital, and that her firm held special status that allowed for such blatant evasions of local labour laws. She went on to discuss her feelings of exploitation in terms related to national identities, and said of her past employers:

> [foreigners], they kind of don't like Guyanese people. So I felt disrespected. Like, "Do you think you [foreigners] could come to

Guyana and exploit Guyanese people?" Even though my passport is Guyanese, I still know about human rights. I still have a foreign mentality. I was so mad that they thought they could come to Guyana and wuk [work] everybody out and have everybody ... like little guinea pigs or test rabbits, or lab rats, and "you just working on us, you know, and you guys are not paying."

Although Shantie anticipated that making a complaint to the state would not benefit her, a group of workers in Linden, a mining town with only one call centre, was reported to have successfully filed such a complaint in September 2015. Workers complained to the ministry of social protection because they had lost their jobs without prior notice. The company was deemed to have violated local labour laws and was asked to compensate workers (*Kaeiteur News* 2015) although enforcement remains uncertain.

Even when companies follow local labour laws, the wages do not allow sustainable livelihoods. The 'Guyanese wage' has both an empirical and an ideological dimension. Empirically, it is a wage that is lower than the one that companies would have to pay to workers doing equivalent work in the US, and it is not linked to the actual cost of living in Guyana. Ideologically, it is a wage paid to workers who have no other alternatives and are conceptualised as people who should be grateful for receiving anything. Bearing the cost of unpaid wages is transferred to workers whose proper place is seen as one of respect for managers and corporations even if the business owners' attempts to generate contracts for Guyana-based companies fail.

Sovereign Customers And Abusive Consequences

In addition to the pace of work and continuous monitoring, one of the most stressful dimensions of working in a call centre is the *irateness* of many callers. M. Korczynski (2007) notes that service work is 'structured by the dual and potentially contradictory logics of bureaucratization and customer orientation' (79). The logic of bureaucratisation prompts organisations to rationalise processes and streamline work in order to reduce costs and increase efficiency. At the same time, customer orientation requires a flexible and resource-rich approach to satisfy the broad range of customer needs. M. Korczynski and U. Ott (2004) argue that management reconciles the dual logics of customer orientation and organisational efficiency by promoting a myth of customer sovereignty. This form of enchantment is promoted such that within the interaction it appears to the customer that he/she is sovereign while at the same time creating space for the frontline worker to guide the customer through the constraints of production (581).

While such sovereignty may be mythical from the perspective of customers, for call centre workers the customer responses to their service have a significant and direct impact on their conditions of work as well as their wages and prospects for future employment. Customers exercise sovereignty in two ways: first, through the exercise of the power that arises from their role as the 'served' during customer-service interactions; and, second, through their regional location in capital-rich countries that are being served by citizens of formerly colonised, poorer countries, which are positioned as labour providers in the global economy.

In the course of telephone conversations with customers asking for information or technical help or to place orders, workers do the emotional labour simultaneously of being empathetic, anticipating, and attempting to meet customer needs, and of managing their own feelings. In addition, they must do all of this while meeting their daily targets. Shannon offered an example:

> In the midst of the conversation someone would be like, "Oh, you know what happened to me today...my dog died ...," but you can't laugh... you gotta be like, "I'm so sorry to hear that...How old was your dog?" That can also make the call overlap the time ...you can get penalised [for that]... if you're too empathetic, they penalise you ..."Oh, this agent was too empathetic; she could have been empathetic but still made the call shorter."

In addition to being empathetic, managing customer anger is seen to be part of all customer service jobs. In transnational customer service exchanges, however, calls are frequently infused with enactments of racialised hierarchies. Despite Guyana's often-cited locational advantage in terms of language, as mentioned earlier, workers in Guyana note that hierarchies of race are often expressed in terms of the focus on the deficiencies of Guyanese accents. Sherry commented: 'When some of the customers pick up on the accent, depending on how you speak to them, when they pick up on the accent and see that it's an outsourced centre, they give you a hell of a time and say, "I can't understand you. You're not speaking English."' Accents are, however, also heard in terms of the places to which speakers belong. Shannon shared an experience in which she was disciplined for being rude to a customer who,

> was cursing and cursing. I was like, "Ma-am, if you keep cursing, I'm going to have to disconnect the call." [The customer said,] "you don't tell me what to effing do." And I warned her again. Then she calmed down. Then she was like, "you know what, I don't know why I call these bullshit places." And then I got really rude. I said, "Ma-am, you need to listen. If you don't listen, you won't get anywhere. You need to shut up and listen."... My quality analyst was listening... and I have to go into the training room and get disciplinary action.

As Shannon's account reveals, customers who make derogatory comments about the 'bullshit' places they are calling are the most difficult to deal with. Marissa noted:

> Sometimes they just hang up. As soon as they realise you are not American, they just hang up. "Where am I calling today?" "You've reached Guyana." They just hang up. And sometimes they say, "Why is it that a call centre that is American has to be all the way in South America, you know, outsourcing, and Americans need jobs?"

As a result of such interactions, workers are continually required to manage their emotions during calls. Odessa described her response to abusive callers:

> I roll my eyes. I sit back. I breathe. Then I start to speak. I say, alright. Then I go into this tone. And I say xyz and try to see what the problem is. You have to relax and let them vent for a couple of minutes. And then they would be like, "Are you there?" And I say, "yes, I'm here. I'm just listening to you." Then they come down because they just want to get that anger out of their system.

This emotional labour serves to get customers into the correct 'mood' so that they can be served by call centre workers. S. Ahmed (2014) notes that 'mood work' is an important part of the construction of nations. She argues that national moods, for example the collective feelings of Americans against outsourcing, serve to identify and name 'moody figures' who are assumed to 'get in the way of attunement' (14). Mood work is done not only by customers who express anger on the telephone, and therefore assert their citizenship right to outsourced jobs, but also by customer service agents like Odessa who, by allowing callers to 'get that anger out,' attempt to transform their moods.

Customer anger about outsourced jobs is often expressed in terms of objections to accents. While workers are often told by customers that their accents are deficient, as we discussed earlier there is no evidence of the sort of widespread training that takes place in Indian call centres and which focuses on accent 'neutralization'. On the contrary, Guyana's locational advantage is seen to lie in the language complementarity between workers and customers. As C. Cowie (2007) has shown, the notion of neutral English that is valorised in customer service work promotes the ideal of a nationless English that is understood by all. In practice, notions of appropriate and inappropriate accents infuse call centre work, and the idea of a 'neutral, globally understood' English is, in fact, code for English spoken by a particular class of people, from particular regions. Most of the training received by workers in Guyana, however, was basic and geared towards using the databases in order to provide information, belying the official promotional material that promises highly skilled and well-trained opportunities. As Julie observed, 'The key skills are just computer knowledge...say, product searching, you should know how to navigate to work in a timely manner to assist the customer. And the way you speak. I guess that's basically it, just the computer knowledge and the way you speak so they could understand you.'

Although basic grammatical tests were administered at some of the sites, no one mentioned receiving the intensive voice and accent training that is common in call centres in other parts of the world. For Shannon,

> when you do the first training, there is a list of words that everyone has to go through and become familiar with ... but they don't constantly check you or come back and say, "Oh, this agent said a word wrong," or "This agent don't pronounce this word correctly" ... If Miami [i.e., offshore quality-control analysts who listen randomly to calls] is listening, they might give a warning.

Joanne remembered that she was simply asked to 'pronounce certain words...words that customers would often use or words that you would have to use with customers.' Audrey recalled being explicitly advised that it would be easier to acquire a British accent in order to be understood, but this was not a job requirement (employees could use computer programmes to practise pronouncing words, but this did not appear to be formally integrated into a consistent training programme). Marlia described the training she received:

> They would just train you – communication – how to talk, how to address a call, customer issues; for example, if [the customers] call and they [didn't] get their phone, well, they gotta do this, that's how

they work you, how they train you. They don't train you on how to talk to a customer. If a customer curses you, there is a script. There is everything in the system. The foreign world, they don't play to curse you out [customers don't hesitate to verbally abuse you at the slightest opportunity]. That's the foreign world. But you have to pick up the script and tell them. But you can't tell them anything without picking up that script.

The English demanded in these transnational service interactions, then, is hegemonic and not universally understood. Parvati pointed out that 'they have an accent to me and I have an accent to them…but if I can speak to you and you can understand me, then we can get the transaction done.' The workers may struggle at times, as Audrey observes: 'The most important thing is to listen to the customer and understand exactly what the customer is saying…for instance, we are calling England, and most of us don't understand the English people when they talk very fast.' But the onus is on the local employees to learn to understand the customers and to adapt their own way of speaking to ensure that they are understood. In the absence of comprehensive training, they must do this largely on their own and incur the consequences of failing to 'speak properly.' Customer rage is significant not only because of the toll it takes on employees required to deal with a continuous stream of abuse, but also because it has a direct relationship to workers' remuneration. Latoya noted, 'you could get a low score for sounding too foreign and not understanding the accent.' During training, workers are told to expect hostility from those at the other end of the call and are taught strategies to defuse this anger. They are encouraged to be empathetic and understanding of customer frustrations and to deal with abusive customers in a calm and detached manner. Susie commented: 'Most of the customers are arrogant, and they weren't listening to me. Some of them, I get them to calm down, and they would listen to me. But some of them are arrogant.' For Marlia, customer feedback can result in an 'autofail' or an immediate dismissal for the day: 'Customers make you go home because when you call the customer back, they say, "I don't like this person and I'm giving them 1." If you give them 1, it's a low score. They pull you off the phone.'

Even in the face of racially specific and sexually explicit harassment, workers are required to educate customers on proper telephone etiquette rather than disconnect the calls. Shannon shared her encounter of a customer who said, 'Hi. Guess what I have today? …I have 8 inches.' After three warnings she was able to finally disconnect this call. During her training,

> they warned you about that. They warned you about a particular lady called the screamer who just used to call in and scream at you. No matter what you are doing or why, she just used to scream. Then they have this old perverted...customer who used to call every month...[and another] who used to want to know the colour of your breasts, if you're black, brown, what colour they are, what size you wear.

Despite these abusive exercises of power, customers give scores to workers, and these scores are treated as decontextualised aggregate measures of performance.

Although workers face possible job termination for speaking back to customers, Shantie offered an instance of when she did so:

> I think my first day I was cursed out. Someone said, "Oh, f**k off." ...I am the type of person I get really offended based on how people speak to me...I think one guy in particular, he was impressed with my persistence because he was trying to insult my job. And I said, "Not because you don't like my job means it's a degrading job. I probably caught you in a bad mood and I apologise for that, but I am not ashamed of my job in any way and I don't think any job should be frowned upon."

Other responses to unsatisfactory working conditions range from occasionally talking back to difficult customers to finding ways of relieving stress on the job, as in the case of one young man who muted his telephone regularly in the face of abuse once he had figured out that he had a three-second span in which to do so. When he came back on the line, he would say, 'I'm sorry about that, I had to cough' (or sneeze or something like that). Alternatively, people simply left the job, even if this was a risky decision to take given the bleak job prospects.

These individualised responses were the only recourse that employees appeared to have. Without exception and despite numerous examples given to us of clear violations of Guyana's labour laws, none of the call centre workers expected to receive any official recourse on their behalf. For instance, during a service call that necessitated her calling another department to assist a customer, Marlia discovered that, unlike agents in other countries employed by the same company, Guyanese workers were required to work on Easter. Her colleague informed her that their local branch had staged a strike and no longer worked on holidays. Marlia reflected that no such protest could occur in Guyana because of the large supply of unemployed educated youth. As in other parts of the world, the industry is completely non-unionised, and so far there appear to be no efforts to organise workers or for employees to seek out a union; as Parvati observed, 'it seems as though these people are so timid … they are fearful they would wake up and hear they don't have a job.' In one case, workers had been laid off without being paid; some had received weeks of training, and others had worked while being continuously promised that they would soon receive their salaries. We were told that several people had gone to look for other employment or had kept up hope that they would receive their monies. A few had brought the matter to the attention of the relevant government officers and ministries, but to no avail. As one of the key informants concluded, 'young people really have nowhere to go. We are like a milking cow. People's rights can be and are violated on a daily basis.' Interviewees repeatedly emphasised that when it came to the call centre industry, it seemed to them that the government was more interested in protecting the interests of employers than in protecting the rights of Guyanese citizens to a living wage. While some recognised the global structural asymmetries at work that gave overseas companies the upper hand, there was an overall sense that this was compounded by a deliberate set of national policies that favoured local elites and foreign capital. Responding to a question about who benefited from call centres, Shantie said:

> for Guyana, the people in the high places like the government and the people the government allows to come into the country to do business…The government body is not making decisions to benefit the citizens as a whole…In school we are taught that a government is a body that is supposed to make laws and rules that would help the citizens; they are not doing that…everything is messed up, they are investing money where they are reaping all the benefits and gains… and the workers…the labourers are being taken for granted.

Given these experiences, none of the current and past employees that we interviewed saw call centres as providing career opportunities for young people. Unlike the women in the Barbados informatics industry interviewed by anthropologist Carla Freeman (2000) in the 1990s, the Guyanese workers do not see themselves as pink-collar employees who actively invest in narratives of class differentiation based upon the work they do. Cynthia reported:

> I kinda enjoy customer service, which is why I am there. But I don't think it's a career thing...basically, well in Guyana, [on] the whole, you have so much qualifications and you still have a hard time to get a job. Call centre is easier. At the end of the day, it doesn't pay a lot, but it's still a job. It's better than just sitting at home.

This is not to say that they do not articulate aspirations to social mobility based on their educational accomplishments. As Shantie reflected, 'I would say that a good job is one that could sustain yourself...you want to buy a car, put down on a house...if you would get a job that could enable you to put down on a car or further your studies or accomplish some of your goals.' However, the call centre was not seen as even approximating the interviewees' idea of a 'good job'; it was described as temporary, something to be done until a better prospect opened up, a place where some fortunate individuals might get promotions that mattered, but where the majority of the workforce faced systematic exploitation with little recourse for protection of their labour rights. Respondents explicitly described the call centre as a 'job of last resort'. As Marlia explained, 'I left [the company] because I felt like a slave. When I say slave, you were not getting...for instance...weekends...I would have to be at work. They give you one day off a week, and you can't choose...you're like a slave, working... Salary is also small, and the people knock you off.' Several workers told us that their family and friends did not see what they were doing as a prestigious occupation but as a low-status job, and a few stated that they were even embarrassed to admit to working there. Marlia reported that she was afraid to even tell people that she was working at a call centre. Marisa said:

> My family, when they heard that I was working at a call centre... everyone was disappointed...because they said, "Man, you're going to UG [University of Guyana] and you have your little CXCs and good grades"...so they didn't think it was the best, but for me it's better than not having a job at all, so for that reason I decided to stay on until something better comes.

Despite having to manage others' disappointment, workers recognise that their choices are limited. Cindy said, 'To be honest with you, [my family] don't like it...but you know as I say...you have to work...I have to get money...Their view for me is to get a government job.' In fact, workers reported the widely held perception that call centres not only provided routinised and low-paying jobs but also exacted a significant emotional toll. As Shannon summarises, 'If someone hears you're working at [a call centre], they say, "Wow, you got patience."'

Conclusion

The call centre industry in Guyana represents a site where multiple sovereignties are manifested and contested. Expressions of state sovereignty, customer sovereignty, and global-capital sovereignty shape the experiences of call centre workers in the industry. In Guyana it would appear that the call centre industry is here to stay for the time being, with the country being identified by both the Guyana government and prospective and existing investors as an excellent location and site for rapid and massive expansion. It is also promoted as a solution to the dilemma facing school leavers, with many high-paying and secure jobs that offer upward mobility and bright futures for career-driven young people. Behind the glossy advertisements, however, lies a story that unfortunately appears to provide little evidence of benefits for local workers. In Guyana, this materialises against a backdrop in which school leavers and graduating students with some level of tertiary education find few jobs to match their skills, and where unsustainably high levels of emigration attest to the overwhelming sense that young professionals can only fulfil their aspirations by leaving. Those who remain have few choices, leading to a situation in which call centres set the rules. Growth, then, is one sided, as Rick presciently observed: 'It's growing because it's a job easy to get in, but I don't think [it's growing] effectively.' Parvati summed up the situation:

> I don't think Guyana benefits on the whole because it's outsourcing whenever it's done ... and it's mostly the investors and whoever is at the top who earn the most ...The agent has to do the work and they are just earning a piece of it ...Like they say, Guyana is a third-world country... Even though we would provide quality customer service, they are not gonna pay us ...These foreign [businesses], coming in and exploiting people at home. I am thinking, as much as they are the advocates for the customer ... to make sure the customer is treated a certain way, ... at the end, who is my advocate? ...There must be somebody who is representing Guyana.

Call centres are sold as a win-win deal for everyone: foreign and local capital, customers, the state, and the Guyanese people. In the final analysis, however, and for the young workers upon whose emotional labour the success of the industry ultimately depends, there is an overwhelming sense that the promissory note they have been issued bears simply the imprint of their exploitation. These expressions of discontent represent cracks in the assumed popular support that underlies the forms of sovereign control at play.

Notes

1. A former British colony, Guyana became independent in 1966.
2. The vast majority of clients are in the US.
3. Foreign exchange earnings have traditionally rested on three primary export sectors – bauxite, rice, and sugar, although, given the size of the Guyanese diaspora, remittances could be added to this list (*Kaieteur News* September 5, 2013).
4. Telecommunications Bill 18 of 2012 – which addresses the liberalisation of telecommunications – remains before a parliamentary select committee. With regard to some of the structural issues with which Guyana is grappling in its move to embrace ICT, a September 2014 report found that of the 27 Caribbean countries surveyed, Guyana had the second-lowest Internet download speeds (after Cuba), 2014, http://www. ict-pulse.com/2014/09/snapshot-actual-internet-download-speeds- caribbean-september-2014.
5. The youth unemployment figures are 46.9 per cent for women and 39.7 per cent for men. See the World Bank Report, http://data.worldbank.org/ indicator/SL.UEM.1524.ZS. Up-to-date and reliable data in Guyana are extremely difficult to find. There have been no recent labour force surveys, and so far preliminary census results include only the most basic demographic information.
6. See, for example, the promotional video at http://www.youtube.com/watch?v=VM2xIQ2KRfo.
7. Ibid.
8. See, for instance, 'Guyana Leads Caribbean as a Call Centre facility,' *Guyana Inc.*, Issue 6.
9. Quoted in a company news report: http://www.qualfon.com/blog/2013/09/04/september-4-2013-georgetown-guyana-qualfon-building-one-of-the-largest-contact-center-campuses-in-the-world-in-georgetown-guyana-and-creating-6000-new-jobs.
10. https://www.youtube.com/watch?v=sl_rDtXtGUo.
11. https://www.youtube.com/watch?v=QJgb5MXrD_U.
12. In just two instances, it was reported that high-performing employees could occasionally spin a wheel to earn a prize, usually a small electronic or durable household item like a toaster.
13. One of the larger firms relied primarily on incoming calls, with which there seemed to be less uncertainty and change in relation to its overseas clients.

References

Ahmed, S. 2014. Not in the Mood. *New Formations: A Journal of Culture/Theory/Politics* 82: 13–28.

Alferoff, C., and D. Knights. 2003. We're All Partying Here: Target and Games, Or Targets as Games in Call Centre Management. In *Art and Aesthetics at Work*, ed. A. Carr and P. Hancock, 70–90. Basingstoke, UK: Palgrave Macmillan.

Ammachchi, N. n.d. Guyana Outsourcing: Positioned For Growth. *Nearshore Americas Blog*. Accessed September 29, 2014. http://www.nearshoreamericas.com/guyanas-outsourcing-sector-brighter-future.

Benhabib, S. 2007. Twilight of Sovereignty or the Emergence of Cosmopolitan Norms? Rethinking Citizenship in Volatile Times. *Citizenship Studies* 11, no. 1: 9–36.

Brown, W. 2010. *Walled States, Waning Sovereignty*. New York, NY: Zone Books.

Cowie, C. 2007. The Accents of Outsourcing: The Meanings of "Neutral" in the Indian Call Centre Industry. *World Englishes* 26, no. 3:316–30.

D'Cruz, P., and E. Noronha. 2006. Being Professional: Organizational Control in Indian Call Centers. *Social Science Computer Review* 24, no. 3:342–61.

Freeman, C. 2000. *High-Tech and High Heels in the Global Economy: Women, Work and Pink Collar Identities in the Caribbean*. Chicago, IL: Duke University Press. http://dx.doi.org/10.1215/9780822380290.

Goldberg, D.T. 2009. *The Threat of Race: Reflections on Racial Neoliberalism*. Oxford, UK: Blackwell Publishing.

Guyana Population and Housing Census. 2012. *Preliminary Report*.

Guyana Chronicle. 2012. Call Centres Burgeoning. July 3. Accessed September 29, 2014. http://guyanachronicle.com/call-centres-burgeoning.

———. 2013. Towards More Employment...Qualfon Turns Providence Sod for 6,000 Jobs Centre – Set to be One of Largest Call Centres in the World. September 5. http://guyanachronicle.com/towards-more-employment-qualfon-turns-providence-sod-for-6000-jobs-centre-set-to-be-one-of-largest-call-centres-in-the-world.

Hardt, M., and A. Negri. 2000. *Empire*. Cambridge, MA: Harvard University Press.

Kaieteur News. 2013. Qualfon Guyana Begins Another Multi- Million Dollar Investment. September 5. Accessed September 29, 2014. http://www.kaieteurnewsonline.com/2013/09/05/qualfon-guyana-begins-another-multi-million-dollar- investment.

———. 2015. 90 Lose Jobs as Linden Call Centre Closes. September 4. Accessed September 29, 2014. http://www.kaieteurnewsonline.com/2015/09/04/90-lose- jobs-as-linden-call-centre-closes.

Klak, T., and G. Myers. 1998. How States Sell Their Countries and Their People. In *Globalization and Neoliberalism: The Caribbean Context*, ed. T. Klak, 87–109. Lanham, MD: Rowman & Littlefield.

Korczynski, M. 2008. Understanding the Contradictory Lived Experience of Service Work: The Customer-Oriented Bureaucracy. In *Service Work: Critical Perspectives*, ed. M. Korczynski and C. L. Macdonald, 73–90. NY: Routledge.

Korczynski, M., and U. Ott. 2004. When Production and Consumption Meet: Cultural Contradictions and the Enchanting Myth of Customer Sovereignty. *Journal of Management Studies* 41, no. 4:575–99.

Korvajärvi, P. 2009. Attracting Customers through Practising Gender in Call-Centre Work. *Work Organisation, Labour & Globalisation* 3, no. 1:131–43.

Lowe, L. 2008. The Gender of Sovereignty. *The Scholar and Feminist Online* 6, no. 3.

Mirchandani, K. 2012. *Phone Clones: Authenticity Work in the Transnational Service Economy*. Ithaca, NY: Cornell University Press.

Mishra, P. 2006. Emigration and Brain Drain: Evidence from the Caribbean. IMF Working Paper 06/25. Washington, D.C.

Ong, A. 2007. *Neoliberalism as Exception: Mutations in Citizenship and Sovereignty*. Durham, NC: Duke University Press.

Salzinger, L. 2003. *Gender in Production: Making Workers in Mexico's Global Factories*. Berkeley, CA: University of California Press.

Sassen, S. 1996. *Losing Control? Sovereignty in an Age of Globalization*. New York, NY: Columbia University Press.

Stabroek Daily News. 2013. Qualfon's New Call Centre to Have 3,500 Seats. September 3. Accessed September 25, 2014. http://www.stabroeknews.com/2013/news/stories/09/03/qualfons-new-call-centre-to-have-3500-seats.

———. 2014. Pro-poor Policies. March 30. Accessed September 25, 2014. http://www.stabroeknews.com/2014/news/stories/03/30/pro-poor-policies.

Stabroek News. 2015. Teleperformance Call Center Operational. October 14. Accessed November 4, 2015. http://www.stabroeknews.com/2015/news/stories/10/14/ teleperformance-call-centre-operational.

Thomas, C. 2014A. Guyana's Recent Population Bombshell. *Stabroek Daily News*, August 3. Accessed September 29, 2014.

———. 2014B. Guyana's 2012 Population Census: Runaway Brain Drain Rules! *Stabroek DailyNews*, August 10. Accessed September 29, 2014. http://www. stabroeknews.com/2014/features/08/10/guyanas-2012-population-census-runaway-brain-drain-rules.

Trouillot, M. 2001. The Anthropology of the State in the Age of Globalization: Close Encounters of the Deceptive Kind. *Current Anthropology* 42, no. 1:125–38. http://dx.doi.org/10.1086/318437.

Van den Broek, D. 2002. Monitoring and Surveillance in Call Centres: Some Responses from Australian Workers. *Labour & Industry* 12, no. 3:43–58. http:// dx.doi.org/10.1080/10301763.2002.10722023.

Vezzoli, S. 2014. The Effects of Independence, State Formation and Migration Policies on Guyanese Migration. International Migration Institute Working Paper Series, No 94. Oxford.

12.
Consolidation and Implications of Discretionary Rule over Guyana's Public Forests, 1992–2015

Janette Bulkan

Introduction

This chapter presents an overview of the management of publicly owned forests during the 23 years of People's Progressive Party (PPP) rule (1992–2015). It is contextualised within the ecological importance of the Guiana Shield frontier forests and the role of Amerindians as rights holders. The discussion takes a longer historical view of forest management, considering the principal changes in this sector under successive post-independence political administrations. It includes a brief review of the status of protected areas, set against key features of forest management, in particular the donor-driven framework for rationalised land use planning and coordination among the natural resources agencies, and the systems of logging allocations and management. As the discussion demonstrates, multiple slippages between law and policy on the one hand and actual practice on the other facilitated, among other distortions, the spatial expansion of the large-scale long-term logging sector without application of the safeguards meant to protect publicly owned assets. As a result, public forests have been dispensed under presidential discretion, and once under licence[1] effectively treated as private property, with little or no attempt made to benefit the Guyanese economy or society.

State Control of Forests

At Independence in 1966, the national government inherited legal and administrative control of state forests and state lands (heretofore crown forests and crown lands). Forests then covered an estimated 85 per cent of Guyana's national territory (18 of 21.5 million hectares (Mha)). The natural resources agencies (Forestry, Mining, Lands and Surveys) held responsibility for the awarding and management of concessions for which no public advertisement or consultation was required, even with the Indigenous Peoples (IP) holding underlying customary land rights (A. Bulkan 2014, 76). The Forest Department (converted into the Guyana Forestry Commission (GFC) in 1979) had the authority to issue forest harvesting licences on state forests only. The Department of Lands and Mines (later converted to the Guyana Geology and Mines Commission (GGMC) had authority to issue prospecting and mining licences in six mining districts overlaid on state forests (and some state lands). The Lands and Surveys Department (later the Guyana Lands and Surveys Commission (GLSC) had the authority to issue agricultural concessions in the state lands category. Logs and lumber extracted from state lands and from Amerindian titled lands from 1976 can only be legally transported outside of those land categories with GFC-issued removal passes.

The state's management authority over all forests in 1966 presented an opportunity for settling Amerindian claims to customary lands, in fulfilment of the 1965 pre-independence agreement; building national wealth through sustainable forest management (SFM); and protecting representative high conservation value (HCV) forests and floral and faunal species. The People's National Congress (PNC) government initiated the settlement of Amerindian land claims, a process that is still ongoing. This chapter focuses on logging concessions and the forestry sector only. The number of and area of natural resources concessions increased during the PNC administrations (1964–92). By 1992 large-scale, long-term logging concessions covered 3.5 Mha or 39 per cent of the 9.1 Mha of forests then categorised as 'State Forests'. What this meant was that the incoming PPP administration had a free hand to develop an integrated land use plan over about 14 Mha of state-claimed and -administered forests (i.e., the remaining state forest and state land areas *not* under large-scale, long-term logging concessions).

There was no lack of donor support in 1992 for developing governance measures, including for continuing Amerindian communal titling, land use planning, forest law and policy reform and support for the professionalisation of the natural resources agencies and personnel. Yet over the following two decades, successive PPP administrations deployed the style of executive control over natural resources that had been practised by the PNC. In practice, the PPP administrations continued the politicisation of the staff of natural resources agencies and the discretionary allocation and management of national patrimony.

The neoliberal policies that were adopted as part of the Economic Recovery Programme (ERP) in 1989 aided the expansion of the cronyism then characteristic of concession allocations in logging and mining (Bulkan 2009). Prospective transnational loggers followed the national custom of seeking out those in power and the go-betweens in the natural resources agencies. Their innovation was to write the secret foreign direct investment (FDI) contracts that brought few long-lasting benefits to the economy but instead transformed forestry into an enclave sector which, *inter alia,* led to intensified forest degradation[2] and the extinction of commercially desirable tree species.

There were few in the pre- and post-independence governments, or in coastlander society more generally, who accepted the inherent rights to territory and resources asserted by their fellow Amerindian citizens (Sanders 1987, 31–54). The general approach to the forest patrimony was extractive in nature. In theory Guyana's relatively small population, and extensive forest cover under the control of the state made and still make the attainment of SFM possible. However, the concentration of power in the executive branch of government after the imposition of the 1980 Constitution on the country facilitated the steady erosion of citizens' rights. All decision-making came to be concentrated in the executive branch. The consequent slippages between official forest laws and policies on the one hand and actual practices on the other cumulatively drove the *de facto* privatisation of publicly owned natural resources.

Guyana's electoral system and ethnic political parties also contribute to such public policy failures. A study by Jana Kunicová and Susan Rose-Ackerman (2005), which investigated parliamentary versus presidential systems of government, and plurality voting versus proportional representation found that the systems most prone to corruption were presidential systems with closed-list proportional representation, which is precisely the form of government adopted in Guyana in 1980 (Lambsdorff 2006, 12). The separation of powers was further restricted in 2007 when the PPP and PNC passed a constitutional amendment which allowed recall by a political party of any member of parliament who was no longer conforming to their party's positions (*Stabroek News* 2007B). This course of action was one of the few expressions of consensus by the two largest parliamentary parties, and it was widely interpreted as further entrenching the power of party leaders and foreclosing any independent action by MPs.

By the end of the PPP's 23-year rule in 2015, the forest areas under logging and mining concessions had expanded, with effective control held by a relatively few players. Evergreen (automatically renewed) large-scale, long-term concessions for logging and gold and diamond mining, in effect, transfer a public property right into private hands with approval necessary only from the executive arm of government. There are no effective checks and balances on presidential power in Guyana. In practice, there is nominal parliamentary oversight of the natural resources sector, unlike Suriname, where the national assembly has to approve the granting of any forestry concession larger than 150,000 hectares (ha). As a result, the clauses of most of the FDI deals are not made public. Taken together with Chinese and Russian ownership of most of Guyana's bauxite deposits, and the concentration of gold and diamond mining concessions in a relatively small percentage of hands, Guyana's key natural resources were largely privatised and offered little public benefit under the PPP administrations.

Legislative protections of Indigenous land rights in particular – within communal titled areas and in customary lands – and of public forests in general have been weakened (Bulkan 2016B, 375–80). President Bharrat Jagdeo's Low Carbon Development Strategy (LCDS), launched in 2009, laden with rhetoric about forest protection, was in practice a means of double-dipping: securing additional payments from inattentive donors while continuing business-as-usual in logging and mining (Bulkan 2016A, 122; 2016E, 98–103). That business-as-usual was extractive and exploitative in essence and reinforced the duality between coastland and hinterland territories and peoples: Creole immigrant populations in the majority on the narrow coastal plain and Creole-dominated governments in charge of land use allocation, versus the Indigenous Amerindians who are the majority populations in the interior forests, mountains and savannahs but whose leaders are shut out of national decision-making processes.

Guiana Shield Frontier Forests

In 1997, the natural forests of the Guiana Shield were regarded as a global treasure: one of four remaining intact 'frontier forests' on the planet, the others being Amazonia, Congo, and Papua New Guinea (Bryant, Nielsen, and Tangley 1997, 15–19). Guiana Shield forests grow on some of the planet's most infertile soils, derived by *in situ* weathering of its Proterozoic metamorphic and igneous rocks. Together with the Brazilian and West African shields, the Guiana Shield is considered one of the planet's oldest land surfaces (Gibbs and Barron 1993, 11, 26, 170–71). Guyana is located at the centre of the Shield which extends westwards to Venezuela and parts of Columbia, eastwards to Suriname and French Guiana and south to the northern bank of the Amazon River in Brazil.

The extreme poverty of the Guiana Shield soils results in forests with unusually high proportions of slow-growing trees with a variety of defensive and nutrient-retaining livelihood strategies. Some 5,562 native flowering plant species have been collected in Guyana's rainforests (Funk et al. 2007). Based on a low number of introduced species in the wild – an estimated 25 – the flora of Guyana was considered to be largely intact and undisturbed in the final decade of the last millennium (ter Steege 2000, 13).

Not surprisingly, many of the trees and other plants which can survive and grow on such infertile soils are specialised and considered endemic to the Guiana Shield, about 50 per cent of an estimated 8,000 species of vascular plants (Lindeman and Mori 1989, 377). Compared with other tropical moist forests, those of the Guiana Shield tend to have few large trees. Mostly they are relatively short, relatively thin, and with relatively hard and heavy timber. These are adaptations to cope with the low levels of plant nutrients and the low water storage capacity in the soil; so trees experience drought or near-drought conditions frequently (Hammond 2005). In 1992, these forests had not been subject to the onslaught of poorly controlled industrial scale logging which had degraded so much of the perhumid forest in the tropics, particularly in Asia (Ross 2001, 54–189).

In spite of Guyana having over 1,000 species of trees (van der Hout 2011,167), logging and log trading have concentrated historically on a very small number of hard, heavy, and decay- and impact-resistant timbers which are preferred for civil and marine construction. Two preferred commercial timbers, the iconic greenheart (*Chlorocardium rodiei)* and purpleheart (*Peltogyne venosa*), grow typically in mono-dominant patches – locally called 'reefs' – on well-defined combinations of slope, soil texture, and soil colour. This clumping or clustering facilitates cut-and-run logging, leading to localised and then generalised commercial extinction of preferred species.

In place from 1988 was the University of Utrecht's long-term forest research programme, concentrated in the logging concessions of Demerara Timbers Limited (DTL). This programme was later expanded with Dutch bilateral aid through Stichting Tropenbos International until 2002. The Tropenbos research showed the vulnerability of individual species: how tenaciously, on these very ancient and nutrient-poor soils, each trophic group captured and retained the sparse pool of nutrients for survival and growth, and how important were the interactions between herbivorous insects and long-lived trees, and between producer and decomposer organisms (ter Steege et al. 1996). From 1992, the government and its agency, the GFC, could have drawn on the research findings of both its predecessor, the Forest Department, and those of Tropenbos, in its planning and management decisions so as to protect species biodiversity and resilience. Instead, the research findings were not translated into *mandatory* rules in the Codes of Practice from 1996 or in concession management contracts (Bulkan and Palmer 2016A, 14–18). Government officials had access to the evidence-based data that indicated localised extinction of the desirable species and the consequent need to enforce rules to protect enough seed-bearing and other trees for future generations. But no mandatory safeguards have been put in place to date.

Settling Amerindian Land Rights

The Indigenous Amerindians who comprise the majority of forest-dependent people had repeatedly asserted indigenous rights to their lands, territories, and resources (LTR) that pre-dated colonial settlement. In 1966, Amerindians numbered only about four per cent of the national population.[3] Anxious about their tenure insecurity, their leaders had lobbied successfully to have the commitment of the independent government to provide their legal ownership or rights of occupancy included in the pre-independence agreement.[4] A decade later, the PNC government issued communal land titles in two principal phases of titling of indigenous lands – to 64 villages in 1976 when the Amerindian Act was revised and to an additional ten villages in 1991, just before the 1992 national election. In 1992, there were 74 Amerindian Villages holding communal titles to 0.8 million Mha or about four per cent of the country's land area (Colchester 1997, 136). The paper titles provided text descriptions of boundaries but only Orealla had been demarcated on the ground.

In its 1992 election manifesto, the PPP had promised that it would 'ensure that titles are given to all Amerindian villages/settlements through their genuine elected councils' (Colchester, La Rose, and James 2002, 17). By 2015, that promise was only partially fulfilled, with communal titles granted to an additional 22 Amerindian villages. In total, 96 Amerindian villages were awarded communal tenure under the *ex gratia* terms of the Amerindian Acts of 1951, 1976, and 2006 to an estimated 3.3 Mha (15 per cent) of national territory, of which an estimated 2.5 Mha were forested (Guyana Forestry Commission and INDUFOR 5). However, the communal land titles remain burdened by state control over rivers and roads, gold mining, and other pre-emptions (Bulkan 2016B, 375–85). Between 42 and 58 Amerindian communities still lack legal communal title.[5]

In a September 2015 report, the NGO 'Rights and Resources Initiative' (RRI) compared data across 64 countries constituting 82 per cent of global land area, aiming to establish a global baseline of data on the legal recognition of Indigenous Peoples' and local communities' land rights (Rights and Resources Initiative 2015, 6). For RRI, the expanded bundle of rights were 'rights of access, the right to withdraw natural resources, management rights, the right of exclusion, the right to due process and compensation in the event of government expropriation, and the right to hold tenure rights for an unlimited span of time' (RRI, 4). RRI noted that the legal communal tenure held by Guyana's Indigenous Villages does not cover the full bundle of rights: 'In Guyana, conversely, Amerindian Village Lands are recognised as indigenous-owned in the national context, but are included here as "designated for" Indigenous Peoples because communities' rights to exclude outsiders from their lands – a key criterion for "ownership" in this framework – are limited' (RRI, 4). In short by the end of the PPP administrations in 2015 while the number of Amerindian communal land title awards had increased, an estimated one-quarter of communities remained untitled, and the titles themselves burdened by pre-emptions.

National Protected Areas System (NPAS)

Guyana was the last country in South America to set up a National Protected Areas System (NPAS 2011). The World Conservation Union (IUCN) recommends that each country should conserve at least 10 per cent of each biome located within national boundaries. Countries have generalised that target as equivalent to formal protection of 10 per cent of national territory. Guyana had only attained one half of that low benchmark by 2015.

Legally Protected Areas covered five per cent of national territory by the end of the PPP regime (Guyana Forestry Commission and Indufor 2013, 5) – Kaieteur (61,000 ha), Kanuku Mountains and Shell Beach (730,000 ha) national parks – totalling (791,000 ha). The wilderness preserve of Iwokrama is about 180,000 ha, under its own Act of Parliament 1996. The Wai Wai Amerindian community of Kanashen has a 625,000 ha community-owned conservation area (COCA). Guyana's Protected Areas Commissioner signalled an interest in including Kanashen's COCA in NPAS which would then increase the national total to eight per cent (Stanley 2015).

Guyana's protected areas are generally *de jure* confirmation of areas already supported by coalitions of internal and external non-governmental organisations (NGOs). Guyana's protected areas neither cover representative sample areas (RSA) of the country's biodiversity nor are linked by ecological migration corridors – a best practice recommendation. Tellingly, successive PPP governments resisted the decade-and-a-half-long petition led by the North Rupununi District Development Board (NRDDB), a community-based organisation formed in 1996, for the country to join the Ramsar Convention for Protection of Wetlands. Ramsar membership would commit Guyana to designate at least one wetland site for inclusion in the List of Wetlands of International Importance (Mistry et al. 2004, 249). Instead, logging and mining concessions in the forests and rice concessions in the Rupununi savannahs, south of the 4th parallel, were issued in areas that the NRDDB had identified as a prime Ramsar site.

The Extension and Management of State Forests

In 1979, under the PNC regime, the Forest Department was converted to the Guyana Forestry Commission (GFC), with enabling legislation for the GFC to engage in commercial activity. Other government departments were similarly transformed, under the umbrella of Guyana State Agencies (GUYSTAC). But, as in the case of the GUYSTAC companies, GFC staff did not receive training in private sector operations. That lack of managerial training, together with the massive staff attrition, import controls and the collapsing economy, all rendered the GFC ineffective both in the field and as a designated commercial enterprise.

Three areas of Crown Lands had been defined as State Forest, totalling 7.7 Mha in the schedule attached to the Forests Act 1953 (Vieira and Richardson 1957, 45). Another 1.4 Mha were converted by Ministerial Order from state lands to state forests, in two tranches in 1969; the orders are no longer accessible. Following the PPP accession to power, the minister issued an order in 1997 extending the state forests south to the Brazilian border by 4.6 Mha and increasing the total state forest area to 13.7 Mha, or two-thirds of national territory. The declared intention at that time was for the southern forest to be reserved for biodiversity and habitat conservation (*Stabroek News* 1997). However, the extension allowed the state, through the GFC, to parcel out and allocate logging concessions in areas then inaccessible for logging.

The forest law in Guyana does not include an inquiry and settlement process to record and assess and confirm or extinguish Indigenous claims to pre-existing resource rights before gazetting state forests (Bulkan and Palmer 2009, 76). The 1997 state forests' extension, without public inquiry, was only acknowledged in GFC statistics in 2008. In that period (1992–97), Malaysian transnational loggers were still negotiating with the Executive arm of government for logging and mining concessions (Colchester 1997; Sizer 1996, 43–46). The expanded area of state forests would facilitate more concession awards to international and some national loggers in the following years.

Rationale and History of Allocating Large-scale, Long-term Logging Concessions

Globally, the large-scale, long-term forest concession model in natural tropical forests gained ground from the 1960s when it was believed that the capital investment required for sustainable forest harvesting and processing of commercial timbers required large areas to defray the investment and operational costs when overall profit margins were small (Grayum 1971, 55–58). The United Nations Food and Agriculture Organization (FAO) provided technical advice and support for two major projects in Guyana: a soil survey project under the ministry of agriculture (Gross-Braun, Derting, and Suggett 1965) and the Forest Industry Development Survey (FIDS) (Grayum 1971). At the time, the FAO promoted the notion of forests as producers of raw material for value-addition through urban-based domestic processing (Westoby 1962, 168–201). Guyana became an exemplar of how complex natural tropical rainforest could be managed systematically, if large enough areas were allocated as long-term logging concessions to private enterprises (Vieira 1980, 31–32). Concessions were to be sized to feed sustainably the associated sawmills and other processing plants, and to be long enough in duration to recoup the high costs of heavy equipment to extract the logs from natural forest with a low frequency of commercial tree species per unit area (Grayum 1971, 50–54).

Until 1973, all logging in Guyana was carried out under short-term licences in an estimated 0.9 Mha of state forests (Schmithüsen 1973, 124), with logs principally processed into lumber for domestic construction and sale to the Caribbean. There was a small historical trade to Europe in railway ties and greenheart baulks for marine piling and civil construction. A joint public-private sector Timber Export Board was created in 1970, the associated act and regulations were passed in 1973 and became operative in 1974. The United Nations Development Fund (UNDP) Special Fund provided two specialists on timber grading devised rules, Flemmich and Booth, who gave training during 1972–73. Also in 1973 the Central Timber Manufacturing Plant (CTMP) was converted into the Forest Industries Corporation (FIC). This incorporated the Forest Department's demonstration mobile sawmill at Winiperu. However, the FIC was an economic failure, with industry run by non-commercial civil servants. A number of factors, including shortage of spare parts, lack of foreign exchange and import licences for their purchase, the difficulty of securing bank credit, and the loss of key staff through emigration caused the collapse of the expatriate Commonwealth Development Corporation (CDC) forestry enterprise at Manaka. CDC had lost money for years, and in 1973 the remaining assets were sold to the government of Guyana, and the enterprise renamed as Guyana Timbers Ltd (Vieira 1980, 25; Welch 1975, 52–53). The local timber industry hunkered down, like the rest of the private sector, to wait for better days.

In 1985, nine large-scale, long-term logging concessions, termed Timber Sales Agreements (TSAs) totalling 830,000 ha were issued administratively to the six dominant national family-owned forestry enterprises (five ethnically East Indian and one Portuguese). Each TSA was for 15 years' duration, and granted exclusive logging access.

In 1989, President Desmond Hoyte embarked on a comprehensive Economic Recovery Programme (ERP), which was a precondition set by the IMF/World Bank before bailing out Guyana's highly indebted and bankrupt economy. *Inter alia*, the ERP opened up Guyana's forests to international logging and mining interests. State-owned loss-making logging enterprises and sawmills were sold at knockdown prices by government officers, without external valuation or due diligence. Some extraordinary one-sided deals were signed in favour of the foreign investor. FDI contracts were negotiated in secret by a few persons only in the executive arm of government, with little or no oversight by the rarely sitting Parliament or by weak and disorganised civil society (Colchester 1997, 101–03). In total, the 13 large-scale concessions issued between 1985 and 1990, during the ERP and before the entry of Asian loggers, covered 1.2 Mha of state forests. In 1991, the year preceding what would be the first 'free-and-fair' elections in 28 years, the government issued seven new TSAs totalling 2.6 Mha – six to three large Malaysian loggers and the seventh, TSA 01/91, to the large-scale Portuguese Guyanese holder of TSA 10/85. The awards, fortuitously timed during the run-up to a general election, more than doubled the existing area allotted to large-scale concessions effected during the PNC administration.

Under the PPP's watch, by December 2015, the area of state forests under concession had more than doubled to 7.4 Mha. Furthermore, three-quarters of that total area was under large-scale, long-term concession licences. In practice, these were treated as a form of private property by the concession holders. The holders of these large-scale, long-term concessions did not build value-added industries that matched the scale of their concessions, nor did they employ Guyanese in significant numbers. Instead, the concession holders concentrated on logging and log export. Further, they were allowed to import Asian logging crews without oversight by any agency as to whether the numbers of foreign workers were within the range specified in their FDIs.

Neither GO-Invest nor the Guyana Revenue Authority (GRA) monitored the (non)compliance of holders of FDI agreements. Go-Invest had been set up to be a one-stop shop for all investors. In practice, FDI arrangements were made by cabinet, not by Go-Invest, and were not publicised either as to the range of possible incentives or as to actual arrangements with individual enterprises. A 2016 forensic audit of Go-Invest used an example of four forestry investors (Baishanlin International Forest Development Inc., Vaitarna Holdings Private Inc., Diamond Tropical Wood Products Inc. and Zhonghao Shipyards Inc.) to show how Guyana had not benefited from over US$9 million in tax concessions. The auditor noted that the failure to monitor the FDI concessions made such typical large-scale abuse by investors possible:

> Go-Invest is a conduit for corporations and other businesses to obtain tax concessions. However, there is also evidence that despite the fact that concessions were granted to many investors, little or no business activity related to the Investment Agreement took place. In some instances, Go-Invest was used by businessmen as an opportunity to obtain products without paying import duty and other taxes, then reselling the goods or keeping them for personal use (Nigel Hinds Financial Services 2016, 13).

Forest Sector Under Cheddi Jagan (1992-97)

In 1992, President Cheddi Jagan proclaimed the need for judicious use of public assets for the greatest good. On May 26, 1993, on the occasion of Guyana's 27th Independence Anniversary, Jagan declared,

> When in opposition, we condemned the indecent haste with which the former regime privatised our national assets at basement prices, and in a manner that lacked transparency and was not in the national interest, we will not do the same. Privatisation and divestment must be approached with due care. I was not elected President to preside over the liquidation of Guyana. I was mandated by the Guyanese people to re-build the national economy and restore a decent standard of life for all Guyanese. In all my political career, I did not succumb to pressure to serve narrow partisan interests; I do not intend to do so now. I will not surrender the interest of the nation for expediency or short-term gain (Jagan 1993).

At the same time, the executive branch of government continued to deal secretly with foreign loggers. Mazaruni Forest Industries Ltd., Solid Timber Sendirian Bhd, Berjaya Group Berhad and Leeling Timber of Asia and the Buchanan Group of Canada were among the logging companies seeking large-scale concessions (Sizer 1996, 43–46). In 1994, Jagan and a large entourage went on a month-long tour of South East Asia, paid for by Barama. That company also paid for additions to the fence around State House, the president's official residence (Forests Monitor n.d.); and in 2001–02, for the renovation of 'Red House', the residence of Prime Minister Jagan in the 1950s (Barama Company Ltd n.d.).

Forest Policy Reform on Paper

Support for the forestry sector from the UK's Overseas Development Agency (ODA) and the Department of International Development (DFID) predated the PPP's assumption to office in 1992. D.A. Black, a British forester, acted as commissioner of forests from 1992 to 1994, and initiated the processes which resulted in the still extant Manual of Procedures for small-scale concessions (Guyana Forestry Commission 1993A) and the forest concession policy (Guyana Forestry Commission 1993B). In 1995, under pressure from foreign donors, the government of Guyana instituted a three-year moratorium on new foreign and local large-scale logging concessions, and a year later introduced no-harvest state forest exploratory permits. Both were conditions for the ODA project to support the institutional reform of the GFC, including developing a capacity for policy and legal reform. This project ran during 1996–2002 and did much to aid institutional reform of the GFC to at least the beginning of a modern service-focused government agency. *Prima facie*, the forestry sector in Guyana then seemed well placed in the late 1990s to avoid the Asian experiences of unsustainable logging and forest corruption, and to benefit from a relatively intact forest estate.

Three scales of forest harvesting in state forests in Guyana are covered by concession-type permits. They range from the small-scale, non-exclusive and bi-annual State Forest Permissions (SFPs, the successors of the wood cutting grants and leases of the colonial period) to the large-scale and long-term TSAs. The third category of forest concession is the Wood Cutting Lease (WCL) that, like the TSA, grants exclusive harvesting rights, but for a shorter period, for three to ten years (extended to ten to 15 years in 2004). In 1993, the GFC laid out the eligibilities and requirements of each type in a forest concessions policy (Guyana Forestry Commission 1993B) (building on the resource information generated by UNDP/SF-FAO FIDS in the late 1960s). The policy explicitly provided for entry-level small-scale, short-term salvage logging, up to large-scale, long-term concessions for sustainable forest management. The 1993 policy is quite clear that the licence holder should be the forest operator (Guyana Forestry Commission 1993B). Four years later, the 1997 national forest policy (Guyana Forestry Commission 1997) repeated the intention that a failing entrepreneur should hand back the logging concession licence for re-auction to a pool of more appropriate enterprises. The GFC applications manual (Guyana Forestry Commission 1993A) requires the GFC staff to carry out due diligence checks on the financial status and technical capability of applicants applying to exploit the public assets of state forests.

Other key benchmarks of the ODA-funded institutional reform project were the National Forest Plan 2001, passage of the Forests (Amendment) (Exploratory Permits) Act 1997 (SFEP) in the national assembly and participatory consultations on the draft Forests Bill of 1996, intended to update the 1953 Forests Act, and institute clear due diligence procedures, including exclusion of forests areas over which there were pre-existing Amerindian land claims. There was complementary support by the Carter Center, in the US, for the multi-stakeholder process over several years that resulted in the National Development Strategy 1996 (Government of Guyana 1996). Kenneth King, a former assistant director general for forestry of FAO, also a Guyanese national, detailed the cross-fertilisation between the latter and the National Forest Policy Statement 1997 (Guyana Forestry Commission 1997) in a review for FAO (King 1998).

King's review for FAO made no reference to corrupt linkages between the state and foreign logging interests which had caught international attention (Colchester 1997; Sizer 1996) and which was an underlying driver for transparent reform of the forest policy process for the Western donors. The United Nations Food and Agriculture Organisation (UN FAO), like the International Tropical Timber Organization (ITTO), steers clear of mention of government corruption (Gale 1998). Nevertheless, the shared hope of Guyanese civil society and external donors was that these initiatives would arrest the government's signing of secret FDI contracts with dubious Asian companies, as had happened during the 1991–96 period, and put the forestry sector on a sound footing by institutionalising a process of transparency and due diligence practices in forest concession awards and management.

Unfortunately the ODA-funded institutional reform project was negotiated between technical staff and never really enthused the real decision-makers in successive PPP political administrations. Consultancy reports and recommendations prepared during this GFC support project are only exceptionally available in the public domain, although some were used to develop GFC procedures that still exist on paper. The ODA project can also be faulted for not preparing summaries of the various projects destined for the GFC, cabinet and the national assembly (Parliament). Those summaries might have stimulated some members of parliament to take an interest in the goings-on in the forestry sector. The agreed policies remained paper documents, useful for waving at foreign delegations. None was put into practice.

Integrated Land Use Planning

A key objective of both the National Development Strategy of 1996 and the National Forest Policy Statement of 1997[6] was the establishment of an integrated land use planning system. In 1996, President Jagan invited the World Resources Institute (WRI), a global research organisation, to study and make recommendations on the forest resources of Guyana, following a similar project in Suriname (Sizer and Rice 1995). Nigel Sizer carried out the WRI study and his report drew attention to the 'lack of government capacity, conflicting institutional mandates, and outdated laws' relating to land use (Sizer 1996, 13). Sizer continued: 'Guyana has no comprehensive laws on land-use planning, monitoring, and enforcement. Instead, much sectoral law and many institutions have evolved, creating conflicts and overlaps in jurisdiction' (13). He recommended 'reform of land allocation and land use planning: Arguably the highest priority for the government as it seeks economic benefits from forest resources is the need to clarify national land-use planning' (15). Sizer's analysis drew extensively from a 1995 'Report on Land Use' authored by Andrew Bishop, at the time Guyana's national coordinator of land use planning (Bishop 1995). Bishop was shortly thereafter appointed by the president to serve as commissioner of the Guyana Lands and Surveys Commission (GLSC), thereby *prima facie* ideally placed to rectify the lack of a national land use plan.

In March 1997, President Cheddi Jagan died during the final year of the PPP's first term in office. Prime Minister Sam Hinds assumed the presidency until December 1997 when the PPP was again victorious at national elections, paving the way for Janet, the wife of Cheddi Jagan, and the PPP presidential candidate, to form the government. Less than two years later, Janet Jagan resigned on account of ill health in August 1999. Sam Hinds was again enlisted in the PPP's stratagems: on this occasion he resigned as prime minister to accommodate the appointment of Bharrat Jagdeo, protégé of Janet Jagan, who could then take over as president. Forest policy reform and integrated land use planning were stillborn in the Jagdeo administrations.

Jagdeo Administrations (1999–2011)

Bharrat Jagdeo further concentrated executive power over all aspects of national decision-making during his 12 years as president. The enduring pattern of ethnic voting at all reasonably 'free and fair' national elections from 1961 (excluding the rigged elections during the 1968–92 period) guaranteed his party's electoral success until 2015 when that dependency came undone by local disaffection and the continuing high rate of East Indian migration to North America. In this section, I detail the progressive normalisation of discretionary practices in the forest sector.

The Setting Aside of Integrated Land Use Planning

In Guyana, integrated land use planning projects last for the duration of donor funds and are never implemented. Initially, the PPP administration had supported the idea of integrated land use planning. The ensuing Guyana Integrated Natural Resources Information Service (GINRIS) project secured German government funding from 1994 for GIS equipment, staff training and participatory development of an inter-agency collaborative mechanism for information sharing and decision-making. The Natural Resources Management Planning (NRMP) body was set up to coordinate the project. When German GTZ funding ended in 2004, GINRIS was systematically dismantled, *after* it had been put in place. The library and equipment were transferred to the GLSC, and trained staff let go. The government never gave a reason for dismantling the mechanism that had been set up to operationalise national land use planning. The decision to disband the NRMP was allegedly made by the executive arm of government, and it provides an indicator of their preference for the non-transparent processes of allocating forestry and mining concessions.

After the discontinuation of GINRIS, inter-agency communication continued in the old way, with allegedly weekly meetings among agency heads comprising the Natural Resources and Environment Advisory Committee (NREAC) – *ad hoc*, secretive, unstructured and dependent on the directives given to agency heads by the executive. By 2015, there were still no procedures for formalising priorities between competing land uses (mining versus agriculture versus forestry). Any system of land use planning that would involve inter-agency sharing of information and facilitate a transparent and rational process of decision-making, and could facilitate efficient subsidiarity in decision-making[7] was and remains anathema to how public affairs are actually conducted in Guyana.

The environmental and social degradation resulting from uncontrolled mining and logging interests were well documented: timber wasted in areas clear-cut for mining before logging, waterways polluted with mercury, fuel and sediment, roads ruined, gaping craters dug up and abandoned (Howard et al. 2011; Miller, Lechler, and Bridge 2003; Mistry et al. 2004; Palmer et al. 2002; Rambajan 1988). Abandoned pits created perfect conditions for propagation of the endemic malarial mosquitoes. The riverbank and river mining, together with pollution of waterways, destroyed potable drinking water supplies and the spawning grounds of fish on which Amerindian communities depended. Indigenous and non-indigenous hinterland communities suffered the impacts but were not organised so as to respond with one voice. These communities are not part of the decision-making processes and have no power to hold the natural resources agencies to account (Bulkan 2013B, 373–77).

Whenever questioned about the basis of their decision-making, top PPP leaders justified their aberration from political campaign promises by referring to 'democratic centralism' (Smith et al. 2003; Smith, Smucker, and Myers 2002). 'Democratic centralism' was the Leninist term used by PPP administrations to describe their governance style. In essence, 'democratic centralism' describes the setting aside of laws and policies by the president and a few persons close to him, to direct a civil service line department or agency, such as the GFC, generally orally, to act or not to act in ways which are contrary to valid legislation or regulations or official procedures and without leaving an audit trail.[8] Such direction is rationalised as being 'in the national interest.' No criteria have been supplied publicly for what that overriding national interest might be. In the case of the PPP, the 'democracy' is limited to a small clique of party political power brokers, not even to all members of the cabinet. In the years out of office (1964–92), the PPP was reputed to be as authoritarian and closed as the then ruling PNC (Majeed 2005).

Fictional Decision-making and Coordinating Bodies

As a result of the ODA projects from 1992 to 2002, Guyana has generally good and eminently workable procedures for forest management on paper. The president (as minister of forestry) and the GFC were keen to publicise these paper procedures, although the volume of press articles and comment from 2000 showed increasing awareness in Guyana that these procedures were not, or were not properly, implemented.[9] After Jagdeo's election to the presidency in 2001, the politically-appointed Commissioner of Forests (CoF), working allegedly with the NREAC, a small politically-appointed body with no status in national law or policy, made the decisive recommendations to the executive arm on concession allocation and on which ones would be monitored. Monitoring teams were dispatched from GFC headquarters, not drawn from the corresponding district forest stations (Bulkan 2009). Many concession holders alleged that monitoring was selectively carried out, and generally only in the case of concession holders who had run afoul of the executive or of the GFC in one form or another (personal communication 2006, 2007, 2013, 2014). A parallel process was put in place at the GGMC where the junior minister of natural resources and the environment and not the closed area committee was the deciding factor in mining concession allocations (Bulkan and Palmer 2016B, 682; Walrond, Heesterman, and Goolsarran 2015, 30). This non-transparent form of governance, inherited from the PNC, was expanded by successive PPP administrations. With such heavy-handed political direction, it is not surprising that the best of the GFC staff trained between 1996 and 2002 turned from 'gamekeeper to poacher' by joining the Asian-owned logging companies or the exodus of the well educated and entrepreneurial from Guyana to North America.

SFEP Legislation Enacted and Disregarded

The State Forest Exploratory Permit (SFEP) legislation had been greeted as a major addition to the Forests Act of 1953 and an achievement for the UK ODA Support Project for the forestry sector, 1996–2002. SFEPs were seen as a step-wise measure towards the achievement of sustainable forest management (SFM): to improve the rationality and quality of bids for large-scale concessions and to provide the GFC with more and better pre-investment data (as recommended by the FAO/FIDS project a quarter-century earlier in 1971). A comprehensive SFEP manual was drafted in 1996 and revised in 1999. The intended 3-year pre-logging SFEPs were supposed to be advertised internationally to attract the most skilled entrepreneurs and highest offers at a premium price. The reason for the US$20,000 application fee, far greater than for all other GFC harvest licences, was to enable the GFC to contract qualified international auditors to conduct due diligence on international applicants. The *SFEP Act* explicitly disallowed transference of effective ownership without the prior consent, in writing, of the GFC.

However, the SFEP legislation was only selectively enforced in the following decades. The 2009 Forests Act subverted the intent of the SFEP

Act by legislating permission for SFEP holders to carry out logging 'for limited commercial purposes to the extent necessary to recoup no more than the appointed percentage of the costs and expenses' (Section 9(2)(b)). Section 9(1)(b) said that 25 per cent would apply in cases where no percentage was specified. In other words, SFEP holders were given *carte blanche* to log as much as they pleased since no benchmarks were set for their costs or expenses. Logging was carried out from the outset in all of the SFEPs awarded from 1997 on.

Perennial Non-payment of Area Fees

In 1985, area fees were imposed on all forest harvesting permits for the first time. Those area fees were among the lowest in the world and TSA fees were lower than the rates levied on the two other types of concession licences (Hunter 2001, 90–97). Yet from the beginning, TSA holders resisted having to pay the area fees that were intended to cover the costs of forest management. In contrast, holders of the small-scale, short-term concessions termed 'State Forest Permissions' (SFPs) paid up annually or risked having their two-year SFPs rescinded (Bulkan 2015, 134–37). Political cronyism over the ensuing 30 years ensured that the big loggers were not penalised for their habitual failures to pay area fees, or to pay on schedule (Goolsarran 2016, 26–47; Guyana Forestry Commission 2005, 58–68, 85). Similarly, the terms and conditions set out for TSAs to carry out SFM were often disregarded in practice (Bulkan 2014A, 415–17).

Landlording in the Logging Sector

The illegal practices of subletting, subleasing, subcontracting and trading in concessions are generally referred to as 'landlording' in Guyana. 'Landlording concessions' describes renting forest harvesting concessions when the original concessionaire finds it technically impossible to operate a log harvest or financially more profitable to get someone else to do the work. Landlording differs from the traditional labour contracting in Guyana ('sprinting') in that the renter takes all effective management decisions relating to the concession. This practice is illegal in Guyana and in many other countries. Concession law and policy indicate that unworkable concessions should be returned to the GFC for re-allocation according to transparent and competitive procedures, or returned to the strategic forest reserve (Forests Act 1953, National Forest Policy 1997, and specific clauses of concession agreements).[10]

In 2001, the GFC Board of Directors granted permission to Guyana Sawmills Ltd, the holder of TSA 7/85 to subcontract the concession to Barama Company Limited (BCL).[11] That marked the first transfer of a forest concession. This action was *ultra vires*, as Condition 13 of TSA makes explicit prohibition of concession subcontracting, except with the prior written permission of the president – not, as claimed by the GFC in several press releases over the course of 2006, the permission of the board or the commissioner of forests.

When news of the Guyana Sawmills-Barama rental deal leaked out, it gave rise to pervasive unease both in the forestry industry and in the wider society (Forte, Cassells, and Mangal 2001). The FDI-benefiting companies, primarily Asian, were seen as being enabled to shape the industry to their ends. But since the Asian loggers effectively controlled the Forest Products Association (FPA), there was no representative body to register a protest. The Asian loggers were the only ones who paid their FPA dues and financially supported the association.[12]

After the precedent of the Guyana Sawmills-Barama rental, landlording practices quickly became entrenched, and grew in scale, allowing four Asian loggers to extend their legal control of forest concessions. By 2008, BCL's control by area increased from 26 to more than 33 per cent; Demerara Timbers Limited (DTL) from eight to over ten per cent, UNAMCO from two to over six per cent, and Jailing (a BaiShanLin subsidiary) from two to over four per cent. The trend continued during the remainder of the PPP's tenure in office. By 2014, BaiShanLin controlled over 1.4 Mha, Barama 1.6 Mha and VHPI/Café Coffee Day 738,000 ha. Those three Asian loggers held at least 3.8 Mha or over 55 per cent by area of all Guyana's forest concessions (Bulkan 2014B). All were focused on log exports, not on in country processing, as advocated by Guyana's national forest policy and the election manifestoes of all the political parties.

Asian loggers also targeted small-scale concessions and Amerindian titled lands, negotiating exclusive access for the purpose of logging or as log buyers. The Asian companies logged seamlessly across the forests without regard to any concession boundary line. For its part, the GFC maintained that renting of concessions was within the ambit of the law, although the law clearly did not allow such activity (Guyana Forestry Commission 2014).

In the 1995–2000 period, chainsaw loggers protested what they described as inequitable concession allocation and monitoring practices. However, by 2001 the GFC had gained control over their fledgling organisations[13] and forestalled any future collective action (Bulkan 2015, 134–35). Cautions from concerned Guyanese and others fell on deaf ears. In a 2003 letter to the *Stabroek News*, an expatriate Guyanese economist, Bishnodat Persaud pointed out another 'embedded longer-term issue that pose[s] such great danger for Guyana...In Guyana's current desperate state, the attention it attracts from Guyanese expatriate and foreign "adventurers" who provide little beyond encouraging corrupt practices; and the large concessions that must be offered to attract investors in the current very unattractive investment climate, which becomes more worrying still, where concessions for natural resource exploitation must be of a long-term nature' (Persaud 2003).

The Guyana Manufacturers and Services Association (GMSA) Wood Sector Sub Group lobbied unsuccessfully from 2003 in meetings convened by the prime minister, (whose portfolio did not include forestry) against landlording and the related practice of uncontrolled exports of prime log species. When one prominent manufacturer described the practices as 'sheer lawlessness' in a *Stabroek Business* special on log exports, the Asian-owned Barama Company Ltd immediately severed commercial relations with him (*Stabroek News* 2004). At that time that wood processor relied on BCL for over half of his lumber supplies (personal communication), providing another indication of BCL's stranglehold over the supply of prime species, and disregard of the local pricing clause (Article 10) in its FDI agreement.[14]

Six points were critical in the private trading of logging concessions: firstly, the renters of large-scale concessions were all Asian loggers, holders of large concessions of their own; secondly, the Asian loggers banked harvesting rights to more and more lands since the state allowed it informally; thirdly, 'rents' payable to the concession holders were a negligible cost compared with the value of the logs exported; fourthly, the only penalty, if any, which accrued to the renter when the concession holders were in arrears for royalties, was a temporary halt in the handing over of timber tags by the GFC; fifthly, the newly acquired concessions could be and were high-graded for the prime timber logs much in demand in India and China, and which were exported at the lowest export prices worldwide for comparable species, with no due diligence measures put in place by regulatory agencies in Guyana; and sixthly, Asians were shifting from employing Guyanese to importing East Asian logging crews (Bulkan and Palmer 2015). None of the beneficiaries of FDI concessions was complying with the promised intentions to set up wood processing industries in Guyana and to train and employ skilled Guyanese workers. The single-minded focus of the renters was to extract prime commercial species for export in log form to Asia.

Timber Tagging and Tracking System Not Used

A timber tagging and tracking system using bar-coded tags (Barne 1999), linked to a concession-based yield allocation system were devised in parallel. However, the GFC failed to purchase bar-code readers or to develop a spatially distributed database for timber production data, and naturally the staff were disinclined to copy out the long numbers from tags on logs. Corruption led to uncontrolled distribution of tags, so that they have been used as a kind of currency in the hinterland (Bulkan and Palmer 2008, 110–15). The United States Agency for International Development (USAID) funded a Proforest (Oxford) consultancy to review the tagging and tracing system in 2006. The ITTO funded a second stage of internationally tendered external consultancies to add operational details to the 1999 recommendations (Guyana Forestry Commission 2007). GFC production data were good enough by late 2007 to support administratively imposed penalties on major logging concessions for forest offences, including logging out of coupe. However, a batch from 2005 to 2012 of the legally mandated GFC annual reports finally submitted to the national assembly in December 2013 detailed no uses of the improved tagging and tracking system (Bulkan and Palmer 2014).

Revision of the GFC Act in 2007 and of the Forests Act in 2009

Using its parliamentary majority, the PPP passed a new GFC Act in July 2007 and a new Forests Act in 2009. The GFC Act set out severe penalties for leakage of information. Although it appeared to contravene the national Constitution's commitment to open government (Articles 13 and 146), it was never challenged in court and it acted as a deterrent to all levels of staff.[15]

The draft Forests Bill tabled in Parliament in 2007 was unconsulted, not the earlier widely-consulted draft of 1996 that had been drawn up by the Barbadian lawyer Toppin-Allahar. A group of civil society members submitted a petition to Parliament listing 127 points of concern with the 2007 draft Forests Bill. The government claimed that a special parliamentary committee considered and consulted widely before rejecting every point raised in the petition. No proof of the alleged consultations was ever placed in the public domain (Martin 2009). The National Assembly passed that unconsulted Forests Act in January 2009. The travesty of justice did not end there. The required presidential assent was delayed by 628 days, and Minister Robert Persaud only signed the commencement order required by section 1 of the Act on August 8, 2012. The GFC and the government have consistently ignored the legal requirements and refer to the Act as the Forests Act 2009, not Forests Act 2012 (*Stabroek News* 2014). The Forests Act 2009 gives the GFC large discretionary powers for making administrative decisions with no guiding criteria and no appeals process. As the GFC failed to prosecute any alleged forest offences in open court, there have been no opportunities for the defendants to challenge the GFC through legal cross-examination.

During the period 2006–08, there was increasing criticism in the independent press of uncontrolled logging and log export, contrary to national policies, and of the abuse by government of forest laws and regulations. President Jagdeo attempted to dampen criticism by two waves of nominal penalties imposed on large-scale loggers in late 2007 and early 2008, but no alleged forest offence was prosecuted in the criminal court and only one case appeared in the civil court, with the GFC as a defendant. The plaintiff, Toolsie Persaud Ltd., won the case (*Stabroek News* 2008A).

No Enforcement of Requirement for TSAs to Carry out Wood Processing in Country

Between 1997 and 2005 an additional 10 large-scale concessions TSAs totalling more than 550,000 ha were awarded, over half to Chinese loggers, without going through the legally required SFEP stage. Five SFEPs totalling more than 500,000 ha were also awarded, all later converted to TSAs. The spatial area of large-scale concessions had increased six-fold in a 20-year period (1985–2000) without any reference to the 1997 National Forest Policy requirement for linkages between large concessions and wood processing industries in Guyana.

Asian loggers and log traders concentrated on the cutting and exporting of a handful of commercially desirable log species, intensifying the localised extinction of prime timbers. Their monopsony also allowed them to set log prices. In spite of the low rates for the few taxes actually paid, Barama with 1.61 Mha of natural forest was massively in arrears of payment by the mid-2000s while simultaneously claiming maximum tax concessions and petitioning for increases (Guyana Forestry Commission 2005). While Barama continued to benefit from generous FDI tax incentives and lax accounting (Ram 2007), from 2000 it reduced its plywood production to only 13 per cent of the installed capacity of 108,000 m3. At the same time, Samling Global, Barama's parent company, leveraged its logging concessions into financial capital by issuing an IPO on the Hong Kong Stock Exchange in 2007 that raised US$369 million (Bulkan and Palmer 2007). Barama's forest concessions in Guyana were a major feature of its IPO; however, Guyana's exchequer did not benefit in any way from the windfall.

During three decades (1992–2015), forestry was transformed into an enclave sector supplying raw logs to Asia and controlled by a handful of secretive Asian loggers and log traders, in flagrant disregard of all national policies for onshore value addition. As the Asian markets for logs of flooring and furniture quality timbers were booming, sawmills and lumber yards relied increasingly on chainsaw operators to supply the sawn wood to be processed for the domestic market. The poorly dressed chain sawn wood triggered the importation of softwood pine lumber from North America into Guyana, which began sometime around 2009. The large-scale pine lumber imports was another bit of evidence of policy failure, in spite of the often-repeated boasts of Guyana having more than 75 per cent cover of natural tropical rainforest and a national forest service for over 85 years.

Selective Logging and Trading of a Few Commercially Desirable Species

Guyana's hard and heavy, dark-coloured timbers constitute only a small proportion of the forest's growing stock but are of such intrinsic value that they are in present danger of being over-harvested, or worse, made commercially extinct. Slow-growing timbers are difficult to manipulate by human action so, following the precautionary principle, logging should be conservative. Unfortunately, successive governments heavily undervalued the forests and the GFC never applied precautions concerning felling cycles for individual species (Guyana Forestry Commission 2002, 8). If there were effective forest management rules, many of these timbers would be placed under CITES protection.

Ignoring forest inventory and floristic knowledge accumulated throughout the twentieth century, the GFC essentially acts as if forest is uniform in species composition and tree stocking. Although there are obvious differences in commercial quality between primary forest and forest which has been logged more than once (Bird and Dhanraj 2001), the GFC treats the forests as uniform for tax purposes, resulting in sharp inequities between concession types. Moreover, the GFC is neither staffed nor motivated, particularly after 2002 when the externally funded projects closed, to take account of forest ecology although it has both GIS capability and yield allocation software, plus the 100 per cent pre-harvesting inventory data for 100-hectare logging blocks submitted by the operators of the long-term forest concessions.

One of the greatest faults was abandoning species-specific estimation of the annual allowable cut (Guyana Forestry Commission 2002, 9). This major failure by the GFC allows unsustainable logging of the commercially preferred species, an error pointed out repeatedly in the press and ignored by the GFC (Bulkan 2007A, 2007B; Bulkan 2016C, 2016D; Kowlessar 2008A, 2008B). In 2006, the only year for which disaggregated data on log exports was made available by the GFC, China imported 78,000 m^3 of Guyana's hard heavy timber logs. The top three species exported – greenheart (25 per cent of total), purpleheart (23 per cent), and mora (14 per cent) – represented 62 per cent of total log volumes in that year. The top ten species by volume accounted for 92 per cent of exports. All top ten species were being sold off for a fraction of their real value and without any field management to protect their regeneration after logging.[16]

Log exporting is hugely profitable to the log traders (Bulkan 2012). Exact estimates are difficult because of secrecy over shipping costs and doubts about the accuracy of Customs declarations and bills of lading. Documentation to circumvent or defraud the US Lacey Act controls against import of illegally produced timber, and the European Union Timber Regulation (EUTR) is easily purchased in Guyana as in Perú (Sears and Pinedo-Vasquez 2011, 614–19). New or tighter regulations by the GFC and the Customs and Trade Administration of the Guyana Revenue Authority involved only partly computerised bureaucracy mixed with hand-completed and typed forms. The additional formalities add almost nothing to international security or the prevention of illegal logging and trade but do expand opportunities for petty corruption. For legitimate traders, these formalities add unpredictable time for document processing before shipment, plus the time and cost to make missing government staff 're-appear' to give their signatures to documents. Operators and shippers known to be close to the apex of power in government were not subject to checks by junior government staff.

Exports of unprocessed logs were 37 per cent of total log production during the period 2009–September 2011. Three prime timbers for flooring and furniture comprised over 66 per cent of the total of 253,000 m^3 of logs of 89 species, all gone to China and India for value-addition. The top six species made up over 75 per cent, and the top 20 timbers made up over 97 per cent, of the exported volume, so the remaining 69 timbers comprised less than three per cent of the total exported. The claim by the big log exporters that they had to export prime timbers in order to persuade the market to accept lesser used species was thus not correct. Other illegalities flourished.

Non-Disclosure of Species' Names or Volumes Exported

The US Lacey Act amended in 2008 and the EUTR enacted in October 2010 both require truthful declarations of species and volumes, and geographical origins, for timber exported into those regions. Instead of following international best practice, the GFC stopped reporting systematically from February 2008 on what timbers were exported in what volumes to which countries. By aggregating all species, the GFC could claim an increase in exports of lesser used species, which conveniently served to deflect attention from exports of the increasingly rare commercially prime species which have been under-managed and over-cut (purpleheart timber over-cut by about 30 times its capacity to regenerate naturally) (Bulkan 2011).

Cocaine in Timber Exports

In mid-March 2011, Jamaican Customs discovered 122 kg of cocaine in bags thrown on top of 130 apparently illegally harvested and illegally exported hard dark heavy flooring wamara logs (*Swartzia leiocalycina*), from Guyana. A Chinese trader had been exporting the logs to processors in China using the documents (Export Licence BER 05602011) of the

Aroaima Forest Producers Association (AFAPA), an association of small-scale loggers. The GFC claimed that it had inspected the logs in Aroaima in Region 10 in mid-February, suggesting that the Trade and Customs Department of the Guyana Revenue Authority (GRA) had failed to inspect the shipment before the container was sealed (*Stabroek News* 2011). This event showed non-compliance with both forest and customs laws. No action was taken then, or ever, by the GFC on the illegal harvest of the logs or the use of a false name on the shipping documents. The shipment to Jamaica was not reported in GFC's monthly trade statistics. In August 2011, the GRA reported the dismissal of one customs officer and suspension of three others in relation to this case (Solomon 2011). Two years later, timber mats to support mechanical diggers in soft ground were found to have been made from illegally harvested timber and to have been stuffed with cocaine for smuggling to the Netherlands concealed in digger mats, confirming continuing lax supervision and enforcement by the GFC and GRA (Bulkan 2013A).

The President's Offer of the Forests of Guyana for Climate Change Mitigation

In late 2006, President Jagdeo become aware of the United Nations Framework Convention on Climate Change (UNFCCC) negotiations on climate change, and the possibility of generating revenue from forest-sequestered carbon. Guyana was already receiving international funding from climate change adaptation funds. An estimated 60 per cent of GDP was lost in 2005 because of unprecedented coastal flooding. The government never provided an audited account of the relief funds that were received. From Jagdeo's point of view, the advent of more substantial international funds for climate change adaptation could be a bonanza.

The president made an offer at a Commonwealth conference on Caribbean investment in 2006, to place all or most of Guyana's natural tropical forests under an international protection regime in the service of climate change mitigation (*Guyana Chronicle* 2006). The basis for this offer seemed to be linked to a long-standing belief in the Office of the President that Guyana's forests are net sequestrators of atmospheric carbon, despite expanded and uncontrolled logging and mining. After the November 2006 announcement, there were several different versions of this offer, and some presidential or ministerial qualifications:

a. assurance to the citizens that there would be no loss of sovereignty over the forests (Office of the President 2008; *Stabroek News* 2007a);
b. assurance that logging (forest degradation) and mineral mining (deforestation) could continue in forests being offered for climate change mitigation (Office of the President 2009);
c. recognition that Amerindians with community land title were exempt from this offer unless they opted for inclusion;
d. no additional regulations for logging and mining but implementation would be required only because of the likelihood of international verification (*Guyana Chronicle* 2009; Persaud 2009);
e. some additional regulations likely;
f. traditional rotational agriculture by Amerindians was neither deforestation nor forest degradation;[17] and
g. land under concessions was exempt from this offer.[18]

President Jagdeo spent the next three years drumming up interest in potential international partners. His own scheme for REDD+ (Reducing Emissions from Deforestation and Forest Degradation) did not depend on estimates of actual deforestation and forest degradation. It was instead based on a fantastical scenario for deliberate destructive logging and mining of 90 per cent of the rain forest at an average rate of four per cent for 25 years, with replacement of the forest by commercial plantation crops. This scenario, developed by McKinsey & Company (Office of the President 2008), valued the forest as the aggregate of the income from its destruction and later agriculture, although there was no public domain evidence of agricultural demand for this forest-covered land. The president proposed that external donors would pay an annual annuity to Guyana in order to prevent this deliberate destruction. His LCDS (Office of the President 2009A) was essentially a wish list of developmental activities to be paid by this annuity. For its own reasons, the government of Norway agreed to fund some projects in the scheme.

Lack of Political Commitment or Practical Action to Set up a Robust Legality Verification System

Guyana and Norway signed a Memorandum of Understanding (MoU) loosely tied to a Reducing Emissions (of forest carbon) from Deforestation and forest Degradation (REDD) scheme, in November 2009 (Government of the Cooperative Republic of Guyana and Government of the Kingdom of Norway 2009). Norway attached several conditions to its proposed five years of annual grants even though Guyana made no formal commitment to reduce or even stabilise its deforestation rate. One of the conditions in the MoU was 'evidence of Guyana entering a formal dialogue with the European Union (EU) with the intent of joining its Forest Law Enforcement, Governance and Trade (FLEGT) processes (European Commission 2003) towards a Voluntary Partnership Agreement (VPA)'. One of the key elements of a VPA is a legality verification system (LVS), to provide assurance that timber imported into the EU from the producer country shall have been produced at least legally if not sustainably.

The Guyana National Bureau of Standards (GNBS) was given the task of developing a national LVS. An undated draft of 16 pages was probably prepared in March 2010 and issued with only minor typing corrections in February 2011 as a formal standard (GYS 496). Compared with the multi-volume LVS prepared in Ghana and Indonesia, the Guyana LVS was sparse. In contrast to the detailed prescriptions in Ghana and Indonesia, the Guyanese standard said nothing at all about the responsibilities of the relevant government agencies, nor how they should coordinate between themselves and with the private sector.

A year later, USAID commissioned an international consultancy on the Guyana national 'Legality Assurance System', which was undertaken in March (Efeca 2011). The report was officially handed over to the junior minister for forestry in October 2011. The GFC registered several disagreements with statements in the report but gave few or no reasons for dispute. The GFC did not take up the redesign offered by Efeca nor post the Efeca report on its website nor engage in public discussion. The Efeca redesign conformed to the general principles of legality verification systems associated with the voluntary partnership agreements of the EU FLEGT action plan. Adopting the re-design would have allowed the GFC to register real forward movement on one of the progress indicators in the Norway–Guyana Memorandum of Understanding (MoU) of November 2009.

In addition to the Efeca study, GFA Consulting Group carried out a scoping mission on the GFC proposal for independent forest monitoring (IFM) (GFA Consulting Group 2011), followed by two annual monitoring visits (GFA Consulting Group 2013, 2014). The mission's initial terms of reference (TORs) in 2011 were only a subset of those proposed by Global

Witness in 2005 (Young 2005, 46–112). GFA failed to notice that the GFC was imposing penalties on forest producers which greatly exceed the legal limit allowed by the Forests Act 2009 for minor administrative mistakes. GFA did notice that the GFC was applying laws and regulations selectively, with the GFC explaining that it had 'policy directives' to exempt (politically favoured) clients from application of law. Exactly who provided these 'policy directives', with what legal authority to circumvent law, was left unstated. The two subsequent monitoring consultancies were process-, not performance-based (Bulkan 2016E).

So the soundly based policy and technical developments in the GFC to 2002 were shown to have been largely left on the shelf for almost a decade, produced at international conferences and to show visitors, but not for general local application against a regime characterised by regulatory capture.[19]

Discretionary Practices Continued Under President Ramotar

Donald Ramotar succeeded Jagdeo as president in December 2011, but his party lost its parliamentary majority by one seat. Nevertheless, President Ramotar continued to rule by discretion. In January 2012, among the first acts of his presidency was to issue TSA 01/12 of 180,000 ha to Toolsie Persaud Timber Traders Inc., a subsidiary of Toolsie Persaud Ltd (TPL). TPL held TSAs 3/85, 4/85, and 11/85, totalling 315,000 ha. Two months later, in March 2012, the CEO of GO-Invest was removed after he refused to grant duty-free concessions to Diamond Tropical Wood Products (DTWP), another TPL subsidiary, on the grounds that it was *ultra vires*. A forensic audit of GO-Invest later found that DTWP 'was granted over GY$60M in concessions to establish a wood processing facility, but it never commenced operation at Diamond, East Bank Demerara' (*Stabroek News* 2017). TPL negotiated with the GFC in 2013 to disengage from TSA 01/12 in exchange for parts of the former SFEPs 02/2005 (Barama Housing, controlled by Barama) and 04/2004 (Guyana Lumber and Timber Ltd). Both these SFEPs had expired in 2007 without completing the pre-logging planning in the exploratory phase since 2004. In short, concessions were awarded to cronies with scant if any reference to the legal requirements.

Conclusion

In 1992, a major PPP advertisement declared: 'What does October 5th 1992 [date of national elections] mean to you?...It means you want a say on how and to whom your resources are divested, instead of the transfer of ownership at rock-bottom prices to foreign interests' (Premdas 1993, 121). That electoral promise did not materialise over the generation in which the PPP held power. The post-independence governments have squandered opportunities for rationalised land use planning and instead have narrowed the range of future options based on a resilient and well-managed forest estate. Decisions on the allocation and management of concessions in logging and mining and later, on the so-called LCDS, became more centralised in the office of the president. By the end of their terms in office, the PPP Administration had little positive to show in exchange for the alienation and unsustainable exploitation of the best-stocked forestlands to loggers. Amerindian land claims were not yet fully settled. Unregulated mining degraded both forests and watersheds. Arguably another worrisome aspect of executive rule by discretion was the way that it had become normalised by 2015. The succeeding A Partnership for National Unity+Alliance for Change (APNU+AFC) administration did not lose much time before settling into the continuation of discretionary rule.

Notes

1. The terms 'forest harvesting licences', 'logging concessions', and 'logging or concession licences' are used interchangeably in Guyana and in this chapter.
2. 'Forest degradation' means leaving the forest after harvesting in a state worse (less productive) than would be the case if the Forests Act, the Forest Regulations, the concession licence conditions and the quite mild GFC *Code of Practice for Timber Harvesting* (first edition 1996, second edition 2002, based on the FAO Reduced Impact Logging [RIL] manual) were to be implemented consistently. N. Sasaki and F.E. Putz propose an expanded definition for forest degradation to include tree 'crown cover (above 40 per cent for closed forest), tree height, tree species composition, and carbon stock', and also other ecosystem services (Sasaki and Putz 2008).
3. In 1964, according to the International Commission of Jurists, the Amerindian population was 29,430 and the national population was 683,030 (Sanders 1987, 8–9).

4. British Guiana Independence Conference, section C of Annex 1 (Bulkan 2016B).
5. Government statements vary on the total number of untitled Amerindian communities.
6. The National Forest Policy of October 1997, section B, subsection 1 (a) states that 'The designation of State Forests shall be based on a comprehensive review of land use policy' (Guyana Forestry Commission 1997).
7. Subsidiarity is an organising principle which enjoins that matters ought to be handled by the smallest, lowest, or least centralised competent authority. The Oxford English Dictionary defines subsidiarity as the idea that a central authority should have a subsidiary function, performing only those tasks which cannot be performed effectively at a more immediate or local level.
8. For example, Dr Luncheon, the head of the Presidential Secretariat (HPS), explained government's illegal granting of a licence and allocation of a frequency to China Central TV in the following way: '...But obviously if they're [National Frequency Management Unit] instructed what do you think they would do? If you were the managing director of NFMU and the HPS called you and said we've just agreed with the People's Republic of China to broadcast the signals and..., they have selected a channel to do so, could you please go ahead and assign a channel, you think he's [the Head of NFMU] going to tell me [Luncheon] that you got to apply and all of those things? I doubt it' (*Stabroek News* 2013).
9. A collection of newspaper articles and letters during this period can be found at http://guyanaforestryblog.blogspot.ca.
10. Landlording is illegal under Condition 2 of 16 of State Forest Permissions – 'This Permit is not transferable without the prior consent in writing of the Commissioner. It may not be assigned or sublet nor may the grantee allow any person to work under it on payment to the Grantee of any consideration whatsoever.'
11. The GFC Board of Directors, which has no legal authority to extend long-term concessions, was allegedly 'persuaded' to allow the subcontracting of this concession to BCL, supposedly as a trial, and without laying out any duration for the subcontract or the safeguards that might have prevented BCL from extending its use of duty-free concessions to its working of subcontracted concessions (interview with former Head of GFC Board 2006). The procedures set out in forest law to regulate the trade in concessions were not used by the GFC, nor was any compensatory premium negotiated or paid by any logger to balance the cost saving of not having to compete for the concession bought over.
12. 'Only a relatively small percentage of the loggers in the sector are members of the FPA and *Stabroek Business* understands that even some of the registered members of the association have been delinquent in the payment of their dues....Meanwhile the source conceded that the FPA itself was in a state of 'confusion' arising out of 'questionable commitment' to the association. The source said that the FPA was effectively controlled by a handful of large

operators in the logging sector and that the larger numbers of loggers are not members of the body. Additionally, the source told *Stabroek Business* that some members of the FPA had been delinquent in the payment of their dues for some time and that there were 'probably only about a dozen paid-up members' of the organisation. 'Part of the problem is that the FPA is not a particularly strong body,' the source said (*Stabroek News* 2008B).

13. Philip Bynoe, the first leader of one of the first three chainsaw logging associations was reported in 2000 as saying: 'We set out to demonstrate the plight of the poor in Region Ten.' He added to this rebuke an accusation that the FPA and the GFC had plotted a monopoly of large logging companies at the expense of the ordinary Guyanese. Furthermore, he claimed log exporting was crippling the industry, as well as threatening the livelihoods of thousands. 'Without exception,' he stated, 'they [exporters] have shifted their export from lumber to logs. This, coupled with the under-invoicing and mislabelling of species, ensures that Guyana's forestry industry is relegated to the role of raw material supplier.' He alleged that for every log exported Guyana receives only 0.001 per cent of its market value and explained that this dumping of logs on the international market for overseas processing restricted Guyana's ability to compete in the lumber and processed wood export market. Bynoe argued that chainsaw logging was the most effective, sustainable and eco-friendly method of farming logs stating, 'from an environmental standpoint the large industry-specific equipment indiscriminately destroys our forest, whereby the chainsaw as a tool of sustainable and affordable forest utilisation is less damaging and more cost-effective' (*Stabroek News* 2008B).

14. Among Barama's minimal obligations included in its FDI agreement was a requirement that the company and the government 'shall discuss and agree on the pricing policy relating to the Company's products which would govern the disposal of any portion(s) of the Company's products on the local Guyanese market, taking into consideration the price(s) and quality of the local Guyanese product(s)' (Article 10).

15. Section 13 of the revised GFC Act restricts access to, disclosure and use of information, and section 27 prescribes atypically severe penalties for infringement, including fines of US$5,000 and imprisonment for one year, and up to ten times those numbers.

16. The disparity between the log export data recorded by customs in Guyana and the prices for logs of equivalent timbers landed in China is around US$320 per cubic metre, a comfortably large amount for minimising inspection. Illegal earnings from this disparity were estimated to be US$3–5 million per month during 2006, when log exports for the year totalled 191,000 m^3.

17. 'The issue of slash and burn was raised and it was agreed that the slash and burn should be treated as part of subsistence farming by Amerindians and not affected by the Strategy,' Office of Climate Change, Stakeholder Consultation Steering Committee Meeting 3, June 23 2009, http://www.lcds.gov.gy.

18. 'The strategy does not include all of Guyana's forest, 10 per cent will be excluded apart from the indigenous lands, private owned lands and land under concession,' Office of Climate Change, Minutes of the Awareness Session for LCDS, July 21 2009, http://www.lcds.gov.gy.
19. State or regulatory capture occurs when a state regulatory agency created to act in the public interest instead acts in favour of the commercial or special interests that dominate in the industry or sector it is charged with regulating (*Wikipedia*).

References

Barama Company Ltd. n.d. Barama Company Limited: Environment and Community. Accessed January 24, 2017 http://www.baramaguyana.com/eng/ec/community.htm.

Barne, John. 1999. *Wood Product Tracking System: Procedure Manual for the GFC by SGS UK Ltd*. Georgetown: Guyana Forestry Commission.

Bird, N. M., and K. Dhanraj. 2001. *SFP Rapid Assessment Procedure: Next Steps*. Georgetown: Guyana Forestry Commission

Bishop, Andrew. 1995. *Collaboration and Consultation on Land Use in Guyana: Short Term Consultancy on Land Use in Guyana*. Georgetown: University of Guyana.

Bryant, Dirk, Daniel Nielsen, and Laura Tangley. 1997. Last Frontier Forests: Ecosystems and Economies on the Edge. http://pdf.wri.org/lastfrontierforests.pdf.

Bulkan, Arif. 2014. *The Survival of Indigenous Rights in Guyana*. Georgetown: University of Guyana.

Bulkan, Janette. 2007A. GFC's Policy Statement on Concessions is Explicit about under-Performing and Inactive Concessions. *Kaieteur News*, July 17.

———. 2007B. Inventories of the Forest Have Been Made since 1908: Data Suggest Purpleheart is about 0.6 per cent of the Tree Population. Stabroek News, July 15. http://www.stabroeknews.com/index.pl/article?id=56524637.

———. 2009. *Slippages between Forestry Concession Policies and Practices in Guyana*. New Haven: Yale University.

———. 2011. It Would Be Good Practice for the GFC and the Forest Products Development and Marketing Council to Join the Global Best Practices in Reporting. *Stabroek News*, August 7. http://www.stabroeknews.com/2011/opinion/letters/08/07/it-would-be-good-practice-for-the-gfc-and-the-forest-products-development-and-marketing-council-to-join-the-global-best-practices-in-reporting.

———. 2012. The Rule of Law?– What Guyana Loses through Export of Timber Logs to Asia. *Stabroek News*, February 6. http://www.redd-monitor.org/2012/02/14/the-rule-of-law-not-in-the-forest-sector-of-guyana-four-articles-by-janette-bulkan-in-the-stabroek-news.

———. 2013A. Persistent Illegalities Allowed by GFC and GRA in Timber Exports – Cocaine in Digger Mats. *Kaieteur News*, March 7. http://www.kaieteurnewsonline.com/2013/03/07/persistent-illegalities-allowed-by-gfc-and-gra-in-timber-exports-cocaine-in-digger-mats.

———. 2013B. The Struggle for Recognition of the Indigenous Voice: Amerindians in Guyanese Politics. The Round Table. *The Commonwealth Journal of International Affairs* 102, no. 4: 367–80.

———. 2014A. Forest Grabbing through Forest Concession Practices: The Case of Guyana. *Journal of Sustainable Forestry* 33, no. 4:407–34.

———. 2014B. Forestry Commission's Attitude towards the Law Is Casual. *Stabroek News*, September 18. http://www.stabroeknews.com/2014/opinion/letters/09/18/forestry-commissions-attitude-towards-law-casual/#Scene_1.

———. 2015. Associations in Name Only: Small Loggers' Associations in Guyana. *International Forestry Review* 17, no. 2:128–40.

———. 2016A. Hegemony in Guyana: REDD-Plus and State Control over Indigenous Peoples and Resources. In *The Caribbean: Aesthetics, World-Ecology, Politics*, ed., C. Campbell and M. Niblett, 118–42. Liverpool: Liverpool University Press.

———. 2016B. Original Lords of the Soil? Amerindian Rights and the Expansion of State Power in Guyana. Environment and History 22, no. 3:351–91.

———. 2016C. Sustainable Management of Guyana's Greenheart Timber. *Kaieteur News*, October 11. http://www.kaieteurnewsonline.com/2016/10/11/sustainable-management-of-guyanas-greenheart-timber.

———. 2016D. Sustainable Management of Guyana's Greenheart Timber. *Guyana Chronicle*, October 11. https://guyanachronicle.com/2016/10/11/sustainable-management-of-guyanas-greenheart-timber.

———. 2016E. The Limitations of International Auditing: The Case of the Norway-Guyana REDD+ Agreement. In *The Carbon Fix: Forest Carbon, Social Justice and Environmental Governance*, ed. S. Paladino and S. J. Fiske, 91–106. London: Routledge.

Bulkan, Janette, and J.R. Palmer. 2007. Lazy Days at International Banks: How Credit Suisse and HSBC Support Illegal Logging and Unsustainable Timber Harvesting by Samling/Barama in Guyana, and Possible Reforms. London: Chatham House. http://www.illegal-logging.info/sites/default/files/uploads/Samling_Barama.pdf.

———. 2008. Breaking the Rings of Forest Corruption: Steps towards Better Forest Governance. *Forests, Trees and Livelihoods* 18, no. 2:103–31.

———. 2009. Scientific Forestry and Degraded Forests: The Story of Guiana Shield Forests. In *Anthropologies of Guayana: Cultural Spaces in Northeastern Amazonia*, ed. N.L. Whitehead and S.W. Aleman, 74–89. Tucson: University of Arizona Press.

———. 2014. Why the National Assembly Should Hold Public Hearings on the Guyana Forestry Commission. *Stabroek News*, January 22. http://www.redd-monitor.org/2014/02/07/why-the-national-assembly-should-hold-public-hearings-on-the-guyana-forestry-commission/#more-14839.

———. 2015. Why Is Govt. so Enamoured of BaiShanLin despite a Catalogue of Illegalities? *Kaieteur News*, May 8. http://www.kaieteurnewsonline.com/2015/05/08/why-is-govt-so-enamoured-of-baishanlin-despite-a-catalogue-of-illegalities.

———. 2016A. Global Ecological Signpost, Local Reality: The Moraballi Creek Studies in Guyana and What Happened Afterwards. *Forests* 7, no. 12:33.

———. 2016B. Rentier Nation: Landlordism, Patronage and Power in Guyana's Gold Mining Sector. *Journal of Extractive Industries and Society* 3, no. 3:676–89.

Colchester, M. 1997. *Guyana: Fragile Frontier: Loggers, Miners and Forest Peoples*. Kingston: Ian Randle Publishers.

Colchester, Marcus, Jean La Rose, and Kid James. 2002. Mining and Amerindians in Guyana. Final Report of the APA/NSI Project on "Exploring Indigenous Perspective on Consultation and Engagement within the Mining Sector in Latin America and the Caribbean". Ottawa: The North-South Institute.

EFECA. 2011. Review of Guyana's Legality Assurance System. Washington, DC.

European Commission. 2003. Forest Law Enforcement, Governance and Trade (FLEGT). Proposal for an EU Action Plan. http://www.illegal-logging.info/uploads/flegt.pdf.

Forests Monitor. n.d. Samling Group. Guyana. Forests Monitor. http://www.forestsmonitor.org/en/reports/550066/550085#samling

Forte, Janette, David Cassells, and Simone Mangal. 2001. Report for [UNDP] PROFOR on Working Groups' Recommendations for Forest Certification: Summary of the Critical Issues Affecting Certification. Georgetown: Iwokrama International Centre for Rainforest Conservation and Development.

Funk, V., T. Hollowell, P. Berry, C. Kelloff, and S.N. Alexander. 2007. Checklist of the Plants of the Guiana Shield (Venezuela: Amazonas, Bolivar, Delta Amacuro; Guyana, Surinam, French Guiana). Contributions from the United States National Herbarium 55, 584.

Gale, Fred. 1998. *The Tropical Timber Trade Regime*. New York: St Martin's.

GFA Consulting Group. 2011. *Guyana - Independent Forest Monitoring Scoping Report*, 89. Hamburg: GFA Consulting Group. http://www.forestry.gov.gy/Downloads/Independent_Forest_Monitoring_in_Guyana_Scoping_Report.pdf.

———. 2013. *Independent Forest Monitoring. Guyana. Summary of First Independent Forest Monitoring*, 43. Hamburg: GFA Consulting Group.

———. 2014. *Independent Forest Monitoring. Guyana. Public Summary Report of Second Independent Forest Monitoring*, 32. Hamburg: GFA Consulting Group.

Gibbs, A.K. and C.N. Barron. 1993. *The Geology of the Guiana Shield*. Oxford: Oxford University Press.

Goolsarran, S.A. 2016. *Report on the Forensic Audit and Review of the Operations of the Guyana Forestry Commission*. Georgetown: Ministry of Finance.

Government of Guyana. 1996. *National Development Strategy 1996–1997*. Georgetown: Ministry of Finance.

Government of the Cooperative Republic of Guyana and Government of the Kingdom of Norway. 2009. *Memorandum of Understanding between the Government of the Cooperative Republic of Guyana and the Government of the Kingdom of Norway Regarding Cooperation on Issues Related to the Fight against Climate Change, the Protection of Biodiversity and the Enhancement of Sustainable Development*. https://www.regjeringen.no/globalassets/

upload/md/vedlegg/klima/klima_skogprosjektet/the-memorandum-of-understanding-guyana-norway-on-redd-081109-signed-091109.pdf
Grayum, G.H. 1971. *Logging and Forest Management. Technical Report Number 12.* Georgetown and Rome: UNDP and FAO.
Gross-Braun, E.H., J. Derting, and R. Suggett. 1965. *Report of the Soil Survey Project of British Guiana VII: A Report to Accompany a General Soil Map of British Guiana.* Rome: FAO.
Guyana Chronicle. 2006. Guyana Can Earn Millions from Carbon Credit Schemes. November 9.
———. 2009. At GGDMA Meeting, President Jagdeo Gives Miners Assurances on LCDS., August 1. https://www.lcds.gov.gy/index.php/documents/climate-change-information/understanding-climate-change/251-guyana-builds-lcds-thrust-in-new-york/file.
Guyana Forestry Commission. 1993A. *Manual of Procedures. Applications for State Forest Woodcutting Permissions.* Georgetown: Guyana Forestry Commission.
———. 1993B. *Policy – Timber Concession.* Georgetown: Guyana Forestry Commission.
———. 1997. *Guyana National Forest Policy Statement.* Georgetown: Guyana Forestry Commission.
———. 2002. *Code of Practice for Timber Harvesting.* 2n ed. Georgetown: Guyana Forestry Commission.
———. 2005. *Guyana's Forest Sector Contribution to GDP: Review of Forest Concession Allocation.* Georgetown: Guyana Forestry Commission.
———. 2007. *Improving the Detection and Prevention of Illegal Logging and Illegality in Shipment and Trade of Wood Products in Guyana. Project Proposal Submitted to ITTO. Serial Number: PD 440/07 Rev. 1(M,1). 51.* Georgetown: Guyana Forestry Commission.
———. 2014. Presentation on the Forestry Sector – (Media). GFC Press Conference. Guyana Forestry Commission, Georgetown, August 13, 2014. https://www.youtube.com/watch?v=H0Q-7zLVk10.
Guyana Forestry Commission and Indufor. 2013. *Guyana REDD+ Monitoring Reporting & Verification System (MRVS), Year 3 Interim Measures Report: 1 January 2012 to 31 December 2012. Version 3.* Georgetown: Guyana Forestry Commission.
Hammond, David S. 2005. *Tropical Forests of the Guiana Shield: Ancient Forests in a Modern World.* Wallingford: CAB International.
Henfrey, C. 1964. *The Gentle People.* London: Hutchinson.
Howard, Joniqua, Maya A. Trotz, Ken Thomas, Erlande Omisca, Hong Ting Chiu, Trina Halfhide, Fenda Akiwumi, Ryan Michael, and Amy L. Stuart. 2011. Total Mercury Loadings in Sediment from Gold Mining and Conservation Areas in Guyana. *Environmental Monitoring and Assessment* 179, nos. 1–4:555–73.
Hunter, Lachlan. 2001. The Forestry Sector in Guyana. Georgetown, Guyana: Guyana Forestry Commission Support Project/UK Department for International Development.

Jagan, C. 1993. Address on Guyana's 27th Anniversary of Independence. Office of the President, Georgetown, May 26, 1993. http://jagan.org/CJ Articles/President/Images/4115a.pdf.

King, Kenneth. 1998. Review of Forest Policies in Guyana. *Forestry policies in the Caribbean. Volume 2: Reports of 28 Selected Countries and Territories. F.F P. 137/2*, 293–322. Rome: FAO.

Kowlessar, Mahadeo. 2008A. Agreements on Carbon Emissions Are Useless without Realistic and Firm National Policies on Forest Management. *Kaieteur News*, December 15. http://www.kaieteurnews.com/2008/12/15/agreements-on-carbon-emissions-are-useless-without-realistic-and-firm-national-policies-on-forest-management.

———. 2008B. For Almost a Decade the GFC Has Failed to Implement Technical Recommendations for Forest Management so How Could It Implement a Post-Kyoto Protocol? *Stabroek News*, December 12. http://www.stabroeknews.com/letters/for-almost-a-decade-the-gfc-has-failed-to-implement-technical-recommendations-for-forest-management-so-how-could-it-implement-a-post-kyoto-protocol.

Kunicová, Jana, and Susan Rose-Ackerman. 2005. Electoral Rules and Constitutional Structures as Constraints on Corruption. *British Journal of Political Science* 35, no. 4:573–606.

Lambsdorff, Johann Graf. 2006. Consequences and Causes of Corruption: What Do We Know from a Cross-Section of Countries? *International Handbook on the Economics of Corruption* 851:3–50.

Lindeman, J.C., and S.A. Mori. 1989. *The Guianas: In Floristic Inventory of Tropical Countries*. New York: The New York Botanical Garden.

Majeed, Halim. 2005. *Forbes Burnham: National Reconciliation and National Unity 1984–1985*. New York: Global Communications Publishing.

Martin, Tusika. 2009. New Forest Bill Replaces 54-Year-Old Legislation. *Kaieteur News*, January 23. https://www.kaieteurnewsonline.com/2009/01/23/new-forest-bill-replaces-54-year-old-legislation.

Miller, Jerry R., Paul J. Lechler, and Gavin Bridge. 2003. Mercury Contamination of Alluvial Sediments within the Essequibo and Mazaruni River Basins, Guyana. *Water, Air, and Soil Pollution* 148, nos. 1–4:139–66.

Mistry, Jayalaxshmi, Andrea Berardi, Matthew Simpson, Odacy Davis, and Lakeram Haynes. 2010. Using a Systems Viability Approach to Evaluate Integrated Conservation and Development Projects: Assessing the Impact of the North Rupununi Adaptive Management Process, Guyana. *Geographical Journal* 176, no. 3:241–52.

Mistry, Jayalaxshmi, Matthews Simpson, Andrea Berardi, and Yung Sandy. 2004. Exploring the Links between Natural Resource Use and Biophysical Status in the Waterways of the North Rupununi, Guyana. *Journal of Environmental Management* 72, no. 3:117–31.

Nigel Hinds Financial Services. 2016. *Forensic Audit of the Guyana Office for Investment (GO-Invest)*. Georgetown: Ministry of Finance.

Office of the President. 2008. *Saving the World's Rainforests Today. Creating Incentives to Avoid Deforestation*. Georgetown: Office of the President.

———. 2009. *Frequently Asked Questions: Transforming Guyana's Economy While Combating Climate Change: A Low-Carbon Development Strategy*. Georgetown: Office of the President.

Palmer, Carol J., J. Lloyd Validum, Bernard Laubach, Harold E Loeffke, Chris Mitchell, Rudy Cummings, and Raul R. Cuadrado. 2002. HIV Prevalence in a Gold Mining Camp in the Amazon Region, Guyana. *Emerging Infectious Diseases* 8, no. 3:330–31.

Persaud, Bishnodat. 2003. The Postponement of the Wilton Park Conference Is a Great Disappointment. *Stabroek News*, June 29. http://guyanaforestryblog.blogspot.ca/2007/09/at-least-22-people-have-expressed.html.

Persaud, Robert. 2009. Low Carbon Strategy Makes It Clear That Areas Already Allocated for Sustainable Forestry Will Continue to Be Harvested. *Stabroek News*, July 6. www.stabroeknews.com/2009/letters/07/06/low-carbon-strategy-makes-it-clear-that-areas-already-allocated-for-sustainable-forestry-will-continue-to-be-harvested.

Premdas, Ralph R. 1993. Guyana: The Critical Elections of 1992 and a Regime Change. *Caribbean Affairs* 6, no. 1:111–40.

Ram, Christopher. 2007. Barama and the Law. *Stabroek News*, June 2.

Rambajan, I. 1988. Reappearance of Unprecedented Falciparum Malaria: 28 Years after the Last Case in the Cuyuni-Mazaruni-Potaro, Guyana, South America. Tropical and Geographical Medicine. 40(3): 269–71. http://www.ncbi.nlm.nih.gov/entrez/query.fcgi?cmd=Retrieve&db=PubMed&dopt=Citation&list_uids=3055569.

Rights and Resources Initiative. 2015. *Who Owns the World's Lands? A Global Baseline of Formally Recognized Indigenous and Community Land Rights*. Washington, DC: Rights and Resources Initiative.

Ross, Michael L. 2001. *Timber Booms and Institutional Breakdown in Southeast Asia*. Cambridge, UK: Cambridge University Press.

Sanders, Andrew. 1987. *The Powerless People: An Analysis of the Amerindians of the Corentyne River*. London: Macmillan Caribbean.

Sasaki, N. and F.E. Putz. 2008. Do Definitions of Forest and Forest Degradation Matter in the REDD Agreement? http://papers.ssrn.com/sol3/papers.cfm?abstract_id=1306431.

Schmithüsen, F. 1977. *Forest Utilization Contracts on Public Land: FAO Forestry Paper 1*. 2d ed. Rome: FAO.

Sears, Robin R. and Miguel Pinedo-Vasquez. 2011. Forest Policy Reform and the Organization of Logging in Peruvian Amazonia. *Development and Change* 42, no. 2:609–31.

Sizer, Nigel. 1996. Profit without Plunder: *Reaping Revenue from Guyana's Tropical Forests without Destroying Them*. Washington, DC: World Resources Institute.

Sizer, Nigel, and R. Rice. 1995. *Backs to the Wall in Suriname: Forest Policy in a Country in Crisis*. Washington, DC: World Resources Institute.

Smith, Zeric Kay, Zoey Breslar, Phyllis Dininio, Jim Holtaway, Ira Lowenthal, and Paul Nuti. 2003. *Democracy, Governance and Conflict Strategic Objective Planning and Design. Prepared by Management Systems International for USAID/Guyana*. Washington, DC: USAID.

Smith, Zeric Kay, Glenn Smucker, and Roxanne Myers. 2002. Guyana. Democracy and *Governance Assessment. Draft 2. Produced for USAID Democracy Center and USAID/Guyana*. Washington, DC: USAID.

Solomon, Alva. 2011. Customs Officer Sacked, Three Suspended over Cocaine in Container – Probe into 'unusual' Assets Ongoing. *Stabroek News*, August 10. https://www.stabroeknews.com/2011/news/stories/08/10/customs-officer-sacked-three-suspended-over-cocaine-in-container.

Stabroek News. 1997. President Signs Order Extending State Forest. September 28.

———. 2004. The Debate over Log Exports…Manufacturer: It's Sheer Lawlessness. August 27.

———. 2007A. Deploying Forest Doesn't Mean Ownership Transfer – President Clarifies. October 17. http://www.stabroeknews.com/2007/archives/10/17/deploying-forest-doesnt-mean-ownership-transfer-president-clarifies.

———. 2007B. MP Recall Bill Passed – Backer, McAllister Abstain. August 10.

———. 2008A. High Court Orders Forestry Commission to Withdraw TPL Closure Notice. July 2. http://www.stabroeknews.com/news/high-court-orders-forestry-commission-to-withdraw-tpl-closure-notice.

———. 2008B. Loggers to Mount Legal Challenge to Forestry Commission Fines – Source Cites Absence of Provision for Penalties in Forestry Legislation. *Stabroek News*, February 15.

———. 2011. Logs in Shipment Where Cocaine Found Were in-Transit in Jamaica – Singh. June 21. http://www.stabroeknews.com/2011/archives/06/21/logs-in-shipment-where-cocaine-found-were-in-transit-in-jamaica-singh.

———. 2013. The Trouble with the Licence for CCTV. *Stabroek News*, February 18. http://www.stabroeknews.com/2013/opinion/editorial/02/18/the-trouble-with-the-licence-for-cctv.

———. 2014. Some Bai Shan Lin Joint Ventures May Be Illegal – Experts. September 1. http://www.stabroeknews.com/2014/news/stories/09/01/bai-shan-lin-joint-ventures-may-illegal-experts.

———. 2017. Audit Says Go-Invest's Failure to Monitor Made 'large Scale Abuse' of Concessions Likely – Finds Country Didn't Benefit from Exemptions to Baishanlin, Vaitarna. February 4. http://www.stabroeknews.com/2017/news/stories/02/04/audit-says-go-invests-failure-monitor-made-large-scale-abuse-concessions-likely.

Stanley, Clifford. 2015. Protected Areas Landmass to Be Increased by 3.2%. Guyana Chronicle, March 1. http://guyanachronicle.com/2015/03/01/protected-areas-landmass-to-be-increased-by-3-2.

ter Steege, Hans. 2000. *Plant Diversity in Guyana: With Recommendations for a National Protected Areas Strategy: Tropenbos Series Number 18*. Wageningen: Stichting Tropenbos.

ter Steege, Hans, René G.A. Boot, Leo C. Brouwer, John C. Caesar, Renske C. Ek, David S. Hammond, P. P. Haripersaud, Peter van der Hout, V. G. Jetten, Arie J. van Kekem, Michelle A. Kellman, Zab Khan, A. M. Polak, Thijs L. Pons, John Pulles, Dorinne Raaimakers, Simmone A. Rose, Joost J. van der Sanden and Roderick J. Zagt. 1996. *Ecology and Logging in a Tropical Rain Forest in Guyana: With Recommendations for Forest Management. Tropenbos Series Number 14*. Wageningen: Stichting Tropenbos.

van der Hout, Peter. 2011. Guyana. In *Sustainable Management of Tropical Rainforests: The CELOS Management System. Tropenbos Series Number 25*, ed. Marinus J.A. Werger, 167–85. Paramaribo: Tropenbos International.

Vieira, V.S. 1980. *Logging in Guyana and Considerations for Improvements*. Georgetown: Guyana National Printers Ltd.

Vieira, V., and H. Richardson. 1957. Forest Conditions, Problems and Programmes in British Guiana. *Caribbean Forester* 18, nos. 1 and 2:44–48.

Walrond, G.W., L.J.L. Heesterman, and J. Goolsarran. 2015. Guyana Geology and Mines Commission Management and Systems Review: Inception Report Mines Division, Land Management Division, Geological Services Division. Unpublished.

Welch, Ivan. 1975. *A Short History of the Guyana Forest Department 1925–1975*. Georgetown: Forest Department.

Westoby, J.C. 1962. Forest Industries in the Attack on Economic Underdevelopment. *Unasylva* 16, no. 4:168–201.

Young, David. 2005. *A Guide to Independent Forest Monitoring*. London: Global Witness.

The Politics of Gender and Sexuality

13.
Madness, Myth, and Masquerade: Cultural Patrimony and Violence Against Disabled Women in Guyana

Savitri Persaud

> 'Old Higue'[1] have to dead and I believe if she was an 'Old Higue' she had to dead.
> – Unnamed resident of Bare Root, East Coast Demerara, Guyana.
> (*Stabroek News*, April 30, 2007)

This chapter analyses how Caribbean myths and the accusation of superstition and spirit/demonic possession function as othering mechanisms that are used to justify violence against disabled women in Guyana. As a consequence, these imputations simultaneously glorify a violent cultural patrimony and venerate representations of a fixed femininity that is rendered powerless. Through the careful examination of the murder of Radika Singh, this chapter shows how the body of a woman with a psychiatric disability was misrecognised and denigrated as the fabled old higue figure of folklore – a female vampiric spirit in Caribbean mythology who has the power of flight, skin-shedding, and total bodily transfiguration. She is capable of morphing into an airborne ball of fire. She flies from house to house and can shrink herself in order to pass through the tiny openings of windows, doors, and roofs, which enables her to gain access to her victims. It is written that the old higue roams the night in spherical fiery form and predominantly preys on the blood of infants and young children as a means of sustenance, and if she is caught she must be beaten and killed as the myth dictates. Singh's presence in another village – directly informed by her psychiatric disability – was transformed by others into this jumbie[2] in order to rationalise and excuse the gendered and ultimately fatal forms of violence committed against her.

Demonic figures like the old higue, who have the ability to indwell in humans and produce oppressive living environments – and jumbies of every description such as the Dutchman/Dutchwoman, wata mama, baccoo, kanaima, bush daidai, churile, moon gazer, and other menacing spirits – are celebrated in the cultural patrimony of Guyana, as demonstrated during the 2014 Mashramani celebrations. Mashramani – also called Guyana Day, Republic Day, and Mash more colloquially – is celebrated annually on February 23 and marks when Guyana became a republic in 1970. The 2014 theme – *Cultural Folklore, Celebrating 44* – lauded this array of folkloric figures, with 44 referencing the number of years since the birth of the Guyanese Republic. This chapter explores how the murder of Singh was made possible when placed side-by-side with a violent cultural patrimony, which dictates that powerful women of myth – constructed as evil and menacing – must die in the name of preserving the nation and its ultimate symbol of futurity, the child. The cultural patrimony of the nation is invoked to excuse gender-based violence, and the old higue legend, as a mythical endowment, is openly celebrated in events that commemorate the nation only when her powers are nullified, as witnessed during Mashramani 2014.

The first section of this chapter unpacks the beating death of Radika Singh. It analyses how the imputation of the old higue – the false accusation that blanketed Singh's body even after her death – bore direct correlation to her murder. It also details how Singh and the old higue were made one and the same, not only by the community where she died but by the media reports which further ensnared her subjectivity through the discursively violent old higue representation. The second section of this chapter analyses the myth of the old higue through a close reading of *Samaan*, a children's story written by Guyanese artist and author Doris Harper-Wills. *Samaan* is a counter narrative that shifts common understandings of the old higue and illustrates the brutality and folly of the human condition when strictly adhering to the dogma of the nation's folklore. The chapter closes by putting myth and the nation's celebration of Mashramani 2014 in conversation with the Singh case. It examines the logics of these myths and the costume presentations at the 2014 Mashramani parade. I argue that the violence enacted on Singh's body was an attempt to expel disability, madness, and representations of a femininity in excess – a femininity deemed too powerful that needed to be killed off both in the fictional and material sense, especially given the reality of Singh's murder. At the same time, the nation – in curating how it commemorated the anniversary of its birth as a republic – chose to reproduce and valorise violence against women through its representations of the old higue mythology.

The Murder of Radika Singh

On the morning of April 28, 2007, the lifeless body of a woman was found at the side of a dirt road aback the community of Bare Root, East Coast Demerara, Guyana (*Stabroek News* April 29, 2007). According to newspaper accounts in all three of Guyana's major dailies, the unidentified woman's body bore marks of violence; her hands and legs appeared to be broken and blood oozed from her mouth (*Guyana Chronicle* April 29, 2007; *Stabroek News* April 30, 2007; *Kaieteur News* April 29, 2007). The three newspapers published accounts from the residents of Bare Root citing a common imputation that became a shorthand reference for this case, namely that the woman – whose body was unidentified days after her death – was an old higue. The initial headlines in the main newspapers read: 'Two Held "Old Higue" Murder' (*Stabroek News* April 29, 2007); 'Residents Beat Suspected "Old Higue" to Death' (*Kaieteur News* April 29, 2007); and 'Villagers Allege Dead Woman was an "Ole Higue"' (*Guyana Chronicle* April 29, 2007). In follow-up reports covering the case, *Stabroek News* referred to this incident of violence as the '"Old Higue" Murder' (April 30, 2007); *Kaieteur News* called it the '"Ole Higue" Killing' (May 1, 2007); and the *Guyana Chronicle* referenced it as the '"Ole Higue" Affair' (May 1, 2007). The body of this dead woman, whose personhood became interchangeable with the old higue, was later identified as Radika Singh – a 55-year-old, Indo-Guyanese housewife and domestic worker with a diagnosed history of mental illness.

As per the early news reports that were published in the first three days after Singh's murder, there were conflicting narratives of how Singh met her death. Some villagers allege that in the early pre-dawn hours of Saturday, April 28, 2007, the woman entered their community and was caught in the act of sucking the blood of an infant (*Stabroek News* April 29, 2007). When the child's mother sounded the alarm that bite marks were found on her son's chest, villagers found and surrounded Singh on the road and meted out a malicious beating against her (*Stabroek News* April 29, 2007). Another community member alleges that before daybreak, two men from the village called out to Singh believing that she was someone they knew (*Stabroek News* April 30, 2007). Residents claimed that Singh was initially not in human form and was 'just a ball of hair' or 'appeared to be a dark ball with long hair' (*Stabroek New,* April 29, 2007). When she responded with growls and snarls, the men requested that other residents come to the scene and render assistance as they were fearful, at which point a woman in distress emerged from her home a short distance away saying that there was a red mark on her baby's chest (*Stabroek News* April 30, 2007). Villagers allegedly surrounded Singh and pelted her with rice, doused her with kerosene in an attempt to burn her, and beat her with a manicole/cabbage[3] broom and pieces of wood, namely paling staves (*Stabroek News* April 29, 2007). It was later revealed that objects had been pushed up into her vagina (*Guyana Chronicle* May 18, 2007). *Kaieteur News* (April 29, 2007) published an image of Singh's mangled body, sprawled out on the ground with her skirt hiked slightly below her waist and a manicole broom positioned beside her head. Grains of rice appeared to be strewn all around her corpse (*Kaieteur News* April 29, 2007).[4] A post-mortem concluded that Singh died of haemorrhaging caused by blunt trauma (*Kaieteur News* May 3, 2007). According to police, while it was rumoured that a child 'get suck', no evidence or formal reports were made to support this claim (*Kaieteur News* May 1, 2007).

On May 1, 2007, newspapers indicated that Radika Singh's body had been identified; her family quickly began an appeal to the public insisting that she was not an old higue (*Stabroek News* May 1, 2007; *Kaieteur News* May 1, 2007; *Guyana Chronicle* May 2, 2007). They disclosed that Singh had had a history of diagnosed mental illness and that she continued to receive psychiatric treatment until her killing (*Stabroek News* May 2, 2007). Singh's family explained that she had had a tendency of wandering away at night from her home in Good Hope, East Coast Demerara, to neighbouring communities, when she refused to take medications intended to treat symptoms of depression (*Stabroek News* May 2, 2007). Two men and one woman were eventually charged with her murder – Roland Spencer, Rayon Bobb, and Aletha Roberts (*Stabroek News* May 3, 2007). All charges were eventually dropped against the three; the prosecution cited insufficient evidence when their star witness stopped attending court and other residents refused to testify against the accused persons in their community (*Stabroek News* April 22, 2008).

The murder of Singh made regional and international headlines (Associated Press May 2, 2007). At the local level and at the height of this case's coverage – from April 29, 2007 to May 18, 2007 – over 50 reports, editorials, and letters to the editor were published in the three dailies, with letters to the editor accounting for the vast majority. In the reports, most of the interviewed Bare Root residents insisted that Singh was an old higue who was deserving of a beating death (*Stabroek News* April 29, 2007; *Kaiteur News* April 29, 2007; *Guyana Chronicle*, April 29, 2007.) Taking into account the opening quotation of this chapter, several villagers of Bare Root vehemently accused Singh of being the mythical creature and relayed their suspicions to reporters:

> She look evil (*Kaieteur News* April 29 2007).
>
> I know 'Old Higue' deh (*Kaieteur News* April 29, 2007).
>
> Is de fuss [first] time I see one (*Kaieteur News* April 29, 2007).
>
> My mother always tell we about it, and she use to tell we when 'Old Higue' sucking you girl child, you does know (*Stabroek News* April 30, 2007).
>
> But you think about it this way if you wake up and see 'Old Higue' sucking you baby what you go do? You have to do something. You ent go stand up and watch it do dat to you child (*Stabroek News* April 30 2007).

Each of the aforementioned interviewees was of the opinion that old higue existed and that Singh was one; such barbarism and violence was justified through the evocation of the phantasm. Faced with her wickedness and nefarious intentions, they had a duty to protect their children, particularly their girl children. Only a small minority of villagers who were interviewed seemed to deviate from this position. One elderly woman registered dismay and anger about Singh's death and disagreement about the old higue accusation: 'I don't believe in that and I don't believe she was any 'old higue'. They were wrong; they should not have killed the woman. They could have chased her out of the village' (*Stabroek News* April 30, 2007). For this aged villager, while the myth of the old higue is purely one of fiction and she condemned the murder of Singh – perhaps because she understands that the old higue accusation can also be directed at elders like her – she recommends that an appropriate call to action would have been to run Singh out of the community. Dissenting opinions from Bare Root, while few, received little coverage. However, common to both sets of opinions – the belief that Singh was the old higue deserving of death and the lone objection raised by an elder – is the shared understanding that Singh's presence, whether old higue or old Indian woman, was rejected. According to most media reports, Singh was recognizable to Bare Root residents only as an outsider who did not belong to this community.

Bare Root, where Singh was killed, is considered to be a community comprised of constituents who are *predominantly Afro-Guyanese*. Singh was an Indian woman from Good Hope, which is thought to be a *primarily Indo-Guyanese* village. As a body out of place, Singh's race and gender, and considerations of community allegiances, are important facets of this case. The three major dailies wrote of the incident as a unique spectacle, divorced of substantive reflections on these dimensions of identity and the history of violence against women in Guyana. *Kaieteur News*, the *Guyana Chronicle*, and *Stabroek News* mention the role of race and gender but avoid any meaningful discourse or considerations of how the two are inextricably bound historically and in the contemporary moment (Trotz 2004, 1–3).

The factors of race, gender, and narrowly drawn village fidelities are key to any meaningful engagement with the tragic violence that Radika Singh suffered. When examining how these communities become racialised spaces, one must survey scholarly debates that analyse the ways in which colonial powers created racial anxieties and conflict between Africans and Indians in Guyana; and later how British and American interventionist foreign policy during the Cold War era perpetuated these racial animosities, especially within the context of Guyana's socialist, anticolonial movement for independence during the 1950s and '60s.[5] I briefly engage with these historical events because it is crucial to grasp the colonial fountainhead of racial conflict in Guyana. During the period of colonisation and after the abolition of slavery throughout the British Empire, Asians (predominantly Indians and Chinese) were brought over to Guyana under the scheme of indentureship to assume work on the sugar plantations just as freed Africans began their struggle for better working conditions, oftentimes preferring alternatives to estate labour. Colonial divide and conquer tactics – the suppression of wages, planter-mediated perceptions of the other through stereotypes – ultimately served the capital interests of Europeans. Discord mounted between Indians and Africans and resulted in violent clashes (Rodney 1981, 180–83). Despite this early history of racialised tensions, Guyanese lived harmoniously in diverse, multi-ethnic villages such as Golden Grove, Buxton, Wismar, Christianburg, and Mackenzie as the colony began its campaign for independence (Wismar Report 1965, 4). The anticolonial movement – initially a multi-racial, socialist endeavour led by Cheddi Jagan and Forbes Burnham, both of the People's Progressive Party (PPP) at the time – quickly became a cause for concern for British and American powers during the Cold War period (Spinner 1984, 57). In 1953, the Churchill Government declared that Guyana was in 'crisis', suspended the constitution, and dispatched troops to the country in an effort to overthrow the democratically elected PPP government; PPP leaders were arrested, and so continued the internal and external destabilisation machinations to partition the core of the PPP along ethnic lines (Spinner 1984, 57).[6] It was not until after the outbreak of violence during the civil disturbances of the 1960s that the ethnic composition of these communities shifted, leading to the perception that the coastal villages are predominantly Indo- or Afro-Guyanese (Wismar Report 1965, 4). Since the disturbances, the country has tried to address the ethnic divisions. However, racial tensions persisted and erupted in violence again during the 1997 and 2000 elections. While racial cleavages endure in Guyana, the 2015 election of a new multiracial coalition government, APNU-AFC, comprised of the parties A Partnership for National Unity (APNU) and the Alliance for Change (AFC) – was a pivotal moment that for some harkens back to the partnership forged by Cheddi Jagan and Forbes Burnham in the early 1950s.

Throughout Guyana's history, the bodies of Indo- and Afro-Guyanese women were constructed as symbolic gatekeepers for their respective communities, and the violence visited on women's bodies also became an attack on their racialised group (Trotz 2004, 7–9). Returning to the Singh case, her Indianness and her death in a community widely considered as predominantly African was raised in some impassioned op-eds and letters. One member of the public, who is identified only as Khan, writes in his letter to the editor: 'Where is the outrage? It is not coincidental that the woman killed on the East Coast was Indian. We all know that this has been happening for years' (*Guyana Chronicle* May 8, 2007). In a column for the *Stabroek News*, sociologist Linden Lewis writes:

> One should also be mindful of the racial and gendered nature of this murder. The violence of this attack was meted out on an Indo-Guyanese woman, who became the focal point of an essentially African legend. In addition, the three persons charged in connection with this crime – one of whom is a woman – are all of African descent. In a racially polarised society, the implications are worth pondering (May 7, 2007).

The sentiments expressed here by Khan and Lewis regarding the murder of Singh directs us to historicise and consider the documented cases of gender-based, racialised violence against Indian women: the woman-murders and violence during the indenture period (Mohapatra 1995, 239); the gang rape of women during the disturbances of 1964 (Wismar Report 1965, 5); and the sexual violence committed against several women during the 1997 and 2000 elections (Trotz 2004, 3) are violent moments in Guyanese history that played out on the bodies of Indian women. Singh was an Indo-Guyanese woman out of place; her Indianness, madness, and threatening femininity – all of which came together in this instance in the menacing figure of the old higue – made her humanity unrecognizable in the village of Bare Root. Singh's murder, in other words, was not a unique spectacle. Her death cannot be divorced from this history of violence and substantive considerations of race, sexuality, and gender.

While the majority of interviewed Bare Root residents did not challenge the idea that Singh was an old higue, closing in around this imputation to protect their own, the general public and wider community seemed, by and large, to recoil in horror. The letters written by the public in response to the murder of Singh were vociferous in condemning the violence, expressing disbelief and shock, remorse and anger, disgust and pity:

> I read it but I don't believe it... This is how cheap life has become; a woman is killed because she wandered into the wrong place and was regarded as the mythical "Ole Higue" (*Kaieteur News* May 8, 2007).

> Now, outrage and shame follows the dastardly murder of a defenseless middle-aged woman whose attackers are claiming she was an 'Ole Higue' (*Kaieteur News* May 9, 2007).

> I was sickened to learn about this poor insane woman's untimely and brutal death... and the dirty, vicious hands that carried out the execution. (*Guyana Chronicle* May 3, 2007).

> This poor helpless creature was guilty of Guyana's two greatest crimes. One, she was of unsound mind; and two, she was poor... Oh what pity! I am sure Radika must be telling the Maker, 'Forgive them Lord, they know not...' (*Guyana Chronicle* May 5, 2007).

Some readers cited common linkages made between the stigma of madness and mental illness to associations of spirit/demonic possession, while others relayed how such connections are indicative of 'backward' societies that choose to live under 'primitive times,' instead of 'marching forward' towards modernity:

> For too long there has been a social stigma attached to mental illness. This stigma has fuelled the superstitious belief that mental sickness is somehow different from physical sickness and that the mentally ill have brought such sickness upon themselves. Some even believe that mental illness is 'demon-possession.' This particular belief resulted in the beating to death of a young woman by a self-styled exorcist a few years

ago. It is social attitudes like these that have led to the underfunding of mental health care institutions in countries like Guyana (*Kaieteur News* May 5, 2007).

> With this incident and a few others in recent years, it seems that a certain section of the Guyanese community is still living under 'PRIMATIVE TIMES' [sic]... Next thing we know these people will be telling us that they killed so and so because, 'de man de possessed by Dutchman or jumbie' or that, 'de lady was a mermaid' or that, 'he bad eye me.' Please, Guyanese people MARCH FORWARD PROUDLY, NOT BACKWARD INTO STUPIDITY [sic] (*Kaieteur News* May 6, 2007).

Ultimately, Singh's subjectivity folded into the legend of the old higue in a sensational narrative that initially painted her as a predator. The myth then became one facet of an evolving discourse that further constructed her as a middle-aged, poor, and mad Guyanese woman of Indian descent who was killed when she became recognizable only as thing of the occult, whose presence necessitated a thrashing. Singh's subjectivity was locked in this duality that failed to acknowledge the fullness of her textured life.

Singh's mental health and the construction of her as a 'poor insane woman' (*Guyana Chronicle* May 3, 2007) of 'unsound mind' (*Guyana Chronicle* May 5, 2007) is a reminder of how people with psychiatric disabilities in Guyana are denigrated and become targets of violence. In my doctoral research, I analysed the relationship between madness, psychiatric disability, and spirit/demonic possession in Guyana.[7] After conducting extensive interviews with medical professionals (nurses, psychiatrists, general practitioners), social service professionals, government officials, religious leaders, and NGO and civil society actors, I found that when people with psychiatric disabilities display behavioural expressions that are not deemed *normal* or *narmal* by Guyanese – behaviours that may seem out of character, unpredictable, and frenzied – they are generally thought to have *tripped off* and are considered mad in the vernacular. One response by the general public is to assume that this madness is linked to spirit possession or that *jumbie gat dem* [demons/spirits have possessed them]. Other Caribbean nations subscribe to similar belief systems (*Jamaica Gleaner*, September 4, 2015; Thachil and Bhugra 2009, 220–23; Maharaj and Parsaram 1999). In Guyana, the long-standing practice of beating out spirits and jumbies – thought more prevalent in Obeah and Shaker religious traditions (Olmos and Paravasini-Gebert 2011, 171) – is utilised through the claim of purging evil and healing illness. Guyanese women and girls with diagnosed mental illnesses, disabilities, and chronic conditions, who were also determined by their communities to be possessed, have been killed through violent interventions intended to exorcise demons. As these following cases will demonstrate, this practice is not specific to one religious or spiritual belief. In 2002, the murder of Kamille Seenauth after an exorcism by 'self-proclaimed' Spiritualist Patricia Alves angered the Georgetown community and is gruesomely remembered by residents as the 'shallow grave' murder (*Jamaica Observer* September 5, 2005; *Guyana Times* November 22, 2012; *Kaieteur News* July 1, 2015). In 2010, 12-year-old Sangeeta Persaud was the subject of an exorcism at Christ Ambassadors Church that was allegedly violent in nature and included the participation of her mother, pastor, and other church members. She later died in hospital (*Kaieteur News* March 31, 2010). In 2014, 20-year-old Todah Richards was killed after an alleged 'ritualistic beating' by her godmother; both women worshipped at Holy Ghost Movement Church, where Richards's father is the pastor (*Kaieteur News* November 27, 2014). According to reports, neighbours allege that 'the church is one where after praying they beat the demon out of their believers' (*Kaieteur News* November 27, 2014). In the cases of Sangeeta Persaud and Todah Richards, we are reminded that intra-community forms of violence also occur, not only inter-community acts of brutality against women and girls as occurred with Radika Singh and Kamille Seenauth. These three additional cases, which share similar circumstances, signal to us that violence against women and girls with disabilities does not exist in a vacuum. These stories belong to this long tradition of gender-based violence in Guyana where disabled, racialised women's bodies, further marked by the abnormality of spirit/demonic possession and rendered evil and dangerous, become targets to expel that which is feared, namely powerful female-gendered figures (when they are thought possessed by folklore characters or other supernatural entities/jumbies), and madness and disability.

The Counter Narrative of The Character Ole Higue in *Samaan*

> In my view, the folklore of a people is at the root of their being, and to cast it aside is to set oneself adrift culturally – an act which one performs at one's own peril.'
>
> Wordsworth McAndrew (*Guyana – A Cultural Look*, 1970)

Who exactly is this strong woman of Guyanese folk culture? One must first come to know her, her power, and her social purchase in Guyana. A.J.

Seymour's *Dictionary of Guyanese Folklore* (1975) provides a comprehensive definition of the old higue legend, specifically how this figure is commonly understood through a powerful and predatory representation as one who must be killed in the name of community safety and survival:

> The story is that the old higue, the Guyanese form of a human vampire, capable of discarding her skin takes the form of an old woman living in a community. At night, she transforms herself into a ball of fire, flies from her own house up into the sky and then lands on the roof of another house where there is a baby in a cradle underneath a sheet whose blood she will suck dry and then go home. The suspicions of the community are soon aroused and the school children cry 'old higue' at her; they make chalk marks, on the bridge to her house, the door, the jalousie window [intended to prevent her from passing into residences]. But the legend goes that she crosses these marks bravely.
>
> Then the community sets a trap. When the ole higue flies abroad another night she finds that the baby in the cradle is clothed in a blue nightgown. There is a heap of rice grains near the cot and the smell of asafoetida.[8] These cast a spell on the ole higue who has to count the grains of rice, and if she loses her way, she has to start counting again.
>
> The light of morning comes and the old higue still has not finished counting the grains of rice. People burst into the room, pick up a cabbage broom and begin to belabour the old higue.
>
> They beat her to death, with great emotion. 'You gwine pay for you sins before you die,' they say.
>
> This is the legendary story of the old higue much feared in villages (48).

The old higue entry, reprinted here in its entirety from the *Dictionary*, synthesises similar retellings of the legend. Poems and stories – predominantly children's tales – written by distinguished Guyanese folklorists and cultural icons like Wordsworth McAndrew[9] and Martin Carter[10] are presented in elaborate elocution performances by young people as a way of demonstrating their *Guyanese-ness* to elders. This *Dictionary* is of particular national and cultural significance because it was formally sanctioned by the state. The publication was produced and funded by the National History and Arts Council and the Ministry of Information and Culture under the Burnham government in 1975. The introduction identifies how the *Dictionary* is 'part of the search for identity' and the 'desire to identify the roots in Guyanese history and society on which we can build a unique and attractive future' (4). It also includes then Prime Minister Burnham's remarks on the importance of articulating the uniqueness of the Guyanese identity: 'The cultural revolution is the expression of what we know, what we are familiar with and what we have experienced, regardless of the origin. It represents a will of a people to express their own way of life' (Seymour 1975, 4). The old higue *Dictionary* entry is one of the more lengthy and detailed definitions, and its prominence underscores how the mythical figure is constitutive of the nation's lore and the peoples' folk identity; she is part of the cultural matrix that informs the 'root of their being' (McAndrew 1970). Her continued folk presence is an assertion of cultural sovereignty. The tellings and retellings of her bloodsucking escapades and bludgeoning are a shared experience among Guyanese across the spectrum of difference. The violent cultural patrimony of how she is always killed off persists even when some tales do not construct her as a predator, like Doris Harper-Wills's *Samaan*,[11] which serves as an important (but tellingly, not as well-known or circulated) counter narrative that refutes typical representations of the old higue in favour of an adventurous and amicable figure (12–17). Nevertheless, the story climaxes with old higue being beaten to death on Guyana Day at the hands of celebrating citizens.

Samaan is a Guyanese children's story about a benevolent and self-sacrificing tree of the same name. The protagonist, 'Ole Samaan', is described as a 'protective', 'mother tree', and a 'friend of everybody', including the elders and spirits that keep her company and alleviate her feelings of loneliness when the children of the village take advantage of her sheltering kindness and abandon her because of her old age (Harper-Wills n.d., 12). 'Fowl Mama', 'Ole Man Papee', 'Baku', and 'Ole Higue' are among Ole Samaan's friends. In this folktale, it is not the jumbies who are depicted as the antagonists, but rather it is the children and their parents – described as the teachers and practitioners of intergenerational violence – who are the monsters. The children repeatedly disrespect the elderly by pelting and insulting them. They defile Ole Samaan's roots, trunk, and branches, disfiguring her with 'ugly writings' etched into her wooden 'flesh': 'Ole Dutch jumbee tree...You does shelter baccoo...Jumbie lef he pipe in ya...Wha' kinda tree this? Stupidee tree this' (13). When Fowl Mama, Ole Man Papee, and Baku stop visiting because the children frighten them, Ole Samaan grows lonely (14). On the night of Guyana Day, Ole Higue makes an appearance and returns to earth after her 'adventures in space' where she previously 'set off for Mars' (14). There is no mention of Ole Higue feasting on the blood of babes. Only Ole Higue's excitement to recount her galactic journey to Ole Samaan and Baku are made clear to the reader; nothing in this tale connects Ole Higue to violence against children or the community. In my feminist reading of the Ole Higue character in *Samaan*, she is presented as an intrepid and independent adventurer capable of not only exploring the world but the universe; her character moves, indeed flies, beyond earthly understandings of being and is shaped by her fearless jaunts throughout the cosmos. One might argue that this old higue can serve as a role model for Guyanese girl children. She is a pioneering, mighty, and well-travelled mythical strong woman of colour who, despite her compulsions to suckle blood and do harm, commits no wrongs against any other character in this story. As Ole Higue tries to change back into human form so that she can tell of her voyage to Mars, she searches for her skin beneath Ole Samaan's roots (14). Unable to locate the skin, Ole Samaan realises that the children must have stolen it:

> Alas, dear Ole Higue, said Ole Samaan, these children of today are not like they used to be long ago. Alas! They have no respect for the old. If they could dig into my skin without a thought about my feelings – I, who have been so kind to them – why wouldn't they destroy your skin if they got hold of it? (14).

Ole Samaan emphasises how the old are abused (dug into, destroyed), scorned, and treated as undesirables. Inherent to Ole Samaan's critique is the implied value and benefit of youth when the attitudes of young people, who become future caregivers, grow hostile towards their elders. Old age and 'old-fashioned ideas... of ancient days' (17) are considered burdensome.

The second half of *Samaan* describes the slaughter of Ole Higue. Unable to find her skin and fearful for her life, Ole Higue scrambles to hide in Ole Samaan's shadow as the children approach during the evening Mashramani celebrations where 'the steelband trampers were passing through the city' and 'had come all the way from Berbice, and were going all the way to Essequibo through Demerara by land' (15). Mischievous Moon thwarts Ole Higue's efforts to seek cover and beams down on her, which enables the children to spot Ole Higue (16). The children inform the other trampers – men, women, and other children. With murderous intentions, they all surround Ole Higue (16). Ole Samaan watches helplessly when the children chant: 'Bring salt, bring pepper! Get chalk, get rice! Quick, quick! Bring a broom!' (16). The women sound rally cries:

> Ole Higue, Ole Higue witch
>
> Burn she, burn she black as pitch
>
> Ole Higue, Ole Higue witch
>
> Burn she, burn she black as pitch (16).

The men then held up Ole Higue's skin and pickled it with vinegar, salt, and pepper, causing it to shrivel up and making it impossible for her to put on her fleshy form (16). Girls drew chalk lines around any hole or hiding place where Ole Higue might have sought safety (16). Boys scattered a path of rice throughout Georgetown leading to Le Repentir Cemetery (16). And 'how they laughed' and 'how they sang' as they all drummed, danced, and viciously attacked Ole Higue, who was on a death march as she followed the morsels of rice to her freshly dug grave (17). All of the humans who were present – women, men, girls, boys – are implicated in the murder of Ole Higue. There is no self-righteousness to be had, especially here, in the killing of Ole Higue, when the people uncritically follow the dictates of their folklore.

After Ole Higue is killed and her burial place covered, Ole Samaan – unable to bear the brutality she witnessed against Ole Higue – protests through self-immolation. The reader is told: 'Samaan realized that the death of Ole Higue was the death of an old-fashioned idea and belief. She knew that the times were changing and she would not fit into this new world... For she, too, was of the ancient days' (17). As Ole Samaan burned, she saw six children who wanted to seek rest and refuge under her branches. They lamented about the killing of Ole Higue and how they bore responsibility. Describing the grisly way in which she was murdered, their dialogue expressed guilt, remorse, and sorrow:

> Ole Higue dead.
>
> Ole Higue dead?
>
> Ole Higue dead.
>
> Dead, dead?
>
> Dead, dead. Beaten on the head.
>
> Bricked until she bled. Ole Higue Dead!
>
> Aren't you glad?
>
> No, we're sad,
>
> Sad, sad...

Now we have no one to tantalise,
Now she's gone we hope you realize,
Even though she's not in fairy tales,
She's the greatest witch we ever had –
Don't mind she black and mad.
Poor us, we have no fairies of our own,
We've looked in books on all the library shelves.
Poor us, we have no witch to call our own.
And now the one we've found, we killed ourselves.
Yes, she's dead.
Dead, dead. Beaten bad and black.
Broomed upon the back.
Oh why they attack,
Ole Higue, the only witch we had to call our own?
She's the greatest witch we ever had,
Don't mind she black and mad (17).

For Ole Samaan, it was the first time that she heard any semblance of reverence expressed about Ole Higue ('Now she's gone we hope you realize / Even though she's not in fairy tales / She's the greatest witch we ever had'), notwithstanding how self-serving the children's regret ('Now we have no one to tantalise' and 'Poor us, we have no witch to call our own') (17). Also foreign to Ole Samaan was how the children's culpability was exposed through self-reflection and the examination of their actions ('Bricked until she bled. Ole Higue Dead! / Aren't you glad? / No, we're sad / Sad, sad...' and 'And now the one we've found, we killed ourselves') (17). This conversation between the children convinced Samaan that her maternal presence was still needed. Before completely lighting herself ablaze, Ole Samaan releases a seed – her son, Young Samaan – after realising that 'these children will need a tree for shelter' (17). *Samaan*, on one level, lays bare the powerful myth of innocence and reasserts how all are implicated and marked. Ole Samaan's sacrifice is also grounded in forgiveness and compassion. This tale – while it works to debunk notions of innocence and how the seemingly bad-minded bad women of myth like Ole Higue are not bad-minded bad women at all – still ends up reproducing normative, gendered lessons of motherly sacrifice (Ole Samaan's self-immolation) in the name of providing maternal care for future generations of Guyanese children. No such altruism or acts of paternal martyrdom is to be expected of jumbies that are often represented as male-gendered figures, like the massacooramaan, Dutchman jumbie, baccoo, kanaima, and moon gazer. The reader is reminded that the tree near D'Urban Park, an open area in the capital city where the children of today play, is Ole Samaan's offspring – birthed at the expense of two powerful female-gendered characters, Ole Higue and Ole Samaan.

Moreover, the line 'Don't mind she black and mad' (17), repeated twice, speaks to harmful representations of Afro-Guyanese women, where blackness and madness are deployed with negative connotations that are also associated with strong women, specifically caricatures of the 'strong black woman' (Harris-Lacewell 2008, 1–2). Recall Lewis's op-ed, which states that the old higue myth is an African legend (Anatol 2015). When, however, the death of the Ole Higue in *Samaan* (who we are told is 'black and mad') is taken up alongside the murder of Singh (who is described as Indian and mad), the myth morphs and moves fluidly across race. Just as the old higue is capable of skin shedding as a racial metaphor (Anatol 2015, 57) and is often an accusation cast and centred on the bodies of Afro-Guyanese women, the myth itself also sheds its skin/its host and assumes the body of an Indo-Guyanese woman, Singh. The legend of the old higue and the way in which this figure can indwell in differently racialised women directs one's attention to the distinctions between *skinfolk* and *kinfolk*, especially when members within the same racialised communities are branded as threats – when they are denounced as the old higue and are rendered non-human; when they are considered incapable of being/becoming citizens. Referencing Zora Neale Hurston's famous line, 'All my skinfolk ain't kinfolk,' Brackette Williams (1991, 76) draws from her experience of conducting fieldwork in Guyana as an African American researcher working, in part, with Afro-Guyanese participants. She discusses insider/outsider relations and distinctions between shared racial identities (skinfolk) and the larger, more intricate system of affinities at play such as gender, class, religion, level of education, marital status, and political affiliation among others (kinfolk) (76–77).

Drawing from her theorising, in my discussion of insider/outsider differences I use skinfolk to mean communities that are forged primarily on the basis of racial solidarities, which play out in the Guyanese context when villages are represented as predominantly Afro- or Indo-Guyanese.

My use of kinfolk implies broader affinities, not solely based on familial/blood relationships or racialised solidarities, but through shared socio-politico-economic principles. Belonging and citizenship within the nation involves a complex set of relations that extend through and beyond race or any single category. In reference to the Radika Singh case, to be sure, Singh was partly accused of being an old higue because she was an Indo-Guyanese woman with a psychiatric disability who was out of place in a largely Afro-Guyanese community (inter-community violence). It is, however, also worth considering how women and girls living in communities that align with their ethnic identity can also become the victims of violence when they are branded as otherworldly, fabled menaces to their said skinfolk community, especially given the instances of intra-community violence in the Sangeeta Persaud and Todah Richards cases. Such violence is ruled justifiable because these women and girls are judged dangerous and are not deemed kinfolk for any number of reasons. They are killed because they do not belong; because their gender expressions may not conform with normative understandings of femininity; because they may be mad; and more generally because they are not considered respectable women of the nation – they cannot fully gain entry into the citizenry due to such non-conformity. When the performance of community-sanctioned violence goes unpunished by the law of the land and the perpetrators face no consequence, that violence is legitimated. The community wields a monopoly on violence when these acts of brutality are buttressed by silence. Further inquiry into the co-construction of madness and disability, race, and gender in the Guyanese and Caribbean contexts is necessary.

The tale of *Samaan* is also of symbolic importance because the climactic event – the killing of the old higue character – occurs on Mashramani (Harper-Wills n.d., 15). The women, men, and children who kill Ole Higue commemorate Guyana Day through an act of communal violence. This violence is a performance of kinship and bonding, staged through national celebration. When citizens openly fête the birth of the Guyanese Republic, in part, through the murder of a female-gendered figure of lore, the cultural patrimony of the nation is used as an alibi for violence against women. How the 'black and mad' Ole Higue character in *Samaan* is slaughtered is a haunting reflection of the material realities faced by women in Guyana. The traditional stories of the old higue, and the protocols that direct how she must be killed via vigilante justice, spurn the gendered power relations that are at play in a nation where women are beaten and killed every day. Women with disabilities – like Singh, Persaud, Seenauth, Richards, and countless others – face situations where the accusation of being mad, evil, or possessed bears a possible death sentence. Ultimately, *Samaan* refutes what is often considered an inconvertible truth – that the old higue is always evil, and that she always preys on children. *Samaan* tells us that she had better things to do.

Masquerading as the Old Higue

Ole Samaan proclaims that the killing of Ole Higue represents the death of an antiquated belief, but the very inclusion of old higue costume presentations along with other influential figures of Guyanese myth in 2014 Mashramani festivities – themed Cultural Folklore, Celebrating 44 – speaks to the enduring relevance of this strong woman of myth.[12] Like the old higue, Mash is a cultural mainstay. Mashramani is an Arawak word that translates to 'the celebration of a job well done', a concept that is derived from Amerindian festivals that occur after harvest (Danns 2014, 72; *Guyana Chronicle* February 23, 2011). Guyana observes its republican status through this annual carnival, and like the national holidays that celebrate ethnic, cultural, and religious multiplicity in the country, Mashramani belongs to this narrative of nation building (Danns 2014, 72). While Mashramani has its origins in Linden, the main celebration is held in Georgetown. Once an annual theme is selected, mas bands (sponsored by the public and private sector) follow suit and create elaborate and brightly coloured garments to outfit their enthusiastic revellers, comprising adults and children alike. On February 23, giant floats parade toward the National Park for judging, and calypso, chutney, reggae, soca, and the sound of steel pans play until dawn. Families come to celebrate and picnic along the procession route in what can be described as a convivial atmosphere.

The theme of 2014 paid homage to the figures of Guyanese folklore. Glitzy fairmaids, verdant bush daidais, silvery Dutchmen and Dutchwomen phantoms, fiery old higues, and other notable characters were well represented in the main carnival and in the children's festival. There were at least three costume iterations of the old higue during the grand parade. Presentations of the old higue saw women revellers encompassed by ornate spheres intended to look like balls of fire. Some wore small bags of rice, while others accented their costumes with intricate flame cut outs and manicole broom fronds. Some creations contrasted greatly. Certain band sections depicted the old higue as a middle-aged hag with claws, fangs, a disfigured face, and whose wrinkled body sprouted blistery embers (see figure 13.1). In the Guyanese context, the old higue, as her name suggests, is usually represented as a middle-aged woman. Mashramani, however, welcomes masqueraders of all ages, especially young people, and some sections of old higue costumes were predominantly donned by younger women (see figure 13.2).

Figure 13.1: Traditional representation of the Old Higue at Mashramani 2014

(Photographer: Kester Clarke, 2014A)[13]

Figure 13.2: Young women don Old Higue costumes at Mashramani 2014

(Photographer: Kester Clarke, 2014B)[14]

These youthful old higues, as contradictory as that description appears, were dressed in tight bejewelled halter crop tops and matching shorts. Their scarlet garb was highlighted with accessories that resembled the manicole broom in the form of a headpiece and sceptre. Their flawless makeup application emphasised their eyes. Rarely is the old higue, as understood in Guyana, presented through aesthetically pleasing portrayals. This costume interpretation – with its gestures towards nubility – is a performance of female agency (Edmondson 2003, 2) that speaks back to the traditional hag iterations that describe the Guyanese old higue as a post-menopausal baby bloodsucker and anti-mother.

And yet, while the old higue is revered at Mashramani 2014 and made manifest through these various costume presentations, such displays in the midst of revelry take on a different significance when read alongside the murder of Radika Singh – the woman who was denounced as an old higue, and killed because the community was convinced that 'Old Higue have to dead' (*Stabroek News* April 30, 2007). A village old higue is fear-provoking, and unlike the masquerading old higues, Singh's visit was not celebrated; her presence alone foreshadowed her death. The imputation of being an old higue took on the status of truth and Singh's powers seemed too real, which at the same time echoes the sentiments of the children in *Samaan*: 'And now the one we've found, we killed ourselves' (Harper-Wills n.d., 17). It must be made clear that what happened on that fateful morning in Bare Root was not the killing of an old higue, but an act of communal violence that resulted in the murder of a defenceless woman named Radika Singh. This brutal act foregrounds how the old higue's presence is revered and fêted only when her power is extinguished and she is transformed into a reified beast of play(ing mas) to commemorate the birth of the Guyanese Republic.

Jennifer Webster, then Minister of Labour, Human Services, and Security, said that her 2014 Mash band and contingent, which made reference to the old higue mythology, signified the restoration of social values by burning out social ills (Non-Aligned Movement News Network with reporting from GINA, February 24, 2014). While Webster did not make mention of any specific social ills, one can assume that violence against women in Guyana is certainly a societal issue that is symbolically represented. The old higue costume presentation by the Ministry, however, in its celebration of the nation, further entraps this female-gendered legend into a narrative where her subjectivity represents the totality of evil, thus necessitating violence and removal. The irony of the ministry's mas band, both the method (burning out) and the target (social ills), is that the vehicle for this (old higue costume representations) reprises legacies of violence against women when we reflect on the brutality that the myth dictates. Furthermore, despite the potentiality and display of a young, liberated sexuality and alternative rendering of the old higue in figure 13.1, the old higue costume presentations at Mash are wind-up demon dolls that are summoned at the nation's whim to wine up (gyrate); and when the song, dance, and play of Republic Day are over, these representations become discarded costumes of yesteryear. The old higue of Mash cannot be the old higue of Harper Wills's legend – the strong woman of Guyanese myth – because we refuse to let her.

'All Are Involved...'

The words of Martin Carter reverberate across this chapter: 'All are involved and all equally responsible, guilty and innocent' (1993, 82). When contemplating the murder of Singh: of how the myth of the old higue became entangled with her body; and of how Guyana's cultural patrimony rejects the complexity of legendary strong women in favour of valorising sanitised representations of the old higue at Mash, we must move to dismantle that most powerful myth of collective innocence, that sense that as protectors of the future (children) we have no choice and only have a responsibility to extinguish the parasitic and destructive life force that is the old higue. It is a lie that persuades us to believe that we had no hand in upholding a patrimony of violence against women when as children we enthusiastically recited McAndrew's (1996) *Ol' Higue* stanzas:

> Is whuh you sayin' deh, you witch?
>
> Done? Look allyou beat de bitch
>
> Whaxen! Whaxen! Pladai! Plai!
>
> Die, you witch you. Die.
>
> Whaxen! Whaxen! Plai![15]

It is this myth of innocence that fuelled the slaughter of Singh and influences the material realities of women in Guyana, particularly those with psychiatric disabilities when they are labelled evil and possessed. What would a rewritten life of the old higue look like? *Samaan* attempted to provide us with such a narrative, but Ole Higue was still brutally killed before she shared the details of her journey to Mars. What did her voyage look like? Did she feel a sense of camaraderie with the blazing sun when she flew out of the Earth's atmosphere? Did she joyride on comets and run races with asteroids? Did she vacation on the moon before finally soaring to the red planet? Those stories are not yet written. And so, it is our task as Guyanese to write them into existence – to refute the vicious fictions that we have historically told ourselves about ourselves and to create fresh narratives of agentive women in myth, ultimately making new meanings and challenging the violence of tired caricatures.

Notes

1. I spell and refer to the old higue as old higue; however, the term is also commonly spelt ol' higue and ole higue, or old haag and old hag to a lesser extent (Seymour 1975, 48).
2. A jumbie is an all-encompassing term used to refer to spirits, demons, and other supernatural entities in the Caribbean, which often bear malicious intent. Seymour defines the jumbie as a 'ghost, spirit of evil disposition' (37).
3. A manicole broom, widely known as a pointer broom, or a cabbage broom, or jumbie broom to a lesser extent, is made from fronds of the manicole tree and

is commonly used to sweep in Guyana and other parts of the Caribbean. The manicole broom is also a specific implement that is used to beat an old higue, as prescribed by the folklore.

4. I have chosen not to reproduce this image or any other newspaper images directly associated with this case given the ways in which these reproductions continue to fix Singh exclusively as an old higue, further perpetuating forms of discursive and representational violence.

5. Given the scope of this chapter, please consult the following sources for detailed accounts of these historical periods and the social and political relations between Indo- and Afro-Guyanese: Walter Rodney, *A History of the Guyanese Working People, 1881–1905* (1981); Basdeo Mangru, *The Elusive El Dorado: Essays on the Indian Experience in Guyana* (2005); Brackette Williams, *Stains on My Name, War in My Veins: Guyana and the Politics of Cultural Struggle* (1991); Ralph Premdas, *Ethnic Conflict and Development: The Case of Guyana* (1995); Thomas Spinner Jr., *A Political and Social History of Guyana, 1945–1983* (1984); British Guiana's Report of the Wismar, Christianburg, and Mackenzie Commission (1965).

6. Consult the 1954 Report of the British Guyana Constitutional Commission (Robertson Commission Report), tasked with investigating the 'crisis' of 1953 (Spinner 1984, 57).

7. See the *Guardian* interview with Farahnaz Mohammed – Guyana: Mental Illness, Witchcraft, And the Highest Suicide Rate in the World, http://www.theguardian.com/global-development-professionals-network/2015/jun/03/guyana-mental-illness-witchcraft-and-the-highest-suicide-rate-in-the-world.

8. Asafoetida, also spelt asafetida or asafetita, is a brown and bitter-tasting resin with a pungent odour that is 'frequently used in Guyana…to protect babies from old higues and as a guard against evil spirits' (Seymour 1975, 7).

9. See Wordsworth McAndrew, 'The Ol' Higue Story,' in *Guyana Folklore: Guyanese Proverbs and Stories*, ed. P.A. Brathwaite (Georgetown, Guyana: n.p., 1966).

10. See Martin Carter, 'Old Higue' from his collection *The Hill of Fire Glows Red* (1951).

11. *Samaan* is found in a children's anthology of fairy tales called *Stories from Guyana*, which was published by the Daily Chronicle Limited. The year of this publication is unknown, but others who have written about this collection's cultural significance estimate that it was printed in the late 1960s or early 1970s (*Guyana Chronicle*, July 20, 2013). This period in the nation's history was one of cultural pride and marked a renaissance for the arts in Guyana. As mentioned, 1970 was the year Guyana became a republic and was the first year of official Mashramani celebrations.

12. Guyana celebrates 44th Independence Anniversary with Mashramani celebration. *Non-Aligned Movement News Network* with sourcing from Guyana's Government Information Agency (GINA), February 24, 2014, http://www.namnewsnetwork.org/v3/read.php?id=MjYwMTc.1

13. Kester Clarke, photographer, Untitled 2014, February 23, https://www.facebook.com/stabroeknews/photos/a.10152197897235053.1073741898.130548565052/10152198192020053/?type=3&theater.
14. Clarke, photographer. Untitled 2014, February 23, https://www.facebook.com/stabroeknews/photos/a.10152197897235053.1073741898.130548565052/10152198571575053/?type=3&theater.
15. See McAndrew, *Ol' Higue*; McAndrew, 'The Ol' Higue Story.'

References

Anatol, Gizelle L. 2015. *Things that Fly in the Night: Female Vampires in Literature of the Circum-Caribbean and African Diaspora*. New Brunswick, NJ: Rutgers University Press.

Carter, Martin. 1951. *The Hill of Fire Glows Red*. Georgetown, British Guiana: The Miniature Poets.

——. 1993. Recent Events Spring from Social Undercurrents. *Kyk-Over-Al Magazine, Special Edition: A Martin Carter Prose Sampler* (May): 44.

Clarke, Kester. 2014A. (Photographer). Untitled [Figure 1.0]. (February 23). https://www.facebook.com/stabroeknews/photos/a.10152197897235053.1073741898.130548565052/10152198192020053/?type=3&theater.

——. 2014B. (Photographer). Untitled [Figure 1.1]. (February 23). https://www.facebook.com/stabroeknews/photos/a.10152197897235053.1073741898.130548565052/10152198571575053/?type=3&theater.

Danns, George K. 2014. The Impact of Identity, Ethnicity and Class on Guyana's Strategic Culture. *American International Journal of Contemporary Research* 4, no. 11 (November): 75–77.

Edmondson, Belinda. 2003. Public spectacles: Women and Politics of Public Performance. *Small Axe* 7 (March): 1–16.

Harper-Wills, Doris. Samaan. In *Stories from Guyana*. Georgetown, Guyana: Daily Chronicle Limited.

Harris-Lacewell, Melissa. 2008. No Place to Rest: African American Political Attitudes and the Myth of Black Women's Strength. *Women and Politics* 23, no. 3. (October): 1–33.

Maharaj, Hari D., and Rampersad Parasram. 1999. The Practice of Psychiatry in Trinidad and Tobago. *International Review of Psychiatry* 11, no. 2/3: 173–83.

Mangru, Basdeo. 2005. *The Elusive El Dorado: Essays on the Indian Experience in Guyana*. Lanham, MD: University Press of America.

McAndrew, Wordsworth. 1966A. The Ol' Higue Story. In *Guyana Folklore: Guyanese Proverbs and Stories*, ed. P.A. Brathwaite's. Georgetown, Guyana: n.p.

——. 1966B. *Ol' Higue*. http://silvertorch.com/c-poetry.html.

——. 1970. Guyana – A Cultural Look. http://www.silvertorch.com/wordsworth-on-culture.html.

Mohapatra, Prabhu. 1995. Restoring the Family: Wife Murders and the Making of a Sexual Contract for Indian Immigrant Labour in the British Caribbean Colonies. *Studies in History* 11, no. 2

Olmos, Margarite Fernández and Lizabeth Paravisini-Gebert. 2011. *Creole Religions of the Caribbean: An Introduction from Vodou and Santería to Obeah and Espiritismo*. New York, NY: New York University Press.
Premdas, Ralph. 1995. Ethnic Conflict and Development: The Case of Guyana. Aldershot, United Kingdom: Ashgate Publishing Limited.
Rodney, Walter. 1981. *A History of the Guyanese Working People, 1881–1905*. Baltimore, MD: Johns Hopkins University Press.
Report of the British Guyana Constitutional Commission (Robertson Commission Report). 1954. http://www.guyana.org/govt/robertson_report.html
Report of the Wismar, Christianburg and Mackenzie Commission of British Guiana. 1965. http://www.guyana.org/features/wismar_report.html.
Seymour, A.J. 1975. *Dictionary of Guyanese Folklore*. National History and Arts Council. Georgetown, Guyana: Ministry of Information and Culture.
Spinner, Thomas J. Jr. 1984. *A Political and Social History of Guyana, 1945–1983*. Boulder: Westview Press.
Thachil, Ajoy, and Dinesh Bhugra. 2009. Globalization and Mental Health – Traditional Medicine and Pathways to Care in the United Kingdom. In *Psychiatrists and Religious Healers: Unwitting Partners in Global Mental Health*, ed. Mario Incayawar et al., 215–28. Hoboken, NJ: John Wiley and Sons.
Trotz, Alissa. 2004. Between Despair and Hope: Women and Violence in Contemporary Guyana. *Small Axe* 15 (March): 1–20.
Williams, Brackette. 1991. *Stains on My Name, War in My Veins: Guyana and the Politics of Cultural Struggle*. Durham, NC: Duke University Press.

14.
Gender, Inclusionary Politics and the Electoral Quota in Guyana: Politics as Usual?

Natalie Persadie

Introduction: Women In Politics

Women and politics have had a historically poor relationship. Female under-representation in parliaments worldwide has been described as symbolising a serious 'democratic deficit' (Phillips 1998, 228). Similarly, the secretary general of the Institute for Democracy and Electoral Assistance noted that the 'under-representation of women in politics undermines the core democratic principle of equal participation and representation' (Leterme 2016). As part of its new sustainable development agenda, the United Nations adopted 17 sustainable development goals (SDGs) in September 2015. One of these focuses on gender equality (SDG5) and reaffirms the organisation's commitment to ensuring women's full and effective decision-making in political life, in recognition of their historical under-representation within this sphere.

The available data clearly demonstrates the need for such measures. On average, only about 23 per cent of women hold seats in lower houses of Parliament around the world, with one notable exception being Rwanda, where women comprise 63.8 per cent of the lower house (Inter-Parliamentary Union 2016). As table 14.1 below shows, the situation in the Anglophone Caribbean reflects this abysmal picture with percentages ranging from 3.1 to 33.3 per cent; just three countries pass the 30 per cent mark. Though electoral gender quotas have been introduced in several countries worldwide to correct this deficit, Guyana is the only country in this group to have done so. But it is not without its challenges.

A period of extensive constitutional reform in the late 1990s to early 2000s in Guyana involved sustained efforts by women to secure representation in the political system. One pioneering result of these efforts was adopting a gender quota to ensure that women comprise a minimum of one-third of the candidates on electoral lists. However, as demonstrated later, this does not necessarily translate into greater numbers of women entering Parliament (Persadie 2014, vii). A recurring question, among many others, is whether the issue of women's political under-representation has been adequately addressed following enactment of the electoral quota law.

Table 14.1: Women's (Under-) representation in National Parliaments in the Independent Anglophone Caribbean

World Rank	Country	Lower or Single House			Upper House or Senate			TOTAL
		Seats*	Women	% Women	Seats*	Women	% Women	Both Houses
32	Grenada	15	5	33.3%	13	2	15.4%	25%
42	Trinidad and Tobago	42	13	31%	31	10	32.3%	31.5%
46	Guyana	69	21	30.4%	---	---	---	30.4%
76	Dominica	32	7	21.9%	---	---	---	21.9%
*	Jamaica	62	11	17.7%	21	5	23.8%	19.2%
107	Barbados	30	5	16.6%	21	5	23.8%	19.6%
107	Saint Lucia	18	3	16.7%	11	3	27.3%	20.6%
132	Saint Kitts and Nevis	15	2	13.3%	---	---	---	13.3%
134	Bahamas	38	5	13.2%	16	4	25.0%	16.6%
135	Saint Vincent and the Grenadines	23	3	13%	---	---	---	13%
148	Antigua and Barbuda	18	2	11.1%	17	7	41.2%	25.7%
177	Belize	32	1	3.1%	13	5	38.5%	13.3%

Figures correspond to the number of seats filled in country parliaments on February 1, 2016, except for Jamaica for which information was compiled independently from the Jamaica Information Service and Jamaica Houses of Parliament for the 2016 election. Jamaica's world rank may have improved based on a comparison with its previous percentage. Other statistics were extracted from the Inter-Parliamentary Union Database, 'Women in National Parliaments.' The last column was added by the author.

This chapter will examine gender and representation in the formal political arena in the pre- and post-1992 period. It will offer some exploratory considerations as to whether or not the requirement of quotas has been effective in increasing actual numbers of women parliamentarians; and discuss some of the challenges that have arisen following enactment of the law. The study will begin with a brief overview of the issue of women's numerical under-representation in Parliament and some of the challenges in changing this, followed by a review of attempts to increase women's political participation across the Caribbean. The focus will then move specifically to efforts of political parties in Guyana during election campaigns in the post-1992 period in addressing gender issues and making Parliament more numerically representative in this regard. I then examine the challenges that arose post-quota adoption, and suggest ways to move political action outside of parliamentary representation to effect gender inclusion. Sources for this study include statements on gender equality from the political parties' manifestos; gender policies of political parties; actual numbers of women in the various parliaments from independence to the present; legislation enacted dealing with women's issues; interviews with key personnel from state and non-state institutions that address women's issues; and the establishment and implementation of the electoral gender quota.

Women's Political Under-Representation

Numerical representation of women in Parliament, at its most basic, simply looks at counting the number of women members of parliament. Increasing these numbers is justified on the basis of ensuring a more representative body by having equal (or less skewed) proportions of men and women (Devlin and Elgie 2008, 237). Women really are a 'political' minority rather than a 'numerical' minority (Halder 2004, 50), as women are known to make up at least half of most populations but are politically under-represented worldwide. Excluding women from the parliamentary arena, however, often means that women's interests are not advanced at that level. According to Dube (2013, 201), the exclusion of women in politics is necessarily an exclusion of their needs and aspirations. A United Nations report (2005, 8–9) advances six arguments for having equal numbers of women in Parliament:

- The justice argument – women account for approximately half the population and therefore have the right to similar numerical representation.
- The experience argument – women's experiences are different from men's and need to be articulated in discussions that result in policymaking and implementation. These different experiences mean that women 'do politics' differently from men.
- The interest argument – the interests of men and women are different, even conflicting, requiring women in representative institutions to articulate their interests.
- The critical mass argument – women are able to achieve solidarity of purpose to represent their interests when they achieve certain levels of representation.
- The symbolic argument – women are attracted to political life if they have role models in the arena. Halder also notes that sometimes women parliamentarians can symbolise potentially expanded political roles for women (50).
- The democracy argument – equal representation of women and men enhances democratisation of governance in both transitional and consolidated democracies.

Such arguments are easily countered when one considers, for example, that equal representation does not translate to equal exercise of power and control (Dube 2013, 207), or that women may feel constrained by party loyalty (Devlin and Elgie 2008, 240), or that party men are reluctant to promote women in the absence of pressure from strong women and feminist groups within its ranks (Halder 2004, 47). The deprecating argument of whether or not competent women would be included where special measures such as quotas are used to ensure greater numbers is unfortunate, but bears little importance. While women may not necessarily always be able to act independently to influence law and policy (50), there really is no obligation (except maybe moral) for women parliamentarians to advance a feminist agenda.

Increasing women's political presence is no simple feat. There are numerous factors that militate against their entry or even their desire to enter into politics. In a study of nearly 4,000 male and female 'potential candidates' for electoral office in the US, Jennifer Lawless and Richard

Fox (2012) argued that women's political under-representation is based largely on the fact that unlike men, they have no political ambition (3). Nomita Halder noted a similar phenomenon in Bangladesh, where she said that women are simply not interested in politics (2004, 28), not taking into account cultural and religious challenges. Moreover, political parties discriminate against women's nomination (28). The American study identified seven reasons in support of this proposition that women lack political ambition, which revolve around the existence of an environment that is highly competitive and biased against women; women believing that they are less qualified to run for office; women being much more risk averse; women reacting negatively to election campaigning; women having less encouragement to run for office; and, of course, women having the responsibility for the majority of childcare and household tasks (Lawless and Fox 2012, 16). On the issues of women's sense of their qualification and lack of encouragement to run for office, a United Nations report made similar findings (United Nations 2005, 16).

The Caribbean Context

A recent Commonwealth report suggests that there is a globally (though not necessarily formally) recognised 30 per cent minimum requirement for women in leadership in both economics and politics (B. Hinds 2015, 5). Hinds also noted different targets such as 40:40:20 (40 per cent of each gender and the remaining 20 per cent of either gender) or 50:50 (5), such as is the legally adopted candidate quota in South Africa (Persadie 2014, 17).

In the Anglophone Caribbean, only Guyana has instituted a gender quota in relation to political leadership, which came about after a period of extensive constitutional reform in the late 1990s to early 2000s. Notwithstanding this ostensibly progressive move, women's numerical presence in the Guyanese Parliament has not exceeded the legal minimum. Numbers for the wider region are generally low, as evidenced by the statistics in table 14.1 above. Nevertheless, there have been discussions in some Caribbean countries such as Jamaica, the Bahamas, Trinidad and Tobago, and Belize, centred around increasing women's political participation.

In March 2011, Jamaica published its national gender policy which recognised that 'women make up 50.7% of the population; however, they are woefully under-represented in the public and private decision-making spheres of the country' (Bureau of Women's Affairs 2011, 9). The policy noted that the government would adopt:

> temporary special measures to accelerate de facto equality between men and women...such as legislated gender quotas, to address the lack of proportional representation of women in Parliament. Such a measure *could* require a thirty per cent (30%) minimum distribution of women among persons appointed to the Senate and the board of public bodies (Bureau of Women's Affairs, 23).[1]

This statement of intent draws on the work of the '51% Coalition'. Established in 2011, this Jamaican alliance of women's organisations and individuals advocating the implementation of a gender quota has among its objectives, 'development and empowerment through equity' (Persadie 2014, 22). In this regard, its goal is for 'a balance of not more than 60 per cent and not less than 40 per cent of either sex on public boards and bodies', including the senate (*Jamaica Observer* 2012). Forbes, in a blog post, specified that while that was the long-term position, in the short term, the immediate target was to increase women's participation to at least 40 per cent of the membership. After the 2015 election, the group reiterated its call for the new government to honour its commitment towards meeting the policy targets for women's inclusion, but, in 2016, the UNDP reported that the country '[fell] short of its own target of having women in 30 per cent of decision-making positions' (Reuters, 'UN Report'; see also Jamaica Houses of Parliament, 'Senators').

The Bahamas made a very brief statement about instituting a gender quota in 2011 at an Organisation for American States forum through its then minister of state for Labour and Social Development. The minister noted that she would support discussions for increasing women's participation in the Bahamian Parliament (Parker 2011A), but there does not seem to have been further exploration of the matter. The issue, however, is not that simple. Women's inclusion in political leadership appears to require 'substantial systematic reform' (Persadie 2014, 22), such as access to campaign financing. While this is perhaps true of many countries, the situation seems to be compounded in the Bahamas by the fact that some believe that the women's movement may not be as engaged as it should be to push the agenda (Parker 2011B).

Trinidad and Tobago has never seen any real move to increase women's political participation. The Network of NGOs of Trinidad and Tobago for the Advancement of Women, a local alliance of NGOs, joined the Women's Environment and Development Organization (WEDO) 50/50 campaign in 2000, which is when WEDO first initiated the movement lobbying towards women's equal participation and representation in governments around the world (Persadie 2014, 24). Statements have also been made in regional and international fora by ministers responsible for women's affairs concerning setting targets for women's increased participation in political leadership, but little seems to have been accomplished beyond these rhetorical declarations (Persadie 2014, 23–24).

Belize finds itself in the unique position of having an approved gender policy from 2002 and a revised, but yet unapproved, 2013 policy (the *Reporter* 2013). Both versions address the issue of women's under-representation in positions of power and decision-making. The 2002 policy recognises that it might be necessary 'to introduce temporary measures to overcome the deeply entrenched barriers to equality' where '[o]ne common measure is the setting of 'quotas' guaranteeing them [traditionally disadvantaged groups] a certain share of opportunities' (Johnson 2002, 5). While noting women's marginalisation in politics, the policy goes on to state:

> At the political level, there has not been uniform consensus about the merit of setting quotas. If a major motivation for women to be more politically involved has been a desire to 'make a difference', or to inject some different perspectives and priorities into policy decision-making, the experience has been rather equivocal (Johnson 2002, 64).

There was no concrete statement on the establishment of any quota but rather a suggestion that there be consultation 'on the merit of setting quotas' (Johnson 2002, 64; 106) and that a cost/benefit analysis be conducted to determine the existence of any such merit (5). Unfortunately, this latter proved unfavourable in this regard, as a 2010 report on the situational analysis of gender issues in Belize reported that the cost/benefit analysis of a gender quota, requested in the original gender policy document, did not find merit for its implementation (64).

The 2013 revised draft states that there has been overwhelming nationwide support for increasing women's political participation at the highest levels of government and reiterated the need for the adoption of temporary special measures (Catzim-Sanchez 2013, 39), although it is not entirely clear how this will work given the unfavourable results of the cost/benefit analysis conducted in 2010, unless some other type of measure is contemplated. In any event, the policy presses political parties to set internal targets and timelines for increasing women's representation (40) and the government to set targets at the national and municipal levels (41). Despite these efforts, nothing has yet translated into practice.

The use of temporary special measures – whether quota or non-quota – to include women in politics is not new, but came to the fore in the 1970s (Krook, 2015, 1). While their proper implementation can ensure women's presence in politics, they are not without challenges. Many women who support the implementation of quota systems, for example, may not necessarily push the gender agenda in Parliament. As Krook points out 'these measures are not feminist quotas but gender quotas – and more properly speaking, sex quotas – that seek merely to increase the number of women in political decision-making, separate from any obligations to change policy outcomes' (2006, 111). Nanivadekar (2006) asked whether elected women owe a primary loyalty to the cause of women only (123). If women pursue too myopic an agenda, they risk further marginalisation in an already very exclusionary arena into which they demanded entry (Persadie 2014, 15).

Jamaica and Trinidad and Tobago provide good examples of the difficulty in pursuing increased women's political participation. Both countries had female prime ministers up to 2016 and 2015 respectively, yet there was no concrete move during their term in office to secure greater participation of women in politics, despite repeated calls by local advocacy groups to do so. Feminist scholars have suggested that women often adopt masculinist norms in order to succeed in such environments (Paxton and Hughes 2007, 13, 16). More particularly, institutions may change women before they can change institutions (13). Vivien Lowndes (2002) noted that institutions are understood as 'stable recurring patterns of behaviour' (91), as 'processes' (101) rather than an actual organisational structure. When women become part of political institutions where male behaviour is considered the norm, they may feel pressured to conform to those norms (Paxton and Hughes 2007, 13), especially where women are few in number (16). This is exacerbated by the fact that '[t]he majority of governing institutions are dominated by men who further their own interests. Male-dominated political institutions of government do not promote women or women's issues' (Dube 2013, 201). Moreover, political parties and their leaders are the major 'gatekeepers' in determining who will be candidates in elected office (United Nations 2005, 16). A Swedish study involving over 30,000 politicians over five election cycles found that 'women's political career advancements are restricted by entrenched male elites' (Folke and Rickne n.d., 2) who are personified by the institution of the party. This does not mean, however, that one woman cannot make a difference; she must have the courage of her conviction.

Nevertheless, institutions are intrinsically problematic from a feminist perspective. If the institutions in question are understood as inherently patriarchal and exclusionary, the (non-)evolution of the 'gender agenda' and limited female representation within political parties and, consequently, Parliament might be explained. Political parties can be viewed as institutions that shape and permit what party members can do. More specifically, these institutions very carefully circumscribe the behaviour of their female members and feminist activity, which may not necessarily coincide with party objectives. This could possibly explain the non-pursuit by the female prime ministers of Jamaica and Trinidad and Tobago with respect to increasing women's political representation in their countries.

Politics and Guyanese Women

From as early as the nineteenth century, women were involved in political activism in Guyana (Woolford 2000, 123), though this can only be understood within the framework of the country's history (Peake 1993, 109). Kimberly Nettles reported, 'Women have been active in voluntary, religious, and political associations in Guiana since its early days as a colonial outpost of the English plantocracy' (2007, 61), but these organisations were largely led by the wives of the white colonial élite. Shortly before Guyana achieved independence, women actively involved in politics created auxiliary arms of their respective parties. According to Roberta Kilkenny:

> The women's organisations of the 1946–1953 period would not merely serve a supportive role in the struggle for political and social justice. Two, in particular, the Women's Political and Economic Organisation (WPEO) [succeeded by] the Women's Progressive Organisation (WPO), would become "comrades-in-arms" with men in that struggle (1984, 1).

These women's organisations were affiliated with the People's Progressive Party (PPP) before Forbes Burnham left in 1955 and created the People's National Congress (PNC) in 1957. The Women's Auxiliary of the

PNC was later to become the Women's Revolutionary Socialist Movement (WRSM), now the National Congress of Women (NCW) (McAlmont 2002). Both organisations, according to Cecelia McAlmont, were headed by the wives of the two political leaders: Mrs Jagan for the then WPEO and Mrs Burnham for the then Women's Auxiliary. The WPEO, in particular, was launched in 1946 'to ensure the political organisation and education of the women of British Guiana in order to promote their economic welfare and their political and social emancipation and betterment' (Kilkenny 1984, 8).[2] In 1976, the WRSM was given parity with the party when the party was restructured and the philosophy of the women's movement changed, with the party leader indicating that the WRSM must lead the campaign for the full emancipation of women (Woolford 2000, 131–32).

Despite what appears to be a strong focus on women's political participation within parties by permitting the establishment of women's arms, McAlmont has observed that, over the years, women from the WPO and NCW had little more than token membership on the Central Executive Committees, the highest decision-making forum of their political parties. Linda Peake also noted that, while some women members are genuinely concerned about the emancipation of women, 'they are constantly constrained by the framework within which they operate' (2002, 119); this 'framework' is the institution of the party at work. Moreover, cross-party caucuses for women to address gender issues were never advanced. This was largely because party interests superseded gender matters once they got into Parliament (George 2012, 2016). A United Nations report noted:

> [P]arty loyalty and identification is often very strong in parliaments and discourages representatives from forming cross-party alliances. Ultimately, women MPs are accountable to their parties first and to women in their constituencies only after they have fulfilled their party's expectations. Women parliamentarians often face the dilemma of having to follow their party's directive, which may not correspond with their wish to articulate demands for women and gender equality (2005, 21).

There were attempts to create such a caucus back in 2011, but they failed, again, because no political party championed such a cause (Persadie 2014, 36–37).

One observer noted the difficulty in getting women to cross party lines 'because the nature of politics kept [them] apart' (Nettles 2007, 69). The blind party loyalty of its members and supporters exacerbated the situation as women would attend meetings once the 'Party' said they must attend (Karen de Souza, in Nettles 2007, 70). This behaviour was credited to a lack of education.³ Additionally, the mobilisation of women by the dominant political parties was less about securing women's rights and more about strengthening the party's position in the country (70). This is reflective of the power of the institution that is the 'Party' and its ability to determine the behaviour of its members and supporters.

Red Thread Foundation for Women (Red Thread), which sought to shift how the political culture was gendered, has the distinction of being the first non-party political women's organisation in Guyana (Peake 1993, 118), a specific response to this party political monopoly (Woolford 2000, 146). Interestingly, though, it was formed largely by activists within the Working People's Alliance (WPA), a political party whose genesis lay in its opposition to the social, political, and economic policies of the Burnham regime (Nettles 2007, 58, 65, 60). Red Thread emerged out of the founders' 'disillusionment with the racialised politics, the lack of economic and social opportunities for women' as well as the 'limiting nature of the political party structure for women's politics and women's empowerment' (Nettles 2007, 76–77). There was a need to create a space to 'raise gender issues without their being relegated to the back burner of party politics' (Peake and Trotz 1999, 184; 179). The organisation was established by a group of Guyanese political activists who wanted to raise women's consciousness; make links across difference (race/ethnicity, class/status); increase women's access to earnings and education; improve community access to running water and food; (re)value women's daily labour and their roles as caretakers and providers; and challenge the prevailing male-centred political culture (Nettles 2007, 58).

Guyanese women have clearly been politically active for a long time but have not had the benefit of political (party) leadership, cross-party caucusing or decision-making power at higher levels within their parties. They were relegated to women's arms of their respective parties or had to form a completely separate non-party group to address pressing women's issues. The formation of women's arms, in particular, seemed to represent placatory moves on the part of the larger political parties to give women a sense of inclusion, but this did not translate at the executive level. As discussed in the next section, this history of tokenism within parties was matched in government, where election promises of addressing women's issues remained unfulfilled after victory at the polls.

Election Promises on Gender Issues in the post-1992 Period

Every election sees the production of manifestos which might include promises to address women's issues in any number of ways, whether as a single statement or in much greater detail. All available manifestos for the period under consideration were reviewed to gauge whether and what promises were made with respect to gender issues.[4] Table 14.2 below shows the various manifestos that were available for review and those that specifically addressed gender issues.

Table 14.2 focuses on the post-1992 era when Guyana resumed electoral democracy up until the last election in 2015. There were no available manifestos for some parties. Reasons for this include the fact that some parties were only recently formed; some parties did not engage in election activity during all election years; some parties existed only briefly; and some parties joined forces for particular elections, such as the APNU and AFC in 2015, a coalition that produced a joint statement.

Table 14.2: Available Party Manifestos with Specific Statements on Gender Issues in the post-1992 Period

YEAR	POLITICAL PARTY							
	PNC	PPP	TUF	AFC	APNU	WPA	AFG	GDP
1992	✓	✓	✓			✓		
1997	✓	✓	★				✓	✓
2001	✓	✓						
2006	✓		✓	✓				
2011		✓	✓	✓	✓			
2015		✓	✓		✓			

Notes:
1. PNC – People's National Congress, now PNC – R; PPP – People's Progressive Party, now PPP/C; TUF – The United Force; AFC – Alliance for Change; APNU – A Partnership for National Unity; WPA – Working People's Alliance; AFG – Alliance for Guyana; GDP – Guyana Democratic Party.
   ✓ Specific statement on gender included, but not necessarily related to increasing women's political participation
   ★ No specific statement on gender

For the purposes of this chapter, only statements concerning increasing women's political participation will be specifically highlighted. During the time period noted for the three long-standing parties (PPP/C, PNC/R, and TUF), it would appear that the PPP/C and TUF have generally consistently included specific promises on gender. The AFC and APNU,[5] while relatively new, have consistently made gender-specific promises since their establishment. Very broadly, many of the manifestos promised to work towards removing the various barriers that inhibit the advancement of women, particularly through legislative means. Specific measures promised include guarantees of gender equality; ensuring maternity leave with pay and better health care; providing day-care centres; protecting women against domestic violence; and strengthening the capacity of arms of government that deal with gender and women's issues. These are among the most important issues facing women and promising to address them can potentially affect how they vote. Notably, these are the very concerns highlighted by women's activist groups. Interestingly, while the groups may not always have been successful in effecting change at the national level on all these matters, their apprehensions are certainly taken into consideration for political purposes. This is unfortunate, but the point is that while their concerns are heard, the take-up appears to be symbolic and aimed at securing votes (not a mandate); there is just no follow through.

In their sole available manifesto, the Alliance for Guyana thought it prudent to liken the challenges faced by women and the differently abled, describing women as 'disabled', despite acknowledging that '[p]ersons with physical, mental and other disabilities are under different and greater handicaps' (1997, 16). This has had the regrettable effect of diminishing the challenges faced by both women and the differently abled. While other manifestos may include women as part of other vulnerable groups in society that require special attention, none have done it as inelegantly as found here.

For the other manifestos produced over the ten-year period ending in 2015, generally very broad and non-committal declarations have been made on gender, making it somewhat challenging to gauge what happens in practice. Earlier manifesto statements are even vaguer. Statements have been made by some of the political parties with respect to increasing women's political participation or further including them in 'power sharing and decision-making at the national level,' as The United Force did in 2006,

2011 and 2015 (TUF 2006, 28; 2011, 27; 2015, 19), but with no concrete target that would be sought. The PNCR-One Guyana, in its 2006 manifesto saw the fuller participation of women and greater opportunities for them as key factors in a successful development programme, but offered no specifics on how this would happen.

The PPP/C acknowledged the need to 'increase the presence of women in leadership and governance in public institutions' in its 2015 manifesto (41), but did not include any targets or specifics as to how this would be achieved. In its 2001 manifesto, that party had recognised its role in paving the way for women's political empowerment (31) through the establishment of the quota, and had promised to continue supporting the Guyana Women's Leadership Institute in its training of women to make them 'more involved in decision making at various levels' (31), but made no specific mention of political decision-making. Their five consecutive terms in government and continued lobbying by non-governmental organisations (NGOs) do not suggest that any practical measures were implemented to achieve increased leadership by women in any arena.

In its 2015 manifesto, APNU and AFC (which came to power in that year's election) made very brief mention of gender equality (38), unlike its 2011 promises to:

> work to effect genuine 50:50 equality in Parliament, and as a proactive step in this direction commits to the global standard for the balance between women and men in governing bodies which is 40/60 – that is, neither sex should have less than 40% or more than 60% representation (16)

in recognition of women's under-representation in positions of power. This is a significant statement given that it was soundly and scathingly rejected during the constitutional reform efforts between the late 1990s and early 2000s. The majority of constitution reform commissioners did not view this favourably either, and a four-member subcommittee report stated, 'I have indicated my firm objection to any such course of action [60:40 gender ratio]... The entrenchment of quotas or ratios in a constitution is not found in any part of the world. *Such institutionalised reverse discrimination will be a forensic nightmare*' (Persaud 1999, 8).[6] The compromise was the adoption of the one-third quota of female candidates to be included on electoral lists (Persadie 2014, 35–36). Such a definitive statement was not repeated in the 2015 APNU and AFC manifesto, which simply 'recognises, supports and celebrates women's leadership, participation and contributions to society' (APNU and AFC 2015, 35). Furthermore, the coalition committed to holding a National Conference of Women within 100 days of being elected into office with a view to drafting a gender policy (8).

The conference was, in fact, one election promise on gender that was kept, but the reviews have been mixed. President Granger noted in August 2015 that gender equality would be a top priority of his administration (*Guyana Chronicle* 2015). The conference report, prepared by the Ministry of Social Protection, identifies eight thematic areas that were addressed, the first among them being gender and governance. Discussions around this theme recognised the under-representation of women in Guyanese politics as well as its very patriarchal nature (Ministry of Social Protection 2015, 11). Recommendations to address these included education, training, and increased gender awareness and sensitivity (12).

While the report included numerous proposals for a way forward, individuals interviewed voiced scepticism about the usefulness of the conference, with one person noting that it was not well organised, and also pointing to 'a striking absence of Indian women' who were not included in the discussion. The report itself documents 15–30 participants per thematic area, raising the question how representative were the conference and the recommendations proposed. One of the main outcomes was supposed to be a national gender policy, but this has not yet been produced. It remains to be seen at what point it will be introduced and what issues it will address.

The Statistics Speak

Political parties may aspire to be truly inclusionary, but the evidence does not match the lofty rhetoric. Table 14.3 provides percentages of women from each party that held seats in the 11 parliaments of the post-independence period. It also provides the total percentage of women in Parliament for the given election year. Numbers from individual parties ranged from zero per cent to 100 per cent, but it should be noted that this latter constituted a total of two representatives. Based on the percentages calculated, the PNC seemed to be increasingly women friendly over the years, even prior to the adoption of the gender quota. Percentages for the newcomers AFC and APNU, for 2006 and 2012 respectively, have exceeded one-third. The PPP, however, peaked at 12 per cent immediately prior to the adoption of the quota, and has never met the one-third expectation.

Table 14.3: Percentage of Women by Party holding seats in Parliament from 1966-2016

PARTY	% OF WOMEN REPRESENTATIVES FOR EACH PARTY FOR EACH PARLIAMENT FROM 1966										
	1966	1969	1973	1981	1986	1992	1998	2001	2006	2012	2015
PNC	**3%**	**11%**	**17%**	**24%**	**32%**	27%	31%	31%	44%	†	†
PPP	0%	10%	6%	9%	11%	**12%**	**12%**	**20%**	**27%**	**26%**	29%
TUF	0%	17%	–	–	0%	0%	0%	–	–	–	–
IP	–	0%	–	–	–	–	–	–	–	–	–
LP	–	–	25%	0%	–	–	–	–	–	–	–
WPA	–	–	–	–	0%	0%	–	100%*	0%*	–	–
AFG	–	–	–	–	–	0%	–	–	–	–	–
ROAR	–	–	–	–	–	–	–	0%	–	–	–
AFC	–	–	–	–	–	–	–	–	50%	33%	**33%**
APNU	–	–	–	–	–	–	–	–	–	37%	
TOTAL %	1%	12%	15%	22%	29%	17%	17%	26%	32%	31%	31%

Notes:

1. PNC – People's National Congress, now PNC–R; PPP – People's Progressive Party, now PPP/C; TUF – The United Force; IP – Independent Party; LP – Liberator Party; WPA – Working People's Alliance; AFG – Alliance for Guyana; ROAR – Rise, Organize and Rebuild; AFC – Alliance for Change; APNU – A Partnership for National Unity
2. In some cases, the parties/coalitions were not yet formed or ceased to be in existence in that particular form, hence ' – '
3. **%** indicates party in government
4. * in coalition with Guyana Action Party
5. † coalition partner with APNU
6. The data in this table was provided by the Parliament Library ('Members of Parliament') in raw form. Percentages calculated also include non-elected members of parliament.
7. The total number of representatives, even excluding non-elected members as identified in the data provided, never added up to the same number. Guyana's parliament is a unicameral legislature with 65 elected members (GECOM, About Guyana). Numbers varied widely.

In McAlmont's 2002 study of women in Parliament under the PNC administration from 1968 to 1985, she noted the low level of women's participation in Guyanese politics, and correlated women's participation in the Guyanese Parliament to their participation in political parties (2–4). She also posited that while women were active voters, they never voted to change the male-dominated leadership structure, which might have been attributable to the gendered division of labour even with the party that 'confined most of the women at Congress to the kitchen' (5), a sentiment reflected by Peake who said the Women's Auxiliary of the PNC served as a domestic unit, catering to the needs of male PNC members (1993, 116). She also remarked that women tend to be concentrated at the lower levels of the political hierarchy (119). In their 1995 report on the status of women in the Commonwealth Caribbean, Alicia Mondesire and Leith Dunn similarly noted the gendered division of labour, where women formed the backbone of political parties, yet, leadership in the party and the state remained firmly in the hands of men (1995, 23). This is consistent with the experience of women worldwide, who face numerous constraints with respect to their entry and participation in politics. Cynthia Barrow-Giles (2011) identified those restraints as including 'debilitating customs, obstructionist attitudes and a patriarchic society' (xv). In Guyana, even with a one-third quota adopted after great effort, no efforts have been made to address the glaring loophole concerning placement of women into Parliament. This is exacerbated by the fact that attempts at cross-party caucusing by women have always failed, very likely on account of the strongly masculinist nature of parliamentary politics and the need to maintain solidarity on positions adopted by parties (Persadie 2014, 37).

The Quota: The Law, The Challenges, The Solution

Even where women show 'an interest in more active participation in electoral politics, the selection process discriminates against them' (Barrow-Giles 2011, xiii; Halder 2004, 28). Guyanese women's exclusion from political participation was so acute that a decision was taken to adopt a quota through the Elections Laws (Amendment) Act, No 15 of 2000:[7] The law mandates in subsections 11B(5) and (6):

> 11B (5) The total number of females on each party's national top-up list shall be at least one third of the total number of persons on that list.

(6) The total number of females on any party's lists for geographical constituencies, taken together, shall be at least one-third of the total number of persons on those lists taken together for the geographical constituencies in which that party is contesting.

So at least one-third of the candidates on party lists prior to elections must be female, in an attempt to ensure that a minimum number of women is included in the process. Notably, however, there is no corresponding stipulation regarding the actual percentage of female representation required in Parliament (Persadie 2014, 40). As pointed out elsewhere, in the absence of any such obligation, political parties generally avoid increasing the share of elected women (Folke and Rickne n.d., 6). Notably, the 2015 election figures fell just under, at about 30 per cent (see table 14.1). This legal factoring of women into political representation came as the result of extensive, concerted and sustained campaigning and networking among and by predominantly middle-class Guyanese women, despite numerous challenges at each step along the way – particularly formal, political and sociocultural male resistance to the idea (see Persadie 2014 generally). Nevertheless, the effort to have this success translated into increased numbers of women parliamentarians has been effectively thwarted by the loophole presented by the wording of the law (Persadie 2014).

Extraction from the List

Though the mandate is that one third of the *candidates* on the list must be women, it is the party leader who selects the parliamentarians. In order for the law to have had the desired effect, it should also have mandated that at least one-third of those selected for parliamentary appointment (extracted off the list of candidates) be women. This omission is what has created the current loophole.

Several interviewees commented on this and the issues that it raised. According to a former parliamentarian, 'There is no extraction requirement...therefore, women's representation can be less; this is a technical loophole.' One Women and Gender Equality Commission (WGEC) commissioner noted the following:

> We acknowledge that we did make a mistake, in that, the niceties of the law, we just said one-third women we would like to see that in Parliament. We did not stress that it applied to the extraction from the list. They would have to have more than one-third women on the list in order to extract one-third.

Admitting to the inadvertent 'blunder', the chair of the WGEC stated 'We assumed one-third means one-third and that one-third referred to extraction as well.' Another women's activist commented:

> If you are electing from a slate that is non-prioritised you could have endless women on it but that does not mean that they would be extracted from the list. The quota system was important to guarantee representation, not that Guyana does not have a history of representation, but the leader of the list has enormous legislative power to extract from the list.

At least one political leader interviewed concurred with others, stating that the problem with the one-third was that there was no further recommendation that when it came to extracting names that one-third would actually be extracted. The totality of the constituency seats would equal one-third. This has the unwitting potential to create a ceiling, as political parties may decide that including one-third women on the list meets the legal requirement, which would automatically limit the number actually extracted and placed in Parliament.

As one interviewee emphatically stated, 'Why would we have wasted our time, effort and intelligence to only have women on the list? That is not what was intended. The point of it is that from the list you get into the house.' A parliamentarian explained that there was a debate as to whether the one-third should be enshrined in the Constitution that included an extraction requirement. She went on to state:

> The agreement was that this was an incremental issue; let us get the parties to comply with the requirement that you must put up one-third on the list to be eligible to contest. The incremental approach was felt to be a better one as Guyana is a multiparty country and some of the parties were very small and would not be able to meet the requirement.

This may have been simply a politically correct way of saying that the downward compromise facilitated parties that would not have agreed to the one-third extraction requirement for women.

Prioritisation

Prioritisation of the list immediately manifested itself as another and directly related issue. Guyana's electoral lists are closed and non-prioritised, meaning that the party leader may choose representatives randomly off the list, regardless of gender or other considerations. While prioritisation of the list came up as an important recommendation in prequota implementation discussions, a former parliamentarian lamented that neither party acquiesced as they were not 'comfortable' with that. Four elections have passed since the adoption of the quota law with no extraction requirement, and no one has moved to address the issue, which suggests a lack of political will to change the status quo of a limited number of women holding seats in Parliament (Persadie 2014, 48–49). It could also reflect a loss of steam to pursue the matter on the part of the civil society groups.

Substantive Representation

Greater representation of women in Parliament might lead to expectations of automatic substantive representation. As Emanuela Garboni noted, however, increased numerical representation of women increases but does not guarantee the possibility of substantive representation, as the influence of the former over the latter is probabilistic rather than deterministic (2015, 87). A study on the effect of increased numbers of women in Rwanda's Parliament, though, notes that 'numbers do count' in that they guarantee the continued presence and normalisation of women's issues on the agenda (in that male MPs also consider them issues worthy of Parliament's consideration), (Devlin and Elgie 2008, 250) as these are now perceived to be 'guaranteed' by the presence of more women (251). Rwanda's special demographic balance needs to be noted to understand this phenomenon, perhaps, as an exception, where immediately post-genocide, approximately 70 per cent of the population was female (242).

Unfortunately, as noted earlier in the discussion of women's political participation in the Caribbean, women in power do not necessarily represent women's issues. In interviews, women who worked assiduously for the quota expressed disappointment that women parliamentarians did not put gender on the agenda, and that simply raising gender issues was sometimes viewed as subversive and disdainful, even by women, including progressive women (and men). In fact, a gender consultant noted that pockets of women in the country did not agree with instituting the gender quota. According to the consultant,

> one middle class woman said that every time the women's movement goes out to fight for something, it creates more pressure [responsibility] for women [to assume both traditional and new roles]. Unfortunately, not all women see women's advancement in the same light.

Nevertheless, those in favour of the quota believe that female parliamentarians play an important role in transforming politics and gendering the political agenda. A former parliamentarian noted, 'You don't want more and more women entering politics just to maintain the status quo; you want them to enter politics to be part of the transformation of how politics is done.' The Chair of the WGEC relayed a similar sentiment: 'You don't want women there just for being there; you want them to be effective, to represent and to champion the issues.'

One social activist expressed disappointment that female parliamentarians were not pushing women's issues:

> Having gotten the women in Parliament, to be honest, we were a bit disappointed. We didn't feel that they fully understood how to put the women's agenda into the parliamentary system, especially given the struggle to get them there in the first place.

The gender consultant agreed with this, observing that, 'Women in parliament are not really doing justice to women's issues. They can do more, but they have to meet with the constituency of women to guide them as to what to present in parliament.' As one interviewee remarked,

> Even when [women] come into positions of power, they are not gender conscious and do not see things through a gender lens

and therefore do not represent women's issues, or even feel inclined to do so.

Describing her observation that women parliamentarians, when asked about substantive representation, respond by saying that if the issues are brought to them they will address them, one interviewee questioned the point of having women representatives if they did not instinctively seek to address women's interests. It was also suggested that only when the international community promotes an issue would it be implemented locally. External pressures could possibly lead to some form of substantive representation if the matter is deemed important enough.

Despite these shortcomings, the gender consultant stated that women's organisations could demand that the WEGC take up substantive issues. This commission was established in 2010 following a recommendation from the constitutional reform process that had taken place a decade earlier. The commission's establishment is part of the ostensible commitment on the part of the government to institutionalise gender equality and ensure that issues affecting the lives of women and girls are given prominence.

In Guyana, substantive representation is also adversely affected by class, race, and ethnic considerations, where there is a clear polarisation of the two main political parties along ethnic lines (Trotz 1996, 180). One interviewee observed that 'everything is driven by race and ethnic loyalties. The electoral system is based on ethnic manipulation.' Notwithstanding the colonial 'ethno-politicization' of Guyana and its persistence into the present, it is too easy to conclude that this is an over-determining situation, since it cannot explain certain moments of political inter-ethnic solidarity (Garner 2008, 35–36, 45). Certainly, the achievement, however limited, of the electoral gender quota, represents one such moment where women were able to mobilise their interests across party and racialised lines.

Nevertheless, the intersection of gender with class and ethnicity/race, determines the manner and impact of women's political participation, mirroring a process of exclusion experienced by other marginalised groups (Kudva 2003, 447). Mondesire and Dunn (1995) postulated that women's numerical power is, indeed, moderated by class, race, gender, and ethnicity in many societies (21). Realistically, though, it may not be possible to elect a woman to represent the unique interests of women *and* be present at the intersection of every social category (Paxton and Hughes 2007, 215). Women do not comprise a homogenous group, but are often represented by 'educated, middle-class, dominant-ethnicity women' (Mansbridge 2005, 634). This is generally true of Guyanese women parliamentarians. Recognising the heterogeneity of 'woman' as a category, a former parliamentarian[8] suggested that the inclusion of gender must properly consider women of different ages, backgrounds, and experiences, such as grass roots women, academics, and young and indigenous persons.

'Paramountcy' of the Party [9]

Another factor that affects increased numerical representation is institutionalism. It is possible to explain the behaviour of women parliamentarians in terms of the institution as represented by their political party (described locally and colloquially as 'party politics'). Furthermore, in the context of these institutions, being affected by factors of ethnicity/race, culture and class (despite specific legislative measures to address this), women seem to be left little choice in political participation and consequent decision-making. Several respondents noted the 'paramountcy' of the party as it affects the behaviour of female members.

According to one social activist, they are constrained by party politics to the point where they are 'owned by the party', which decides what they can do or say. One interviewee noted that 'when women MPs go in Parliament they will speak with the voice of their political party.' The leader of the WPA noted, 'Most of the progressive women I speak to say that women become parliamentarians and support the party whip and do not pursue women's issues. They suck their teeth at [view disdainfully] parliamentary representation of women.'

Another interviewee explained that in Guyana it is the party that is supreme, not women's issues. She continued, 'There is no interest in having a caucus; there is no championing of this particular cause by any of the parties.' It can be concluded that without the party's support, women shy away from forming a caucus. She also observed that 'immature, tribal politics' is what passes for politics in Guyana. 'Tribal' here, of course, reflects the ethno-politicised nature of the system. Others expressed similar sentiments: the party system is too strong, and race/party will often determine how parliamentarians behave, with the more vocal women even going so far as to act as 'guard dogs' for the parties in Parliament. One example that was highlighted was of then education minister, Priya Manickchand, who started with widespread consultations in 2008 on changing the law with respect to violence against women, and was able to elicit public response on the issue (Persadie 2014, 49). She was described as having become 'partyocratised', so much so that that this consultative behaviour waned over time (49). Some others felt 'that women want to be a part of a party' rather than to represent women.

The gender consultant suggested that when women MPs go to Parliament 'they speak with the voice of their political party' and that their 'parties tell them what to support. The fear of victimisation causes them to toe the party line.' Others voiced their frustration that women allowed themselves to become party pawns and consequently toed the party line as they were nurtured to think that if they want to get ahead politically this is what they had to do. In the same vein, they accepted the 'soft' ministries – social development, health, gender (see also Dube 2013, 205; United Nations 2005). No different from men in this regard, they are motivated by self-interest. Women who speak out are marginalised. Fear of job loss and discrimination were described as keeping women in check. This is 'the institution' at work. Gail Teixeira, PPP/C parliamentarian, was identified as one woman parliamentarian who promoted the gender agenda without fear of repercussion from her party's leadership, even risking her job by promoting the Medical Termination of Pregnancy Bill in Parliament. Her party was not happy with this move (neither was the Catholic lobby). Yet, her 'critical act' (Dahlerup 2006, 513) helped make the law a reality.

The comments on women's constrained political behaviour generally corroborate the fact that *inter alia*, institutionalism, in the form of party politics and even blind party loyalty, as well as patriarchy, continue to negatively affect women's desire and ability to participate in Guyanese politics in a way that would positively change the lived situation of women.

The Role of NGOs

NGOs are extremely important in advocating gender equality and women's rights. Women's NGOs question the status quo privileging men, which ultimately affects the possibility of the distribution of power benefiting women. Social transformation of this type is a much lengthier process with less readily visible results, which explains why the successes of women's NGOs tend to be low-key and difficult to attain (Meyer and Prügl 1999, 16), as evidenced by the quota adoption and associated challenges. NGOs create space for themselves within civil society, 'one of the most familiar grounds for feminist activists and women's NGOs' (Marchand and Runyan 2000, 20). Within this space, NGOs provide alternative decision-making structures that claim to allow for 'greater participation and broader democracy than other top-down institutional forms' (Tinker 1999, 94–95). Their most essential role is perhaps that of agents of change. Historically, it has been NGOs and private citizens, rather than states, which have served as prominent conduits of pressure and influence on state activity and policy regarding human rights (Clark 1995, 512). This influence can only be effective where these groups unify their efforts. This is reflective of what took place in Guyana around the adoption of the quota, as well as with other activities related to women's rights. It also highlights the tremendous potential that exists to push for the placement mandate.

In fact, NGOs were largely responsible for the amendments to the Sexual Offences Act in 2010 in Guyana (Persadie 2014, 50), but it is noted, with concern, that the Act is 'gender neutral' (Government of the Republic of Guyana, 13), even though the persons against whom these crimes are committed are largely female. Pamela Paxton and Melanie

Hughes postulated that the use of gender neutral language 'actually hides substantive gender inequality' and makes women invisible (2007, 3). Legal scholar, Tracy Robinson (2000), likened this attempt at gender neutrality to 'gender-blind or virtual equality', where equality is an abstraction causing women to appear as de-gendered, unsexed bodies, resulting in a failure to adequately address the substantive inequality that they face (4). Equality must recognise difference if it is to be meaningful.

NGOs also assist in educational efforts, such as explaining legal rights to the public in more simplified terms, as was done for the Sexual Offences Act (George 2012, 2016) and the Domestic Violence Act (Rockcliffe 2012). Between 1989 and 1991 CARICOM introduced a package of model legislation in six critical areas related to women's issues, which may have provided the foundation for some of these pieces of enacted legislation, especially given their year of enactment. The six issues that the model legislation package covered included citizenship, domestic violence, equal pay, inheritance, sexual harassment, and sexual offences. In 1991, CARICOM drafted additional model legislation that addressed equal opportunity and treatment in employment and maintenance. Since legislation was enacted in Guyana concerning such issues shortly after CARICOM drafted the model legislation, it is reasonable to surmise that CARICOM's efforts were highly influential in the process. No women parliamentarians, however, attempted to rectify the various flaws in these pieces of legislation to advance women's issues, suggesting again that increasing women's seats in Parliament does not necessarily equate to advancing women's issues in the country (Persadie 2014, 50).

Other pieces of legislation were enacted in the post-quota era, five of which specifically safeguard the rights of women (see Government of the Republic of Guyana 2014, 12–14), but it remains unclear what role Guyanese women parliamentarians actually played in the process of having these enacted.

Anecdotal evidence suggests that female parliamentarians have not necessarily introduced legislation that would benefit women but that it is the NGO movement that has been largely instrumental in driving this agenda (CARICOM-driven legislation aside). This was seen with the Sexual Offences Act, though it should be noted enactment would not have been possible without the unwavering support of then minister of human services and social security Priya Manickchand. In 2008, she spearheaded a nationwide 'Stamp It Out' campaign to deal with violence against women and children (Persadie 2014, 49). Ministerial support, together with sustained NGO efforts, was therefore crucial to achieving this success. While difficult, it is this type of meaningful and consistent collaboration between parliamentarians, whether female or male, and civil society, that can effect positive change for women.

Conclusion: Politics as Usual?

Women's unequal access to political space is deeply entrenched in strongly masculinist institutions, customs and beliefs across the world. While constructions of masculinity and femininity are both present in political institutions, the masculine ideal underpins institutional structures, practices and norms, shaping 'ways of valuing things, ways of behaving and ways of being...as well as constraining the expression and articulation of marginalised perspectives' (Mackay, Kenny and Chappell 2020, 582).

In Guyana, this has been further imbued by the colonial ethno-politicisation of social groups. Racial and ethnic considerations have become the foundation of political behaviour in Guyana under which class and culture and, lastly, gender are subsumed. Indo-Guyanese women, for example, are deemed to be more politically conservative than their Afro-Guyanese peers and therefore less willing to participate in politics or even show public support. This would be a direct consequence of their race/ethnicity, class and cultural heritage. Undoubtedly, even 'gender' is ranked (Paxton and Hughes 2007, 25) such that women fall to the lowermost echelons of the entire hierarchy.

Couched in this framework, it is not surprising that the rhetoric of inclusion has not translated into practice in any real manner. Political parties have permitted the creation of women's arms, but their work does not necessarily influence the work of the party, while the converse is true. Moreover, the statistics, as shown in table 14.3, leave much to be desired. Election after election has not seen any appreciable increase in women parliamentarians, despite promises made to change this. The numbers hover around the accepted one-third for the odd party, but generally fall below this level. Even the implementation of the 'true spirit' of the quota has been skilfully circumvented by the (what must be deliberate) legal loophole of not including a placement mandate with an accompanying sanction. Perhaps the adoption of the quota was merely a 'symbolic gesture' (Driscoll and Krook 2009, 243): it cost little and did not significantly improve the number of women in Parliament. For the few women who do make it into Parliament, their behaviour is generally constrained by party politics. The unequal balance of power enables men to determine the conditions of women's access to the political system (Driscoll and Krook 2009, 242) and their behaviour therein, which might include them having to toe the party line.

Nevertheless, it is clear that female parliamentarians play a key role in transforming politics and gendering the political agenda. Substantive representation, perhaps best measured through the enactment of legislation that advances women's rights, is possible, regardless of the number of female parliamentary representatives, as changes can be made once any issue is deemed significant enough. It only takes a few to push a particular topic for it see to legislative fruition. It can be done, and has been achieved in Guyana, as seen by the results of the collaborative efforts between parliamentarians and civil society concerning the enactment of the Sexual Offences Act.

What next? The reality is that the situation is unlikely to change in the near future, unless there is some exogenous shock to the system. Nevertheless, the feminisation of the party lists is certainly one step forward in the right direction. Ideational modification becomes crucial in eliminating deeply institutionalised and gendered notions of political representation. Education and gender sensitivity training starting with the very young are required for this transformation. This is where NGOs shoulder an incredibly important responsibility as agents of change. They allow the space for alternative views which are not always welcomed in traditional political parties and can help create an environment more conducive to gender inclusiveness. The leader of the WPA noted in 2012 that it now falls to civil society to work with parliamentarians and do educational work.

The work of NGOs and continued education and training provide answers outside of parliamentary representation with respect to gender equality generally and, more specifically, increasing women's participation in politics. The Guyana's Women Leadership Institute, as well as other organisations, play a critical role in actively involving more women in politics which is supplemented by the activities of the Women's Affairs Bureau (Persadie 2014, 55). As stated by Neema Kudva:

> The extent of women's formal participation in politics is an important marker for women's empowerment. The premise is that increasing women's participation in political processes, as both voters and candidates, will change the nature and functioning of public institutions, which will ultimately influence future development decisions and create a more equitable, gender-responsive and humane society (2003, 446).

This must be the goal.

Acknowledgements

The author wishes to thank the various people who helped in the data gathering stage, including everyone who so kindly afforded her the opportunity to interview them. These include Diana Swan-Lawrence, CEO, Women and Gender Equality Commission; Hazel Halley-Burnett, gender consultant; Justice Roxane George; Karen de Souza, founding member, Red Thread; Indranie Chanderpal, Freedom House; and Manzoor Nadir, The United Force. The author also wishes to express her gratitude to those who assisted with data collection, including Gwyneth George, university librarian, University of Guyana; Sandrene Harris, librarian, University of Guyana, and her staff; Michael Munroe, documentation research officer, Parliamentary Library and his staff; Kim Chung, communications supervisor, Congress House; and Allison Simmons, reference librarian, National Library. Many thanks also go to the editors of this collection for the invitation to contribute this chapter.

Notes

1. Emphasis added. 'Could' allows for upward flexibility, but it remains to be seen how this will be interpreted and implemented.
2. Birbalsingh commented that despite Mrs Jagan's important role in the PPP, this role was not 'associated with feminist issues in particular' (2007, 22). Such a conclusion would seem to suggest that she must have kept her PPP and WPEO interests separate, as she held the position of general secretary of the WPEO, which was 'concerned with the general conditions in the country, particularly in areas such as health, housing, and education, which had disproportionate effects on women and children' (D. Hinds 2011, 197). Mrs Jagan was well known for her feminist activity.
3. Analyses of voter behaviour for the 2016 US election results show this is not necessarily true, though.

4. Unfortunately, not all manifestos were available for review; neither were all available from all political parties for the period under review. Only those parties for which manifestos were available were included in the table. Political party headquarters generally only had recent manifestos. Indranie Chanderpal, for example, stated that the manifestos for the PPP were lost during the Freedom House fire of 2002 during a period of political unrest. Searches at the Caribbean Research Library of the University of Guyana yielded some of the earlier ones (before 2001). Other repositories of similar types of information, such as the Guyana Elections Commission (GECOM), the National Archives, and the National Library did not have any. The Parliament Library had very few.
5. This usage of distinct identities reflects the Parties' 2015 manifesto, in which they are treated separately and referred to consistently as 'APNU & AFC', and is also consistent with the APNU website where the AFC is not a named as a coalition partner.
6. Emphasis added.
7. While such exclusion is true for most other countries, Guyana's peculiar sociopolitical history made this decision possible during a period of extensive constitutional reform and widespread consultation (see Persadie generally).
8. It was with great sadness that the author learned in January 2016 of Deborah Backer's passing.
9. This is a play on Forbes Burnham's institution of the PNC as supreme over all other parties, institutions, and state agencies (Rose 2002, 194).

References

Alliance for Change. 2006. *Action Plan for Change and Development for Guyana*. Georgetown: Alliance for Change.

———. 2011. *Change is Coming: Action Plan for Guyana*. Georgetown: Alliance for Change.

Alliance for Guyana. 1997. *Guyana for Guyanese: Manifesto of the Alliance for Guyana WPA – GLP – Citizens*. Georgetown: Alliance for Guyana.

Backer, Deborah. 2012. Interview with author. Georgetown, Guyana.

Barrow-Giles, Cynthia. 2011. The Struggle for Women's Political Participation in the Caribbean. In *Women in Caribbean Politics*, ed. Cynthia Barrow-Giles, xi–xv. Kingston: Ian Randle Publishers.

Birbalsingh, Frank. 2007. *The People's Progressive Party of Guyana 1950–1992: An Oral History*. Hertfordshire: Hansib Publications.

Bureau of Women's Affairs (Gender Affairs) Kingston, Jamaica and the Gender Advisory Committee. 2011. *National Policy for Gender Equality (NPGE): Jamaica*. Kingston, Jamaica: The Bureau of Women's Affairs (Gender Affairs).

Catzim-Sanchez, Adele. 2010. *National Gender Policy: Situation Analysis of Gender Issues in Belize*. Belize City: National Women's Commission.

———. 2013. The Revised National Gender Policy (Updated Version 2013). National Women's Commission, Belize City.

Chanderpal, Indranie. 2012. Interview with author. Georgetown, Guyana.
Clark, Ann Marie. 1995. Non-Governmental Organizations and Their Influence on International Society. *Journal of International Affairs* 48, no. 2 (Winter): 507–25.
Dahlerup, Drude. 2006. The Story of the Theory of Critical Mass. *Politics & Gender* 2, no. 4: 511–22.
De Souza, Karen. 2016. Interview with author. Georgetown, Guyana.
Devlin, Claire, and Robert Elgie. 2008. The Effect of Increased Women's Representation in Parliament: The Case of Rwanda. *Parliamentary Affairs* 61, no. 2:237–54.
Driscoll, Amanda, and Mona Lena Krook. 2009. 'Can There be a Feminist Rational Choice Institutionalism?' *Politics & Gender* 5, no. 2:238–45.
Dube, Thulani. 2013. Engendering Politics and Parliamentary Representation in Zimbabwe. *Journal of African Studies and Development* 5, no. 8 (December): 200–07.
Folke, Olle and Johanna Rickne. n.d. Female Representation but Male Rule? Elite Entrenchment, Gender Quotas and the Political Glass Ceiling. Accessed July 23, 2017. http://www.lse.ac.uk/government/research/resgroups/PSPE/pdf/Folke.pdf.
Forbes, Marcia. n.d. The 51% Coalition – Development & Empowerment through Equity. *Marcia Forbes: Media Matters*. Accessed November 15, 2016. http://www.marciaforbes.com/article/51 – coalition – %E2%80%93 – development – empowerment – through – equity.
Garboni, Emanuela Simona. 2015. The Impact of Descriptive Representation on Substantive Representation of Women at European and National Parliamentary Levels. Case Study: Romania. *Procedia – Social and Behavioral Sciences* 183:85–92.
Garner, Steve. 2008. *Guyana 1838–1985: Ethnicity, Class and Gender*. Kingston: Ian Randle Publishers.
GECOM. 2016. About Guyana. Accessed April 5, 2016. http://www.gecom.org.gy/guyana.html.
George, Roxane. 2012. Written comments sent via email.
———. 2016 and 2012. Interview with author. Georgetown, Guyana.
Government of the Republic of Guyana. 2014. *National Review of the Implementation of the Beijing Declaration and Platform for Action (1995) and the Outcomes of the Twenty – third Special Session on the General Assembly (2000)*. Georgetown: Government of the Republic of Guyana.
Guyana Chronicle. 2015. President Calls for Comprehensive Approach to Gender Equality. August 28. Accessed April 2, 2016, from http://guyanachronicle.com/president – calls – for – comprehensive – approach – to – gender – equality.
Guyana Democratic Party. 1997. *The Way Forward! Programmes & Policies for a Prosperous Guyana*. Georgetown: Guyana Democratic Party.
Halder, Nomita. 2004. Female Representation in Parliament: A Case Study from Bangladesh. *New Zealand Journal of Asian Studies* 6, no. 1: (June): 27–63.

Halley-Burnett, Hazel. 2016 and 2012. Interview with author. Georgetown, Guyana.

Hinds, Bronagh. 2015. *Strategies for Increased Participation of Women in Leadership across the Commonwealth*. London: Commonwealth Secretariat.

Hinds, David. 2011. Janet Jagan and the Politics of Ethnicity in Guyana. In *Women in Caribbean Politics*, ed. Cynthia Barrow-Giles, 195–208. Kingston: Ian Randle Publishers.

Inter-Parliamentary Union. 2016. Women in National Parliaments. Updated February 1, 2016. Accessed March 4, 2016. http://www.ipu.org/wmn – e/world.htm.

Jamaica Houses of Parliament. 2016. Senators. Accessed April 9, 2016. http://www.japarliament.gov.jm/index.php#.

Jamaica Information Service. 2016. Members of Parliament. Accessed April 9, 2016. http://jis.gov.jm/government/members – of – parliament.

Jamaica Observer. 2012. All Woman. 1-year-old 51% Coalition Working to Address Gender Imbalance. Accessed November 15, 2016. http://www.jamaicaobserver.com/magazines/allwoman/1–year–old– 51–Coalition–working–to–address–gender–imbalance.

Johnson, Robert. 2002. *National Gender Policy: Belize*. Belize City: National Women's Commission.

Kaieteur News. 2016. Govt to Present National Gender Policy this year. Accessed April 2, 2016. http://www.kaieteurnewsonline.com/2016/02/01/govt-to-present-national-gender-policy- this-year.

Kilkenny, Roberta. 1984. Women in Social and Political Struggle: British Guiana, 1946–1953. Presented at the Sixteenth Annual Conference of Caribbean Historians, Barbados, April 8–13.

Krook, Mona Lena. 2006. Gender Quotas, Norms, and Politics. *Politics & Gender* 2, no. 1:110–18.

——. 2015. *Gender and Elections: Temporary Special Measures beyond Quotas*. Conflict Prevention and Peace Forum. CPPF Working Papers on Women in Politics No. 4, Rutgers University.

Kudva, Neema. 2003. Engineering Elections: The Experiences of Women in Panchayati Raj in Karnataka, India. *International Journal of Politics, Culture and Society* 16, no. 3 (Spring): 445–63.

Lawless, Jennifer, and Richard Fox. 2012. *Men Rule: The Continued Under-Representation of Women in US Politics*. Washington, DC: Women & Politics Institute.

Leterme, Yves. 2016. How We Work to Promote Gender Equality. *International IDEA*. Accessed March 2016, from http://www.idea.int/about/secretary – general/how – we – work – to – promote – gender – equality.cfm.

Lowndes, Vivien. 2002. Institutionalism. In *Theory and Methods in Political Science*, ed. David, 90–108. Marsh and Gerry Stoker. Basingstoke: Palgrave MacMillan.

Mackay, Fiona, Meryl Kenny and Louise Chappell. 2010. New Institutionalism through a Gender Lens: Towards a Feminist Institutionalism? *International Political Science Review* 31, no. 5:573–88.

Mackay, Fiona and Petra Meier. 2003. Institutions, Change and Gender-Relations: Towards a New Feminist Institutionalism? Prepared for the Joint Sessions of European Consortium of Political Research 2003, Workshop 23.

Mansbridge, Jane. 2005. Quota Problems: Combating the Dangers of Essentialism. *Politics & Gender* 1, no. 4:622–38.

March, James, and Johan Olsen. 2005. Elaborating the "New Institutionalism". Working Paper, No. 11 of March 2005. Arena, Centre for European Studies, University of Oslo.

Marchand, Marianne, and Anne Runyun. 2000. Feminist Sightings of Global Restructuring: Conceptualizations and Reconceptualizations. In *Gender and Global Restructuring: Sightings, Sites and Resistances*, ed. Marianne Marchand and Anne Runyun, 1–22. London: Routledge.

McAlmont, Cecilia. 2002. Guyanese Women in Non-Governmental Organisations: The period before 1975. *Stabroek News*, November 14. Accessed March 30, 2016. http://www.landofsixpeoples.com/news022/ns2111414.htm.

———. 2011. The Participation of Guyanese Women in Politics and Parliament during the Administration of the People's National Congress. *History in Action* 2, no. 1 (April): 1–7.

McCormack, Mike. 2012. Interview with author. Georgetown, Guyana.

Meyer, Mary, and Elisabeth Prügl. 1999. Gender Politics in Global Governance. In *Gender Politics in Global Governance*, ed. Mary Meyer and Elisabeth Prügl, 3–18. Lanham, MD: Rowman and Littlefield.

Ministry of Social Protection. 2015. National Gender Policy Conference Report Theme: 'Equal Rights for All: Be Good to People.' Arthur Chung Convention Centre, Liliendaal, Guyana.

Mondesire, Alicia and Leith Dunn. 1995. *Towards Equity in Development: A Report on The Status of Women in Sixteen Commonwealth Caribbean Countries*. Georgetown: CARICOM.

Nadir, Mansoor. 2016. Interview with author. Georgetown, Guyana.

Nanivadekar, Medha. 2006. Are Quotas a Good Idea? The Indian Experience with Reserved Seats for Women. *Politics & Gender* 2, no. 1:119–28.

Nettles, Kimberly. 2007. Becoming Red Thread Women: Alternative Visions of Gendered Politics in Post-independence Guyana. *Social Movement Studies* 6, no. 1 (May): 57–82.

Parker, Khyle. 2011A. Gender Quotas: Do They Work? *Bahamas Weekly*, April 19. Accessed November 15, 2016. http://www.thebahamasweekly.com/publish/bis – newsupdates/Gender_Quotas_Do_They_Work15535.shtml.

———. 2011B. Minister Open to Gender Quota, Region Focuses on Gender Parity. *Bahamas Weekly*, April 11. Accessed November 15, 2016. http://www.thebahamasweekly.com/publish/international/Minister_Open_To_Gender_Quota_Region_Focuses_On_Gender_Parity15381.shtml.

Parliament Library of Guyana. 2016. Members of Parliament from 1966 to Present. Copy with author.

Partnership for National Unity, A. 2011. *A Good Life for All Guyanese*. Georgetown: Partnership for National Unity.

Partnership for National Unity, A, and Alliance for Change Coalition (APNU and AFC). 2015. *Manifesto: Elections 2015.* Georgetown: APNU & AFC.
Paxton, Pamela, and Melanie Hughes. 2007. *Women, Politics and Power: A Global Perspective.* Los Angeles, CA: Pine Forge Press.
Peake, Linda. 1993. The Development & Role of Women's Political Organizations in Guyana. In *Women & Change in the Caribbean: A Pan-Caribbean Perspective*, ed. Janet Momsen, 109–31. Kingston: Ian Randle Publishers.
Peake, Linda, and D. Alissa Trotz. 1999. *Gender, Ethnicity and Place: Women and Identities in Guyana.* London: Routledge.
People's Progressive Party. 1964. *Manifesto: General Election – December 7, 1964.* Georgetown, Guyana: People's Progressive Party.
Persadie, Natalie. 2014. Getting to One-Third? Creating Legislative Access for Women to Political Space in Guyana. In *Politics, Power and Gender Justice in the Anglophone Caribbean: Women's Understandings of Politics, Experiences of Political Contestation and the Possibilities for Gender Transformation IDRC Research Report 106430 – 001*, by Principal Investigator Gabrielle Jamela Hosein and Lead Researcher Jane Parpart. Ottawa, ON Canada: International Development Research Centre.
Persaud, Vidyanand. 1999. Addendum to the Report of the Sub-Committee to the Constitution Reform Committee. No. 5, June 15.
Phillips, Anne. 1998. Democracy and Representation: Or, Why Should it Matter Who our Representatives Are? In *Feminism and Politics*, ed. Anne Phillips, 224–40. Oxford: Oxford University Press.
PNC. 1992. *Development, Social Harmony and Prosperity with Hugh Desmond Hoyte.* Georgetown: Peoples' National Congress.
———. 1997. *The PNC Plan for a Stronger Guyana.* Georgetown: Peoples' National Congress.
———. 2001. *The Modernisation of Guyana with the PNC Reform.* Georgetown: Peoples' National Congress.
PNCR – 1G. 2006. *Move Forward with 1 Guyana.* Georgetown: Peoples' National Congress.
Pollard, Magda. 2012. Interview with author. Georgetown, Guyana.
PPP/Civic. 1997. *Consolidating Democracy and Unity for Continuous Progress.* Georgetown: Peoples' Progressive Party.
———. 1992. *Time for Change, Time to Rebuild. Manifesto Elections 1992.* Georgetown: Peoples' Progressive Party.
———. 2001. *Let's Protect Our Gains and Accelerate Progress Together.* Georgetown: Peoples' Progressive Party.
———. 2011. *Working Together for a Better Tomorrow.* Georgetown: Peoples' Progressive Party.
———. 2015. *Our Vision: Guyana Version 2.0.* Georgetown: Peoples' Progressive Party.
Radzik, Vanda. 2012. Interview with author. Georgetown, Guyana.
The *Reporter*. 2013. WIN Belize supports 2013 Gender Policy. July 22. Accessed November 15, 2016. http://www.reporter.bz/general/win – belize – supports – 2013 – gender – policy.

Reuters. 2016. UN Report: Jamaica Slow to Put Women in Positions of Political Power. VOA. March 9. Accessed November 18, 2016. http://www.voanews.com/a/un – report – jamaica – slow – to – put – women – in – positions – of – political – power/3227968.html.

Robinson, Tracy. 2000. Fictions of Citizenship, Bodies without Sex: The Production and Effacement of Gender in Law. *Small Axe* 7 (March): 1–27.

Rockcliffe, Abena. 2012. Red Thread Produces 'household guide' on Sexual Offences Act. *Kaieteur News*, DATE. Accessed October 19, 2012. http://www.kaieteurnewsonline.com/2012/09/29/red – thread – produces – household – guide – onsexual – offences – act.

Roopnaraine, Rupert. 2012. Interview with author. Georgetown, Guyana.

Rose, Euclide. 2002. *Dependency and Socialism in the Modern Caribbean: Superpower Intervention in Guyana, Jamaica, and Grenada, 1970–1985*. Lanham, MD: Lexington Books.

Singh, Moneeta. 2000. Janet Jagan: An Outstanding Woman in Guyanese Politics. In *An Introductory Reader for Women's Studies in Guyana*, ed. Hazel Woolford, 153–58. Georgetown Guyana: CAFRA Guyana Chapter.

Steinmo, Sven. 2001. Institutionalism. In *International Encyclopedia of the Social and Behavioral Sciences*, ed. Nelson Polsby. London: Elsevier Science.

Swan-Lawrence, Diana. 2016. Interview with author. Georgetown, Guyana.

Tinker, Irene. 1999. Nongovernmental Organizations: An Alternative Power Base for Women? In *Gender Politics in Global Governance*, ed. Mary Meyer and Elisabeth Prügl, 88–104. Lanham, MD: Rowman and Littlefield.

Trotman, Anande. 2012. Interview with author via Skype.

Trotz, Alissa. 1996. Gender, Ethnicity and Familial Ideology in Georgetown, Guyana: Household Structure and Female Labour Force Participation Reconsidered. *European Journal of Development Research* 8, no. 1 (June): 177–99.

United Force, The. 1964. *Highway to Happiness: A Declaration of Ideas and Policies for Guianese Progress*. Georgetown, United Force.

———. 1992. *Manifesto for the Nineties: Towards a Brighter Future: Highways to Happiness II*. Georgetown: United Force Guyana.

———. 1997. *Leadership into the Twenty First Century*. Georgetown: United Force.

———. 2006. *The Road to Prosperity*. Georgetown: United Force.

———. 2011. *Agenda for Development*. Georgetown: United Force.

———. 2015. *Manifesto 2015: Action Agenda*. Georgetown: United Force.

United Nations. 2016. Sustainable Development Goals: 17 Goals to Transform Our World. Department of Public Information. Accessed March 8, 2016. http://www.un.org/sustainabledevelopment/sustainable-development-goals.

———. 2005. *Equal Participation of Women and Men in Decision-Making Processes, with Particular Emphasis on Political Participation and Leadership, Division for the Advancement of Women (DAW), Department of Economic and Social Affairs (DESA), Economic Commission for Africa (ECA), Inter-Parliamentary Union (IPU). EGM/EPDM /2005/REPORT*. Report of the Expert Group Meeting, Addis-Ababa, Ethiopia, October 24–27.

Woolford, Hazel. 2000. African-Guyanese Female Politicians: 1946–1992. In *An Introductory Reader for Women's Studies in Guyana*, ed. Hazel Woolford, 119–52. Georgetown: CAFRA Guyana Chapter.

WPA. 1985. *WPA Manifesto for the Redemption, Reconstruction and Rebirth of Guyana.* Georgetown: Working Peoples' Alliance.

———. 1992. *WPA Manifesto: Justice, Opportunity, Security for a Multiracial Guyana.* Georgetown: Working Peoples' Alliance.

15.
'Push Ya' Body': Imaginaries of the 'Bush' and the Amerindian Body in the Guyanese State

Shanya Cordis

On September 3, 2015, Guyana's newly elected A Partnership for National Unity and the Alliance for Change (APNU-AFC) coalition government convened a public forum with attendees from all sectors – distinguished government and state officials, civil society, non-governmental organisations, and international dignitaries – calling for inter-ethnic unity, reconciliation, and social cohesion.

As the overhead lights darkened and warm yellow light illuminated the centre of the brimming amphitheatre, the murmuring conversations fell to a hush; the sound of drums echoed and reverberated staccato rhythms. Several dancers descended the stairs to the makeshift stage, green skirts twirling and assembling into a seated circle. A woman pursued the set of dancers, her fiery red skirt flaring around her body, undulating with purposeful steps to the beat. A seemingly disembodied voice pierced the darkness, narrating the story of the emergence of the earth:

> ...and then came the children of the sun, strong like the drum. And the children walked across the land to every corner of the earth...and they were one.

The drums momentarily quieted, the dancers' lithe movements emulating the softened rhythm as the narrator continued:

> They went from place to place and gave the lands they wandered many names. But the earth was one *and they were one.*[1] Over time, these "children" dispersed across the lands, losing contact with each other: They changed and forgot that they had brothers and sisters all across the Earth, so that when they saw each other again, they thought they were strangers and they fought with each other and enslaved one another and tried to hurt one another. And some of them found a beautiful land, filled with waters, with rivers, with creeks, with waterfalls and rapids. The land of many waters...Guyana.

A male dancer in flowing white pants mirrored the female dancer's arabesque motions, until he, alone, remained:

> And through times they fought with each other because they had forgotten they were one. But one of their own remembered, and sacrificed himself so that they could all remember. He was named Kaie, and his legend lives on in the name of the falls over which he went, the beautiful and majestic Kaieteur.

***

So begins the *social cohesion roundtable*, a mythical reimagining of the nation's origins and a projected pathway toward healing the lingering wounds of divisive racial violence between dominant African and (East) Indian groups, or *Creoles*.[2] Notably, this violence is reconciled through indigenous sacrifice in the figure of Kaie. During his opening address, newly elected Guyanese President David A. Granger reiterated his promise to eliminate 'ethnic insecurity', and 'deepen national consciousness' by engendering socio-economic and class parity through targeted initiatives to address 'spatial segregation' between the centrally populated coast and the interior, or hinterlands to the south.[3]

The coalition government's national elections' win ostensibly signalled a 'democratic transformation'[4] that would revitalise an ailing Guyanese nationalism and the bankrupt promise of full independence, in effect exorcising the haunting afterlife of colonialism. The new government advanced a discourse of reconciliation along racial/ethnic and political lines as the fulcrum of a cohesive society, generating favourable conditions for economic development that would advance the 'good life' for all Guyanese citizens. Paramount in this vision of harmonious bounty, the land prefigures as an inheritance for all to share equally. Oriented around the principle of an 'inclusionary democracy', the newly created ministry of social cohesion suggested a multi-racial, multicultural society transcending the separatism of the past and moving towards realising the national motto, 'One Nation, One People, One Destiny'. This principle reflects the national anxiety surrounding the inherited stains of colonialism that continue to shape the post-independence ethno-political landscape (Williams 1991; Premdas 1995).

With notable exceptions, questions of space (Hennessey 2013; Trotz and Roopnaraine 2009) and the racialised gendered female body (Peake and Trotz 1999; Trotz 2004) remain absent in our efforts to comprehend what is at stake in how identity and difference are produced in the post-1966 Guyanese state. Indigenous peoples occupy a marginal position in the Guyanese imaginary and scholarship, which remain largely overdetermined by framings of ethno-political conflict between dominant African and Indian groups. Even less attention has been given to the undergirding representations of the geospatial landscape of the hinterland as 'bush,' and the ascribed racial-sexual images of the peoples who dwell there. As I will argue, these ideologies maintain Amerindian marginalisation, with particular gendered implications for the Amerindian woman.

Drawing on ethnographic fieldwork and interviews I conducted in the lower Cuyuni-Mazaruni (Region 7) from January 2015 to June 2016, and analysis of indigenous recognition policies implemented at the inception and post-independence period of 1966, this chapter attends to the impacts of shifting recognition policies toward Amerindians within increasingly neoliberal forms of governance in Guyana. It maps how spatial and social orderings maintain indigenous marginalisation, placing them within what I refer to as zones of corporeal-spatial precarity. While Amerindians in Guyana are ostensibly rights-bearing subjects through indigenous state recognition, I argue that spatial (re)ordering (through collective land titling processes) and representations of Amerindian peoples coalesce to subject them to national imperatives of social cohesion, integration, and national progress and development. This reading of Guyana's landscape gestures toward rethinking territory not as a static abstraction but rather as multiscalar processes that illuminate how state power works *through* spatial acts that make governable the indigenous population, what Marjo Lindroth has termed 'biopolitical collectivities' (Lindroth 2014, 342, 346). These land/body processes manifest in gendered and racialised ways, naturalising and (em)placing particular bodies to specific spaces, most visible in the segmented coast/hinterland cartography. In the following sections, I examine what I call the unthought position of indigenous peoples in the national imaginary. As such, this chapter challenges the hegemonic assumption that recognition necessarily secures indigenous self-determination; rather, it extends an inherited colonial condition that marginalises indigenous livelihoods.

Kaie's Sacrifice and the Unthought Position

At the level of discourse, the opening cultural exposition at the *social cohesion roundtable* reveals what might be called the unthought position of the Amerindian subject[5] within the national imaginary: a figure situated in a simultaneous position of hypervisibility and invisibility. The showcase depicts the possibility of a historically elusive cohesion, yet paradoxically, the very inclusivity it purports to represent by foregrounding the elements of *Guyaneseness* –primarily Africans, (East) Indians, and Amerindians – is tenuously achieved by this 'absence/presence' of the Amerindian subject, Kaie. Based on Guyanese poet A.J. Seymour's famous poem, *The Legend of Kaieteur*, the showcase reimagines Seymour's version, which is itself a retelling of the local indigenous Patamona legend. The poem narrates the legend of Kaie, a Patamona leader, who in an act of heroic sacrifice to Makonaima, the Great Spirit, paddles over the roaring falls (known today as the iconic Kaieteur Falls) in order to save his people and restore peace between two warring indigenous nations. In other versions, it is disease and not war that has afflicted the Patamona nation, calling for Kaie's death to appease Makonaima. In another, perhaps less romantic version, members of Kaie's nation push his canoe over the falls, having grown tired of caring for an old man whose feet have become diseased with chigoes. Seymour himself foregrounds the heroic deed – Kaie's sacrifice to restore peace between the 'savage Caribishi'[6] and his Patamona peoples, in which Kaie becomes immortalised in the landscape as a jutting rock at the outcrop of the world's widest single drop waterfall. Kaie's (re)imagined sacrifice as the impetus for reconciliation between the two warring 'nations', (in this case African and Indian 'nations'), points to the unthought position of the Amerindian subject in national development discourses that purport to foster inclusion. It is telling that Kaie's bodily (and spiritual) sacrifice is the enabling condition for Guyanese advancement – the redeemer of an elusive postcolonial futurity.

Even as a promising vision of alterity from inherited colonial racial/sexual hierarchies, in which they 'remember they were one,' the narrative excludes the Amerindian figure from the realisation of this oneness through a symbolic and literal death: Kaie's role as a sacrificial hero is represented as a voluntary disappearance into the land. Kaie, as a racial-spatial figure and embodiment of a pre-colonial moment, becomes the catalyst for the rebirth of a new *Guyaneseness*. The subsequent (dis)placement of Kaie through his self-sacrifice reflects the notion that his radical alterity, presumably untouched by colonial and post-independence discord, makes him the perfect conduit for the collective healing of a fractured nation. Further, it elides colonial and indigenous social and political entanglements and depoliticises indigenous issues by framing them as merely *cultural bearers* with no political investments in the contemporary political landscape (Moreno 2009, 145–53).

The placement of the indigenous subject within this narrative not only reflects 'coastlander ambivalence' about the hinterland and how it should be managed and incorporated but also the power of the state, and those who benefit, to re-place indigenous landscapes (Trotz and Roopnaraine 2009, 25; Hennessy 2013, 1245). As argued in one analysis of the hinterland as captured within coastlander subjectivity, namely 'porkknockers'[7] circulating discourses, these stories conjure the time-space of the interior and through its circulation as 'a story about a story about a story' construct a body of meaning (Trotz and Roopnaraine 2009, 23). Similarly, the showcase functions as a myth about a myth about a myth, in which Patamona people's meanings of Kaieteur Falls as a *living place* is displaced and reimagined within the coastlander imaginary. Through a sense of nostalgic benediction, Kaie represents Guyanese oneness *and* essentialising difference, revealing a search for Guyanese spirit through the Amerindian figure.

Kaie's sacrifice, noble in its pure act of selflessness, functions as paradox; while Kaie lives on in the place of Kaieteur Falls, immortalised in the cartography of the land, he ultimately does not live to partake in the reconciliation engendered through his self-effacement. In the *spirit* of oneness, Kaie facilitates a social cohesion that ultimately excludes him. Recast as open-handed sacrifice, performed with humble and infallible acquiescence reminiscent of colonial tropes of Amerindians as docile, noble *Others*, it reinscribes the very racial/spatial hierarchy it seeks to dissolve. Rather than integrate, the story re-establishes the Amerindian subject at the bottom of an enduring colonial racial hierarchy. This (re) imagining begs the question, what place do indigenous peoples truly have within development discourse and how does Guyana envision itself to itself? What does it mean to imagine social cohesion through the act of Amerindian sacrifice? Through ethnography and interviews conducted in several Amerindian villages in the lower Cuyuni-Mazaruni region and discursive analysis of indigenous governing policies, the following sections map how ideas of the 'bush' and the neoliberal spatial logics that inform indigenous recognition enable the state to retain territorial authority over indigenous geographies.

The Gold Bush Gateway

In the 'gold bush gateway', where the dark waters of the Essequibo, Mazaruni, and Cuyuni rivers converge and diverge, overlapping river boundaries serve as highways to the backdam[8] where speedboats, guided by skilful boat captains, traverse the river channels. The mythical search for the lost city of gold, *El Dorado*, chronicled in Walter Raleigh's infamous 1596 account *Discoverie of Guiana*, indelibly marks the social imaginary of the region. Known administratively as Region 7, the Cuyuni-Mazaruni is home to the mining town of Bartica, where Creole coastlanders, Brazilians, and Amerindians alike pursue the possibility of vast wealth. After many years of observation and journeys during the rainy and dry seasons, young men draw on embodied knowledge in order to read the river's cyclical rhythms to navigate powerful speedboats through tumultuous rapids and rocky terrain. This labour is undeniably dangerous as I observed during several speedboat ventures through the Cuyuni River, where shattered remains of boats broken up by jutting rocks and perforated and splintered wood lay abandoned in the river. A lone shop served as a brief rest stop for boatmen carrying miners into the backdam. Long iron boats sloshed through the river at much slower speeds, emptied out grey whales filled with barrels of fuel from Bartica to unknown destinations up the river to replenish ongoing dredge operations. This flow of traffic is interspersed with logging activities, as timber of various species were cut in uniform pieces to form a floating raft; men alternately lounged on thick logs, or stood, feet bracing the wood, while water deflected light into weathered, fatigued faces. Alongside the constant movement and humming were moments of deep silence.

'When people hear bush, they see gold,' a villager from the mouth of the Cuyuni River told me thoughtfully as we navigated the river, 'whitened' from 'missiles' (river mining dredges). The rumbling murmur of the 15-HP speedboat gently propelled us forward. Despite the village's complaints to the Ministry of Amerindian Affairs[9] about missiles in the waterway, they remained a constant presence, altering the cartography of the river with huge mounds of sediment 'beaches' formed as a result of the powerful suctioning force of gravel pumps, which vacuumed material from the riverbed in search of gold.[10] 'I hear a man from Georgetown has a claim to this river,' he said as he waved his arm in a sweeping gesture. As a riverine community, the village heavily relied on the river for subsistence fishing and farming and everyday activities like cooking, bathing, and washing clothes. During the unusually dry season, many turned to the river for drinking water. However, the government continues to grant licensing 'claims' for dredging operations. These claims are designated sections of the river cordoned off by fluid boundaries rather than rigid land coordinates, making it difficult to decipher if missiles actually operate within bounds.

The village received its land title in 2015, immediately preceding the national elections in May. Despite having secured land title, the village had no decision-making input on the locations of river or land dredges, as water and subsurface minerals remain property of the state. The village was undergoing the second phase of securing absolute collective title: demarcation of the land. Officials from the Lands and Surveys Commission, along with select members of the community, would venture inland on both sides of the river to cut boundary lines into the land, an endeavour that drew on the collective memory of village land use. Despite providing a detailed description, nearly a third of the village was left out of the land title, putting villagers in the position where they will need to re-apply for an extension of lands they already occupied, with no guarantee of its approval.

The former toshao, Trevor Stephens, in a personal conversation, relayed the uncertainties the village continued to face, even with village title.[11] We sat in the shade of a coconut tree overlooking the river. He leaned over, swiftly drew several vertical lines indicating the river and drew a larger rectangular outline – the boundary of the village lands.

'When I was village toshao, we talked about applying for title [for the village], which some didn't agree with, you know.' Many had viewed individual leasing as more 'secure' than title. Yet as Stephens described, 'it's just like you renting the land from the state, so there's no guarantee, where[as] a title is you own land, ...but a *lease* is like you renting an apartment.' He paused, then explained that while titled villages exercised a certain level of control and self-governance, the discovery of subsurface mineral resources in the area, whether on land or water, made the village vulnerable to land annexation for the expansion of extractive industries, which could mean village relocation or remapping of its boundaries.

> Some people look at it as we got we rights, yes, but when you get this reservation you still don't get control because if they find a piece of gold here, people can come in and take back a piece of land on the reservation. But…you got to try and push ya' body.

He then remarked incredulously that another village down the river had recently undergone land demarcation several years after receiving titled status. Similarly, their boundaries did not accurately reflect the provided description. Half of the village was left out of the demarcation process.

These accounts reflect colonial and post-1966 governments' policy of rescinding land titles when new diamond or gold shouts signalled the potential for mineral wealth, particularly in the Upper Mazaruni District (Amerindian Peoples Association (APA) 1999; APA, Upper Mazaruni Amerindian District Council, and the Forest People's Programme 2000). Further, it underscores the contested and sometimes arbitrary nature of mapping. As a small-scale miner remarked: 'governing bodies such as the GGMC[12] and the Lands and Surveys Commission have poor communication [between government entities],'[13] exacerbating ongoing land conflicts not only between indigenous communities and miners but also *between* miners through overlapping boundaries and inaccurate demarcations. Underlining these mapping practices is a colonial cartography that frames indigenous land struggles as a problem to be managed.

Moreover, much of the local economy was oriented toward the demands of miners traversing through the riverine community; from chicken farms to rum shops, mining dominated the local economy. Stephens explained that many of the jobs available to villagers revolved around the mining industry and, to a lesser extent, forestry, with the majority of medium and large-scale operations conducted by coastlanders or Brazilians with the capital to buy expensive equipment such as excavators. Describing his experiences working 'topside,'[14] he nodded emphatically: 'The backdam is another world. It's a world within a world.' His statement echoed the imaginary of the hinterland as a 'cowboy landscape' of excess plagued by lawlessness, disorder, and violence, but also teeming with untapped wealth. These images underline much of the discourse surrounding the 'bush', an imaginary of the interior that extends to the bodies occupying that space. As another villager recounted, perceptions of the bush shape how Amerindian people are treated: 'when they see [that] you [are] from the interior, they try to take advantage because you come from "gold bush" area. Some would make joke and say the bush must be burning' (upon seeing Amerindians in the coastal capital of Georgetown). These 'bush'/hinterland and coastal imaginaries reflect a bifurcated landscape, in which Amerindians are portrayed as out of place.

In his analysis of the coastlander imaginary toward the hinterland, T. Roopnaraine (in Trotz and Roopnarine 2009) examines the experiences of porkknockers.[15] Through bodily experiential knowledge, a 'physical hardening of the flesh' and gradual acquisition of the knowledge required to labour and live in the hinterland, he argues that *being* in the hinterland constitutes a hermeneutic 'shaped by the collision of a coastlander ontology with a world of radical difference, both physically and culturally' (Trotz and Roopnaraine 2009, 25). Through a process of self-transformation, coastlanders reconcile 'a series of contradictions and negative polarities' that underline their ambivalence toward the hinterland: 'thus poverty becomes wealth, disorientation becomes familiarity, the wild becomes the dominated and constraint becomes freedom.'[16] In the next section, I examine how this ambivalence manifests within indigenous recognition policies, revealing the coloniality of recognition[17] that structures state-indigenous relations and delimits indigenous self-determination.

(Post)Colonial Legalities and the Amerindian Act

The Guyanese state's ambivalence toward the hinterland has its origins in the policy of 'benign neglect' which Dutch and British colonisers adopted toward the interior, with the exception of a few trading posts. Rather, colonial authorities concentrated sugar and rice plantations on the coastal strip of land, which was expanded through the exploitation of enslaved Africans and later, indentured Indians' labour. Though indigenous lands had not been ceded or relinquished to the British colonial administration through conquest or treaty, nonetheless, as 'empty lands' they were annexed as Crown Lands. This unofficial policy of benign neglect shifted with the 1902 Aboriginal Indians Protection Ordinance which established ten reservations and appointed a Protector of Indians as guardian of the indigenous population. The succeeding 1910 Aboriginal Indian Ordinance further entrenched a guiding principle of paternalism and asserted colonial power and sovereignty, denigrating indigenous groups to the status of wards of the state. These ordinances did not confer reservation ownership, but rather were 'designated as safe zones and could therefore be recovered by colonial officials' (Ifill 2009, 6).

The subsequent Amerindian Ordinance of 1951 granted provisions for state management of indigenous peoples, erecting what Butt-Colson has called the 'administrative annexation' of Amerindian peoples and their territories' (cited in Colchester 2005, 280–81). The Act reconfigured residence patterns through an imposed centralised democratic system of governance, whereby reservations were renamed Amerindian Districts and fell under the management of the Department of the Interior (280–81). During independence negotiations with British authorities, one condition agreed upon regarding the land rights of Amerindian peoples was the granting of 'legal ownership to the lands where they were "ordinarily resident or settled,"' explicitly linking the transferal of colonial sovereignty to the emerging Guyanese state (Annex C, Section L of 1965 Guyana Independence Agreement).

The 1966 Amerindian Lands Commission (ALC) conducted a comprehensive survey of Amerindian land claims, publishing a report in 1969 that made recommendations for land titling for the majority of Amerindian communities. However, the recommendations reflected substantially smaller territorial claims than those made by Amerindian communities to the commission, calling on the government to grant 24,000 square miles of land out of a requested 43,000 square miles (Amerindian Lands Commission 1969). As part of the encompassing power of colonialism, 'the colonial state had stealthily assimilated the Amerindians as its subjects and then claimed frontiers against other colonial states, on the basis of extending the protections of British law and order over them' (Colchester 2005, 279).

Not until the international controversy of the Mazaruni hydropower project in 1976, and subsequent indigenous mobilisation against the proposed project, did the state act to uphold its legal obligation outlined in the independence agreement with the amendment of the 1951 Amerindian Act. Significantly, the amended Act 'provid[ed] Amerindians with community title and the right to administer their areas through their captains and councils' (Colchester 2005, 285). The 1976 amendments included limited self-governance through democratically elected Village Councils; however, under the law, the state reserved the right to remove captains and councillors and replace them at their discretion, and granted the minister authority to suspend, change, or revoke any created village council rules.[18] Lauded by the predominantly Afro-Guyanese People's National Congress (PNC) Forbes Burnham government as a progressive step toward hinterland integration and indigenous recognition, the ordinance reinforced state control over indigenous territories and reconfigured indigenous governance according to a statist model. Notably, the PNC government relied on the ALC report in their configuration of the new Act, under which nearly 48 other villages did not receive collective title (APA 1998).

Further, this post-independence period of cooperative socialism asserted governing policies designed to facilitate economic production and had the lasting effect of 'respatializing' the interior (Hennessy 2013). Marked by a pronounced ideological shift, following more than a decade of socialism under the Forbes Burnham PNC rule in the 1960s, the government swiftly moved toward structural adjustment and neoliberal development under a predominantly Indo-Guyanese regime, the People's Progressive Party (PPP) in 1992. The corresponding expansion of resource extraction, development, and environmental conservation initiatives not only inserted indigenous communities into the global economy but also yielded significant social, economic, and environmental impacts on Amerindian communities (Forte and Melville 1989; Colchester 1997; Canterbury 1998; Colchester, LaRose, and James 2002; Bulkan and Bulkan 2006).

The preoccupation of post-independence governments to construct a cohesive Guyanese nationalism, apparent in the lexicon of security, reveals the state's ongoing anxieties over the hinterland and Amerindian sovereignty. The spatial distance between the post-independence administrations on the coast and the remote living space of the indigenous were perceived as potentially undermining the nationalistic project to create a cohesive or imagined national identity amenable to economic development and international investments. As Brackette Williams contends, ideological struggles over the production of Guyanese identity 'aimed to *place* groups within a single sociocultural and political order and to legitimate their right to participate in all aspects of society and economy...[that] proposed particular and competing intersections of territorial nationalism and cultural identities' (Williams 1991, 168, original emphasis).

Land, its acquisition and control, undergirds the state's anxiety over consolidating state sovereignty not only against internal threats but also against ongoing claims to nearly two-thirds of Guyana's territory by Venezuela and Suriname. As such, the 1976 Amerindian Act adopted 'atomized' processes of land titling, as cooperative socialism advanced a holistic agenda of 'spatial and cultural consolidation' based on the villagisation scheme implemented in coastal communities to streamline agricultural development (Hennessy 2013, 1257). These processes reformulated contiguous spaces of shared territories of distinct Amerindian identities into porous boundaries, effectively fragmenting large swathes of territory and dividing the population into titled and untitled segments, leaving apertures of state land in between them.

Though cooperative socialism shifted to a neoliberal consolidation, the titling model of the previous period informed the 2006 Amerindian Act, which outlines the composition and function of village councils to 'provide for the planning and development of the Village' (13(1)(c), and 'manage and regulate the use and occupation of Village lands' (13)(1)(e). Further, it extols the extent of the powers of the elected toshao and village council, whose rights to make rules, or any amendments to these rules, must obtain two-thirds vote from the village *as well as* approval by the minister, making councils vulnerable to the directives of the government of the day. To acquire communal land title, 'a community may apply in writing to the Minister for a grant of State lands provided it has been in existence for at least twenty-five years; and at the time of the application and for the immediately preceding five years, it comprised at least one hundred and fifty persons.'[19] Indigenous communities that have traditionally inhabited land prior to colonial and state rule, must apply to the state to legitimate their 'traditional occupation and use' of the land.

Moreover, the language of *ownership*, as evinced in the Independence Agreement and subsequent Amerindian Acts, frames recognition of Amerindian land claims through Eurocentric conceptualisation of land, as propertied ownership. This perception of land delimits and displaces distinct cultural and spiritual attachments and embodied relationships to the land. As one villager proclaimed, 'land is we life'; not mere hyperbole, it signals indigenous modes of interdependence with the land. Though seemingly more progressive than other commonwealth/CARICOM countries such as Belize and Suriname, statutory recognition of indigenous land titles in Guyana paradoxically, reproduces a condition of coloniality, facilitating the erosion of indigenous control over their lands and territories and marginalising indigenous interests, knowledges, and voices. The state arbitrates indigenous relations to the land, qualifying the extent of actual recognition, codification, and realisation of indigenous land rights, even as it prioritizes economic ventures that undermine indigenous self-determination. This socio-spatial reconfiguration of territory demonstrates how state power functions *through* legal mechanisms, placing indigenous peoples within what might be called *corporeal-spatial precarity*.

Consequently, with the increasing presence of foreign and multilateral companies at the level of large-scale ventures, this reordering of indigenous lands through regimes of legality constrains village autonomy and governance and engenders land and resource grabbing, expansive annexation for extractive industries, and landlordism.[20] Similar to its colonial predecessors, post-independence governments merely extended this logic of protectionism and intervention which limit the rights and property of Amerindians through its uncritical reinscription of inherited colonial policies and ideologies about the hinterland and its communities. This ongoing grinding away of indigenous lands and sovereignty constitute indigenous dispossession; that is, legal and spatial techniques of power, such as contested demarcation and titling processes that obscure local knowledges, collective memory, and sense of place; the separation of indigenous territories into 'titled' and 'untitled' lands; increased vulnerability to the environmental and social impacts of mining and logging activities – all of which enable the shift of lands into state control for neoliberal development. Perceived as inhabiting an inherently neutral and objective domain, this chapter demonstrates how legalities – specifically, recognition – function as a mechanism of control that subjects indigenous peoples to vectors of state power as part of a continuum of more explicit, violent expressions of dispossession.

To the extent that post-independence governments censure indigenous demands for a recognition policy that reflects indigenous epistemologies, indigenous communities are forced to directly engage, indeed adapt to, a legal regime that masks its own complicity with the dominant Western eurocentric episteme and that perpetuates skewed, narrow definitions of what constitutes Amerindian community, livelihood, and being. Through recognition policies that advance neoliberal economic expansion, the state continues to dispossess Amerindian communities of their collective lands and territories, even as it distances itself from the colonial violence of the past through discourses of cohesion, unity, progress, and the 'good life' for all. The next section considers how perceptions of the land are not mere abstract projections, but manifest on the contours of the indigenous body through specific racial-sexual configurations, with particular consequence for the Amerindian woman.

The 'Buck' Woman

How the interior landscape is imagined, and how the bush takes shape within the national imaginary as a polarising, redemptive space, is inextricably linked to the racial-sexual Amerindian female body. In the final section, I examine how the 'bush' as a 'space that bears the projection of man's desire, like the woman's body,' (Jackson 2005, 95) is constructed alongside the racial-sexual image of the 'buck woman' as a subjecting force over the landscape to be possessed. The term 'buck', a colonial image[21] of the Amerindian subject-as-less than human, associates Amerindians with being closer to nature, indeed, intertwined with an uncivilised landscape.

One afternoon in one of the village's shops, I sat on a turquoise wooden bench with a resident, 'gyaffing,'[22] the shade cast by the thin zinc roof providing minimal protection from the heat radiating through it. Known as 'Uncle David' in the village, he was one of several black inhabitants of the Amerindian village, identified for his rumbling voice and impressive stature. He had worked for several decades in various parts of the interior. Perfunctorily, he described the limited occupations available to residents. Although mining was the dominant form of labour for many men in the village, it was often small-scale ventures or as individual 'pork knockers', and while the village owned a small logging concession 'it was not possessed' properly. With a tilted head, he explained that some of the women, predominantly middle-aged and older, worked individual farms, as there were no designated communal farms. Many of the young women in the village did not work outside of the household, and largely depended on the income generated by their partners' labour in the backdam, whether as boat captains, shunting fuel, or as part of mining or logging operations. According to him, the impacts of mining on the community could be characterised as cycles of 'cohesion and disruption'. Men remained home in between the typical six-week mining cycle and when demand for mining labour decreased. As such, women often bore the brunt of maintaining the household.

When I asked him about his thoughts on the experiences of women in the hinterland, he acknowledged the prevalence of sexual violence, rape, and domestic abuse, yet paused when I asked about the nation's growing attention to trafficking in persons (TIP) cases, largely viewed as an impediment to national progress. His eyes obscured behind dark shades, his shoulders rose and fell with his deep breathing. He conceded that while there were incidents of trafficking, the majority of cases actually comprised women who voluntarily 'picked fare' in the backdam. Although there were under-aged girls who left school or ran away from home, he recognised this as a consequence of extreme conditions of poverty, which sometimes led parents to 'encourage their young daughters to work bush,' where 'advantage' might happen. He readily acknowledged that while 'predators' further exploited these women and girls, the situation was at times misrecognised as coerced prostitution or unwilling sex work. 'After a time the sex part doesn't mean nothing because she get customed to it, she body suit…' He motioned with his hands, outward and in, a tightening gesture that conjured a feminine silhouette. 'She body become[s] accustomed to it.' With a resigned expression, he noted that from 'time memorial', prostitution formed 'part of the thing [mining]…entertainment and dem thing would always happen.' Prostitution constituted a part of 'bush work', which belied gendered and sexualised notions of the female body as an important aspect of the entertainment for miners alongside the prevalence of sporting (drinking), drug trafficking, and crime.[23] Other residents, women and men alike, shared similar sentiments about the presence of women in the backdam as being associated with sexual availability.

What does it means for the female body to be perceived as predisposed – even 'suited' – for sexual labour and exploitation as a composite part of working the bush? In tandem with the overidentification of the 'bush' as a productive cultural or economic resource of the state, these ambivalent imaginaries of the space of the bush are imbued with colonial feminisation of the interior as a space to subdue, tame, and beat back. As bodies are maps of power and identity (Haraway 1990; Lefebvre 1991[1974]), examining the discursive representations of Amerindian women reveals the way gendered and racialised identities become reproduced and expressed as natural; in turn, this process shapes how particular bodies are treated.

Notably, perceptions about Amerindian women cannot be extricated from the racial-sexual representations of Afro- and Indo-Guyanese women, and the pervasive heteropartriarchal violence women experience across difference.[24] As Linda Peake and Alissa Trotz (1999) argue, the reproduction of racialised identities relies on gendered practices and representations that are constituted and challenged across various sites. Although their analysis primarily attends to the representational construction of Indo- and Afro-Guyanese women, this work provides a way to read the mapping and placement of the Amerindian woman as crucial to the maintenance of racial/ethnic boundaries and the processes through which hierarchical social orders are reinscripted in relation to place and territory.

The circulation of the Amerindian woman as 'buck' and innately hyper-sexualised was reflected in the experiences a middle-aged Amerindian woman related to me. While attending a workshop in Georgetown addressing sexual violence and trafficking in persons, she described her dismay at overhearing another female participant state, 'all buck women know to do is f**k, f**k, f**k...women in Guyana, especially Amerindian women, are treated like sexual objects.' For the 'buck woman', geographic domination is worked out through reading and managing her specific racial-sexual body. The view of women and girls as commodities is linked to the image of the sexualised 'buck' woman as predisposed for sexual labour; as backward bodies marked as less than, they are then considered violable and 'rapeable'. By extension, because they are perceived as extensions of the geographical space of the hinterland, Amerindian women (and lands) are imagined as exploitable and disposable.

Further, depictions of the Amerindian woman as the emblematic figure of trafficking cases obfuscates a complex analysis of the structural forms of exploitation and conditions they encounter and, paradoxically, reinscribes a condition of hypervisibility and invisibility. Whether as 'coerced prostitute', voluntary sex worker, or 'trafficked victim', or a congruent conflation, the Amerindian 'buck woman' becomes a floating signifier, an integral part of how the 'bush' is imagined as a landscape of cowboy lawlessness, disorder, and gratuitous violence *and* as a redemptive panacea of wealth and economic potential for the advancement of national development. Geopolitical divisions between the coast and the hinterland prevent a more expansive understanding of TIP and sexual violence cases. This limited framework effaces the reality that coastlander women are also trafficked *into* the hinterland. Despite numerous reports of the disproportionate vulnerability of Amerindian *and* Afro-Guyanese women to sexual violence, these circulating discourses frame the coast as a neutral space,[25] hindering an intersectional analysis of gender and sexual violence more broadly. These violences cannot be understood only in terms of interactions between coastlander men and Amerindian women, but also in terms of the gender-sexual constructs that shape relations between Amerindian men and women *and* between Creole men and women. As Trotz demonstrates, the hinterland, and the Amerindian woman, come into the purview of the state as a means to create an environment amenable to foreign investment and funding from multilateral and bilateral creditors by addressing TIPs as a problem of the hinterland, one that 'underscore[s] the legitimacy of the state machinery on both a local and international stage' (Trotz and Roopnaraine 19).

Moreover, underlining the ambivalence about whether trafficking in persons is actually misrecognised prostitution is the assumption that bodies 'picking fare', are impure and dirty 'bad women' are inviolable and unrapeable as it is seen by dominant heteropatriarchal and respectability norms that these bodies are incapable of integrity. Consequently, violence against Amerindian women is inextricably situated within sex/gender colonial hierarchies of power and post-independence hinterland development policies and neoliberal economic expansion. Rather than mere pathological, derivative effects of the moral degradation associated with mining, gender violence against Amerindian women is *integrally* related to her racial-sexual body ('buck woman') as being a naturalised extension of the 'bush' landscape. As Katherine McKittrick (2006) poignantly states, 'geographic domination, then, is conceptually and materially bound up with racial-sexual displacement' (xvii). The uneven geographical distribution of particular groups, through colonial racial-sexual and economic hierarchies and the 'simultaneous naturalisation of bodies and places' must be unsettled if we are to create and imagine decolonial land/body relationships, as the present landscape is 'both haunted and developed by old and new hierarchies of humanness.'[26] In the contemporary Guyanese landscape, the *where* of indigenous geographies and indigenous subjectivities is disciplined through seemingly natural stabilities, of fixed boundaries and places, of naturalised 'bush' and 'buck'. As one Amerindian woman expressed to me during a workshop I conducted deconstructing these circulating representations: 'These images of us as 'buck' and the idea that we can't represent ourselves are not true...we are beautiful, intelligent, and...we are the *First Peoples*.' Her refutation of these circulating representations signals self-making processes that reassert Amerindian *living presence* and self-determination, as unevenly subjugated bodies, in particular the Amerindian woman, also constitute a body-space element of resistance to dominance.

Conclusion

Through ethnography and an attention to the unthought position of Amerindians that informs colonial and post-independence governing policies, I have argued that indigenous recognition and circulating ideas about the 'bush' and the Amerindian 'buck woman' facilitate the expansion of a state territorial sovereignty guided by neoliberal logic, placing indigenous peoples within spaces of 'corporeal-spatial' precarity. The aim has not been to disparage the pragmatic implications of ascertaining recognition for indigenous communities; rather, I have sought to problematise what recognition actually engenders. Rather than a transformation of state-indigenous relations, it demonstrates a reconfiguration of state power.

Ultimately, the struggle over land and resources, then, is more than a contest over territorial possession. It is about shifting dynamics of power as 'projecting perceptions and policies, laws, and institutional relations onto natural environments and human landscapes' (Colchester 2005, 271). If a truly transformative Guyanese social and political landscape is to emerge, reimagining other ways of being outside inherited colonial projections of the land and indigenous bodies – such as imaginaries of reconciliation grounded in Amerindian sacrifice – demands grounded, rather than metaphorical centring, of indigenous livelihoods, epistemologies, and relational ways of being.

Notes

1. Original emphasis.
2. 'Creole' refers to the 90 per cent of the Guyanese population, primarily descendants of enslaved Africans and indentured Indian labour forces as distinct from any of the indigenous groups in Guyana. Yet, the term itself obfuscates the ethnic differentiation created under British colonialism that remains paramount in Guyanese society.

3. Ethnographic notes from my attendance at President Granger's opening address at the *Social Cohesion Roundtable* in Georgetown, Guyana, September 2015.
4. Ibid.
5. The term Amerindian is a colonial term that obscures distinctions between indigenous nations in Guyana. It is widely used in local context, often interchangeably with 'Indigenous' and 'First Peoples'. However, it, along with the nine indigenous nations model, elides the transnational dimensions of Amerindian social and political relationships across the fixed geographical boundaries of the modern Guyanese nation-state, such as economic and cultural exchanges across geographic borders in Makushi and Wapishana communities on the Guyana–Brazil border, for example. This chapter does not necessarily depend on disaggregating those differences. For further critique of the commonly accepted nine-tribes model in Guyana, see Hornborg and Hill, *Ethnicity in Ancient Amazonia: Reconstructing Past Identities from Archaeology, Linguistics, and Ethnohistory* (Boulder: University Press of Colorado, 2011). Further, the communities with which I conducted research reflect how territorial ascriptions do not necessarily align with distinct indigenous groups, though there are regions with more defined ethnic presence such as the Akawaio in the upper Mazaruni and others. For example, in this ethnographic context, several indigenous groups lived within one particular village, in part from migration from other regions in search of economic livelihood, and intermarriage across distinct ethnic and national affiliations.
6. A.J. Seymour, *The Legend of Kaiteur* references the Carib nation of Guyana, invoking historical and contemporary stereotypical representations of Caribs as warring, 'cannibalistic' societies.
7. Porkknockers are primarily coastlanders who venture into the bush as freelance small-scale gold and diamond miners.
8. The term backdam here refers to the sites of mining and other extractive labour further inland, often remote areas with no substantive built environment.
9. Following the 2015 national elections, the ministry was renamed the Ministry of Indigenous Affairs.
10. Mining regulations permit river dredging up to 20 metres on both riverbanks, with missile dredging being cited as a concern for the turbidity of rivers being mined and the potential for disfiguring channels of the river. See Thomas, Clive, *Too Big to Fail: A Scoping Study of the Small and Medium Scale Gold and Diamond Mining Industry in Guyana* (unpublished paper, 2009), 22.
11. *Toshao* refers to the democratically elected village leader of a titled Amerindian village.
12. Guyana Geology and Mines Commission.
13. Personal conversation with a female miner from Georgetown.
14. 'Topside' refers to a geographical area further up the Cuyuni River near the Venezuela–Guyana border, an interior area where mining, fuel shunting, and other activities occur.
15. T. Roopnaraine (in Trotz and Roopnarine 2009) provides an excellent analysis of coastlander porkknockers' sense-making of the 'bush' as reflecting a coastlander ontology. While Amerindians involvement in the mining sector

often occurs in exploited positions, additional research on Amerindian perceptions of mining as a potential avenue for indigenous self-determination and development is necessary.
16. Ibid.
17. I define 'coloniality' as the living legacy of colonialism that shapes the contemporary moment, in which race, gender, class, and political hierarchies imposed by European colonialism, structure our social world. My conceptualisation of coloniality of recognition draws from Anibal Quijano's analysis of the constitution of America and global capitalism as a Euro-centred colonial/modern world power and Maria Lugones's crucial critique and expansion of Quijano's analysis through an examination of the constitutively gendered nature of modern/colonial formations. See Anibal Quijano, 'Coloniality of Power and Eurocentrism in Latin America,' *International Sociology* 15, no. 2(2000): 215–32 and Maria Lugones, 'The Coloniality of Gender' *Worlds & Knowledges Otherwise* no. 2 (Spring 2008):1–17. For a similar argument regarding indigenous recognition in Canada, see Glen Coulthard, *Red Skin, White Masks: Rejecting the Colonial Politics of Recognition* (Minneapolis, MN: University of Minnesota Press, 2014).
18. The Amerindian Act 1976 Part IV(14). The act refers to 'Minister' without specifying which minister.
19. Section VI (60)(1)(a)(b).
20. See J. Bulkan,*"Red Star over Guyana": Colonial-style Grabbing of Natural Resources but New Grabbers*, (conference paper presented at the International Conference on Global Land Grabbing, University of Sussex, 2011).
21. Dutch colonisers referred to indigenous peoples as 'buck' (bok), which means antelope or goat in Dutch. See Mary Noel Menezes, *The Amerindians in Guyana, 1803–1873: A Documentary History* (London: Cass, 1979).
22. To 'gyaff' is to talk, engage in informal, long-ranging conversations.
23. For an excellent analysis of the circulating discourses surrounding women as 'victims' or 'voluntary agents' in the sex trade, see Ruth Goldstein, 'Semiophors and Sexual Systems: the Circulation of Words and Women,' *Pragmatics & Society* 6, no. 2 (2015): 217–39.
24. It is beyond the scope of this chapter to thoroughly examine the interconnected, yet distinct experiences of indigenous and creole women in the Guyanese context.
25. Guyana Human Rights Association Report. *Getting Serious: Detecting and Protecting Against Crimes of Sexual Violence in Guyana* (2007).
26. Ibid.

References

The Amerindian (Amendment) Act 1976.
The Amerindian Act 2006, Chapter 29:01. Laws of Guyana.
Amerindian Lands Commission. 1969. *Report by the Amerindian Lands Commission*. Georgetown, Guyana: Amerindian Lands Commission.

Amerindian Peoples Association. 1998. A Plain English Guide to the 1976 Amerindian Act. Georgetown, Guyana: Amerindian Peoples Association.

———. 1999. *Amerindians and the law in Guyana 1580–1999. APA Information Sheet for National Captain's Conference, April 26–30.* Georgetown, Guyana: Amerindian Peoples Association.

———. 2000. Upper Mazaruni Amerindian District Council, and the Forrest Peoples Programme. *Indigenous Peoples, Land Rights, and Mining in the Upper Mazaruni.* Georgetown, Guyana: Guyana Law Association,

Baines, Stephen Grant. 2005. Indigenous Autonomies and Rights on the Brazil-Guyana Border: Makushi and Wapishana on an International Border. *Série Antropologia.*

Bulkan, Janette. 2013. The Struggle for Recognition of the Indigenous Voice: Amerindians in Guyanese Politics. *The Round Table* 102, no. 4:367–80.

Bulkan, J., and A. Bulkan. 2006. These Forests Have Always Been Ours: Official and Amerindian Discourses on Guyana's Forest Estate. In *Indigenous Resurgence in the Contemporary Caribbean: Amerindian Survival and Revival*, ed. M. Forte, 135–54. New York: Peter Lang.

Canterbury, D., ed. 1998. Guyana's Gold Industry: Evolution, Structure, Impact, and Non-wage Benefits. *Transition*, Special Issue No. 27–28. Georgetown, Guyana: Institute of Development Studies, University of Guyana.

Colchester, Marcus. 1997. *Guyana: Fragile Frontier. Loggers, Miners, and Forest Peoples.* London: Latin American Bureau and the World Rainforest Movement.

———. 2005. Maps, Power, and the Defense of Territory. In *Communities and Conservation: Histories and Politics of Community-Based Natural Resource Management*, ed. J. Peter Brosius, Anna Lowenhaupt Tsing, and Charles Zerner, 271–304. Walnut Creek, CA: AltaMira Press.

Colchester, M., J. La Rose, and K. James. 2002. *Mining and Amerindians in Guyana: Final Report of the APA/NSI project on Exploring Indigenous perspectives on consultation and engagement within the mining sector in Latin America and the Caribbean.* Ottawa, Canada: North-South Institute.

Coulthard, Glen. 2014. *Red Skin, White Masks: Rejecting the Colonial Politics of Recognition.* Minneapolis: University of Minnesota Press.

Ferguson, James. 1994. *The Anti-Politics Machine: 'Development,' Depoliticization, and Bureaucratic Power in Lesotho.* Minneapolis, MN: University of Minnesota Press.

Forte, J., and I. Melville, ed. 1989. *Amerindian Testimonies.* Boise, ID: Boise State University.

France, Hollis. 2005 Continuity or Change? Structural Adjustment Decision-making in Guyana (1988–97): The Hoyte and Jagan Years. *Social and Economic Studies* 54, no. 1:83–128.

Gibson, Kean. 2003. *The Cycle of Racial Oppression in Guyana.* Lanham, MD: University Press of America.

Goldstein, Ruth. 2015. Semiophors and Sexual Systems: the Circulation of Words and Women. *Pragmatics & Society* 6, no. 2:217–39.

Greene-Roesel, J. 1996. Power, Identity, and Development: The Decline and Rise of Amerindian Agency in North West Guyana. PhD dissertation, University of Cambridge, Cambridge, UK.

Greenidge, C.B. 2001. *Empowering a peasantry in a Caribbean Context: The Case of Land Settlement Schemes in Guyana*. Barbados: University Press of the West Indies.

Haraway, Donna. 1990. *Simians, Cyborgs, and Women: The Reinvention of Nature*. 1st ed. New York: Routledge.

Hennessey, Logan. 2013. Re-Placing Indigenous Territory: Villagization and the Transformation of Amerindian Environments Under 'Cooperative Socialism' in Guyana. *Annals of the Association of American Geographers* 103, no. 5:1,242–65.

Hinds, D. 2009. Ethnopolitics and Fractured Nationalism in Guyana. In *Anthropologies of Guayana: Cultural Space in Northeastern Amazonia*, ed. N.L. Whitehead and S.W. Alemán, 154–66. Tucson, AZ: University of Arizona Press.

Hintzen, Percy C. 2004. Creoleness and Nationalism in Guyanese Anticolonialism and Postcolonial Formation. *Small Axe* 8, no.1:106–22.

Hornborg, Alf, and Jonathan D. Hill. 2011. *Ethnicity in Ancient Amazonia: Reconstructing Past Identities from Archaeology, Linguistics, and Ethnohistory*. Boulder: University Press of Colorado.

Ifill, Melissa. 2009. The Indigenous Struggle: Challenging and Undermining Capitalism and Liberal Democracy. PhD Dissertation, Department of Sociology, University of Guyana.

Jackson, Shona N. 2005. Subjection and Resistance in the Transformation of Guyana's Mytho-Colonial Landscape. In *Caribbean Literature and the Environment: Between Nature and Culture*, ed. Elizabeth M. DeLoughrey, Renèe K. Gosson, and George B. Handley, 85–98. Charlottesville: University of Virginia Press.

Lefebvre, Henri. 1991[1974]. *The Production of Space*. 1st ed. Oxford, OX, UK; Cambridge, MA: Wiley-Blackwell.

Lindroth, Marjo. 2014. Indigenous Rights as Tactics of Neoliberal Governance: Practices of Expertise in the United Nations. *Social & Legal Studies* 23, no. 3:341–60.

Lugones, M. 2008. The Coloniality of Gender. *Words & Knowledges Otherwise*, 2 (Spring), 1–17.

McKittrick, Katherine. 2006. *Demonic Grounds: Black Women and the Cartographies of Struggle*. Minneapolis, MN: University of Minnesota Press.

Menezes, Mary Noel. 1977. *British Policy towards the Amerindians in British Guiana, 1803–1873*. Oxford: Clarendon Press.

———. 1979. *The Amerindians in Guyana, 1803–1873: A Documentary History*. London: Cass.

Mentore, George. 2007. Guyanese Amerindian Epistemology: The Gift from a Pacifist Insurgence. *Race & Class* 49, no. 2:57–70.

Moreno, María del Carmen. 2009. Guyana's Amerindians: Post-Independence Identity Politics, and National Discourse. In *Anthropologies of Guyana:*

Cultural Spaces in Northeastern Amazonia, ed. N.L. Whitehead and S.W. Aleman, 145–53. Tucson, AZ: University of Arizona Press.
Peake, Linda, and D. Alissa Trotz. 1999. Gender, Ethnicity and Place: Women and Identities in Guyana. In *Routledge Studies in Development and Society*. London: Routledge.
Premdas, R. 1995. *Ethnic Conflict and Development: The Case of Guyana*. Aldershot: Avebury.
Quijano, Aníbal. 2000. Coloniality of Power and Eurocentrism in Latin America. *International Sociology* 15, no. 2:215–32.
Roopnaraine, T. 1995. Shout on the Border: Minerals, Social Tension, and the Frontier. *Journal of Archaeology and Anthropology* 10:36–42.
———. 1996. Freighted Fortunes: Gold and Diamond Mining in the Pakaraima Mountains, Guyana. PhD dissertation, University of Cambridge, Cambridge, UK.
Seymour, A.J. and CARIFESTA I – 1972. *The Legend of Kaieteur* (Performance Booklet). CARIFESTA I – 1972. The University of Florida: Digital Library of the Caribbean.
Thomas, Clive. 2009. *Too Big to Fail: A Scoping Study of the Small and Medium Scale Gold and Diamond Mining Industry in Guyana*. Unpublished paper, 22.
Trotz, Alissa and T. Roopnaraine. 2009. Angles of Vision from the Coast and Hinterland of Guyana. In *Anthropologies of Guyana: Cultural spaces in Northeastern Amazonia*, ed. N.L. Whitehead and S.W. Alemán, 235–53. Tucson, AZ: University of Arizona Press.
Trotz, D. Alissa. 2004. Between Despair and Hope: Women and Violence in Contemporary Guyana. *Small Axe* 8, no. 1:1–20. https://doi.org/10.1215/-8-1-1.
Vadjunec, J.M., M. Schmink, and A. Greiner. 2011. New Amazonian Geographies: Emerging Identities and Landscapes. *Journal of Cultural Geography* 28, no. 1:1–20.
Williams, Brackette F. 1991. *Stains on My Name, War in My Veins: Guyana and the Politics of Cultural Struggle*. Durham, NC: Duke University Press.

Lenses of Hope: Alternative Engagements with the State

16.
Lenses of Hope: Investigating the Social Economy as a Paradigmatic Shift Through the Wowetta Women's Agro-Processing Cassava Enterprise

Hollis France

Introduction

The Amerindian-state relationship in post-colonial Guyana in the last 50 years can at best be characterised as significant and intrusive. The Guyanese state has always maintained a considerable presence in hinterland communities where Amerindians primarily reside, but this engagement has not necessarily been empowering and beneficial for Amerindians as a group. However, despite the reaches of the post-colonial state at every turn to impose development ontologies antithetical to Amerindian development, Amerindians remain resilient in the face of this adversity.

From the inception of the post-colonial state the two dominant political parties, first the People's National Congress (PNC) and then the Peoples Progressive Party (PPP)[1] employed state resources as a means to solidify their political agendas and projects in Amerindian communities. Villagisation saw some Amerindian communities being awarded collective titles to land, but 'the new boundaries of the villages were not always contiguous, leaving gaps of state land in between them. These exclusions and divisions left the majority of interior land in the hands of the state' (Hennessy 2013, 1,251). This political project, incentivised by economic interests, was initiated by the PNC to buttress its state-led development project of agricultural cooperatives, and later continued under the leadership of the PPP, in the 1990s, in an effort to augment its neoliberal extractive industry export-oriented development focus. Under the PNC regime, access to state land was often afforded to small-scale and some large-scale coast landers in the mining and logging sectors, while under the PPP the shift was made towards attracting large-scale multinational corporations engaged in mining and logging. The nestling of state lands used for mining and logging between Amerindian villages often resulted in grave environmental degradation, from diminishing wildlife and fisheries to polluted water ways. Additionally, during the reign of the PNC the failure of agricultural cooperatives to produce financially viable and sustainable development in Amerindian communities ignited the creeping exodus of community members. This outward migration was further exacerbated by the PPP's decision in 1992 to fully embrace and open up the mining and timber industries to foreign investment.

To the casual observer the model of villagisation, initiated by the PNC and later re-inscribed in the neoliberal polices of the PPP, might appear as merely a competing economic arrangement contrasting with generations of Amerindian subsistence economies. Heralded as the first major post-independence development model, Amerindians were expected to engage in monocrop cultivation with crops such as blackeyed peas, peanuts, cabbage, tomatoes, and potatoes in exchange for low wages and inputs such as seeds, fertilisers, and pesticides from the government (Hennessy 2013, 1,247–51). However, when one closely extrapolates the attendant economic factors of villagisation it becomes clear that this was not just offering a different economic model of development, but in fact militating against many aspects of Amerindian communal ideologies and economic arrangements. Side by side with the traditional, the village model created top-down hierarchies of social and economic control. Communities were brutally (in the moral and operational sense) cut off from each other, so that successive governments could control access to natural resources and dole out concessions based on the perceived benefits to the national economy. Amerindian households were transformed into wage earning units and left dependent on obtaining goods through a cash economy 'without obvious means of paying for them' (Colchester 1997, 137), as cash employment opportunities gradually dwindled in communities. Wage earning also magnetically enticed Amerindians away from their sacred and valuable rituals, leaving them little or no time to practice those rituals, as they were seduced by the goods that wage labour could provide them. Further, it seemed that the 'magical hand' of the extractive industry was pulling away not only the men folk from their communities but also the younger Amerindians. Of course, in the hierarchy of the economy, imposed first by the PNC and consolidated under the PPP, is the image of government representatives being the lords and masters in this schema.

However, this transformational drama is far from complete without an interrogation of the various responses by Amerindians to the foregoing social and cultural impositions that accrued. Amerindians have not all willingly accepted being 'acted upon' or 'acted for', and their communities have and continue to demonstrate a capacity born of their own agency. Migratory push factors as responses to diminishing wage earning opportunities (Flores 2011; Trotz and Roopnaraine 2009), although instrumental in eroding Amerindian cultural values, have seen a number of communities responding by maintaining communal values and rituals that they hold dear. It is this response which this chapter explores in order to understand how some groups have rejected neoliberal ontologies of top down, business as usual approaches to development.

Employing a case study of the Wowetta Women's Agro-processing Cassava Enterprise, this chapter illustrates how a group of indigenous women are attempting to transform their landscape which threatens their traditions and has produced vulnerabilities and insecurities for themselves and their community over time.[2] From their decision-making practices, to the strategies they utilise to organise their production networks, their efforts speak to the ongoing struggle these women are engaged in to activate a social economy predicated on collectivist norms and the overall wellbeing of their community. They seek to jettison the universalising one model market-driven solution enshrined in the dominant neoliberal top-down development policies and practices. They reject the 'one size fits all' demands of the 'bottom line', 'business as usual', 'imperatives of the market' neoliberal status quo approach to development, which in turn produces individualising norms. This is not to suggest that the experiences of the Agro-processing Cassava Enterprise have been linear, or that they have been completely inoculated against or sheltered from the heavily incentivised individualising appeals of market driven approaches. The political economy of Guyana in which these women are embedded presents many challenges to their success in activating an alternative to the neoliberal hegemony. Guyana's continued deepening of its global capitalist linkages – that is the export-oriented platform of timber and mining, and its equally challenging racialised political environment seen in the electoral competition between the two dominant ethnicities of Afro- and Indo Guyanese – threaten to derail many of the achievements of the Wowetta Agro-processing Cassava Enterprise. Hence, this chapter demonstrates the practices which give voice to alternative development possibilities, while simultaneously recognising the limitations produced when interfacing in a deeply entrenched market economy and a contentious political environment. What follows is a track along the map of developmental paradigms to understand where the Wowetta model is positioned in the purview of ontological discourses. This excursion is intended to investigate cultural phenomena that bifurcate the existing developmental pathways (or show where the roads diverge), and offer a different perspective to models found along the main road of neoliberal ontological explanatory accounts.

Mainstream Income-Generating Models as a Pathway to Development

At first glance, the temptation may exist to squarely situate the Wowetta Women's Agro-processing Cassava Enterprise within the confines of the mainstream neoliberal narrative regarding income-generating enterprises. After all, as poor, indigenous, rural women located in the global south, all these social identities make the Wowetta Women prime subjects for the application of the narrative peddled by national and global policy elites who view income-generating enterprises as the saviour of the poor. Such enterprises have attracted the support of international development agencies, governments, and non-governmental organisations (NGOs), and are being heralded as potential panaceas for addressing and ameliorating poverty in the global south generally, and among women in particular (Balkenhol 2007). Income-generating enterprises, which come under the general rubric of micro-financing[3] are viewed as pathways to integrate and bring those marginalised by neoliberal restructuring back into the fold of the mainstream market economy. This process of formalisation, to which Timothy Mitchell refers, is informed by the expectations that poor and marginalised groups can be turned into capitalist individual entrepreneurs (2005). It is argued that by fusing private sector market driven approaches with individualised self-help grassroots practices, the poor can exit out of poverty (Bateman and Chang 2012, 14). In other words, as seasoned community development activist John Pearce (2009) has observed, many international donors and their governmental counterparts have attempted to co-opt community-generated, income-producing enterprises in order to reorient them from collective community action towards individual social entrepreneurs that employ private enterprise-styled business models. This microcredit financing approach, of which agro-processing is usually a part, has been celebrated by the international community as a path to sustainable economic development – especially for those excluded from more traditional economic mechanisms (Yunus 2006). The growing captivation with micro-financing by the policy elites reached its pinnacle in 2005 which the United Nations designated as the 'Year of Micro-financing'.[4]

Originally, these micro-financing models used 'solidarity lending' – lending to individuals as members of a collective. Within the solidarity lending framework, individuals borrow as members of a group, all of whom are jointly aware of the status of each other's loans, and are somewhat jointly responsible for repayment, as further loans will not be made to that group in the case of a default. In other words, it socialises responsibility while individualising reward. However, even in this 'kinder, gentler' development model, individual success comes with massive externalised costs, which are papered over in development discussions (Boudreaux and Cowen 2008; Roodman 2012). Soon after, however, micro-financing shifted from the realm of solidarity lending to individual client financing in tiny informal sector enterprises. Initially, micro-financing entities were subsidised by both national governments and the international development community. But as neoliberal policy elites felt conflicted by the employment of subsidies to finance micro loans, a gradual shift towards the commercialisation of loans emerged. Micro-financing was reconstituted and turned over to the privately owned, for-profit commercial institutions. The commercialisation track record thus far of micro-financing is one 'marked out by huge client over-indebtedness, rapidly growing client defaults, massive client withdrawals' (Bateman and Chang 2012, 16).

While the practice of combined subsidised and commercialised loans continues to trend, the attractiveness of microcredit schemes receives the majority of its momentum from the normalising and stabilising message communicated by the individual achievement of the 'winner.' It is the expectation of neoliberal supporters that the 'winner' will become the advocates and most vocal supporters of these private provisioning microcredit schemes. After all, they are the most invested, and hence will seek to maintain the status quo. Their individual successes are made highly visible with the attached message that individual efforts through market-driven mechanisms (not state intervention) will deliver the poor out of poverty. In actuality, as Milford Bateman and Ha-Joon Chang express, micro-financing dampens resistance to alternatives to the neoliberal globalising agenda (2012, 30). This, in turn, helps to normalise and stabilise neoliberal practices as the preferred outcomes for alleviating poverty and, thus, serves as a containment strategy (Bateman and Chang 2012; Hickel 2015).

Charting an Alternative Income-Generating Model

Despite these cheerleading efforts promoted by neoliberal policy elites regarding income-generating schemes, marginalised and poor communities like Wowetta are pushing back. No longer willing to accept being 'acted upon' or 'acted for', marginalised and poor communities at various scales are demonstrating a capacity born of their own agency. This is evidenced in the group's adoption of a philosophy of life that calls for urgent attention to alternative possibilities.

This alternative model seeks to dis-incentivise individual risk-taking, takes into account 'externalities' produced by micro-financing schemes, and tacitly or overtly argues that the community's good is not at all (or certainly not) external to the good of the individual. These motivations are captured by the term 'social economy'.[5] A fundamental principle governing the social economy is recognition among its participants of the need to 'internalize the externalities' that are often neglected in the neoliberal hegemonic discourse regarding development. John Pearce (2009, 23) argues that community social enterprises take seriously the idea of 'working for the common good', hence constantly appraising how their actions and policies impact the "'triple bottom line" – the impact on people, on the environment and on the (local) economy'. Actors within the social economy, therefore, appear to reject the primacy of profit maximisation and its ensuing neoliberal individualising norms. They strive instead to engender norms, practices and policies that are shaped by ethical commitments to equality, democracy, and more ecological ways of living together. Therefore, those engaged in the social economy are not interested in 'business as usual' 'bottom-line' imperatives that appear to dictate the success of mainstream enterprises (Cameron 2010; Gibson-Graham 2006B). Rather, the participants within the social economy are seeking a new model of sustainable and inclusive development (Lechat 2009, 160).

Central to fulfilling this vision of an economy built on an ethic of care, marginalised and poor communities are shifting their organisational structures of production, participation, and engagements with the market. They are putting into place practices geared towards de-centring mainstream narratives which prioritise market-driven economic practices of wage labour, commodity market exchanges, and capitalist enterprises as the only viable practices for achieving growth and prosperity (Gibson-Graham 2006A, 58). Instead, these affected communities are embracing diverse economic practices – alternative and non-market (transactions, labour arrangements) and non-capitalist enterprises which they view as contributing to overall well-being, unlike the current neoliberal model. Through their embrace of a set of diverse economic practices they challenge 'capitalicentrism' (Gibson-Graham 2006B) embedded in the European modernity model (Escobar 2010), which privileges capital as the central organising principle of economic life, thus masking and making invisible the diverse non-capitalist practices and activities in which the majority of the world's population participates on a daily basis. Therefore, marginalised and poor communities, particularly indigenous communities, are engaged in what noted Latin American scholar, Arturo Escobar, reads as ontological struggles emanating from a desire to move beyond dualistic worldviews to spaces represented by relational worldviews (Escobar 2010, 5). Current indigenous mobilisations seek to eschew the naturalisation of capital as the only form of economy, and the assumption that all other economic practices are inconsequential to societal well-being. The 'either/or' divide obfuscates the diverse and multi-forms of economic practices and economies indigenous people operate in, from capitalist, alternative capitalist, non-capitalist practices to solidarity, cooperative, and social communal to moral economies. Activating a relational ontology and placing it at the centre of development narratives and practices would bridge exclusionary and reductionist divides such as 'nature and culture...civilized and Indian, colonizer and colonized and developed and underdeveloped' (Escobar 2010, 39). Furthermore, by enacting a relational ontology, indigenous populations are recognising the importance of interdependence to ensure that their actions and decisions are not divorced from impacts on their communities.

Case Study: Wowetta Women Agro-Processing Cassava Enterprise

This case study examines the community initiated Cassava Income-Generating Agro-processing Enterprise among the Makushi indigenous women of Wowetta in the North Rupununi of Guyana. Employing participant observation, surveys, and semi-formal interviews, this case study specifically seeks to unpack how the Wowetta Cassava Income-Generating Enterprise, challenges the business as usual, capital-centric, market-driven approach to development. To assess their local economic impact an inventory of formal, informal, and non-market economic practices and activities were taken. The data collected suggest emerging innovative labour arrangements and diverse market relationships. A searchlight was also directed at the factors contributing to the women's decision to work in the enterprise. The data collected indicate that their choices reflect different ethical commitments to both intrinsic (e.g. social relevance of the job) and extrinsic (e.g. necessity of income) incentives. This framework provides a more complete picture than standard political economic analyses which only measure extrinsic incentives. Additionally, the sustainability of the Cassava Enterprise was assessed by investigating the perceptions of community members regarding community 'buy in'. While the data collected suggest mixed perceptions by men and women regarding practices such as women working outside of the home for an income, there is a general consensus that women working in the Cassava Enterprise are a valuable asset to maintaining and reproducing Makushi culture. Finally, the ecological leg of the triple bottom line exploring the relationship between the enterprise's economic practices and its carbon footprint reveal the incorporation of traditional knowledge regarding land use and inputs promoting stewardship rather than exploitation of nature.

Genesis of Wowetta Women's Agro-processing Cassava Enterprise

The Wowetta Women's Agro-processing Group was formed in 2009 operating under the umbrella of Wowetta Business Enterprises Incorporated. It began as part of a rural electrification programme with funding from the Canadian International Development Agency (CIDA), and executed by OLADE, the Latin American Organization for Energy; the University of Calgary and the Guyana Energy Agency (GEA). The funding extended to the purchasing of graters and solar systems. The Wowetta community currently experiences the outward migration of young adult men and women pursuing economic opportunities, the movement of child farm labour into state-sponsored educational institutions, and a reduction in subsistence farming activities. Effects of these shifts which the community face include decreased food supplies as male labour is lost and the cash contributions they may have made to purchasing consumables vanish (Dilly 2003, 62). The primary goal of the Wowetta Cassava Enterprise is to provide income-generating employment for women through the cassava processing operation, currently focused on the production of farine.[6] This has resulted in changes within the egalitarian gender relations between men and women concerning household provisioning, previously moulded on the traditional distribution of labour in agriculture. As Barbara Dilly argues, the cooperative ethos traditionally found in food production among Makushi men and women was significantly transformed beginning in the 1970s with the nationalist Cooperative Socialist period in Guyana (see Hennessy 2013), and was intensified in the current neoliberal period with increasingly men being 'drawn away from their families and communities into individual wage-labor employment opportunities' (Dilly 2003, 61). This transformed the societal/gender landscape and set the stage for women in communities like Wowetta to find alternative pathways to meet their needs.

Originally, the women's agro-processing enterprise consisted of 49 members in total, of which five served on the executive committee. Men within the community also benefit from income-generating opportunities as craftsmen, who are able to sell their products to the group (e.g. matapees, sifters and generally all technologies necessary for the production operation), as well as through direct employment as handymen and for transportation. Without the labour of the handymen or the products of the craftsmen, the enterprise would be unable to carry out its function. This decision-making on the part of the women in the cassava enterprise to establish backward linkages with individual producers (men) in the community illustrates the construction of a shared ethical space in which all parties recognise that interdependence is necessary to create a successful enterprise that promotes community well-being. Therefore, the inclusivity of other economic subjects, which has always been the backbone of Makushi cooperative gender relations, is sustained. Rather than simply embracing the externalities produced by national and global development policies, i.e., the exodus of males from the community, the women have chosen to internalise these possible outcomes. Instead of seeking employment in Brazil or in the mines, the traditional craft knowledge can be passed on to younger men who, in turn, can provide the necessary production technologies and be involved in their community development, while still earning an income, albeit (or 'if') less than they might earn in urban centres or mining towns.

Production Process

The core product produced by the Women's Group is farine, while other cassava products that are produced periodically are cassava bread, tapioca, and casareep. Among the Makushi and Amerindians across the Rupununi region, farine is a staple food and is key to ensuring food security for the local population. Virtually every family produces it for personal consumption, and those able to produce on a slightly larger scale may be involved in local cash sales. As the Women's Group owns an 11-acre farm, planted with the Amazon variety of cassava, they do not currently purchase any cassava; reaping it is considered a core part of their work.

Typically, farine is produced over the course of three days starting with cassava reaping. During the first part of the week, the women go to the farm, located in the nearby forest, an approximate 30-minute walk from the cassava processing house, to pull bitter cassava[7] to produce the yeast necessary for processing and making farine. Upon arriving, the women identify cassava ready to be pulled by the maturity of the cassava branches. They then cut the branches leaving approximately one-fourth of the stem so that they can use their hands to then pull the tuberous cassava out of the ground. The branches chopped off are then cleaned of any leaves, and approximately one-fourth of the branch which now looks like a stick is replanted. Once reaped, the cassava is transported to the cassava house primarily by 'warishi', a basket-like apparatus made out of palm leaves which is worn like a backpack and/or via a donkey. When it arrives, the women fetch several buckets of water from the well, and begin the process of soaking the cassava for three days in a large drum. On the third day they repeat the entire process, up to the point of returning to the cassava house with raw cassava to mix with the soaked cassava. The women have devised the formula of 11 pounds of soaked cassava (which produces the yeast) mixed with four pounds of raw cassava to produce 11 pounds of farine.

Soaked cassava (yeast)	Raw cassava	Farine
1lb	4 lbs	1lb

In order to net 600 pounds of farine it is necessary to pull 600 pounds of cassava for soaking to produce the yeast and then mix it with approximately 2,400 pounds of raw cassava.

Upon returning to the cassava house, an immediate division of labour transpires. Some women fetch water from a nearby well, while others begin the scraping process of the raw cassava (that is, using knives or potato peelers to remove the tough skin). After the women responsible for fetching water complete their tasks they then join in with the women who began the scraping process. When scraping is completed the cassava is washed and the grating process begins, which is followed by the mixing of the grated cassava with the yeast from the cassava soaked three days previously. The mixed content is placed in a large wooded container and left overnight. The following day, if handymen are not available to collect firewood for the parching process, some women will set out to the forest to collect firewood, while others begin matapeeing.[8] Approximately three matapees are in use at any one time. After the juice is extracted the substance remaining in the matapee is then sifted in preparation for parching. In the meantime, some women will be engaged in arranging firewood beneath the large tin pans in which the parching is done and then lighting a fire. The parching process for each large basket of sifted cassava lasts approximately two to three hours. The farine, which is the parched product, is then placed in large rice bags and transported for sale at the village shop.

Diverse Economic Practices: Workers and Markets

As noted above, the Wowetta Women's Agro-processing Cassava Enterprise is firmly committed to the community enterprise principle of localising decision-making regarding the local economy. The enterprise's rotating labour arrangements and tiered market engagements confirm how the organisation of economic practices captures their ethical commitments.

Labour Arrangements

The Wowetta Women's enterprise operates on both a paid employment and voluntary (in-kind) basis. Paid employment is restricted to those strictly involved in the cassava processing, and to the handymen/craftsmen/transportation directly involved in supporting the process. This arrangement is necessary to achieve one of its primary mandates of increasing local employment opportunities. Unlike mainstream business enterprises, the workers are more than just employees, and the enterprise reflects this. For example, during the first two years of the enterprise all workers were paid the standard going rate in the indigenous communities of GY$2,000, the equivalent of US$10 per day regardless of total output, hours spent during the processing phase, or their role in the processing. The mere fact that everyone was paid the same wage was driven by an expectation that every worker would contribute equally, and the belief that every member had a stake in the viability of the production process as a means of providing and keeping jobs in the community.

By 2011, this wage system was revised to address differential labour contributions to overall production output. At both the general women's group meeting and a larger Wowetta community-wide meeting, an agreement was secured for workers to agree to work three weeks in succession, and then be paid on a monthly basis. A group of five women (including the supervisor) produce farine from Monday to Wednesday during the first three weeks of the month, with each batch targeting a minimum production of 500 pounds. The fourth week will be for rest, and at the start of the following month a new group of women will begin the next three-week rotation. Assuming that the target of 500 pounds per week is produced, the women will receive GY$18,000 (US$90) per month, which is equivalent to what they were being paid before. However, if additional farine is produced, additional payments will be distributed among the five women working. These additional payments are set in increments of 10 pounds, and paid at a rate of $60/pounds (e.g. an extra 100 pounds of farine would result in an additional payment of $6,000 (US$30) split amongst the five women, such that each would take home an additional GY$1,200 (US$6).

This new 'pay for production' system, as characterised by a 2011 report prepared by the Secure Livelihood Programme of Voluntary Service Overseas (VSO) Guyana, is intended to address the free-rider tendency among some members, whereby some women showed up as early as 4:00 a.m. to begin the production process while others arrived between 9:00 and 10:00 a.m. yet expected to be compensated at the same daily rate. Additionally, by working for three weeks per month and having the following month off from cassava production, the women are afforded opportunities to attend to their individual farms and other household and family duties that may have been neglected. The decision made by the women and the community reflects an ethos of fairness and recognition of a commitment by the community to ensuring that other aspects of members' livelihoods are equally integrated. In other words, the community is cognizant of the disastrous potential in the over-dependence on the production of one crop, and its consequences for overall livelihood activities. Whereas paid employment is restricted to members directly engaged in the cassava production process, committee members operate on a voluntary (in kind) basis and are not paid to manage the enterprise. These positions are currently held by members of the community who may or may not have public sector jobs. For example, the past chairperson of the Wowetta Women's Group was also the Community Development Officer (CDO) for North Rupununi, Region 9, while the chairperson in 2014 was a stay-at-home mother. The former treasurer was responsible for the day-to-day operations of the village shop, and the current secretary is also the health officer for the village. These women, recognising that one worked in the home, primarily engaged in public sector jobs that demand a substantial amount of their time, have been willing to carve time out of their busy schedules to support the women involved in cassava production and the smooth operation of the community enterprise. They recognise that the women's success is tied to overall community development and the vitalisation of the local economy.

The activity of 'Matroman' is another dimension of the voluntary (in kind) labour arrangement that illustrates overall community commitment to taking greater responsibility and increased involvement in decision-making in the local economy. When land needed to be cleared, cut, cleaned, ploughed and fields planted, as was required at the beginning of the enterprise, and as new land is acquired, the women put out calls to the community inviting men, women and children to participate. The women engaged directly in cassava production cook and provide the fermented cassava drink 'Cari' in return for the community's labour. The ethos of a shared responsibility for community development is reflected in the 'Matroman' activity, whereby community members commit their time so that benefits will be secured not just for the women involved in cassava production, but to additionally support and facilitate overall community development. Furthermore, the activity itself helps to maintain and sustain Makushi cultural patterns of cooperation. However, one person lamented, 'some community members want to be paid in cash now when calls go out for cleaning up farm land' (interview with Wowetta community member, July 2014).

The Wowetta women exemplify how community enterprises can develop labour arrangements to reflect ethical commitments. Their goal of increasing local employment for women means that workers directly engaged in the cassava production process are paid, while their commitment to participation shapes the conditions of employment for workers. They ensure fairness in tying workers' wages to production and are dedicated to making sure that workers' participation in cassava production does not erode other livelihood activities and practices tied to the functioning of the local economy. Furthermore, a commitment to participation shapes the conditions of community involvement – such as with the 'Matroman' and the voluntary in-kind service of the Women's Group executive committee members. As Jenny Cameron asserts, these kinds of labour arrangements demonstrate the work innovations open to community enterprises and reflect the variety of labour practices available that can be employed to embrace their ethical commitments (2010, 4).

Given that conventional capitalist market engagements can produce gradual alienation from subsistence livelihood practices and household, family and community responsibilities, the women of the cassava enterprise selected a rotating labour system to cushion these disruptions. However, during the course of the enterprise the number of women participating on a regular basis dwindled gradually from the initial 22 full-time members to five dedicated and consistent participants, with the other original members participating on a less consistent basis. Many young women in the village find it more financially lucrative to travel to mining areas or to Brazil to engage in domestic work, than to stay in the village and work in the cassava enterprise. During interviews conducted with both men and women in the community, many lamented that the cassava enterprise offered 'little money'. As one young woman, who worked more on a part-time rather than full-time basis in cassava production related, 'sometimes my children will ask me, "mommy why don't you go and do some cassava work so we could have little money to buy sweetie (candy)?" And my husband would say, "why you going to do cassava work for such little money?"' (interview with Wowetta community member June 2013). Repeatedly, community members stated that 'cassava work is hard work, and it only brings in little money.' Interestingly enough, men in the community noted that, despite the labour-intensive nature of cassava work and its meagre remuneration, they would still encourage their mothers, daughters, and wives to participate in the cassava enterprise, because it helped to pass on traditional knowledge about cassava production.

Market Relationships

The Wowetta Women's Group cassava income-generating enterprise is innovating market arrangements which reaffirm their commitment to developing the local economy *on their terms*. These market arrangements go beyond formal market transactions while simultaneously embracing alternative and non-market transactions (Gibson-Graham 2006B, chapter 3).

After a batch of farine is completed it is transported to the Village Shop for sale. The cassava produced by the Wowetta Women's Group is in high demand both locally and further afield, and sells for GY$140 per pound (US$0.70). Primary formal market sales are made through the village shop to local residents, to surrounding communities, and to two businesspeople that regularly pass through. Many of these local sales are in small quantities. Both surrounding communities and local villagers purchasing farine generally do so after their individual homemade supply is depleted. The two businessmen purchase farine in large quantities and re-sell further afield in mining areas at five to six times the original price (see also Cobb 2011, 18).

Given the large quantities purchased by the two businesspeople versus small individual purchases locally, farine for local consumption by Wowetta villagers is usually unavailable. In 2013 the women began discussions about the possibilities of developing a two-tier pricing system, one for villagers and the other for businesspeople from outside of the community. This two-tier pricing structure holds the possibility of ensuring local demand for farine is met and affordable. Nonetheless, the women along with the Village Council collectively agreed that from every batch of farine processed two bags would be set aside for local sales, while the remaining would be sold to businesspeople from outside the community. These recent deliberations by the women and the community at large highlight their commitment first and foremost to the development of the local economy. To ensure that unnecessary hardships are not met by villagers, the community enterprise is willing to sell below the going market price. This further demonstrates that the collective well-being of the community is preferred over the bottom line approach associated with traditional capitalist business practices.

The Wowetta Women's Group also engages in alternative market transactions which continue to diversify and expand markets based on solidarity principles of fair trade. These range from participating in regional food fairs such as the annual Rupununi Expo held in Lethem, and the national trade show GuyExpo convened in the capital city, Georgetown. At these regional and national events, the women showcase their cassava-based products (farine, cassava bread, cassareep, and tapioca). In addition to providing an opportunity for them to achieve product visibility, these spaces develop direct relationships between the women (producers) and consumers. These direct engagements equip them to educate the buying public about how their purchasing power can leverage support for more equitable models of commercial partnerships. Moreover, these face-to-face encounters, listed as a core solidarity principle of fair trade,[9] help the women to avoid a middle person. This, in turn, enables them to retain a larger part of their products' value. A second layer of solidarity principle practices by the Wowetta women is demonstrated in the development of long-term commercial partnerships established with retailers. To make this a reality, the Wowetta women engaged in a number of capacity-building initiatives supported by international and national NGOs such as CUSO International; the Inter-American Institute for Agricultural Cooperation (IICA); and Women's Agro-Processors Development Network (WADN).[10] These initiatives range from providing support in business planning, to assisting the women to obtain their food handling certificates, to matching the women with local organisations as developmental partners. As a result, the Wowetta women were successful at negotiating fair prices directly with the New Guyana Shop, operated by the Guyana Marketing Corporation (GMC), an agency of the Ministry of Agriculture, to sell their diversified cassava product offerings. The sale of these products in the New Guyana Shop allows the Wowetta enterprise to make its products available on a regular basis in the central urban area of Guyana. But beyond visibility, and the ability to make consumers conscious about supporting ethical trade practices, the placement of the Wowetta cassava enterprise's products communicates a cultural expression of the Makushi way of life, and its contribution to local food security.

The numerous non-market transactions associated with the cassava income-generating enterprise help to sustain the enterprise and the generate community participation and engagement. For example, during the initial phase of the enterprise they were approached by the Guyanese Government to provide cassava biscuits for the nursery and primary schools in Wowetta. The provision of cassava biscuits was to be coordinated with peanut butter purchased from one of the surrounding communities' income-generating enterprises. This project was viewed by the government as one that linked the assets of communities in the Region #9 area to further economic development. However, the women soon found that the price the government was willing to purchase cassava biscuits at was unsustainable for the enterprise. In turn, the government abandoned their commitment to purchasing cassava biscuits from the Wowetta Women's Group. The women then made a strong commitment to produce cassava biscuits periodically for the village schools. As the chairperson of the Women's Group indicated, 'It's our children. If we don't feed them who will?' (interview July 2012).

As this statement and the decision to go ahead and produce cassava biscuits for the village children without government support suggest, this act of gift giving was seen as an ethical commitment to taking responsibility for the children of the community. Regardless of the extra time and hours that would be spent, without cash payment to produce cassava biscuits, the women felt that they could not see their children go hungry. Furthermore, in instances where alternative snacks were provided by the government, they felt these snacks were often alien to the diets of Amerindian communities, contributing in the long term to diseases associated with processed foods. Some women also suggested that cassava biscuits themselves represented Makushi cultural traditions that were important to sustain.

All of the above diverse market activities indicate that the cassava income-generating enterprise is 'redefining markets as something different than an instrumental relationship in which the producer tries to extract the highest price for their product, and the purchaser tries for the lowest price' (Cameron 2010, 5). For the Wowetta Women's Group the market is not about making as much money as possible without considering how differential pricing systems can mean the difference between full and limited access to food. Their use of alternative and non-market transactions demonstrates how a community that has lived the reality of being unable to afford the cash purchase of necessities is attempting to provide more equitable solutions.

Implications: The Way Forward

This case study suggests that community enterprises which employ innovative economic practices can offer alternative pathways to the current hegemonic economic development model. The creative labour arrangements and market relationships discussed suggest an ethic of care: the overall well-being of the local community is at the front and centre of the enterprise's approach to economic development. This is in sharp contrast to the capitalicentric/business-as-usual model of economic development subscribed to by policy elites in which the focus on income-generating enterprises is the pathway into formal paid employment. As Ash Amin points out, this expectation of community enterprises is unrealistic (2009B, 46). Through research on social enterprises in the UK, Amin concludes that the ethic of care and social participation are the values and motivations that distinguish community/social enterprises from public and private sector organisations.

Expanding on this observation Jenny Cameron suggests that community/social enterprises need to be given the space to operate in their own distinctive way. She further warns that given the overemphasis by policy elites on the business end of community/social enterprises, the risk exists 'that mainstream business practices are being overvalued, thereby undermining other features that may well be the very strength of community and social enterprises – for example, the ethic of care and social participation that Amin refers to' (2010, 8).

In the case of the Wowetta Women's group, the space to operate in their own distinctive way is signified by the various innovative and creative labour arrangements and market relationships. These practices all point to what David Barkin refers to as 'selective market engagements' (Barkin 2001),[11] whereby community enterprises are in the driver's seat determining on their own terms 'when and how to engage in markets' (Kay 2008, 930). These ethical spaces of engagement carved out and developed by the Wowetta women are predicated on achieving autonomy and self-sufficiency. However, this introduces the question: how can the women protect their achievements from being jeopardised by the intrusion of the state apparatus? As noted by Cameron (2010), Amin (2009A), Pearce

(2009), and Bateman and Chang (2012), the neoliberalising agenda of the state often attempts to shift the norms and practices of community-based enterprises from collectivist community goals towards individualising entrepreneurial market 'bottom line' business-as-usual models.

To date, the women face challenges of reliable transportation of the cassava from the farm to the processing site, and of the finished product from the rugged terrain of the hinterlands, where Wowetta is located, to customers further afield. The challenge going forward for the Wowetta women will not only be to seek substantial financial, infrastructural, and human capital commitments from the state but to also transform and reconfigure community-state relations.

In many instances, the system of political patronage continues to stymie development in Amerindian communities due to the lack of both transparency and accountability. Both the PPP and the PNC have traditionally allocated state funds to Amerindian communities based on votes the party received at the polls. Given the 'counting at the place of the poll' during elections, the ruling party 'knows in which villages it garnered the majority of votes' (Bulkan 2013, 374). It is armed with this knowledge that the PPP for the past 23 years, like its predecessor the PNC, engaged state resources particularly at election time to win over Amerindian communities. These resources, whether one refers to them as 'goodies' (Kissoon 2015) or 'handouts' (Abraham 2014) were often delivered to village councils, which either kept vehicles, building material, or generators for their own personal use or distributed them based on perceived favouritism to certain members of the community. Audits under the newly elected coalition government are uncovering the lack of records regarding who got what and when (Audit Office of Guyana 2015, 105–20).

The last election on May 11, 2015 witnessed a shift in the Guyanese political landscape with a victory by a coalition government – A Partnership for National Unity (APNU) and the Alliance for Change (AFC). The new coalition government appears committed to engaging in a participatory partnership with Amerindian communities. Their thrust appears to seek to disrupt the binary opposition of the 'bush' and 'town', the former associated with a space inhabited by Amerindians, to be controlled and feared, and the later as a space where directives to the former are given and expected to be obeyed (see Jefferson 2012).[12] If this is indeed the case, then the Wowetta women's group finds itself in a position to identify and represent its external resource needs to the state, coupled with the possibility of forging 'enabling power' practices which have been contrary to the 'power over' engagements historically characterising Amerindian/state relations (France 2015).

Conclusion

The Wowetta Women's Group community income-generating enterprise provides us with a paradigmatic shift regarding approaches to economic development. Its practices de-centre the capitalicentric/business as usual model of economic development and makes visible diverse and alternative models of economic development. It challenges the incentivising of individual rewards which often jeopardises overall community well-being. In return, the women offer diverse and alternative models where both communal and individual good can be enacted and actualised. Through creative and innovative rotating labour arrangements and tiered market engagements the group exemplifies movement beyond seeing work as just another pay check but also, or instead, establishes the value of voluntary in-kind and participatory work practices. These arrangements also envision market engagements as possessing power beyond the laws of supply-and-demand and making profits. Instead, they present an opportunity for communities to put in place safeguards that ensure that markets will work *for them* instead of solely acting *on them*. The paradigms, codes and folk norms of the Wowetta community seem more likely to endure as they are able to cling to the traditional values they hold dear.

Notes

1. Historically, political rule in Guyana has been dominated by first the Afro-Guyanese political party, the Peoples National Congress – PNC 1966–92, and then the Indo-Guyanese dominated party, the Peoples Progressive Party – PPP 1992–2015 (Hinds 2009; Gafar 2003; Mars 2001; Hintzen 1989).
2. The ethnographic fieldwork informing this paper took place in Wowetta from 2012 to 2014.
3. As defined by Bateman and Chang, 'microfinance is actually the generic term covering all varieties of micro-financial interventions, such as microcredit, microsavings, microinsurance, micro-franchising, and so on' (2012, 13).
4. http://www.un.org/press/en/2004/dev2492.doc.htm.
5. The term social economy refers to socialising the market to ensure it works for people, the environment, and produces an ethic of care. Ash Amin notes, the social economy 'is understood as commercial and non-commercial

activity largely in the hands of the third-sector or community organisations that gives priority to meeting social (and environmental) needs before profit maximisation' (Amin 2009B, 4). Variant terms often linked with the term social economy, but often more geographically and place-based defined are: moral economy, third sector, solidarity economy and cooperatives.

6. Farine is one by-product of bitter cassava. It is granular in consistency and called a cereal.
7. Manihot is the scientific name given to cassava. There are generally two types of cassava: sweet and bitter. Bitter cassava contains high levels of cyanide that must be extracted by both squeezing (or matapeeing) and cooking before consumption. As Elias, Rival, and Mckey point out, 'Bitter cassava is characterised by high cyanogenic-glucoside content of the tuberous roots' (2000, 242). Cassava production has been a part of Amerindian practices for the past 300 years (Renvoize 1972).
8. Matapeeing is the process of squeezing out the cyanide content from the bitter cassava. The matapee which is a cylindrically shaped object is constructed from the palm tree by craftsmen in the village.
9. See Bisailon et al. *Fair Trade and the Solidarity Economy: The Challenges Ahead*: workshop report for evolving definitions of fair trade and core principles (2005, 5). Despite the evolving definition, 'direct relationships between producers and consumers, avoiding intermediaries and speculators' remains at the heart of all definitions.
10. The Women's Agro-Processors Development Network, founded in 2011, consists of 11 member groups of small scale agro-processors located in rural and indigenous communities in Guyana. They are a regional affiliate of the Caribbean Network of Rural Women Producers (CANROP).
11. David Barkin provides a framework based on the three principles – autonomy, self-sufficiency, and production diversification – which communities may wish to consider as they search for alternative pathways to neoliberal development (Barkin 2001, 33). He recommends that the key to unlocking autonomy (which is not about isolation) and self-sufficiency (not absolute) is 'selective market engagement'.
12. The coalition party is also very much aware that the shifting Amerindian demographics highlights their potential to swing elections. They make up 10.5 per cent of the Guyanese population and are superseded by Indo-Guyanese who make up 38.9 per cent of the population, followed by Afro-Guyanese at 29.2 per cent. and the mixed population at 19.9 per cent (Guyana Bureau of Statistics 2016).

References

Abraham, Medino. 2014. What if the Amerindians Could Unite and Have Their Own Political Party? Letter to the editor, *Stabroek News*, December 10.
Amin, A. 2009A. Extraordinarily Ordinary: Working in the Social Economy. *Social Enterprise Journal 5*, no. 1:30–49.

———. 2009B *The Social Economy: International Perspectives on Economic Solidarity.* London: Zed.
Audit Office of Guyana. 2015. *Report of the Auditor General on Public Accounts of Guyana and the Accounts of Ministries/Departments/Regions for the Fiscal Year End 31 December 2014.* Georgetown: Audit Office of Guyana.
Balkenhol, Bernd. 2007. Policy Implications. In *Microfinance and Public Policy: Outreach, Performance and Efficiency,* ed. B Balkenhol, 213. London: Palgrave Macmillan.
Barkin, David. 2001. La Nueva Ruralidad y la Globalizaci´on. In *La Nueva Ruralidad en América Latina: Maestría en Desarrollo Rural 20 años,* vol 2, ed. E. Pérez and M.A. Farah, 21–40. Bogotá: Pontificia Universidad Javeriana.
Bateman, Milford, and Ha-Joon Chang. 2012. Microfinance and the Illusion of Development: From Hubris to Nemesis in Thirty Years. *World Economic Review* 1:13–36.
Bisaillon, Verinique, Corinne Gendron, and Marie-France Turcotte. 2006. Fair Trade and the Solidarity Economy: The Challenges Ahead Summary of the Fair Trade Workshop's Activities. Les cashiers de la Chaire-collective recherché. http://www.crsdd.uqam.ca/Pages/docs/pdfCahiersRecherche/2006/05-2006.pdf.
Boudreaux, Karol, and Tyler Cowen. 2008. The Micromagic of Microcredit. *The Wilson Quarterly* (Winter): 27–31.
Bulkan, Janette. 2013. The Struggle for Recognition of the Indigenous Voice: Amerindians in Guyanese Politics. *Round Table* 102, no. 4:367–80.
Cameron, Jenny. 2010. Business as Usual or Economic Innovation? Work, Markets and Growth in Community and Social Enterprises. *Third Sector Review,* Special Issue on Social Enterprise and Social Innovation 16, no. 2.
Cobb, Heather. 2011. *Market Assessment: Farine, Cassava Bread & Other Cassava Products. Wowetta Women's Group, Wowetta Village, North Rupununi, Region #9, Guyana.* Report prepared for VSO Guyana.
Colchester, Martin. 1997. *Guyana: Fragile frontier. Loggers, Miners, and Forest Peoples.* London: Latin American Bureau and the World Rainforest Movement.
Dilly, Barbara. 2003. Gender, Culture, and Ecotourism: Development Policies and Practices in the Guyanese RainForest. *Women's Studies Quarterly* 31, no. 3/4:58–75.
Elias, Marianne, Laura Rival, and Doyle Mckey. 2000. Perceptions and Management of Cassava *(Manihot Esculenta* Crantz) Diversity among Makushi Amerindians of Guyana (South America). *Journal of Ethnobiology* 20, no. 2:239–65.
Escobar, Arturo. 2010. Latin America at a Crossroads: Alternative Modernizations, post-liberalism, or Post-development? *Cultural Studies* 24, no. 1:1–65.
Flores, John. 2011. The Changing Face of the Guyana-Brazil Frontier. Unpublished Paper. University of the West Indies, St Augustine.
France, Hollis. 2015. Moving beyond a Politics of Optics and towards a Politics of Empowerment. *Stabroek News,* In the Diaspora, May 25. http://www.stabroeknews.com/2015/features/in-the-diaspora/05/25/moving-beyond-a-politics-of-optics-towards-a-politics-of-empowerment-for-our-amerindian-sisters-and-brothers.

Gafar, John. 2003. *Guyana: From State Control to Free Markets*. Hauppauge, NY: Nova Science.

Gibson-Graham, J.K. 2006A. *The End of Capitalism (As We Knew It): A Feminist Critique of Political Economy*. 2nd ed. Minneapolis: University Of Minnesota Press.

———. 2006B. *A Postcapitalist Politics*. Minneapolis: University Of Minnesota Press.

Guyana Bureau of Statistics. 2016. *The Cooperative Republic of Guyana. Population and Housing Census 2012. National Census Report*. Georgetown: Guyana Bureau of Statistics.

Hennessy, Logan. 2013. Re-Placing Indigenous Territory: Villagization and the Transformation of Amerindian Environments under 'Cooperative Socialism' in Guyana. *Annals of the Association of American Geographers* 103, no. 5:1,242–65.

Hickel, Jason. 2015. The Microfinance Delusion: Who Really Wins? *Guardian*, June 10. http://www.theguardian.com/global-development-professionals-network/2015/jun/10/the-microfinance-delusion-who-really-wins.

Hintzen, Percy. 1989. *The Costs of Regime Survival: Racial Mobilization and Control of the State in Guyana and Trinidad*. Cambridge: Cambridge University Press.

Hinds, David. 2009. Ethnopolitics and Fractured Nationalism in Guyana. In *Anthropologies of Guayana: Cultural Spaces in Northeastern Amazonia*, ed. N.L. Whitehead and S.W. Alemán, 154–66. Tucson, AZ: University of Arizona Press.

Jefferson, Ben. 2012. The Particularity of Place in Derek Walcott's Bush. *Modern Horizon Journal*, June. http://modernhorizonsjournal.ca/june2012issue.

Kay, Cristóbal. 2008. Reflections on Latin American Rural Studies in the Neoliberal Globalization Period: A New Rurality? *Development and Change* 39, no. 6:915–43

Kissoon, Freddie. 2015. The PPP and the Amerindian Vote. *Kaieteur News*, features/columnist. June 16.

Lechat, Noell. 2009. Organizing for the Solidarity Economy in South Brazil. In *The Social Economy: International Perspectives on Economic Solidarity*, ed. A. Amin, 159–75. London: Zed.

Mars, Perry. 2001. Ethnic Politics, Mediation, and Conflict Resolution: The Guyana Experience. *Journal of Peace Research* 38, no. 3:353–72.

Mitchell, Timothy. 2005. The Work of Economics: How a Discipline Makes Its World. *European Journal of Sociology* 46, no. 2:297–320.

Pearce, John. 2009. Social Economy: Engaging as a Third System? In *The Social Economy: International Perspectives on Economic Solidarity*, ed. A. Amin, 22–38. London: Zed.

Renvoize, Benoit. 1972. The Area of Origin of Manihot Esculenta as a Crop Plant – A Review of the Evidence. *Economic Botany* 26, no. 4:352–60.

Roodman, David. 2012. *Due Diligence: An Impertinent Inquiry into Microfinance*. Baltimore: Brookings Institute Press.

Trotz, Alissa and Terry Roopnaraine. 2009. Angles of Vision from the Coast and Hinterland of Guyana. In *Anthropologies of Guyana: Cultural Spaces in*

Northeastern Amazonia, ed. N. L. Whitehead and S.W. Alemán, 235–53. Tucson: University of Arizona Press.

United Nations. 2004. UN Launches International Year of Microcredit 2005. Press release. http://www.un.org/press/en/2004/dev2492.doc.htm.

Yunus, Muhammad. 2006. Poverty is a Threat to Peace. Nobel Lecture. http://www.nobelprize.org/nobel_prizes/peace/laureates/2006/yunus-lecture-en.html.

17.
Inundated with Facts: Flooding and the Knowledge Economies of Climate Adaptation in Guyana

Sarah E. Vaughn

Introduction

Between December 2004 and February 2005, coastal Guyana experienced multiple storms which resulted in over 60 inches of rain (Blommestein 2005). The storms were unprecedented, measured against engineers' records that estimated seven inches as the average monthly rainfall. Extensive flooding unfolded across Regions 3, 4, and 5 where 62 per cent of the nation's population resides (roughly 520,000 people). Many of these residents include farmers who have since become fluent in translating their concerns about canals to state officials and civil engineers. At state-sponsored community meetings, their conversations have focused on the construction of the Hope Canal, a six-mile-long earthen drainage channel that was to become a first line of defence against seasonal flooding. However, many farmers felt that the canal diverted attention away from their more immediate needs. They described daily struggles with 'secondary arteries' clogged with weeds and lack of access to 'back dams'. Curbing flood waters, they argued, required intimate knowledge about the canal's possibilities as much as about its constraints. With dry land at a minimum, the Hope Canal forced farmers, state officials, and engineers to rethink what counts as collective survival along Guyana's coastal floodplain.

There are several ways in which the Hope Canal matters to flooding. Designated as a drainage channel, it also supports the system of water storage in nearby dams. This arrangement required state officials and engineers to develop a canal design that could account for both drainage flow and intensified rainfall due to climate change. Guyana's ministry of agriculture subsidised costs for the canal by collaborating with engineering firms in the local private sector. The collaborations were related to an ongoing World Bank project which involved the ministry creating new hydraulic models of dams (Morton and Guzmán 2014).

These collaborations have come to undergird a new kind of knowledge economy in Guyana. Eager to experiment with engineering measures, state officials and engineers actively recognise that intense storms related to climate change have undercut their abilities to manage flooding. The state-sponsored community meeting with farmers is just one example of a public forum where ordinary citizens have debated the practical importance of both drainage and the kinds of expertise needed to adapt to climate change. With these deliberations, climate change has become a window of opportunity for reimagining state-private partnerships in the development of large-scale infrastructure.

In this chapter I track the ways the Hope Canal constitutes the day-to-day economic relations of climate adaptation in Guyana. The Hope Canal is a site where both techno-scientific and environmental agendas tentatively coalesce around the circulation of capital between the state and local private engineering firms. I suggest that in climate adaptation, complex environmental processes shape expert and public understandings of public services and their value. In doing so, I offer an alternative perspective to the emerging literature on climate adaptation that emphasises its market processes as solely based in 'cost-effective' technological solutions (Oels 2006; Evans and Reid 2014). Instead, I follow Melinda Cooper's (2010) call to interpret climate change as 'a function of [people's] relative degrees of confidence' in the market to tame environmental risks (176).

I take climatological events, such as floods, not as problems for climate adaptation projects to overcome but as starting points for understanding market processes. I suggest that climate adaptation projects comprise what Naomi Klein (2008) calls 'disaster capitalism', the trend of states using catastrophes to empower capitalist interests and the private sector. In this regard, climate adaptation offers an extraordinary example of neoliberalism in practice: markets are both causes and solutions to the state's limited capacity to effectively avert environmental disasters. But climate adaptation projects also generate kinds of possible worlds that link people to credible scenarios about what it means to live with vulnerability.

In the next section of this chapter, I develop the idea that climate adaptation projects do not merely respond to but are also shaped by environments. In the following three sections, I suggest that an environmental focus on disaster capitalism has three advantages. First, it pushes the concept of disaster capitalism beyond attention to how the bureaucratic provision of infrastructure generates profit. I show that the economic-political utility of infrastructure is not always self-evident. In their local geographies, infrastructures can be physically transformed by environmental processes to shape how people recognise themselves as economic-political actors (Anand 2011). Second, it forces us to abandon neat notions of expertise and its public and private performative dimensions. Like other kinds of infrastructure (Larkin 2013), Guyana's earthen canals and dams often 'breakdown', meaning that they can erode under pressure due to intense flooding. Their failure can reproduce forms of knowledge and patron-clientship that do not necessarily correspond to their intended function. Third, an environmental focus reveals that the compensatory measures that inform climate adaptation projects are not merely economic but epistemic, a point often under-theorised in critical analyses of disaster capitalism. In particular, I draw on the experiences of displaced farmers to argue that their sensory interactions with the canal help them re-imagine vulnerable landscapes as sites of knowledge production.

This chapter is based on 17 months of ethnographic and archival research between 2009 and 2010 in Guyana, and shorter visits in 2011 and 2014. I conducted over 30 interviews with engineers affiliated with the Hope Canal's construction and interviews with six of the 20 landowners directly affected by its construction. In addition, I attended meetings held by the state related to the design and modelling of the Hope Canal, spent time with landowners living and farming on their compromised land, and attended community-led workshops about flooding across the country, all being events that inform this chapter.

Environments of Disaster Capitalism

Across the social sciences many scholars have engaged Naomi Klein's concept of disaster capitalism as a means to describe the global ascent of neoliberal orders (Cavanagh 2017; Gunewardena and Schuller 2008; Ortner 2016; Dole et al. 2016; Hickel and Khan 2012). They have examined how the post-Second World War configuration of EuroAmerican free market policies direct humanitarian and military spending especially in (post) colonial, war-torn, and (post)socialist states. These policies, Klein argues, are directly related to the way states issue executive orders to usher in free market policies that would have probably met resistance from citizens under normal circumstances. The concept of disaster capitalism thus presents disasters as differentially produced by socio-political processes over time.

The analytical benefit of bringing the concept of disaster capitalism to bear on politics is considerable. It reveals that public policies based in market fundamentalism can (but not always) lead to the under-provision of public services for disaster preparedness and relief (Somers 2008). Ordinary citizens assume greater risks as individuals, learning to strategically rely on a mix of state and privatised networks for services such as health care and insurance (Roberts 2010). In such scenarios, vulnerability is turned into a market opportunity, while state funding fuels capital accumulation and a style of intervention based in the 'economization' of public services (Harvey 2007).

In her recent book *This Changes Everything: Capitalism vs. The Climate* (2015), Klein details disaster capitalism from the perspective of perhaps the greatest threat to neoliberalism – climate change. She argues that disaster capitalism is an issue that shapes the ways states not only respond to but define climate change as a problem. She notes:

> Climate change has never received the crisis treatment from our leaders, despite the fact that it carries the risk of destroying lives on a vastly greater scale than collapsed banks or collapsed buildings. The cuts to our greenhouse gas emissions that scientists tell us are necessary in order to greatly reduce the risk of catastrophe are treated as nothing more than gentle suggestions, actions that can be put off pretty much indefinitely. Clearly, what gets declared a crisis is an expression of power and priorities as much as hard facts (6).

States, in other words, view cutting carbon emissions as disrupting the status quo management of economic institutions and related infrastructure (see also Fletcher 2012; Bumpus and Liverman 2008). Klein is not always clear about which states or governmental agencies are responsible for climate inaction, or the specifics behind how they purportedly avoid responsibility. However, she does emphasise that in both Global North and Global South contexts, ordinary citizens have responded by campaigning for the de-privatisation of public services – including those for energy (see also Howe and Boyer 2016). They have brought forth referendums with the hope of urging lawmakers to invest in local management strategies that rely on renewables. At the same time, Klein (2015) argues that 'energy privatization reversals' matter as much for economic reform as for rebuilding the public sphere (97–98). She writes,

> every time a new, record-breaking disaster fills our screens…we have more reminders of how climate change has the potential to provide a direct and quick way to invest in the publicly owned bones of our societies, made brittle by decades of neglect (102).

I interpret Klein as pointing to the open-ended relationships between the public and private sectors that climate change underscores. For instance, there are cases when there is not a big enough profit margin for private partners to team up with the state in large-scale infrastructure development. She cites the efforts of the French government in 2014 to curb air pollution by making public transit free for three days. The French government viewed this measure as 'temporary', because overall prices needed to be lowered to balance the state's budget while encouraging public transit into the future (109). Indeed, disaster capitalism may be economically driven, but it can be informed by a variety of concerns including accessibility (see also Lakoff 2013). Moreover, the issue of accessibility suggests that state-private partnerships are structured by moral assumptions about the kinds of market mechanisms needed to avert disasters (MacKenzie 2009).

Questions of value and the meaning of public services have been no less fraught within the context of drainage management since the 2005 disaster in Guyana. Timing the release of water from the coast's main dam called the East Demerara Water Conservancy (EDWC) into canals was crucial during the disaster. If water was released when the tide was high, Georgetown would have been inundated not only with water from the EDWC but also the sea. Engineers devised a plan that allowed them to release water into the nearby Mahaica River. While this strategy saved Georgetown, it further exacerbated flooding in rural communities. Engineers' fragmented response was suggestive of a changing climate generating further uncertainty about the structural integrity of the EDWC.

After the 2005 disaster, the World Bank sponsored the Conservancy Adaptation Project (CAP). Under CAP, Guyanese and foreign engineers created hydraulic models that took into account the impacts of climate-related storms and sea-level rise on the EDWC. One outcome of these models was the recommendation for a drainage channel that has a direct route to the Atlantic Ocean. While some technical assessments for the Hope Canal were completed under the World Bank, the majority of its planning fell under a separate project directed by the Ministry of Agriculture and National Irrigation and Drainage Authority (NDIA).

The nearly US$20 million project was financed with tax payer dollars and the PetroCaribe Fund (*Guyana Chronicle Online* 2016).[1] Similar to other large-scale infrastructure development projects in Guyana, the ministry hired local private engineering firms for additional technical support. Between 2009 and 2015, private engineering firms built the canal and its adjacent bridge. An audit completed by an independent consulting group found that the project was millions of dollars over budget and that the ministry did not keep an asset register (*Stabroek News Online* 2016). In particular, the auditor raised questions about whether the government relied too much on private contractors as opposed to using already available NDIA staff and equipment to build the canal.

The Hope Canal is similar to Klein's example of French public transit because they are both responses to climate change, but the Hope Canal departs from it in a significant way. The Guyanese state actively recognises that economic planning for large-scale infrastructure cannot control but is dependent on changes in the surrounding environment due to climate change. Hydraulic models informed engineers' vision for the canal and their civic commitments to protect the public. But so too did the economy, playing an important role in establishing divisions in expert labour between the World Bank, the ministry, and local private engineering firms. These distinctions are important because they demonstrate that climate adaptation is informed by different styles of calculative reasoning. As David Graeber (2014) argues, principles of property *and* conviviality shape the way knowledge is produced, circulated, and disseminated in market economies. But Graeber admits that these principles do not map on evenly to all persons and things, particularly in times of disaster (67–70).[2] Importantly, then, climate adaptation projects are place-making (Massey 2005). They strive to align experts' and the public's competing visions about the entanglements of place-based ecology, infrastructure, and risk. At the same time, they re-contextualise the jurisdictions of expertise across state-private domains. This chapter is an attempt to map these jurisdictions as both experts and the public struggle to define what counts as climate adaptation and the role of large-scale infrastructure in protecting the coastal floodplain.

While Klein's notion of disaster capitalism treats environments as objects on which experts and economic institutions intervene, I ask what happens if we saw environments playing an active role in climate adaptation. Central to an environmental imaginary of disaster capitalism is that scientific tools such as hydraulic models and environmental assessments strive to identify ongoing or potential shifts in ecosystems (Beck 2008; Tsing 2015). Throughout this chapter, I pay close attention to the ways experts and the public attempt to account for the impact of climate change on floods. I show that the zones where economy and environment meet form less a rigid barrier than a fluid boundary in climate adaptation. This boundary is organised as much by ecological, atmospheric, and hydrological dynamics, as by infrastructures, including dams and canals historically used for plantation agriculture in Guyana. Recent research into civil engineering underscores the idea that climate-related flooding has the capacity to transform the material dimensions and use-value of dams and canals (Whatmore 2013). More than ecological events, floods infringe on landscape operations. Floods shed light on the ways in which infrastructure becomes entangled with the disparate forms of marketisation captured in Klein's notion of disaster capitalism.

In the rest of this chapter, I trace the economic activities and landscapes that make climate adaptation a neoliberal practice in Guyana. I argue that the Hope Canal is not only a response to the 2005 disaster but part of a changing local ecology that is enfolding environmental processes less confidently than ever into the economy. In effect, climate-related flooding has become a platform for both experts and ordinary citizens to question the efficacy of state-private partnerships in large-scale infrastructure development. In the context of climate adaptation, we see that disaster capitalism is a fragmented process that unfolds across competing claims to expertise and economic relations. I show that with the construction of the Hope Canal theoretical ideas about the relationship between environment and economy materialise, and when flooding occurs, such ideas are put to the test and refined.

Disasters and Political Economies

The Hope Canal is a product of more than just the 2005 disaster. Its construction is part of the ministry of agriculture's efforts to expand the Mahaica-Mahaicony-Abary Scheme (MMA Scheme). The initial plans for the MMA Scheme were proposed by state-sponsored engineers in the early 1950s. The MMA Scheme was intended to enhance flood management and agricultural development through three river-based dams. Engineers envisioned that these three dams would connect to the East Coast region's largest dam, the EDWC.

While the MMA Scheme grew out of India's Damodar Valley Corporation model of damming, it was also rooted in local concerns about decolonisation (Camacho 1960, 5).[3] Political events surrounding the colony's 1953 constitutional suspension underscored its importance. British colonial authorities surmised that 'expansive flood protection' was the only way to 'give more people the feeling of having a real stake in the country' (Colonial Office 2003, 21). This pledge to freedom through flood-control was a response to escalating tensions between Afro-Guianese and Indo-Guianese over under-employment in the sugar sector. At the same time, authorities looked to create political conditions that could protect the interests of British-based sugar firms after independence. They envisioned that the MMA Scheme's system of individual leasehold titling based on selective crop rotations would lessen these tensions (Camacho 1960).[4] The MMA Scheme was a result of free market agricultural policies that sought to de-centralise agricultural planning and production. But, with independence in 1966, under the rule of the People's National Congress (PNC), efforts at de-centralisation came to a halt. Beginning in the early 1970s, the PNC embraced cooperative socialism and extensive nationalisation of the agricultural industry. The PNC envisioned that revenue available to the state would increase enormously through profits generated by the state corporate sector. Yet, as Percy Hintzen (1989) notes, the PNC implemented policies that tied the country's agricultural industry firmly to export earnings and the need for large amounts of finance capital (183–93). These policies increased the debt burden on the country and dictated a programme of state expansion that limited investments in dams and canals. Even the MMA Scheme's resident engineer warned that its subsidiary infrastructure would amount to US$140 million and would 'definitely need foreign financing' (Veramallay 1976, 97). With inadequate financing, only one of the three MMA dams was completed under the PNC.

With the death of Forbes Burnham in 1985 his successor, Desmond Hoyte, became committed to completing the MMA Scheme. The Hoyte government implemented an Economic Recovery Program (ERP) under pressure from the World Bank to re-open the economy to foreign capital and divest public enterprises. However, the sugar sector remained majority state-owned with some measures put in place for selective foreign investments. This staggered transition was partially crystallised by the emergence of local private contracting and engineering firms that could readily provide labour and materials to collaborate with state agencies. Between 1988 and 1991, the ERP set an annual production target for sugar at 240,000 metric tons and strived to base 17 per cent of the annual gross domestic product in agriculture (Canterbury 2007). However, these goals were not met, which forced the government to expand the scope of the ERP.

By 1992, a national election was held and the People's Progressive Party (PPP), a staunch critic of the PNC's development policies particularly in the agriculture sector, came into office in coalition with a 'civic' component (the PPP/C). The PPP/C government developed the ERP primarily around the rice sector with considerations for non-traditional commodities, including fruits and vegetables. With the help of the Inter-American Development Bank (IDB), the PPP/C created water user associations mostly in areas of the MMA Scheme. Since then, their water fees and allocation schedules have been based on water usage on individual plots, crop rotations, and state budgets for canal dredging (Mott McDonald and Ministry of Agriculture 2003). To date, the second MMA dam has been completed alongside other agricultural programmes that mobilise similar campaigns about the links between infrastructure development and responsible citizenship.

Despite these heavy capital investments in the MMA Scheme, the damage wrought by the 2005 disaster was unprecedented. In addition to flood waters causing the EDWC's embankment to crack, 17 of 19 water supply pumping stations were submerged during the disaster. Sewage and agricultural chemicals were introduced into water supplies (Bloomstein 2005, 49). These toxins, alongside canals already clogged with garbage, contributed to the threat of water-borne diseases and contaminated waters. Months after the disaster, state officials circulated elaborate reports about how they planned to repair the EDWC. Within these documents plenty of slippages exist in theories, data, and models about what counts as a disaster. Records show that on average, a major flood engulfs the East Coast region every decade. However, state officials still noted fears about factors that are outside of their control: that climate change will make future floods 'more catastrophic' (Mott McDonald 2005).

In this respect, the 2005 disaster was symptomatic of the post-1992 ERP measures that helped privatise infrastructure development in Guyana. On the one hand, many noted that the flood's damage was an effect of the state's piecemeal contracts since 1992, with local private engineering firms, to complete the MMA Scheme. On the other, many pointed to ordinary citizens' tendency to litter in canals and their expectation that it was the state's duty to clean them or at least if they could not, to hire private contractors to do so (Pelling 1996). Everyone, state officials and ordinary citizens; rural and urban; rich and poor; PNC and PPP, were seemingly to blame for the 'ongoing political and social collapse of infrastructure' (Westmaas 2005; Trotz 2010). The disaster demonstrated how with the threat of intensified rainfall Guyana's irrigation and drainage system cannot prevent but accommodates flooding.

In the aftermath of the 2005 disaster, ordinary citizens bear the burden of hardships that are in the statistical aggregate, while state agencies lack confidence about their capabilities to avert flooding. But beyond this explicit policy of risk is a mode of governance that relies on ordinary citizens to become socially and politically committed to climate adaptation. In the next two sections, I elaborate on the various activities state officials, engineers, and ordinary citizens depend on to build new canals. But even as these infrastructures put tremendous demands on the state and private sector to interact in prescribed ways, they are often undercut or rearranged to fit dynamic environmental conditions. This was particularly the case when the government attempted to assess the environmental conditions suitable for building the Hope Canal. I now turn to these moments.

Structural Forces

At their core, climate adaptation projects comprise practices that are influenced by multiple economic arrangements, including development policies and trade agreements, as Guyana's MMA Scheme and PetroFund indicate (see also Pelling 2010). Climate adaptation, however, also gains traction through the way lending institutions and nation-states generate ideas of 'place-ness' brought on by planetary climatological risks. For instance, CAP was supported by the World Bank's Global Environmental Facility agency (Morton and Guzmán 2014). A first of its kind for both the ministry and private engineering firms in Guyana, engineers were eager to work on CAP, designing the Hope Canal to be the first in the country's history solely dedicated to draining flood waters. For the World Bank, CAP was its first project in the Caribbean to target 'strengthening infrastructure for adaptation' (6). Moreover, the timing of CAP was significant in the World Bank's history, as it had not been in the business of directly targeting environment or infrastructure but economic development projects (Sande Lie 2015). By the end of CAP in 2013 its agenda began to shift, with the establishment of separate 'Climate Change Action' and 'Global Infrastructure Facility' programmes across its network, and the launch of a similar project to CAP in Suriname.

In this respect, Hope Canal collaborations between the ministry, local private engineering firms, and the World Bank have shifted understandings of drainage from a problem of national to planetary security. There are two latent consequences to this shift. First, the ministry supports the expansion of the local private engineering sector to justify the cost of innovative infrastructure development. Second, and relatedly, it makes tacit knowledge – intuitive and experiential understandings of flooding – central to public and private sector collaborations (Elyachar 2012). In other words, climate adaptation projects, while justified in worlds that are imagined through the market and national revenues, are bound-up with global environmental processes that threaten to destroy these very worlds.

The Hope Canal supplements the historic and strategic importance of the MMA Scheme to the coastal floodplain. If the MMA Scheme was intended to improve flood management for the purpose of agricultural production, then the Hope Canal exceeds this circuit of exchange and distribution. To understand contemporary climate adaptation in Guyana one cannot limit its analysis to capitalist expansion in the agricultural sector. Aspirations for climate adaptation are not iterative, nested in neat economic transactions, but shift depending on networks of government expertise and the public's support of them.

From its inception in 2010, the Hope Canal was met with opposition by some in the Guyanese engineering community. This opposition was led by the Guyana Association of Professional Engineers (GAPE). A group that comprised engineers and related professionals, many members had either practised or studied engineering in both the local private and public sectors as well as abroad. They called on the ministry to complete an environmental assessment, a report about the anticipated impacts of the canal on surrounding land. In a number of lengthy newspaper editorials, opponents described the Hope Canal as problematic because it was being built in an area with an ample amount of pegasse (peat), a highly-permeable type of soil. They argued that pegasse was a difficult, if not unreliable, medium for canal construction. They called the canal an extravagant expense, and feared that sections of it would be prone to collapsing just as the EDWC had during the 2005 disaster.

But this point was not ignored by engineers who worked on the Hope Canal. They took extensive measures to accommodate pegasse, using construction materials such as geotextiles to reinforce the canal's foundation. In a number of interviews, engineers explained to me their frustration with pegasse but overall sense of responsibility to the Guyanese public. As one engineer noted:

> We do a lot to look at these things [soils and the land]…we can't build this canal and let it blow when it fill[s]-up with rainwater and you know then, everybody will come and say it blew in a spot where we bloody well knew we have pegasse…I mean, if you leave it [the canal] there for about ten years it will harden and dry and it should be fine. In the meantime we reinforce it and get this done to better the coast.

The ministry held press conferences to explain the immediate environmental significance of the canal despite the hazards of pegasse. At these press conferences engineers asserted that the 2005 disaster was evidence of the havoc climate change was having on Guyana. According to their calculations, the threat of a 10,000 year flood event is the threshold they had to consider to effectively manage the EDWC's water supply (Mott McDonald 2005). With perennial flooding now exacerbated, they surmised that the Hope Canal was a quick fix, given that completing the MMA Scheme's third dam would be more labour, capital, and time intensive. Ultimately, the ministry reasoned that the canal was a risk worth taking – citing climate change as more dangerous than pegasse – and proceeded with no environmental assessments. Analyses of pegasse and drainage capacity were not the only environmental assessments that opponents of the canal envisioned. They also hoped to write a report about the 'social vulnerabilities' the Hope Canal could create for coastal populations. GAPE members and those of civic groups organised informational sessions about the canal. At these meetings university lecturers presented technical analyses of the canal to diverse audiences of students, engineering professionals, activists, and landowners who lived near the canal's construction site. The canal was expected to cut across a major roadway and a schoolyard. Some argued that the canal would impact people's use of roads and basic movement, which could compromise their abilities to go to work or impose excessive transportation fares. Others feared that with the canal so close to settlements, it was not only prone to collapsing due to water pressure but from indirect wear and tear.

This debate about environmental assessments was in no small part one about the value of tacit knowledge to climate adaptation. Pegasse's permeability is not merely an environmental indicator of the Hope Canal. It also has an experiential dimension, indexed by engineers' trials and errors building *and* ordinary citizens confronting floods. This means that both ordinary citizens and engineers' tacit knowledge are important resources for 'preserv[ing] the state's public resources' (Elyachar 2012, 79). Not only do public forums such as press conferences and university lectures help facilitate the circulation of tacit knowledge but so too do private gatherings. Retired ministry engineers often met at each other's homes or social clubs to discuss the canal. Relying on personal field notes and copies of old government reports, they brainstormed design measures for the third MMA Scheme dam and alternative drainage schedules to improve the EDWC. Memories about past efforts managing the MMA Scheme and EDWC were circumscribed by their fears about the Hope Canal's potential collapse. The retired engineers' discussions about pegasse often turned into material for strategising ways to present their findings to state officials at Parliament sessions. Pegasse was transformed into a matter of political mobilisation that muddied distinctions between the way state agencies, private engineering firms, and the general public accounted for flooding. And while their political aspirations never materialised, head ministry of agriculture officials routinely called on many of these critics to help build the canal.

The Hope Canal offers an example of how climate adaptation emerges in the shadow of its ideal self. At every scale, from the atmosphere to the underground, the Ministry of Agriculture and its opponents have anxiously constructed and tabulated different flood scenarios. These scenarios raise complex questions about the ideological coherence of neoliberalism, unravelling the myth of a hollowed-out public sector. Here, the notion of the public sector is not completely evacuated, as ordinary citizens and private engineering firms meet the state halfway to help facilitate climate adaptation. Guyana is not unique in this regard. It has been well documented elsewhere that neoliberal economic policies are not only structural forces that affect people's life-chances but also remake people's sense of optimism in the state (Berlant 2011). Read one way, the Hope Canal is a classic case of disaster capitalism. The state has used climate change and a past disaster to shore-up international donor funding and partnerships with the local private engineering sector. I have emphasised, however, that the Hope Canal undermines the neat bureaucratic accounting of the relations between environment and economy. Moreover, it is not clear whether the Hope Canal is any more or less prone to failure than the EDWC since its CAP-sponsored improvements. The planning for climate adaptation, then, depends on ordinary citizens presenting evidence to the state as to why infrastructure development is not an economic or technical risk worth taking. In turn, market arrangements take shape around the roles of ordinary citizens as knowledge producers in an economy that relies on tacit knowledge to support the technical planning of infrastructure. To illustrate how these arrangements work, I turn to farmers evicted for the Hope Canal's construction and its effects on their land's productivity.

Sensory Engagements

The environmental connections of disaster capitalism can be equally traced through the tactics the state used to compensate farmers displaced by the Hope Canal. Compensation, while seemingly a means of redistributing economic resources and land, also reveals the embodied and lived dimensions of market activities. In particular, farmers' sensory interactions with the Hope Canal are moments when they re-imagine vulnerable landscapes as sites of not only (dis)possession but knowledge production.

The Hope Canal's site is circumscribed by a complicated system of land tenure and agriculture in the villages of Hope/DuchFort. During the late-colonial period this area was once home to one of the premier sugar estates of the London-based Booker and Brothers Company. The estate's grid of irrigation and drainage supported not only a sugar plantation but day labourers' logies (houses). Adjoining these logies, day labourers had small plots to cultivate cash crops. With independence and the nationalisation of the sugar industry, the Hope Estate declined and the integrated canal grid for sugar and cash crops collapsed. As Eusi Kwayana, a prominent activist and opponent of the socialist government, explains:

> [The socialist government] introduced compulsory labor at Plantation Hope, a coconut plantation...At Plantation Hope he [Forbes Burnham, the executive president] lorded it over the people.... He sent typists, office workers, professionals into the cane field in 1977, to break a sugar strike. They messed up the cultivation. They knew nothing about it...He was mostly the hero of middle-class Africans [Afro-Guyanese] (Naipaul 2003, 76–77).

Today, Hope farmers, especially those of Indo-Guyanese descent, view themselves as doubly marginalised. They were once a population outside the socialist government's broader agenda of purported Black nationalism and then remained outside the post-1992 Indo-Guyanese government's agriculture policies which emphasised the rice sector.[5] In short, Hope farmers have come to experience floods as events shaped by both shifting rainfall patterns and state divestments in cash crops.

The modern sociological consensus – from all sides of the ideological spectrum – is that cash crop lands have historically been the sites for the formation of non-serialised political identities. Marilyn Silverman (1980) has described this much of post-independence rural villages. She writes, 'the political sphere [in rural communities] came to reflect the heightened competition as a result of scarce resources, class interests and vertical economic cleavages... Local politics [was] organized by factionalism' (3). This phrasing begs the question of what counts as a calculated and a symbolic 'cleavage', or vulnerability. Since the Hope/DuchFort villages are located outside of the MMA Scheme, there has been relatively little infrastructure development since the 1970s. Small-scale farming, therefore, has historically required a systematic response to floods that spurs a 'bottom-up' and collective strategy of welfare. In this way, the area has become both the site for various kinds of affective and monetary economies rooted in vulnerability.

Engineers built the Hope Canal across several farm plots. Within the first months of its construction, Hope/Duchfort farmers took their concerns about the canal to the Guyana Human Rights Association. In the thick of this political mobilisation, some threatened to sue the government. They argued that because the state did not conduct an environmental assessment the canal violated Article 13 of the Constitution: 'that the principal objective of the political system of the State is to establish an inclusionary democracy by providing increasing opportunities for the participation of citizens, and their organisations in the management and decision-making processes of the State.' Farmers' appeal to Article 13 suggests that consultation is not a self-evident process when they have to consider both the promises of climate adaptation and the possibility of disaster. Here, environmental assessments are not only a measure of safety as GAPE argued, but a tool for re-establishing relations of accountability.

Their grievances, however, never made it to the court. The ministry of housing offered the displaced new plots and payments for their evictions. State officials calculated the value of land plots relative to the going rate of other agricultural plots in the country and not the actual fertility of land plots. In effect, the ministry's practice of accounting did not directly address the specific needs of farmers but offered them a blank slate to start anew. The ministry hoped that by relocating these farmers 'untapped' fertile land would be put to use. A cash crop farmer named Roy, who worked closely with the Guyana Human Rights Association, explained the paradoxes of compensation:

> It's like this: they take this piece of land and there's a coconut tree. I make G$5,000 per month on this coconut tree. And now to cultivate back a piece of land and put back a coconut tree it would take you about three months. Now you calculate that by month and that's how much they are supposed to pay you. This canal is taking the barren food we have, which is our backbone....[We] take [cash crops] to the market and sell to get the family going, and everything. But too with some other crops like these, coconut, this crop is [also] our backbone it comes from our fore-parents, come to us and this probably might be our savings. And so you know if we fall short, our crop – whether the dry or rainy season – we have something to raise us (personal interview, July 2014).

The ethical and technical weight on Roy's shoulders is heavy. He interprets economic losses due to flooding as more predictable than the losses he suspects of the Hope Canal and the state's relocation programme. Ruptured kin relations, hunger and longing, rainfall, and the canal are all bound together. His embodied reading of the canal re-theorises compensation beyond issues of capital, property, and (re)payments. Instead, he realises compensation as involving a kind of affective labour enacted across and *with* landscapes. Climate adaptation projects and economy, just like land and vulnerability, are enfolded into one another. In her work on Hurricane Katrina, Vincanne Adams (2012) calls attention to the integral role of affective labour to disaster capitalism:

For those residents of New Orleans who were still hoping to get back to their homes...the process of recovery by the market has produced an emotional surfeit, an affective surplus, in which the need has become a circulating resource defined by its affective registers. Affect here is not just the visceral and emotional suffering felt and worn by people...[it] is also a fiscal potential, with its call for emotional responsiveness and inducement to action (209–10).

Roy further adds to this notion of 'fiscal potential' by suggesting that affective labour is as much human-oriented, as it relies on sensory interactions with the environment. Roy's new piece of land is just feet away from the embankment of the canal. Spend a few moments in this bordered space and you begin to feel the subtle distinctions in the moisture content and the permeability of the soil adjacent to the canal. He makes efforts to figure out how to transverse the canal's six-foot embankment without causing it damage or letting excess soil infringe on his plot. Otherwise, he finds that his crops retain less water, and that his makeshift trenches become clogged. Even during the canal's construction Roy's knowledge of the land aided engineers. In the months leading-up to the canal's completion engineers dug a channel to improve Hope/DuchFort farmers' system of 'secondary trenches'. Since then, engineers have relied on the feedback of farmers to deal with flooding. The canal's operation now depends upon engineers' and farmers' exchange of knowledge about the insecurity of pegasse and water supply in the Hope Canal network.

Roy's sentiments about the Hope Canal demonstrate that people engage with climate adaptation projects in piecemeal ways. The Hope farmers' mobilisation was routinely positioned in the private press as a challenge to the post-1992 state's *over reliance* on farmers to monitor flooding. In other words, the passion that the Hope Canal provoked in farmers like Roy seems impossible to reconcile with notions of simple resistance or disdain for the state. Neither is climate adaptation solely a matter of canals and their technological efficacy. Rather, what is important here is the new configuration of responsibility Hope farmers have toward each other, engineers, land, pegasse, and infrastructure.

As a knowledge practice, climate adaptation remakes people's sensory interactions with places, just as it remakes expectations about the abilities of markets to tame environmental risks. We are reminded, then, that climate adaptation is a categorical act. It encourages us to pay close attention to embodied practices through which economic concepts, including state-private partnerships, public services, and planning, get side-tracked or likewise gain traction in the world.

Conclusion

Climate adaptation has been accompanied worldwide by larger questions about the state, and if it is possible for it to act in the interests of citizens in light of climate change's disparate and multi-scalar threats (Nyamwanza and Bhatasara 2015). At stake are not only the material dimensions of politics, but competing ideas about economic planning and the role state–private partnerships might play in financing infrastructure. The possibilities of these collaborations emerge around imagined scenarios about the entangled 'fragility' of infrastructure and markets to climate change (Connolly 2013).

In the aftermath of Guyana's 2005 disaster, the stakes of flooding are high. While the Hope Canal has brought the potential opportunity for new kinds of drainage, it has also upended people's historical understandings of the relationship between environment and economy. The state's planning for infrastructure, once almost exclusively focused on agriculture, is now increasingly shaped by costs associated with climate related disasters. What has developed out of this new arrangement of drainage are fragmented opportunities for ordinary citizens, particularly cash crop farmers, to make a living. Yet we also see that new kinds of political engagements that cut across and challenge logics of class, race, and party politics have formed. Of course, flooding together with capitalist markets in many contexts produce vulnerable people. This is an insight New World and dependency school theorists alongside Walter Rodney's historiography of colonial Guiana have long ago explicated. Nevertheless, the point of rereading the debates about flooding in Guyana through the lens of disaster capitalism is not to measure the historic gap between the promise and reality of (post) colonial governments. Rather, it can help us better understand how traces of those debates are left out of or still affect Guyana's political formations around flooding in the present.

I have argued that what is distinctive about climate adaptation projects as a neoliberal practice is its knowledge economy. Under climate adaptation, the state depends on ordinary citizens and the private sector as 'technical' surrogates. By this I mean two things. In Guyana, state agencies have effectively orchestrated the expansion of the local private engineering sector. Alongside this growth is a parallel knowledge economy based in tacit forms of knowledge that help both experts and the public learn to identify the impacts of climate-related flooding. In the process, we see that not all forms of tacit knowledge are made equal or are easily translated into something called climate adaptation. As a consequence, entangled feelings of appeasement, anxiety, distrust, and aspiration inform the production of expertise across society. This means that the 'public sector' is not exhausted by disastrous events but works in ways that simultaneously constrain and create opportunities for people to imagine ways to engage the state. Paying attention to these opportunities is one way to bring to the forefront the environmental dimensions of disaster capitalism. In doing so, scholars are in a better position to understand how state apparatuses take shape through disastrous events and the vulnerabilities that neoliberal policies often undergird.

Notes

1. The PetroCaribe Fund was established between Guyana and Venezuela in 2005–06. The agreement involves Venezuela selling oil at a concessionary rate and providing loans to Guyana and other CARICOM and Latin American countries. Under the trade agreement, Guyana supplies rice to Venezuela, and the proceeds are used to pay rice farmers. Alongside these payments, the government has used US$15 million from the fund to pay for the Hope Canal.
2. David Graeber insists that market economies function because they are passed in a 'plurality' of economic relations. Following Marcel Mauss's theory of gift exchange, he emphasises that markets are not impersonal machines but are made and remade through people's life experiences. For Graeber, there are three moral grounds for economic relations: communism, exchange, and hierarchy. His aim is to show that these moral grounds not only help people cope when markets fail or do not provide security, but are entangled worldviews that help people think of alternative ways of organising society. Within the context of climate adaptation projects, the moral grounds for economic relations are not only subject to human actions but are made meaningful because of disasters and the potential of their occurrence.
3. The Damodar Valley Cooperation had a model of damming that took inspiration from the Tennessee Valley Authority, see D'Souza 2003. More than a pursuit at postcolonial development and the American welfare state, these schemes laid the foundation for global institutional arrangements in engineering management and consulting.
4. This is not to say that the MMA Scheme was the only land settlement the state facilitated during the independence period. A variety of other smaller settlements included Garden of Eden and Mara Land.

5. Many historians of this period identify Burnham's co-operative socialism as expanding regimes of state bureaucracy, and so employment for all professional Guyanese, but particularly for the urban Afro-Guyanese middle class. At the same time, the government's inability to secure funding for agriculture contributed to the divestment in rural-based employment, a sector traditionally populated by Indo-Guyanese. Thus, historians debate whether racial antagonism was rooted in Burnham's brand of co-operative socialism or was an effect of short-sighted economic planning.

References

Adams, Vincanne. 2012. The Other Road to Serfdom: Recovery by the Market and the Affect Economy in New Orleans. *Public Culture* 1, no. 24:186–216.

Anand, Nikhil. 2011. Pressure: The PoliTechnics of Water Supply in Mumbai. *Cultural Anthropology* 4, no. 26:542–64.

Beck, Ulrich. 2008. *World at Risk.* Malden: Polity Press.

Berlant, Lauren. 2011. *Cruel Optimism.* Durham: Duke University Press.

Blommestein, Eric. 2005. *Guyana: Socio-Economic Assessment of the Damages and Losses Caused by the January–February 2005 Flooding, a United Nations Development Program (UNDP)/Economic Commission for Latin America and the Caribbean (ECLAC) Report.* Georgetown, Guyana: ECLAC-UNDP.

Bumpus, Adam G. and Diana M. Liverman. 2008. Accumulation by Decarbonization and the Governance of Carbon. *Economic Geography* 84, no. 2:127–55.

Camacho, R.F. 1960. The Mahaica-Mahaicony-Abary Water Control Project: Stage 1, the Control of the Abary. Georgetown: Drainage and Irrigation Department.

Canterbury, Dennis. 2007. Caribbean Agriculture under Three Regimes: Colonialism, Nationalism and Neoliberalism in Guyana. *Journal of Peasant Studies* 1, no. 34:1–28.

Cavanagh, Connor J. 2017. Resilience, Class, and the Antifragility of Capital. *Resilience: International Policies, Practices, and Discourses* 5:1–19.

Collier, Stephan. 2013. Neoliberalism and Natural Disaster. *Journal of Cultural Economy* 3, no. 7:273–90.

Colonial Office. 2003. *Report of the British Guiana Constitutional Commission 1954*, ed. Odeen Ishmael. Georgetown: GNI Publications. .

Connolly, William. 2013. *The Fragility of Things: Self-Organizing Processes, Neoliberal Fantasies, and Democratic Activism.* Durham, NC: Duke University Press.

Cooper, Melinda. 2010. Turbulent Worlds: Financial Markets and Environmental Crisis. *Theory, Culture & Society* 2–3, no. 27:167–90.

Dole, Christopher, Robert Hayashi, Andrew Poe, Austin Sarat, and Boris Wolfson, eds. 2016. *The Time of Catastrophe: Multidisciplinary Approaches to the Age of Catastrophe.* New York: Routledge.

D'Souza, Rohan. 2003. Damming the Mahanadi River: The Emergence of Multi-Purpose River Valley Development in India (1943–46). *Indian Economic & Society History Review* 1, no. 40:81–105.

Elyachar, Julia. 2012. Before (and After) Neoliberalism: Tacit Knowledge, Secrets of the Trade, and the Public Sector in Egypt. *Cultural Anthropology* 1, no. 27:76–96.
Evans, Brad, and Julian Reid. 2014. *Resilient Life: The Art of Living Dangerously.* New York: Polity.
Fletcher, Robert. 2012. Capitalizing on Chaos: Climate Change and Disaster Capitalism *Ephemera: Theory & Politics in Organization* 12, no. 1/2:97–112.
Graeber, David. 2014. On the Moral Grounds of Economic Relations: A Maussian Approach. *Journal of Classical Sociology* 14, no. 1:65–77.
Gunewardena, Nandini and Mark Schuller. 2008. *Capitalizing on Catastrophe: Neoliberal Strategies in Disaster Reconstruction.* Lanham: Altamira Press.
Guyana Chronicle Online. 2016. Hope Canal Project Understated by $700M. Staff reporter, June 11.
Harvey, David. 2007. *A Brief History of Neoliberalism.* Oxford: Oxford University Press.
Hickel, Jason and Arsalan Khan. 2012. The Culture of Capitalism and the Crisis of Critique *Anthropological Quarterly* 85, no. 1:203–77.
Hintzen, Percy. 1989. *The Costs of Regime Survival: Racial Mobilization, Elite Domination and Control of the State in Guyana and Trinidad.* Cambridge: Cambridge University Press.
Howe, Cymene and Dominic Boyer. 2016. Aeolian Extractivism and Community Wind in Southern Mexico. *Public Culture* 28, no. 279:215–35.
Klein, Naomi. 2008. *The Shock Doctrine: The Rise of Disaster Capitalism.* New York: Picador Press.
———. 2015. *This Changes Everything: Capitalism vs. The Climate.* New York: Simon & Shuster.
Lakoff, Andrew, ed. 2013. *Disaster and the Politics of Intervention.* New York: Columbia University Press.
Larkin, Brian. 2013. The Politics and Poetics of Infrastructure. *Annual Review of Anthropology* no. 42:327–43.
MacKenzie, Donald. 2009. Making Things the Same: Gases, Emission Rights and the Politics of Carbon Markets. *Accounting, Organizations and Society* 34, no. 3/4: 440–55.
Massey, Doreen. 2005. *For Space.* London: Sage.
Morton, John, and Armando Guzmán. 2014. *Implementation Complementation and Results Report for a Conservancy Adaptation.* Georgetown, Guyana: World Bank.
Mott McDonald. 2005. *Infrastructure Rehabilitation: Short to Medium Term Plan.* Georgetown, Guyana: Mott McDonald.
Mott McDonald and Ministry of Agriculture. 2003. *Guyana Drainage and Irrigation Systems Rehabilitation Project.* Georgetown, Guyana: Mott McDonald and Ministry of Agriculture.
Naipaul, V.S. 2003. *The Writer and the World: Essay.* New York: Vintage.

Nyamwanza, Admire and Sandra Bhatasara. 2015. The Utility of Postmodern Thinking in Climate Adaptation Research. *Environment, Development, and Sustainability* 17, no. 5:1,183–96.
Oels, Angela. 2006. Rendering Climate Change Governable: From Biopower to Advance Liberal Government? *Journal of Environmental Policy and Planning* 7, no. 3:185–207.
Ortner, Sherry. 2016. Dark Anthropology and Its Others: Theory since the Eighties. *Hau: Journal of Ethnographic Theory* 6, no. 1:47–73.
Pelling, Mark. 1996. Coastal Flood Hazard in Guyana: Environmental and Economic Causes. *Caribbean Geography* 1, no. 7:3–22.
———. 2010. *Adaptation to Climate Change: From Resilience to Transformation*. London: Routledge.
Roberts, Patrick S. 2013. Private Choices, Public Harms: The Evolution of National Disaster Organizations in the United States. In *Disaster and the Politics of Intervention*, ed. Andrew Lakoff, 42–69. New York: Columbia University Press.
Sande Lie, Jon H. 2015. *Developmentality: An Ethnography of the World Bank–Uganda Partnership*. Oxford: Berghahn Books.
Silverman, Marilyn. 1980. *Rich People and Rice: Factional Politics in Rural Guyana*. Leiden: EJ Brill.
Somers, Margaret R. 2008. *Genealogies of Citizenship: Markets, Statelessness, and the Right to Have Rights*. Cambridge: Cambridge University Press.
Stabroek News Online. 2016. Flooding and the NDIA Audit. Staff writer, June 13.
Trotz, Alissa. 2010. Shifting the Ground Beneath Us. *Interventions* 1, no. 12:112–24.
Tsing, Anna. 2015. *The Mushroom at the End of the World: On the Possibility of Life in Capitalist Ruins*. Princeton, NJ: Princeton University Press.
Vaughn, Sarah E. 2012. Reconstructing the Citizen: Disaster, Citizenship, and Expertise in Racial Guyana. *Critique of Anthropology* 4, no. 32:359–87.
Veramallay, Ashton Isardatt.1976. An Evaluation of Water Resource Developments in Guyana: With Application to Selected Drainage and Irrigation Projects. PhD diss., Iowa State University.
Westmaas, Nigel. 2005. History: Mother of All Floods. *Guyana Review* (March): 19–21.
Whatmore, Sarah J. 2013. Earthly Powers and Affective Environments: An Ontological Politics of Flood Risk. *Theory, Culture, & Society* 7/8, no. 30:33–50.

18.

Journeying Towards LGBTIQ+ Equality in Guyana[1]

Vidyaratha Kissoon

Manifestos

'Jagdeo didn' change the law, you tink Granger gun change it?' the man asked from the kitchen in a joking voice. The restaurant is a popular one, good food at low cost in Georgetown.

The kind of restaurant where from the kitchen, the cooks could talk to the people who are eating through the door. It is a hot Thursday afternoon. A man had brought up the matter of a transgender woman jumping up to 'wine' on a stage during one of the shows for the Republic anniversary. 'You could imagine what gun happen if you gie dem dey rights?' a woman asked from behind the counter. There were murmurings and smiles from the people who were eating. Everybody had become involved as in that interesting Guyana way in minibuses, waiting rooms and other places, where one person could throw a topical subject in the air and everybody could participate, smiling and nodding their heads but not dissenting.

The people in the restaurant probably did not know that the 2015 Election manifestos of both Bharrat Jagdeo's party – the PPP/Civic – and David Granger's APNU+AFC coalition made promises to deal with discrimination against 'dem' – lesbian, gay, bisexual, and transgender citizens. APNU+AFC made 'A Commitment to Gender Equality', which imagined that there should be no discrimination based on sexual orientation:

> APNU+AFC recognise that Gender equality is an intrinsic basic human right and are committed to eradicating all forms of gender bias and gender-based violence. We commit to putting in place measures which will ensure that all vulnerable groups in our society, including women, children, persons with disabilities, rural and indigenous women, youth, the elderly and the sick and those marginalised because of sexual orientation are protected and not discriminated against.[2]

In its manifesto, the PPP/C also agreed with APNU+AFC that no Guyanese should be discriminated against because of their sexual orientation:

> The People's Progressive Party/Civic is building a country in which no one should feel left out from development. We want to give a good life to all citizens so that they can live with dignity and security. As such, we aim to address the needs and meet the expectations of all our people with particular concern for our children, women, indigenous people, single parents and the vulnerable. *We believe that all Guyanese must be free to make choices and must not be discriminated against because of their ethnicity, gender, religion or sexual orientation.*[3]

The promise in the manifesto happened not only in Guyana. In Trinidad and Tobago, in 2015, the People's Partnership also promised an end to discrimination on the grounds of sexual orientation:

> The People's Partnership is committed to all citizens enjoying equal human rights under the law and to ensuring that there is no discrimination on the bases of race, religion, gender, place of residence political affiliation or sexual orientation.[4]

The promise of the manifestos did not generate any outrage or prayers at the time. Voters probably knew that manifestos have no meaning anyway. The usual election time divisions of race and ethnicity were not affected by the apparent unity across the two major political parties in Guyana on non-discrimination on the grounds of sexual orientation.

How did Guyana get to this stage of manifesto promises for non-discrimination on the basis of sexual orientation? Was this a sign of some radical democratic progress which recognised that all citizens were equal?

History

Lesbian, gay, bisexual, transgender, intersex, and queer (LGBTIQ+)[5] citizens of Guyana have had to find ways to live around the homophobia grounded in legislation and religion. Intersex persons have been identified in some historical reports, where there are some references to records and punishments and other events.

In 1835 'John', an apprentice, was sentenced to death for sodomy. Governor Carmichael-Smyth pardoned John on condition that he left British Guiana.[6] The pardon was reportedly given because the governor thought discussions on the offence on sodomy would corrupt youth.

In 1898, the surgeon superintendent, Dr Harrison, who accompanied the *Mersey* bringing labourers from India to British Guiana, wrote:

> September 25: No 696, Nobibux, m., 20 years, and No 351 Mohangu, m, 22 years, were caught about midnight by a sirdar named Rambocus committing sodomy. When brought up before the captain and myself they both confessed their guilt. Nobibux stated that for the last 10 years he had allowed men to commit acts of beastliness: he had no doubt induced Mohangu to do this criminal act. Nobibux was put in irons and Mohangu, after blistering his penis, was made to holystone [scrub the decks] from 6 a.m. to 6 p.m. daily.[7]

In 1903, 19 year old Rukmini on the ship Clyde, was listed as 'hermaphrodite.'[8]

In 1959, the *Guiana Graphic* of July 12, reported on the all men wedding of the Year:

> ANOTHER strange 'wedding'...an all men affair...sent the down-town Charlestown area into a furore on Friday night as thousands blocked the traffic to get a glimpse of the 'yellow tie' men. The cutting of the three-tier cake was carried out without police intervention, unlike the last time when they were arrested and charged.

The *Guiana Graphic* of April 1, 1966 carried a story about 65 year old Caroline Vaughn from New Amsterdam. The doctors discovered from examining her body after her death that she was 'neither male nor female.'

On January 9, 1968, the *Guiana Graphic* (renamed *Guyana Graphic* after independence) carried a story about young Compton Bowen, who was sent by Magistrate Aubrey Bishop for psychiatric treatment for wearing a miniskirt. The prosecutor noted that Bowen was 'swaying his hips from side to side like a woman.'

In 1978, 12 years after independence, Guyana was beginning to feel the effects of the Forbes Burnham government. Walter Rodney was mobilising opposition to the dictatorial regime. The *Citizen* newspaper of January 26, 1978 (reprinted in the *Guyana Chronicle* on Sept 12, 2014) carried a headline 'Sex Operation Successful – Dream Come True', reporting that 'Guyana's second transsexual in 13 months is now resting at the Georgetown Hospital after what was described as a successful operation.' The patient said that she wanted to be called Sabrina. Sabrina still lives in Guyana. She told one of my colleagues that as far as she was concerned 'Burnham paid for my operation.' The Georgetown Hospital did not charge.

In February 1978, police were chasing thieves through a yard. They claimed they found two men having sex. This was happening as the Co-operative Republic continued to experience its birthing pains. The state-owned *Guyana Chronicle* had news of the upheavals around the world – the ending of Idi Amin's dictatorship, Maurice Bishop's New Jewel Movement, and the People's Revolutionary Government in Grenada, and the new impositions of the Islamic Republic of Iran on its citizens.

A headline in the *Guyana Chronicle* of April 4, 1979 that 'Counsel wants law to permit Homo Relations'[9] must have been an interesting distraction from the other headlines. According to the report,

> Barrister-at-Law Stanley Moore has said that the criminal law in Guyana should be amended to permit homosexual relations between consenting adults. He said that the United Kingdom had already amended laws to permit this. Mr. Moore, a lecturer on criminal law at the University of Guyana, was at the time making a plea in mitigation before Principal Magistrate Owen Fung-kee-Fung for former Ministry of Labour employee Wendell Brotherson, who pleaded guilty to committing an act of gross indecency with another male person. In a plea for leniency the counsel said that it was wrong for the law to seek to suppress the natural sexual urgings of individuals with homosexual tendencies. He argued that a homosexual was a person who was born with a deformity for which he or she was not responsible and to condemn such a person would be like condemning a person born with a deformed lip palate or limbs. The lawyer said that he would agree that the law should continue to frown on homosexual acts between adults and children or young persons, adding that to his mind such persons should be dealt with severely.

During an interview with me in his office in Guyana in September 2016, Moore laughed at the irony of the circumstances: 'The police were chasing thieves, and it seems they abandoned their pursuit in favour of two men who were not harming any one. One would have thought the thieves would have been more of a threat.' He noted that the comments were made because he 'had a duty to give the best defence and this is what I did.'

There are few reports of lawyers in the Caribbean calling for a repeal of the sodomy laws in their defence of clients who were charged under those laws. As Moore noted, 'I don't recall any backlash or condemnations arising from my comments. I was doing radio programmes and in the public. I think some persons might have said "Stanley there are more important things to worry about"'. Stanley Moore went on to become a minister of home affairs in Guyana and subsequently attorney general in Montserrat. He served as a judge in the Eastern Caribbean Supreme Court, and in the Supreme Courts of Botswana and of Swaziland. Justice Moore remembers that the gay community was visible 'often in court on various matters'.

Living with the Laws which Discriminate

Guyana preserved a number of offences criminalising acts of same-sex intimacy at independence and when it became a republic. The most draconian one is that of buggery, for which a maximum sentence of life imprisonment may be imposed on conviction.[10]

Buggery is undefined in the statute, but as interpreted by judicial decisions it is committed by sexual intercourse *per anum*, involving penetration by the male sexual organ. Although the offence may be committed by male/female couples, various courts have accepted that such prohibitions impact disproportionately on male homosexuals.[11] There is no requirement for lack of consent, and the act is punishable whether committed in public or private. It is thus a sweeping offence that captures consensual sexual intercourse between adults in private. Attempted buggery and assault with intent to commit buggery are also crimes, punishable on conviction by up to ten years' imprisonment.[12] Another section (352) also punishes indecent assault committed on one male by another, but this offence requires the use of force and thus does not apply to consensual same-sex intimate acts.

Statute also criminalises what is termed 'acts of gross indecency', including procuring or attempting to procure a male person to commit gross indecency with another male person, any of which are punishable on conviction by up to two years' imprisonment.[13] Gross indecency applies to acts committed by one male person against another, and like buggery it does not require force or the absence of consent, nor does it matter whether the act takes place in public or private. Any sexual act short of penetration of the anus would be captured by this offence. There are no recent reports of anyone being charged under these laws for consensual sex. Prior to the reformed Sexual Offences Act of 2010, the laws were enforced for acts of rape.

Guyana's Summary Jurisdiction (Offences) Act, Chapter 8:02, provides in section 153(1)(xlvii) that it is an offence 'being a man, in any public way or public place, for any improper purpose, [who] appears in female attire or being a woman, in any public way or public place, for any improper purpose, [who] appears in male attire.' This law is referred to as the cross-dressing law. The cross-dressing law and loitering laws have been used to harass transgender sex workers especially. In February 2009, 41 years after

Compton Bowen was sent for psychiatric treatment for wearing a miniskirt, Chief Magistrate Melissa Robertson-Ogle convicted and fined seven men for the same offence.[14]

In February 2010, Quincy McEwan, Seon Clarke, Joseph Fraser, and Seyon Persaud, along with the Society against Sexual Orientation Discrimination (SASOD), joined to challenge the constitutionality of the cross-dressing law. They argued that the law violates many provisions of the amended Constitution of Guyana, including the rights to equality and non-discrimination found in Articles 149 and 149D.[15] In September 2013, the court ruled that cross-dressing was not a crime unless it was done for an improper purpose.[16] The court did not agree that the laws were discriminatory. In his judgment acting Chief Justice Chang asserted,

> It is instructive to note that it is not a criminal offence for a male to wear female attire and for a female to wear male attire in a public way or place under section 153(1)(xlvii). It is only if such an act is done for an improper purpose that criminal liability attaches. Therefore, it is not criminally offensive for a person to wear the attire of the opposite sex as a matter of preference or to give expression to or to reflect his or her sexual orientation.[17]

Given the ambiguity in the condition of 'improper purpose' which the court refused to strike down, the claimants appealed. The claimants argued that while the position of the acting Chief Justice may seem to be a satisfactory resolution of the case, in that he ruled affirmatively that cross dressing as an expression of one's sexual orientation is not per se prohibited, the difficulty that persisted was a very concrete one of not knowing for sure what an improper purpose means. The ambiguity in the provision, the claimants argued, leaves trans persons in particular in great uncertainty as to what is allowed and gives state officials – like police on the beat and magistrates in court – wide discretion in their interpretation and application of the law.

The court of appeal did not agree with these arguments and in February 2017 dismissed the appeal. However, the court of appeal explicitly affirmed the acting chief justice's ruling that cross-dressing as an expression of a person's sexual orientation is not prohibited. In refusing to strike down the law, the court expressed great concern that criminals could dress as female in order to rob unsuspecting persons. The claimants have since appealed further to the Caribbean Court of Justice, Guyana's final court of appeal. The appeal succeeded in November 2018.

In July 2010, in Belize, Caleb Orozco filed a challenge to the sodomy laws of Belize which are enshrined in section 53 of the Criminal Code of Belize. The decision was handed down in 2016 by Guyana born Chief Justice Kenneth Benjamin, who ruled that section 53 of the Criminal Code is inconsistent with the Constitution of Belize. In April 2018, in Trinidad and Tobago, Justice Devindra Rampersad ruled that the sodomy laws of Trinidad and Tobago are unconstitutional.

The Guyana cross-dressing case and the Belize case were supported by the University of the West Indies (UWI) Rights Advocacy Project (U-RAP). The project team includes lecturers from the Faculty of Law who are from different Caribbean countries, including Guyana. The U-RAP project is an example of Caribbean organising to challenge LGBTIQ+ discrimination.

In 1997, the informal network Caribbean Forum for Lesbians, All-sexuals and Gays (C-FLAG) was convened to respond to the HIV/AIDS epidemic. C-FLAG evolved into CARIFLAGS – the Caribbean Forum for Liberation and Acceptance of Genders & Sexualities with a secretariat, at the time of writing this chapter, in the SASOD office in Guyana.

Organising

Prominent theatre worker, the late Andre Subryan, founded Artistes in Direct Support in 1992 with Margaret Lawrence, Desiree Edghill, and the late Robert Narain. They produced the play 'One of our sons is missing' by Trinidadian Godfrey Sealey. The play was about a bisexual young man who contracts HIV/AIDS. There were no protests at the time, though Desiree Edghill recalls that the small audience of about 50 persons seemed to be laughing when the actors were crying. Artistes in Direct Support produced the play again in December 2015 for Andre Subryan's 15th death anniversary. According to Desiree Edghill, 'It was played to a packed theatre and people were crying.'

Andre Subryan became active in forming a network of Guyanese living with HIV/AIDS. He also convened a network of gay men and used his house as a space to discuss HIV/AIDS and related health and safety matters. Robert Singh recalls that Andre Sobryan was very determined that men who have sex with men had access to condoms and other services. Robert Singh recalled that Andre Subryan had attended a workshop with other Caribbean representatives of networks who were concerned about HIV and men who have sex with men. Robert Singh recalls Subryan's house as being a kind of drop-in centre. The network was informally called the Rainbow Crew. An organisation, Guyana Rainbow Foundation (Guybow) was later registered. Colleen McEwan, the current Executive Director of GuyBow, recalls that the focus at the time was on building community, providing health education, and access to health services. They did not get involved in any discussion on advocating for changes in laws. They had relationships with the Genito-Urinary Medical Clinic at the Georgetown Hospital. I remember in 1995, that the clinic was providing counselling services for men who have sex with men.

2001 Constitutional Reform

The 2000/2001 Constitutional Reform process opened the discussion on recognising the equality of LGBTIQ+ citizens, after the model of the South African state. In January 2001, the National Assembly voted unanimously to include sexual orientation as one of the grounds of non-discrimination in the Constitution. Following the mobilisation within some sections of the religious community against this development, Bishop Juan Edghill and other Christians prayed and fasted with President Bharat Jagdeo, who then refused to assent to the Constitutional Amendment Bill.

There was discussion in the letters to the editor columns in the newspapers which stated not only opposition to the bill but also support for reform of the laws. On Feb 1, 2001 in a letter in the *Stabroek News* titled 'Gay rights', the writer Dr Lee Garnett wrote that slavery was endorsed by early Christians and that 'History is repeating itself with the oppression of Gays & Lesbians. Ironically the people who were once oppressed are seemingly now doing the persecuting.' Parliament was dissolved for elections without this matter being resolved or assent being given, and the life of the Bill including the amendment expired.

In 2002, a University of Guyana Social Work student, Clayton Newman, decided to do some research on young gay men he met in Georgetown. He agreed to share the research outside of the university with persons who were interested in activism. His research showed that the young gay men he spoke with yearned for acceptance from family and community. Also in 2002, a young human rights activist from India, Sanjay Kabir Bavikatte, started teaching in the Faculty of Law at the University of Guyana. He had been involved in activism in India around rights of sexual and gender minorities, and in Guyana continued to engage both his students and the wider public (through the letters column of the newspapers) in debates around these rights. The letter columns at the time were also full of discussion not only about difference in sexual orientation but also about race and ethnicity.

> **PRAYER AND FASTING**
>
> Page 20 SUNDAY STABROEK, January 21, 2001
>
> THE LEADERS OF THE CHRISTIAN COMMUNITY CALL THE NATION OF GUYANA TO REPENT, FAST, AND PRAY FOR GOD'S INTERVENTION TO STOP THE LEGALISATION OF HOMOSEXUALITY AND ALL OTHER FORMS OF SEXUAL IMMORALITY WHICH WOULD CONTRIBUTE TO THE DESTRUCTION OF OUR SOCIETY AND INVITE GOD'S JUDGMENT ON GUYANA.
>
> **The duration of the fast will be from Monday January 22 to Wednesday January 24, 2001.**
>
> JONAH 3:5 & 10 "... SO THE PEOPLE OF NINEVEH BELIEVED GOD AND PROCLAIMED A FAST, AND PUT ON SACKCLOTH, FROM THE GREATEST OF THEM TO THE LEAST OF THEM ... AND GOD SAW THEIR WORKS, THAT THEY HAD CEASED FROM THEIR EVIL WAYS, AND HE ABANDONED HIS PLAN TO DESTROY THEM."
>
> Regarding Constitution (Amendment) (No. 5) Bill 2000 passed by the Parliament of Guyana on Thursday, January 4, 2001: The leaders and members of the Christian Community adamantly oppose the recent amendment to the Constitution of Guyana whereby discrimination is prohibited on the basis of sexual orientation and marital status. (See section 15 of the 2000 Bill).
>
> As Christians, we believe, in accordance with the teaching of the Holy Bible*, that the act of sexual intercourse is only approved by God and beneficial to the individual, the family and the society when practiced between a man and woman who are married to each other, and that sexual intercourse in every other circumstance - fornication, adultery, homosexuality, lesbianism, paedophilia, bestiality - is abhorrent to God and counter-productive to the welfare of the individual, the family and the society. We are convinced that any law which promotes and protects the practice of sexual intercourse outside of marriage will result in a further decay of the moral fabric of our society with all of its attendant economic and social problems and costs.
>
> In particular, the entire Christian Community joins with all God-fearing Guyanese in opposing the inclusion within the Constitution of Guyana, the highest legal instrument of our land, of official endorsement and national approval of sexual perversion under the guise of removal of discrimination based on "*sexual orientation*". We recognize that to protect homosexuality/lesbianism in the highest law of the land would serve to further erode family values and undermine the social and moral fabric of our society while giving impetus to the introduction of values and behaviours that are alien to the values, culture and traditions of our peoples.
>
> In keeping with our duty to work for the protection and prosperity of this nation, we are bound to always teach, by word and act, against conduct and laws which are in contravention of the laws of God. However, if the aforementioned amendment to the Constitution is permitted to stand, teaching and acting against corrupt and ungodly sexual practices will be rendered an act of discrimination and thus illegal.
>
> Furthermore, the Christian Community is firmly opposed to the inclusion in the Bill of the clause which states that "*no person's religion or religious belief shall be vilified*" (Section 8). This clause, if retained, will effectively render it illegal to speak against practices and beliefs which are contrary to the teachings of the Bible.
>
> Clearly, the noted portions of Section 8 and Section 15, besides facilitating destruction and chaos in our society, amount to an interference of the right to free speech and the right not to be discriminated against on the basis of religion.
>
> In the light of all the above, we call for the immediate removal of the above-mentioned phrases and clauses from our Constitution.
>
> * Scriptures that oppose homosexuality:
> Leviticus 18:22 - Thou shall not lie with mankind, as with womankind: it is an abomination.
> Leviticus 20:13 - If a man also lie with mankind, as he lieth with a woman, both of them have committed an abomination, they shall surely be put to death, their blood shall be upon them.
> Romans 1: 26-27 - For this cause God gave them up unto vile affections: for even their women did change the natural use into that which is against nature. And likewise also the men, leaving the natural use of the woman, burned in their lust one towards another, men with men working that which is unseemly, and receiving in themselves that recompence of their error which was met.
>
> **A NATIONAL CALL**

Full Page Advertisement, Sunday Stabroek, January 21 2001

In April 2003, the first public forum was organised on sexual orientation as a fundamental right, and in May 2003, the political parties agreed to restore the discussion about sexual orientation with all of the other rights bills that had been outstanding. Some of the law students at the University of Guyana organised themselves as Students against Sexual Orientation Discrimination, just as the Sexual Orientation Bill was coming to Parliament for a second time. They engaged the members of parliament who were supposed to discuss the amendment to the constitution. There was a forum at the National Library on June 7, 2003 which was recorded by the Guyana Broadcasting Corporation. This date is used as the founding date of SASOD. According to Joel Simpson, writing in the *Stabroek News*,[18]

> But for the small group at the National Library that Saturday, it was an opportunity to have an informed, reasoned discussion about including "sexual orientation" as grounds for discrimination in Article 149 of the Guyana's [sic] constitution. It was this very lack of rational debate that spurred the birth of this student lobby group at the time.

The Hansard of July 24, 2003 reveals no indication that parliamentarians listened to the legal arguments put forward by the students. Instead, the then Leader of the Opposition Robert Corbin is reported in the Hansard as saying '…our constituency has spoken firmly…that the inclusion of these two words is unacceptable at this point in history… I, like Joshua, stand on the side of the Georgetown Ministers Fellowship and the Evangelical Church on this issue…' The Georgetown Ministers Fellowship had prepared a 16-page dossier on the evils of homosexuality.

In the parliamentary sitting of July 24, 2003, the late Deryck Bernard, a PNC MP, also asserted his Christian faith and reflected on the intention of the Constitutional Reform Commission to 'thoughtfully and consciously attempt to expand fundamental rights in the country…in terms of what human rights thinking around the world meant…and no intention to undermine the social structures, morals and values of our country.' Other members of parliament spoke about the procedure for the bill. PPP/C MP Dr Leslie Ramsammy remarked on President Jagdeo's refusal to assent to the 2001 amendment:

> The President, in his wisdom, agreed that there is a problem and responded positively to those who lobbied and advocated for a revision of those provisions. We ought to admire, not only the wisdom of the President, but the courage of the President to say to the National Assembly, after we had passed the Bill unanimously, that we must reconsider the Bill.

None of the MPs from the PPP/C, ROAR, or GAP/WPA quoted any of their religious beliefs but focused on the problematic process to deal with the bill and made indirect references to the strong lobbying. Parliament decided to send the second bill back for 'consensus building and consultation'. The consensus building and consultation never happened.

Some students preferred to contribute anonymously. Two students, a young man 'D', and a young woman collaborated online to create the SASOD logo, and to develop the first Internet resources – the email address, the Yahoo Group, and the first website. This use of the Internet contributed to the visibility of the work and helped to virtually ground SASOD, which was operating without a physical office space for many years.

The students focused on completing their studies after the 2003 debacle in Parliament. In 2005, the students, former students and supporters reorganised and decided on the bold project, 'Painting the Spectrum', the English-speaking Caribbean's first LGBTIQ+ Film festival.

The link between university knowledge and community activism was further exemplified by Jermaine Grant. He participated in several Model United Nations (UN) and Organization of American States (OAS) General Assemblies as part of the University of Guyana International Affairs Association, and then represented SASOD at the OAS civil society forum and General Assembly in 2007 at Panama City, Panama. SASOD went on to win the International Red Ribbon Award in 2014 and has continued to engage in various activities.

In January 2012, Guyana Trans United (GTU) was inaugurated. It provides services to and advocacy on behalf of the transgender community and has been involved in advocacy for the rights of trans citizens. Guybow organises lesbian, bisexual, and transgender women and allies and has been engaging with the religious and other sections of the community. Another organisation, Friends across Differences, existed briefly.

Intersectionality

The first Universal Periodic Review (UPR) for Guyana was concluded in 2010. The UPR process highlighted three issues – corporal punishment of children, the death penalty and the laws criminalising same-sex relationships. SASOD organised a UPR public forum on August 17, 2010. The panel included U-RAP co-founder, Arif Bulkan, who spoke on the death penalty,[19] Namela Henry who spoke to the homophobic discrimination, and the author of this chapter, who spoke about corporal punishment. This forum connected and brought together different organisations and individuals working on separate human rights issues. SASOD's experience with the UPR and with human rights mechanisms subsequently led to the convening of the Guyana Equality Forum (GEF) in May 2011. The GEF is described as a 'network of civil society organisations working cohesively to achieve equal rights and justice for all Guyanese.'[20] It has lobbied the government on dealing with discrimination against LGBTIQ+ citizens, indigenous citizens, persons with disabilities and youth. The GEF and SASOD have engaged different members of the post-2015 Government on related issues.

The Ministry of Education in October 2017 posted a press release with the headline 'Government Reaffirms Its Support for LGBTQ Community.'[21] Minister of Education Nicolette Henry participated in an event organised by the British High Commission. She spoke assertively against bullying of LGBTIQ+ children, but she has not abolished corporal punishment in Guyana's schools even though she has the power to do so.

The University of Guyana organised another event around education reform, in Guyana, in January 2018. None of the speakers at the event seemed to address abolishing corporal punishment,[22] but there was wide media coverage of the calls by the GEF to end discrimination against LGBTIQ+ children.

More work probably needs to be done with the government on understanding intersectionality as it deals with the human rights of children and other citizens.

Who Else Spoke Out and Supported the Work?

In 2003, the Guyana Human Rights Association (GHRA) joined in the call for the constitutional amendment. GHRA issued a comprehensive press release[23] before the parliamentary discussion. In that release, the GHRA shared a quote from Justice Albie Sachs, of South Africa, on the inclusion of sexual orientation in the Constitution of South Africa, to wit: 'The manner in which discrimination is experienced on grounds of race, sex, religion or disability varies considerably. In the case of gays, history and experience teach us that it is the denial of full moral citizenship in society because you are what you are, that impinges on the dignity and self-worth of a group.' The connection with post-Apartheid South Africa was important. Many of the opponents to the inclusion of sexual orientation as a ground of non-discrimination in the Constitution of Guyana argue that equality for LGBT citizens is a 'European' thing, so it was important to show that other post-colonial societies were rejecting the homophobia of the colonial powers.

In October 2004, Assistant Secretary-General of the United Nations (UN), Guyanese-born lawyer Bertie Ramcharan, also stated his support for law reform at a public human rights forum which included the prime minister and other members of parliament. On International Human Rights Day in 2007, the GHRA invited SASOD to make a presentation. This presentation was then published in the December 14, 2007 edition of *Dayclean*, the organ of the Working People's Alliance – the first time that any political party in Guyana had endorsed LGBTIQ+ activist positions.

In May 2005, the late Grenadian scholar Professor Simeon C. R. McIntosh became the most prominent Caribbean legal scholar to speak in the public domain to the needed changes, in an article published in the *Barbados Advocate* titled 'Homosexuality: A constitutional question'. At the time, he was dean of the faculty of law at UWI, Cave Hill. Other commentators such as Sir Ronald Sanders, Ralph Ramkarran, politicians, and newspaper columnists around the Caribbean have also challenged the discrimination which exists in the Caribbean and Guyana.

Other support in Guyana came from different places. The first film festival had the support of the 3HCD/Video Club and Sidewalk Cafe. In November, 2005, the recently opened Oasis Cafe agreed to host an evening of 'Readings from the Spectrum: Lesbian and Gay Writings'. In addition to publishing the notice for the event, a young journalist in the *Stabroek News* published the entire text of the epic poem in prose form of Alan Moore's 'The Mirror of Love', which looked at the history of same-sex love.[24] This kind of support from the media has been critical to the work.

Role of Media

The newspapers in Guyana had been carrying LGBTIQ+ related content from the early reports in the *Guiana Graphic* to the Helen Haynes advice columns. The letters columns were used after January 2001 by both supporters and opponents of gay rights. In 2003, the government-owned radio station aired and broadcast the first public forum, which resulted in an article in the *Guyana Chronicle* with an opening sentence 'A giant has been awakened.'

A young TV talk show host on *MTV65* owned by members of the PPP, invited the new activists to talk about the constitutional amendments because at the time he felt that the 'opposition' voices were being given more space. That vibrant discussion that ensued among Ramon Gaskin, who supported the constitutional amendment, Juan Edghill, who opposed it, and Joel Simpson from SASOD, must be one of the most memorable in Guyana around any human rights issue. Regrettably, the radio station and the government-owned TV station were not so consistent in terms of how they involved activists from that 2003 debate.

In May 2006, Petronella Trotman was arrested and charged for cross-dressing. SASOD connected with her and on May 17, 2006, she spoke on the state radio about her ordeal. What was poignant about that evening was the nature and possibility of acceptance in Guyana as signified by the interaction between the security guard at the state-owned National Communications Network (NCN) and Petronella. According to the security guard, Petronella's skirt was too short and did not fit the dress code. A covering was found, and the security guard then allowed Petronella in with the longer 'skirt'.

The media reporting is usually based on the decisions of individual journalists, many of whom decided to take their own risks to report on LGBTIQ+ issues. The media in Guyana have been generally fair in their reporting of the activism, though there have been inconsistencies over the years. One newspaper, for example, which had at least two editorials supporting LGBTIQ+ rights, has from time to time not published any letters or notices of events like the SASOD film festival. The 2007 film festival had the broadest range of coverage in radio, television, and print at the time. There is a tendency to sensationalise some reports, while at the other times there is balanced reporting. Some news reports started using the feminine pronoun to refer to male to female transgender citizens.

Diaspora

The engagement of the Guyanese and Caribbean diaspora included the support of filmmakers Philip Pike, Michelle Mohabeer, Richard Fung, Sean Drakes, Renata Mohammed, Andil Gosine, Gavin Ramotar, Antoine Craigwell, and others. Diaspora contributions extend to support from artistes like Nhojj.

LGBTIQ+ Guyanese returning home have expressed surprise at the work being done, and some have used the space created by the film festival to speak about their reconciliation with their memories of leaving Guyana. This has even gone beyond the Guyanese community; it was interesting one year when a young American from Ohio credited Guyana with giving him the courage to come out to his parents. Diaspora engagements now extend to research, such as a paper about SASOD presented at the 2013 Caribbean Studies Association Conference in Grenada by a young Canadian/Guyanese student.

Encounters With God

The opposition to equality for Guyanese LGBTIQ+ has been in the form of objections on religious grounds. However, different sections of the religious community have had different positions on the issues of discrimination against LGBTIQ+ Guyanese. The Roman Catholic church in Guyana issued a position in 2001, opposing discrimination in any form while stating their objection to gay marriage. Other writers such as Jesuit Priest Father Malcolm Rodrigues in 2001, and Reverend Patricia Sheeratan in 2003, also supported the calls for discrimination to be outlawed. In June 2010, the Inter-Religious Organization (IRO) through its spokesperson Mr Juan Edghill condemned the SASOD Film Festival. He used the offices of the Ethnic Relations Commission (ERC) to express his homophobia. He was then chairperson of the ERC. This condemnation resulted in some important statements. First, the co-chairperson of the IRO at the time, Swami Aksharananda, wrote a response in which he distanced himself from the IRO position and called for reason and respect for life. He was later joined by Pandits Rajin Balgobin and Deodat Tillack, who also shared similar views in an article in the April, May, June 2011 issue of *Hinduism Today* magazine that discussed the diverse views of Hindus. Roman Catholic Bishop Francis Alleyne has, on more than one occasion, apologised to the LGBT community. In Trinidad and Tobago, Pandita Indranie Rampersaud also showed support for LGBTIQ+ equality even as some other Hindu leaders expressed different opinions. The supportive religious positions from Hindus, Christians and others for LGBTIQ+ equality have been expressed in Trinidad and Tobago, Jamaica and other parts of the Caribbean, and challenge the 'united religious' homophobic narrative.

Other condemnations of the IRO position came from Women's activist group Red Thread member Wintress Whyte, and businessman Clinton Urling (who was then president of the Georgetown Chamber of Commerce and Industry). There was a feeling among many persons that Mr Edghill and the IRO deserved a vocal and public condemnation for the abuse of state resources allocated to the office of the Ethnic Relations Commission.[25] A senior Caribbean civil servant asked members of SASOD to reflect on the Civil Paths to Peace Initiative to promote respect and understanding which had been recently launched by the Commonwealth Foundation. And so it was that co-chairpersons Namela Henry and Joel Simpson responded a few days later, noting

> In a society which is marred by conflict and the abuses of power, it is not easy to try alternative ways of engagement which are not meant to destroy or humiliate. But, try we must and in the spirit of the Film Festival's mission to promote discussion and education about the diversity of sexual orientations and gender identities in this country, we therefore make ourselves available to dialogue with the IRO and with any other interested parties about their concerns.

The IRO never responded.

'Is it Homophobic to Say that Homosexuality is a Sin?'

A statement from the Christian Community in Guyana on the proposed decriminalisation of homosexuality notes that,

> We also believe...that we are called to embrace and reflect God's love and compassion for humanity as outlined in the Bible which demands that we reject the acts of violence and hostility meted out to some homosexuals and other attitudes or actions that devalue and diminish our humanity as God intended.

The statement affirms in addition that 'It is evident that homosexuality is an offense to religion, morality and public convenience.'

This experience of loving is manifested in the experience of LGBTIQ+ people who are then threatened with the 'fyah' which reportedly destroyed Sodom. Fyah – in 2013 – in the form of the acid thrown on Sandy Jackman as she dealt with her family duties; and fyah in the cigarette lighter flame held by 'loving' citizens to the locks of Ryon Rawlins as he walked down Regent Street going about his business, with a reminder of his apparent sin in the chants of 'bun batty man'. A gay teacher living in a rural area in Guyana told me that he did not have much faith in laws and was looking instead at fundamental changes in the education of regular people.

Ravi Dev was a member of parliament when he participated in the first public forum in April 2003. In his reflections on the ten years since that forum, he said he believed the discussion on sexual orientation and gender identity is one which is related to the general discussions on diversity and difference and who has moral superiority over whom. This moral superiority, in this instance, was often expressed in the violence and discrimination that seemingly has no redress.

In 2017 and 2018, Christian Bishop Apostle London organised marches in Linden and Georgetown against sodomy. He and his followers were loud in their calls for the government to enforce the sodomy laws.

How then can the views of 'regular people' who oppose discrimination against LGBTIQ+ Guyanese be given prominence in the national discussion about laws and policies?

In April 2013, I visited the Wedding Expo and used the opportunity to poll the issue of gay marriage. I asked 13 exhibitors how they felt about offering wedding and honeymoon services to same-sex couples. Eleven of the exhibitors said they had no problem (a few had already done so) while two persons said that offering services to same-sex couples would conflict with their faith.

A survey conducted by the Caribbean Development Research Services Inc (CADRES)[26] published in 2013 concluded that 58 per cent of Guyanese were tolerant of homosexuals, while 17 per cent were undecided and 25 per cent were homophobic.

Caribbean Community

In 2004, Caribbean and other LGBTIQ+ activists, concerned with the growing popularity of homophobic lyrics, initiated the 'Stop Murder Music' Campaign to bring pressure to bear on private and public sector groups in the Caribbean, North America, and Europe to respond to these lyrics. Guyanese joined the campaign by writing to the Ethnic Relations Commission since they believed 'that sexual orientation is one of the forms of diversity in a plural society and that therefore the ERC holds a constitutional mandate to encourage respect for the rights of gay and lesbian people in Guyana.' One year after the appeal, the ERC said it had no mandate to deal with the matter.

The *Jamaica Outpost*, a newsletter which ran in Kingston between October 2004 and June 2005, as well as the *Free Forum* magazine edited by the late Deni James of the organisation Men Who Have Sex with Men No Political Agenda (MSMNPA) in Trinidad and Tobago carried articles from Guyana.

The Regional HIV/AIDS mechanisms interrogated the laws fuelling discrimination and the years 2004 and 2005 saw discussions in different countries, including Guyana, about the need for repeal of 'sodomy laws'. Some Caribbean minsters of health, including Guyana's Dr Leslie Ramsammy, supported these calls, which were rejected by their governments.

In 2007, Trinidadian activist Colin Robinson wrote that:

> In a field in which international human rights advocacy and HIV response work have been the dominant forms of LGBTIQ+ organising, SASOD's breathtaking cultural and political programmes have distinguished themselves by their inventiveness, analysis, balance, and skilful use of limited resources. SASOD's work and imaginativeness reflect the best Caribbean political and cultural traditions and they make me proud to be a gay Caribbean man.

In 2008, the late Dr Robert Carr, who was based in Jamaica, also stated that he wished there was a 'SASOD in every Caribbean country'.

In 2008, Jamaican Prime Minister Bruce Golding made international headlines with his position of 'No Gays in my cabinet'.[27] The position was milder than the vehement calls from other leaders around the world for discrimination against LGBTIQ+ citizens. The positions of Caribbean and other leaders seemed to shift away from Mr Golding's. In 2010, Cuban leader Fidel Castro was reported to have expressed regret for the persecution of homosexuals in the revolution, stating in an interview with Mexican newspaper *La Jornada* 'fueron momentos de una gran injusticia, ¡una gran injusticia (there were moments of great injustice, a great injustice)!'[28]

In 2011, on the eve of an election, Jamaican Prime Minister Portia Simpson Miller implied she had no intention of prying into anyone's personal life. In 2014, current Jamaican Prime Minister Andrew Holness seemed to say he would allow gays in his cabinet.[29]

If Not Changing the Laws, Then What?

On August 9, 2012, the words 'Lesbian' and 'Bisexual' and 'Transgender' were probably used for the first time in Guyana's Parliament as Prime Minister Samuel Hinds moved the motion to form a Parliamentary Select Committee to consider The Decriminalization of Consensual Adult Same Sex Relations and Discrimination Against Lesbians, Gays, Bi-Sexual And Transgender Persons. Opposition MP Volda Lawrence questioned in her speech 'Offences against Morality,' 'What has happened to Guyana, the [sovereign] state and why do we have to repeal our laws because a few European delegations proposed that we do that?'[30]

In 2014, Presidential Advisor on Governance Gail Texeira spoke at a Canadian High Commission reception saying that it would take a long time for gay rights.[31] This seemed to start a fascinating trend of government officials speaking at social events organised by foreign delegations speaking about non-discrimination without committing to changing anything. In 2016, Ms Lawrence, now minister of public health, spoke against discrimination against LGBTIQ+ at the British High Commission – a European function.[32] What was the change since 2012 about the appeal to the homophobic sovereign nation?

Quincy McEwan from Guyana Trans United recalled a 2015 meeting convened by the PPP/C before the elections. The then General Secretary Clement Rohee who was also minister of home affairs chaired the meeting of LGBTIQ+ organisations and allies to talk about what changes were needed. Some of the participants had questioned Minister Rohee about his lack of action in providing real change in affording protection to LGBTIQ+ citizens.

Gender Neutral Legislation and Policies Around Non-Discrimination

The Women's Movement in the Caribbean had started advocating in the 1990s for changes to the legislation which affected women. In 1996, the Domestic Violence Act was passed in Guyana. The Domestic Violence Act was described as 'gender-neutral'. The Act also makes it possible for a person to file for orders against partners or former partners of the same-sex. The Sexual Offences Act (2010) is also gender neutral. The act describes the offences using the term person rather than male or female. Non-consensual same-sex activity can now be penalised under this Act.

Help and Shelter, a non-governmental organisation (NGO) which provides services for survivors of domestic violence and other forms of gender-based violence and child abuse, states in its code of conduct for employees:

- Homosexuality
  - » We will apply our counselling skills and strategies to deal with issues of abuse and violence professionally and impartially whatever our individual feelings towards homosexuality and same sex relationships may be.

» We will not attempt to change people's sexual orientation.

The University of Guyana's Code of Conduct for staff states:

> 12. Treat students, other staff and members of the community equitably, fairly and courteously, irrespective of differences in culture, race, gender, nationality, age, religion, disability, marital status, sexual inclination, political orientation, education, life experiences, options and/or beliefs.

The 2017–18 Code of Conduct for students recommends:

> SHOW tolerance towards colleagues, lecturers and other University workers, and desist from exhibiting prejudice based on race, ethnicity, sexual preference, gender, religion, political persuasion, socio-economic status or other human condition.

In 2008, the National Domestic Violence Policy acknowledged that domestic violence between same-sex partners needed specialist attention. In 2011, the Ministry of Health launched a policy against stigma and discrimination, calling on health officials not to discriminate on the grounds of sexual orientation. In 2014, a project funded by the UNDP sought to build capacity of municipalities to respond to HIV/AIDS. The Municipalities of New Amsterdam and Linden signed declarations which sought to:

- Respect the dignity and worth of every person, without distinction on the basis of race, colour, sex, gender, sexual orientation, gender identity, language, religion, property, birth or other status
- Renounce homophobia and support the rights and dignity of all persons regardless of their gender, sexuality or employment to care, treatment and support as human rights.

The election manifestos in 2015 seemed to indicate that these changes would become laws.

In 2018, the Ministry of Finance, National Procurement and Tender Board Vendor Form gave applicants the options of male, female and other for the field 'Gender.'

The Referendum that Might Have Been

One of the first projects that SASOD engaged in was funded through the Global Fund/Ministry of Health in 2006. The SASOD website at the time was funded through the project and had to be branded with the coat of arms of Guyana. Cynics might ask whether the government was funding a revolution against itself. Whenever President Jagdeo was asked about the issue of law reform, his response was always framed in the position of 'no discrimination' even as he remained non-committal on law reform.

In March 2011, Cabinet Secretary Dr Roger Luncheon noted that 'Cabinet reflected on social responses to homosexuality and reiterated its position of not supporting discrimination of those whose sexual orientation offended contemporary social norms and also consequently any advocacy of such lifestyles.'

It seemed that the politicians were becoming comfortable with the idea that since the laws were not being enforced, then there would be no need to generate prayer and fasting in trying to change any of the laws. And well-meaning persons who abhorred homosexuals could preach to love the sinner without changing any of the laws to love the sin.

In 2012, the report 'Collateral Damage: The Social Impact of Laws Affecting LGBT Persons in Guyana' was produced by Christopher Carrico with U-RAP. The interviewees noted that the existence of the laws made them regulate their behaviour at the workplace so as to ensure access to livelihood. The report concluded that 'the laws against sodomy, same sex sexual activity and crossdressing are not harmless laws, and that it is likely that the laws against loitering have been invoked arbitrarily to target the LGBT population.'

In January 2016, President Granger was reported as saying that 'I am prepared to respect the rights of any adult to indulge in any practice which is not harmful to others.' He did not reportedly use any specific language to talk about which adults and which practice. First Lady Sandra Granger has on several occasions spoken out against discrimination against LGBTIQ+ youth and individuals.

On May 15, 2017, the Attorney General Basil Williams at an event against homophobia funded by the 'Europeans'[33] stated that 'the government noted that the Guyanese people are to decide in a referendum whether homosexuality should remain a criminal offence.' There was some consternation about the proposed referendum and Minister of State Joseph Harmon subsequently noted that 'This is not an issue that has been ventilated at Cabinet and Cabinet has made no decision on that matter and so the question of a referendum, when it will occur and all of that, that is really not on the cards.'[34]

So it seems the people in the restaurant who were smiling and nodding about the fears of 'gie-ing dem dey rights' would not have a chance to go to the ballot to keep the laws which discriminate against LGBTIQ+ citizens. Meanwhile, though, it seems that the people in Guyana who are serious about the intention of the 2015 Manifesto promises will be trying to find ways to make sure those promises are fulfilled.

Notes

1. This chapter adapts and updates an article that was first presented in 'From Madness to Mainstream – "Gay rights" in Guyana,' Part I and Part 2, published in the Diaspora Column of the *Stabroek News* on June 24, 2013 and July 1, 2013, respectively.
2. 'A Joint Manifesto – A Good Life for All' APNU+AFC 2015 Manifesto.
3. 'Our Vision : Guyana Version 2.0' PPP/C 2015 Manifesto.
4. 'Courageous, Caring, Compassionate Leadership: The People's Partnership Plan 2015'.
5. There are different ways of referring to the spectra of sexual orientations and gender identities. For the purposes of this chapter, LGBTIQ+ (Lesbian, gay, bisexual, transgender, intersex, queer and other non-conforming persons) is used.
6. C. Anderson, 'Execution and its Aftermath in the Nineteenth-Century British Empire,' in *A Global History of Execution and the Criminal Corpse, Palgrave Historical Studies in the Criminal Corpse and its Afterlife*, ed. R. Ward (London: Palgrave Macmillan, 2015).
7. Research shared by Gaiutra Bahadur, author of *Coolie Woman: An Odyssey of Indenture* (Chicago: University of Chicago Press 2013) and available on the IRN collection of the Digital Library of the Caribbean at http://ufdc.ufl.edu/AA00007501/00001/citation.
8. Gaiutra Bahadur, *Coolie Woman*.
9. 'Counsel Wants Law to Permit Homo Relations,' *Guyana Chronicle*, April 4, 1979 and reprinted in *Tales from Way Back When* by Clifford Stanley in *Sunday Chronicle*, March 7, 2014, http://dloc.com/AA00048305/00001/citation.
10. Criminal Law (Offences) Act, Chapter 8:01, s. 353.
11. *National Coalition for Gay and Lesbian Equality v Minister of Justice* CCT 11/98 (CC South Africa), per Ackermann, J. at [28]-[32]; *Lawrence v Texas* (2003) 539 US 558 (US Supreme Court) per O'Connor, J. at 583.
12. Criminal Law (Offences) Act, Chapter 8:01, s. 352.
13. Ibid., 351.
14. 'He Wore Blue Velvet...? Seven Fined for Cross-dressing,' *Stabroek News*, February 10, 2009.
15. 'McEwan, Clarke, Fraser, Persaud & SASOD v Attorney General of Guyana,' http://www.u-rap.org/web2/index.php/2015-09-29-00-40-03/mcewan-others/item/1-mcewan-clarke-fraser-persaud-sasod-v-attorney-general-of-guyana.
16. http://sasod.blogspot.com/2013/09/joint-media-release-from-thesociety.html.

17. *McEwan et al v Attorney General,* #21-M/2010, decision dated September 6, 2013.
18. Joel Simpson 'SASOD at 10 Coming Full Circle,' *Stabroek News,* June 10, 2013, https://www.stabroeknews.com/2013/features/in-the-diaspora/06/10/sasod-at-10-coming-full-circle.
19. Iana Seales, 'Death Penalty "Spectacular Failure" in Crime Fight,' *Stabroek News,* August 18, 2010, https://www.stabroeknews.com/2010/news/stories/08/18/death-penalty-%e2%80%98spectacular-failure%e2%80%99-in-crime-fight.
20. 'About - Guyana Equality Forum,' http://equality.gy/about/ accessed April 22, 2018.
21. 'Government Reaffirms Its Support for LGBTQ Community,' Ministry of Education press release, https://www.education.gov.gy/web/index.php/mediacenter/item/3127-govt-reaffirms-its-support-for-lgbtq-community.
22. 'Corporal punishment in schools should be highlighted in education reform forum,' letter to the editor, Vidyaratha Kissoon, *Stabroek News,* February 4, 2018 https://www.stabroeknews.com/2018/opinion/letters/02/04/corporal-punishment-in-schools-should-be-highlighted-in-education-reform-forum.
23. Available at http://ufdc.ufl.edu/AA00062735/00001.
24. 'The Mirror of Love,' The Scene, *Stabroek News,* November 19, 2005.
25. 'The SASOD Film Festival and the IRO,' editorial, *Stabroek News,* July 5, 2010, https://www.stabroeknews.com/2010/opinion/editorial/07/05/the-sasod-film-festival-and-the-iro.
26. 'Survey Report: Attitudes towards Homosexuals in Guyana (2013),' *Caribbean IRN* Blog, http://caribbeanirn.blogspot.com/2013/07/survey-report-attitudes-towards.html.
27. https://www.youtube.com/watch?v=cLDqM-A4tH4.
28. http://www.jornada.unam.mx/2010/08/31/mundo/026e1mun.
29. https://76crimes.com/2014/05/05/jamaican-politician-i-would-allow-gays-in-cabinet.
30. http://parliament.gov.gy/media-centre/speeches/offences-against-morality/#.WqnObedG3IV
31. 'No Fast Track to Gay Rights in Guyana – Teixeira,' *Demerara Waves,* July 14, 2014, http://demerarawaves.com/2014/07/02/no-fast-track-to-gay-rights-in-guyana-teixeira.
32. http://guyanachronicle.com/2016/03/18/lawrence-bats-for-lgbt-community.
33. 'Attorney General Calls for Referendum on Legality of Homosexual Intimacy at IDAHOT Event,' *SASOD* website, http://www.sasod.org.gy/sasod-blog-attorney-general-calls-referendum-legality-homosexual-intimacy-idahot-event.
34. Denis Chabrol, 'No Decision on Referendum to Scrap Buggery Law – Harmon,' *Demerara Waves,* June 2, 2017, http://demerarawaves.com/2017/06/02/no-decision-on-referendum-to-scrap-buggery-law-harmon.

References

Anderson, Clare. 2015. Execution and its Aftermath in the Nineteenth-Century British Empire. In *A Global History of Execution and the Criminal Corpse*, ed. Richard Ward. London: Palgrave Macmillan.

Bahadur, Gaiutra. 2013. *Coolie Woman: The Odyssey of Indenture*. Chicago: University of Chicago Press.

Carrico, Christopher. 2012. *Collateral Damage: The Social Impact of Laws Affecting LGBT in Guyana*. Barbados: University of the West Indies.

Contributors

Diana ABRAHAM is an ABD doctoral candidate at the Faculty of Environmental Studies, York University, Toronto. While her doctoral inquiry examined the effects of the migration of the tertiary educated on the economic and social development of less developed countries, her thesis research focused on the impact of the migration of qualified teachers on the delivery of public education in Guyana. Diana is a retired senior consultant with the government of Ontario with several years' experience in the development of programmes and services related to the settlement of immigrants and refugees. She is also an adjunct faculty member at the Department of Social Work, York University.

Arif BULKAN (PhD Osgoode) is a senior lecturer in the Faculty of Law at the University of the West Indies, St Augustine campus, where he lectures Criminal Law, Constitutional Law, and Caribbean and International Human Rights Law. Before that he practised law in Guyana from 1990 to 2004. He is the author of *The Survival of Indigenous Rights in Guyana* (IDS, UG, 2014) and co-author with Tracy Robinson and Adrian Saunders of *Fundamentals of Caribbean Constitutional Law* (Sweet and Maxwell 2015). His research focuses on constitutionalism and governance, the protection of fundamental rights, and indigenous rights doctrines.

Janette BULKAN (PhD Yale) is an assistant professor in the Department of Forest Resources Management in the Faculty of Forestry, University of British Columbia, Canada. She was coordinator of the Amerindian Research Unit, University of Guyana, from 1985 to 2000. For over 20 years, she has conducted collaborative research with Indigenous Peoples and local communities in Guyana. Her research interests are forest governance, collaborative natural resource management, concession systems, community forestry and third-party forest certification systems. Janette serves on the Editorial Board of the *Journal of Sustainable Forestry* and on the Editorial Advisory Board of the *Journal Archaeology and Anthropology*. She is a member of the Governing Council of the Commonwealth Forestry Association (CFA) and of the Policy and Standards Committee of the Forest Stewardship Council (FSC).

Shanya CORDIS is an assistant professor of Anthropology at Spelman College with a focus on Native American and Indigenous Studies and African and African Diaspora Studies. A first generation Guyanese-American of black and indigenous (Warau and Lokono) heritage, her research focus includes indigeneity across the Americas and the Caribbean, black and indigenous political subjectivities and social movements, gender violence, and critical feminist geographies. Her forthcoming manuscript, tentatively titled *Unsettling Dispossession: Gender Violence and Indigenous Struggles for Land in Guyana* examines the relationship between (neo)colonial recognition, territorial conflicts, and indigenous gendered dispossession in Guyana.

Hollis FRANCE is an associate professor at the College of Charleston (Charleston, South Carolina) in the Department of Political Science and the Latin American and Caribbean Studies Program. At the College of Charleston, she is the director of the Gender and Sexuality Equity Center (GSEC). Her current research focuses on diverse and social economies as alternative development models, and the intersections of gender and political economy. Her ongoing fieldwork is centred on the North Rupununi of Guyana where she works among Makushi communities engaged in community-based development projects. In Charleston, she is currently working on the Illumination Project, which creates a process, grounded in trust and legitimacy, to strengthen and broaden collaboration between the police and the citizens they serve.

Anand GOOLSARRAN is a fellow of the Chartered Association of Certified Accountants with a Masters and PhD in Business Administration. He has over 30 years of professional experience in public sector financial management at both the national and international levels, and served as the auditor general of Guyana from 1990 to 2004. He was the executive secretary of the United Nations Board of Auditors and of the Panel of External Auditors from 2005 to 2012, and also chief resident auditor of the United Nations Peacekeeping Operations in Sierra Leone and Liberia for two years. He was the president of the Transparency Institute Guyana Inc from 2013 to 2014 and is a weekly columnist in the independent daily newspaper, the *Stabroek News*. He is the author of several published works, including two books entitled *Improving Public Accountability: The Guyana Experience 1985–2007* and *Public Accountability at the Crossroad: The Guyana Experience*.

Clement HENRY recently completed the requirements for the Doctor of Philosophy in International Relations at the University of the West Indies, St Augustine. His dissertation is entitled 'A Theoretical and Empirical Analysis of the Dimensions of Human Security: The Case of Guyana.' Clement is also a graduate of the University of Guyana and Andrews University, Berrien Springs, Michigan. He is currently the project manager for the Citizen Security Strengthening Programme in the Ministry of Public Security and an executive board member of the National Data Management Authority and Youth Challenge Guyana. He has served as head of Policy and Research in the Ministry of Home Affairs in Guyana for seven years and as social management and community development specialist for the E-Government Unit, Ministry of the Presidency. His publications include: 'An Analysis of the Effectiveness of Foreign Aid Flows to Guyana,' in *Selected Essays in Contemporary Caribbean Issues*, edited by Anatol and Kirton. His research interests include human and citizen security, poverty, digital poverty, development and economic growth, and development finance.

Percy C. HINTZEN is currently a professor in the Department of Global and Sociocultural Studies and director of the African and African Diaspora Studies Program at Florida International University, and Professor Emeritus at the University of California, Berkeley. He earned his PhD in Comparative Political Sociology from Yale University. His research and publications examine relationships among modernity, political economy, and the production of difference. His primary fields of enquiry are postcolonial studies, globalisation, and development.

Iman KHAN is the director of Business Development and Communications at Corum Holdings in Georgetown, Guyana. She holds various private sector posts such as council member of the Georgetown Chamber of Commerce and advisor to the president of the American Chamber of Commerce of Guyana. She has researched and written chapters on policy, politics, and neoliberalism in the Caribbean.

Tarron KHEMRAJ is the William G. and Marie Selby Professor of Economics at New College of Florida, the honours college of the State University System of Florida. He is currently a columnist at *Stabroek News*, Guyana. Tarron was formerly an economist at the Bank of Guyana and once served as a research associate at the Caribbean Centre for Money and Finance.

Vidyaratha KISSOON has been associated with the work to achieve LGBT equality in Guyana since 2001. He was part of the Society against Sexual Orientation Discrimination until his resignation in June 2012.

Esther M. MCINTOSH is a Governance and Development specialist with experience managing and implementing local governance initiatives in South and Central Asia, East-Central Africa, the Pacific, and the Caribbean. She currently serves as the Deputy Director on a Decentralisation and Citizen Participation Partnership facility between the governments of Papua New Guinea and Australia. She holds a masters degree from the Institute of Development Studies, University of Sussex (United Kingdom) and is completing her PhD at the University of Leiden (The Netherlands). She has published papers on a number of subjects related to local government in her areas of interest that include minority participation and post conflict transitions.

Kiran MIRCHANDANI is professor in the Adult Education and Community Development Program at the University of Toronto. Her research and teaching focuses on gendered and racialised processes in the workplace; critical perspectives on organisational development and learning; criminalisation and welfare policy; and globalisation and economic restructuring. She is the author of *Phone Clones: Transnational Service Work in the Global Economy* (2012), co-author of *Criminalizing Race,*

Criminalizing Poverty: Welfare Fraud Enforcement in Canada (2007), and co-editor of *Borders in Service: Enactments of Nationhood in Transnational Call Centers* (2016).

Wazir MOHAMMED is an associate professor of Sociology at Indiana University East in Richmond, Indiana. He holds a BS in Communication from the University of Guyana, and an MA and PhD in Sociology from Binghamton University. His interests include the intersection of Atlantic slavery, particularly with the rise of slavery in the age of abolition, the second slavery in Cuba, Brazil, and the US with the persistence of ethnic divisions and marginalisation of the descendants of slaves in the African Diaspora of the Caribbean and the Americas. His research makes the connection between land control, land use, and land ownership and the continuing marginalisation of the majority of the working people in postcolonial societies. Wazir was formerly a social and political justice activist in Guyana as a member and later co-leader of the Working People's Alliance.

Natalie PERSADIE is assistant professor in the Design and Manufacturing Engineering Unit at the University of Trinidad and Tobago, as well as a part-time lecturer at the University of the West Indies where she has taught a number of law-related subjects in various Faculties. She obtained a PhD in International Studies from the University of Birmingham, UK. Natalie does consulting in environmental, legal and technical work, as well as pro bono work for NGOs, CBOs, and clubs. She researches and publishes on a variety of topics, including gender and the law, environmental law, industrial relations, business law, and company law. Current research interests include sustainability, manufacturing policy, and entrepreneurship.

Savitri PERSAUD is a PhD candidate in the Department of Social and Political Thought at York University. Her doctoral dissertation examines discourses of mental health and madness, disablement, and violence in Guyana, the Caribbean, and Caribbean diasporas. She was born in Guyana and spent part of her childhood in Moblissa, located off of the Linden Highway; and in Belle Vue, West Bank Demerara, before migrating to Toronto, Canada.

Rishee THAKUR is senior lecturer in the Department of Government and International Affairs at the University of Guyana, Berbice Campus. His teaching and research are in the areas of public policy and political theory. He is co-editor of a forthcoming collection on 'Decentralising a Troubled State: Local Government Reform in Guyana'.

Alissa TROTZ is professor of Women and Gender Studies, and Caribbean Studies, at New College, University of Toronto. She is also associate faculty at the Dame Nita Barrow Institute of Gender and Development Studies, University of the West Indies (Barbados). Her published work addresses such topics as Caribbean migration and diaspora; the gendered politics of neoliberalism, social reproduction and women's activism; history, memory and violence; and transnational feminisms. She edits a weekly newspaper column, 'In the Diaspora,' *Stabroek News*, Guyana.

Sarah Elizabeth VAUGHN is an assistant professor in the Department of Anthropology at the University of California, Berkeley. Her primary field is the critical study of climate change. She has engaged climate change through both ethnographic and archival research of the geotechnical engineering sciences, flooding, sea defence, and at the intersection of mining and forest mapping. At stake is the way climate change generates problem spaces and claims to expertise in Guyana and the circum-Caribbean.

Index

Page numbers in boldface refer to tables and page numbers in italics refer to figures.

ABC for Local Government Elections, The, 82n10
Aboriginal Indian Ordinances, 437
Abraham, Diana, xviii, xix
Adams, Vincanne, 494
Adamson, Alan, 97
African-Guyanese people: desire to emigrate among, 142; marginalisation of, xii, 105–6, 126, 144; mistrust in judicial system, 142; political attitudes of, 139–42; violence of, xvi, 106; voting preferences, 107–8, **108**, 109–10. *See also* maroon communities
African liberation army: violence of, 18–19
African Society for Cultural Relations with Independent Africa (ASCRIA), 189–90
agriculture: contract relationships, 233n32; cooperatives, 455, 456; costs of, 99; drainage and irrigation, 223, 224; historical development of, 93; internal market, 100; lack of diversification, 217; nationalisation of, 486; in neoliberal economy, 225–26; polder system in, 99; prospects of, 230; rapid development of, 187. *See also* farming; rice industry; sugar industry
Ahmed, S., 315
Aksharananda, Swami, 291n10, 515
Alexander, Jacqui, 170
Alkire, Sabina, 243
Alleyne, Francis, 515
Alliance for Change (AFC): emergence of, 145; ethnic identification with, **108**; manifesto on gender issues, **405**, 407–8; motion of no-confidence against Ramotar's government, 12; popular support of, xxviii, 92, **108**, 109; women representative in parliaments, **409**
Alliance for Guyana (AFG), 405, 406, **409**
Ally, Fazal, 226
Ally, Hydar, 16
Alves, Patricia, 378
Americas Watch, 197
Amerindian Acts, 67, 330, 331, 437–38, 439, 440
Amerindian Lands Commission (ALC), 438
Amerindian people: communal values, 457; crop cultivation, 456; cultural exchanges, 447n5; dependence on forests, 330; economic practices, xxv, 447n5, 456, 461; environmental insecurity of, xx, 341, 439; legal status of, xx; marginalisation of, 431; nine-tribes model, 447n5; occupations, 442; population statistics, xxviii, 355n3, 475n12; recognition policies, 326, 431, 437, 440–41, 446; rights to territory and resources, xxiv, 331; state's relationship with, xxiii–xxiv, xxv, 439, 455; villagisation of, 455, 456
Amerindian village communities: collective land titles of, 331, 435–36, 440, 455; constrain of autonomy of, 441; exodus

of members, 456; government control over, 456; impact of mining on, 436, 442–43; interviews with, 442; land claims, 438, 440–41; political patronage of, 473; reliance on river, 435
Amerindian women: as 'buck,' image of, 444, 446, 448n21; circulating representations of, 445–46; decision-making practices, 457; economic activities, 457–58; prostitution, 443; sexual violence against, 444–45; social status of, xxiv, 444; trafficking in persons (TIP) cases, 443, 445
Amin, Ash, 472
Amnesty International, 26
Anand, Sudhir, 243
Andaiye (women activist), 137, 138, 162, 172, 175n43, 175n45
Anglophone Caribbean states, 3–4, 5, 29n5
anticolonial movement, 374
Anti-Money Laundering and Countering of Financing of Terrorists Act (2009), 56–57, 58–59
anti-violence activism, xvii, 165
APNU-AFC coalition government, xxxi, 429, 473, 501–2
Arnstein, Sherry, 76
Artistes in Direct Support, 507
asafoetida, 379, 391n8
Atoyan, Ruben, 272
Audit Act (2004), 54–55
auditor general office: audit of public accounts by, 38–40, 41; autonomy of, 54, 59; constitutional amendments concerning, 50; criticism of, 41–42; fiscal reports of, 42, 43; lack of integrity, 23–24; mandate of, 44, 54; recommendations on government's financial management, 40

authoritarianism, xxviii, xxix–xxx, xxxi–xxxii, 3, 4, 9

Bahamas, 94, 95, **95**, **96**, 399
Balgobin, Rajin, 515
Barama Company Limited (BCL), 344, 345, 348, 356n11, 357n14
Barbados, 94, 95, **95**, **96**, 180, 319
Bare Root village, 371, 372, 373, 376
Barkin, David, 472, 475n11
Barrow-Giles, Cynthia, 410
Bartica, town of, 434
Bateman, Milford, 459
bauxite industry, 37, 114, 150n26, 229, 271–72, 328
Bavikatte, Sanjay Kabir, 508
Belize, 305, **395**, 398, 400–401, 507
Benjamin, Anna, 26
Benjamin, Kenneth, xxxi, 507
Bernard, Deryck, 510
Bernard, Desiree, 133, 156
bi-communal societies, xvi, 91, 97, 98, 115
Bishop, Andrew, 339
Black, D.A., 337
Black Bush Polder LSS, 224
Botswana, 94, **95**, 96, **96**
Brama, Nandlall, 122
British Guiana: nationalist movement, 180–81, 182; path to independence, 182–83
British Guiana Rice Development Company (BGRDC), 224
Broek, D. Van den, 311
Brotherson, Wendell, 504
Buchanan, James M., 68
Bulkan, Arif, xi, xiii, xiv, xvi, xxiii, xxxi, 511
Bulkan, Janette, xx
Burnham, Forbes: criticism of US administration, 191; death of, x; education policy, 270; establishment of People's National Congress, 155; intolerance to criticism, xxxi;

nationalist views of, 186; political career, 6, 8, 81n7, 439; remarks on Guyanese identity, 380; socialist policy, 374, 498n5; support base of, 184
Bush, George, 196
'bush,' circulating ideas about, 434, 436–37, 446
business-processing outsourcing firms (BPOs), 301
Bynoe, Ivan, 68, 77
Bynoe, Philip, 356n13, 357n13

Calder, Jason, 104
call centres: analysis of, 299–300; economic niche of, 301–2; feminization of, xx, 310; geography of outsourced, 303; growth of, 297, 306–7, 321; Guyana's strategic advantage for, 303–4, 306; promotion of, 321–22; recruitment advertisements of, 299–300; as site of multiple sovereignties, 321
call centre workers: communication with abusive callers, 315, 317–18; customer service, 314, 315; customers' feedback, 305, 318; demographics, 301, 307; exploitation of, 312–13; grammatical tests for, 316; high turnover of, 311–12, 313; holidays, 318; incentives for, xx, 309, 322n12; insecurity of, 319; interviews with, 297–98, 300; linguistic advantage of, 304–5, 315–16; public shaming of, 311; qualities of good, 310–11; recruitment of, 299–300; social status of, 319; stress of, 313, 320–21; training programme, 316–17; wages of, 307, 308–10, 320; work environment, 311, 314–15, 318–19
Cameron, Jenny, 469, 472

canals: littering of, 488. *See also* Hope Canal
Caribbean Community (CARICOM), 66, 94, 129–30, 156, 203, 303, 418
Caribbean Development Research Services Inc (CADRES), 517
Caribbean Financial Action Task Force (CFATF), 55, 56, 57
Carney, Judith, 218, 231–32n15, 232n16
Carnoy, Martin, 272
Carr, Robert, 518
Carter, Jimmy, 1, 197, 198, 199
Carter, Martin, 120, 170, 379, 389
cassava, 463, 464, 465, 467, 468–69, 470, 471, 475n7
Castro, Fidel, 518
Central Tender Board, 49, 50
Central Timber Manufacturing Plant (CTMP), 334
chainsaw logging, 344, 348, 357n13. *See also* logging concessions
Chanderpal, Indranie, 422n4
Chang, Ha-Joon, 459
Chang, Ian, xxx
Cheema, G., 74
Choy, Talia, 68, 77
Chronicle, xxxi, 26
Churchill, Winston, 181
civil society organisations, 77, 78–79
Clarke, Seon, 506
Clementi, Cecil: *Constitutional History of British Guiana*, 216
climate adaptation projects: economic relations of, 480, 484, 494; environment and, 480–81, 485; financial support of, 488; as knowledge practice, 495–97; role of state in, 496. *See also* Hope Canal
climate change, 351, 480, 482, 483
coastal region, xxv–xxvi, 92–93, 437
Collier, Paul, 109
Collymore, Clinton, 83n15

colonialism: legacy of, 3–4; as root of racial conflict, 374
coloniality of recognition, 437, 448n17
colonial underdevelopment trap: economic outcome of, 114; pro-ethnic voting and, 112–14, 115; roots of, 93, 99–101, *100*; schematic representations of, *100*, *113*; theory of, 92, 99
Commission of Inquiry for the Guyana Sugar Corporation, 229
Commission of Inquiry into the Wismar disturbances (1964), 159, 162
Committee for the Defence of the Constitution, 21
Common External Tariff (CET), 226
Community Development Councils, 65
Conservancy Adaptation Project (CAP), 483, 488–89
Constantine, Collin, 102
Constitutional History of British Guiana (Clementi), 216
constitutional reform, xiv, xxviii–xxix, 10, 13–14, 66
Constitution of 1980: amendments, 12; on authority of local government, xv, 65, 74, 75; characteristics of, xiii, 7, 10–11; on education, xix; on executive power, 7; on 'integrity' of the public service, 15; on limits of president's term, 12; on no-confidence procedure, 12; on political system of the State, 75; on presidential authority, xxx; on presidential elections, 11–12; on public finances, 22
Cooper, Melinda, 480
cooperative socialism, 486, 498n5
Corbin, Robert, 510
Cordis, Shanya, xxiii, xxiv
corruption, 2, 3, 45, 47
Costa, Emilia Viotti da, 210

Council of Freely Elected Heads of Governments, 197
Cowall, Sally, 196
Cowie, C., 316
Craigwell, Antoine, 514
Creole nationalism, 183–84, 189
Creoles, 328, 430, 445, 446n2
Cricket World Cup, 23
crime, 2, 121, 135–36, 138, 350–51, 505. *See also* Mash jail break
Crook, R.C., 72, 74
cross-dressing: decriminalization of, 505–6, 507
Crown Lands, 214–15, 221–22, 333
Cuba: sugar industry in, 210
cultural patrimony, 369, 370, 380, 385, 390
customer sovereignty, myth of, 313–14
Customs Act, 71
Customs and Excise Department, 17, 48
Customs Duties (Amendment) Bill, 71
Cuyuni River community, 434, 435
Cyril Potter College of Education, 281

D'Aguiar, Peter, 186
Damodar Valley Cooperation model of damming, 486, 497n3
Danns, George K., 106, 112, 116n2
Darke, Bernard, 2
Davies, Michael, 19
D'Cruz, P., 310
Deadly Ethnic Riot (Horowitz), 122
'Demerara Crystals,' 211, 231n5
Demerara Timbers Limited (DTL), 330, 344
DeMerieux, Margaret, 24
democracy, 62, 139, 188
Dev, Ravi, 112, 125, 148n13, 516
development, concept of, 94
Diamond Tropical Wood Products (DTWP), 354
Dictionary of Guyanese Folklore (Seymour), 379–80
Dilly, Barbara, 463

disaster capitalism, 480, 481–82, 492, 494–95
discount rate: in pro-ethnic voting model, 109, 110, 111, 112, 114; in theory of investment, 116–17n7
Doctrine of Paramountcy (Declaration of Sophia), 64–65
Domestic Violence Act, 165, 173n15, 418, 519
drainage management, 483–84, 496
Drakes, Sean, 514
Dunn, Leith, 410, 415

East Demerara Water Conservancy (EDWC), 483
East Indian masses (EIMs). *See* Indian-Guyanese people
economic crisis, 37–38, 191–93
economic development: between 1957 and 1964, 186–87; alternative models of, 474; broad indicators of, 94–95; comparative analysis of, 93, 94–97; ethno-political mobilisation and, 107; financial indicator of, **95**; geographic factor in, 97–98; Gini coefficient of, 95–96, **96**; global capitalist system and, 97–98; HDI score for, 95–96, **96**; historical overview of, 97–99; monetary indicator of, 94; oil discovery and, 114; post-1992, 103–7; public perception of, 141; suppression of wages and, 98, 101, 102; two vicious cycles of, **102**, 103
Economic Recovery Programme (ERP): effect of, 140, 229; formulation of, 38; implementation of, 132, 150n22, 301, 334–35, 486–87; objectives of, 238–39, 272
economic relations: moral grounds for, 497n2
economic security, 252, **253**
economy: as appendage to global capitalist system, 224; criminalization of, 136; dependence on foreign aid, 191, 193–95, 290n3; liberalisation of, xvii, xviii, 225; period of growth of, 271; principle of social, 460, 474n5; structural changes, xviii, 101–2. *See also* agriculture
Edghill, Desiree, 507
Edghill, Juan, 508, 514, 515
Edmonstone, Charles, 218
education: constitutional provisions on, xix, 271; expansion of primary and secondary, 187; government policy in, xviii–xix, 288, 289–90, 291n11; historical background of, 270–72; as path out of poverty, 237; principles of public, 270–71. *See also* private schools; public schools; teachers
Elected Oligarchy (EO), xi, xv, 91, 104
election of 1953, 155
election of 1964, ix, 186
election of 1968, 63
election of 1992, 1–2, 65, 105, 122, 155, 197, 199–200, 487
election of 1994, 65, 70
election of 1997: audit of, 130; contestation of the outcome of, 131, 203; international observers of, 127, 129–30; political parties in, 125–26; political unrest after, 127, 128–29, 155–56, 201; question of validity of, 129, 149n18, 149n21, 155; racial tensions during, 66, 126; results of, 105, 127, 128, **130**, 130–31, 155
election of 2001, 105, 131, 132–34, 139–40, 155, 200–201
election of 2011, xiii, xxvii–xxviii
election of 2015, xxviii, 375, 429
elections: call for fair and free, 198–99; as condition for political representation, 74; gender quota, 395, 410–11; international

support of democratic, 197, 201–2; issue of legitimacy of, 203–4; and violence, 124–36
Elections Amendment Act, 130
electoral fraud, xii, 6
electoral lists, 411–13
electoral system: establishment of, 121, 122; ethnic manipulation as basis of, 415; 'first past the post' (FPTP) principle of, 4–5; legislative framework, 64, 197; proportional representation, 5–6, 186; reforms of, 130, 131, 196, 197; restoration of democratic, xii; substantive representation, 415; Westminster tradition in, xv, 5–6, 15
Elgie, Robert, 9
Enron, 44
environmental degradation, 340–41, 456
environmental security, 255, **255**, 257
Escobar, Arturo, 461
Espinet, Ramabai, 170, 175n45
ethnic cleansing, 104
Ethnic Relations Commission (ERC), 13, 515, 517
ethno-political mobilisation, 104, 107–8, 114–15
European Union Timber Regulation (EUTR), 349, 350
Evans, Peter, 114
ExxonMobil, xxxi, 114

Falleti, Tulia, 70
family: Eurocentric idea of, 160; feminist analysis of, 169; gender inequalities within, 157; scholar analysis of, 169–70
farine (by-product of bitter cassava), 463, 464, 465, 466, 469, 475n6
Farmer's Register of the Guyana Rice Development Board (GRDB), 227
farming, 99–100, 226, 227–28

Feed, Clothes, and House Ourselves programme (FCH), 190
Fiji, 94, **95**, **96**, 97
Filkin, G., 72
finances, xiv, 37–38, 47, 48, 56, 94, 193, 196. *See also* public financial management; taxation
Financial Action Task Force (FATF), 55
Financial Administration and Audit (FAA) Act, xiv, 43–44
Financial Intelligence Unit (FIU), 56, 58
Fiscal Management and Accountability (FMA) Act, 50–51, 59
flooding: climate change and, 485, 487; damage cause by, 479, 487–88; defense against, 479–80, 481; impact on landscapes, 485; impact on sugar industry, 493; population affected by, 479
folk culture, 378–79
food security, 229, **253**
Forde, Henry, 129
foreign investments in, xix–xx, 132, 190, 302, 305–6
forest degradation, 327, 352, 355n2
forest harvesting licences. *See* logging concessions
Forest Industries Corporation (FIC), 334
forest industry: concession policy, 337, 342; decision-making process, 341–42; employment in, xx–xxi, 335; environmental impact, 340–41; foreign investments, xxi, 327, 328, 335–36, 344; under Hoyte administration, 334–36; under Jagan administration, 336–39; under Jagdeo administration, 339–51; landlording practices in, 343, 344, 345, 356n10; log trading areas, 329; management of, 334; under Ramotar administration, 354; regulations, 342–43, 349–50; taxation, 349

Forest Industry Development Survey (FIDS), 333
Forest Products Association (FPA), 344, 356n12
forests: commercial quality of, 348–49; Guiana Shield, 328–29; land-use planning and, 339; management of state, xx, xx–xxi, 325–28, 332, 333–34, 341, 342; national policy on, 337–38; privatisation of, xx; proposal for independent monitoring of, 353–54; protection of, 326, 351–52; research programme of, 330; territory covered by, 325
Forests Acts, 333, 338, 342, 346–47
Fox, Richard, 397–98
Franc, Elsie Le, 241
France, Hollis, xxiv, xxv
Fraser, Joseph, 506
Fraser, Mark, 123
freedom of expression: government attacks on, 27, 33n52
Freeman, Carla, 319
Fung, Richard, 514

Gampat, Ramesh, 93
Garboni, Emanuela, 413
Garnett, Lee, 508
Gaskin, Ramon, 514
gay marriage: Catholic church's objection to, 515; public opinion poll on, 517
gay rights: struggle for, 508–9
gender equality: political party manifestos on, xxii, 501–2. *See also* women
George, Roxane, xxx
Georgetown, city of: danger of flooding, 483; street demonstrations, 133–34; violence in, 10, 128–29, 134, 147, 171
Gilzean, A.R., 220
Girvan, Norman, xi

Global Women's Strike, 168
Go-Invest, 301, 335, 336, 354
Gold, Judith, 272
Goldberg, D.T., 299
'gold bush gateway,' myth of, 434
Golding, Bruce, 5, 518
Goolsarran, Anand, xiv, 23
Gopal, Latchmin, 279
Gosine, Andil, 514
government: accountability mechanisms, xiv, 21; alternative ('shadow') institutions of, 78; corruption and, 2, 3; evaluation of performance of, 47–48; failures of, 28; influence of ruling party on, 17; opposition to, 2, 19; public perception of, 141; reforms of, 15; restructure of bureaucratic sector, 195
Graeber, David, 484, 497n2
Granger, David A., xxix, xxix–xxx, 408, 430, 521
Granger, Sandra, 521
Grant, C. H., 64
Grant, Jermaine, 511
Great Britain: intervention of Guyana, 121, 181–82, 184, 191, 374–75
gross domestic product, 38
Guiana Shield forests, 328–29
Gurkha (newspaper), 148n13
Guyana: British intervention of, 121, 181–82, 184, 191, 374–75; constitutional system of, 6–9, 28; democratic transformation, ix, 1, 430; demographics, xxviii; economic, political, and social prospects, 125, 147–48n2, 305–6; ethnic conflicts, xii, xvii, 106, 116n4; foreign relations, 190, 198, 303–4, 352–53; gender and sexuality in, xvi–xvii; geographical location of, xix–xx; historical background, 63; human development ranking, 3; independence of, 63; international

status of, 122; investment opportunities, 301–3, 304; literacy rate, 273, 303; patronage system, 91–93; periods of political turmoil, ix–xi; post-war political settlement, 121; power structure, xiii–xv; protected areas, 332; survey of political attitudes, 139–42
Guyana Action Party/Working People's Alliance, 201
Guyana Chronicle, 83n15
Guyana Cooperative Agricultural and Industrial Development Bank (GAIBANK), 224
Guyana Credit Corporation (GCC), 224
Guyana Day commemoration, 385
Guyana Elections Commission (GECOM), xxix–xxx, 127, 132–33, 200
Guyana Equality Forum (GEF), 512
Guyana Forestry Commission (GFC), 332, 337, 344, 346, 348–49, 353–54, 356n11, 357n15
Guyana Human Rights Association (GHRA), 512, 513
Guyana Indian Foundation Trust (GIFT), 156, 162
Guyana Indian Heritage Association (GIHA), 19, 136–37, 138, 157
Guyana Integrated Natural Resources Information Service (GINRIS) project, 340
Guyana Living Conditions Survey, 239
Guyana Marketing Corporation (GMC), 470
Guyana Multiple Indicator Cluster Survey (MICS), 259n4
Guyana National Bureau of Standards (GNBS), 353
Guyana Rainbow Foundation (Guybow), xxvi, 508, 511
Guyana Revenue Authority (GRA), 17, 25, 48, 59
Guyana Rice Corporation, 224

Guyana Rice Development Board (GRDB), 227
Guyana Sawmills Ltd, 344
Guyana's Women Leadership Institute, 420
Guyana Telephone and Telegraph (GT&T), 23
Guyana Times, 26
Guyana Trans United (GTU), xxvi–xxvii, 511
Guyanese Action for Reform and Democracy (GUARD), 196, xxxiin8
Guyanese identity, 432–33
Guyanese society: polarization index, **96**, 97
Guyanese wage, 308, 313

Halder, Nomita, 398
Hall, Stuart, 164
Hamilton, Joseph, 133
Harmon, Joseph, 521
Harper-Wills, Doris, 370, 380. *See also Samaan*
Harvey, David, 224
Haynes, Helen, 513
Haynes, W., 82n7
health care, 187, **254**, 257
Help and Shelter organisation, 165, 175n38, 519–20
Henry, Clement, xviii, xx
Henry, Namela, 511, 516
Henry, Nicolette, 512
Henry-Lee, Aldrie, 241
Herdmanston Accord, 10, 66, 69, 71, 129, 156, 203
Heywood, A., 74
Hidalgo, C.A., 101
Hill, Cave, 513
Hinds, David, xxxi, 112, 116n2, 137, 398
Hinds, Samuel, 84n22, 339, 518
hinterland, 437, 439, 445, 455
Hintzen, Percy, xvii, xviii, xxvii, xxxi, 63, 116n2, 486
HIV/AIDS, xxvi, 507–8

Holness, Andrew, 518
homophobia, 502–3, 516, 517
homosexuality: call to repeal laws on, 504, 506; opposition to legalization of, *509*, 510, 516–17; persecution of, 502–3, 504, 505
'Homosexuality: A constitutional question' (McIntosh), 513
Hope Canal: as case of disaster capitalism, 492; construction of, 479, 484, 485; effect on farmers, 492, 493–94, 495; effect on sugar industry, 492–93; environmental assessment debates, 490–91; government support of, 489; hazards of pegasse, 490, 491; impact on coastal populations, 490–91; opponents of, 489–90; technical aspects of, 484, 496
Horowitz, David, 122
Horowitz, Donald, 97
Household Income and Expenditure Surveys, 239
House of Israel (quasi-religious group), 2
Hoyte, Desmond: economic policy, 38, 272, 334–35, 486–87; on 'ethnic cleansing,' 104–5; foreign policy, 198; international pressure on, 196–97, 198; media policy, 25; as opposition leader, 128, 134, 144; political reforms, 38; restoration of democracy by, x; on sugar crisis, 230
Hughes, Melanie, 417–18
Hughes, Nigel, xxix
Human Development Index (HDI), 94, 95, **96**
Human Rights Commission, 14
human security: classifications of, **251**; definition of, 244–45; dimensions of, 245, **246**, 249; government expenditure on, 258; indicators of, 245, **246, 248**, 249; levels of, **251**, 252; method of computing, 249–50, **250**; vs. nation-state security, 245; regional differences of, 252–58, **253**; threats to, 245
Hurston, Zora Neale, 384

ideology of Marxism/Leninism, 189, 190
immigrant groups, 98–99
income-generating enterprises, 458–59
Independent Party, **409**
Indian-Guyanese people: in agricultural labour force, 222; civic competence of, 140; confidence in government, 141; desire to emigrate among, 142, 152n43; perception of judicial system, 142; political attitudes of, 139–42, 184; in public sector, 15–16, 105; of Region Six, 152n43; surveys of, 140–42; violence against, xiii, 18–19, 106, 136–37, 145–46, 154, 156; voting preferences, 107–8, **108**, 109–10
Indo-Guyanese women: relation to family, 164; sexual assault of, 159; violence against, 157, 158, 160, 161–63, 166, 169
infrastructure development projects, 484
Inland Revenue Department, 17, 48
Institute of Chartered Accountants of the Caribbean (ICAC), 52
Integrated Financial Management and Accounting System (IFMAS), 55, 59
Integrity Commission, 24, 45, 46–47, 59
Inter-American Commission on Human Rights, 27
Inter-American Convention against Corruption (IACAC), 45, 60n23
Interim Management Committees (IMCs), 79
Interim Management Councils, 24
International Federation of Accountants (IFAC), 52

International Foundation for Electoral Systems (IFES), 65, 82n10, 197, 198
International Labour Organization (ILO), 272
International Monetary Fund (IMF), 37, 38, 193, 195, 209, 269
International Public Sector Accounting Standards (IPSAS), 52
International Tropical Timber Organization (ITTO), 338
Inter-Religious Organization (IRO), 515, 516
interventionism, 178, 188, 194–95, 204
Ishmael, Odeen, 64

Jackman, Sandy, 516
Jagan, Cheddi: comment on black people, 106; constitutional reform of, xiv, 186; death of, 1, 126, 339; economic policy, 199, 374; education policy, 270; forest policy, 336; interest in community governance, 65; political career, ix, x, 18, 155, 184, 339; support base of, 184; trips to the US, 199
Jagan, Derek, 18
Jagan, Janet, xi, xxii, 1, 126, 127–28, 172n5, 421n2
Jagdeo, Bharrat: attacks on independent media, 33n53; authoritarian style, xiv, xxxi, 10, 14, 19, 29n9; dialogue with opposition, 134–35; economic policy, 113, 272; electoral victory, 131, 133, 339, 342; forest protection initiative, 351–52; governance reforms, 15; Low Carbon Development Strategy, xxi, 335; as opposition leader, xxix; political rallies, 33n53; position on LGBTIQ+ rights, xxvi, 508; presidency of, xi, 14, 15
Jaguar Committee for Democracy, 148n13
Jamaica, 94, **95**, 96, **96**, 180, 398–99, 401
James, Deni, 517
James, Rudy, 7
Jennings, Zellynne, 273, 288
Joint Task Force on Local Government: challenges of, 67, 83n15; establishment of, 66, 69; functions of, 66–67; public consultations, 82n14; recommendations, 83n19; representatives from political parties, 66, 82n12; task force of, 82n13
Judicial Services Commission (JSC), 11, 20–21
judiciary branch of government, 19, 20–21, 142
jumbie, 369, 377, 380, 384, 390n2. *See also* spirits

Kaie's sacrifice, 429–30, 432–33
Kaieteur Falls, 433
Kaieteur News (newspaper), 25–26, 27, 33n55
Kennedy, Edward, 197
Kesic, Vesna, 174n26
Khan, Iman, xix
Khan, Roger, 2, 18, 19, 29n3
Khemraj, Tarron, xi, xv, xvi, 99
kidnappings, 122, 123, 124
Kilkenny, Roberta, 402
King, Kenneth, 338
Kingsbury, Arthur, 244
Kissoon, Frederick, 16, 29n9, 106
Kissoon, Vidyaratha, xxvi, xxvii
Klein, Naomi, 480, 481, 483; *This Changes Everything: Capitalism vs. The Climate*, 482
knowledge economy, 480
Korczynski, M., 313
Korvajärvi, P., 310

Krook, Mona Lena, 401
Kudva, Neema, 421
Kunicová, Jana, 327
Kwayana, Eusi, 137, 138, 159, 189, 492

labour force, xvii–xviii, 98–99, 101
Lamming, George, xxv
lands: communal, xx; demarcation of, 436; indigenous, 330, 441, 442; laws, 214–15, 221, 222; management of, xx, xxi; as means of labour control, 217; price of, 221; restrictions on acquisition of, 214–15, 231n13; state control over, 440; theft of, 228
Land Settlement Schemes (LSS), 224
land titling, 436, 440
land-use planning, 339, 340
Langrod, P.G., 62
Latin American Public Opinion Project (LAPOP), 108
Lawless, Jennifer, 397
Lawrence, Margaret, 507
Lawrence, Volda, 518
Legally Protected Areas, 332
Lewis, Lincoln, xxxi
Lewis, W. Arthur, 101
LGBTIQ+ citizens: activism, xxvii; government's position on status of, 508, 518–19, 521; homophobia towards, 502, 512, 516; international support of, 514–15, 517–18; living with HIV, 507–8; media reports on stories of, 502–4, 513–14; non-discrimination policies, 519–20; public debates on rights of, 508–11; public opinion about, 521–22; public support of, 511–14; religious opposition to equality of, 515–16; social and legal status of, xxvi
LGBTIQ+ Film festival, 511
Liberator Party, **409**
Linden, town of, xii, 25, 167

Lindroth, Marjo, 431
Lipjhart, Arend, 125
Local Authorities (Elections) (Amendment) Act, 70, 83n16
Local Democratic Organ Act, 65
local government: challenges of, xiv–xv, 65–66; characteristics of, 79; civil society groups and, 75, 84n27; community participation in, 76, 80–81; definition of, 81n1; elections of, xv, 24, 62, 64, 68–69, 73, 75, 80; informal mechanisms of, 70; international scrutiny of, 66, 83n21, 84n22; legislative framework, 64, 65, 67, 70, 81n5, 83n17; national actors and, 72–73; non-state actors and, 80–81; perceptions of, 76–78; political parties and, 69–70, 73–74; as precondition for democracy, 74, 75; proportional representation in, 83n16; reform process of, 69–70, 71–74, 80, 83n19; scholarship on, 64, 75, 76, 81n2; state institutions and, 73, 80, 81–82n7; structures of, 64, 65; weakness of, 76, 80, 82n8; women's participation in, 77, 84n35
Local Government Act, 79, 85n37
Local Government Board, 64
Local Government Commission, 65
log export: criminal activities and, 350–51; criticism of practice of, 329–30, 357n13; disparity of data about, 357n16; legality verification system (LVS) of, 353; market for, 349, 350; non-compliance with laws and regulations, 351; volume of, 349–50
logging concessions: area fees on, 343; foreign control of, 344; illegal subletting, 343; long-term, 326, 328, 334, 335; management of,

328, 330, 355; moratorium on new, 337; negotiations of, 333, 335; private trading of, 345–46; profitability of, 348; short-term, 334; small- and large-scale, 335, 337, 344
Lomé Convention, 230, 234n33
London, Apostle, 517
Loomba, Ania, 159
Lorde, Audre, 169, 170
Low Carbon Development Strategy (LCDS), xxi, 328, 335
Lowndes, Vivien, 401
Lugones, Maria, 448n17
Luncheon, Roger, 16, 17, 134, 356n8, 521
Lyttleton, Oliver, ix

Mahaica-Mahaicony-Abary Scheme (MMA Scheme), 485–86, 487, 488, 489, 491, 497n4
Mani, Lata, 162
Manickchand, Priya, xxiii, 292n20, 292n21, 416, 418
manicole broom, *388*, 390n3
manihot. *See* cassava
Manor, J., 74
maroon communities, 217–18
Marx, Karl, 214
Marxist movement, 155
Mash jail break, 121, 123, 124, 148n3
Mashramani festivities (Guyana Day), xxii, 370, 386, *387*, 387–88, *388*, 389
mass media, xiii, 25–26, 33n53, 106
matapeeing process, 465, 475nn7–8
Mauritius, 94, **95**, **96**, 97
Mazaruni hydropower project, 438
McAlmont, Cecilia, 403, 410
McAndrew, Wordsworth, 378, 379; *Ol' Higue*, 390
McEwan, Colleen, 508
McEwan, Quincy, 506, 519
McIntosh, Esther, xiv, xv
McIntosh, Simeon C. R., 513

McIntyre, Alister, 120, 129
McKittrick, Katherine, 445
Men Against Violence Against Women, 165
Men Who Have Sex with Men No Political Agenda (MSMNPA), 517
micro-financing, 459–60, 474n3
Mighty Rebel (music band), 105
Miller, Portia Simpson, 518
mining sector, 447n10, 448n15
Mirchandani, Kiran, xix
'Mirror of Love, The' (Moore), 513
Mitchell, Keith, 129
Mitchell, Timothy, 458
Mohabeer, Michelle, 514
Mohammed, Renata, 514
Mohammed, Wazir, xvii, xviii, xxv
Mondesire, Alicia, 410, 415
Montalvo, Jose, 95
Moore, Alan, 513
Moore, Dale, 123
Moore, Stanley, 504
Mothers in Black, 165, 175n38
Moyne Commission of inquiry, 232n21
Mulroney, Brian, 197
Municipal District Councils Act, 81n5
Mustapha, Zulfikar, xxx
Myers, Roxanne, 84n35, 104
myths, Caribbean, 369–70, 390

Nanivadekar, Medha, 401
Narain, Robert, 507
Nascimento, Kit, 149n15
Nash equilibrium in game theory, 110, 111, 112. *See also* prisoners' dilemma game
Nath, Dwarka, 232n17
National Congress of Local Organs, 66
National Congress of Women (NCW), 403
National Democratic Institute (NDI), 65, 66, 197
National Development Strategy (NDS), 273, 338, 339
National Domestic Violence Policy, 520

National Heritage Commission, 71
National Industrial and Commercial Investments Ltd (NICIL), 22–23, 113, 230
National Irrigation and Drainage Authority (NDIA), 484
nationalism, 158, 178, 179, 180–83, 184, 185
National Procurement and Tender Administration Board (NPTAB), 50, 53
National Protected Areas System (NPAS), 331
National Women's Rights Campaign, 165
Natural Resources and Environment Advisory Committee (NREAC), 340
neighbourhood democratic councils (NDCs), 65, 79, 84n35, 85n38, 233n23
neocolonialism, 178
Nettles, Kimberly, 402
Newman, Clayton, 508
non-governmental organisations (NGOs), 78, 85n36, 417–18, 470
normal profit, 100–101
Noronha, E., 310
North Rupununi District Development Board (NRDDB), 332

Office of the Ombudsman, 24
oil industry, xxxi, 114
Ole Higue: as folklore figure, xxi–xxii, 370, 373, 377, 379–80, 384, 390n1; as literary character, 385, 386, 390
Ole Samaan (literary character), 380, 381, 382, 383, 384
O'Loughlin, C., 223, 227, 232n19
'One of our sons is missing' play, 507
Ong, Aihwa, 298
opposition. *See* political opposition
Orozco, Caleb, 507

Other Countries and Territories Route (OCT), 226
Ott, U., 313

parliamentary systems, 6, 9, 19
Parliament of Guyana: presidential control over, 4, 7–8, 10; procedure of removal of members of, 18; prorogations of, 10, 12, 57; sectoral committees, 12–13; Speaker's role in, 18, 19
Parris, Haslyn, 133
A Partnership for National Unity (APNU), xxviii, xxviii–xxix, 91, 375, **405**, 407–8, **409**
party paramountcy system, 6, 116n2
Patriotic Coalition for Democracy (PCD), xxxii, 195
patronage politics, 91, 92–93, 104
Patterson, James, xxx
Paxton, Pamela, 417
Peake, Linda, 444
Pearce, John, 458
Pelling, Mark, 76, 79
People's National Congress (PNC): anti-Indianism of, 185; contestation of the results of elections, 127–28, 129, 200; economic policy, 190–91, 192, 193, 439, 486; electoral performance, 125, 133, 134, 147, 155, 188, 199–200; ethnic policy, 104–5; extremism of, 106, 137; foundation of, x, 184; idea of 'shared governance,' 145; international alliances, 192; leadership, 131, 155; left wing radicalism, 189; local government reform and, 64, 69; as opposition force, 202, 203; political coalitions of, 6, 191; political impasse and, 143–44; public sector reforms, 150n26; seats in Parliament, 145, 408,

409, 410; support base of, 105, 128, 184, 186, 188, 189; Women's Auxiliary of, 402–3

People's Progressive Party (PPP): anticolonial agenda of, 180–81; attitude to opposition, 145; constitutional reform and, xiv; criticism of, 187; democratic centralism, 341; domestic policy, 186–87; election promises, 354–55; electoral performance, ix–x, xxvii–xxviii, 125–26, 127, 131, 132, 155, 181, 199–200, 201; ethnic mobilisation strategy of, 106–7; ideology of, 104; international support of, 202; local government reform and, 69; non-cooperation campaign, 191; pro-business position of, xv; public perception of, 141, 183; removal from power, 182, 184, 375; seats in Parliament, **409**; support base of, xvi, 105, 108, 184, 201, 202

People's Progressive Party-Civic (PPP/C), xii, xxxii*n*8, 1, 2, 3, **405**, 407, 501–2. *See also* PPP/C government

per capita income, 38, 94, **95**

Perreira, Esther, 149n21

Persadie, Natalie, xxii, xxiii

Persaud, Bishnodat, 345

Persaud, Robert, 347

Persaud, Sangeeta, 378

Persaud, Savitri, xxi

Persaud, Seyon, 506

personal security, **254**, 255, 258

Petro Caribe deal, 226, 227, 233n28

PetroCaribe Fund, 484, 497n1

Pettit, Jethro, 237, 257

Phantom Squad, xii, 2

Pike, Philip, 514

police force, 7, 11, 202

political attitudes, survey of, 139–42, 151nn40–42

Political Economy Analysis (PEA), 63, 81n3

political impasse, 120, 142–43

political opposition: economic victimisation of, 25, 32n46; growing power of, 195–96; law suits against, 24–25; online vilification of, 26; overseas campaign, 196; suppression of, 24–25

political parties: competition for control over the state, 103–4; contribution to 'zero sum' politics, 150–51n33; dominant, 474n1; election promises on gender issues, **405**, 405–8, 422nn4–5; ethnic identification with, **108**; ethno-political mobilisation strategy, 104–5; international alliances of, 192; local government reform and, 68–70, 71–72; racialized identities of, 184–85, 199–200; relations between, 70–71, 72, 92, 150–51n33; selection of parliamentarians by, 411; as self-interested agents, 68; women mobilisation by, 403–4

political security, 255, 257

political system, xiii–xiv, xxxi–xxxii, 1–2, 68, 115

population: dispersion of, 92–93; emigration of, 302, 306; ethnic composition of, 187–88, 375; life expectancy, 95, **95**; negative growth rate of, 302

Population and Housing Census, 302

porkknockers, 433, 437, 447n7, 448n15

Post, Richard, 244

Potter, Lesley, 220, 221, 222

poverty: absolute vs. relative, 242; alleviation strategies, 238, 241; assumptions about, 236; capability approach to assessment of, 243–44; definition of, 236, 242; dimensions of, xviii, 238, 243; education as path out of, 237; extreme, 236–37, 239; human security factor in assessment of, 249; moderate, 239; monetary measures of, 241–43; non-monetary indicators of, 243; percent of population living in, 236–37, *240*; progress in reduction of, 239–40; public perception of, 141; recommendations for tackling, 258–59; regional variations of, xviii, *240*, 241

Poverty: A Study of Town Life (Rowntree), 241

Poverty Reduction Strategy Paper (PRSP), 238, 241

poverty study: 17-indicator instrument, 245, **246**; confirmatory factor analysis technique of, 247–48, **248**, 249; data-collection method, 245, 246–47, 258, 259n4, 267; findings of, 249–51, *252*; limitations of, 258; modelling process, **268**; overview of, xviii, 238–341; questionnaire, 263–66

power sharing, 115, 144

PPP/C government: authoritarian rule, 1–2, 24; constitutional reforms, 9–10; economic policy, 113, 202, 487; forest management, 325; local government elections and, 24, 65, 69; media policy, 25, 26–27; political propaganda, 26; suppression of opposition, 24–25; system of patronage, 91

Pradoville 2, 23

Premdas, Ralph, 81n6, 116n2, 116n4, 120, 147–48n2

presidential powers: over appointment to administrative offices, xxix–xxx, xxx–xxxi, 8, 10–11; over cabinet of ministers, 7, 28; over judicial branch, 11; over legislative branch, 7–8, 10; over Service Commissions, 11, 15; to veto legislations, 19

prisoners' dilemma game, 107, 109–12, 115

private schools: cost of, 288–89; elitism of, 292n21; quality of education in, 279, 292n20, 293n22; student enrollment, 292n20, 293n23; teachers' migration to, 278; working conditions at, 278–79, 291n8

Private Sector Commission, 202–3

Procurement Act, 46, 52, 53

pro-ethnic strategic voting: dominant groups in, 91; outcomes of, 112; prisoners' dilemma game, 107–12; subjective discount factor, 109, 110, 111, 112, 114

Programme Performance Statements, 47

psychiatric disabilities: link to spirit possession, 377–78; violence against people with, 377

public accounts: annual financial reporting of, 40–43; audit of, 38–39; definition of, 50; overdraft of, 51–52

Public Accounts Committee (PAC), 41–42, 43, 59

public financial management: accounting standards, 41, 52; auditor general's recommendations for, 40; audit regulations, 54–55; constitutional amendments related to, 50; electronic accounting, 55; evaluation of, 56–57; public accountability of, 37, 59; reporting system, 40–43, 55

public procurement process, 49–50, 59, 61n40

public schools: access to primary, 273;

automatic promotion of students, 284, 292n17; establishment of school boards, 279–80; funding of, 288, 289; government spending on, 272–73; impact of the austerity measures on, 269–70, 272–73, 274; infrastructure, 275–76, 278–79, 290–91n6, 291n7; issue of 'extra lessons,' 275, 290n5; lack of students' interest in, 288; non-government organisations and, 280; prestige of, 273; privatisation of, 279; process of 'freeing,' 270; quality of education in, 279, 281, 287; Secondary School Entrance Examination, 291nn9–10; spending on, 271; students' graduation rate, 289; study of, 269–70, 290n1. *See also* teachers

public sector: appointments to, 15–16; contract employees, 16, 30n17; formal privatisation of, 17; job loss in, 150n22; politicisation of, 16; reform of, 150n26; salaries and benefits in, 16; size of, 271

Public Service Commission, 7, 11

Puerto Rico, 98, 180

Queen's College, 280

Quijano, Anibal, 448n17

racialised identities, xvi, 444

racialised spaces, 374

racial tensions, 146, 147, 158–60, 374, 375

Radika Singh's murder: charges laid in relation to, 372; conflicting narratives of, 371–72; press coverage of, 371, 372, 373; public response to, 375, 376–77; public responsibility for, 389–90

Raleigh, Walter, 434

Ramcharan, Bertie, 513

Ramkarran, Ralph, 18, 513

Ramotar, Donald, xxviii, 12, 71–72, 113, 354

Ramotar, Gavin, 514

Rampersad, Devindra, 507

Rampersaud, Pandita Indranie, 515

Ramphal, Shridath, 129

Ramsahoye, Fenton, 196

Ramsammy, Leslie, 29n3, 510, 518

Ramsar Convention for Protection of Wetlands, 332

Reagan, Ronald, 191

reconciliation, discourse of, 430

REDD+ (Reducing Emissions from Deforestation and Forest Degradation) scheme, 352

Red Thread (women's NGO), 154, 164, 165–67, 168, 171, 175n39, 404

Reducing Emissions from Deforestation and forest Degradation (REDD) scheme, 352

regional democratic councils (RDCs), 65

religious traditions, 377–78

Renshaw, John, 237

Reynal-Querol, Marta, 95

rice: history of cultivation of, 209, 220–21, 231–32n15, 232n16; planters' attitude to, 218–19, 220; slavery and production of, 217–18

Rice Development Company (RDC), 224

rice industry: colonial legacy and, 230; cooperative movement and, 224; cross-cultural cooperation in, 223–24; decline of, 114, 226–28; economic liberalisation and, 226; emergence and evolution of, 219, 220–21; global competition, 101, 224–25; government assistance to, 224; growth of, 221–22, 223–24, 226; impact on national economy, 229; labour force, 219–20; land ownership and tenure, 225, 227–28, 233n23; number of

farmers in, 223, 232n19, 233n29; production figures, 225; small-farming, 222–24, 227–28; sugar crisis and, 221
Rice Producers Association, 223
Richards, Todah, 378
Rights Advocacy Project (U-RAP), 507
'Rights and Resources Initiative' (RRI), 331
Rise, Organise and Rebuild (ROAR), 92, 125, 148n13, 201, **409**
RISE Guyana (Rise Organise and Rebuild Guyana), xxix
Roach, Lancelot, 123
Robertson-Ogle, Melissa, 506
Robinson, Colin, 518
Robinson, Tracy, 418
Rodney, Walter, xii, 97, 210, 496; *History of the Guyanese Working People*, xvii, xxv
Rodrigues, Malcolm, 515
Rohee, Clement, 519
Rondinelli, A., 74
Roopnaraine, Rupert, 155, 289
Roopnaraine, T., 437, 448n15
Rose-Ackerman, Susan, 327
Rowntree, Benjamin Seebohm, 241
rural electrification programme, 462
Russell, William, 220
Rwanda, 394, 413
Ryan, Selwyn, 2

Sachs, Albie, 513
Salzinger, L., 308
Samaan (Harper-Wills): in children anthology, 370, 391n11; Ole Higue character in, 380, 381–84; overview, 380–81; symbolic importance of, 385
Sanders, Ronald, 513
Sealey, Godfrey, 507
Secure Livelihood Programme of Voluntary Service Overseas (VSO) Guyana, 466
security, concept of, 244. *See also* human security
Seecharan, Clem, 97
Seenauth, Kamille, 378
Seeraj, Dharamkumar, 227
self-determination, ideology of, 178
semi-presidential system, 6, 9
Sen, Amartya, 243, 244
Sexual Offences Act, xxiii, 417, 519
Sexual Orientation Bill, 510–11
Seymour, A. J.: *Dictionary of Guyanese Folklore*, 379; *The Legend of Kaieteur*, 432
shared governance, idea of, 142, 143, 145
Sheeratan, Patricia, 515
Silverman, Marilyn, 64, 493
Simpson, Joel, xxvii, 510, 514, 516
Singapore, 94, **95**, 95–96, **96**
Singh, Carl, xxx
Singh, Chaitram, 116n2
Singh, Claudette, 131
Singh, Doodnauth, 149n21
Singh, Joe, 202
Singh, Paul, 82n8
Singh, Radika: accusation of being an old higue, 369, 385, 388–89; identity of, 374; mental health of, xxi, 372, 377. *See also* Radika Singh's murder
Singh, Rajesh, 138
Singh, Robert, 507
Sizer, Nigel, 339
skinfolk, 384–85
slavery, 211, 217–18, 231n2
social cohesion roundtable, 429–30, 432–33
Social Impact Amelioration Programme (SIMAP), xviii, 238, 239
societal security, 255–57, **256**
Society against Sexual Orientation Discrimination (SASOD), 506, 511–12, 520
soil survey project, 333
Solarz, Stephen J., 197

Solomon, Frank, 123
Souza, Karen de, 167
sovereignty, 178, 188, 298–99
speedboat ventures through Cuyuni River, 434
Spicker, Paul, 242
spirits, 377
Sri Lanka, 94, **95**, **96**, 97
Stabroek News, 25–26, 122–24, 132, 136, 142, 155, 162, 345, 508
'Stamp It Out' campaign, 418–19
Staritz, Cornelia, 272
State Forest Exploratory Permit (SFEP) legislation, 342–43
State Forest Permissions (SFPs), 337, 343, 347
Stephens, Trevor, 435, 436
Structural Adjustment Program (SAP), 272, 273, 279–80, 288
Students against Sexual Orientation Discrimination (SASOD), xxvi–xxvii, 510
Subryan, Andre, 507
subsidiarity, principle of, 355–56n7
sugar belt towns, 209
Sugar Duties Act, 212–13
sugar industry: annual production target, 487; colonial legacy in, 229, 230; competitiveness of, 98, 100; corrupt practices in, 229; crisis of, 114, 222, 228–29; in Cuba, 210; history and evolution of, 209; impact on national economy, 229; internal market, 100; labour force, 98, 101, 210, 211, 212, 213–14; land ownership, 229; normal profit rates, 100–101; polder system's effect on, 98; quality of products in, 211; technical improvements, 211; wages suppression in, 100
Sukul, Rabi, 20
Summary Jurisdiction (Offences) Act, 505–6

Sunday Stabroek, 509
Suriname, 94, **95**, 96, **96**
Surujbally, Steve, xxix

Taeuber, Irene, 98
taxation, 48–49
teachers: attrition rates, 274–78, 286; impact on children, 285–86; lack of appreciation, 277; leave without notice, 285; migration of, 277–78; in private schools, 278–79; psychological pressure on, 287; qualifications of, 282–84; replacements of, 281–82, 284; responsibilities of, 292n18; salaries of, xix, 274–75, 291n8; shortage of, 275, 285, 286, 292n19; sources of supplementary income, 274–75; stress level of, 286–87; training, 280–81, 284, 292n16; volunteers, 280; working conditions, 275–76, 278–79, 284–85, 290–91n6, 291n7
Teaching Services Commission, 7, 11, 281
Teixeira, Gail, 416
telecommunication, liberalisation of, 322n4
Teleperformance USA, 302
tendering procedures, 49
Texeira, Gail, 519
Thakur, Rishee, xvi
Thatcher, Margaret, 191
This Changes Everything: Capitalism vs. The Climate (Klein), 482
Thomas, Clive, 2, 135, 238, 239
Thomas, C.Y., xi
Thomas, Jayan Jose, 116n2
Tillack, Deodat, 515
timber manufacturing and trade, 329, 334, 346, 348, 349
Timber Sales Agreements (TSAs), 334, 343, 347

Tocqueville, Alexis de, 84n28
Toolsie Persaud Ltd, 354
Toolsie Persaud Timber Traders Inc., 354
Torres, Carlos, 272
Trinidad and Tobago: economic development, 94, **95**, **96**, 97; gender equality manifesto, 502; homophobia, 515; privatisation of the postal service, 17; sodomy laws, 507; women's political participation in, 399–400, 401
Trinidad and Tobago for the Advancement of Women, 399–400
Trotman, Petronella, 514
Trotz, Alissa, xvi, xvii, xix, 444, 445
Trump, Donald, 33n53
Tullock, Gordon, 68, 74

underdevelopment: cycles of, **102**, 103. *See also* colonial underdevelopment trap
unemployment, 150n22, 302, 307, 308, 322n5
The United Force (TUF), 6, 184–85, 186, 201, **405**, 406–7, **409**
United Nations: reports on women parliamentarians, 396–97, 403; sustainable development goals, 394
United Nations Convention against Corruption (UNCAC), 45, 60n24
United Nations Food and Agriculture Organization (FAO), 229, 333, 338
United Nations Framework Convention on Climate Change (UNFCCC), 351
United States: anti-communism, 180; foreign relations, 46, 59, 180, 191; as global economic power, 179–80; immigration to, 180; involvement in Guyana affairs, 182, 196–97; Lacey Act, 350; land use in, 116n5; Sarbanes-Oxley Act, 44
Universal Periodic Review (UPR) for Guyana, 511–12
University of Guyana's Code of Conduct, 520
University of the West Indies Rights Action Project (U-RAP), xxvii
Upper Mazaruni District, 436
Urling, Clinton, 516

Value Added Tax Act amendments, 48
Vaughn, Sarah, xxv, xxvi
villages: councils, 85n37; dependence on sugar monoculture, 217; fragmentation of, 215–16, *216*, 217; land cultivation, 216; plan of, *216*
violence: anti-Indian, 134, 145, 156–57, 172n11; calls to end, 124; Caribbean debates on, 158; elections and, 124–36; ethnic, 106, 136–38, 145–46, 152n42, 157; gendered, 155–57; against police, 168; politically motivated, 133–34, 155–57; post-electoral, 154; poverty and, 167; racial, xvi, 134, 159–60; roots of, 146, 157, 172–73n11; scale of, 156, 173n11; scholarly literature on, 173n16; sexual, 444–45; statistics of, 124; weapons used in, 123, 124
violence against women: creation of male identities and, 160; with disability, 369; domestic, 158, 161; effects of, 161; forms of, 161; in hinterland, 443; justification of, 385; letters to local newspapers about, 160–61; politically motivated, 158, 159; public response to, 161; religious, 378; sexual, 375–76; struggle against, 162–63, 171. *See also* Radika Singh's murder
Volunteer Services Organisation (VSO), 280

voting: bloc, 63; independent, 92; preferences, 107–8, **108**; racialized, xii, 91–92; swing, 115–16. *See also* pro-ethnic strategic voting

Watts, Harold, 236
weather, 479, 480
Webster, Jennifer, 389
West Indies, 178–79, 180
Whyte, Wintress, 516
Williams, Basil, 521
Williams, Brackette, 384, 439
Williams, Eric, 98
Williams, Paul, 244
Wilson, Stacey-Ann, 112
Wolfers, Arnold, 244
women: colonial stereotypes of, 164; communal identification of, 162; with disabilities, societal attitudes towards, 386; economic activities, xxiv–xxv; gendered and racialised inferiority of, 159; impact of economic crisis on, 157–58; labour movement, 166–67, 168; as mothers, recognition of, 168; perception of bodies of, 375, 443; racial differences among, 163–64; social activism, 169; social status of, xxi, 158; street protests, 157; as victims, stereotype of, 174n26
Women against Violence Everywhere (WAVE), 171
Women and Gender Equality Commission, xxii
women in politics: in Anglophone Caribbean states, 394, **395**, 398, 399; colonial ethno-politicisation of, 419; future of, 420–21; in local government, 77, 84n35; measures to include, 401; NGOs and, 420–21; overview, xxii–xxiii, 402; political institutions and, 401–2, 415–16; quota systems for, 401, 410, 411–12, 419–20; study of, 395, 397–98; under-representation of, 394–95, 396–98
women parliamentarians: arguments for having equal numbers of, 396–97; constrained behaviour of, 416–17, 420; political agenda of, 413–14; promotion of gender issues by, 417; as representatives of political parties, 403–4, 415–16; in Rwanda, study of, 413; selection of, 411–12; statistics of, 408–10, 419, 420; substantive representation, 413–15, 420
Women's Agro-Processors Development Network, 475n10
Women's Environment and Development Organization (WEDO), 400
women's organisations, 163, 402–3
Women's Political Organization (WPO), 163
Women's Revolutionary Socialist Movement (WRSM), 163, 403
Wood Cutting Lease (WCL), 337
wood processing industries, 347–48
working class, 181
Working People's Alliance (WPA), xii, 92, 404, **409**, 513
World Bank, 38, 193, 195
WorldCom, 44
World Conservation Union (IUCN), 331
World Resources Institute (WRI), 339
'World Union of Guyanese,' 196
Wowetta community, 462
Wowetta Women's Agro-processing Cassava Enterprise: autonomy of, 472; capacity-building initiatives, 470; case study of, xxiv–xxv, 457, 461–62, 472–73; challenges of, 473; decision-making practices, xxv, 465; ethical commitments, 468, 471, 472; focus on community well-

being, 474; formation of, 462; as income-generating enterprise, 458; involvement of men into, 463–64; labour arrangements in, 465–69; market relationships, 469–72; in neoliberal narrative, 458; non-market transactions, 471; organizational structure of, 463; paid labour, 467; participation in regional food fairs, 470; pricing system, 469–70; primary goal of, 463; products of, 464–65; relations with the government, 471; shared responsibility, 467; wage system, 466

Youth Challenge Guyana (YCG), 280

Zeihan, Peter, 116n5
Zheng, Buhong, 243

www.ingramcontent.com/pod-product-compliance
Lightning Source LLC
Chambersburg PA
CBHW070004010526
44117CB00011B/1424